Maine

AN EXPLORER'S GUIDE

Maine

AN EXPLORER'S GUIDE

CHRISTINA TREE & ELIZABETH ROUNDY RICHARDS

Principal Photography by Kim Grant

Tenth Edition

The Countryman Press
Woodstock, Vermont

Dedications
To Timothy and Yuko, married in Maine,
and to their dreams for daughter Aki Maya Kodama Davis-Tree.
—C.T.
To the memory of Nancy Gilles.
—E.R.R.

ISBN 0-88150-492-0
ISSN 1533-6883

Maps by Mapping Specialists, Ltd., Madison, WI,
© 2001 The Countryman Press
Interior design by Glenn Suokko
Cover design by Joanna Bodenweber
Front cover photograph by Paul Rezendes
Back cover photographs of Red's Eats by Kim Grant,
and The Portland Museum of Art by Steve Rosenthal

Published by The Countryman Press
P.O. Box 748, Woodstock, Vermont 05091

Distributed by W. W. Norton & Company, Inc.,
500 Fifth Avenue, New York, NY 10110

Printed in the United States of America
10 9 8 7 6 5 4 3 2 1

Explore With Us!

We have been fine-tuning *Maine: An Explorer's Guide* for the past 20 years, a period in which lodging, dining, and shopping opportunities have more than quadrupled in the state. As we have expanded our guide, we have also been increasingly selective, making recommendations based on years of conscientious research and personal experience. We describe the state by locally defined regions, giving you Maine's communities, not simply her most popular destinations. With this guide you'll feel confident to venture beyond the tourist towns, along roads less traveled, to places of special hospitality and charm.

WHAT'S WHERE

In the beginning of the book you'll find an alphabetical listing of special highlights and important information that you may want to reference quickly. You'll find advice on everything from where to buy the best local lobster to where to write or call for camping reservations and park information.

LODGING

We've selected lodging places for mention in this book based on their merit alone; **we do not charge innkeepers for inclusion.** We're the only travel guide that tries personally to check every bed & breakfast, farm, sporting lodge, and inn in Maine, and one of the few that do not charge for inclusion.

Prices: Please don't hold us or the respective innkeepers responsible for the rates listed as of press time in 2001. Some changes are inevitable. The 7 percent state rooms and meals tax should be added to all prices unless we specifically state that it's included in a price. We've tried to note when a gratuity is added, but it's always wise to check before booking.

Smoking: Maine B&Bs, inns, and restaurants are now generally smoke-free, but many lodging places still reserve some rooms for smokers and, depending on their license, some restaurants still offer a smoking area. If this is important to you, be sure to ask when making reservations.

RESTAURANTS

In most sections please note a distinction between *Dining Out* and *Eating Out*. By their nature, restaurants included in the *Eating Out* group are generally inexpensive.

KEY TO SYMBOLS

🎗 Special value. The blue-ribbon symbol appears next to selected lodging and restaurants that combine quality and moderate prices.

✐ Child-friendly. The crayon symbol appears next to lodging, restaurants, activities, and shops of special interest or appeal to youngsters.

♿ Handicapped access. The wheelchair symbol appears next to lodging, restaurants, and attractions that are partially or completely handicapped accessible.

🐾 Pets. The dog-paw symbol appears next to lodgings that accept pets.

Author's Choice: The gray-shaded entries scattered throughout this are our best recommendations for don't-miss things to see and do.

We would appreciate any comments or corrections. Please write to Explorer's Guide Editor, The Countryman Press, P.O. Box 748, Woodstock, VT 05091; or e-mail countrymanpress@wwnorton.com.

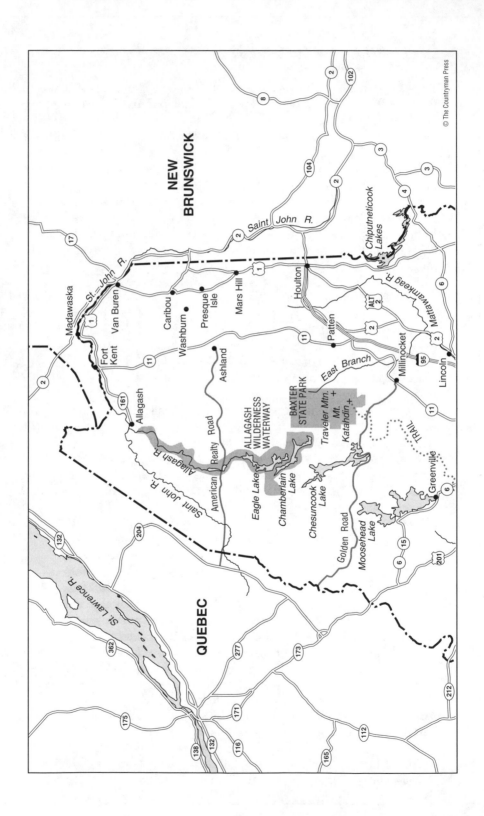

© The Countryman Press

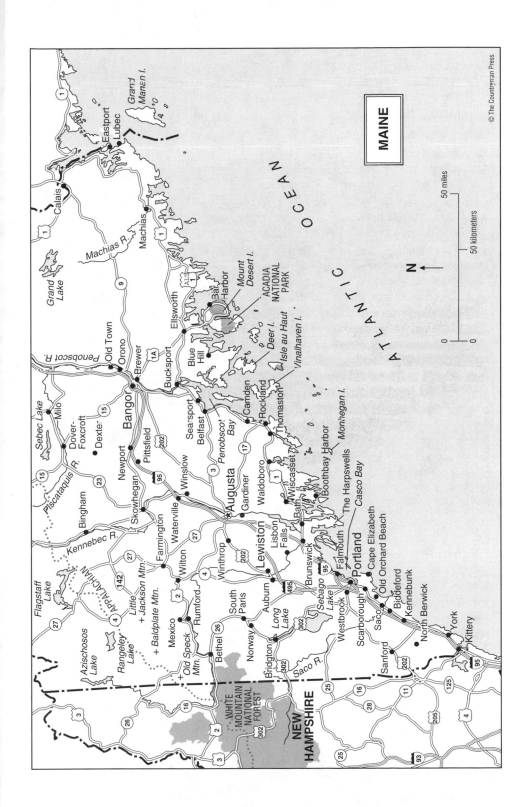

MAINE

© The Countryman Press

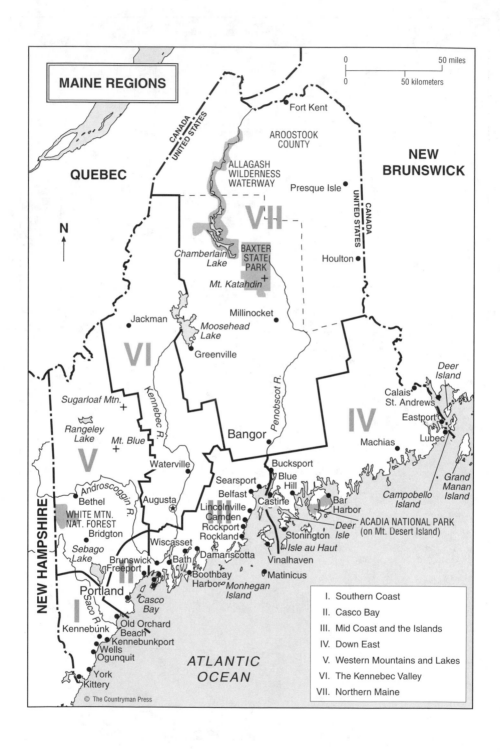

MAINE REGIONS

QUEBEC

N

NEW BRUNSWICK

CANADA
UNITED STATES

Fort Kent

AROOSTOOK
COUNTY

ALLAGASH
WILDERNESS
WATERWAY

Presque Isle

VII

CANADA
UNITED STATES

Chamberlain
Lake

BAXTER
STATE
PARK

Mt. Katahdin +

Houlton

Millinocket

Jackman

Moosehead
Lake

Greenville

Deer
Island

Calais
St. Andrews

Sugarloaf Mtn. +

Kennebec R.

VI

Penobscot R.

Eastport

IV

Rangeley
Lake

Mt. Blue +

Bangor

Machias

Lubec

V

Waterville

Bucksport

Grand
Manan
Island

Androscoggin R.

Bethel

WHITE MTN.
NAT. FOREST

Bridgton

Augusta

Searsport
Belfast

III

Lincolnville

Camden

Rockport
Rockland

Blue
Hill

Castine

Deer
Isle

Campobello
Island

Bar
Harbor

Stonington

ACADIA NATIONAL PARK
(on Mt. Desert Island)

Wiscasset

Sebago
Lake

Brunswick
Freeport

Bath

Damariscotta

Isle au Haut

Vinalhaven

NEW HAMPSHIRE

II

Boothbay
Harbor

Monhegan
Island

Matinicus

Portland

Saco R.

Casco
Bay

I

Kennebunk

Old Orchard
Beach

Kennebunkport

Wells

Ogunquit

ATLANTIC
OCEAN

York

Kittery

© The Countryman Press

I.   Southern Coast

II. Casco Bay

III. Mid Coast and the Islands

IV. Down East

V. Western Mountains and Lakes

VI. The Kennebec Valley

VII. Northern Maine

0   50 miles

0   50 kilometers

Contents

Introduction

He who rides and keeps the beaten track studies the fences chiefly.
—*Henry David Thoreau, The Maine Woods, 1853*

Over the past 20 years *Maine: An Explorer's Guide* has introduced hundreds of thousands of people to many Maines.

When this book first appeared, it was the first 20th-century guidebook to describe New England's largest state region by region rather than to focus only on the most touristed communities, listed alphabetically. From the start, we critiqued places to stay and to eat as well as everything to see and to do—based on merit rather than money (we don't charge anyone to be included).

The big news, however, isn't that *Maine: An Explorer's Guide* was first but that readers constantly tell us that it remains the best Maine guidebook—that despite current competition, this "Maine Bible" gets better with each edition.

And it should. With each new edition we build on what we know, still spending months on the road, checking every lodging we include, making sure it's a place we would personally like to stay.

Initially, back in 1981, this didn't seem like a tall order. Chris's three sons—ages three, six, and eight—helped her research reasonably priced rental cottages, ice cream stands, and beaches. The guide, however, quickly grew as inns, B&Bs, and other lodging options proliferated, along with things to do and see, dining venues, and shopping options. The book also soon included all the parts of Maine in which a visitor can find a campsite or commercial lodging, from Matinicus to Madawaska and from the White Mountains to the island of Monhegan, not to mention all of Route 1 from Kittery to Fort Kent.

After the first couple of editions it became obvious that no one person could explore this immense and richly textured state during one summer and fall. Maine writer Mimi Steadman came to the rescue in 1986, and when she stepped down in 1994 Bangor native Elizabeth Roundy Richards came on board as coauthor.

We now describe more than 500 places to stay, ranging from campgrounds to grand old resorts and including farms as well as B&Bs and inns—in all corners of the state and in all price ranges. We have also checked out a similar number of places to dine and to eat (we make a distinction between dining and eating), and, since shopping is an important part of everyone's travels, we include special stores we encounter. We have opinions about everything we've found, and we don't hesitate to share them. In every category we record exactly what we see.

Chris was born in Hawaii and bred in Manhattan, and she has been living in Massachusetts since she came there to work for the *Boston Globe* in 1968. She is addicted to many Maines. As a toddler she learned to swim in the Ogunquit River and later watched her sons do the same in Monhegan's icy waters—and then learn to sail at summer camp in Raymond and paddle canoes on the Saco River and down the St. John. Her number-two son was recently married on Little Cranberry Island off Mount Desert. For the *Globe*, she continues to write about a variety of things to do in Maine, from skiing at Sugarloaf and Sunday River and dogsledding into a North Woods sporting camp to llama trekking and horseback riding in Bethel to sea kayaking off points from Portland to Pembroke and windjamming on Penobscot Bay. Increasingly, too, she finds herself writing about Maine's art and artists (of which there are more per capita in Maine than in any other state). She values her vantage point from Boston, far enough away to give her the perspective on what it means to be a visitor, yet near enough to comfortably and continually explore Maine.

Elizabeth was born and raised in the Bangor area, and she took Maine for granted, never appreciating its beauty and uniqueness until she returned after moving out of state for a few years. She has lived in the Bangor area, Augusta, Bar Harbor, and the Portland area and has spent time in "camps" on lakes with her family as a child; one of her favorite spots remains a large lodge overlooking the ocean on Sandy Point, where she spent many special summers. She, too, thought she knew Maine, but in the course of this research realized that she was wrong, that there are many less traveled areas that even a native can overlook, places she had avoided with misconceived notions of how they would be, only to be pleasantly surprised. She also discovered some amazing history she had been missing but won't soon forget.

We are both fascinated by Maine's history in general and its tourism history in particular. It seems ironic that back in the 1920s, "motor touring" was hailed as a big improvement over train and steamer travel because it meant you no longer had to go where everyone else did— over routes prescribed by railroad tracks and steamboat schedules. In Maine cars seem, however, to have had precisely the opposite effect. Now 90 percent of the state's visitors follow the coastal tourist route as faithfully as though their wheels were grooved to Route 1.

Worse still, it's as though many tourists are on a train making only express stops—at rush hour. At least half of those who follow Route 1 stop, stay, and eat in all the same places (such as Kennebunkport, Boothbay or Camden, and Bar Harbor)—in August.

Tourism has always been driven by images. In the 1840s Thomas Cole, Frederick Church (both of whom sketched and painted scenes of Mount Desert), and lesser-known artists began projecting Maine as a romantic, remote destination in the many papers, magazines, and children's books of the decade. While Henry David Thoreau's *The Maine Woods* was not published until 1864, many of its chapters appeared as magazine articles years before (Thoreau first climbed Katahdin in 1846), and in 1853 *Atlantic Monthly* editor James Russell Lowell visited and wrote about Moosehead Lake.

After the Civil War, Maine tourism boomed. Via railroad and steamboat, residents of cities throughout the East and Midwest streamed into the Pine Tree State, most toting guidebooks, many published by rail and steamboat lines to boost business. Male "sports" in search of big game and big fish patronized "sporting camps" throughout the North Woods. Thanks to the rise in popularity of fly-fishing and easily maneuverable canoes, women were able to share in North Woods soft adventure. Splendid lakeside hotels were built on the Rangeley Lakes and Moosehead, and farms took in boarders throughout the Western Lakes region. Along the coast and on dozens of islands, hotels of every size were built, most by Maine natives. Blue-collar workers came by trolley to summer religious camp meetings, and the wealthy built themselves elaborate summer "cottages" on islands and around Bar Harbor, Camden, and Boothbay Harbor. Developments and sophisticated landscaping transformed much of the previously ignored sandy Southern Coast.

Although it's difficult to document, it's safe to say that Maine attracted the same number of visitors in the summer of 1900 that it did in 2000. This picture altered little for another decade. Then came World War I, coinciding with the proliferation of the Model A.

The 1922 founding of the Maine Publicity Bureau (the present Maine Tourism Association), we suspect, reflects the panic of hoteliers (founder Hiram Ricker himself owned three of the state's grandest hotels: the Mount Kineo House, the Poland Spring House, and the Samoset). Over the next few years these hotels went the way of passenger service, and "motorists" stuck to motor courts and motels along Route 1 and a limited number of inland routes.

By the late 1960s, when Chris began writing about Maine, much of the state had all but dropped off the tourist map, and in the decades since she has chronicled the reawakening of most of the old resort areas. Whale-watching and whitewater rafting, skiing and snowmobiling, windjamming and kayaking, outlet shopping, and the renewed popularity of country inns and the spread of B&Bs have all contributed to this reawakening. Maine is, after all, magnificent. It was just a matter of time.

Recently the extent of waterside (both coastal and inland) walks open to the public has dramatically increased. It's interesting to note that this phenomenon of preserving and maintaining outstanding landscapes—from Ogunquit's Marginal Way to the core of what's now Acadia National Park—was also an offshoot of Maine's first tourism boom.

A major change in this edition of *Maine: An Explorer's Guide* is the increase in web sites we include for lodging places as well as chambers of commerce, attractions, and activities. Web site visuals can now amplify our own descriptions. We assume that readers understand the difference between promotional images on the web and information based on the experience of personally seeing and choosing among what's out there. This book is now, in effect, a sophisticated, unbiased, and—we hope—the ultimate Maine search engine.

While the number of Maine guidebooks has proliferated too, we remain proud of the depth and scope of this one. We strive not only to update details but also to simplify the format and to sharpen the word pictures that describe each area.

This book's introductory section, "What's Where in Maine," is a quick reference directory to a vast variety of information about the state. The remainder of the book describes Maine region by region. The basic criterion for including an area is the availability of lodging.

Note that "off-season" prices are often substantially lower than those in July and August. September is dependably sparkling and frequently warm. Early October in Maine is just as spectacular as it is in New Hampshire and Vermont, with magnificent mountains rising from inland lakes as well as the golds and reds set against coastal blue. It's also well worth noting that the inland ski resorts of Sunday River near Bethel and the Sugarloaf area are "off-season" all summer as well as fall.

Maine is almost as big as the other five New England states combined, but her residents add up to less than half the population of greater Boston. That means there is plenty of room for all who look to her for renewal—both residents and out-of-staters.

It's our hope that, although this book should help visitors and Maine residents alike enjoy the state's resort towns, it will be particularly useful for those who explore off the beaten track.

We would like to thank Ann Kraybill in particular at The Countryman Press for shepherding this monster manuscript through the many stages of production. We would both also like to thank Charlene Williams, Nancy Marshall, and Nat Bowditch for their unfailing response to all cries for help with gathering information throughout Maine, as well as New Brunswick's Lee Heenan.

Chris owes thanks, as always, to Virginia Fieldman in Jonesboro, also to Robert Godfrey of Eastport. Moving down the coast, heartfelt thanks are due to Joel and Leslie Harlow of Sullivan Harbor, Nicole Purslow of Hancock, Helene and Roy Harton of Bar Harbor, Sue Bonkowski and Toby Strong of Southwest Harbor and Gerrie Sweet of

Northeast, Cynthia Leif and Frances Jo Bartlett of Islesford, Jill Hoy and Charlotte Cosgrain of Stonington, Ann and Bob Hamilton of Brooklin, Jim and Sally Littlefield and Bette Noble of Brooksville, and Nancy and Bruce Suppes of Stockton Springs. In Rockland, thank you Shari Closter; Ken, Ellen, and Susan Barnes; and Regan and John Cary. On Vinalhaven, thank you Fred and Bena Pillsbury, Phil Crossman, and Roy Heisler. On Monhegan, thanks go to the friendly staff of the revitalized Trailing Yew. Thanks also to Kim Maxcy in Damariscotta, to the Phinney family in New Harbor, to Mary and Frank Shorey of Bailey's Island, and to Susan and Bill Menz of South Harpswell. In Portland, thanks to Jessica Turner, Jessica Roy, and Dale Northrup; in Kennebunkport, to Karen Arel and Sandra Severance; in Ogunquit, to Eleanor Vadenais and the Andrews family; in York, to Sue Antal and Lou Hogan. Thanks, too, to New Brunswick's Valerie Kidney and to Laura Buckley of Grand Manan. Last but not least, wholehearted thanks are due the world's most helpful and long-suffering husband, William A. Davis.

Elizabeth owes thanks to Catherine Pullen in Freeport, Nick Bayard in Bath, Jamie Kleinstiver in Boothbay Harbor, Heather Mackey and Peter Smith in Camden, Vicki Farrell in Calais, Maureen Aube in Oxford Hills, Julia Reuter in Bethel, Evelyn McAllister in Rangeley, Cheryl Fullerton at Sugarloaf, Peter Thompson and Dawn Stickney in Augusta, Toni Blake in Greenville, Joan Moscone in Millinocket, Louise Howard in Bangor, Kim Douston in Fort Kent, and Kate McCartney in Caribou. She also thanks her new husband, Craig, for his unwavering support and assistance.

We would also like to thank all the people who have taken the time to write about their experiences in Maine. We can't tell you how much your input—or simply your reactions to how we have described things—means to us. We welcome your comments and appreciate all your thoughtful suggestions for the next edition of *Maine: An Explorer's Guide*. Note the postcard in this book for that purpose. You can also contact us directly by e-mail: ctree@traveltree.net or emroundy@aol.com.

What's Where in Maine

AREA CODE
The area code throughout Maine is 207.

ABENAKI
See *Wabanaki*.

ACADIANS
Acadians trace their lineage to French settlers who came to farm and fish in Nova Scotia in the early 1600s and who, in 1755, were forcibly deported by an English governor. This "Great Disturbance," dispersing a population of some 10,000 Acadians, brutally divided families. In a meadow overlooking the St. John River at Madawaska's **Tante Blanche Museum,** a large marble cross marks the spot on which several hundred displaced Acadians landed in 1787. **Village Acadien,** a dozen buildings forming a mini–museum village just west of Van Buren, only begins to tell the story. Acadian scholarship is centered at the University of Maine, Fort Kent. While the sizable Franco-American communities in Biddeford, Lewiston, and Brunswick have a different history (their forebears were recruited from Quebec to work in 19th-century mills), they have shared a long repression of their culture and recent resurgence of pride in a shared French heritage. **La Kermesse,** held in late June in Biddeford, is a major Franco-American festival, as is the **Festival de Joie** in Lewiston.

Contact the Maine Acadian Heritage Council (728-6826) for more information.

AGRICULTURAL FAIRS
The season opens in late June and runs through the first week of October, culminating with the large, colorful, immensely popular (traffic backs up for miles) **Fryeburg Fair.** Among the best traditional fairs are the **Union Fair** (late August) and the **Blue Hill Fair** (Labor Day weekend). The **Common Ground Country Fair** (late September, at the fairgrounds in Unity) draws Maine's back-to-the-earth and organic gardeners from all corners of the state. Request a pamphlet listing all the fairs from the Maine Department of Agriculture (287-3491), 28 State House Station, Augusta 04333; www.mainefoodandfarms.com.

AIRPORTS AND AIRLINES
Portland International Jetport (774-7301), with connections to most large American and Canadian cities, is served by eight carriers: Continental Airlines (1-800-525-0280), Delta Air Lines (1-800-221-1212), United Airlines (1-800-241-6522), U.S. Airways (1-800-428-4322), American Airlines (1-800-433-7300), Air Nova, TWA (1-800-221-2000), and Northwest Airlink (1-800-225-2525). **Bangor International Airport** (947-0384; www.flybangor.com), serving

northern and Down East Maine, also offers connections to all parts of the U.S. via American Eagle/BEX, U.S. Airways (1-800-428-4322), PanAm, and Delta Connections (1-800-221-1212). Colgan Air operates U.S. Airways flights (1-800-428-4322) to **Hancock County Regional Airport** (Trenton/Bar Harbor), **Augusta State Airport,** and **Knox County Regional Airport** (Rockland/Owls Head). **Northern Maine Regional Airport** (Presque Isle) is served by Business Express (1-800-433-7300) and U.S. Airways (1-800-428-4322).

AIR SERVICES

Also called flying services, these are useful links with wilderness camps and coastal islands. Greenville, prime jumping-off point for the North Woods, claims to be New England's largest seaplane base. In this book flying services are also listed under *Getting There* or *Getting Around* in "Rangeley Lakes Region," "Moosehead Lake Area," "Katahdin Region," and "Washington County and the Quoddy Loop." Check *Getting There* in "Rockland/Thomaston Area" for air taxis to several islands, including Vinalhaven, North Haven, and Matinicus.

AMTRAK

Passenger service has been in the works for over a decade and has again been postponed due to the Big Dig near Boston's North Station. In fall 2000 they were projecting that service would begin in April 2001. We'll see. The service, when it finally begins, will include stops in Wells, Old Orchard Beach, and Portland. Phone 1-800-USA-RAIL or look them up on the web at www.amtrak. com.

AMUSEMENT PARKS

Funtown/Splashtown USA in Saco is Maine's biggest, with rides, water slides, and pools. **Aquaboggan** (pools and slides) is also

KIM GRANT

on Route 1 in Saco. **Palace Playland** in Old Orchard Beach is a classic, with a carousel, a Ferris wheel, rides, and a 60-foot water slide. **York's Wild Kingdom** at York Beach has a zoo and amusement area.

ANTIQUARIAN BOOKS

Maine is well known among book buffs as a browsing mecca. Within this book we have noted antiquarian bookstores where they cluster along Route 1 in Wells and in Portland. **Maine Antiquarian Booksellers** publishes a printed directory of more than 80 members. Request a copy by calling 645-4122. You can also download it at their web site: www.mainebooksellers.org.

ANTIQUES

A member directory listing more than 100 dealers is produced by the **Maine Antiques Dealers' Association, Inc.** The association maintains an active web site listing members as well as auctions: www.maineantiques. org. Another useful resource is the monthly *Maine Antiques Digest* (www.maineantiques digest.com), available in many bookstores.

APPALACHIAN TRAIL (AT)

The 275 Maine miles of this 2,144-mile Georgia-to-Maine footpath enters the state in the Mahoosuc Range (see the "Bethel Area" map), accessible there from Grafton Notch State Park (the Mahoosuc Notch section is extremely difficult), and continues north into the Rangeley and Sugarloaf areas, on up through the Upper Kennebec Valley to Monson. West of Moosehead Lake it runs through Gulf Hagas and on around Nahmakanta Lake, through Abol Bridge to Baxter State Park, ending at the summit of 5,267-foot Mount Katahdin. Hikes along the trail are noted within specific chapters; lodging places catering to AT through-hikers include **Mrs. G's B&B** and **Harrison's Pierce Pond Sporting Camps** in Bingham, **Shaw's Boarding House** in Monson, and **Little Lyford Pond Camps** near Gulf Hagas. For a list of publications, write to Appalachian Trail Conference, P.O. Box 807, Harpers Ferry, WV 25425-0807.

APPLES
Fall brings plenty of pick-your-own opportunities across the state, and many orchards also sell apples and cider. For a list of orchards, contact the Department of Agriculture (287-3491). Information about orchards, mail order, and recipes can also be found on the Department of Agriculture's web site: www.getrealmaine.com. In York the **Parsons Family Winery** is putting an old orchard to new uses.

AQUARIUMS
The **Department of Marine Resources Aquarium** in Boothbay Harbor displays regional fish and sea creatures, many of them surprisingly colorful. The stars of the show are the sharks and skates in a large touch tank. The **Mount Desert Oceanarium** is a commercial attraction with several locations in the Bar Harbor area.

ART ASSOCIATIONS AND COUNCILS
In recent years there has been a proliferation of regional associations and councils dedicated to promoting the arts within a specific area. Many of these organizations are producing detailed listings of arts-related organizations, individual artists, and businesses in the arts, in conjunction with the **Maine Arts Commission.** The commission has a searchable database on the web (www.mainearts.com) that can help you find area councils and listings. **Cultural directories** are currently available for central Aroostook, Rangeley Lakes, Lincoln County, Hancock County, and the Brunswick area. More are in the works.

ARTISTS AND ART GALLERIES
Maine's dramatic coastal and island scenery, her lakes and mountains, have drawn major artists since the mid–19th century, and the experience of art as a major part of the Maine visitor's experience has dramatically increased in recent years. Within each chapter we describe a good percentage of the commercial galleries that have proliferated throughout the state but especially in Portland, Rockland, Northeast Harbor, Stonington, Blue Hill, and Eastport. Several recent art books are also popularizing the

© ERIC HOPKINS

work of dozens of significant artists; a standout is *Art of the Maine Islands* by Carl Little and Arnold Skolnick (Down East Books). Artist-owned galleries, which have become destinations in their own right, are found in Sullivan and Stonington and on the islands of Monhegan, North Haven, and Little Cranberry. For weeklong summer art workshops, see our *To Do—Special Learning Programs* listings in Stonington (see "Deer Isle, Stonington, and Isle au Haut") and Rockland (see "Rockland/Thomaston Area"). For summer art programs, see *Camps, for Adults.*

ART MUSEUMS

The **Portland Museum of Art (PMA)** is one of the country's fine smaller museums with a strong collection of works by impressionist and postimpressionist masters as well as Winslow Homer. The collection of Maine art has been significantly augmented in recent years and special exhibits are frequently outstanding. The **Farnsworth Art Museum** and its **Center for the Wyeth Family in Maine** in Rockland, moreover, has a stellar collection of Maine art, as well as frequent special exhibits that draw art lovers from around the country. The **Ogunquit Museum of American Art,** the **Bowdoin College Museum of Art** in Brunswick, and the **Colby College Museum of Art** in Waterville (see "Augusta and Mid-Maine") are all described within their respective chapters. Seven of the state's museums have formed a partnership called the **Maine Art Museum Trail** and publish a brochure describing each of these museums. A copy can be requested at 1-800-782-6497, or peruse their web site: www.maineartmuseums.com.

BALLOONING

Hot-air balloon rides are available across the state from **Balloons over New England** (499-7575; 1-800-788-5562) in Kennebunk-

KIM GRANT

port, **Hot Fun** (799-0193) in South Portland, **Balloon Rides** (1-800-952-2076) in Portland, and **Sails Aloft** (623-1136) in Augusta.

BEACHES

Less than 5 percent of the Maine coast is public, and not all of that is beach. Given the summer temperature of the water (from 59 degrees in Ogunquit to 54 degrees at Bar Harbor), swimming isn't the primary reason you come to Maine. But Maine beaches (for instance at York, Wells, the Kennebunks, Portland, Popham, and Pemaquid) can be splendid walking, sunning, and kite-flying places. At **Ogunquit** and in **Reid State Park,** there are also warmer backwater areas in which small children can paddle. Families tend to take advantage of the reasonably priced cottages available on lakes, many of them just a few miles from the seashore (see *Lakes*). Other outstanding beaches include 7-mile-long **Old Orchard Beach** and, nearby, state-maintained **Crescent Beach** on Cape Elizabeth; **Scarborough Beach** in Scarborough, **Ferry Beach** in Saco, and **Sand Beach** in Acadia National Park. The big, state-maintained freshwater beaches are on **Lakes Damariscotta, St. George, Sebec, Rangeley, Sebago,** and **Moosehead;** also on **Pleasant Pond** in Richmond. All state beaches include changing facilities, rest rooms, and showers; many have snack bars. The town of Bridgton has several fine little lakeside beaches.

BED & BREAKFASTS

We have visited hundreds of B&Bs and been impressed by what we have seen. They range from elegant town houses and country mansions to farms and fishermen's homes. Prices vary from $45 to $475 (on the coast in August) for a double and average $100 to $150 in high season on the coast. With few exceptions, they offer a friendly entrée to their communities. Hosts are usually delighted to advise guests on places to explore, dine, and shop. "The Maine Guide to Inns and Bed & Breakfasts," published by the Maine Tourism Association, is free and can be picked up at visitors centers or requested by calling 1-800-533-9595.

BICYCLING

Mountain biking is particularly popular on the carriage roads in **Acadia National Park.** Four ski areas also specialize in summer mountain biking: **Sunday River** in the Bethel area and **Shawnee Peak** in Bridgton offer lift-assisted, high-altitude trails; **Lost Valley** in Auburn opens its trails to mountain bikers, and **Sugarloaf/USA** offers rentals and trail maps to trails on and off the mountain. Biking on the Kineo peninsula is also popular, as is biking on several islands off the coast, especially those in Casco Bay. Bicycle touring is, however, limited. Route 1 is too heavily trafficked, and rural roads are generally narrow, curved, and have no shoulder, making them unsuitable for bicycling. Dedicated recreation paths are beginning to appear, notably in Portland and Brunswick/Bath. Bicycling also makes sense in heavily touristed resort areas in which a car can be a nuisance; rentals are available in Ogunquit, Kennebunkport, Portland, Camden, Southwest Harbor, Northeast Harbor, and Bar Harbor; also in Bethel and Rangeley. Hostelling International maintains nominally priced, bicyclist-geared hostels described in "Bar Harbor and Ellsworth"

and "Oxford Hills and Lewiston/Auburn." Also check out *25 Bicycle Tours in Maine* by Howard Stone (Backcountry Guides).

The "Maine Bicycle Map" published by the Maine DOT represents a massive effort to identify roads throughout the state that are scenic, wide shouldered, and relatively little trafficked; for a copy, phone 287-6600. You can also check the Internet at www.state.me.us/mdot/biketours.htm for a description of 21 tours ranging from 20 to 100 miles. The **Bicycle Coalition of Maine** (BCM; 623-4511; www.bikemaine.org) serves as a conduit for information about both off- and on-road bicycling throughout the state, and maintains a calendar of bicycling events; request an information packet from BCM, P.O. Box 5275, Augusta 04332.

BIRDING

The **Maine Audubon Society** (781-2330; www.maineaudubon.org), based at Gilsland Farm in Falmouth, maintains a number of birding sites and sponsors nature programs and field trips, which include cruises to Matinicus Rock and to Eagle Island. (For details about the **National Audubon Ecology Camp** on Hog Island, see "Damariscotta/Newcastle and Pemaquid Area.") **Laudholm Farm** in Wells, **Biddeford Pool, Scarborough Marsh, Merrymeeting Bay,** and **Mount Desert** (see www.mainebirding.net) are also popular birding sites. **Monhegan** is the island to visit. The **Moosehorn National Wildlife Refuge** (454-3521) in Washington County represents the northeastern terminus of the East Coast chain of wildlife refuges and is particularly rich in bird life. We recommend *Birder's Guide to Maine* by Elizabeth Cary Pierson, Jan Erik Pierson, and Peter D. Vickery (Down East Books). (Also see *Puffin-Watching* and *Nature Preserves, Coastal* and *Inland*.) The official state bird is the chickadee.

KIM GRANT

BLUEBERRYING

Maine grows 98 percent of America's low-bush blueberries. More than 65.5 million pounds are harvested annually from an estimated 25,000 acres. There are absolutely no human-planted wild blueberry fields. Low-bush blueberry plants spread naturally. Few growers allow U-pick, at least not until the commercial harvest is over. (One exception is **Staples Homestead Blueberries** in Stockton Springs.) Then the public is invited to go "stumping" for leftovers. On the other hand, berrying along roads and hiking paths is a rite of summer. The **blueberry barrens**—thousands of blueberry-covered acres—spread across Cherryfield, Columbia, and Machias (site of the state's most colorful blueberry festival in August) in Washington County. For more about Maine's famous fruit, write: Wild Blueberry Association of North America, 59 Cottage Street, Bar Harbor 04609; call 1-800-add-wild; or click on www.wildblueberries.com.

BOATBUILDING

WoodenBoat School (359-4651) in Brooklin (see "Blue Hill Area") offers more than 75 warm-weather courses, including more than 24 on various aspects of boat-building. The **Maine Maritime Museum** in Bath offers an apprenticeship program; the **Landing School of Boatbuilding and Design** in Kennebunk offers summer courses in building sailboats; the **Appren-**

ticeshop Boat Building School (594-1800) in Rockland offers 2-year apprentice programs and 6-week (or longer) internships; and the **Washington County Technical College Marine Trades Center** at Eastport attracts many out-of-staters.

BOAT EXCURSIONS

You don't need to own your own yacht to enjoy the salt spray and views, and you really won't know what Maine is about until you stand off at sea to appreciate the beauty of the cliffs and island-dotted bays. For the greatest concentrations of boat excursions, see "Boothbay Harbor Region," "Rockland/ Thomaston Area," and "Bar Harbor and Ellsworth"; there are also excursions from Ogunquit, Kennebunkport, Portland, Belfast, Camden, Castine, and Stonington. (Also see *Coastal Cruises; Ferries, in Maine* and *to Canada; Sailing;* and *Windjammer Cruises.* See "Sebago and Long Lakes Region" and "Augusta and Mid-Maine" for lake excursions.) A partial list of more than 50

KIM GRANT

cruises, ferries, and deep-sea-fishing options is published in the Maine Tourism Association's annual free magazine, "Maine Invites You" (see *Information*).

BOOKS

Anyone who seriously sets out to explore Maine should read the following mix of Maine classics and guidebooks: *The Maine Woods* by Henry David Thoreau, first published posthumously in 1864, remains very readable and gives an excellent description of Maine's mountains (we recommend the Penguin edition). Our favorite relatively recent Maine author is Ruth Moore, who writes about Maine islands in *The Weir, Spoonhandle,* and *Speak to the Wind* (originally published in the 1940s and reissued by Blackberry Books, Nobleboro); happily, the 1940s books by Louise Dickinson Rich, among which our favorites are *The Coast of Maine: An Informal History* and *We Took to the Woods,* are now published by Down East Books in Camden, along with Henry Beston's 1940s classic *Northern Farm: A Chronicle of Maine.* Sarah Orne Jewett's classic, *The Country of the Pointed Firs and Other Stories* (W. W. Norton), first published in 1896, is still an excellent read, set on the coast around Tenants Harbor. The children's classics by Robert McCloskey, *Blueberries for Sal* (1948), *Time of Wonder* (1957), and *One Morning in Maine* (1952), are as fresh as the day they were written. John Gould, an essayist who wrote a regular column for the *Christian Science Monitor* for more than 50 years, has published several books, including *Dispatches from Maine,* a collection of those columns, and *Maine Lingo* (with Lillian Ross), a humorous look at Maine phrases and expressions. E. B. White has some wonderful essay collections as well, along with his ever-popular children's novels, *Charlotte's Web* and *Stuart Little.*

Recent classics set in Maine include Carolyn Chute's *The Beans of Egypt, Maine* (1985), *Letourneau's Used Auto Parts* (1988), and *Merry Men* (1994), and Cathie Pelletier's *The Funeral Makers* (1987) and *The Weight of Winter* (1991). *Maine Speaks,* an anthology of Maine literature published by the Maine Writers and Publishers Alliance (see "Brunswick and the Harpswells"), contains all the obvious poems and essays and many pleasant surprises; *The Maine Reader,* edited by Charles and Samuella Shain, is an anthology of writing from the 1600s to the present.

Guides to exploring Maine include the indispensable *Maine Atlas and Gazetteer* (DeLorme) and, from Down East Books, *Birder's Guide to Maine* by Elizabeth Cary Pierson, Jan Erik Pierson, and Peter D. Vickery; *Walking the Maine Coast* by John Gibson; and *Islands in Time: A Natural and Cultural History of the Islands of the Gulf of Maine* by Philip W. Conkling. Serious hikers should secure the *AMC Maine Mountain Guide* (AMC Books); also *50 Hikes in the Maine Mountains* by Cloe Chunn and *50 Hikes in Coastal and Southern Maine* by John Gibson (both Backcountry Guides). Also worth noting, though it's out of print and may be hard to find: *Maine,* by Charles C. Calhoun (Compass American Guides), complements this guide with its superb illustrations and well-written background text.

BUS SERVICE

Concord Trailways (1-800-639-3317) serves Portland, Brunswick, Bath, Wiscasset, Damariscotta, Waldoboro, Rockland, Camden, Belfast, Searsport, Bangor, and the University of Maine at Orono (when school is in session). **Greyhound Bus Lines/Vermont Transit** (1-800-221-2222) serves Augusta, Lewiston, Waterville, Portland, and Bangor.

CAMPING

Almost half of Maine lies within "unorganized townships": wooded, privately owned lands, most of which are open to the public on the condition that basic rules be observed. These rules vary with the owners. See "The North Woods" chapters for details about camping within these vast fiefdoms, and also for camping in **Baxter State Park** (see *Green Space* in "Katahdin Region") and along the **Allagash Wilderness Waterway** (see *To Do—Canoeing* in "Aroostook County"). For camping within **Acadia National Park,** see "Acadia National Park." For the same within the **White Mountain National Forest,** see "Bethel Area." For private campgrounds, the booklet "Maine Camping Guide," published by the Maine Campground Owners Association (782-5874; www.campmaine.com), lists most privately operated camping and tenting areas. Request a copy from MCOA, 655 Main Street, Lewiston 04240. Reservations are advised for the state's 13 parks that offer camping (see *Parks, State*). We have attempted to describe the state parks in detail wherever they appear in this book (see Damariscotta, Camden, Cobscook Bay, Sebago, Rangeley, and Greenville). Note that though campsites can accommodate average-sized campers and trailers, there are no trailer hook-ups. **Warren Island** (just off Islesboro) and **Swan Island** (just off Richmond) offer organized camping, and primitive camping is permitted on a number of islands through the **Maine Island Trail Association** (MITA; see *Islands*). Within this book we occasionally describe outstanding campgrounds.

CAMPS, FOR ADULTS

The **Appalachian Mountain Club** (617-523-0636; www.outdoors.org) maintains a number of summer lodges and campsites for adults and families seeking a hiking and/or canoeing vacation. Intended primarily for members, they are open to all who reserve space, available only after April 1. The full-service camps in Maine (offering three daily meals, organized hikes, evening programs) are at **Echo Lake** on Mount Desert and **Cold River Camp** in Evans Notch (near the New Hampshire border within the White Mountain National Forest). The Rockland-based **Hurricane Island Outward Bound School** offers a variety of adult-geared outdoor adventures on Hurricane Island (off Vinalhaven), in Newry (near Bethel), and in Greenville, as well as throughout the country. The **National Audubon Ecology Camp** on Hog Island off Bremen offers a series of weeklong courses (see "Damariscotta/Newcastle and Pemaquid Area"). The **University of Maine at Machias** offers summer ornithology workshops. Photographers should check out the **Maine Photographic Workshops** in Rockport; also see *Boatbuilding* (**WoodenBoat** offers much more than boatbuilding) and check **Elderhostel** (617-426-7788), which offers a variety of programs throughout Maine for everyone over age 60. Art courses include **Merle Donovan's Maine Coast Workshops** in Rockland and the **Stonington Painter's Workshop** in Stonington. The most prestigious summer arts workshop in Maine is the **Skowhegan School of Painting and Sculpture** (474-9345 or 212-529-0505). Also see the **Haystack Mountain School** under *Crafts*.

CAMPS, FOR CHILDREN

More than 200 summer camps are listed in the exceptional booklet published annually by the Maine Youth Camping Association (581-1350), P.O. Box 455, Orono 04473. Also check the online guide www.camppage.com for listings.

KIM GRANT

CAMPS, RENTAL

In Maine *camp* is the word for a second home or cottage. See *Cottage Rentals* for inexpensive vacation rentals.

CANOEING, GUIDED TRIPS

The slow-moving, shallow **Saco River** is great for beginners and offers a number of well-maintained camping sites. Several outfitters in the Fryeburg area (see *To Do* in "Sebago and Long Lakes Region") offer rentals and shuttle service, and **Saco Bound,** just over the New Hampshire line, offers guided tours. The **Moose River** near Jackman (see *To Do* in "The Upper Kennebec Valley and Moose River Valley") offers a similar camping/canoeing trip, and **Sunrise Canoe Expeditions,** based on Cathance Lake (see *To Do* in "Calais and the St. Croix Valley") offers guided trips down the Grand Lake chain of lakes and the St. Croix River. Also see www.maineoutdoors.com.

CANOEING THE ALLAGASH

The ultimate canoe trip in Maine (and on the entire East Coast, for that matter) is the 7- to 10-day expedition up the Allagash Wilderness Waterway, a 92-mile ribbon of lakes, ponds, rivers, and streams in the heart of northern Maine's vast commercial forests. Since 1966 the land flanking the waterway has been owned (500 feet back on either side of the waterway) by the state of Maine. Amid considerable controversy, the state has recently decided to make vehicle access to the waterway easier. We still advise using a shuttle service. The general information numbers for the Allagash Wilderness Waterway are 941-4014 and 435-7963. A map pinpointing the 65 authorized campsites within the zone (and supplying other crucial information) is available free from the Bureau of Parks and Lands (287-4984), State House Station 22, Augusta 04333. A more detailed map, backed with historical and a variety of other handy information, is DeLorme's "Map and Guide to the Allagash and St. John." Anybody contemplating the trip should be aware of blackflies in June and the "no-see-ums" when warm weather finally comes. For further information, see *Camping* and *Guide Services,* and check out www.maineoutdoors.com. Also see *To Do—Canoeing* in "Aroostook County."

CHILDREN, ESPECIALLY FOR

Throughout this book, restaurants, lodgings, and attractions that are of special interest to families with children are indicated by the crayon symbol *✐* in the margin.

CLAMMING

Maine state law permits the harvesting of shellfish for personal use only, unless you have a commercial license. Individuals can take up to ½ bushel of shellfish or 3 bushels of hen or surf clams (the big ones out in the flats) in 1 day, unless municipal ordinances further limit "the taking of shellfish." Be sure

KIM GRANT

to check locally at the town clerk's office (source of licenses) before you dig, and make sure there's no red tide. Some towns do prohibit clamming, and in certain places there is a temporary stay on harvesting while the beds are being seeded.

COASTAL CRUISES

Cruise is a much used (and abused) term along the Maine coast, chiefly intended to mean a boat ride. "Maine Invites You" has a list of over 50 cruises, ferries, and deep-sea-fishing choices, most of them described in the appropriate chapters of this book. We have also tried to list the charter sailing yachts that will take passengers on multiday cruises and have described each of the windjammers that sail for 3 and 6 days at a time (see *Windjammer Cruises*).

COTTAGE RENTALS

Cottage rentals are the only reasonably priced way to go for families who wish to stay in one Maine spot for a week or more (unless you camp). Request the booklet "Maine Guide to Camp and Cottage Rentals" from the Maine Office of Tourism (1-800-533-9595), or contact the Maine Tourism Association (623-0363; www.maine tourism.com). We recommend contacting local real estate agencies. Printouts are available for a small fee by writing to the Maine Department of Business Regulation, Central Licensing Division, State House Station 35, Augusta 04333 (287-2217). Many local chambers of commerce also keep a list of available rentals.

COVERED BRIDGES

Of the 120 covered bridges that once spanned Maine rivers, just 9 survive. The most famous, and certainly picturesque, is the **Artists' Covered Bridge** (1872) over the Sunday River in Newry, northwest of Bethel. The others are: **Porter Bridge**

(1876), over the Ossipee River, 0.5 mile south of Porter; **Babb's Bridge,** rebuilt after burning in 1973 , over the Presumpscot River between Gorham and Windham; **Hemlock Bridge** (1857), 3 miles northwest of East Fryeburg; **Lovejoy Bridge** (1883), over the Ellis River in South Andover; **Bennett Bridge** (1901), over the Magalloway River, 1.5 miles south of the Wilson's Mills post office; **Robyville Bridge** (1876), Maine's only completely shingled covered bridge, in the town of Corinth; the **Watson Settlement Bridge** (1911), between Woodstock and Littleton; and **Low's Bridge,** carefully reconstructed in 1990 after a flood took the 1857 structure, across the Piscataquis River between Guilford and Sangerville.

CRAFTS

"Maine Cultural Guide," available free from the **Maine Crafts Association** (780-1807; www.mainecrafts.maine.com), 15 Walton Street, Portland 04103, is a geographical listing of studios, galleries, and museums throughout Maine. **"Directions,"** published by the **Maine Crafts Guild** (P.O. Box 10832, Portland 04104), lists members by category and the annual schedule of shows. **United Maine Craftsmen, Inc.** (621-2818), also sponsors several large shows each year. **Haystack Mountain School of Crafts** (see "Deer Isle, Stonington, and Isle au Haut") is a summer school nationally respected in a variety of crafts. They offer 3-week courses beginning mid-June and continuing through mid-September. Applicants must be more than 18 years old; enrollment is limited to 65. Work by students is displayed in the visitors center, which also serves as a forum for frequent evening presentations. The surrounding area (Blue Hill to Stonington) contains the largest concentration of Maine craftspeople, many of whom invite visitors into their studios.

MAINE OFFICE OF TOURISM

DOGSLEDDING

Although racing is a long-established winter spectator sport, the chance actually to ride on a dogsled is relatively recent and growing in popularity. In Newry, Polly Mahoney and Kevin Slater at **Mahoosuc Mountain Adventures** (824-2073) offer multiday treks with their huskies. In the Moosehead Lake region Stephen Medera's **Song in the Woods** (876-4736) offers full-day trips on which you actually do the driving; we were surprised at how smoothly the dogs responded to our commands on a 10-mile woods road.

EVENTS

We have listed outstanding annual events within each chapter of this book, and leaflet guides to events are published by the state four times a year. Events are listed on the web: **www.visitmaine.com.**

FACTORY OUTLETS

Individual outlet stores seem to be popping up throughout the state, but if a full day of shopping is what you are after, Kittery and Freeport are still your best bets (see "Kittery and the Yorks" and "Freeport").

FALL FOLIAGE

Autumn days tend to be clear, and the changing leaves against the blue sea and lakes can be spectacular. Many inns remain open through foliage season, and the major resort towns all offer excellent dining, shop-

ping, and lodging through Columbus Day weekend. Off-season prices prevail, in contrast with the rest of New England, at this time of year. Check the Maine Office of Tourism web site, www.visitmaine.com, for frequently updated foliage reports and suggested routes.

FARM B&BS

The Maine Farm Vacation B&B Association describes its 17 members in its brochure, and at www.mainefarmvacation.com. This is a promotional association, not an officially approved and inspected group. Properties vary widely. Some offer plenty of space, animals, big breakfasts, friendly, informal atmosphere, but others are not working farms. The properties are scattered across Maine. Though we haven't made it to all of those listed yet, the ones we have seen are recommended in their regions. We wish there were some in Aroostook County. Brochures are available from RR 3, 377 Gray Road, Route 26, West Falmouth 04105 (797-5540; fax, 797-7599; quakerbb@aol.com).

FARMER'S MARKETS

The **Maine Department of Agriculture** (Division of Market and Production Development, 28 State House Station, Augusta 04330; 287-3491; maine.grown@state.me.us) lists on their web site (www.mainefoodand farms.com) more than 50 markets. A list can also be found in "Maine Invites You" (see *Information*).

FERRIES, TO CANADA

Portland to Yarmouth, Nova Scotia: **Prince of Fundy Cruises** offers nightly sailings (departing 9:30 PM) late April through the Columbus Day weekend. The ferry itself is a car-carrying cruise ship with gambling, restaurants, and cabins aboard (1-800-482-0955 in Maine; 1-800-341-7540 from elsewhere in the United States). **Northumberland/Bay Ferries** (1-888-249-7245) operates a high-speed catamaran ("The Cat") between Bar Harbor and Yarmouth (spring through fall). Note that it's very possible to use these ferries as part of a loop: going on one and returning on the other. Mid-June through mid-September **East Coast Ferries Ltd.** (506-747-2159), a small car ferry based on Deer Island, serves Eastport (30 minutes) and Campobello (45 minutes), and the small provincial (free) **Deer Island–L'Etete Ferry** (506-453-2600) connects Deer Island with the New Brunswick mainland. The 65-car **Coastal Transport Ltd. Ferry** (506-662-3724) runs year-round from Blacks Harbour, not far east of L'Etete, to the island of Grand Manan.

FERRIES, IN MAINE

Maine State Ferry Service (1-800-491-4883), Rockland 04841, operates year-round service from Rockland to Vinalhaven and North Haven, from Lincolnville to Islesboro, and from Bass Harbor to Swan's Island and Frenchboro. They also run once a month (more in summer) from Rockland to Matinicus. For private ferry services to Monhegan, see "Boothbay Harbor Region" and "Midcoast Islands"; for the Casco Bay islands, see "Portland Area"; for Matinicus, see "Midcoast Islands"; and for Isle au Haut, see "East Penobscot Bay Region."

FILM

Northeast Historic Film (1-800-639-1636; fax, 469-7875) is based at "The

KIM GRANT

Alamo," a vintage 1916 movie house (P.O. Box 900, Bucksport 04416) that Northeast Historic Film has restored. This admirable group has created a regional moving-image archive of films based on or made in New England that were shown in every small town during the first part of the 20th century. Films also record life in the lumbering and fishing industries. Request the catalog "Videotapes of Life in New England." The **International Film/Television Workshops** in Rockport offers a variety of weeklong courses in various aspects of film. The **Maine International Film Festival** is a 10-day event, with over 60 films shown at the Waterville Opera House and the Railroad Square Cinema. For details, check out their web site at www.miff.org.

FIRE PERMITS

Maine law dictates that no person shall kindle or use outdoor fires without a permit, except at authorized campsites or picnic grounds. Fire permits in the organized townships are obtained from the local town warden; in the unorganized townships, from the nearest forest ranger. Portable stoves fueled by propane gas, gasoline, or sterno are exempt from the rule.

FISHING

"The Maine Guide to Hunting and Fishing," published by the Maine Tourism Association (623-0363) and available by phoning 1-800-533-9595, is a handy overview of rules, license fees, and other matters of interest to fishermen. Detailed descriptions of camps and rustic resorts catering to fishermen can be found in the chapters under "Western Mountains and Lakes Region" and "The North Woods," and in "The Upper Kennebec Valley and Moose River Valley." A 1-day fishing license cost nonresidents $10 in 2000; 3-, 7-, and 15-day licenses are also available at most general stores and sporting-goods outlets or by writing to the Maine Department of Inland Fisheries and Wildlife (287-2571), 284 State Street, Augusta 04333.

FORTS

To be married to a fort freak is to realize that there are people in this world who will detour 50 miles to see an 18th-century earthworks. Maine's forts are actually a fascinating lot, monuments to the state's unique and largely forgotten history. Examples: **Fort William Henry** at Pemaquid, **Fort Edgecomb** in Edgecomb, **Fort George** in Castine, **Fort Knox** near Bucksport, **Fort McClary** in Kittery, **Fort O'Brien** near Machias, **Fort Kent** in Fort Kent, **Fort Popham** near Bath, and **Fort Pownall** at Stockton Springs.

GOLDEN ROAD

This legendary 96-mile road (almost entirely gravel) is the privately owned high road of the North Woods, linking Millinocket's paper mills on the east with commercial wood-

KIM GRANT

lands that extend to the Quebec border. Its name derives from its multimillion-dollar cost in 1975, but its value has proven great to visitors heading up from Moosehead Lake, as well as from Millinocket to Baxter State Park. It's also used by the whitewater rafting companies on the Penobscot River and the Allagash Wilderness Waterway, and for remote lakes like Chesuncook. Expect to pay a user fee for your vehicle and to pull to the side to permit lumber trucks to pass. The road is exceptionally maintained, even (especially) in winter.

GOLF

"Maine Invites You" (see *Information*) lists golf courses across the state. We list them under *To Do* within each chapter. The major resorts catering to golfers are the **Samoset** in Rockport, the **Bethel Inn** in Bethel, **Sebasco Harbor Resort** near Bath, the **Country Club Inn** in Rangeley, and **Sugarloaf/USA** in the Carrabassett Valley.

GORGES

Maine has the lion's share of the Northeast's gorges. There are four biggies. The widest is the **Upper Sebois River Gorge** north of Patten, and the most dramatic, "Maine's Miniature Grand Canyon," is **Gulf Hagas** near the Katahdin Iron Works (see "Katahdin Region"). Both **Kennebec Gorge** and **Ripogenus Gorge** are now popular whitewater rafting routes.

GUIDE SERVICES

In 1897 the Maine legislature passed a bill requiring hunting guides to register with the state; the first to register was Cornelia Thurza Crosby (better known as "Fly Rod" Crosby), whose syndicated column appeared in New York, Boston, and Chicago newspapers at the turn of the 20th century. Becoming a Registered Maine Guide entails passing one of several specialized tests—in hunting, fishing, or one of a growing number of recreational categories, including whitewater rafting, canoeing, or kayaking—administered by the Maine Department of Inland Fisheries and Wildlife. There are currently some 3,000 Registered Maine Guides, but just a few hundred are full-time professional guides. The web site of the 500-member Maine Professional Guides Association is www.maineguides.org.

Also see *Hunting* and *Fishing*.

HANDICAPPED ACCESS

Within this book, handicapped-accessible lodging, restaurants, and attractions are marked with a wheelchair symbol &. Maine, by the way, offers an outstanding handicapped skiing program, both cross-country and alpine; phone 1-800-639-7770.

HIKING

For organized trips, contact the Appalachian Mountain Club. The Maine chapter can be reached at P.O. Box 720, Oakland 04963; www.gwi.net/amcmaine. The Boston office (617-523-0636; www.outdoors.org) is another good source of information. In addition to the *AMC Maine Mountain Guide* (available from AMC Books Division, Department B, 5 Joy Street, Boston, MA 02108) and the AMC map guide to trails on Mount Desert, we recommend investing in *50 Hikes in Coastal and Southern Maine* by John Gibson and *50 Hikes in the Maine Mountains* by Cloe Chunn (both from Backcountry Guides), which offer clear, inviting treks up hills of every size throughout the state. The *Maine Atlas and Gazetteer* (DeLorme) also outlines a number of rewarding hikes. Also see *Appalachian Trail.*

HISTORY

Within this book Maine's rich history is told through the places that still recall or dramatize it. See *Wabanaki* in this section for sites

KIM GRANT

that tell of the long precolonial history. For traces of early-17th-century settlement, see our descriptions of **Phippsburg, Pemaquid,** and **Augusta.** The French and Indian Wars (1675–1760), in which Maine was more involved than most of New England, are recalled in the reconstructed English Fort William Henry at **Pemaquid** and in historical markers scattered around **Castine** (Baron de Saint Castine, a young French nobleman married to a Penobscot Indian princess, controlled the coastal area we now call "Down East"). A striking house built in 1760 on **Kittery Point** (see *To See—Scenic Drives* in "Kittery and the Yorks") evokes Sir William Pepperrell, credited with having captured the fortress at Louisburg from the French, and restored buildings in **York Village** (same chapter) suggests Maine's brief, peaceful colonial period.

In the Burnham Tavern at **Machias** you learn that townspeople captured a British man-of-war on June 1, 1775, the first naval engagement of the Revolution. Other reminders of the Revolution are less triumphant: At the Cathedral Pines in **Eustis** and spotted along Route 202 in the **Upper Kennebec Valley,** historical markers tell the poignant saga of Colonel Benedict Arnold's ill-fated 1775 attempt to capture Quebec. Worse: Markers at Fort George in Castine detail the ways in which a substantial patriot fleet utterly disgraced itself there. Maine's brush with the British didn't end with the Revolution: The Barracks Museum in **East-**

port tells of British occupation again in 1814.

Climb the six steep floors of the newly restored **Portland Observatory** (built 1807) and hear how Portland ranked second among New England ports, its tonnage based on lumber, the resource that fueled fortunes like those evidenced by the amazingly opulent **Colonel Black Mansion** in Ellsworth and the elegant **Ruggles House** way Down East in Columbia Falls. In 1820 Maine finally became a state (the 23rd) but, as we note in our introduction to "The North Woods," not without a price. The mother state, her coffers at their usual low, stipulated an even division of all previously undeeded wilderness, and some 10.5 million acres were quickly sold off, vast privately owned tracts that survive today as the unorganized townships.

Plagued in 1839 by boundary disputes that were ignored in Washington, the new, timber-rich state built its own northern forts (the **Fort Kent Blockhouse** survives). This "Aroostook War" was terminated by the Webster-Ashburton Treaty of 1842, a deal that we note in our introduction to "Washington County and the Quoddy Loop" because it gave Campobello and Grand Manan to Canada (the story goes that it was a foggy night and Webster couldn't see how much nearer the islands are to Maine than to New Brunswick). In 1844 the state built massive **Fort Knox** at the mouth of the Penobscot River (see "Bucksport"), just in case. Never entirely completed, it makes an interesting state park. This era was, however, one of great prosperity and expansion within the new state.

We note in the introduction to "Brunswick and the Harpswells" that it can be argued that the Civil War began and ended there. Unfortunately the state suffered heavy losses: Some 18,000 young soldiers from Maine died, as Civil War monuments remind us. The end of the war, however, ushered in a boom decade. Granite from Maine islands (see "The Fox Islands: Vinalhaven and North Haven") fed the demand for monumental public buildings throughout the country, and both schooners and Down Easters (graceful square-rigged vessels) were in great demand (see the **Penobscot Marine Museum** in "Belfast, Searsport, and Stockton Springs" and the **Maine Maritime Museum** in "Bath Area").

In the late 19th century many Maine industries boomed, tourism included. We describe Maine's tourism history in our introduction because it is so colorful, little recognized, and so much a part of what you see in Maine today.

Maine, the Pine Tree State from Prehistory to the Present by Richard Judd, Edwin Churchill, and Joel Eastman (University of Maine Press) is a good, recent, readable history (paperback).

HORSEBACK RIDING

Northern Maine Riding Adventures (see "Moosehead Lake Area") offers entire days and overnights as well as shorter stints in the saddle, and special-needs riders are welcomed. Also check "Old Orchard Beach, Saco, and Biddeford" "Boothbay Harbor Region," "St. Andrews and Grand Manan," "Bethel Area," "Rangeley Lakes Region," and "Sebago and Long Lakes Region."

HORSE RACING

Harness racing can be found at **Scarborough Downs** (883-4331), Route 1 (exit 6 off the Maine Turnpike), April through November. The **Bangor Raceway** is open late May through late July. Many of the agricultural fairs also feature harness racing. Contact the Maine Harness Racing Commission (287-3221) for more information, or check the web site of the Maine Harness Racing Promotions Board at www.maine harnessracing.com for schedules.

HUNTING

Hunters should obtain a summary of Maine hunting and trapping laws from the Maine Department of Inland Fisheries and Wildlife (287-3371), 284 State Street, Augusta 04333. For leads on Registered Maine Guides who specialize in organized expeditions, contact the sources we list under *Fishing; Guide Services; Canoeing Guided Trips;* and *Camping.* You might also try the **Moosehead Lake Region Chamber of Commerce** (695-2702). "The Maine Guide to Hunting and Fishing," published annually by the Maine Tourism Association (1-800-533-9595), is filled with information and ads for hunting lodges, guides, and the like.

INFORMATION

The Maine Office of Tourism maintains a web site: www.visitmaine.com. Unfortunately, however, there's no staff person to answer specific questions. The information line—1-800-533-9595—connects with a fulfillment clerk at L. L. Bean, who will send you the thick four-season guide "Maine Invites You." They will also send—if you request them—useful specialized booklets: "Maine Guide to Hunting and Fishing," "Maine Guide to Camp & Cottage Rentals," and "Maine Guide to Inns and Bed & Breakfasts," all published by the **Maine Tourism Association,** which maintains its own web site: www.mainetourism.com. You can also e-mail them at mtainfo@mainetourism.com. MTA also operates unusually well-stocked and -staffed welcome centers at its southern gateway at Kittery (439-1319) on I-95 northbound (also accessible from Route 1); just off coastal Route 1 and I-95 in Yarmouth (846-0833); both northbound and southbound on I-95 in Hampden near Bangor (862-6628/6638); in Calais (454-2211); and in Houlton (532-6346). There is also an information center on the New Hampshire line on Route 302 in Fryeburg (935-3639).

KIM GRANT

The Maine Tourism Association has welcome centers on Route 2 in Bethel (shared quarters with the White Mountain National Forest information staff: 824-4582) and at their administrative offices in Hallowell (623-0363). Also see *Web Sites.*

INNS

Each edition of this book has become more selective as the number of places to stay increases. We personally inspected hundreds of inns and B&Bs. Our choices reflect both what we have seen and the feedback we receive from others. *Best Places to Stay in New England* by Christina Tree and Kimberly Grant (Houghton Mifflin) also includes a wide range of places to stay in Maine. The Maine Innkeepers Association maintains a web site of their members at www.maine inns.com. The "Maine Guide to Inns and Bed & Breakfasts" is also a useful resource (see *Information,* above).

ISLANDS

In all there are reportedly 3,250 offshore Maine islands, most uninhabited. We describe each of the islands that offer overnight lodging—Chebeague, Great Diamond,

Long, and Peaks Islands in Casco Bay; Monhegan, Vinalhaven, North Haven, Islesboro, and Matinicus along the Midcoast; and Isle au Haut, Islesford, Swan's Island, and Grand Manan (N.B.) in the Down East section—in varying detail. In Casco Bay the ferry also serves Cliff Island (summer rentals are available); and Eagle Island, former home of Admiral Perry, is served by daily excursion boats from Portland. For information on public and private islands on which low-impact visitors are welcome, contact the **Maine Island Trail Association** (596-6456; www.mita.org; P.O. Box C, Rockland 04841). MITA maintains 80 islands and charges $40 for membership, which brings with it a detailed guidebook and the right to land on these islands. **The Island Institute** (594-9202; www.islandinstitute.org), which spawned MITA, now serves as an umbrella organization for the island communities; with the $40 membership come its publications: *Island Journal, Working Waterfront,* and *Inter Island News.*

KIM GRANT

LAKES

Maine boasts some 6,000 lakes and ponds, and every natural body of water over 10 acres is theoretically available to the public for "fishing and fowling." Access is, however, limited by the property owners. Because paper companies and other land-management concerns permit public use (see *Camping*), there is ample opportunity to canoe or fish in solitary waters. Powerboat owners should note that most states have reciprocal license privileges with Maine; the big exception is New Hampshire. For more about the most popular resort lakes in the state, see Bridgton, Rangeley, Moosehead, and the Belgrade Lakes. The state parks on lakes are **Aroostook** (camping, fishing, swimming; Route 1 south of Presque Isle), **Damariscotta Lake State Park** (Route 32; Jefferson), **Lake St. George State Park** (swimming, picnicking, fishing; Route 3 in Liberty), **Lily Bay State Park** (8 miles north of Greenville), **Peacock Beach State Park** (swimming, picnicking; Richmond), **Peaks-Kenny State Park** (Sebec Lake in Dover-Foxcroft), **Rangeley Lake State Park** (swimming, camping; Rangeley), **Range Pond State Park** (Poland), **Sebago Lake State Park** (swimming, picnicking, camping; near Bridgton), **Mount Blue State Park** (Weld), and **Swan Lake State Park** (Swanville). Families with small children should note the many coastal lakes surrounded by reasonably priced cottages (see *Cottage Rentals*).

LIGHTHOUSES

Maine takes pride in its 63 lighthouses. The most popular to visit are **Portland Head Light** (completed in 1790, automated in 1990, now a delightful museum featuring the history of lighthouses) on Cape Elizabeth; **Cape Neddick Light** in York; **Marshall Point Light** at Port Clyde; **Fort Point Light** at Stockton Springs; **Pemaquid Point** (the lighthouse keeper's house is now a museum, there's an art gallery, and the rocks below are peerless for scrambling); **Owls Head** near Rockland (built 1826); **Bass Harbor Head Light** at Bass Harbor; and Lubec's **West Quoddy Head,** the start of a beautiful shore path. On **Monhegan** the lighthouse keeper's house is a seasonal museum, and at **Grindle Point** on Islesboro there is also an adjacent seasonal museum.

True lighthouse buffs also make the pilgrimage to **Matinicus Rock,** the setting for several children's books. Lighthouse aficionados tell us that getting to **East Quoddy Head Lighthouse** on the island of Campobello, accessible at low tide, is the ultimate adventure; it is also a prime whale-watching post. Captain Barna Norton (497-5933) runs charters from Jonesport to lighthouses on Libby Island, Moose Peak, Nash Island, and Petit Manan, as well as to Machias Seal Island (see *Puffin-Watching*).

KIM GRANT

LITTER

Littering in Maine is punishable by a $100 fine; this applies to dumping from boats as well as other vehicles. Most cans and bottles are redeemable.

LLAMA TREKKING

The principle is appealingly simple: The llama carries your gear; you lead the llama. From the **Telemark Inn** (836-2703), surrounded by semiwilderness west of Bethel, Steve Crone offers day and multiday treks. At **Pleasant Bay Bed & Breakfast** (483-4490) in Addison guests can walk the property's waterside trails with the llamas, and at **Maine-lly Llamas Farm** (929-3057) in Hollis guests can also take a nature trek with llamas. **Hidden Acres Llama Farm** (549-5575) in Jefferson, near the northern tip of Damariscotta Lake, offers a one-bedroom apartment and the chance to participate in farm activities as well as to take llamas on treks over mountain trails.

LOBSTER POUNDS

In another era this term referred to the saltwater holding areas in which lobsters were literally impounded, but in tourist talk *lobster pound* now usually means a no-frills seaside restaurant that specializes in serving lobsters and clams steamed in seawater. The Pemaquid Peninsula (see "Damariscotta/

Newcastle and Pemaquid Area") is especially blessed: Check out **Shaw's** in New Harbor and the nearby **Pemaquid Co-op,** and, in Round Pond, both **Muscongus Bay Lobster** and **Round Pond Lobster.** Not far from Rockland look for **Cod End** in Tenants Harbor, **Miller's Lobster Company** on Spruce Head, and **Waterman's Beach Lobsters** in South Thomaston. Other lobster-eating landmarks include **Robinson's Wharf** at Townsend Gut near Boothbay, the **Lobster Shack** in Cape Elizabeth near Portland, **Young's Lobster Pound** in East Belfast, the **Lobster Pound** in Lincolnville Beach, **Union River Lobster Pot** in Ellsworth, **Trenton Bridge** on Route 3 at the entrance to Mount Desert Island; on Mount Desert Island **Beal's** is in Southwest Harbor and **Thurston's,** which we prefer, is in Bernard. Minutes from Freeport's outlets, the **Harraseeket Lunch & Lobster Company** in South Freeport is a find. On the Southern Coast the **Ogunquit Lobster Pound** on Route 1 in Ogunquit is now a full-service restaurant, but waterside **Chauncey Creek** in Kittery is still no frills (BYO everything from salad to wine) and a good value. **Nunan's Lobster Hut** in Cape Porpoise and **Fisherman's Catch** in Wells Harbor are also the real thing.

THE MAINE FESTIVAL

Maine's biggest, splashiest cultural happening of the year, the festival is held for 4 days around the first weekend in August at Thomas Point Beach in Brunswick. Performing artists are from everywhere, but the Maine folk artists are definitely local, as are the craftspeople; children's entertainment, a food garden, and plenty of outdoor sculpture are also part of the scene. Sponsored by Maine Arts (772-9012; 1-800-639-4212; www.mainearts.org).

MAINE GROWN

Locally produced food includes venison and beeswax as well as blueberries, Christmas wreaths, smoked seafood, teas, beer, wine, maple syrup, and lobster stew, to name just a few. The Maine Department of Agriculture, Food and Rural Resources (287-3491; www.getrealmaine.com) publishes several helpful guides.

MAINE MADE

Maine craftspeople and entrepreneurs produce an ever-increasing variety of specialty foods, handcrafted furniture and furnishings, apparel, toys, and much more. Request a "Maine Made" catalog (1-800-541-5872; www.mainemade.com).

MAINE PUBLIC BROADCASTING

Public broadcasting is represented statewide with both television and radio. Programs and services can be found on the Maine Public Broadcasting web site at www.mpbc.org. The five stations of Maine Public Television are: Channel 10 in Augusta, Channel 12 in Orono, Channel 13 in Calais, Channel 10 in Presque Isle, and Channel 26 in Biddeford. In addition to many national public broadcasting programs, local programming includes *Home, The Story of Maine,* documenting Maine history and subjects of specifically Maine interest; *Made in Maine,* a profile of businesses in Maine; *Maine Watch,* highlighting important issues in Maine each week; and the *Maine State Concert Series,*

featuring concerts by some of Maine's best performing artists. **Maine's six public radio stations** can be found on the dial at 89.7 in Calais, 90.1 in Portland, 90.9 in Bangor, 91.3 in Waterville, 106.1 in Presque Isle, and 106.5 in Fort Kent. In addition to popular National Public Radio programs, MPR also offers the radio version of *Maine Watch; Maine Things Considered,* a news program highlighting state news; and *Maine Stage,* a classical music series.

MAINE TURNPIKE

For travel conditions and construction updates, phone 1-800-675-PIKE, or check www.maineturnpike.com. Tolls are now a flat rate (no more tickets), paid when getting on—and sometimes off—the turnpike. Heading north, the first booth is in York. If you remain on the turnpike all the way to Augusta, you will pass through two other booths requiring a toll (New Gloucester and just outside Augusta). Unless you need to exit at Gray or Lewiston/Auburn, it's cheaper and quicker to follow I-95 (exit 9) rather than the Maine Turnpike (I-495) north to Augusta and Bangor.

MAPLE SUGARING

Maine produces roughly 8,000 gallons of syrup a year, and the Maine Department of Agriculture (287-3491; www.getrealmaine. com) publishes a list of producers who welcome visitors on **Maine Maple Sunday** (also known as Sap Sunday) in late March.

MARITIME MUSEUMS

The **Maine Maritime Museum** in Bath stands in a class by itself and should not be missed. The **Penobscot Marine Museum** in Searsport is smaller but still substantial, focusing on the merchant captains and their experiences in far corners of the world. The **Kittery Historical and Naval Museum** is also worth checking. For an overview of the state's sea-related sites, request a copy of the "Maine Maritime Heritage Trail" brochure from 1-888-MAINE45 (623-8428), ext. 45.

MOOSE-WATCHING

The moose, the state animal, has made a comeback from its near-extinct status in the 1930s and now numbers more than 20,000. Your chances of spotting one are best in early morning or at dusk on a wooded pond or lake or along logging roads. If you are driving through moose country at night, go slowly because moose typically freeze rather than retreat from oncoming headlights. For details about commercial moose-watching expeditions, check "Rangeley Lakes Region" and "Moosehead Lake Area." The Moosehead Lake Region Chamber of Commerce sponsors **"Moosemainea"** mid-May through mid-June, with special events and a huge moose locator map. Suspicious that this promotion coincided with Moosehead's low tourist season, we queried the state's moose expert, who assures us that moose are indeed most visible in late spring.

MUSEUMS

Also see *Art Museums, Museum Villages, Maritime Museums,* and *Wabanaki.* Easily the most undervisited museum in the state, the **Maine State Museum** in Augusta has outstanding displays on the varied Maine landscape and offers historical exhibits ranging from traces of the area's earliest people to rifles used by State of Mainers in Korea; it also includes exhibits on fishing, agriculture, lumbering, quarrying, and shipbuilding. The **Seashore Trolley Museum** in Kennebunkport and the **Owls Head Transportation Museum** near Rockland are family finds (inquire about special events at both). Our favorites also include the **Peary-MacMillan Arctic Museum** at Bowdoin College in Brunswick, the **Wilson Museum**

KIM GRANT

in Castine, and the **L. C. Bates Museum** in Hinckley, easily the state's most old-time museum, filled with stuffed animals and Indian artifacts and surpassingly lively (see "The Upper Kennebec Valley and the Moose River Valley"). The **Lumberman's Museum** in "Katahdin Region" and the **Rangeley Lakes Region Logging Museum** are both glimpses of a recently vanished way of life in Maine's North Woods. The museum at the **Colonial Pemaquid Restoration** in Pemaquid, presenting archaeological finds from the adjacent early-17th-century settlement, is also unexpectedly fascinating. Click onto www.maine museums.org and/or request a free copy of "Maine Museums and Archives" (60 Community Drive, Augusta 04330; 623-8424, ext. 296).

MUSEUM VILLAGES

York Village, with its Old Gaol, school, tavern, church, and scattering of historic houses open to the public, represents one of the country's earliest preservation efforts and adds up to a picture of 18th-century life in coastal Maine. **Willowbrook** at Newfield, by contrast, is a 19th-century village center consisting of 31 buildings that have been restored through the efforts of one man. **Norlands,** in Livermore, is a former estate with a neo-Gothic library, school, and farm buildings, all evoking rural life in the 1870s. **Sabbathday Lake Shaker Community and Museum** is the country's last functioning Shaker religious community, but visitors are welcome to walk the grounds, visit the small museum/gift shop, and attend seasonal Sunday services in the meetinghouse.

MUSIC CONCERT SERIES

Bowdoin Summer Music Festival in Brunswick (725-3322) is the state's most prestigious and varied chamber music series, and the **Kneisel Hall Chamber Music Festival** (374-2811) in Blue Hill is its oldest chamber music festival, also still outstanding. The **Mount Desert Festival of Chamber Music** (276-5039), the **Bar Harbor Festival** (288-5744), and the **Arcady Music Festival** (288-3151) are all highlights of the season on Mount Desert. The **Sebago/Long Lakes Region Chamber Music Festival** in North Bridgton (627-4939) is noteworthy, and **Bay Chamber Concerts,** presented in the Rockport Opera House (236-2823), are popular in the Camden/Rockport area. A series of outdoor picnic concerts are performed at the **Round Top Center for the Arts** (563-1507) in Damariscotta, while the **Machias Bay**

Chamber Concerts in Machias (255-3889) are held in the town's Congregational church. There is, of course, the **Portland Symphony Orchestra** (842-0800), which also has a summertime pops series, and the **Bangor Symphony Orchestra** (942-5555; 1-800-639-3221). Music lovers should also take note of the **Annual Rockport Folk Festival** in mid-July, the **Downeast Jazz Festival in Rockland** every August, the **Lincoln Arts Festival** of classical and choral music held throughout the Boothbay Harbor region in summer months, and the **Bluegrass Festival** at Thomas Point Beach in September. Click on www.mainemusic.org for daily updated musical events in Maine.

MUSIC SCHOOLS

Notable are the **Bowdoin Summer Music Festival** (see *Music Concert Series*); **Kneisel Hall** in Blue Hill (call 374-2811 only after June 24; prior inquiries should be addressed to Kneisel Hall, Blue Hill 04614); the **Pierre Monteux Memorial School** in Hancock (442-6251); **Salzedo Summer Harp Colony** in Camden (236-2289); **New England Music Camp** in Oakland (465-3025); **Maine Summer Youth Music** at the University of Maine, Orono (581-1254); and **Maine Music Camp** at the University of Maine, Farmington.

NATURE PRESERVES, COASTAL

From **Kittery's Brave Boat Harbor Trail** to the **Bold Coast Trail** way down in Washington County not far from West Quoddy Light, oceanside walking trails have multiplied in the last few years. Within each chapter we describe these under *Green Space* or *To Do—Hiking.* On the Southern Coast the **Wells National Estuarine Research Reserve** at Laudholm Farm includes two barrier beaches. On Casco Bay the Maine Audubon Society headquarters at **Gilsland**

KIM GRANT

Farm in Falmouth includes 70 acres of nature trails; Maine Audubon also offers canoe tours and many summer programs at their **Scarborough Marsh** nature center and maintains picnic and tenting sites at **Mast Landing Sanctuary** in Freeport. Along the Midcoast both the **Boothbay Region Land Trust** and the **Damariscotta River Association** now maintain a number of exceptional preserves, and **Camden Hills State Park** includes miles of little-trafficked trails with magnificent views. Down East in the Blue Hill area the 1,350-acre **Holbrook Island Sanctuary** in West Brooksville is a beauty, and in Ellsworth, 40-acre **Birdsacre** includes nature trails and a museum honoring ornithologist Cordelia Stanwood. **Acadia National Park,** the state's busiest preserve, offers 120 miles of hiking paths on Mount Desert, also trails on **Isle au Haut** and at **Schoodic Point. Schoodic Mountain** north of Sullivan is one of the area's most spectacular hikes. Right across the line in Washington County the 6,000-acre **Petit Manan National Wildlife Refuge,** based in Steuben, includes two coastal peninsulas and 24 offshore islands. Near Jonesport **Great Wass Island** (accessible by land) is maintained by the Maine Chapter of The Nature Conservancy, a beautiful preserve with a 2-mile shore trail. **Western Head,** near Machias, is now maintained by Maine Coast Heritage Trust; Maine's Bureau of Parks and Lands maintains a 5½-mile **Bold**

Coast Trail along the high bluffs west of Cutler; **West Quoddy Light State Park** includes a splendid 2-mile shore trail. **Roosevelt Campobello International Park** also includes many miles of shore paths, and **Cobscook Bay State Park** (see "Eastport and Cobscook Bay") and **Moosehorn National Wildlife Refuge** (see "Calais and the St. Croix Valley") also offer hiking trails. Two islands that maintain magnificent hiking trails are **Monhegan** and **Vinalhaven.** The Maine Chapter of The Nature Conservancy (729-5181) has published *Maine Forever,* a "Guide to Nature Conservancy Preserves in Maine." The Maine Coast Heritage Trust (729-7366) also makes available several useful brochures about its holdings.

NATURE PRESERVES, INLAND

In the Rangeley area the **Rangeley Lakes Heritage Trust** has, in recent years, preserved more than 10,000 acres, including 20 miles of lake and river frontage and 10 islands; the **Stephen Phillips Memorial Preserve Trust** maintains a number of campsites on its land along Lake Mooselookmeguntic. In the Sugarloaf area the Maine Bureau of Parks and Lands now offers detailed maps to trails within the 35,000-acre **Bigelow Preserve.** Within each chapter we describe nature preserves along with state parks under *Green Space* or *To Do—Hiking.* Among our favorites are Vaughan Woods (see "Kittery and the Yorks"), a 250-acre state preserve with wooded hiking trails along the Salmon River and trails to the top of **Mount Kineo** overlooking Moosehead Lake. **Baxter State Park** (see "Katahdin Region") is, of course, the greatest inland preserve.

PARKS AND FORESTS, NATIONAL

Acadia National Park (288-3338; www.

KIM GRANT

nps.gov/acad), which occupies roughly half of Mount Desert Island, plus scattered areas on Isle au Haut, Little Cranberry Island, Baker Island, Little Moose Island, and Schoodic Point, adds up to more than 40,000 acres offering hiking, ski touring, swimming, horseback riding, canoeing, and a variety of guided nature tours and programs, as well as a scenic 27-mile driving tour. Note that an entry fee is charged to drive the Park Loop Road. Camping is by reservation only at Blackwoods, and first-come, first-served at Seawall. See "Acadia National Park" for details. The **White Mountain National Forest** encompasses 41,943 acres in Maine, including five campgrounds under the jurisdiction of the Evans Notch Ranger District (824-2134), Bridge Street, Bethel 04217. For details, see "Bethel Area."

PARKS, STATE
The Bureau of Parks and Lands (287-3821; www.state.me.us/doc/parks.htm), 22 State House Station, Augusta 04333, can send a packet of information describing each of the 32 parks and the 12 (plus the Allagash Wilderness Waterway) that offer camping facilities. We have described parks as they appear geographically. In 2000 day-use fees were between $1 and $2.50 per adult; children 5–11, $.50; free for children under 5 and for seniors over 65. The camping fee was $9–13 for residents, $11–17 for nonresidents. There is also a $2-per-night reserva-

tion fee for camping. Call the reservations hotline (1-800-332-1501 within Maine; 207-287-3824 from outside the state) at least 7 days in advance to make a campground reservation, or use the online registration form. (Also see *Lakes.*)

PETS
Throughout this book, lodgings and selected other places that accept pets are indicated with the dog-paw symbol 🐾. Please note that most lodgings require a reservation and a deposit or additional fee. Always call ahead when traveling with your pet.

PLOYES
This traditional Acadian pancake/flatbread, as delicate as a crêpe, is a specialty throughout the St. John Valley. The **Bouchard Family Farm** produces a line of French Canadian food products: 1-800-239-3237.

POPULATION
Approximately 1.2 million.

PUFFIN-WATCHING
Atlantic puffins are smaller than you might expect. They lay just one egg a year and were heading for extinction around the turn of the 20th century, when the only surviving birds nested either on Matinicus Rock or Machias Seal Island. Since 1973 the Audubon Society has helped reintroduce nesting on Eastern Egg Rock in Muscongus Bay, 6 miles off Pemaquid Point, and since 1984 there has been a similar puffin-restoration project on Seal Island in outer Penobscot Bay, 6 miles from Matinicus Rock. The best times for viewing puffins are June and July or the first few days of August. The only place from which you are allowed to view the birds on land is at Machias Seal Island, where visitors are permitted in limited numbers. Contact **Barna and John Norton** (1-800-454-5467) in Jonesport and **Andrew Patterson**

(259-4484) in Cutler. With the help of binoculars (a must), you can also view the birds from the water via tours with **Atlantic Expeditions** (372-8621) out to Matinicus Rock and Seal Island from Rockland, and around Eastern Egg Rock with **Cap'n Fish** (633-3244) from Boothbay Harbor and **Hardy Boat Cruises** (1-800-278-3346) from New Harbor. The **National Audubon Society Ecology Camp** (see "Damariscotta/Newcastle and the Pemaquid Area") also offers programs at their facility near Eastern Egg Rock. Click onto www.maine birding.net.

RAILROAD RIDES AND MUSEUMS

Boothbay Railway Village delights small children and offers railroad exhibits in its depot. Elsewhere on the Midcoast rail fans can take excursions with the **Belfast & Moosehead Lake Railroad Company** in Belfast and the **Maine Coast Railroad** in Wiscasset. In Portland the **Maine Narrow Gauge Railroad Company & Museum** combines displays and a 3-mile shoreside excursion. Inland, the **Sandy River & Rangeley Lakes Railroad** in Phillips in the Rangeley region operates short excursions one Sunday per month in summer.

RATES

Please do not regard any prices listed for *Lodging* as set in stone. Call ahead to con-

firm them. Rates are those in effect as we go to press. MAP stands for Modified American Plan: breakfast and dinner included in rate. AP stands for American Plan: three meals included in rate. EP stands for European Plan: breakfast included in rate. B&B stands for bed & breakfast: continental breakfast included in rate.

ROCKHOUNDING

Perham's Maine Mineral Store at Trap Corner in West Paris displays Maine minerals and offers access to its four quarries. The store also offers information about other quarries and sells its own guidebooks to gem hunting in Oxford County and throughout the state. Open year-round 9–5 daily except Thanksgiving and Christmas. For other rockhounding meccas, check "Bethel Area." Thanks to the high price of gold, prospectors are back-panning Maine streambeds; a list of likely spots is available from the Maine Geological Survey (287-2801), Department of Conservation, 22 State House Station, Augusta 04333.

SAILING

Windjammers and yacht charter brokers aside, there are a limited number of places that will rent small sailing craft, fewer that will offer lessons to adults and children alike. The **Mansell Boat Company,** Southwest Harbor, rents sailboats by the day or longer. Learn-to-sail programs are offered by **WoodenBoat School** in Brooklin and in Camden by both the **Camden Yacht Club** and **Bay Island Sailing School.** Sailboat rentals and daysails are listed throughout the book. (Also see *Windjammer Cruises.*)

SEA KAYAKING

Sea kayaking is the fastest-growing sport along the coast of Maine, and outfitters are responding to the demand, offering guided half-day and full-day trips, also overnight and

KIM GRANT

multiday expeditions with camping on Maine islands. When paddling a kayak, you're so low that you can stare down a duck or a cormorant, or study the surface of the water and its kaleidoscopic patterns. Maneuverable in as little as 6 inches of water, kayaks are ideal craft for "gunkholing" (poking in and out of coves). The leading outfitters are **Maine Island Kayak Company** (1-800-796-2373; www.maineislandkayak.com) on Peaks Island off Portland, and **Maine Sport Outfitters** (236-8797) in Rockport, both of which specialize in multiday camping trips and offer introductory lessons. Others that we have checked out include **H₂Outfitters** (833-5257) on Orrs Island near Brunswick, **Tidal Transit** (633-7140) in Boothbay Harbor, **Outward Bound School** (1-800-341-1744) in Rockland, **Granite Island Guide Service** (348-2668; www.graniteislandguide.com) in Deer Isle, **Coastal Kayaking Tours** (288-9605) in Bar Harbor, **Moose Look Guide Service** (963-7720) in Gouldsboro, **Machias Bay Sea Kayaking** (259-3338; www.machiasbay.com) in East Machias, and **Tidal Trails** (726-4799; www.nemaine.com/tidaltrails) in Pembroke. **L. L. Bean Sea Kayak Symposium,** held in early July in Castine (by reservation only), is New England's oldest and still its biggest annual kayaking event: a 2-day program geared to neophytes and all levels of ability, with lessons and equipment demonstrations. For reservations and info about L. L. Bean's kayaking programs, call

1-888-552-3261; also click onto www.llbean.com and check out **Outdoor Discovery Schools.** *Sea Kayaking along the New England Coast* by Tamsin Venn (Appalachian Mountain Club) includes detailed guidance to kayaking routes from Portland to Cobscook Bay as well as an overall introduction to the sport. Dorcas Miller's comprehensive new guidebook *Kayaking the Maine Coast, A Paddler's Guide to Day Trips from Kittery to Cobscook* (Backcountry Guides) is an excellent resource for kayak owners and competent kayakers.

SKIING, CROSS-COUNTRY
The **Maine Nordic Ski Council** (1-800-SKI-XCME; www.mnsc.com), P.O. Box 645, Bethel 04217, is a great source of information about conditions, ski centers, and outfitters. **Carrabassett Valley Touring Center** at Sugarloaf is the largest commercial Nordic network in the state. Bethel, with four trail networks **(Sunday River Inn,** the **Bethel Inn, Carter's X-C Ski Center,** and **Telemark Farm)** offers varied terrain. The town of Rangeley also maintains an extensive trail network that enjoys dependable snow cover. The most adventurous touring is found in the Katahdin/Moosehead area in Maine's North Woods. **The Birches Resort** in Rockwood and **Little Lyford Pond Camps** near Brownville Junction offer guided wilderness tours. **Mahoosuc Mountain Adventures** in the Bethel area also offers guided trips with dogsleds toting gear for overnight camping.

SKIING, DOWNHILL
Ski Maine Association (761-3774; www.skimaine.com) lists information about mountains in Maine, snow conditions, and more on their web site. **Sugarloaf/USA** in the Carrabassett Valley and **Sunday River** in the Bethel area, both owned by the Bethel-based American Skiing Company,

KIM GRANT

vie for the title of Maine's number-one ski resort. The two are very different and actually complement each other well. Sugarloaf is a high, relatively remote mountain with New England's only lift-serviced snowfields on its summit and a classy, self-contained condo village at its base. Sunday River, just 1 hour north of Portland, consists of eight adjoining (relatively low-altitude) mountains; snowmaking is a big point of pride, and facilities include a variety of slope-side condo lodging. **Saddleback Mountain** (in the Rangeley area) is a big, relatively undeveloped mountain with a small, enthusiastic following. **Mount Abram** (also in the Bethel area) is a true family area with a strong ski school and some fine runs. **Shawnee Peak** in Bridgton is a medium-sized, family-geared area that offers night as well as day skiing. **Squaw Mountain** in Greenville and the **Camden Snow Bowl** in Camden are also medium sized but satisfying.

SNOWMOBILING
Maine has reciprocal agreements with nearly all states and provinces; for licensing and rules, contact the Department of Inland Fisheries and Wildlife (287-2043), 41 State House Station, Augusta 04330. The **Maine Snowmobile Association** (MSA; 622-6983; www.mesnow.com), P.O. Box 77, Augusta 04332, represents over 280 clubs and maintains some 12,500 miles of an ever-expanding cross-state trail network. Aroostook County, given its reliable snow condi-

tions, is an increasingly popular destination. **Sled Maine** (1-877-2SLED-ME; www.sledme.com) is a visitor-geared group supplying information on destinations with lodging, rentals, and guided tours as well as trails. The Upper Kennebec Valley and Jackman as well as the entire Moosehead and Rangeley Lake areas are snowmobiling meccas. For maps and further information, write to the Snowmobile Program, Bureau of Parks and Lands, 22 State House Station, Augusta 04333; MSA maintains a trail-conditions hotline: 626-5717.

SPORTING CAMPS
The Maine sporting camp is a distinctly Maine phenomenon that began appearing in the 1860s—a gathering of log cabins around a log lodge by a lake, frequently many miles from the nearest road. In the 19th century access was usually via Rangeley or Greenville, where "sports" (urbanites who wanted to hunt wild game) would be met by a guide and paddled up lakes and rivers to a camp. With the advent of floatplanes, many of these camps became more accessible (see *Air Services*), and the proliferation of private logging roads has put most within reach of sturdy vehicles. True sporting camps still cater primarily to fishermen in spring and hunters in fall, but since Au-

SLED MAINE

gust is neither a hunting season nor a prime fishing season, they are increasingly hosting families who just want to be in the woods by a lake in summer. True sporting camps (as opposed to "rental camps") include a central lodge in which guests are served all three meals; boats and guide service are available. The **Maine Sporting Camp Association** (www.mainesportingcamps.com), P.O. Box 89, Jay 04239, publishes a truly fabulous map/guide to its more than 50 members. Also see *In the Maine Woods: An Insider's Guide to Traditional Maine Sporting Camps* by Alice Arlen (Countryman Press).

THEATER, SUMMER

The **Ogunquit Playhouse** (646-5511) is among the oldest and most prestigious summer theaters in the country, and the **Arundel Barn Playhouse** (985-5552) in Kennebunk is the newest. The **Hackmatack Playhouse** in Berwick (698-1807) and **Biddeford City Theater** (282-0849) are other Southern Coast options. In Portland note the **Portland Stage Company** (774-0465), and in Brunswick the **Maine State Music Theater** and **Children's Theatre Program** on the Bowdoin campus (725-8769). Farther along the coast look for the **Camden Civic Theatre** based in the refurbished Opera House in Camden (236-2281), **The Belfast Maskers** in Belfast (338-4427), the **Surry Opera Company** in Surry (667-2629), the **Acadia Repertory Theatre** (244-7260) in Somesville, and **Downriver Theater Productions** (255-4997) in Machias. Inland look for the **Theater at Monmouth** (933-2952), **Lakewood Theater** (474-7176) in Skowhegan, **DeerTrees Theatre** (583-6747) in Harrison, and **Celebration Barn Theater** (743-8452) in South Paris.

THEATER, YEAR-ROUND

Penobscot Theatre Company in Bangor

offers a variety of winter productions (947-3333). Other companies are the **Chocolate Church Arts Center** in Bath (442-8455), the **Camden Civic Theatre** in Camden (236-2281). **Portland Stage Company** (774-0465) presents a series of productions at 25A Forest Avenue, Portland. The **Portland Players** (799-7337) present a winter season of productions, as does the **Public Theatre** (782-3200) in Auburn. In Brunswick the **Theater Project** (729-8584) performs year-round. Most universities and colleges also offer performances throughout the school year.

TRAFFIC AND HIGHWAY TRAVEL TIPS

Maine coastal travel has its sticky wickets. By far the worst is the backup at the tolls at the entrance to the Maine Turnpike as well as those not far south in New Hampshire. Avoid passing through these tolls, if at all possible, on Friday evening, Saturday morning, and Sunday evening from June through September and on Columbus Day weekend. Within this book we have offered suggested ways around lesser bottlenecks at Brunswick, Wiscasset, and Camden. It's also worth noting that it doesn't necessarily take longer to reach a Down East than a Midcoast destination. It's all thanks to the way the highways run. The quickest way to reach Rockland or Camden from points south is, for instance, up I-95 to Brunswick and then coastal Route 1. Belfast and east through Blue Hill peninsula destinations, however, can be reached in roughly the same time by taking I-95 to Augusta and then Route 3 to coastal Route 1. You can reach Ellsworth (gateway to Mount Desert and points east) in equal time by traveling I-95 to the Maine Turnpike to Bangor and then down Route 1A.

WABANAKI

Wabanaki means "people of the dawn." It's

the name of Native Americans who have lived in Maine and eastern Canada for many thousands of years, judging from shell heaps and artifacts found in areas ranging from the coastal Damariscotta/Boothbay and Blue Hill areas to the Rangeley Lakes in western Maine. Ancient pictographs can be found on the Kennebec River and around Machias Bay. An excellent exhibit, *12,000 Years in Maine,* in the **Maine State Museum** in Augusta depicts the distinct periods in this history and features the Red Paint People, so named for the red pigments found sprinkled in their burial sites. They flourished between 5,000 and 3,800 years ago and are said to have fished from large, sturdy boats. Similar displays at the **Robert Abbe Museum** on Mount Desert include awls, pear-shaped net weights, and weights for sophisticated "atlatl" spears. Two North Woods sites are said to have been sacred to these people: the Katahdin Iron Works, in Brownville Junction, source of the pigments found in their burial sites; and Mount Kineo on Moosehead Lake, source of the flintlike volcanic stone widely used for arrowheads. Early French missions at Mount Desert and Castine proved battlegrounds between the French and English, and by the end of the 17th century thousands of Wabanaki had retreated either to Canada or to the Penobscot community of Old Town and to Norridgewock, where Father Sebastian Rasle insisted that the Indian lands "were given them of God, to them and their children forever, according to the Christian oracles." The mission was obliterated (it's now a pleasant roadside rest area), and by the end of the French and Indian Wars only four tribes remained. Of these the Micmacs and Malecites made the unlucky choice of siding with the crown and were subsequently forced to flee (but communities remain near the Aroostook County–Canadian border in Presque Isle and Littleton, respectively).

That left only the Penobscots and the Passamaquoddies.

In 1794 the Penobscots technically deeded most of Maine to Massachusetts in exchange for the 140 small islands in the Penobscot River, and in 1818 Massachusetts agreed to pay them an assortment of trinkets for the land. In 1820, when Maine became a state, a trust fund was set aside but ended up in the general treasury. The state's three reservations (two belonging to the Passamaquoddies and one to the Penobscots) were termed "enclaves of disfranchised citizens bereft of any special status." Indians loomed large in Maine lore and greeted 19th-century tourists as fishing and hunting guides in the woods and as snowshoe and canoe makers and guides, while Native American women sold their distinctive sweetgrass and ash splint baskets and beadwork at the many coastal and inland summer hotels and boardinghouses.

In 1972 the Penobscots and Passamaquoddies sued to reclaim 1½ million acres of land allegedly illegally appropriated by the state, and in 1980 they received an $80.6 million settlement, which they have since invested in a variety of enterprises. The Indian Island Reservation in Old Town is presently home to 500 of the tribe's 2,000 members, and the **Penobscot Nation Museum** there, while small, is open regularly and well worth checking. The Passamaquoddy tribe today numbers 2,500 members, roughly divided between the reservations at Indian Township on Schoodic Lake and at Pleasant Point, near Eastport, site of the **Waponahki Museum and Resource Center** and of **Indian Ceremonial Days,** held annually in mid-August to celebrate Passamaquoddy culture and climaxing in dances in full regalia.

The **Hudson Museum** at the University of Maine, Orono, has a small display on local tribes and hosts an annual early-December **Maine Indian Basketmakers Sale and Demonstration,** featuring the work of all four tribes. A similar sale is held in Bar Harbor in early July. The **L. C. Bates Museum** in Hinckley (see "Upper Kennebec Valley and Moose River Valley") displays ancient artifacts and 19th- and early-20th-century craftsmanship, and **Nowetah's American Indian Museum** in New Portland (see "Sugarloaf and the Carrabassett Valley") displays a large collection of authentic basketry. Contact the Maine Indian Basketmakers Alliance (P.O. Box 3253, Old Town 04468; 859-9722; miba@mint.net) for a copy of the "Wabanaki Cultural Resource Guide."

WATERFALLS
The following are all easily accessible to families with small children: **Snow Falls Gorge** off Route 26 in West Paris offers a beautiful cascade (ask for directions at Perham's Gem Store); **Smalls Falls** on the Sandy River, off Route 4 between Rangeley and Phillips, has a picnic spot with a trail beside the falls; **Jewell Falls** is located in the Fore River Sanctuary in the heart of Portland; **Step Falls** is on Wight Brook in Newry off Route 26; and just up the road in Grafton Notch State Park is **Screw Auger Falls,** with its natural gorge. Another Screw Auger Falls is in Gulf Hagas (see *Gorges*), off the Appalachian Trail near the Katahdin Iron Works Road, north of Brownville Junction. **Kezar Falls,** on the Kezar River, is best reached via Lovell Road from Route

35 at North Waterford. An extensive list of "scenic waterfalls" is detailed in the *Maine Atlas and Gazetteer* (DeLorme). Check out 90-foot **Moxie Falls** at The Forks.

WEB SITES
We include web sites for lodging places as well as chambers of commerce, attractions, and activities. We are delighted that web site visuals can now amplify our verbal descriptions and hope that you will agree that this book is the ultimate Maine search engine.

WEDDINGS
At this writing no one conduit exists for information about the ever-increasing number of services (photographers, musicians, carriage operators, caterers, and florists, as well as inns and venues) geared to helping couples wed near Maine water. Several chambers of commerce, notably York, Kennebunkport, Boothbay, and Camden, are particularly helpful. Within the book we note properties that specialize in weddings. A Maine marriage license currently costs just $20.

WHALE-WATCHING
Each spring humpback, finback, and minke whales migrate to New England waters, where they remain until fall, cavorting, it sometimes seems, for the pleasure of excursion boats. One prime gathering spot is **Jeffrey's Ledge,** about 20 miles off Kennebunkport, and another is the **Bay of Fundy.** For listings of whale-watch cruises, see "The Kennebunks," "Portland Area," "Bar Harbor and Ellsworth," and "Washington County and the Quoddy Loop." The East Quoddy (Campobello) and West Quoddy (Lubec) lighthouses are also prime viewing spots.

WHITEWATER RAFTING
Whitewater rafting is such a spring-through-fall phenomenon in Maine today that it's dif-

ALLAN MCDONALD

ficult to believe it only began in 1976, coincidentally the year of the last log drive on the Kennebec River. Logs were actually still hurtling through Kennebec Gorge on that day in the spring of 1976 when fishing guide Wayne Hockmeyer (and eight bear hunters from New Jersey he had talked into coming along) plunged through it in a rubber raft. At the time Hockmeyer's rafting know-how stemmed solely from having seen *River of No Return,* in which Robert Mitchum steered Marilyn Monroe down the Salmon River. Needless to say, Hockmeyer's **Northern Outdoors** and the more than a dozen other major outfitters now positioned around the tiny village of The Forks, near the confluence of the Kennebec and Dead Rivers, are all well skilled in negotiating the rapids through nearby 12-mile-long Kennebec Gorge. Numbers on the river are now strictly limited, and rafts line up to take their turns riding the releases—which gush up to 8,000 cubic feet of water per second—from the Harris Hydroelectric Station above the gorge. Several rafting companies—notably **Northern Outdoors, New England Outdoor Center, Crab Apple White Water,** and **Unicorn Rafting Expeditions**—have fairly elaborate base facilities in and around The Forks, while **Wilderness Expeditions** offers facilities both there and at The Birches Resort, a family-geared resort on nearby Moosehead Lake. Several outfitters—including **Northern Outdoors, Wilderness Expeditions, New England Outdoor Center,** and **Unicorn**—have established food and lodging facilities for patrons who want to raft the Penobscot near Baxter State Park. **North American Whitewater Expeditions,** based in The Forks, rafts six different New England rivers. Some 80,000 rafters of all ages and abilities now raft in Maine each year. For information about most outfitters, contact **Raft Maine** (1-800-723-8633; www.raftmaine. com).

KIM GRANT

WINDJAMMERS

In 1935 a young artist named Frank Swift fitted a few former fishing and cargo schooners to carry passengers around the islands of Penobscot Bay. At the time there were plenty of these old vessels moored in every harbor and cove, casualties of progress. Swift called his business **Maine Windjammer Cruises,** and during the next two decades it grew to include more than a dozen vessels. Competitors also prospered throughout the 1950s, but the entire windjammer fleet almost faded away with the advent of rigorous Coast Guard licensing requirements in the 1960s. The 1970s and 1980s saw the rise of a new breed of windjammer captain. Almost every one of those now sailing has built or restored the vessel he or she commands. Members of the current Maine windjammer fleet range from the *Stephen Taber* and the *Lewis R. French,* both originally launched in 1871, to the *Heritage,* launched in 1983, to the *Kathryn B* (a luxury version of the others), launched in 1996.

Taber co-captain Ellen Barnes recalls her own joy upon first discovering the windjammers as a passenger: "No museums had gobbled up these vessels; no cities had purchased them to sit at piers as public-relations gimmicks. These vessels were the real thing, plying their trade as they had in the past with one exception: The present-day cargo was people instead of pulpwood, bricks, coal, limestone, and granite."

Windjammers offer a sense of what the

Maine coast and islands are all about. Most sail with the tide on Monday; where they go depends on the wind and the tide. Passengers help haul a line and then lounge around the decks, gradually succumbing to the luxury of steeping in life on the face of Penobscot Bay. Supper is hearty Yankee fare, maybe fish chowder and beef stew with plenty of fresh corn bread. Before or after supper, passengers can board the vessel's yawl for a foray into the nearest village or onto the nearest road (most landlubbers feel the need to walk a bit each day).

Choosing which vessel to sail on is the most difficult part of a windjammer vacation. All have ship-to-shore radios and sophisticated radar, and some offer more in the way of creature comforts; some are known for their food or a captain with great jokes or songs. In relevant chapters we have described each vessel in the kind of detail we devote to individual inns. Windjammers accommodate between 12 and 44 passengers. Excessive drinking is discouraged on all the vessels, and guests are invited to bring their musical instruments. Children under 14 are permitted only on some vessels. See "Rockland/Thomaston Area" and "Camden/Rockport Area" for details and toll-free numbers for the various vessels. Questions you might like to ask in making your reservation include the following: (1) What's the bunk arrangement? Double bunks and cabins for a family or group do exist. (2) What's the cabin ventilation? Some vessels offer cabins with portholes or windows that open. (3) What's the rule about children? Several schooners schedule special family cruises with activities geared to kids. (4) What's the extent of weatherproof common space? It varies widely. (5) Is smoking allowed? (6) Is there evening entertainment of any kind?

The **Maine Windjammers Association** (1-800-807-WIND; www.sailmainecoast.com) represents all the major windjammers, which claim to be "the largest fleet of merchant ships operating under sail in America."

I. SOUTHERN COAST

Kittery and the Yorks
Ogunquit and Wells
The Kennebunks
Old Orchard Beach, Saco, and Biddeford

KIM GRANT

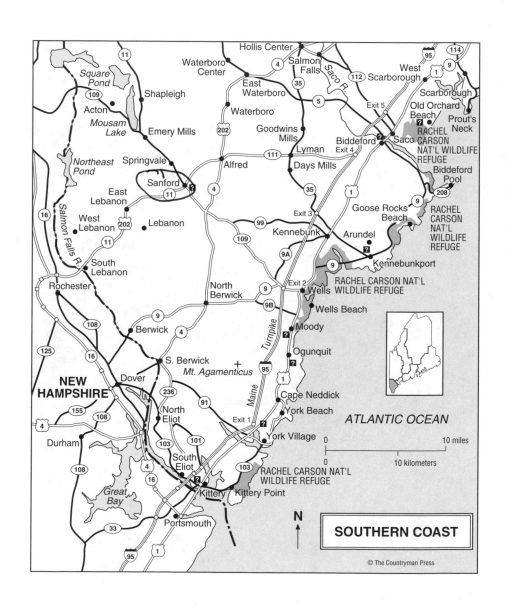

SOUTHERN COAST

© The Countryman Press

Southern Coast

The smell of pine needles and salt air, the taste of lobster and saltwater taffy, the shock of cold green waves, and, most of all, the promise of endless beach—this is the Maine that draws upward of half the state's visitors, those who never get beyond its Southern Coast. The southern Maine coast comprises just 35 miles of the state's 35,000 coastal miles but contains 90 percent of its sand.

Beyond their sand these resort towns—and the villages within them—differ deeply. York Village and Kittery are recognized as the oldest communities in Maine; Wells dates from the 1640s, and Kennebunkport was a shipbuilding center by the 1790s. All were trans formed in the second half of the 19th century, an era when most Americans—not just the rich—began to take summer vacations, each in his or her own way.

Maine's Southern Coast was one of the country's first beach resort areas, and it catered—as it does today—to the full spectrum of vacationers, from blue-collar workers to millionaires. Before the Civil War, Old Orchard Beach rivaled Newport, Rhode Island, as the place to be seen; when the Grand Trunk Railroad to Montreal opened in 1854, it became the first American resort to attract a sizable number of Canadians.

While ocean tides are most extreme way Down East, the ebb and flow of tourist tides wash most dramatically over this stretch of Maine. Nowhere are the 1930s-era motor courts thicker along Route 1, now sandwiched between elaborate '90s condo-style complexes with indoor pools and elevators. Most of the big old summer hotels vanished by the 1950s, the era of the motor inns that now occupy their sites. But in the past few decades hundreds of former sea captains' homes and summer mansions have been transformed into small inns and bed & breakfasts, rounding out the lodging options. Luckily, the lay of the land—salt marsh, estuarine reserves, and other wetlands—largely limits commercial clutter.

GUIDANCE

The **Coalition of Southern Maine Chambers of Commerce** maintains a toll-free number that connects with each of the six chambers: 1-800-639-2442. Request the free booklet guide. Check the web site: www. southernmainecoast.com.

Kittery and the Yorks

The moment you cross the Piscataqua River you know you are in Maine. You have to go a long way Down East to find any deeper coves, finer lobster pounds, rockier ocean paths, or sandier beaches than those in Kittery and York.

Both towns claim to be Maine's oldest community. Technically Kittery wins, but York looks older . . . depending, of course, on which Kittery and which York you are talking about.

Kittery Point, an 18th-century settlement overlooking Portsmouth Harbor, boasts Maine's oldest church and some of the state's finest mansions. The village of Kittery itself, however, has been shattered by so many bridges and rotaries that it seems to exist only as a gateway, on the one hand for workers at the Portsmouth Naval Shipyard and on the other for patrons of the outlet malls on Route 1. The Kittery Historical and Naval Museum is worth searching out, as are the dining, strolling, and swimming spots along coastal Route 103.

In the late 19th century artists and literati gathered at Kittery Point. Novelist William Dean Howells, who summered here, became keenly interested in preserving the area's colonial-era buildings. He, his friend Sam Clemens (otherwise known as Mark Twain), and wealthy summer people began buying up the splendid old buildings in York, where the school, church, burial ground, and abundance of 1740s homes made up Maine's oldest surviving community.

In 1900 Howells suggested turning the "old gaol" in York Village into a museum. At the time you could count the country's historic house museums on your fingers. In the Old Gaol of today you learn about the village's bizarre history, including its origins as a Native American settlement called Agamenticus, one of many settlements wiped out by a plague in 1616. In 1630 it was settled by English colonists, and in 1642 it became Gorgeana, America's first chartered city. It was then demoted to the town of York, part of Massachusetts, in 1670. Fierce Native American raids followed, but by the middle of the 18th century the present colonial village was established, a crucial way station between Portsmouth and points east.

York is divided into so many distinct villages that Clemens once observed, "It is difficult to throw a brick . . . in any one direction without

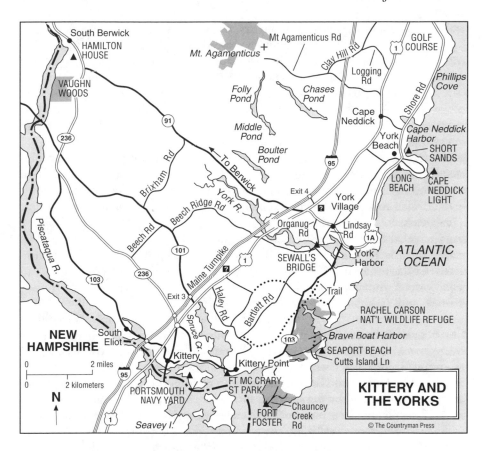

danger of disabling a postmaster." Not counting Scotland and York Corners, York includes York Village, York Harbor, York Beach, and Cape Neddick—such varied communities that locals can't bring themselves to speak of them as one town; they refer instead to "the Yorks."

The rocky shore beyond York Village was Lower Town until the Marshall House was opened near the small gray sand beach in 1871 and its address was changed to York Harbor. Soon the hotel had 300 rooms, and other mammoth frame hotels appeared at intervals along the shore. All the old hotels are gone. All, that is, except the 162-room Cliff House, which, although physically in York, has long since changed its address and phone to Ogunquit, better known now as a resort town. Still, York Harbor remains a delightful, low-key retreat. The Marshall House has been replaced by the modern Stage Neck Inn, and several dignified old summer "cottages" are now inns and B&Bs. A narrow, mile-or-so path along the shore was first traced by fishermen and later smoothed and graced with small touches such as the Wiggly Bridge, a graceful little suspension bridge across the river and through Steedman Woods.

Landscaping and public spaces were among the consuming interests of the 19th-century summer residents, who around the turn of the century also became interested in zoning. In *Trending into Maine* (1935) Kenneth Roberts noted York Harbor's "determination to be free of billboards, tourist camps, dance halls and other cheapening manifestations of the herd instinct and Vacationland civilization."

A York Harbor corporation was formed to impose its own taxes and keep out unwanted development. The corporation's biggest fight, wrote Roberts, was against the Libby Camps, a tent-and-trailer campground on the eastern edge of York Harbor that "had spread with such funguslike rapidity that York Harbor was in danger of being almost completely swamped by young ladies in shorts, young men in soiled undershirts, and fat ladies in knickerbockers."

Libby's Oceanside Camp still sits on Roaring Rock Point, its trailers neatly angled along the shore. Across from it is matching Camp Eaton, established in 1923. No other village boundary within a New England town remains more clearly defined than this one between York Harbor and York Beach.

Beyond the campgrounds stretches 2-mile Long Sands Beach, lined with a simpler breed of summer cottage than anything in York Village or York Harbor. There is a real charm to the strip and to the village of York Beach, with its Victorian-style shops, boardwalk amusements, and the Goldenrod—known for its taffy Goldenrod Kisses. This restaurant is still owned by the same family that opened it in 1896, about the time the electric streetcar put York Beach within reach of the "working class."

During this "trolley era" a half-dozen big hotels accommodated 3,000 summer visitors, and 2,000 more patronized boardinghouses in York Beach. Today's lodgings are a mix of motels, cottages, and B&Bs. There are beaches (with free or metered parking), Fun-O-Rama games and bowling, and York's Wild Kingdom, with exotic animals and carnival rides. York Beach, too, has now gained "historic" status, and the Old York Historical Society, keeper of the half-dozen colonial-era buildings open to the public in York Village, now sponsors York Beach walking tours.

GUIDANCE

The **Kittery Information Center** (439-1319), Maine's gatehouse in a real sense, is on I-95 northbound in Kittery, with exhibits on Maine regions and products and a desk staffed by Maine Tourism Association employees, who dispense advice on local as well as statewide lodging, dining, and attractions. You can also check out regional web sites and lodging by computer. Open daily except Christmas and Thanksgiving, 8–6 in summer months, otherwise 9–5 (bathrooms open 24 hours daily). The rest area also includes vending machines and picnic tables under the pines.

Gateway to Maine Chamber of Commerce (439-7545; 1-800-639-

9645), upstairs over the Weathervane Restaurant, Route 1. Phone queries answered 10–2 weekdays, year-round. Office open 9–5 weekdays.

York Chamber of Commerce (363-4422; via the Southern Maine link, 1-800-639-2442; www.yorkme.org), 571 Route 17, York 03909. On Route 1 just off exit 4 northbound (York), a handsome information center (with rest rooms) modeled on a Victorian summer "cottage" is open daily year-round, 9–5 (later on summer weekends).

GETTING THERE

Trailways (1-800-639-3317) serves Portsmouth, New Hampshire, some 12 miles south. **Little Brook Airport** in Eliot serves private and charter planes.

GETTING AROUND

From late June through Labor Day, 10 AM–8 PM, an **open-sided trolley** links York Village, Harbor, and Beach with Cape Neddick and Long Sands Shopping Plaza. Narrated tours are offered every hour. For details, check with the chambers of commerce (see *Guidance*). A trolley also serves the Kittery outlets during peak periods.

MEDICAL EMERGENCY

York Hospital 24-Hour Emergency Services (363-4321), Lindsay Road, York Village. **911** also works here.

TO SEE

In Kittery

Kittery Historical and Naval Museum (439-3080), Route 1, just north of the Route 236 rotary. Open Tuesday through Saturday, 10–4 June through Columbus Day, then Wednesday and Saturday until December. Inquire about open house during Christmas shopping season. $3 adults, $1.50 ages 7–15. A fine little museum filled with ship models, naval relics from the Portsmouth Naval Shipyard, and exhibits about the early history of this stretch of the Southern Coast. Displays include archaeological finds, ship models, early shipbuilding tools, navigational instruments, trade documents, and mariner's folk art, including samples of work by Kittery master ship's carver John Haley Bellamy (1836–1914). The lens from Boon Island Light is also displayed. Inquire about visiting the nearby Portsmouth Naval Shipyard, established in 1806 and responsible for building half of all American submarines during World War II.

Fort McClary, Route 103. A state park open seasonally (grounds accessible year-round). A hexagonal 1846 blockhouse on a granite base, it was the site of fortifications in 1715, 1776, and 1808. The site was first fortified in the early 18th century to protect Massachusetts's vessels from being taxed by the New Hampshire colony. This is a good place to picnic, overlooking Portsmouth Harbor, but the formal picnicking area is across the road.

For **Fort Foster,** see *Green Space—Parks.*

For **Hamilton House,** the **Sarah Orne Jewett House,** and **Kittery Point,** see *Scenic Drives.*

In York

Old York (363-4974; www.oldyork.org). The nonprofit Old York Historical Society maintains seven historic buildings, open to the public from mid-June through mid-October, Tuesday through Saturday 10–5, Sunday 1–5; $7 adults, $6 seniors, $3 ages 6–16 ($15 per family) includes admission to all buildings. The society also sponsors walking tours and special events, and offers a local historical research library and archives in its headquarters, a former bank building at 207 York Street in the middle of York Village. Begin your tour at the **Jefferds Tavern Visitors Center,** Route 1A, a 1759 building moved from Wells in 1939. Watch the orientation video for Old York and purchase tickets to other museum buildings and tours. Exhibits change, and food is frequently cooking on the hearth at the tavern kitchen. The **Old School House** next door, an original, mid-18th-century York school, contains an exhibit on education of the period. **Old Gaol** (Jail), York Village center. Dating from 1719 and billed as the oldest remaining public building of the English colonies, it once served the whole province of Maine and continued to house York County prisoners until 1860. You can inspect the cells and jailer's quarters and learn about York's early miscreants. Many were hanged at the gallows on Stage Neck (site of the present hotel by that name). **Emerson-Wilcox House,** Route 1A. Dating in part from 1742 and expanded over the years, period rooms and gallery space trace the development of domestic interiors and decorative arts in York from the Revolutionary period to the 1930s. Exhibits include furniture, ceramics, glass, and a complete set of bed hangings embroidered by Mary Bulman in 1745. **Elizabeth Perkins House,** Lindsay Road (at Sewall Bridge—a replica of the first pile bridge in America, built on this spot in 1761). Our favorite building, this 1730 house is down by the York River. It is still filled with colonial-era antiques and with the spirit of Elizabeth Perkins (it's preserved to look the way it did when she died in 1952), the real powerhouse behind York's original Historic Landmarks Society. It was Miss Perkins who saved the Jefferds Tavern. **John Hancock Warehouse and Wharf,** Lindsay Road. An 18th-century warehouse with exhibits of 18th-century life and industry on and around the York River. **George Marshall Store** (a former chandlery at which large schooners once docked), 140 Lindsay Road, houses changing exhibits. **First Parish Church,** York Village. An outstanding, mid-18th-century meetinghouse with a fine cemetery full of old stones with death's heads and Old English spelling. **Civil War Monument,** York Village.

In York Harbor and York Beach

Sayward-Wheeler House (603-436-3205), 79 Barrell Lane, York Harbor. Open June through October 15, weekends 11–4; tours on the hour. $4

KIM GRANT

Fort McClary

adults, $3.50 seniors, $2 children 12 and under. Maintained by the Society for the Preservation of New England Antiquities (SPNEA). A fine, early-18th-century house built by Jonathan Sayward—merchant, shipowner, judge, and representative to the Massachusetts General Court—who earned the respect of the community despite his Tory leanings. It remained in the same family for 200 years and retains its Queen Anne and Chippendale furnishings, family portraits, and china brought back as booty from the expedition against the French at Louisburg in 1745. Accessible from York's Shore Path, near the Wiggly Bridge (see *Green Space—Walks*).

Nubble Light, York Beach. From Route 1A (Long Beach Avenue), take Nubble Road out through the Nubble (a cottage-covered peninsula) to Sohier Park at the tip of the peninsula. It includes a parking area, rest rooms, and a seasonal information center and overlooks an 1879 lighthouse perched on a small island of its own.

York's Wild Kingdom (363-4911; 1-800-456-4911), York Beach. Rides open daily at noon, Memorial Day weekend through Labor Day weekend (weekends only in June and September); zoo is open 10–5. This is a combination amusement area and zoo with paddleboats, midway rides, and over 200 animals, including some real exotica. There are also mini-golf and both pony and elephant rides. It's $14.75 adults, $10.75 children 4–10, and $3.50 ages 3 and under for zoo/ride admission. Zoo only: $11.75 adults, $8.25 children, $1 ages 3 and under.

KIM GRANT

Nubble Light

SCENIC DRIVES
Kittery Point, Pepperrell Cove, and Gerrish Island. From Route 1, find your way to Route 103 (see map on page 51) and follow its twists and turns along the harbor until you come to the white **First Congregational Church** and a small green across from a striking, privately owned Georgian-style house. An old graveyard overlooking the harbor completes the scene. Park at the church (built in 1730, Maine's oldest), notice the parsonage (1729), and walk across the road to the old **graveyard**. The neighboring magnificent house was built in 1760 for the widow of Sir William Pepperrell, the French and Indian War hero who captured the fortress at Louisburg from the French. Knighted for his feat, Pepperrell went on to become the richest man in New England. For a splendid view of the harbor, continue along Route 103 to Fort McClary, and for the same view combined with good food, stop up the road at Cap'n Simeon's Galley (see *Dining Out*) in Pepperrell Cove, where everyone seems to be named Frisbee. It's hidden behind **Frisbee's Market,** in business since 1828, claiming to be America's oldest family-run grocery store (also known for its handmade corned beef). Four large hotels once clustered in this corner of Kittery, but today it's one of the quietest along the Southern Coast. You sense layerings of history here. At the back of the parking lot across from Frisbee's a seemingly forgotten tomb is inscribed with a plaque commemorating Colonel William Pepperrell, born in Devonshire in 1646, died in Kittery in 1734, and Sir William Pepperrell (1696–1759). Just beyond you can still see the foundations of one of the former summer hotels. Turn right beyond Pepperrell

Cove and follow Gerrish Island Lane to a T; then take Pocahontas (the name of another vanished hotel) to World War I–era **Fort Foster,** now a park (see *Green Space—Parks*). Also see **Chauncey Creek Lobster Pound** (under *Where to Eat—Lobster Pounds*) and **Seapoint Beach** (under *Green Space—Beaches*). Route 103 winds on by the mouth of the York River and into York Harbor.

South Berwick. A short ride north of the Route 1 outlets and clutter (see map on page 51) transports you to a bend in the Salmon Falls River that is capped by a splendid 1780s Georgian mansion, restored through the efforts of local author Sarah Orne Jewett; a formal garden and riverside trails through the woods add to the unusual appeal of this place. From Kittery, take either Route 236 north from the I-95 Eliot exit or Route 101 north from Route 1 (through high farmland to join Route 236). From York, take Route 91 north. Hamilton House and **Vaughan Woods** are the first left after the junction of Routes 236 and 91 (Brattle Street); follow signs. **Hamilton House** (384-5269) is open June through October 15, Wednesday through Sunday 11–4, with tours on the hour ($4 adults, $3.50 seniors, $2 children 12 and under); grounds open every day dawn to dusk, Sunday-afternoon garden concerts in-season. The foursquare Georgian mansion built in 1785 on a promontory above the river had fallen into disrepair by the time Sarah Orne Jewett was growing up in nearby South Berwick; she used it as the setting for her novel *The Tory Lover,* and persuaded wealthy friends to restore it in 1898 (the same period that William Dean Howells was involved in restoring nearby York Village). The Society for the Preservation of New England Antiquities also maintains the **Sarah Orne Jewett House** (384-5269) farther up Route 236, smack in the middle of the village of South Berwick at the junction with Route 4. This is another fine 1774 Georgian house that has been preserved to look much as the author knew it. She actually grew up in the house next door, now the town library. A joint ticket to the two houses is $6.

TO DO

BOAT EXCURSIONS
Lobstering trips (call between 5 and 6 PM: 363-3234), Town Dock #2, York Harbor. Tom Farnum offers 1-hour lobstering trips around York Harbor in his 22-foot wooden lobster skiff.

Isles of Shoals Steamship Co. (603-431-5000) in Portsmouth, New Hampshire, offers daily cruises in-season to the Isles of Shoals, stopping at Star Island, site of a vast old white summer hotel that's now a Unitarian conference center. Visitors are welcome to this barren but fascinating place, webbed with walking trails. The ride on the 90-foot replica of an old steamboat takes 1 hour each way.

Also see "Ogunquit and Wells" for excursions from Perkins Cove.

York Beach

FISHING
Check with the **York Chamber of Commerce** (see *Guidance*) about the half-dozen deep-sea-fishing boats operating from York Harbor. Surf casting is also popular along Long Sands and Short Sands Beaches and from Sohier Park in York. The **York Parks & Recreation Department** (363-1040) offers a 4-week introduction to fly-fishing. **Eldredge Bros. Fly Shop** (363-9269), 1480 Route 1, Cape Neddick, is a full-service outfitter offering a variety of guided freshwater and saltwater trips.

FRIGHTS
Ghostly Tours (363-000), 250 York Street (Route 1A), York Village, next to Rick's Restaurant. Late June through Halloween, Monday through Saturday. Candlelight tours through Old York Village guided by a hooded ghost-tale teller.

GOLF
York Corner Golf (363-5439), Route 1, York. Nine holes, par 3.

The Ledges Golf Club (351-3000; www.ledgesgolf.com), 1 Ledges Drive (off Route 91), York. Fully opened with 18 holes in 1999, this is a destination course for much of southern Maine. Carts, pro shop, favored by local residents.

HORSEBACK RIDING
Mount Agamenticus Riding Stables (361-2840), summit of Mount Agamenticus (turn off Route 1 at Flo's Hot Dogs). Open daily late June through Labor Day, 8–8: 1-hour trail rides, extended rides, corral rides, private lessons.

SCUBA DIVING
York Beach Scuba (363-3330), Railroad Avenue, York Beach. Guided dives

around Nubble Light, boat dives, rental equipment, and instruction are all offered.

SEA KAYAKING
Harbor Adventures (363-8466) in York Harbor and **Excursions** (363-0181), based in Cape Neddick, both offer guided tours.

York Recreation Department (363-1040) offers rentals, guided tours, and a 6-week-long summer program.

SUMMER YOUTH PROGRAMS
 York Parks & Recreation Department (363-1040) offers summer baseball, basketball, mountain biking, and dance programs for younger children and teens. The office is in Recreation Hall, Church Street, York Beach.

GREEN SPACE

BEACHES
In Kittery
Seapoint Beach, Kittery, is long with silky soft sand. Parking is residents-only right at the sand, but there's limited public parking 0.5 mile back up Curtis Island Lane (off Route 103).

 Fort Foster, Gerrish Island (see *Parks*) is shallow a long way out and also has low-tide tidal pools with crabs and snails.
In York
Long Sands is a 2-mile expanse of coarse gray sand stretching from York Harbor to the Nubble, backed by Route 1A and summer cottages, great for walking. Metered parking the length of the beach and a bathhouse midway. Lifeguard in high season.

 Short Sands is a shorter stretch of coarse gray sand with a parking lot (meters), toilets, and a fenced-in playground. At low tide look for starfish, snails, and crabs. The Victorian-era village of York Beach is just behind it.

York Harbor Beach is small and pebbly, but pleasant. Very limited parking.

 Cape Neddick Beach, Shore Road just east of Route 1A, is smallest of all, at the river's mouth, sheltered, and a good choice for children.

PARKS
Fort Foster Park, Kittery. Beyond Pepperrell Cove, look for Gerrish Island Lane and turn right at the T onto Pocahontas Road, which leads, eventually, to this 92-acre town park. The World War I fortifications are ugly, but there is a choice of small beaches with different exposures, one very popular with windsurfers, also extensive walking trails and picnic facilities. Fee.

Piscataqua River Boat Basin (439-1813), Main Street, Eliot. Open May through October. Boat launch, picnic area, beach, rest rooms.

Mount Agamenticus (363-1040), York. Open weekdays 8:30–4:30. Just 580 feet high but billed as the highest hill on the Atlantic seaboard between York and Florida. A defunct ski area now owned by the town of York, it can be reached by an access road from Mountain Road off Route 1 (turn at Flo's Hot Dogs; see *Eating Out*). The summit is cluttered by radio and TV towers, but the view is sweeping. Rocks mark the grave of St. Aspinquid, a Native American medicine man who died at age 94 in 1682; according to the plaque, 6,723 wild animals were sacrificed here at the wise man's funeral. See *To Do* for details about mountain biking and horseback riding. Inquire about the pleasant trail to the summit.

Vaughan Woods, South Berwick. A 250-acre preserve on the banks of the Salmon Falls River; picnic facilities and nature trails. The first cows in Maine are said to have been landed here at Cow Cove in 1634. See directions under *To See—Scenic Drives.*

Sohier Park, Route 1A, York. See Nubble Light under *To See—In York Harbor and York Beach.* A popular picnic and scuba diving spot.

Goodrich Park, York. A good picnic spot on the banks of the York River, accessible from Route 1 south; look for the entrance just before the bridge.

Mason Park, Route 1A, York Harbor, adjoining Harbor Beach. Created in 1998 when several classic York Harbor cottages were destroyed in accordance with the wills of their former owners. Another possible picnic spot.

WALKS

Shore Path, York Harbor. For more than a mile, you can pick your way along the town's most pleasant piece of shorefront. Begin at the George Marshall Store (see *To See—In York*) and walk east along the river and through the shady Steedman Woods. Go across the Wiggly Bridge (a mini–suspension bridge), then continue across Route 103, past the Sayward House, along the harbor, down the beach, and along the top of the rocks. Route 103 cuts through the middle of this walk, offering convenient access in either direction.

Brave Boat Harbor Trail, York. One of the few walkable segments in the 10-part Rachel Carson National Wildlife Refuge: A 2-mile trail begins at the pullout on Brave Boat Harbor Road off Route 103. It offers a little history and a lot of birds.

LODGING

Note: York Beach offers many **summer cottage rentals,** and rentals can also be found elsewhere in town. Check with the **York Chamber of Commerce** (see *Guidance*) for individual rentals as well as reliable Realtors.

In Kittery, Eliot, and South Berwick

The Inn at Portsmouth Harbor (439-4040; www.innatportsmouth.com), 6 Water Street, Kittery 03904. Open year-round. Terry and Kim O'Mahoney bought what was called, until fall 1998, Gundalow Inn. The 1890s brick

The Wiggly Bridge in York

village house just off the Kittery green is across the road from the Piscataqua River, within walking distance (across the bridge) of downtown Portsmouth, New Hampshire. Common rooms now feature English antiques and Victorian watercolors, and the five guest rooms are carefully, imaginatively furnished; all have private baths (some with claw-foot tubs), phones with data ports, and cable TV. $135–155 in-season includes a full breakfast. From $85 off-season. No smoking.

🐑 **High Meadows Bed & Breakfast** (439-0590; www.HighMeadowsBnB. com), Route 101, Eliot 03903. Technically in Eliot, this pleasant retreat is really just a few miles off Route 1. Open April through October. A 1736 house with four nicely furnished rooms, all with private baths. Our favorite is what we call the sea chest room. Common space includes a comfortable common room with a woodstove and a formal living room with a fireplace; a wicker-furnished porch overlooks landscaped grounds. Walking trails lead through the surrounding 30 acres. No children under 12. Rooms are $80–90, less off-season; full breakfast and afternoon snack included.

The Academy Street Inn (384-5633), 15 Academy Street, South Berwick 03908. A 1903 mansion just off the main drag in an attractive village, handy to the Piscataqua River, the Sarah Orne Jewett House, and Hamilton House (see *To See—Scenic Drives*). Paul and Lee Fopeano offer five spacious guest rooms (private baths); a full breakfast is served at the dining room table. There's plenty of space for relaxing—a large porch as well as parlor. $65–85.

INNS

In York Village and York Harbor

🐾♿ **Dockside Guest Quarters** (363-2868; 1-800-270-1977; www.docksidegq.

com), P.O. Box 205, Harris Island Road, York 03909. Open daily May through October, weekends the rest of the year. Two generations of the Lusty family imbue this fine little hideaway with a warmth that few inns this size possess. Situated on a peninsula in York Harbor, it offers the best views of any lodging in town. The very best is from the porch of the gracious, 19th-century Maine House, which is the centerpiece of a 7-acre compound that includes four newer, multiunit cottages, and the **Dockside Restaurant** (see *Dining Out*). In all there are 26 guest rooms—including several with gas fireplaces and 6 apartment/suites with kitchenettes—all with private decks and water views. Breakfast is served buffet-style in the Maine House. It's a nominally priced, "continental plus" (fruit compote, baked goods, and such), muffins-and-juice breakfast, laid out on the dining room table—a morning gathering place for guests who check the blackboard weather forecast and plan their day. Guests can use the house fishing equipment and bicycles, rowing skiff or Boston whaler, or take advantage of regularly scheduled harbor and river cruises. Special lodging and cruise packages are offered June through October. Two-night minimum stay during July and August. $78–199 in high season, $65–114 off-season.

Stage Neck Inn (363-3850; 1-800-222-3238), York Harbor 03911. Open year-round. An attractive 1970s complex of 58 rooms built on the site of the 19th-century Marshall House. Located on its own peninsula, the inn offers water views (by request), a formal dining room (see *Dining Out*), a less formal **Sandpiper Grille,** tennis courts, an outdoor pool, a small indoor pool, and a Jacuzzi. The lobby, sitting room, and main dining room are formal; a frequent conference site. $190–285 per room in-season; from $120 off-season; no meals included.

    ♿ **York Harbor Inn** (363-5119; 1-800-343-3869; www.yorkharborinn.com), Box 573, York Street Route 1A, York Harbor 03911. Open year-round. The beamed lobby is said to have been built in 1637 on the Isles of Shoals. An exclusive men's club in the 19th century, this is now a popular dining spot (see *Dining Out*), and the **Wine Cellar Pub Grill,** with an elaborately carved bar, is a local gathering place. The 33 rooms all have private baths and air-conditioning, several in the old house have working fireplaces, some in the newer, neighboring Yorkshire House have Jacuzzis and sitting areas, and most have water views. $89–269 double, continental breakfast included; the neighboring **Harbor Cliffs Inn,** a former summer mansion, is now another adjunct to the inn proper but one with its own elegant common rooms and several suites, the most luxurious accessed by a spiral staircase and walled-in windows overlooking the harbor (there's also a balcony) as well as a gas fireplace and whirlpool bath. $212–299, including continental breakfast. Inquire about the many special packages.

BED & BREAKFASTS
In York Harbor 03911

♁ **Inn at Harmon Park** (363-2031; santal@gwi.net), P.O. Box 495. This shingled 1899 Victorian in the middle of the village of York Harbor, within walking distance of the beach and Shore Path. It's attractive and airy, with a comfortable living room with a fireplace and a front porch with rockers. The four guest rooms vary, from the small Celia Thaxter in the back with its water view (nice if you are alone) to the suite with working fireplace (nice if you aren't). All are bright and thoughtfully furnished in wicker, antiques, and beds dressed with antique quilts. All have private baths, also radios, small TVs, and VCRs. Room diaries are filled with praise for Sue Antal, who is, incidentally, a justice of the peace and knows all the most beautiful spots (indoors and out) to arrange weddings in the area. $79–119 ($59–99 off-season) includes a full, healthy breakfast. The entire house is also available for weekly rental.

Edwards' Harborside Inn (363-3037), P.O. Box 866. Open year-round. Nicely sited across from York Harbor Beach with a long wharf of its own, this solidly built summer mansion is owned by Jay Edwards, a third-generation innkeeper. Breakfast is served in one of the most pleasant rooms in the area: a sunporch with an unbeatable view of the harbor. Many of the 10 guest rooms (8 with private baths) also have water views, and all are air-conditioned and have TVs; the York Suite is a lulu, with water views on three sides and a Jacuzzi overlooking the water, too. Rooms $90–120 and suites from $270 in July and August, $70–190 in shoulder months, $50–160 in winter.

Tanglewood Hall (351-1075; www.tanglewoodhall.com), 611 York Street, P.O. Box 490. Open May through mid-October. This shingled 1880s summer mansion was a summer home of bandleader Tommy Dorsey and his brother Jimmy. Set in gardens and woods, it offers three nicely decorated guest rooms. The spacious York Harbor Suite ($140) has a gas fireplace and conservatory, and all three have private baths and feather beds. New innkeepers Bonnie and Bill Alstrom were in the process of adding another ground-floor room ("The Library") when we stopped by; the octagonal game/music room and many-windowed dining room are pleasant. Breakfast is very full, served by candlelight.

🍁 **Bell Buoy** (363-7264), 570 York Street (Route 1A). Open year-round. Wes and Kathie Cook have restored a spacious 19th-century summer "cottage," offering plenty of common space, rooms with private baths, and a two-room suite. $80–100 in-season includes a full breakfast in the dining room or, weather permitting, on the large porch. No view but within walking distance of Long Sands Beach (a real plus, given the challenge of parking). Off-season: $70–85.

In York Beach 03910

🍁 **The Katahdin Inn** (363-1824; in winter, 617-938-0335), 11 Ocean Avenue Extension. Open mid-May through October. "Bed and beach" is the way innkeeper Rae LeBlanc describes her pumpkin-colored 1890s guest house overlooking Short Sands Beach and the ocean. Eight of the 11 guest rooms have water views. Number 9 on the third floor is small and white with a window and a skylight that seem to suspend it above the water. All rooms have a small fridge. More water views from the living room and two porches (one enclosed), which are equipped with games for poor weather. From $75 (shared bath) to $95 for a large room, private bath; less off-season. No breakfast but morning tea and coffee.

♿ **View Point** (363-2661), 229 Nubble Road, P.O. Box 1980. Office open daily in summer, selected days off-season. A nicely designed, oceanfront, condominium-style complex overlooking the Nubble Lighthouse. All nine suites have a living room, kitchen, porch or patio, gas fireplace, phone, cable TV, CD stereo, VCR, washer/dryer. From $175 for a one-bedroom unit to $425 for three-bedroom units. Weekly rates available.

♿ **The Anchorage Inn** (363-5112; www.anchorageinn.com), Route 1A, Long Beach Avenue. A total of 179 motel-style rooms, most with water views across from Long Sands Beach. For families, this is a good choice; facilities include indoor and outdoor pools, rooms that sleep four, TV, small fridge. In high season $124–325 (for a spa suite) and in low season $57–250; inquire about packages.

In Cape Neddick 03902

Cape Neddick House (363-2500; www.capeneddickhouse.com), 1300 Route 1, P.O. Box 70. Open year-round. Although it is right on Route 1, this Victorian house (in the Goodwin family for more than 100 years) offers an away-from-it-all feel and genuine hospitality. There are four guest rooms with private baths, plus one suite with a working fireplace, all furnished with antiques. Breakfast is an event—maybe strawberry scones and ham with apple biscuits—served on the back deck (overlooking garden and woods), in the dining room, or in the homey kitchen. A six-course dinner—from stuffed mushrooms to raspberry cheesecake, all cooked on the 80-year-old Glenwood woodstove—can be reserved in advance. $85–120 double, depending on room and season.

❋ **Country View Motel & Guesthouse** (363-7160; 1-800-258-6598; www.countryviewmotel.com), 1521 Route 1, Cape Neddick. Open year-round. True to its name, this complex faces one of the few remaining meadows on this stretch of Route 1, an anomaly like this big old house. Margaret Bowden offers six rooms with private baths ($50–85 in-season with continental breakfast) in the house itself and 16 units in the two-story motel (beyond the swimming pool), varying from standard units (with direct-dial phones, cable TV, and air-conditioning) to a two-story apartment ($80–180 in-season). Pets are $10 each per night.

WHERE TO EAT

DINING OUT

Cape Neddick Inn and Gallery (363-2899), Route 1, Cape Neddick. Open year-round for dinner; closed Monday and Tuesday from Columbus Day through mid-June. A combination art gallery and restaurant that's been York's leading restaurant since it opened in 1979 and was totally revamped by owner Glenn Gobeille and chef Michele Duval in 1998. White linen tablecloths and napkins set the tone, and a pianist plays 5 nights a week. The menu is large and varied. Entrées might include wasabi- and sesame-crusted halibut and ginger- and juniper-marinated duck braised in a sweet and tart gooseberry sauce with a summer melon and Bermuda onion salad. The desserts are spectacular. Reservations suggested. $17–25.

The York Harbor Inn (363-5119), Route 1A, York Harbor. Open year-round for lunch and dinner, also Sunday brunch. Four pleasant dining rooms, most with views of water. The menu is large. The seafood chowder is studded with shrimp, scallops, crabmeat, and haddock ($5.95 a cup); milk-fed veal and fresh seafood are the specialties. Dinner entrées might include Yorkshire lobster supreme (lobster stuffed with a scallop and shrimp filling, $28.95) and veal Swiss (sautéed with shallots, mushrooms, and a demi-glace with Swiss cheese, $23.95). Sunday brunch is big. The wine selection is large. Downstairs in the inviting **Cellar Pub Grill** (open 4–11 PM) the menu runs to burgers, soups, sandwiches, and salads.

✎ **Dockside Restaurant** (363-2722), off Route 103, York Harbor. Open for lunch and dinner late May through Columbus Day except Monday. Reservations suggested for dinner. Docking as well as parking. The view of York Harbor from Phil and Anne Lusty's glass-walled dining room and screened porch is hard to beat. Understandably, the decor is nautical and the menu features seafood: at lunch, fish-and-chips, also chicken potpie or a smoked turkey BLT; at dinner, bouillabaisse (including half a lobster), lobster, scrod, and more; roast stuffed duckling is also a house specialty. Children get a "Dockside Vacation" coloring book to use while waiting. Dinner entrées $9.95–19.95.

Harbor Porches (363-3850), Stage Neck Road, York Harbor. Open year-round for breakfast, lunch, and dinner. The gilded-era decor evokes the glory days of the Marshall House, a grand hotel that occupied this site for many decades, and the glass walls overlook the open ocean. The menu is traditional, from seafood-stuffed sole and pan-seared scallops to grilled sirloin. Entrées $18.95–23.95.

✎ **Cap'n Simeon's Galley** (439-3655), Route 103, Pepperrell Cove. Open year-round for lunch and dinner and Sunday brunch; closed Tuesday mid-October through Memorial Day. A special place with a water view. You enter through the original Frisbee's Store (the building is said to date back to 1680; the store opened in 1828) to a spacious dining area with picture windows overlooking the cove and beyond to Portsmouth Harbor. Seafood is the specialty, but you can get anything from a grilled cheese sandwich ($2.75) to a New York choice sirloin steak ($13.95). Try the broiled scallops or fisherman's seafood platter (all seafood is fried in 100 percent vegetable oil).

Mimmo's (363-3807), Route 1A, Long Sands, York Beach. Open for breakfast and dinner June through September and for dinner only the rest of the year; closed on Christmas and Thanksgiving. Named for its colorful chef Mimmo Basileo, this trattoria is a hot spot in summer (reservations necessary). Tables are closely packed, the water view is limited to the front dining room, and the menu ranges from eggplant parmigiana through a variety of pastas to seafood *coastazurro* (mussels, shrimp, haddock, and calamari sautéed with garlic). Entrées $15.95–17.95; BYOB.

Note: Also see **Clay Hill Farm** and the **Cliff House** under *Dining Out* in "Ogunquit and Wells."

LOBSTER

The Lobster Barn (363-4721), Route 1, York. Open year-round for lunch and dinner. A pubby, informal, popular dining room with wooden booths and a full menu. Specialties such as scallop and shrimp pie earn this place top marks from locals. In summer, lobster dinners (in the rough) are served under a tent out back. Lobster is priced daily.

Chauncey Creek Lobster Pound (439-1030), Chauncey Creek Road, Kittery Point. Open daily 11–8 in summer, weekends in October. Owned by the Spinney family since the 1950s, serving lobster in rolls and in the rough, steamed clams and mussels, chowders, baked beans, a chicken dinner, and pizza. There is also a raw bar. An average lobster dinner with steamers is reasonably priced, but don't expect any extras. The locals bring their own bread, wine, and anything they want that isn't on the menu. Tables line a pier on a tidal river, walled by pine trees. There's also inside seating. Weekdays you can usually get a table, but on summer weekends expect a wait.

Cape Neddick Lobster Pound (363-5471), Route 1A (Shore Road), Cape Neddick. Open March through November for lunch and dinner. Situated at the mouth of a tidal river, this attractive modern building with dining inside and out (on a deck) has the look of having always been there. Besides lobster and clams, the menu offers a wide choice of everything from pasta and sandwiches, soups and salads, to filet mignon and bouillabaisse. Dinner entrées from $12.95. Fully licensed.

Warren's Lobster House (439-1630), 1 Water Street, Kittery. Open year-round; lunch, dinner, and Sunday brunch; docking facilities. A rambling, low-ceilinged, knotty-pine dining room overlooking the Piscataqua River and Portsmouth, New Hampshire, beyond. An old dining landmark with 1940s decor. The salad bar features over 50 selections (a meal in itself), and the specialty is "Lobster, Lobster, and More Lobster" (priced daily). The menu is, however, large and varied with several beef dishes and plenty of seafood; crab-stuffed chicken is just $12.50.

Fox's Lobster House (363-2643), Nubble Point, York Beach. Open daily in-season 11:45–9. A large, tourist-geared place with a water view and a pricey menu, ranging from $11.95 for fried clam rolls to $25.95 for a shore dinner: lobster, chowder, steamers, fries, and salad.

York Beach Fish Market (363-2763), Route 1A, York Beach. Billed and generally agreed to be the best lobster rolls in York Beach. Eat in the new booths or walk to the beach to enjoy. Crab rolls, chowder, hot dogs, and more also served.

Foster's Downeast Clambake (263-3255; 1-800-552-0242; www.fosters clambake.com), P.O. Box 486, York Harbor 03991. This is all about lobster bakes for groups, either at their place or yours, anywhere in the world (including the White House).

EATING OUT

The Goldenrod (363-2621; www.thegoldenrod.com), York Beach. Open Memorial Day through Labor Day for breakfast, lunch, and dinner. Still owned by the Talpey family, who first opened for business here in 1896—just in time to serve the first electric trolleys rolling into York Beach from Portsmouth and Kittery. It's still one of the best family restaurants in New England; same menu all day 8 AM–10:30 PM, but lunch and dinner specials are served up at time-polished, wooden tables in the big dining room with a fieldstone fireplace as well as at the old-style soda fountain. Their famous Goldenrod Kisses (saltwater taffy) are cooked and pulled in the windows. A wide selection of homemade ice creams and yogurts, good sandwiches (where else can you still get cream cheese and olives or nuts? And for $2.25?).

Fazio's (363-7019), 38 Woodbridge Road, York Village. Open daily for dinner from 4 PM. This popular trattoria is decorated with original murals and photos of Annette Fazio's mother. The menu is traditional— fettuccine carbonara (pancetta, cheese, cream, cracked pepper, and egg) and chicken Francese (white wine and lemon sauce served with cheese pasta); also interesting daily specials. The pasta is made daily. Pastas: $7.99–10.50; other entrées: $11.25–16.95 (the higher price is for *bistecca*, the restaurant's signature dish). Children's menu. **La Stalla Pizzeria,** part of the family, is a source of pizzas, also subs and salads, from 11 AM.

Lunch Break (363-6039), Route 1 south, York. Open Monday through Saturday year-round, 7 AM–3:30 PM. No credit cards. Easy to miss because it's in a house set back from the road, this pleasant little restaurant offers good taste in both senses. We lunched well on chowder and half a BLT (with provolone), listened to patrons chatting with chef-owner Cathy Cole, and eyed the delectable-looking tortilla salad at the next table. In summer, dining includes tables on the deck.

Carla's Bakery & Café (363-4637), 241 York Street, York Village. Open weekdays 6 AM–3:30 PM, Saturday 7 AM–1 PM. A find, delivering soups, salads, and sandwiches made with fresh ingredients from the local food co-op and suppliers. Launched by the popularity of her almond scones and orange and blueberry muffins, Carla has honed her skills at culinary school. The results include delectable quiches and salads, sandwiches with roasted vegetables and homemade Boursin, as well as hand-

The Goldenrod

cut chicken salad with grapes, lettuce, and mango chutney. Coffees include espresso.

Cap'n Simeon's Galley (see *Dining Out*) is also the best bet in Kittery for a fried scallop roll or burger at lunch.

Flo's Hot Dogs, Route 1. Open only 11–3 and not a minute later. The steamers are just $1.50, but that doesn't explain the long lines, and it's not Flo who draws the crowds because Flo has passed away. This is just a great place. It's even fun to stand in line here. Request the special sauce.

Bob's Clam Hut (439-4233), Route 1, Kittery. Open year-round. The best fried clams on the strip. Here since 1956 and now, finally, with indoor seating.

Rick's All Seasons Restaurant (363-5584), 240 R York Street, York Village. Open daily from 4 AM for breakfast until 2:30 PM weekdays, closing earlier on weekends, for dinner only Wednesday and Thursday until 8 PM. Prices are unbeatable, and specialties include omelets, quiche, and a range of side orders like corned beef hash and hot apple pie with cheese. Rick Ciampa has been operating this town gossip center since 1980.

SNACKS

Brown's Ice Cream (363-4077), Nubble Road, a quarter mile beyond the lighthouse, York Beach. Seasonal. All ice cream is made on the premises. Exotic flavors, generous portions.

Pie in the Sky Bakery (363-2656), Route 1, Cape Neddick, York Beach. Open Monday through Saturday except January; hours vary off-season. The purple house at the corner of River Road is filled with delicious smells and irresistible muffins, pies, scones, and breads, all baked here by John and Nancy Stern.

Also see **The Goldenrod** under *Eating Out* for Goldenrod Kisses (saltwater taffy) and ice cream.

ENTERTAINMENT

Ogunquit Playhouse (see *To See* in "Ogunquit and Wells") is the nearest and most famous summer theater.

Hackmatack Playhouse (698-1807), in Berwick, presents summer-stock performances most evenings; Thursday matinees.

Seacoast Repertory Theatre (603-433-4472; 1-800-639-7650), 125 Bow Street, Portsmouth, New Hampshire. Professional theater productions.

York Beach Cinema (363-2074), 6 Beach Street, York. First-run movies.

SELECTIVE SHOPPING

ANTIQUES

A half-dozen antiques dealers are spotted along Route 1 between **Bell Farm Antiques** in York and **Columbary Antiques** (group shop) in Cape Neddick. Stop in one and pick up the leaflet guide to the couple of dozen member shops between York and Arundel.

TJ's (363-5673), 1287 Route 1, Cape Neddick. In a class of its own. All reproduction antiques, including fine arts and fabrics. Operated by interior designers Jerry Rippletoe and Tony Sienicki.

Also see **York Village Crafts** under *Crafts.*

ART GALLERIES

York Art Association Gallery (363-4049/2918), Route 1A, York Harbor. Annual July art show, films, and workshops.

CRAFTS

York Village Crafts (363-4830), 211 York Street, York Village. Open daily 9–5. Housed in the vintage 1834 church in the center of York Village, more than 100 displays of crafts, art, books, and antiques.

River Place (351-3266), 250 York Street, York Village, features fine crafted pottery, prints, ceramics, and jewelry, clothing; also books, cards, and games.

SPECIAL STORES

Stonewall Kitchen (352-2713; 1-800-207-JAMS; www.stonewallkitchen. com), Stonewall Lane, Route 1, York. What began as a display of offbeat vinegars at a local farmer's market in 1991 is now a mega specialty food business with a big wholesale and mail-order component. Owners

Jonathan King and Jim Stott are quick to claim, however, that all their products—from roasted garlic and onion red pepper jelly or raspberry peach champagne jam through sun-dried tomato mustard to fresh lemon curd and dozens of vinegars, chutneys, barbecue sauces, and specially packaged children's jelly—are still made with homemade care and concern. Through a window you can view the jams and jellies, sauces, and such being squirted through shiny tubes into the company's signature jars. Better, you can sample them in the spiffy new open-kitchen-style shop that's part of this new corporate campus. Right beside the York Chamber of Commerce information center on Route 1, just off Maine Turnpike exit 4. Cookbooks, crockery, and gadgets are also sold.

Gravestone Artwear (1-800-564-4310), 250 York Street, York Village. This departure point for Ghostly Tours (see *To Do—Frights*) is a trove of ghostly and graveyard-related products, from carvings to cards, T-shirts, and more.

Rocky Mountain Quilts (363-6800; 1-800-762-5940), 130 York Street (Route 1A), York Village. Open May through October daily 10–5, call off-season. Betsey Telford not only makes and restores quilts but also sells antique quilts, blocks, and fabrics from the late 1700s to the 1940s (more than 300 in stock, "from doll to king"); decorating accessories as well.

Knight's (361-2500; www.mainequiltshop.com), 1901 Route 1, Cape Neddick. A wide choice of bright fabric, quilt supplies, and small quilted gifts (but no quilts) are sold here. Inquire about quilting classes.

Alpaca Fields (363-4385), 116 Beech Ridge Road, York. The alpacas are on view, along with yarn spun from the fleece of these gentle animals. The store sells sweaters and blankets, also locally made pottery, slippers, and alpaca teddy bears from Peru.

The Museum Shop, 196 York Street (Route 1A), York Village. Open May through December, Tuesday through Saturday 10–5, Sunday 1–5. The museum shop for the **Old York Historical Society.**

YORK OUTLET MALLS

Note: For the Kittery shopping strip, take I-95, exit 3. At this writing the 120 discount stores within a 1.3-mile strip of Route 1 in Kittery represent a mix of clothing, household furnishings, gifts, and basics. All purport to offer savings of at least 20 percent on retail prices, many up to 70 percent. Open daily year-round; hours vary; call 1-888-KITTERY or click onto www.thekitteryoutlets.com. The strip is divided into a series of malls, with the **Kittery Trading Post** (439-2700; www.kitterytrading post.com) as the original anchor store. A local institution since 1926, the sprawling store is always jammed with shoppers in search of sportswear, shoes, children's clothing, firearms, outdoors books, and fishing or camping gear. The summer-end sales are legendary, and many items are routinely discounted.

WINERY

The Parsons Family Winery (363-3332), Brixham Road, York. Open Monday through Saturday 10–5, Sunday noon–5. From Route 1 in York, take Route 91; go 4.8 miles, turn left onto Brixham Road, and look for the big white farmhouse that's now an apple winery. The winery also sells locally crafted products, but this place is all about the orchards that once covered this landscape for miles around and the wine that one family (farming in this spot for 280 years) began producing in 1996. Tours and tastings are offered. Four apple varietals are made at this writing, along with blueberry, peach, pear, and raspberry wines, not to mention old-fashioned hard cider ("like what Grandad made, only smoother"). Visitors are welcome and will learn about local history; you need not buy wine.

SPECIAL EVENTS

Note: Be sure to pick up the area's unusually lively "Summer Social Calendar" at the York Chamber of Commerce (see *Guidance*).

June: **Strawberry Festival,** South Berwick.

July: **Independence Day celebrations,** in York—parades, cannon salutes, militia encampment, crafts and food fair, picnic, and dinner; Kittery—**Seaside Festival** at Fort Foster's Park. **Band concerts,** Wednesday evenings at Short Sands Pavilion, York Beach. **Old York Designers' Show House** sponsored by the Old York Historical Society. **York Days Celebration** *(last days of month, see August)*—raffle, puppet shows, skits.

August: **York Days Celebration** *(beginning of the month)*—flower show, church supper, concerts, square dances, parade, and sand-castle contest. **Seacoast Crafts Fair** *(late in the month).*

Late September: **House Tours. Eliot Festival Days.**

October: **Harvest Fest,** York Village *(the weekend after Columbus Day weekend, usually coinciding with peak foliage here)*—an ox roast, oxcart races, hay- and horse rides, militia encampment, music, and live entertainment.

November: **Lighting of the Nubble** (Sunday of Thanksgiving weekend), Sohier Park, 5:45–7 with a shuttle bus from Ellis Park (363-1040). The famous lighthouse is illuminated in sparkling white lights for the Christmas season.

December: **Christmas Open House Tours. Kittery Christmas Parade and Tree Lighting** and **York Festival of Lights Parade** *(first weekend in December).*

Ogunquit and Wells

Ogunquit and Wells share many miles of uninterrupted sand, and the line between the two towns also blurs along Route 1, a stretch of restaurants, family attractions, and family-geared lodging places. The two beach resorts are, however, very different.

Named for the English cathedral town, Wells was incorporated in 1653 and remains a year-round community of 10,000 with seasonal cottages, condo complexes, and campgrounds strung along the beach and Route 1—parallel strips separated by a mile-wide swatch of salt marsh. Wells is a resort for families, the place to find a reasonably priced weekly rental.

Ogunquit was part of Wells until 1980 but seceded in spirit long before that, establishing itself as a summer resort in the 1880s and a magnet for artists in the 1890s through the 1940s. It remains a compact, walk-around resort village clustered between its magnificent beach and picturesque Perkins Cove; these two venues are connected by the mile-long Marginal Way, an exceptional shore path. The village offers a vintage movie house and the Ogunquit Playhouse, one of New England's most famous summer theaters. Most of Ogunquit's big old wooden hotels were razed during the 1960s and replaced by motor inns. With the 1980s came condos, B&Bs, more restaurants, and boutiques. Luckily, the decade also brought trolleys-on-wheels to ease the traffic crunch at Perkins Cove and the beach. With a year-round population of 1,000 and summer beds for 2,500 visitors, Ogunquit regularly draws 35,000 on a summer weekend, 45,000 on holiday weekends. Our favorite time here is September and October.

Natural beauty remains surprisingly accessible in both Ogunquit and Wells. Given the vast expanse of sand, you can always find an uncrowded spot, and Wells harbors more than 4,000 acres of conservation land, much of it webbed with trails (see *Green Space—Nature Preserves*).

GUIDANCE

Ogunquit Chamber of Commerce (646-2939; www.ogunquit.org), P.O. Box 2289, Route 1 (beside the Ogunquit Playhouse). Open October through May, Monday through Saturday 9–5, until 8 on Friday and Saturday in July and August. It's stocked with pamphlets and offers rest rooms.
Wells Chamber of Commerce (646-2451; 1-800-639-2442; www.wells chamber.org), 136 Post Road (Route 1, northbound side) in Moody.

Open daily Memorial Day through Columbus Day, 9–5, weekdays the rest of the year.

GETTING THERE

By car: Coming north on I-95, take exit 4 (York) and drive up Route 1 to the village of Ogunquit. Coming south on the Maine Turnpike/I-95, take turnpike exit 2 (Wells).

By train: **AMTRAK** service from Boston's North Station was promised for 1996, then '97, then '98, then 1999, but actually seems possible for 2001. A station to serve the Southern Coast is under construction in Wells, just off the turnpike. Stay tuned.

Brewster's Taxi (646-2141), billed as serving Ogunquit since 1898, offers local and long-distance service.

GETTING AROUND

Seasonal **open-sided trolleys** make frequent stops throughout the village of Ogunquit, Perkins Cove, at the beach, and along Route 1. They connect with the trolleys that circulate up and down Route 1 and through the beach and lodging areas in Wells. Fare is nominal. Trolley stops are mapped, and maps are available from the chambers of commerce.

PARKING

Park and walk or take the trolley. In summer this is no place to drive. There are at least seven public lots; rates are $7 per day. There is also free parking (2-hour limit) on Route 1 across from the Leavitt Theatre just north of Ogunquit Square or adjacent to Cumberland Farms. Parking at the main entrance to Ogunquit Beach is $2 per hour ($8 per day at the other entrances; see *Green Space—Beaches*). In Wells parking at the five public lots is $8 per day; monthly permits are available from the town office. Perkins Cove has hellish European-style meters; minimum $2 (good for 1 hour).

PUBLIC REST ROOMS

In Ogunquit: At Footbridge Beach, Main Beach, Perkins Cove, Jacob's Lot, and the Dunaway and information centers.

In Wells: At the Jetty, Wells Harbor Pier, Wells Beach, and Drakes Island parking areas.

MEDICAL EMERGENCY

Ambulance/Rescue Squad (646-5111), town of Ogunquit. **York Hospital** (363-4321), 24-hour emergency, 15 Hospital Drive, York Village. For ambulance service in Ogunquit, phone the fire department: 646-5111; **911** works here.

Wells Ambulance (646-9911). In Wells you may be nearer to **Southern Maine Medical Center** (283-3663), 1 Mountain Road, Biddeford.

TO SEE

Perkins Cove, Ogunquit. This is probably Maine's most painted fishing cove, with some 40 restaurants and shops now housed in weathered

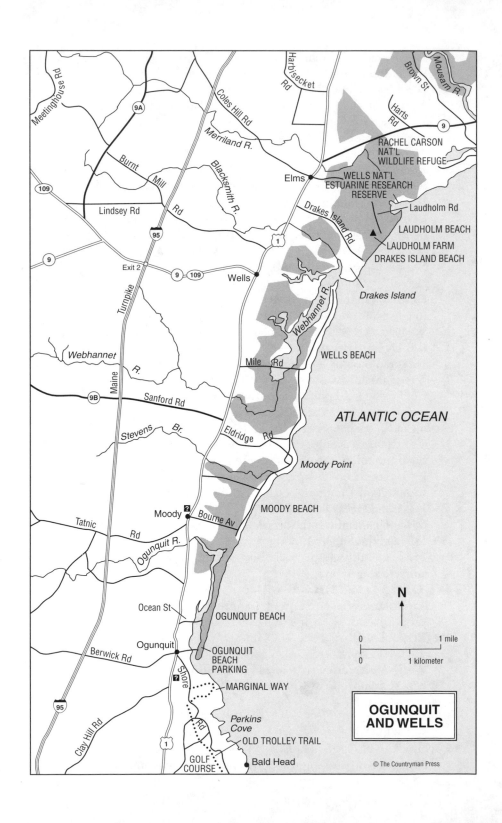

OGUNQUIT
AND WELLS

© The Countryman Press

fish shacks. It is the departure point for the area's excursion and fishing
boats, based beside the famous draw-footbridge. Parking is nearly impossible in summer, but public lots are nearby, and the trolley stops
here regularly. The cove can also be reached on foot via the Marginal
Way (see *Green Space—Walks*).

Ogunquit Museum of American Art (646-4909), Shore Road, Ogunquit
(0.4 mile west of Perkins Cove). Open July through October, 10:30–5
daily; Sunday 2–5. $4 adults, $3 seniors, free under 12. Built superbly of
local stone and wood with enough glass to let in the beauty of the cove it
faces, the museum displays selected paintings from its permanent collection, which includes the strong, bright oils of Henry Strater and other
onetime locals such as Reginald Marsh; also Thomas Hart Benton,
Marsden Hartley, Edward Hopper, Rockwell Kent, and William and
Marguerite Zorach. Special exhibitions feature nationally recognized
artists.

Museum at Historic First Meeting House (646-4755), Route 1, Wells
(opposite Wells Plaza). Open for tours June through October, Tuesday,
Wednesday and Thursday 10–4, Saturday 10–1, otherwise Wednesday
and Thursday 10–4. The Wells-Ogunquit Historical Society displays old
photos, memorabilia, ship's models, and such. Nominal admission.

🖉🕭 **Wells Auto Museum** (646-9064), Wells. Open daily Memorial Day through
Columbus Day, 10–5. More than 80 cars dating from 1900 to 1963,
including a 1919 Stutz Bearcat and a 1941 Packard convertible, plus
nickelodeons, toys, and bicycles. Rides in antique cars are offered.

🖉 **Ogunquit Playhouse** (646-5511; www.ogunquitplayhouse.org), Route 1
(just south of Ogunquit Village). Open mid-June through Labor Day.
Billing itself as "America's Foremost Summer Theater," this grand old
summer-stock theater (now air-conditioned) opened for its first season
in 1933 and continues to feature top stars in productions staged Monday
through Friday at 8 PM; Saturday at 8:30 PM; matinees are Wednesday at
2:30 PM; Saturday at 10:30 AM for kids, Sunday concerts at 7 PM. Usually
we describe summer stock under *Entertainment* near the end of a
chapter; this is a must-see.

TO DO

BICYCLING
Wheels & Waves (646-5774), 578 Post Road (Route 1), Wells. Rents bikes;
also a source of wet suits and skateboards.

BOAT EXCURSIONS
From Perkins Cove
Finestkind (646-5227). Scenic cruises to Nubble Light, cocktail cruises,
and "lobstering trips" (watch lobster traps hauled, hear about lobstering). Both the ***Ugly Anne*** (646-7202) and the ***Bunny Clark*** (646-2214)
offer deep-sea-fishing trips. The excursion boat ***Deborah Ann*** (361-

Perkins Cove

9501) offers 4½-hour whale-watching cruises out to Jeffrey's Ledge.

FISHING FROM SHORE

Tackle and bait can be rented at Wells Harbor. The obvious fishing spots are the municipal dock and harbor jetties. There is surf casting near the mouth of the Mousam River. Also see "Kittery and the Yorks" and "The Kennebunks."

GOLF

Merriland Farm (464-5008; www.merrilandfarm.com), 545 Coles Hill Road off Route 1. Nine-hole, par-3 course on a working farm. Also a café serving Memorial Day weekend to early fall, 8–4 (see *Selective Shopping—Special Shops*).

Maplewood Farm Driving Range (641-8393), Landholm Farm Road, Wells. Putting green, sand traps, 20 tees and grass for wood or iron play. Also see "Kittery and the Yorks."

MINI-GOLF

Wells Beach Mini-Golf, next to Big Daddy's Ice Cream, Route 1, Wells. Open daily in-season 10–10.

Wonder Mountain, Route 1, Wells. A mini-golf mountain, complete with waterfalls; adjoins **Outdoor World.**

Sea-Vu Mini Golf (646-7732) is another Route 1 option in Wells.

SEA KAYAKING

World Within Sea Kayaking (646-0455; www.worldwithin.com), 746 Ocean Avenue, Wells. Registered Maine Guide Andrew French offers guided estuary and ocean tours from the Norseman Resort, Ogunquit. Also see "Kittery and the Yorks."

TENNIS
Three public courts in Ogunquit. Inquire at **Dunaway Center** (646-9361).
Wells Recreation Area, Route 9A, Wells. Four courts.

GREEN SPACE

BEACHES
Three-mile-long **Ogunquit Beach** offers surf, soft sand, and space for kite
flying, as well as a sheltered strip along the mouth of the Ogunquit
River for toddlers. It can be approached three ways: (1) The most popular way is from the foot of Beach Street. There are boardwalk snacks,
changing facilities, and toilets, and it is here that the beach forms a
tongue between the ocean and the Ogunquit River (parking in the lot
here is $2 per hour in-season). (2) The Footbridge Beach access (take
Ocean Street off Route 1 north of the village) offers rest rooms and is
less crowded. (3) Eldridge Street, Wells. Be sure to park in the lot provided. Walk west onto Ogunquit Beach, not to Moody Beach, now private above the high-water mark.
Wells Beach. Limited free parking right in the middle of the village of
Wells Beach; also parking at the east end by the jetty. Wooden casino
and boardwalk, clam shacks, clean public toilets, a cluster of motels,
concrete benches—a gathering point for older people who sit while
enjoying the view of the wide, smooth beach.
Drakes Island, Wells. Take Drakes Island Road off Route 1. There are
three small parking areas on this spit of land lined with private cottages.
NATURE PRESERVES
Wells National Estuarine Research Reserve at Laudholm Farm (646-
1555), Laudholm Road (off Route 1, just south of junction with Route
9, Wells; look for the sign between the Lighthouse Depot and the Maine
Diner), managed by the Laudholm Trust. The reserve consists of 1,600
acres of estuarine habitat for the area's wildlife. *Estuarine,* by the way,
describes an area formed where ocean tides meet freshwater currents
(an estuary). The reserve is divided into two parts, each with its own
access point. Grounds include meadows and two barrier beaches at the
mouth of the Little River and Laudholm Farm, a former estate that
began as a saltwater farm in the 1620s. Owned by the Lord family from
1881 until 1986 (George C. Lord was president of the Boston & Maine
Railroad), it was farmed until the 1950s. This is a birder's mecca. The
farm itself now includes a visitors center (open May through October,
Monday through Saturday 10–4, Sunday noon–4; otherwise, weekdays
only) with a slide show, exhibits, rest rooms, and parking ($2 in July and
August, weekends mid-June through September). Seven miles of trails
meander through fields, woods, and wetlands (bring a bathing suit if
you want to swim at the beach). The Laudholm Trust grounds are open
year-round (gates open daily at 8 and remain open until 8 in summer

months; otherwise, until 5). Inquire about guided trail walks, also about Laudholm Farm Day (last Saturday in July) and Laudholm Nature Crafts Festival on the weekend after Labor Day.

Rachel Carson National Wildlife Refuge (operated by the U.S. Fish and Wildlife Service), off Route 9 on the Wells-Kennebunk line. See the description under *Green Space—Nature Preserves* in "The Kennebunks."

WALKS

Marginal Way. In 1923 Josiah Chase gave Ogunquit this windy path along the ocean. A farmer from the town of York, just south of here, Chase had driven his cattle around rocky Israel's Head each summer to pasture on the marsh grass in Wells, just to the north. Over the years he bought land here and there until, eventually, he owned the whole promontory. He then sold off sea-view lots at a tidy profit and donated the actual ocean frontage to the town, thus preserving his own right-of-way. There is very limited parking at the mini-lighthouse on Israel's Head.

✐♿ **Wells Harbor.** Here is a pleasant walk along a granite jetty and a good fishing spot. There is also a playground and gazebo where concerts are held.

Old Trolley Trail. An interesting nature walk and cross-country ski trail; begins on Pine Hill Road North, Ogunquit.

Mount Agamenticus is a defunct ski area and the highest hill on the Atlantic between Florida and Bar Harbor, Maine. Take the Big A access road off Agamenticus Road, Ogunquit. See "Kittery and the Yorks" for details and information about horseback riding there.

LODGING

Note: Room rates drop more precipitously here the day after Labor Day than any other place we know in Maine, a factor to consider because September is such a pleasant month here, usually still warm enough for beaching and far less crowded than August.

All listings are in Ogunquit 03907 unless otherwise noted.

RESORT

♿ **The Cliff House** (361-1000; www.cliffhousemaine.com), Shore Road, P.O. Box 2274. Open late March through mid-December. The present innkeeper, Kathryn Weare, a great-granddaughter of the indomitable lady who opened The Cliff House in 1872, is overseeing a dramatic expansion begun during winter 2000–2001 and lasting several years. Older buildings are giving way to new: a series of interconnected buildings in which all rooms will have ocean views. The tower-topped, mansard-roofed Cliffscape Building, which opened in 1990, will remain the centerpiece of this 160-room, 70-acre resort. Its multitiered lobby and dining rooms make the most of this oceanside roost atop Bald Head Cliff, and the atmosphere is a blend of amenities (including an indoor lap pool) and family antiques. Stop by at least to dine or view the waves crashing on Bald Head Cliff. Bear in mind that this resort has weathered many changes. During World War II it was literally drafted—as a radar station, keeping a 24-hour vigil for Nazi submarines. When the Weares were finally permitted back on their property, they found it a shambles. Discouraged, Charles Weare placed an ad in a 1946 edition of the *Wall Street Journal:* "For sale. 144 rooms. 90 acres, over 2,500 feet ocean frontage for just $50,000." There were no takers. High-season summer rates range from $170 for a motel-like unit with a limited view to $240 for a one-bedroom suite. Inquire about off-season rates and many packages. Facilities include outdoor and indoor pools, a sauna and Jacuzzi, an exercise room, a game room, tennis courts, and a summertime trolley into the village and to the beach.

RESORT MOTOR INNS

Our usual format places inns before motels, but in the 1960s some of Ogunquit's leading resorts replaced their old hotel buildings with luxury "motor inns."

🐾& **Sparhawk** (646-5562), Shore Road, Box 936. Open mid-April through late October. The 51 oceanfront motel units, each with a balcony, overlook the confluence of the Ogunquit River and the Atlantic Ocean and the length of Ogunquit Beach. The 20 units in neighboring Ireland House (with balconies canted toward the water) are combination living room/bedroom suites. The Barbara Dean and Jacobs Houses, formerly village homes, add another 11 suites and four apartments, some with gas fireplaces and Jacuzzis. The Little White House is a two-bedroom house overlooking the ocean. Guests register and gather in Sparhawk Hall; a continental breakfast is served here, and there are books and comfortable spaces to read and to study local menus. Recreation options include a pool, shuffleboard, croquet, tennis, and privileges at the local golf course and fitness center. One-week minimum stay, July through mid-August; $155–295 in high summer, $75–215 in spring and fall.

🐾& **Aspinquid** (646-7072; www.aspinquid.com), Box 2408, Beach Street. Open mid-March through mid-October. A picture of the old Aspinquid hangs outside the check-in counter of this condo-style complex just across the bridge from Ogunquit Beach. Built in 1971 by the owners of the old hotel, the two-story clusters still look modern. They are nicely designed and range in size from motel units to two-room apartments; all have two double beds, phones, and TVs; most have kitchenettes. Sliding doors overlook the water, and you can hear the surf pounding on Ogunquit Beach. Facilities include a pool, a lighted tennis court, a sauna, a spa, and a fish pond with a waterfall ideal for peaceful reading and relaxation. Rates vary with the season: from $115 in-season, $55–145 in spring and fall.

INNS AND HOTELS

🐾 **Beachmere** (646-2021; 1-800-336-3983; www.beachmereinn.com), Box 2340. Open late March through mid-December. Sited on the Marginal Way with water views, this complex consists of an expansive mansion and a two-story motel-style annex angled in such a way as not to detract from the main house and so that almost all units have water views; there are also rooms in Mayfair and Bullfrog Cottages 0.5 mile away on Israel's Head Road. This has been owned by female members of the same family since 1937. All rooms have kitchenettes and cable TV, and most have private balconies, decks, or terraces; many are large enough to accommodate families. In the mansion no two rooms are alike, and three have working fireplaces. Common space is limited to one small room, but the large inviting grounds overlook Ogunquit Beach, and smaller beaches are a few minutes' walk. High-season rates, $120–210, drop in the off-season and after Columbus Day to as low as $70–110.

☙ **The Grand Hotel** (646-1231), 102 Shore Drive. Open mid-April through November. An attractive three-floor, 28-suite hotel across the road from the shore but with water views from upper floors. Outfall from the 1980s real estate boom, this was built as a condominium complex, but it makes a great small hotel. All suites have two rooms, with wet bar, fridge, color cable TV, and private sundeck or balcony; fireplaces on the top floor. There's an elevator, an interior atrium, and an indoor pool. $170–220 in high season, $90–200 right after Labor Day, from $70 off-season.

♿ **The Colonial** (646-5191; 1-800-233-5191), 61 Shore Road, P.O. Box 895. Open April 16 through October 18. This 80-room complex, owned for many years by Chet and Sheila Sawtelle, includes a four-story 1887 summer hotel, the last of more than a dozen similar hotels that once lined this mile of shore (the last that's still operating as a hotel). It's an inviting, informal place with a large old-fashioned lobby filled with flower-patterned sofas and armchairs (too bad the breakfast room features a soda machine). The guest rooms we checked are pleasant, some with ocean views, ranging $79–99 in July and August, $42–55 right after Labor Day. Depending on the season, a studio apartment is $45–125, and two-room family suites (with efficiency unit) run $50–149. All rooms have private baths, air-conditioning, and direct-dial phones. Only some upstairs rooms in the hotel have sea views, but the location is good—steps from the Marginal Way and midway between the village and Perkins Cove.

BED & BREAKFASTS

The Trellis House (646-7909; 1-800-681-7909; www.trellishouse.com), 2 Beachmere Place, P.O. Box 2229. Open year-round. This is a find. Pat and Jerry Houlihan's shingled, turn-of-the-20th-century summer cottage offers appealing common areas, including a wraparound screened porch (where breakfast is served in nice weather) and comfortable seating around the hearth. Upstairs are three guest rooms, all with full private baths, one with a water view. The most romantic room is a cottage in the garden, but the four rooms in the carriage house also have a squirreled-away feel; we prefer the upstairs to the downstairs rooms there; all rooms have air-conditioning. This is one of those places where guests—whether they come alone or in couples—mingle without stiffness. The Houlihans are genuine hosts. $105–140 in-season, from $75 off-season,

Marginal Way in Ogunquit

includes a breakfast (served anytime between 8:30 and 10) that might include a fruit compote and zucchini pie, or maybe apple-cinnamon French toast and sausage. The inn is handy both to the village and to Perkins Cove via the Marginal Way.

Marginal Way House and Motel (646-8801; 363-6566 in winter), Box 697, 8 Wharf Lane. Open late April through October. Ed and Brenda Blake have owned this delightful complex since 1968. Just a short walk from the beach and really in the middle of the village, it is hidden down a back, waterside lane. There are old-fashioned guest rooms with private baths in the inn itself, and six standard motel rooms in a small, shingled, waterside building, as well as seven one- and two-bedroom apartments. The landscaped grounds have an ocean view. High season $93–195, low $42–122; apartments are rented only by the week in high season.

Morning Dove (646-3891; www.morningdove.simplenet.com), P.O. Box 1940, 30 Bourne Lane. Open year-round. On a quiet side street off Shore Road, within walking distance of everything, is this carefully restored 1860s farmhouse. We like the feel of the living room with its white marble fireplace, and of the seven nicely decorated guest rooms (five with private baths); the innkeepers are Jane and Fred Garland. $85–140 in-season, $65–90 off-season, full breakfast included.

🎖 **Ye Olde Perkins Place** (361-1119), 749 Shore Road (south of Perkins Cove), Cape Neddick 03902. Open late June through Labor Day. Overlooking the ocean, Prim and Dick Winkler's 1717 homestead has six guest rooms (four baths). Away from the village but within walking distance of Perkins Cove and right above a pebble beach in a pretty cove. $60–70 per room (2-night minimum); coffee, juice, and muffins included. No credit cards.

Above Tide Inn (646-7454; www.abovetideinn.com), 26 Beach Street. Open May 15 through October 15. Location! Location! Sited right at the start of the Marginal Way and steps from the bridge leading over to Ogunquit Beach, also steps from village shops and jutting right out into the water. The nine rooms are all shaped differently, each with a sitting area, all brightly, simply, tastefully furnished and equipped with a small fridge, TV, and shower or bath. All but one room have water views. Mid-July through Labor Day rates are $130–185; $85–120 off-season, continental breakfast included.

Beach Farm Inn (646-8493; www.beachfarminn.com), Eldridge Road, Wells 04090. Open year-round. This handsome old house has been taking in guests since the 19th century, when it still also served a working salt-marsh farm. Now an imaginative, hardworking trio have restored the living room and dining room to Victorian elegance, added a state-of-the art kitchen, and spiffed up the sunporch on which is served a full breakfast featuring fresh eggs, fruit, and baked goods. Amenities include a guest pantry and swimming pool, and the four rooms in the house have all been artfully decorated. At present they share two baths but more baths are promised. There are also two efficiency cottages. $70–125 per couple June through September and holiday weekends, including breakfast; less off-season. $10 surcharge for 1-night stays.

COTTAGES

We have noted just a few of the dozens of cottage, condominium, and motel complexes that line Route 1. The helpful Wells Chamber of Commerce (see *Guidance*) keeps track of vacancies in these and in many private cottages.

✎ **The Dunes** (646-2612; www.dunesmotel.com), Box 917, 260 Route 1. Open May through October. Owned by the Perkins family for more than 60 years, this is really a historic property, the best of the coast's surviving "cottage colonies," as well as a great family find. The 36 units include 19 old-style white cottages with green trim, scattered over well-kept grounds fronting on the Ogunquit River, with direct access to Ogunquit Beach by rowboat at high tide and on foot at low tide. Most cottages have fireplaces. All rooms have refrigerators and color TVs. One- and two-bedroom cottages are $130–160 in-season (June 19 through Labor Day), $95–100 off-season. Two-week minimum stay in July and August in the larger cottages, 1 week in the others. Rooms (also scattered) are $85–150 in-season, $68–90 off-season.

🏵✎ **Cottage in the Lane Motor Lodge** (646-7903; www.cottageinthelane. com), 84 Drakes Island Road, Wells 04090. There are 11 housekeeping cottages, all facing landscaped grounds under the pines (an artistic play structure and a pool form the centerpiece); salt marsh beyond. It's a ¾-mile walk or bike ride to the beach. The quiet setting borders the Rachel Carson Wildlife Refuge and Laudholm Farm (see *Green Space— Nature Preserves*). $525–565 per week for a three-room cottage accommodating four, and $645–725 for a four-room cottage good for up to six people; less in mid- and low season as well as off-season.

🐾🦽 **The Seagull Motor Inn and Cottages** (646-5164; www.seagullvacations. com), 1413 Post Road (Route 1), Wells 04090. Open late April through late October. Facilities include 24 motel units, 24 one- and two-bedroom cottages with screened porches, a pool, a playground, and lawn games on 11 acres. Having spent four summer vacations here as a child (more than 40 years ago), Chris Tree is happy to report that the place has survived its recent sale to Carrie McBride and David Moulton and remains a family value, with plenty of common space, a water view, and a loyal following. Rentals are nightly or by the week, $350–840 for housekeeping cottages. Motel units are $46–92.

MOTELS

Riverside Motel (646-2741; www.riversidemotel.com), P.O. Box 2244, Shore Road. Open late April through late October. Just across the draw-footbridge and overlooking Perkins Cove is this trim, friendly place with 41 units; also four rooms in the 1874 house. The property has been in Harold Staples's family for more than 100 years. All rooms have color TVs and full baths, and all overlook the cove; continental breakfast is included and served in the lobby around the fireplace or on the sundeck. $50–140, depending on season and location of room. Three-day minimum July 28 through August 17.

WHERE TO EAT

DINING OUT

Arrow's (361-1100; www.arrowsrestaurant.com), Berwick Road, Ogunquit. Dinner 6–9, late April through October. Reservations recommended. Considered one of the best—and most expensive—restaurants in Maine, with an emphasis on fresh local ingredients. A 1765 farmhouse up a windy wooded road is the setting for nouvelle-inspired dishes with an emphasis on the preparation of vegetables grown in the adjoining 6-acre garden. Chef-owners Clark Frasier and Mark Gaier have earned top accolades, making this a destination restaurant from Boston and Portland. You can dine à la carte or select from the $75 tasting menu, beginning with a creamy crab spring roll with sweet chili sauce, Maine lobster claw with a ginger vanilla sauce, and greens with champagne vinaigrette and parsnip chips, and dining on grilled venison with a celery root pancake, horseradish-enriched stock, fiddleheads, and black truffle potato chips, followed by a selection of local cheeses and a selection of Lucia's desserts. Entrées $35.95–37.95.

Hurricane Restaurant (646-6348), Perkins Cove. Year-round, 11:30 AM–10:30 PM daily. "Our view will blow you away—our menu will bring you back" is the boast of the most popular place to dine in Ogunquit, not to mention Perkins Cove. Reservations recommended. Dining rooms maximize the ocean view. Maine lobster chowder is a house specialty ($8), and a dinner staple is lobster cioppino with littleneck clams, scallops, and a fillet of fresh finfish in a Pernod and saffron tomato broth served with a sweet red pepper *roille.* The dinner menu is big and ranges from pork chops to pheasant to filet mignon (over caramelized mashed banana). Save room for desserts like mile-high cheesecake or warm fruit and berry cheesecake. Lunch options include soups and salads and "small plates" like pan-fried crabcakes with shaved onion salad and chèvre ($13) or grilled wild boar sausage pizza with fresh tomato and aged provolone ($9). Dinner entrées $16–35.

98 Provence (646-9898; www.98provence.com), 98 Shore Road, Ogunquit. Open April through December 1 for dinner (5:30–9:30) except Tuesday. A classic French restaurant featuring Provençal cuisine. You might begin with duck foie gras baked in parchment paper ($12) and dine on pan-roasted duck breast with ginger and orange sauce ($26). Entrées $21–30. Needless to say, the wine list is extensive.

Gypsy Sweethearts (646-7021), 18 Shore Road, Ogunquit Village. Open May through October. Dinner nightly in-season and breakfast weekends; closed Monday off-season. Fine, multiethnic dining in a charming old house that all Ogunquit regulars hit at least once in their stay. Chef-owner Judy Clayton's specialties include light seafood dishes like shrimp Margarite and chicken breast in citrus sauce; early-bird specials (5:30–6). Award-winning wine list. Entrées from $13.95 for a vegetarian dish to $23.95.

Clay Hill Farm (361-2272; www.clayhillfarm.com), Agamenticus Road (north of Ogunquit Village). Open year-round for dinner but closed Monday and Tuesday in winter. A gracious old farmhouse set in landscaped gardens halfway up Mount Agamenticus, with valet parking and an elegant decor; geared to functions but with a reliable menu that might include veal Piccata with fettuccine, tournedos of beef, and potato pancakes piled high with roasted vegetables drizzled with horseradish aioli and topped with shoestring sweet potatoes. Entrées $16–23.

Cliff House (361-1000), Bald Hill Cliff, Shore Road, Ogunquit. Open for breakfast and dinner most of the year, for lunch in July and August. The dining room is in the Cliffscape Building, with dramatic ocean views. Unique creations like lobster tails lightly breaded in hazelnuts and sautéed in lemon-wine butter and beef tournedos sauced with truffle demiglaze and blue cheese, served with roasted tomato-herb bread pudding. Entrées $18–33. Sunday breakfast buffet (7:30 AM–1 PM) is a deal.

The Old Village Inn (646-7088), 30 Main Street, Ogunquit. Open all year but not all nights off-season. Check. This village landmark includes various Victorian-style dining rooms (one in the rear with a fireplace) and an English pub-style bar with an equally varied menu, ranging from pastas and stir-fries to roast rack of lamb, filet mignon, and the lobster of the evening. Entrées $13.95–21.95.

Jonathan's Restaurant (646-4777; www.johnathans.com), 2 Bourne Lane, Ogunquit. Open year-round. There are two entirely distinct parts to this place, both hugely popular. The downstairs restaurant consists of a series of dimly lit, nicely decorated rooms (one with a 600-gallon tropical aquarium) hung with work by local artists and surrounded by landscaped gardens. The food is reliably good. Choices range from vegetarian pasta or polenta to grilled veal sirloin. Entrées $15–25. For more about what happens upstairs, see *Entertainment*.

Poor Richard's Tavern (646-4722), 125 Shore Road. This local dining landmark has moved several times over the past 30 years but remains a favorite. Chef-owner Richard Perkins prides himself on his lobster stew and Infamous Lobster Pie, and offers a large menu ranging from meat loaf to charbroiled fillet of salmon. Entrées $11.95–24.95.

Blue Water Inn (646-5559), Beach Street, Ogunquit. The view of the Ogunquit River is hard to beat, and the specialty is fish—mako shark as well as mackerel and haddock and the shore dinner. Entrées $11.95–17.95.

Grey Gull Inn (646-7501; www.thegreygullinn.com), 475 Webhannet Drive, Moody Point, Wells. Open year-round for dinner. Across the road from the ocean, a dependable dining room with minimal atmosphere. Entrées range from pastas (from $10.95) to coquilles Saint-Jacques ($18.95) and rack of lamb ($22.95).

LOBSTER POUNDS

Note: Maine's southernmost beach resorts are the first place many visitors sample real "Mane Lobstah" the way it should be eaten: messily, with bib, broth, butter, and a water view.

Barnacle Billy's, Etc. (646-5575), Perkins Cove. Open April through mid-October for lunch and dinner. What began as a no-frills lobster place (the one that's still next door) has expanded to fill a luxurious dining space created for a more upscale restaurant. Lobster and seafood dishes remain the specialty, and it's difficult to beat the view combined with comfort, which frequently includes the glow from two great stone fireplaces. Full bar; entrées from $12.95 for grilled chicken to $18.95 for a boiled lobster. You can also order lobster at the counter and wait for your number, dine on the outdoor deck, order burgers.

Lobster Shack (646-2941), end of Perkins Cove. Open April through mid-October, 11–9 in-season. A genuine old-style, serious lobster-eating place since the 1940s (when it was known as Maxwell and Perkins); oilcloth-covered tables, lobster by the pound, steamer clams, good chowder, house coleslaw, also reasonably priced burgers, apple pie à la mode, wine, beer. If only everything didn't come in Styrofoam.

Ogunquit Lobster Pound (646-2516; www.ogunquitlobsterpound.com), Route 1 (north of Ogunquit Village). Open Mother's Day through Columbus Day weekend and winter weekends for dinner. Expanded gradually over the years, this log landmark still retains its 1930s atmosphere and is still all about selecting your lobster and watching it (if you so choose) get steamed in the huge outdoor pots. "Steamers" (steamed clams) are the other specialty. The large menu, however, now ranges from angelhair pasta to filet mignon with wild mushroom ravioli. Beer and wine are available. Don't pass up the deep-dish blueberry pie. Entrées $8.95 for teriyaki chicken to $25.50 for surf and turf. Children's menu.

🦞 **Fisherman's Catch** (985-2698), 134 Harbor Road, Wells Harbor. Open Mother's Day through Columbus Day, 9–8 daily. Set in a salt marsh, with rustic tables; a traditional seafood place with unbeatable prices. Our kind of place. Good chowder and really good lobster stew, homemade crabcakes, baked haddock with rice or french fries. Lobster dinners, children's menu, beer on tap.

EATING OUT

Café Amore (646-6661), 102 Shore Road, Ogunquit. Open mid-March through mid-December. In-season 7 AM–3 PM, closed selected days. A thoroughly cheerful place, good for a leisurely breakfast or an afternoon cappuccino. Specialty omelets (try the "In Your Teeth": spinach, mushrooms, onions, and cheese), many variations on eggs Benedict, waffles, French toast, and specialty sandwiches (maybe "Capri": lettuce, provolone, and veggies in a tortilla roll-up).

Lord's Harborside Restaurant (646-2651), Wells Harbor. Open April through November for lunch and dinner, closed Tuesdays in spring and fall. A big, ungarnished dining room with a harbor view and a reputation for fresh fish and seafood. Lobster (fried, boiled, and baked).

Jake's Seafood (646-6771), Route 1, Bourne Avenue, Moody. Open for all three meals year-round. Specializes in good American cooking, fresh seafood, homemade ice cream.

Congdon's Donuts Family Restaurant (646-4219), Route 1, Wells. Open from 6:30 AM year-round. Fresh muffins, breads, pastries, and doughnuts; also ice cream made on premises and a full menu for lunch and dinner.

🦞 **Billy's Chowder House** (646-7558), Mile Road, Wells. Open daily late January through early December. Overlooking Wells Harbor and salt marsh, a rambling old family favorite with a big menu, a famous chowder, and a selection of fried seafood, steamed shellfish, broiled scallops, and, of course, boiled lobster. There is also plenty of meat on the menu, including a hot dog and fries (but you have to be under 12). Exotic drinks are a specialty.

Maine Diner (656-4441), Route 1, Wells. Open year-round 7 AM–9 PM, near the junction of Routes 1 and 9. A classic diner with a large menu for all three meals, plus beer, wine, take-out; breakfast all day, great corned beef hash, and outstanding clam chowder. The homemade chicken potpie takes a few minutes longer, but it's worth the wait.

🦞 **Gourmet Express** (646-2989), Ogunquit. Sue Pollard's service—pizzas, roll-ups, stuffed baguettes, eggplant parmigiana, pastas, and a children's menu to match—is a real find for everyone whose accommodations include a small table, let alone all those people with cooking facilities who are too tired to go out or cook. Good, reasonably priced food, free delivery. Ask about the dessert of the day.

SNACKS

Bread & Roses Bakery (646-4227), 28 Main Street, Ogunquit. A pleasant source of muffins, coffee, and delectable pastries.

Scoop Deck (646 5150), Eldridge Road (just off Route 1), Wells. Memorial Day through Columbus Day. Mocha almond fudge and dinosaur crunch (blue vanilla) are among the more than 40 flavors; the ice cream is from Thibodeau Farms in Saco. Also yogurt, cookies, brownies, and hot dogs.

ENTERTAINMENT

THEATERS

Hackmatack Playhouse (698-1807), Route 9, Berwick. Stages live performances throughout the year. **Hope Hobbs Gazebo** at Wells Harbor Park offers summer Saturday-night concerts. **Jonathan's** (646-4777; 1-800-464-9934), 2 Bourne Lane, Ogunquit. Open April through October. Upstairs over this popular restaurant is a performance space featuring nationally known performers most nights in-season.

✒ **Booth Theater** (646-8142; www.boothproductions.com), at the Betty Doon, 5 Beach Street, Ogunquit. A black-box theater (based in Worcester, Massachusetts, in winter) with productions Monday through Saturday, June through August. The theater seats 74, and the productions vary from musicals to dramas. Inquire about children's matinees and magic shows.

Leavitt Fine Arts Theatre (646-3123), 40 Main Street, Ogunquit Village. Open early spring through fall. An old-time theater with new screen and sound; showing first-run films since 1923.

Ogunquit Playhouse. Such a must-see part of Ogunquit that we describe it under *To See.*

SELECTIVE SHOPPING

ANTIQUARIAN BOOKS

Boston book lovers drive to Wells to browse in this cluster of exceptional bookstores along Route 1. They include **Douglas N. Harding Rare Books** (646-8785), 2152 Post Road, open year-round, which is huge and excellent with some 90,000 titles, including rare finds, maps, and prints. **The Book Barn** (646-4926), at South Street, specializes in old paperbacks, comic books, baseball cards, and collectors' supplies. **East Coast Books** (646-3584), Depot Street at Route 109, has a large general collection, autographed copies, and art and historical books. **The Arringtons** (646-4137), 1908 Post Road (Route 1), specialize in military subjects as well as vintage paperbacks and postcards.

Noel's Antique Shop in Wells

KIM GRANT

ANTIQUES SHOPS
Route 1 from York through Wells and the Kennebunks is studded with antiques shops, among them: **MacDougall-Gionet** (646-3531), open 9–5 Tuesday through Sunday; a particularly rich trove of country furniture in a barn; 60 dealers are represented. **R. Jorgensen Antiques** (646-9444) has nine rooms filled with antique furniture, including fine formal pieces from a number of countries.

ART GALLERIES
In addition to the Ogunquit Museum of Art (under *To See—Museums*), there is the **Ogunquit Art Association** (646-8400), Shore Road and Bourne Lane, Ogunquit. Open Memorial Day through September, Monday through Saturday 11–5 and Sunday 1–5. The gallery showcases work by members; also stages frequent workshops, lectures, films, and concerts. Ogunquit's galleries (all seasonal) also include: **June Weare Fine Arts** (646-8200), Shore Road; open mid-May through mid-October, 10–4. Original prints, paintings, and sculpture. In Perkins Cove look for the **George Carpenter Gallery** (646-5106). A longtime area resident, Carpenter paints outdoors in the tradition and style of New England's 1920s marine and landscape artists. **Hearthstone at Stonecrop Gallery** (361-1678), Shore Road at Juniper Lane, three doors south of the Ogunquit Museum; landscape paintings and handsome stoneware by a husband and wife, displayed in their unusual gallery/home. **Shore Road Gallery** (646-5046), 112 Shore Road; open daily Memorial Day through Columbus Day weekend. Fine arts, jewelry, and fine crafts by nationally known artists.

SPECIAL SHOPS
Perkins Cove, the cluster of former fish shacks by Ogunquit's famous draw-

footbridge, harbors more than a dozen shops and galleries. Our favorites are the **Carpenter Gallery** (see *Art Galleries*); **Dock Square Clothiers** (646-8548), featuring natural-fiber clothing; and **Books Ink.** (646-8393), a collection of toys, games, cards, wine, books, and other things owner Barbara Lee Chertok finds interesting or educational. Sit on the terrace and look over the cove.

Ogunquit Camera (646-2261), at the corner of Shore Road and Wharf Lane in Ogunquit Village. Open year-round, and features 1-hour film developing. A great little shop that's been here since 1952. It's also a trove of toys, towels, windsocks, beach supplies, and sunglasses.

Harbor Candy Shop, 26 Main Street, Ogunquit. Seasonal. Chocolates and specialty candies are made on the spot; there's also a selection of imported candies.

Merriland Farm (646-5040), 545 Coles Hill Road (off Route 1), Wells. This 200-year-old farm offers a view of Wells that was here for centuries before its sandy shore was developed. In addition to operating a café specializing in pies and berry shortcake and a nine-hole golf course (see *To Do—Golf*), this is a place to pick cultivated high-bush blueberries in July and August and to buy jams, raspberry vinegar, and gift baskets.

Lighthouse Depot (646-0608), Route 1 north, Wells. Look for the lighthouses outside (just before turnoff for Laudholm Farm). Open year-round, closed Sundays off-season. Billed as "the largest selection of lighthouse gift items in the world," this is two floors filled with lawn lighthouses, lighthouse books, ornaments, jewelry, paintings, replicas, and much more. Inquire about the monthly *Lighthouse Digest.*

Ogunquit Round Table (646-2332), 24 Shore Road, Ogunquit. We are delighted to see this friendly full-service bookstore prospering. Well stocked, it fills the first floor of an old house and offers plenty of space for browsing.

SPECIAL EVENTS

April: Big **Patriot's Day celebration** at Ogunquit Beach.

June: **Ogunquit Chamber Music Festival** *(first week);* **Laudholm Farm Day** *(midmonth).* **Wells Week** *(end of the month)*—a weeklong celebration centering on Harbor Park Day; boat launchings, a chicken barbecue, a sand-sculpture contest, and a crafts fair.

July: **Independence Day fireworks** at Ogunquit Beach. **Sand-castle-building contest** *(midmonth).*

August: **Sidewalk art show, Great Inner Tube Race, Kite Day,** all in Ogunquit.

September: **Open Homes Day,** sponsored by the Wells Historical Society. **Nature Crafts Festival** at Laudholm Farm *(second weekend).* **Capriccio,** a celebration of the performing arts, Ogunquit.

December: **Christmas parade** in Wells; **Christmas by the Sea** in Ogunquit.

The Kennebunks

The Kennebunks began as a fishing stage near Cape Porpoise as early as 1602, but the community was repeatedly destroyed by Native American raids. In 1719 the present "port" was incorporated as Arundel, a name that stuck through its lucrative shipbuilding and seafaring years until 1821, when it became Kennebunkport. Later, when the novel *Arundel* by Kenneth Roberts (born in Kennebunk) had run through 32 printings, residents gave the old name to North Kennebunkport.

That the Kennebunks prospered as a shipbuilding center is obvious from the quantity and quality of its sea captains' and shipbuilders' mansions, the presence of its brick customs house (now the library), and the beauty of its churches.

In his 1891 guidebook, *The Pine-Tree Coast,* Samuel Adams Drake notes that "since the beginning of the century more than eight hundred vessels have been sent out from the shipyards of this river." He recalls: "When I first knew this place, both banks of the river were lined with shipyards . . . all alive with the labor of hundreds of workmen," but by the 1890s, Drake notes, shipbuilding is "moribund" and Kennebunkport has become "a well-established watering-place."

In 1872 this entire spectacular 5-mile stretch of coast—from Lord's Point at the western end of Kennebunk Beach all the way to Cape Porpoise on the east—was acquired by one developer, the Sea Shore Company. Over the next couple of decades no fewer than 30 grand hotels and dozens of summer mansions evolved to accommodate the summer visitors that train service brought. The Kennebunks, however, shared the 1940s to 1960s decline suffered by all Maine coastal resorts, losing all but a scattering of old hotels. Then the tourist tide again turned, and over the past few decades surviving hotels have been condoed, inns have been rehabbed, and dozens of B&Bs and inns have opened.

You can bed down a few steps from Dock Square's lively shops and restaurants, 2 miles away in the quiet village of Cape Porpoise, or out at Goose Rocks, where the only sound is the lapping of waves on endless sand. Most B&Bs are, however, the former sea captains' homes grouped within a few stately streets of each other, within walking distance of both Dock Square and the open ocean.

This is the least-seasonal resort town on the Southern Coast. Most

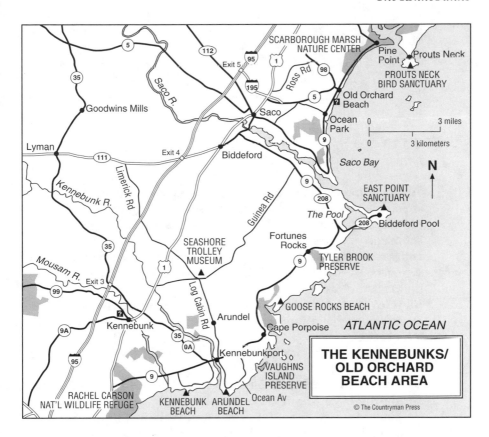

inns and shops remain open through Christmas Prelude in early December (see *Special Events*), and many never close.

GUIDANCE

Kennebunk/Kennebunkport Chamber of Commerce (967-0857; 1-800-982-4421; www.kkcc.maine.org), P.O. Box 740, Kennebunk 04043. Open daily in summer, weekdays year-round, plus Saturdays during special events like Christmas Prelude. The information center is in a yellow building on Route 9 just east of its junction with Route 35 (at the light in Lower Village). There's plenty of parking in the rear of the building. Staff are unusually helpful, and the chamber publishes an excellent free guide. A seasonal desk in maintained in **The Brick Store Museum** (see *To See—Museums*) in Kennebunk.

Kennebunkport Information and Hospitality Center (967-8600). Open May through mid-December. Rest rooms and information at Dock Square.

GETTING THERE

By air: You can fly your own plane into **Sanford Airport;** otherwise, **Portland International Jetport** (see "Portland Area") is served by **Lilley's Limo** (773-5765) and **Mermaid Transportation** (1-800-696-

2463), which also serves Boston and Manchester, New Hampshire.

By car: Drive up I-95 to exit 3 and take Route 35 into Kennebunk, on to Kennebunkport and Kennebunk Beach. Coming up Route 1, take Route 9 east from Wells.

By train: See **AMTRAK** in "What's Where in Maine"; service is scheduled to begin in 2001, stopping near Maine Turnpike exit 3 in Wells (stay tuned).

GETTING AROUND

Kennebunk is a busy commercial center straddling the strip of Route 1 between the Mousam and Kennebunk Rivers. A 10-minute ride down Summer Street (Route 35) brings you to Kennebunkport. Then there are Kennebunk Beach, Cape Porpoise, Goose Rocks Beach, Cape Arundel, and Kennebunk Lower Village. Luckily, free detailed maps are readily available.

Intown Trolley Co. (967-3686), Kennebunkport, offers narrated sightseeing tours with $7 tickets good for the day, so you can also use them to shuttle between Dock Square and Kennebunk Beach.

Bicycles work well here and are a good way to handle the mile between Dock Square and Kennebunk Beach (see *To Do—Bicycling*).

PARKING

A municipal parking lot is hidden behind the commercial block in Dock Square. Good luck!

MEDICAL EMERGENCY

Southern Maine Medical Center (283-7000), Medical Center Drive (off Route 111), Biddeford. **Kennebunk Walk-in Clinic** (985-6027), Route 1 north, Kennebunk. **911** works here.

TO SEE

MUSEUMS

The Brick Store Museum (985-4802; www.brickstoremuseum.org), 117 Main Street, Kennebunk. Open most of the year, Tuesday through Saturday 10–4:30. $6 adults, $5.50 seniors, $2 students and children, no charge 6 and under. This block of early-19th-century commercial buildings, including William Lord's **Brick Store** (1825), is used for changing exhibits of fine and decorative arts and marine collections. You enter through the gift store. The permanent collection upstairs has been completely redesigned for 2001, focusing on four distinct chapters in the town's history: early settlement, shipbuilding and shipping, the late-19th-century resort era, and what's happened since. Inquire about guided walks.

✍ **Seashore Trolley Museum** (967-2800; www.trolleymuseum.org), Log Cabin Road, located 3.2 miles up North Street from Kennebunkport or 2.8 miles north on Route 1 from Kennebunk, then right at the yellow blinker. Open daily, rain or shine, Father's Day through Columbus Day, weekends in May and through October; call to check on special events. $7.25 adults, $5.25 children, and family rates. This nonprofit museum has preserved the history of the trolley era, displaying more than 200 vehicles from the world over. The impressive collection began in 1939, when the last open-sided Biddeford–Old Orchard Beach trolley was retired to an open field straddling the old Atlantic Shore Line railbed. The museum now owns 300 acres as well as cars shipped here from London, Budapest, Rome, and Nagasaki, among other cities. A nearly 4-mile round-trip excursion on a trolley takes visitors out through woods and fields, along a stretch once traveled by summer guests en route to Old Orchard Beach.

Kennebunkport Historical Society (967-2751). Based in the Town House School on North Street, Kennebunkport. Open year-round, Wednesday through Saturday 1–4. Displays local memorabilia; maritime exhibits are housed in the adjoining office of the Clark Shipyard. The society maintains the **Nott House,** open mid-June through Columbus Day, Tuesday through Friday 1–4. A Greek Revival mansion with Doric columns, original wallpapers, carpets, and furnishings. $3 adults. Also see *To Do—Walks.*

HISTORIC SITES

Wedding Cake House, Summer Street (Route 35), Kennebunk. This privately owned 1826 house is laced up and down with white wooden latticework. The tale is that a local sea captain had to rush off to sea before a proper wedding cake could be baked, but he more than made up for it later.

South Congregational Church, Temple Street, Kennebunkport. Just off Dock Square, built in 1824 with a Christopher Wren–style cupola and belfry; Doric columns added in 1912.

Louis T. Graves Memorial Library (967-2778), Main Street, Kennebunkport. Built in 1813 as a bank, which went bust, it later served as a customs house. It was subsequently donated to the library association by artist Abbott Graves, whose pictures alone make it worth a visit. You can still see the bank vault and the sign from the customs collector's office. Upstairs, the book sale room is full of bargains.

First Parish Unitarian Church, Main Street, Kennebunk. Built between 1772 and 1773 with an Asher Benjamin–style steeple added between 1803 and 1804, along with a Paul Revere bell. In 1838 the interior was divided into two levels, with the church proper elevated to the second floor.

Kennebunkport Maritime Museum & Shop (967-3218). Open May 15 through October 15, 10–4. Admission fee. This "museum" occupies the former boathouse in which Booth Tarkington wrote. The last remnants of the schooner *Regina* and a collection of early-19th-century scrimshaw and other nautical memorabilia are displayed. There is a museum shop.

SCENIC DRIVE

Ocean Avenue, starting in Kennebunkport (see map on page 91), follows the Kennebunk River for a mile to Cape Arundel and the open ocean, then winds past many magnificent summer homes, including **Walker's Point,** former president Bush's summer estate (it fills a private 11-acre peninsula). Built by his grandfather in 1903, its position was uncannily ideal for use as a president's summer home, moated by water on three sides, yet clearly visible from the pull-out places along the avenue. Continue along the ocean (you don't have to worry about driving too slowly, because everyone else is, too). Follow the road to **Cape Porpoise,** site of the area's original 1600s settlement. The cove is still a base for lobster and commercial fishing boats, and the village is a good place to lunch or dine. Continue along Route 9 to Clock Farm Corner (you'll know it when you see it) and turn right on Dyke Road to **Goose Rocks Beach;** park and walk. Return to Route 9 and cross it, continuing via Goose Rocks Road to the **Seashore Trolley Museum** (see *To See—Museums*) and then Log Cabin Road to Kennebunkport.

TO DO

BALLOONING
Balloons over New England (499-7575; 1-800-788-5562), based in Kennebunkport, offers champagne flights year-round. $200 per person. Also see *To Do* in "Portland Area."

BICYCLING
Cape-Able Bike Shop (967-4382), Townhouse Corners (off Log Cabin Road), Kennebunkport. Billed as Maine's biggest bike shop, Cape-Able rents a variety of bikes, including tandems and trail-a-bikes; owner Peter Sargent is the local biking guru, source of maps and advice. Open most of the year; in summer months Monday through Saturday 9–6, closed Monday off-season. The lay of this land lends itself to exploration by bike, a far more satisfying way to go in summer than by car since you can stop and park wherever the view and urge hit you. Inquire about the **Bridle Path** (an old trolley-line route) and **Wonderbrook Parkland.**

Pups & Pedals (967-1198), The Yellow House, Lower Village, Kennebunk. Rental bikes are retros (coaster brakes only) and tandems.

BOATBUILDING SCHOOL
The Landing School of Boat Building and Design (985-7976), River Road, Kennebunk, offers a September-to-June program in building sailing craft. Visitors welcome if you call ahead.

BOAT EXCURSIONS
See *Fishing, Sailing,* and *Whale-Watching,* and check with the chamber of commerce (see *Guidance*).

CARRIAGE RIDES
Rockin Horse Stables (967-4288), 245 Arundel Road, Kennebunkport. Tours of Kennebunkport's historic district (25 minutes) in a spiffy white

vis-à-vis carriage with burgundy-colored velvet seats and antique lanterns are offered by Vincent Thelin.

DAY CAMP

𝒮 **Kennebunk Beach Improvement Association** (967-2180; September through May, 967-4075) offers weekly sessions for 3- to 18-year-olds, featuring swimming, sailing, rowing, fishing, golf, tennis, arts and crafts, photography, and sand-castle building.

FISHING

Deep-sea fishing is available on the charter boat *Lady J* (985-7304).

Guided fly- and spin-fishing are offered through Northeast Angler (967-5889), an Orvis distributor in Lower Village, Kennebunk.

GOLF

Cape Arundel Golf Club (967-3494), Kennebunkport, 18 holes. These are the local links former president Bush frequents. Open to the public except 11–2:30. **Webhannet Golf Club** (967-2061), Kennebunk Beach, 18 holes. Open to the public except 11:30–1. **Dutch Elm Golf Course** (282-9850), Arundel, 18 holes; cart and club rental, lessons, pro shop, snack bar, putting greens.

𝒮 **Hillcrest Pitch & Putt and Driving Range** (967-4661), Kennebunk. Open daily 9–dusk; balls and clubs furnished.

Also see *To Do—Golf* in "Kittery and the Yorks."

SAILING

Several schooners and yachts offer daysails; check with the chamber of commerce (see *Guidance*).

TROLLEY RIDE

See **Seashore Trolley Museum** under *To See—Museums.*

WHALE-WATCHING

This is a popular departure point for whale-watching on Jeffrey's Ledge, about 20 miles offshore. If you have any tendency toward seasickness, be sure to choose a calm day. Chances are you'll see more than a dozen whales. Frequently sighted species include finbacks, minkes, rights, and humpbacks. The ***Nautilus*** (967-0707), a 65-foot boat carrying up to 100 passengers, offers narrated trips daily from May through October. ***First Chance*** (967-5507) also offers whale-watching and sunset cruises.

WINTER PASTIMES

CROSS-COUNTRY SKIING

Harris Farm (499-2678), Buzzell Road, Dayton. A 500-acre dairy farm with more than 20 miles of trails. Equipment rentals available. Located 1.5 miles from the Route 5 and Route 35 intersection.

SLEIGH RIDES

Vincent and Susan Thelin of **Rockin Horse Stables** (967-4288), 245 Arundel Road, Kennebunkport, offer half-hour to 40-minute sleigh rides on their 100-acre farm; $10 adults, $6 children; group rates.

GREEN SPACE

BEACHES

The Kennebunks discourage weekend day-trippers by requiring a permit to park at major beaches. Day and seasonal passes must be secured from the chamber of commerce, town hall, police department, or local lodging places. You can also park in one of the town lots and walk, bike, or take a trolley to the beach.

Goose Rocks Beach, a few miles north of Kennebunkport Village on Route 9, is the area's most beautiful beach: a magnificent, wide, smooth stretch of silver-white sand backed by the road.

Kennebunk and **Gooch's Beaches** in Kennebunk are both long, wide strips of firm sand backed by Beach Avenue, divided by Oak's Neck. Beyond Gooch's Beach, take Great Hill Road along the water to **Strawberry Island,** a great place to walk and examine tidal pools. Please don't picnic. Keep going and you come to **Mother's Beach,** small and very sandy.

Arundel Beach, near the Colony Hotel at the mouth of the Kennebunk River, offers nice rocks for climbing.

Parsons Beach, south of Kennebunk Beach on Route 9, requires no permit, but it's impossible to park nearby in-season; off-season it's a splendid place for a walk.

NATURE PRESERVES

 ♿ **Rachel Carson National Wildlife Refuge** (646-9226). Headquarters for this approximately 50-mile, nearly 5,000-acre preserve are just south of the Kennebunkport line at 321 Port Road (Route 9) in Wells. Office open weekdays, 8–4:30. The preserve is divided among 10 sites along Maine's Southern Coast. Pick up a leaflet guide to the mile-long, wheelchair-accessible nature trail here. (Also see **Laudholm Farm** described under *Green Space—Nature Preserves* in "Ogunquit and Wells.")

Kennebunkport Conservation Trust, P.O. Box 7028, Cape Porpoise 04014, maintains several properties. These include the **Tyler Brook Preserve** near Goose Rocks, the 148-acre **Emmons Preserve** along the Batson River (access from unpaved Gravelly Road, off Beachwood Road), and the **Vaughns Island Preserve,** which offers nature trails on a wooded island separated from the mainland by two tidal creeks. Cellar holes of historic houses are accessible by foot from 3 hours after to 3 hours before high tide.

The Nature Conservancy (729-5181) maintains 14-acre **Butler Preserve** on the Kennebunk River, including Picnic Rock, and the **Kennebunk Plains Preserve** (1,500 acres of blueberry plains in West Kennebunk; take Route 99 toward Sanford).

East Point Sanctuary, off Route 9 (east of Goose Rocks Beach) in Biddeford Pool. A 30-acre Maine Audubon Society preserve, well known to birders, who flock here during migrating seasons. Beautiful any time of year. From Route 9 turn right just beyond Goose Rocks Beach onto Fortune Rocks Beach Road to Lester B. Orcutt Boulevard; turn right, drive almost to the end, and look for a chain-link fence and AUDUBON sign. The trail continues along the golf course and sea.

WALKS

Henry Parsons Park, Ocean Avenue, is a path along the rocks leading to Spouting Rock and Blowing Cave, both sights to see at midtide. A great way to view the beautiful homes along Ocean Avenue.

St. Anthony Monastery and Shrine (967-2011), Kennebunkport. Some 20 acres of peaceful riverside fields and forests on Beach Road, now maintained by Lithuanian Franciscans as a shrine and retreat. Visitors are welcome; gift shop. Ask about summer lodging in the **Guesthouse.**

LODGING

The Kennebunks represent one of the Maine coast's largest concentrations of inns and B&Bs; some 80 lodging places belong to the chamber. These, however, add up to just 1,400 rooms, all of which are filled on August weekends. For this reason, we list a number of options in different price ranges ($65–399 in-season); this is still just a fraction of what's available. These lodging places tend to stay open at least through the first two weekends in December, when the town celebrates Christmas Prelude, and many are open year-round.

All listings are in Kennebunkport 04046 unless otherwise noted.

RESORT HOTEL

🐾✂️♿**The Colony Hotel** (967-3331; 1-800-552-2363; www.thecolonyhotel.com), 140 Ocean Avenue and King's Highway. Open May through October. With 123 rooms (all with private baths) in three buildings, this is among the last of New England's coastal resorts that are still maintained in the grand style. It's set on a rise, overlooking the point at which the Kennebunk River meets the Atlantic. It's been owned by the Boughton family since 1948; many guests have been coming for generations. Amenities include a saltwater pool, a private beach, an 18-hole putting green, and a social program. A 3-night minimum is required for weekend reservations for July and August. $175–425 single or double per day includes a full breakfast and 25 percent discount on lunch, dinner, or Sunday brunch; $25 per extra person (children too), plus $5 per person service charge. Worth it. Pets are $25 per day.

TOP-DOLLAR INNS AND B&BS

Captain Lord Mansion (967-3141; www.captainlord.com), P.O. Box 800. Open year-round at the corner of Pleasant and Green Streets. This splendid mansion, built in 1814, is one of the most romantic inns around. The three-story, Federal-era home is topped with a widow's walk from which guests can contemplate the town and sea beyond.

Other architectural features include a three-story suspended elliptical staircase and pine doors that have been painted trompe l'oeil–style to simulate inlaid mahogany. There are 16 meticulously decorated rooms, 15 with gas fireplaces, some with high four-posters and canopy beds— and all with antiques and private baths. The Merchant Captain's Suite boasts what's probably the largest, most elaborate bathroom in Maine. The gathering room is also very elegant, but the full breakfast is an informal affair, served in the large country kitchen. Since 1978 hosts Bev Davis and Rick Litchfield have devoted their considerable energies to making this one of Maine's outstanding inns. Phebe's Fantasy, a separate building, has four more rooms with fireplaces. $175–399 per room in high season, breakfast and tea included; $125–325 off-season.

White Barn Inn (967-2321; www.whitebarninn.com), P.O. Box 560C, Beach Street. Open year-round. The "barn" is now an elegant dining room (see *Dining Out*) attached to the inn. Built in 1820 as a farmhouse, later enlarged as the Forest Hills Hotel, this complex midway between Dock Square and Kennebunk Beach has no view, and the least-expensive rooms are small, but it represents the height of Southern Coast luxury and formality. Choose an antiques-furnished room in the original farmhouse, a suite in the carriage house (four-poster king beds, fireplaces, and marble baths with whirlpool tubs), a cottage suite with its specially crafted furnishings, a double-sided fireplace, Jacuzzi, and steam shower, or the former loft suite of owner Laurie Bongiorno. Guests breakfast in the inn's original, old-fashioned dining room, and common space consists of a sitting room and the landscaped pool area. The 25 rooms vary in size, decor, plumbing, and niceties like fireplaces; $230–560 per couple includes breakfast, afternoon tea, and use of touring bikes. Inquire about special packages.

The Beach House (967-3850; www.beachhseinn.com), 211 Beach Avenue, Kennebunkport. Open year-round. Laurie Bongiorno (see above) and his associates have spiffed up this formerly modest B&B across the street from Kennebunk Beach. The old sitting room and dining room remain comfortable but have obviously been decorated by a top designer. The eight rooms are $210–290 April through November; less off-season.

Note: The 20-room 19th-century **Breakwater Inn** on the Kennebunk River has also been recently acquired by Laurie Bongiorno et al. and will undoubtedly have been dramatically upscaled by the 2001 season.

MODERATELY EXPENSIVE INNS AND B&BS
On the water

Cape Arundel Inn (967-2125; www.capearundelinn.com), 208 Ocean Avenue, P.O. Box 530A, Kennebunkport 04046. Open mid-April through December. The most dramatic location in town, facing the open ocean with just Walker's Point (the islandlike estate of former president Bush) interrupting the water view. One of the area's 19th-century mansion

ROBERT DENNIS

Dock Square during Christmas Prelude

"cottages," this has been an inn for some time but has become one of the coast's best places to stay only in the past couple of years, since Jack Nahil, former owner of the White Barn Inn and present owner of On The Marsh Tavern (see *Dining Out*), began transforming it room by room. Nahil has added windows (as if there weren't already enough) to maximize the views and has obviously enjoyed painting and decorating each of the seven rooms in the main house and six in the adjacent motel (a 1950s addition but weathering nicely with picture windows facing the water, parking in back, TVs). A carriage-house water-view suite (up a long flight of stairs) has a deck and sitting area, a fridge, and a microwave. All rooms have phones, and the living room is comfortably elegant, hung with interesting art, some of it his own. The dining room, which is open for dinner to the public (see *Dining Out*), gets rave reviews. $200–250 in-season; from $135 off-season; includes a light breakfast.

✎ **Tides Inn By-the-Sea** (967-3757; www.tidesinnbythesea.com), 252 Kings Highway, Goose Rocks Beach, Kennebunkport 04046. Open May through October. Away from Dock Square but right across from the area's best beach: wide, firm enough for running, long, and silvery. This is one of the area's best-kept secrets—a small, very Victorian inn built by Maine's foremost shingle-style architect, John Calvin Stevens, in 1899. Guests have included Teddy Roosevelt and Sir Arthur Conan Doyle. Owned since 1972 by Marie Henriksen and now run jointly with her daughter Kristin Blomberg, it is one of the area's most popular places to eat (see *Dining Out*), but guests also have plenty of comfortable sitting space around the fireplace downstairs. Rooms in the main building are furnished with antiques, and we recommend going for the high-end

rooms with both private bath and view. We were lulled to sleep by the sound of the waves in Room 24, a third-floor aerie with an ocean view from the bed. $115–165. This is one place that manages to be both romantic and a family find. Next door, **Tides Too** offers a one-bedroom apartment ($1,500 per week in-season; from $265 per night). Inquire about Emma Foss (the ghost).

The Ocean View (967-2750; www.theoceanview.com), 171 Beach Avenue, Kennebunk Beach 04043. Open April through mid-December. Bob and Carole Arena's painted lady is right across from Kennebunk Beach. The main house has four bright oceanfront guest rooms and one suite, a comfortable TV room, and a living room with fireplace and a sunny breakfast room with a view of the ocean across the street. A separate building houses four pretty water-view suites with sitting areas, color TVs, and private terraces. All rooms offer bathrobes, a CD player, ceiling fans, a mini-fridge, and a phone. Breakfasts are consciously healthy as well as full. "Breakfast in bed" is served to guests in suites. High-season rates run $210–295; low, $130–235.

🐾⌀ **Seaside Motor Inn & Cottages** (967-4461; www.kennebunkbeach.com), P.O. Box 631, Gooch's Beach 04046. The motor inn is open year-round; cottages are rented May through October. An attractive complex formed by a 1720s homestead, a 1756 inn, a modern 22-room motor inn, and 10 housekeeping cottages—all set in 20 landscaped acres on a private beach next to one of Maine's best public strands. This property has been in the Gooch-Severance family for 13 generations. The homestead, which was built as a tavern (the tavern keeper operated the ferry across the mouth of the Kennebunk River here), is now rented as a cottage. The cheery breakfast room (a buffet breakfast is set out for motor-inn guests) is a former boathouse for the 19th-century inn that stood here until the 1950s. Motor-inn rooms are large, with two queen beds and cable TV recessed in highboys. All have private phones and balconies or patios. Cottages vary in size and view. Cottages are per month in July and August, per week the rest of the season. One-week minimum in oceanfront rooms and 2-day minimum in terrace-side rooms in high season. $179–199 per night; less off-season. Pets are accepted in some cottages.

Bufflehead Cove Inn (967-3879; www.buffleheadcove.com), Box 499, off Route 35, Kennebunkport 04046. Open April through December. This is a hidden gem, sequestered on 6 acres at the end of a dirt road, overlooking an 8-foot tidal cove, but less than a mile from the village of Kennebunkport. It's a Dutch colonial–style home in which Harriet and Jim Gott raised their children. Harriet is a native of nearby Cape Porpoise, and Jim is a commercial fisherman. There are five pretty guest rooms and a suite, some with hand-painted or stenciled wall designs. The Hideaway features a fireplace that opens into the bedroom on one side and into the sitting area on the other. The living room has a hearth and deep window seats; you'll also find an inviting veranda, and woods and orchard to explore. $115–295 includes a full breakfast and after-noon wine and cheese.

The Inn at Harbor Head (967-5564; www.harborhead.com), 41 Pier Road, Cape Porpoise 04046. Open year-round. Dick and Eve Roesler offer three rooms and two suites (both with fireplaces) in their ram-bling, shingled home overlooking Cape Porpoise harbor. The Summer Suite has a view of the picturesque harbor from the bath as well as from the bed. Most rooms have water views and hand-painted seascapes on the walls; all are decorated with florals and antiques. Guests share the dock, terrace, and sitting rooms; there is an inviting fireplace in the library. Fresh-baked goods top off large breakfasts; afternoon tea or wine and cheese are served. Beach passes and towels provided for nearby Goose Rocks Beach. No smoking, no TV. $190–330 per room in-season, $130–260 in winter.

In Kennebunkport 04046

Kennebunkport Inn (967-2621; 1-800-248-2621; www.kennebunkport inn.com), 1 Dock Square, P.O. Box 111. Open year-round; dining room closed November through April. Originally an 1890s mansion, but an inn since 1926. Although just a skip from Dock Square, it's set back from the hubbub. The feel here is of a small, personable European hotel, the kind with one innkeeper (Rick Griffin) behind the check-in desk and the other (Martha Griffin) supervising the well-respected kitchen. There are 34 rooms, some with river views, three with gas fireplaces. The inn has three sections—the main house; a 1980s Federal-style addition; and a 1930s river house, with smaller rooms and stenciled walls. Each room is individually decorated with antiques, and all have TVs, private baths, and air-conditioning; many have water views. In summer a small pool on the terrace is available to guests. The cocktail lounge is dark and friendly with a huge old bar and green-hooded lights; evening pi-ano music. Special packages include meals and a lobster cruise. High-season rates $99.50–299 per room, off-season $79.50–289.

Inn on South Street (967-5151; 1-800-963-5151; www.innonsouthst.com), South Street, P.O. Box 478A. Open year-round. A Greek Revival home on a quiet street preserves a sense of the era in which it was built. Inn-keeper Jack Downs is a retired professor with a keen interest in the China trade, and the living room decor includes the kind of Chinese furniture and furnishings a Kennebunkport sea captain might well have brought back. There are three guest rooms and a suite. Our favorite room, named for "Mrs. Perkins," has a fireplace, a pine four-poster bed with a canopy, Oriental rugs, a new bath, and a portrait of its namesake tucked in the closet. The first-floor suite has its own sitting room, a four-poster bed and wood-burning stove, a bath with Jacuzzi, a kitchen, and a porch overlooking the herb garden. Breakfast is either in the din-ing room or on the terrace by the landscaped garden in the back; after-noon tea is also served, and is included in rates that run $105–175 for a double room, $105–185 for a fireplace room, $185–250 for the suite.

   よ **The Captain Fairfield Inn** (967-4454; 1-800-322-1928; www.captain fairfield.com), P.O. Box 2690, corner of Pleasant and Green Streets. Open year-round. There is a sense of light and space both inside and out—plenty of comfortable, gracious common spaces and a lawn that stretches back across the width of the block into that of the neighboring Inn on South Street (see above). The nine bedrooms all have queen beds and private baths and are tastefully furnished; four have gas fireplaces, and the Library Suite has a double whirlpool as well. Innkeepers Janet and Rick Wolf offer a four-course breakfast, perhaps featuring Maine blueberry crêpes, pumpkin pancakes, or skillet frittatas. $165–250 in high season, $110–225 in low; $25 per extra person. Off-season specials.

Old Fort Inn (967-5353; 1-800-828-FORT; www.oldfortinn.com), P.O. Box M. Open mid-April through mid-December. Sequestered in a quiet corner of Kennebunkport just off Ocean Avenue with spacious grounds, the site of an 1880s resort. The 16 guest rooms are in a stone and brick carriage house, and each is furnished with carefully chosen antiques (innkeepers David and Sheila Aldrich know antiques) and equipped with color TVs, phones, air-conditioning, and wet bars. There is a sitting room in the carriage house, and another—even more spacious and inviting—in the neighboring barn, which also doubles as a reception area and antiques shop. The property includes a landscaped pool, a tennis court, horseshoes, and shuffleboard. A path leads down to the ocean. Unsuitable for children under 12. Two-night minimum during high season. $150–350; less off-season. Rates include a full buffet breakfast.

  🐾 **The Captain Jefferds Inn** (967-2311; 1-800-839-6844; www.captain jefferdsinn.com), 5 Pearl Street, Box 691. This strikingly handsome, Federal-era mansion has received a thorough makeover thanks to Dick and Pat Bartholomew and their daughter Jane. Each of the 15 guest rooms is now named for one of their favorite places in the world, like Assisi, a suite with a king-sized iron bed, a gas fireplace, a large Italian tiled bathroom, and an indoor garden with a fountain ($260). Our favorite is actually Florida, a bright contemporary room with a skylight over the bed and two trapezoidal doors overlooking the garden ($155). The four rooms in the carriage house are less formal than the main house, which offers several elegant common rooms. A three-course breakfast is served either by candlelight in the dining room or on the terrace, and tea is served in the afternoon. Dick is a veterinarian who genuinely loves dogs. Kate, a golden retriever, is in residence, and guest dogs are accepted by reservation; $20 extra. $135–285 year-round.

  🐕 **Maine Stay Inn and Cottages** (967-2117; 1-800-950-2117; www.mainestay inn.com), Box 500A, 34 Maine Street. Open year-round. The 1860 house is big, white, and distinctive, with a large cupola. It offers four guest rooms—each with private bath, one with a fireplace and deck—and two suites, both with fireplaces. What sets this place apart from the other gracious B&Bs in Kennebunkport are the 11 cottages of varying sizes sequestered in nicely landscaped grounds, 6 with fireplaces, 3 with double whirlpool tubs, 5 with efficiency kitchens. This is one of the few attractive places for families to stay within walking distance of Dock Square. A full breakfast is served and might include blueberry blintzes or apricot scones (cottage guests have the option of breakfast delivered in a basket). All guests can enjoy a full afternoon tea in the attractive living room or on the wraparound porch. Carol and Lindsay Copeland are warm hosts, eager to help you make the most of your stay. $160–235 in-season; $95–190 off-season.

  ⟁ **The 1802 House** (967-5632; 1-800-932-5632; www.1802inn.com), P.O. Box 646-A, 15 Locke Street. Open year-round. Ron and Carol Perry offer six guest rooms furnished with antiques, also a three-room suite with a fireplace, fridge, and double shower, and a Roman garden room with a double whirlpool tub overlooking a private deck. Most rooms have queen-sized four-posters and fireplaces, and many have whirlpool tubs. The house is away from town on the edge of the Cape Arundel Golf Club, with an out-in-the-country feel, shaded by large pines. A ship's bell calls guests to a very full breakfast. Common rooms are airy and comfortable; cozy corners for winter. $149–389 in high season, $119–349 in low.

MODERATELY PRICED INNS AND B&BS

🐾🍽️ **The Green Heron** (967-3315; www.greenheroninn.com), P.O. Box 2578, 126 Ocean Avenue. Open except for deep winter (January through early February). Within walking distance of both village and shore, this old guest house is filled with the spirit of a friendlier, simpler day. The 10 rooms are attractive, clean, and bright, individually decorated, and equipped with private baths, air-conditioning, and color TVs. There is also a coveside cottage. The famous breakfast (see *Eating Out*) is included in the guest rates. Ownership has remained in the Reid family for many decades. The front porch is an inviting evening gathering place, and the paved path overlooking the creek leads to steps to a tiny gravel beach. In-season: $105–125 double; $165 for Shanon Cottage; children's rates. Both children and pets are welcome.

Charrid House (967-5695), 2 Arlington Avenue. Open year-round. Maine native Ann Dubay's cedar-shingled house, squirreled away in the heart of the Port's 19th-century neighborhood of "cottages," was built in 1887 as the "casino" that went with the elite Kennebunk River Club (subsequently moved from next door to its present site on Ocean Avenue). A short block from Henry Parsons Park (see *Green Space—Parks*). The two upstairs guest rooms (one with twin maple beds and the second with a queen) share a bath, sitting room, and sunroom. The house is charming, furnished with antiques, and nicely landscaped. Breakfast is served on the front sunporch. A studio apartment is also available in summer. $70 per room includes a full breakfast.

Chetwynd House Inn (967-2235), P.O. Box 130TN, Chestnut Street.

Open year-round. In 1978 Susan Chetwynd opened Kennebunkport's first B&B, a gracious 1840s home near Dock Square. The four antiques-furnished guest rooms have private baths and TVs; a top-floor two-room suite has skylights and a river view. Generous breakfasts—maybe ham and cheese omelets and a quarter of a melon with peaches, blueberries, and bananas—are served family-style at the dining room table; afternoon refreshments are offered in the sitting room/library. $99–169.

Harbor Inn (967-2074; www.harbor-inn.com), 90 Ocean Avenue, P.O. Box 538A. Kathy and Bob Jones, longtime Port residents and owners of Cove House (see below), have acquired this fine old house and thoroughly brighented it, filling it with flowers and an airy, hospitable air. The five rooms and two-room suite (all with private baths) are furnished with a mix of family antiques, paintings, and prints, and the long porch is lined with wicker. A full buffet breakfast is set out in the Ivy Room. It's a short walk to the ocean, a longer but pleasant walk to Dock Square. $95–140 for rooms. Woodbine Cottage in the rear is $140–150.

🎖 **Cove House Bed & Breakfast** (967-3704; www.covehouse.com), 11 South Main Street. This 18th-century colonial house is down by Chick's Cove on the Kennebunk River, within walking distance of a beach and easy bicycling distance of Dock Square. The three pleasant guest rooms have private baths; there's a book-lined living room with a woodstove. $80–117, $20 per extra person, includes breakfast.

The Waldo Emerson Inn (985-4250; www.waldoemersoninn.com), 108 Summer Street (Route 35), Kennebunk 04043. This is a special house, built in 1748 by a shipbuilder who inherited the land and original 1753 cottage (the present kitchen) from Waldo Emerson, the great-uncle of the famous poet and essayist. Ralph Waldo Emerson summered in this house for many years. There are four cozy guest rooms, all with private baths and antiques. A quilt store is attached, and the Wedding Cake House (see *To See—Historic Sites*) is next door. $85–115 per couple includes a full breakfast.

OTHER LODGING

Yachtsman Lodge and Marina (967-2511; 1-800-9-YACHTS; www.yachtsmanlodge.com), P.O. Box 2609, Ocean Avenue. Open late April through late October. This is a beautifully positioned property, right on the Kennebunk River, a short walk from Dock Square. Under the same ownership as the White Barn Inn, The Beach House, and the Breakwater. Rooms have recently been tastefully decorated. They offer private riverside patios. Slip space for boats available at the marina. $129–235.

Schooners Inn (967-5333), P.O. Box 709, Ocean Avenue. Open seasonally. Every room has a water view, some with balconies and skylights, and each is named after a schooner and furnished with Thomas Moser furniture. Amenities include an elevator, cable TV, phones; the master suite has a raised sitting area, whirlpool bath, and private deck. $155–275 high season; less off-season.

🐾🐱⚓♿**Shorelands** (985-4460; 1-800-99-BEACH; www.shorelands.com), P.O. Box 3035, Route 9. Open April through October. A family-owned, family-geared motel and cottage complex of four guest rooms, two apartments, and 25 cottages within walking distance of Parsons Beach. Facilities include outdoor pool, indoor hot tub, yard games, horseshoes, basketball, and grills. $59–155 in-season, $39–99 off-season, weekly rates, off-season packages.

WHERE TO EAT

DINING OUT
Cape Arundel Inn (967-2125) Ocean Avenue, Kennebunkport. Open mid-April through December for dinner (closed Sunday evenings). This dining room should be called "Windows on the Ocean" because that's the view, with just one piece of land in sight: former president Bush's estate, Walker's Point. Jack Nahil, the resort's most highly respected restaurateur (The White Barn Inn is his creation), is now focusing his energies on this one superb dining room. The à la carte menu includes "first plates" like applewood-smoked and bacon-wrapped sea scallops with red lentil and spinach salad ($9.75) and entrées like grilled Atlantic salmon fillet with braised white beans and roasted vegetables ($23.95).

White Barn Inn (967-2321), Kennebunk Beach. Open for dinner year-round except January. Rated among New England's top restaurants and set in an open-beamed 19th-century barn with a three-story glassed rear wall, overlooking extravagant seasonal floral displays. Walls are hung with original art, tables are set with silver and fine linens, and the fare is characterized as contemporary and regional. The five-course menu changes frequently, but you might begin with a lobster spring roll or boneless quail breast, and dine on grilled beef tenderloin with a local lobster mushroom crust and a merlot sauce. Palate cleansers are served throughout the meal to prepare you for the next course. The service is formal and attentive. $73 prix fixe plus tax, beverage, and gratuity.

Kennebunkport Inn (967-2621), Dock Square, Kennebunkport. Open April through December. Breakfast and dinner daily May through October. Elegant fare in two lacy dining rooms. Entrées range from pan-seared chicken breast to the inn's signature bouillabaisse: lobster, shrimp, scallops, swordfish, mussels, and clams in a tomato-fennel broth, served with hot pepper sauce on the side. Lighter fare is served in **Martha's Vineyard** (Martha Griffin is the owner-chef), a pleasant garden just off Dock Square and a good place for a glass of wine with grilled bruschetta and mussels. Entrées $19–31.

On The Marsh Tavern (967-4500), Route 9, Lower Village, Kennebunk. Open daily for dinner; closed January to mid-March. Continental dining with style, overlooking a salt marsh. Entrées $19–28.

The Belvidere Room at the Tides Inn By-the-Sea (967-3757), Goose

Rocks Beach, 6 miles northeast of Dock Square. Open mid-May through mid-October for breakfast and dinner. The preferred tables are on the sunporch with ocean views. The monkfish and Maine shrimp gumbo is a great start, and entrées usually include turbans of sole (stuffed with scallops, crabmeat, and shrimp) ($24.95), and homemade pasta ($18.95). Come early enough to walk Goose Rocks Beach before or after.

Windows on the Water (967-3313), Chase Hill, Kennebunkport. Open year-round for lunch, dinner, and Sunday brunch (noon–2:30). A dining room with views of the port through arched windows, screened terrace or alfresco dining, and live entertainment on Friday and Saturday. Seafood is the specialty and the food is excellent. Lobster-stuffed potato is popular at lunch. Light-fare selection for smaller appetites. Reservations are a must for dinner. Dinner entrées $20–38. Brunch is a good value.

✍ **The Colony** (967-3331), Ocean Avenue, Kennebunkport. The elegant dining room at this grand old resort is open to the public for all three meals. Menu selections change each night and might include North Atlantic haddock baked with crab, fresh lemon, and fresh thyme ($16.50) and filet mignon ($19). Sunday brunch is served 11–2, with a changing theme (such as "Christmas in July") each week and the Friday-night buffet is popular at $26 (reservations recommended). Evening pub and children's menus are also available.

Seascapes (967-8500), Pier Road, Cape Porpoise. Open for lunch and dinner daily May through October, closed some days in shoulder seasons. Seascapes combines a great location (on a working fishing pier) with well-known local management (Angela LeBlanc). Specialties include roasted lobster and "Christina's Shrimp." Entrées $18.95–29.

Mabel's Lobster Claw (967-2562), Ocean Avenue, Kennebunkport. April through late October, open for lunch and dinner. An informal favorite with locals, including former president Bush. Reservations recommended for dinner. The specialty is lobster, pure or richly dressed with scallops, shrimp, and fresh mushrooms in a creamy Newburg sauce, topped with Parmesan cheese. The lunch special is a lobster roll with Russian dressing and lettuce in a buttery, grilled hot-dog roll. Dinner entrées $15.95–25.95, but you can always get a hamburger ($6.95).

Grissini (967-2211), 27 Western Avenue, Kennebunk. Open year-round, except January, for dinner. A northern Italian trattoria created by the owner of the White Barn Inn, this is a 120-seat, informal, and trendy restaurant with seasonal outdoor terrace dining and an à la carte menu. You might dine on *rigatoni bolognese* (tube pasta in a veal, pork, and tomato sauce; $15.95) or osso buco (braised veal shank; $17.95) with a house salad ($4.50).

Kennebunk Inn (985-3351), 45 Main Street, Kennebunk 04043. Open daily for dinner. The inn itself is an 1820s building expanded in the later 19th century into the middle-of-Maine-Street (Route 1) inn that's revived its old

KIM GRANT

The Clam Shack in Kennebunkport

reputation for fine dining under ownership by John and Kristen Martin
and chef Dave Ruitenberg. The dining room is low-beamed and formal
and the menu is ambitious. You might begin with crispy potato *galette* roped
with a chive crème fraîche and smoked salmon and dine on herb-roasted
breast of duck over a Shiitake mushroom and port wine sauce or marinated
and grilled loin of lamb set with balsamic-roasted shallots. The wine list is a
point of pride. Entrées $16–20.

LOBSTER AND CLAMS

Nunan's Lobster Hut (967-4362), Route 9, Cape Porpoise. Open for dinner May through October. This low, shedlike landmark packs them in
and charges, too. This is the place for a classic lobster feed—there are
sinks with paper towels to wipe off the melted butter. Lobster, clams,
and pies are the fare. No credit cards.

The Lobster Pot (967-4607), 62 Mills Road, Cape Porpoise. A full-service
restaurant open for lunch and dinner, good for a cheeseburger and fried
seafood, steak, or pasta primavera, but it's lobster most people come
for. Beer and wine served.

The Clam Shack (967-3321/2560), Kennebunkport (at the bridge). Clams, lobsters, and fresh fish. A year-round seafood market and seasonal take-out stand that's worth the wait. Other seafood markets include **Preble Fish** (967-4620) and **Cape Porpoise Lobster Co.** (967-4268), both in Cape Porpoise, where the locals get their fish and steamed lobster to go. **Port Lobster** (967-2081), Ocean Avenue, Kennebunkport. Live or cooked lobsters packed to travel or ship, and lobster, shrimp, and crab rolls to go (several obvious waterside picnic spots are within walking distance).

Also see **Mabel's Lobster Claw** under *Dining Out*.

EATING OUT

🦉💅 **The Wayfarer** (967-8961), 1 Pier Road, Cape Porpoise. Open from 6:30 AM for breakfast, lunch, and dinner. Closed Mondays off-season. The atmosphere is upscale coffee shop with a counter and booths, and the food is superb: haddock chowder, spicy pan-blackened swordfish steak, or the night's roast (maybe turkey or Yankee pot roast). Smaller portions on some meals are available for kids. All meals include salad, starch, and hot rolls. BYOB from the general store across the road.

Alisson's (967-4841), 5 Dock Square, Kennebunkport. Open at 6:30 for breakfast; also serves lunch and dinner. A pub and grill "where the nicest people meet the nicest people," the true heart of Dock Square. Our lunch favorite is the salad in a monster tortilla shell with chili, salsa, and sour cream, topped with Monterey jack. Dinner entrées include lobster ravioli and some good vegetarian options as well as "A Fish Called Wanda" (the ultimate fish sandwich). **The Market Pub** is Dock Square's meeting place.

The Green Heron (967-3315), Ocean Avenue, Kennebunkport. *The* place for breakfast, a long-standing tradition, served on a glassed-in, waterside porch. The menu is vast and varied.

💅 **Federal Jack's Restaurant & Brew Pub** (967-4322), 8 Western Avenue, Kennebunk Lower Village. Open for lunch and dinner, offering a variety of handcrafted ales. The original Shipyard Ale brewery, squirreled away on the river, with parking right in the thick of things. The restaurant is upstairs, spacious, sleek, and sunny, with windows and seasonal terrace dining on the river. The menu is large, complementing the English-style ales. Hummus and chicken Caesar wraps and large salads as well as burgers and fried fish, good seafood pasta. Live acoustic music on weekends.

Bartley's Dockside (967-5050; www.kportmaine.com), by the bridge, Kennebunkport. Since 1977 this friendly family-owned place has been a reliable bet for moderately priced meals—from lunchtime chowders and stews to a dinner bouillabaisse. What's gotten out of control recently is the demand for Mrs. B.'s wild Maine blueberry pie. People frequently come in asking if they can just have pie, and they can't. Thirty blueberry pies are enough to bake every day, and they tend to get scarfed up by lunch and dinner patrons.

Leedy's Restaurant (324-5856), Alfred Square, Alfred. Open 7 AM–8 PM, until 9 on weekends (Sunday it opens at noon). This is the kind of place you walk into and know immediately that everything is going to taste good. Straight-shooting, all-American cooking specializing in seafood and prime rib.

ENTERTAINMENT

Arundel Barn Playhouse (985-5552), 53 Old Post Road (just off Route 1 by the Blue Moon Diner), Arundel. Opened in 1998 in a totally revamped barn, this is a thoroughly professional classic summer theater with performances late every evening (with the exception of days between productions), June through late August, matinees Wednesday and Friday; tickets $16–20.

Hackmatack Playhouse (698-1807), Route 9, Beaver Dam, Berwick. Local actors, rave reviews.

Maritime Productions (967-0005; 1-800-853-5002), otherwise known as Kennebunk Theater Cruise, departing nightly June 5 through October 18 from Performance Marine by the bridge in Dock Square. This 2-hour cruise features dramatic renditions of Seafaring Legends, Haunts, and Folklore; beer, wine, and light fare served.

River Tree Arts (985-4343) stages local productions and happenings.

Thursday-night summer concerts are performed at 7 PM on the lawn of the South Congregational Church in July and August (rain location: Community House; 985-4343).

Also see **Federal Jack's** under *Eating Out; Entertainment* in "Ogunquit and Wells."

SELECTIVE SHOPPING

ANTIQUES SHOPS
The Kennebunks are known as an antiques center with a half-dozen shops, representing a number of dealers, most on Route 1.

ART GALLERIES
You'll find some 50 galleries, most of them seasonal; **Mast Cove Galleries** (967-3453) on Main Street, Kennebunkport, is touted as the "largest group gallery in the area." Pick up a free copy of the annual "Guide to Fine Art, Studios, and Galleries," published by the **Art Guild of the Kennebunks** and available at the chamber of commerce and most galleries.

FARMS
Russel Acres Farm and Produce/Orchard Dell Deer Farm (985-2435), 1797 Alewife Road, Kennebunk. A red-deer breeding farm with a 1754 farmhouse. Visitors welcome; venison, quail, pheasant, rabbit, free-range chicken, and ice cream sold. Route 35, 2 miles west of I-95, exit 3.

✎ **Harris Farm** (499-2678), Buzzell Road, Dayton. July through October
visitors are welcome to tour the dairy barn; fresh milk, eggs, and produce
sold. Pick-your-own pumpkins on the last Sunday in September and the
first in October; a short, pleasant ride up Route 35; call for directions.

SPECIAL SHOPS

Kennebunk Book Port, 10 Dock Square, Kennebunkport. Open year-round.
The oldest commercial building in the port (1775) is one of the most pleasant bookstores in New England. Climb an outside staircase into this inviting mecca, which is dedicated to reading as well as to buying. Helpful handwritten notes with recommendations from staff make browsing even easier.
Books about Maine and the sea are specialties.

Tom's of Maine Natural Living Store (985-294), in the Lafayette Center,
Storer and Main Streets, Kennebunk. Open daily year-round. This is the
outlet for a variety of Tom's of Maine products made in town. Inquire about
factory tours.

Brick Store Museum Shop (985-4802), 117 Main Street, Kennebunk. A selection of books, handmade quilts, pottery, Indian baskets, painted boxes,
and the like.

Port Canvas (967-2717), Dock Square, Kennebunkport. Open year-round.
Canvas totes, suitcases, and hats, all made in Kennebunkport.

The Good Earth, Dock Square, Kennebunkport. Open daily May through October, varying hours; closed January through March. Stoneware in unusual
designs—mugs, vases, and bowls. Great browsing in the loft showroom.

Clay Art (967-1177), 127 Ocean Avenue, Kennebunkport. A studio/gallery featuring Monique Bousquet's hand-built porcelain.

KBC Coffee & Drygoods (967-1261), 8 Western Avenue, Kennebunkport.
Hidden away down on the river beneath Federal Jack's (see *Eating Out*),
this is a source of Kennebec Brewing Company ales and brew gear as well
as souvenir clothing and gifts; also good for cappuccino and pastry.

SPECIAL EVENTS

February: **Winter Carnival Weekend** *(first weekend);* **hay- and sleigh
rides** on Saturday all month. Weekend **February Is for Lovers** events
(967-0857).

March: **Kennebunkport tours and food show. Annual Kennebunk
Fun Run.**

June: **Bed & Breakfast Inn and Garden Tour. Blessing of the Fleet.**

July: Old-fashioned **picnic, fireworks, and band concert.**

August: **Riverfest** *(first Saturday).* **Kennebearport Teddy Bear Show**
(second Saturday).

September: **Old-Time Fiddlers Contest** *(second Saturday).*

December: **Christmas Prelude** *(first and second weekends)*—Dock Square
is decked out for Yuletide, and there are champagne receptions, church
suppers, concerts, and carols; holiday fairs and open houses.

Old Orchard Beach, Saco, and Biddeford

When Thomas Rogers was granted 12 acres of land in 1657 and planted a fruit orchard, he undoubtedly had no idea his holding would one day become a resort area so popular that its year-round population would multiply by 10 in the summer.

In 1837 E. C. Staples first recognized the region's potential as a summer playground. From taking in boarders on his farm for $1.50 a week, he moved to building the first Old Orchard House. His instincts proved right, for rail travel brought a wave of tourists to the beach from both the United States and Canada.

The Grand Trunk Railroad did away with the long carriage ride from Montreal, and Canadians discovered that the Maine shore was a great place to vacation. The area is still a popular destination for French Canadian visitors, and you are likely to hear French spoken almost anywhere you go.

When the first pier at Old Orchard Beach was built in 1898, it stood 20 feet above and 1,800 feet out over the water and was constructed entirely of steel. The pavilions housed animals, a casino, and a restaurant. In the decades that followed, the original pier was rebuilt many times after being damaged by fire and storms, until a wider and shorter pier of wood was built in 1980. The pier continues to be a focal point in the community and a hub of activity.

An amusement area appeared in 1902 and grew after World War I. The 1920s brought big-name bands such as those led by Guy Lombardo and Duke Ellington to the Pier Casino, and thousands danced under a revolving crystal ball.

Fire, hard economic times, the decline of the railroad and steamboat industries—all took their toll on Old Orchard Beach over the years. Though the 7 miles of sandy beach and the amusement park near the pier endured, the 1980s saw the area deteriorate and succumb to a younger, wilder crowd.

In the early 1990s the citizens decided to reclaim their town. A major revitalization plan widened sidewalks, added benches and streetlights, and passed and enforced ordinances that prevent "cruising" (repeatedly driving the same stretch of road). The result is a cleaner, more appealing, yet still lively and fun vacation spot. For families, it can't be beat, with the beach, amusement park rides, mini-golf just down the road, the kind of food kids love everywhere, and reasonable lodging rates.

The area is also well known for the camp meetings held beginning in the late 1800s, first by Methodists, then by the Salvation Army. These meetings continue throughout the summer in the Ocean Park community today.

Biddeford and Saco are often called the twin cities, and no two Maine towns are more different or more closely linked. Saco is a classic Yankee town with white-clapboard mansions lining its main street. Biddeford is a classic mill town with a strong French Canadian heritage and mammoth 19th-century brick textile mills that have stood idle since the 1950s. A few years back the largest mills were renamed Saco Island and slated for redevelopment as a combination hotel, office, shop, and condo complex. That project has yet to become a reality. The buildings have been seeing increased development, but there's still a lot of un-used space. Still, Biddeford is worth visiting, especially for La Kermesse, the colorful Franco-American festival in late June. Saco's Route 1 strip of amusement parks is a big draw for those with children.

Parts of Scarborough's 49 square miles belong more in Casco Bay descriptions, but Pine Point and its surrounding area is the easternmost tip of Old Orchard Beach, and is often a less crowded, quieter spot to visit. A large saltwater marsh in Scarborough is also good for quiet re-laxation and exploring by canoe.

GUIDANCE

Old Orchard Beach Chamber of Commerce (934-2500; 1-800-365-9386; www.oldorchardbeachmaine.com), P.O. Box 600 (First Street), Old Orchard Beach 04064, maintains a year-round walk-in information center (open 8:30–4:30 weekdays, also Saturday and Sunday from June through August) and offers help with reservations.

Biddeford-Saco Chamber of Commerce & Industry (282-1567; www.biddefordsacochamber.org), 110 Main Street, Saco Island, Suite #1202, Saco 04072. Stocks many local brochures; helpful, friendly staff.

The Southern Maine Coast Tourism Association (1-800-639-2442), a cooperative effort among the area chambers, can also be a helpful resource.

GETTING THERE

By air: **Portland International Jetport** is 13 miles north, and rental cars are available at the airport. You can also fly your own plane into Sanford Airport.

By car: Exits 5 and 6 off the Maine Turnpike (I-95) take you easily to the center of Old Orchard Beach. You can also find the town from Route 1 (turn by the large flea market).

GETTING AROUND

From many accommodations in Old Orchard Beach, you are close enough to walk to the pier, the town's center of activity. The **Biddeford-Saco-OOB Transit** also takes you right to the center of town; call 245-5408 for schedules. **Mainely Tours** (774-0808) offers excursions to Portland, and will pick up and drop off at all area motels and campgrounds.

PARKING

An abundance of privately owned lots can be found in the center of Old Orchard Beach. Most charge $2–4 for any length of time—10 minutes or all day. There are meters on the street if you don't mind circling a few times to catch an available one, but at 15 minutes for a quarter, you're better off in lots if you plan to stay long.

MEDICAL EMERGENCY

Southern Maine Medical Center (283-7000), Biddeford.

VILLAGES

Ocean Park is a historic community founded in 1881 by Free Will Baptists and well known for its outstanding religious, educational, and cultural programs. The Ocean Park Association (934-9068; www.oceanpark.org) sponsors lectures, concerts, and other events throughout the summer in the cluster of old, interesting buildings known as Temple Square. Within the community, there is also a recreation hall, shuffleboard, and tennis courts, an old-fashioned ice cream parlor, and a smattering of gift shops. The entire community is a state game preserve, and you can find great walking trails through cathedral pines. A comprehensive guide to programs and recreation is put out by the association.

Pine Point. This quiet and less crowded end of the beach offers a selection of gift shops, restaurants, lobster pounds, and places to stay.

Camp Ellis. At the end of a quiet peninsula where the Saco River blends with the ocean. Residents fight a constant battle with beach erosion, and some of the homes are frighteningly close to the shore. Fishing trips, whale-watching, a long breakwater great for walking, interesting shops, and a couple of good restaurants.

TO SEE AND DO

FOR FAMILIES

The Route 1 strip in Saco and nearby Old Orchard Beach makes up Maine's biggest concentration of kid-geared "attractions." Be prepared to pay.

✎ **Funtown/Splashtown USA** (284-5139), Route 1, Saco. Open daily (depending on the weather) mid-June through Labor Day, weekends in spring and fall. Water activities and a large amusement park. In addition to the 100-foot wooden roller coaster "Excalibur," the park has bumper cars, New England's largest log flume, plenty of carnival rides, hydrofighter, kiddie rides, antique cars.

✎ **Aquaboggan Water Park** (282-3112), Route 1, Saco. Open June through

Labor Day. Several water slides, including a new high-thrills slide with mats or tubes, "Aquasaucer," swimming pool, bumper boats, mini-golf, arcade, shuffleboard, toddler area, wave pool.

✑ **Pirate's Cove Adventure Golf** (934-5086), 70 First Street, Old Orchard Beach. Thirty-six up-and-down mini-golf holes, waterfalls, ponds. Two separate courses available.

✑ **Palace Playland** (934-2001), 1 Old Orchard Street, Old Orchard Beach. Open daily June through Labor Day. For more than 60 years, fun seekers have been wheeled, lifted, shaken, spun, and bumped in Palace Playland rides. There's a carousel (though it no longer contains the original 1906 horses), a Ferris wheel, a 60-foot-high (Maine's largest) water slide, and a roller coaster. You can pay by the ride, or buy an all-day pass.

✑ **Village Park** (934-7666), Old Orchard Beach. On the other side of the pier, across the road from Palace Playland. Arcade, games, kiddie rides. All-day passes available.

GOLF

Dunegrass (934-4513), 49 Ross Road, Old Orchard Beach, 27 holes (a 9-hole course and an 18-hole course are both available here).

Biddeford-Saco Country Club (282-5883), 101 Old Orchard Road, Saco, 18 holes.

Willowdale Golf Club (883-9351), off Route 1, Scarborough, 18 holes.

HORSEBACK RIDING

✑ **Horseback Riding Plus** (883-6400), 338 Broadturn Street, Scarborough. Guided trail rides and beach rides for adults; kiddie and pony rides.

MUSEUMS

York Institute Museum (282-3031), 371 Main Street, Saco. Open Tuesday, Wednesday, and Friday 1–4, Thursday noon–8. Also open Saturday and Sunday noon–4 June through August. $4 adults, $3 seniors, $1 under 16, free under 6. Larger than it looks from the outside, and very well maintained. Rotating exhibits, original paintings, furniture, decorative arts, tools, and natural history specimens. Inquire about frequent lectures, tours, and special exhibits. The institute's **Dyer Library** next door has an outstanding Maine history collection.

Harmon Historical Museum, 4 Portland Avenue, Old Orchard Beach, is open Tuesday through Saturday 1–4, June through September, and by appointment. Home of the Old Orchard Beach Historical Society, the building is full of exhibits from the town's past. Each year, in addition to the regular school, fire, and aviation exhibits, there is a special exhibit on display. Pick up the timeline of the area's history and the walking map of historic sites.

RACING

Scarborough Downs (883-4331), off I-95, exit 6, in Scarborough. The largest harness-racing facility in New England. Live harness racing, as well as thoroughbred and harness racing via simulcast. **Downs Club Restaurant** (883-3022) is open for dinner and Sunday brunch.

Beech Ridge Motor Speedway (883-5227), Holmes Road, Scarborough. Summer stock-car racing every Saturday night.

SAILING

Saco Bay Sailing (283-1624). Offers sailing excursions from Camp Ellis.

SCENIC DRIVES

From Saco (see map on page 48), there's a loop that heads out Route 112, past the **Way-Way General Store** (see *Selective Shopping*). On the left a few miles out is the **Saco Heath Preserve** (see *Green Space— Nature Preserves*), worth a stop to explore. From there, continue on Route 112 until it intersects with Route 202. Turn left and stay on 202 until you see the intersection with Route 5. Turn left again and follow Route 5 along the river, back to the center of Saco.

TENNIS

The Ocean Park Association (934-9068) maintains public tennis courts, open in July and August.

GREEN SPACE

BEACHES

Obviously, **Old Orchard Beach** is the big draw in this area, with 7 miles of sand and plenty of space for sunbathing, swimming, volleyball, and other recreation.

Ferry Beach State Park is marked from Route 9 between Old Orchard Beach and Camp Ellis, in Saco. The 100-plus-acre preserve includes 70 yards of sand, a boardwalk through the dunes, bike paths, nature trails, a picnic area with grills, lifeguards, changing rooms, pit toilets. Even in the middle of summer it isn't terribly crowded here. $2 per person, free under age 12.

Bay View Beach, at the end of Bay View Road near Ferry Beach, is 200 yards of mostly sandy beach; lifeguards, free parking.

Camp Ellis Beach, Route 9, Saco. Some 2,000 feet of beach backed by cottages; also a long fishing pier. The commercial parking lots fill quickly on sunny days.

Pine Point, Route 9 (at the very end), Scarborough, is small and un-crowded, with a lobster pound and restaurant. The larger beach area just a bit closer to Old Orchard, with snack bar, changing room, and bathrooms, charges $5 for parking in the adjacent lot.

HIKING

Saco Trails, P.O. Box 852, Saco 04072, publishes a booklet called "Take a Hike in Saco," which lists several trails that are maintained for hiking.

NATURE PRESERVES

Scarborough Marsh Nature Center (883-5100), Pine Point Road (Route 9), Scarborough. Open daily mid-June through Labor Day, 9:30–5:30. The largest salt marsh (3,000 acres) in Maine, this is a great place for quiet canoe exploration. This Maine Audubon Nature Center offers canoe rentals, exhibits, a nature store, and guided walking and canoe

A view through dune grass

KIM GRANT

tours throughout the summer.

Saco Heath Preserve, Route 112, Saco. Maybe this small Nature Conservancy preserve isn't crowded because nobody knows it's there, but it shouldn't be overlooked. The sign is hard to spot, but look for it on the right-hand side a few miles out of Saco. A quiet, peaceful walk through a peat bog on a wooden boardwalk.

East Point Sanctuary (781-2330), Lester B. Orcutt Boulevard, Biddeford Pool. Open sunrise to sunset year-round. A 30-acre Maine Audubon Society preserve with trails, a view of Wood Island Light, and terrific birding in spring and fall.

LODGING

INNS AND BED & BREAKFASTS

The Carriage House (934-2141), 24 Portland Avenue, Old Orchard Beach 04064. Open year-round. Just off the main drag, this Victorian home with carriage house offers eight pretty rooms furnished in period antiques in the main house, all with shared baths. We particularly like the downstairs room with an antique brass bed. The carriage-house suite is large and private, with a kitchen and TV. Also available is a five-room apartment with a deck. Common areas include a sauna, Jacuzzi, and a few exercise machines. $50–100 in-season.

The Atlantic Birches Inn (934-5295; 1-888-934-5295; www.atlanticbirches. com), 20 Portland Avenue, Old Orchard Beach 04064. A lovely Victorian, shingle-style home, built in the area's heyday. Guest rooms, named after former grand hotels, are bright and cheerful with a mix of old and new furnishings. There is space for relaxing in the living room and on the large front porch shaded by white birches. The "cottage" next door offers three rooms and two kitchenette suites with separate entrances. The in-ground pool is perfect on a hot day. $85–130 in high season, less off-season, includes a breakfast of muffins or coffee cake, fruit salad, cereal, coffee, and juice (cottage breakfast is muffins, coffee, and juice).

🐾🍽 **Crown 'n' Anchor Inn** (282-3829; 1-800-561-8865), P.O. Box 228, Saco 04072-0228. This is a rare find: a Greek Revival, pillared mansion built in 1827 by a local lawyer and sold in 1841 to Stephen Goodale, in whose family it remained until 1925. Obviously, these were all well-to-do folk, and Stephen's son George became a Harvard professor of botany, involved with the planning and execution of the university's botanical museum (he was the man who commissioned those famous glass flowers). Hosts John Barclay and Martha Forester continually strive to improve and update their property. Common space, lovely for weddings and receptions (they host several each season), includes a double living room, the front room returned to its traditional look as a "receiving parlor." All rooms are painstakingly restored, each with an elegant bathroom. The Normandy Suite with its two working fireplaces and Jacuzzi bath is particularly nice, as is the barn room (it's hard to believe it was once a stable). Throughout the inn is a large, intriguing collection of British royal family memorabilia. The inn is just up the street from the York Institute and a 10-minute drive from Saco's relatively uncrowded sands (see *Beaches*). A candlelight breakfast is served on fine china in the small but formal dining room. Pets accepted. $75–125 in-season ($10 less off-season).

🐾🍽 **Country Farm** (282-0208), 139 Louden Road, Saco 04072. Open year-round. Nothing fancy, just a 150-acre working farm (cattle, goats, several kittens, and a horse) that's been in the same family for several generations with two clean, comfortable guest rooms (shared bath) and plenty of space to wander—down to the shore of the Saco River. Arlene and Norman Gonneville seem to enjoy their guests, children included. $45 for two, including full breakfast. $10 per additional guest.

🍽 **Maine-lly Llamas Farm** (929-3057), Route 35, Hollis. May through November. John and Gale Yohe offer comfortable guest rooms and a chance to learn about the farm or take a nature trek with their gentle llamas. Rooms are in the carriage house, with a separate staircase, part of an apartment that can be rented with kitchen for $110, including breakfast for up to five guests; otherwise, $55 single, $65 double with breakfast. Guided llama treks are $20 per hour for two llamas, $10 for each additional llama.

OTHER LODGING

Old Orchard Beach offers an overwhelming number of motel, cottage, and condominium complexes both along the beach and on main roads. The chamber of commerce publishes a helpful "Old Orchard Beach Vacation Planner" (see *Guidance*). A word of caution—some of these establishments have been around for years, with no renovations and poor upkeep. We strongly recommend looking at a room before making reservations. Generally, condominiums on the beach are better kept, and many have reasonable rates.

Aquarius Motel (934-2626; www.aquariusmotel.com), 1 Brown Street, Old Orchard Beach 04064. A small, family-owned and -operated 14-room motel that's exceptionally clean, and right on the beach. The patio is a great place to relax after a day of sight-seeing. Wes and Barb Carter are friendly and eager to help travelers plan their stay. Rates are $85–140 (for a two-room unit with three double beds and kitchenette) in-season. Many special rates in early spring and late fall. Three-night minimum on holiday weekends.

Ocean Walk Hotel (934-1716; 1-800-992-3779; www.oceanwalkhotel.com), 197 East Grand Avenue, Old Orchard Beach 04064. Forty-four well-kept rooms, from studios to oceanfront suites. The top-floor rooms in one building have very high ceilings, giving them a light, airy, spacious feel. $120–200 in-season.

Sea View (934-4180; 1-800-541-8439), 65 West Grand Avenue, Old Orchard Beach 04064. Forty-nine rooms, some with oceanfront views. Pretty landscaping, with an outdoor pool and a beautiful fountain in front. Rooms are modern, bright, and clean. Two-bedroom suites with kitchenettes are also available. $70–190 in-season.

The Gull Motel & Inn (934-4321), 89 West Grand Avenue, Old Orchard Beach 04064. An attractive motel, clean and family oriented. The inn is right on the beach, with a great porch. Cottages also available by the week. $65–115 in high season; cottages $850 per week.

✐ **Billowhouse** (934-2333; 1-888-767-7776; www.billowhouse.com), 2 Temple Avenue, Ocean Park 04063-7543. This 1881 Victorian guest house is Mary and Bill Kerrigan's retirement project. Completely renovated yet with old-fashioned charm. There are three ground-level efficiency apartments and six more kitchenette units in the adjoining motel. The five B&B rooms include a large fourth-floor room with a play loft for children. Rooms in the guest house share a deck overlooking the ocean; the beach is just steps away. Private baths. $80–150 in-season, with discounts for extended stays, breakfast included for B&B guests only; $52–110 off-season.

CAMPGROUNDS

Camping is a budget-minded family's best bet in this area. There are at least a dozen campgrounds here (more than 4,000 sites in the area), many geared to families and offering games, recreational activities, and trolley service to the beach in-season. Following are a couple of recommendations; check with the chamber (see *Guidance*) for a full listing.

🚲♿ **Bayley's Camping Resort** (883-6043; www.bayleys-camping.com), 27 Ross Road, West Scarborough 04074. Just down the road from Pine Point, you hardly have to leave the grounds to have a terrific vacation. Paddleboats, swimming pool, Jacuzzi, horseback riding, fishing, game room, special programs for children and adults—the list goes on and on. Four hundred sites and four rental trailers. $31.50–42 depending on hook-ups; lower rates in spring and fall.

🚲♿ **Powder Horn** (934-4733; 1-800-934-7038; www.mainecamping.com), P.O. Box 366, Old Orchard Beach 04064. A 450-site campground with plenty of recreation options—playgrounds, shuffleboard, horseshoes, volleyball, rec hall and game room, mini-golf, trolley service to the beach in-season. $24–33 per night.

WHERE TO EAT

DINING OUT
Cornforth House (284-2006; www.cornforthhouse.com), 893 Route 1, Saco. Open for dinner Tuesday through Saturday and seasonal Sunday brunch. This brick Federal farmhouse was recently remodeled and features a series of small dining rooms with working fireplaces. The atmosphere is casual, yet intimate. Meals are prepared with an emphasis on fresh local ingredients. Wine-tasting dinners held monthly, and they have a 100-bottle wine list. $12–21.

🚲 **Village Inn** (934-7370), 213 Saco Avenue, Old Orchard Beach. Open for lunch and dinner, with a large and varied menu. Also offers a seasonal breakfast buffet. Lunch specials include fried seafood, pastas, and chicken cordon bleu. At dinner choices range from seafood specialties and lobster to surf and turf or pasta. Children's menu. $6.95–17.95.

🚲♿ **Joseph's by the Sea** (934-5044), 55 West Grand Avenue, Old Orchard Beach. Open April through December. Serving breakfast and dinner daily in-season; hours vary the rest of the year, so call ahead. The dining rooms overlook the water, or you can dine on the garden patio. Dinner entrées include grilled Tuscan swordfish and pepper-crusted filet mignon. Children's menu $3.50–5.95. Entrées $13.95–23.95.

The Landmark (934-0156), 28 East Grand Avenue, Old Orchard Beach. Open for dinner at 5 PM and Sunday brunch from April 1 through the end of December. Daily June through August; otherwise, closed on Mondays. Fine dining in a 1910 Victorian house. Menu specialties include roast duckling, lobster stew, and homemade desserts. $11.95–17.95.

EATING OUT
🍴 **Danton's Family Restaurant** (934-7701), Old Orchard Beach Street. Easy to overlook on the main road amid all the souvenir shops and take-out stands, but don't. Established in 1946, this little place is still a great

alternative to the pier snacks. Home-cooked meals for breakfast, lunch, and dinner at very reasonable prices. Daily lunch specials might include macaroni and cheese, fish-and-chips. Try the homemade pies.

🎖 **Chowderheads** (883-8333), Oak Hill Plaza, Intersection of Routes 1 and 114, Scarborough. Open for lunch and dinner daily. The award-winning seafood chowder is thick, hearty, and delicious. Specialties include swordfish and salmon steak dinners, salmon pie, and fried seafood dinners. Portions are quite generous.

Hattie's (282-3435), Biddeford Pool. *The* gathering spot in Biddeford Pool for breakfast and lunch, and it's a find. Former president Bush knows it well.

Bufflehead's (284-6000), 122 Hills Beach Road, Biddeford Pool. Open year-round daily for all three meals. Indoor and outdoor seating with a great view. The menu includes seafood, pasta, burgers, and pizza.

Wormwoods (282-9679), Camp Ellis Beach, Saco. Open daily year-round for all three meals. A large, friendly, old-fashioned place at the beginning of the breakwater. They go all out decorating for the seasons, and can be counted on for good food, especially seafood. Half portions are available for those with smaller appetites.

TAKE-OUT

Near the pier and on the main drag of Old Orchard Beach are an abundance of take-out stands and informal restaurants serving pizza, burgers, hot dogs, fried seafood, fried dough, pier fries, ice cream, and more. Our favorites are **Bill's** for pizza, **Lisa's** for pier fries.

Rapid Ray's (282-1847), 179 Main Street, Saco. A local icon for more than 40 years. Quick and friendly service from people who seem to know almost everyone who walks through the door. Burgers, hot dogs, lobster rolls, fries, onion rings, and the like at great prices.

LOBSTER POUNDS

Bayley's Lobster Pound (883-4571), Pine Point, Scarborough. A popular place for lobster and seafood.

Lobster Claw (282-0040), Route 5, Ocean Park Road, Saco. Lobsters cooked outside in giant kettles, stews and chowders, cozy dining room, and take-out available. Twin lobster specials, also steamers, fried seafood. Lobster packed to travel.

ENTERTAINMENT

The Ballpark (934-1124), Old Orchard Beach. Once a professional baseball stadium, the park now features a mix of entertainment throughout the summer, including sporting events, concerts, fairs, festivals, and family shows.

City Theater (282-0849), Main Street, Biddeford. This 660-seat, 1890s theater offers a series of live performances.

Saco Drive-In (284-1016), Route 1, Saco. Double features in spring, summer, and fall.

SELECTIVE SHOPPING

✎ **Way-Way General Store** (283-1682), 93 Buxton Road (Route 112). Worth
a short drive out of your way to see this little piece of history in a small red-
and-white, stone-and-tile building. Small and chock-full of things. Local
children simply call it "the candy store," due to an amazing array of penny
candy.

Cascade Flea Market, Route 1, Saco. One of Maine's largest outdoor flea
markets, open daily in summer.

Stone Soup Artisans (283-4715), 228 Main Street, Saco. Quality crafts
from more than 60 artisans.

SPECIAL EVENTS

Late June: **La Kermesse,** Biddeford—parade, public suppers, dancing, and
entertainment highlighting culture and traditions.

Early July: **Beachfest**—major sand-sculpture exhibit and competitions, entertainment, male and female physique contests, Frisbee tournament, more.

June through Labor Day: **Fireworks** near the pier every Thursday at 9:30 PM.

August: Ocean Park **Festival of Lights** and **Salvation Army camp meetings**
under the new pavilion in Ocean Park. **Beach Olympics,** featuring competitions, music, displays, and presentations to benefit the Maine Special
Olympics.

September: **Classic car weekend,** Old Orchard Beach.

December: **"Celebrate the Season by the Sea" tree-lighting ceremony**
with sleigh rides, refreshments, holiday bazaar, caroling, and a bonfire on
the beach.

II. CASCO BAY

KIM GRANT

Portland Area

Lively, walkable, sophisticated, Maine's largest city is still a working port. Greater Portland (230,000) accounts for one-quarter of Maine's total population, but Portland proper is a 3½-mile-long peninsula (population 64,000) facing Casco Bay. Visitors head first for the Old Port, more than five square blocks built exuberantly during the city's peak shipping era and now laced with restaurants, cafés, shops, and galleries.

Portland's motto, *Resurgam* (I shall rise again), could not be more appropriate. The 17th-century settlement was expunged twice by Native Americans, then once by the British. Finally it prospered as a lumbering port in the 1820s—as still evidenced by its many Federal-era mansions and commercial buildings like the granite-and-glass Mariner's Church in the Old Port, built in 1820 to be the largest building in the capital of a brand-new state. Then it happened again. On Independence Day in 1866 a firecracker flamed up in a Commercial Street boatyard and quickly destroyed most of the downtown. Again the city rose like the legendary phoenix, rebuilding quickly and beautifully, this time in sturdy brick. The buildings were replete with the flourishes to be expected at the core of northern New England's shipping, rail, and manufacturing businesses.

These very buildings, a century later, were "going for peanuts," in the words of a real estate agent who began buying them up in the late 1960s. The city's prominence as a port had been eclipsed by the opening of the St. Lawrence Seaway, and its handsome Grand Trunk Station had been demolished. Down by the harbor artists and craftspeople were renting shop fronts for $50 per month. They formed the Old Port Association, hoping to entice people to stroll through the no-man's-land. That first winter they strung lights through upper floors to convey a sense of security, and they shoveled their own streets, a service the city had ceased to provide to that area. At the end of the winter they celebrated their survival by holding the first Old Port Festival, a street fair that is still held each June.

More recently it is Congress Street that has come back from the brink. Shadowing a ridge above the Old Port, this was the city's fashionable shopping and financial strip in the first half of the 20th century. The present Maine Bank & Trust Building was the tallest building in all

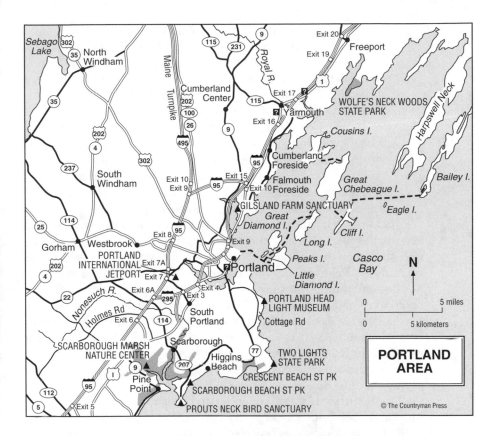

New England when it was built in 1909. By the mid-1990s, however, the three department stores here had closed and foot traffic has shifted to the Maine Mall. Now, however, it's back.

The glass-and-timber Portland Public Market, filled with dozens of vendors selling Maine produce and food products, is now just off Congress Street, near Monument Square. The Maine College of Art (MECA) has replaced Porteus Department Store in a five-story beaux-arts building and maintains the street-level Institute of Contemporary Art. With a student body of 400 (twice what it was two years ago) and a far larger continuing-education program, MECA has had an visual impact up and down Congress Street, which is now called the Arts District. Contemporary art galleries continue to proliferate around the Portland Museum of Art, especially along the recently iffy area between Congress and Longfellow Squares, blocks also now filled with antiques stores and restaurants.

Longfellow Square, in turn, abuts the gracious residential blocks of the West End. Spared by the fire that destroyed the Old Port, its leafy streets are lined with town houses and mansions in a range of graceful architectural styles (an increasing number are B&Bs).

It's been noted that the Portland Peninsula is (English) saddle shaped, with promontories at both ends. The Western Promenade was laid out as an overlook for the West End way back in 1836, as the Eastern Promenade was at the opposite end of the peninsula, along the verge of Munjoy Hill, overlooking Casco Bay. In the 1890s, with the help of Boston's Olmsted brothers, Deering Oaks Park and a greenbelt along Back Cove were added. Bikeways and walkways continue to expand.

Portland's Old Port also continues to thrive, and on its fringes new semi-high-rise, redbrick buildings blend with the old and link the Old Port with Congress Street. Condominiums now line a wharf or two, but Portland remains a working port. In 2000 it landed 18,000 pounds of fish and served 378 ships, including 45 cruise ships.

It's also a departure point for the ferry to Yarmouth (Nova Scotia) and for the fleet of Casco Bay liners that regularly transport people, mail, and supplies among Casco Bay's Calendar Islands. These range from nearby Peaks Island—offering rental bikes, guided sea kayaking, lodging, and dining—to Cliff Island, more than an hour's ride, offering sandy roads and a remote feel. In summer these ferries bill their longer runs as Casco Bay Cruises, and add Music Cruises and a lazy circuit to Bailey Island. Excursion lines also service Eagle Island, preserved as a memorial to Arctic explorer Admiral Peary. The waterfront is, moreover, the departure point for deep-sea fishing, harbor cruises, and daysailing.

South Portland (SoPo), connected to Portland proper by the soaring new Casco Bay Bridge, is a city in its own right (Maine's fourth largest). While it is best known as home of the Maine Mall, its waterfront has become far more visitor friendly in recent years, with the Spring Point Lighthouse and Portland Harbor Museum as a focal point and a burgeoning number of restaurants and galleries.

Beyond South Portland lies Cape Elizabeth, home of the vintage-1791 Portland Head Light and its museum. Visitors come to see the lighthouse but stay to walk and swim at the beaches. Nearby Scarborough to the south and both Falmouth and Yarmouth, just north of the city, also offer surprisingly secluded seaside reserves for walking, boating and birding. While visitors tend to discover Portland on their way up the coast in summer, increasingly they are returning in winter to spend a few days.

GUIDANCE

Convention and Visitors Bureau of Greater Portland (772-5800; www.visitportland.com), 305 Commercial Street, Portland 04101, publishes "Greater Portland Visitors Guide," listing restaurants, sights, museums, and accommodations. It also keeps a list of cottage rental sources. The walk-in information center is open daily year-round. The CVB also maintains a seasonal kiosk in Congress Square and a center (775-5809) at the Portland International Jetport.

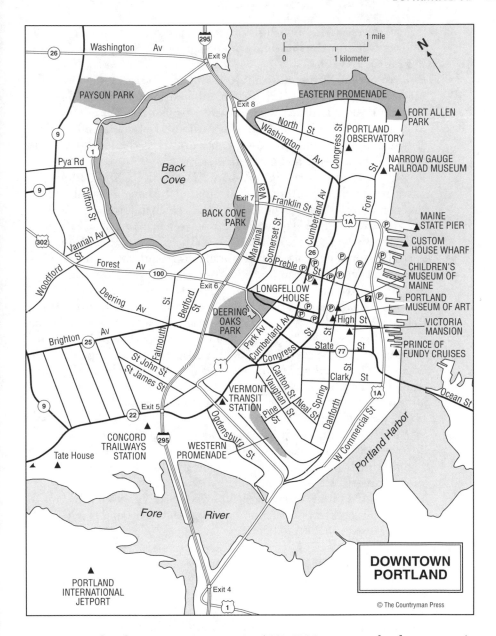

DOWNTOWN PORTLAND

© The Countryman Press

Portland's Downtown District (772-6828; www.portlandmaine.com),
400 Congress Street, Portland 04101, offers information about performances, festivals, and special events. They publish a guide to services,
attractions, dining, and lodging. For current entertainment, weather,
and dining ratings, click onto **www.portland.com,** maintained by the
Portland Press Herald.

The Maine Tourism Association (846-0833) staffs a major state information center on Route 1 in Yarmouth, just off I-95, exit 17.

Also see **Greater Portland Landmarks** under *To See—Guided Tours.*

GETTING THERE

By air: **Portland International Jetport** (774-7301) is served by Delta Air Lines (1-800-221-1212), Continental Airlines (1-800-523-3273), United (1-800-241-6522), U.S. Airways (1-800-428-4322), Northwest Airlink (1-800-225-2525), American Airlines (1-800-433-7300), TWA (1-800-221-2000), and Air Nova. **Car rentals** at the airport include National, Avis, Hertz, and Budget.

By bus: **Vermont Transit** (772-6587; 1-800-55-BUSES) offers frequent service between Portland, Boston, and Maine's coastal and inland points, using the Greyhound terminal, which unfortunately is dingy and inconvenient to downtown and ferries (see map on page 127). **Concord Trailways** (828-1151; 1-800-639-3317) stops en route from Boston to Bangor or coastal points at a bright and clean station just off I-95; buses offer movies, music, and a nonstop express to Boston and its Logan Airport. It's a $5 taxi ride from the bus station to downtown.

By ferry: Canadians can cruise to Portland aboard the **Prince of Fundy Cruises Limited** ferry, *Scotia Prince,* out of Yarmouth, Nova Scotia (775-5616; seasonally, 1-800-482-0955 in Maine; 1-800-341-7540 outside Maine). Overnight cruises are offered early May through October. Prices vary, depending on the season, cabin, or special package. Restaurants, shops, live entertainment, and a casino are some of the features passengers enjoy aboard. The luxury cruise vessel accommodates 1,500 passengers in 800 cabins, plus 250 cars.

By car: From I-95, follow I-295 and signs for the ferry. The **Convention and Visitors Bureau** information center (see *Guidance*) is at 305 Commercial Street between the Old Port and the ferry terminal and is easy to miss.

By train: **AMTRAK service** (1-800-USA-RAIL; www.amtrak.com). The Downeaster from Boston's North Station to Portland is scheduled to begin service in 2001. Check.

GETTING AROUND

The **Metro** (774-0351) bus transfer system serves greater Portland. Metro city buses connect airport and city, as well as offering convenient routes around the city.

PARKING

Portland meters are $.25 per half hour but, as we have discovered the hard way, you get a $10 ticket after 2 hours, which climbs to $15 if you keep feeding the meter. The city urges visitors to use its many parking garages. The **Fore Street Garage** (439 Fore Street) puts you at one end of the Old Port, and the **Custom House Square Garage** (25 Pearl Street), at the other. **The Casco Bay Garage** (Maine State Pier) and **Free Street Parking** (130 Free Street, just up from the art museum) are also handy. The **Gateway Garage** next to the Eastland Park Hotel is large and convenient, as is the **Portland Public Market Garage** (Preble Street), which offers the first 2 hours free with a purchase in the market.

MEDICAL EMERGENCY

Portland Ambulance Service: 911. **Maine Medical Center** (871-0111), 22 Bramhall Street, Portland. **Mercy Hospital** (879-3000), 144 State Street.

TO SEE

MUSEUMS

 ♿ **Portland Museum of Art** (775-6148; for a weekly schedule of events and information, 773-ARTS; www.portlandmuseum.org), 7 Congress Square, Portland. Open Tuesday, Wednesday, and Saturday 10–5, Thursday and Friday 10–9, and Sunday noon–5; closed New Year's Day, July 4, Thanksgiving, and Christmas. $6 adults, $5 students (with ID) and seniors, and $1 children 6–12. Tours daily at 2 PM. Maine's largest art museum offers an extensive collection housed in a striking building designed by I. M. Pei. Featured American artists include Winslow Homer, Edward Hopper, Rockwell Kent, Louise Nevelson, Andrew and N. C. Wyeth, John Singer Sargent, and Marguerite Zorach; European works by Renoir, Degas, Prendergast, Matisse, and Picasso are also usually on view. Like many modern museums, this one incorporates glimpses of its environs. Minutes after studying Winslow Homer's 1868 painting *Artists Sketching in the White Mountains*, for instance, you can see Mount Washington itself (80 miles northwest of Portland) framed in a second-floor window. Changing exhibits are frequently worth the trip.

Center for Maine History, 485 Congress Street. Maintained by the Maine Historical Society (879-0427). The center includes the **Wadsworth-Longfellow House, Maine History Gallery,** and **historical-society library,** open June through October, Tuesday through Sunday 10–4 (closed July 4 and Labor Day; gallery and library open in winter, Wednesday through Saturday noon–4). $6 adults for the house and gallery, $2 children under 18. Allow 45 minutes for a guided tour of the house. Built in 1785 by the grandfather of Henry Wadsworth Longfellow, this was the first brick dwelling in town. Peleg Wadsworth was a Revolutionary War hero, and the entire clan of Wadsworths and Longfellows was prominent in the city. Remarkably enough, the house retains most of its original furnishings as well as a sense of the poet who spent his childhood here.

    The house is now part of a 1-acre campus with changing exhibits and an interesting museum store. A lovely small garden is hidden behind the house, and there is another a couple of doors down behind the granite First Parish Church (#425), marking the site on which Maine's constitution was drafted in 1819.

Portland Head Light

🖋️♿ **The Museum at Portland Head Light** (799-2661; www.portlandheadlight. com), 1000 Shore Road in Fort Williams Park, Cape Elizabeth. Open June through October, 10–4, and November, December, April, and May weekends 10–4. $2 per adult, $1 children 6–18. This is the oldest lighthouse in Maine, first illuminated in 1791 per order of George Washington. It is now automated, and the former keeper's house has been transformed into an exceptional lighthouse museum. Bring a picnic; there are tables with water views as well as the ruins of an old fort in the surrounding **Fort Williams Park,** just 4 miles from downtown Portland: Take State Street (Route 77) south across the bridge to South Portland, then left on Broadway and right on Cottage Street, which turns into Shore Road.

Institute of Contemporary Art/MECA (879-5742), 522 Congress Street. Changing exhibits are frequently worth checking; free. The ICA is a street-level gallery at the Maine College of Art (MECA), where there are 400 full-time students with many times that number enrolled in continuing-studies programs.

🖋️ **Maine Narrow Gauge Railroad Co. & Museum** (828-0814; http://mngrr. rails.net), 58 Fore Street, Portland. Open year-round, daily 10–4. The museum and gift shop are free; excursion fares are $5 round-trip adult, $4 seniors, $3 children. Hard to spot if you aren't looking for it: Drive through the complex of brick buildings and park on the waterside. The octagonal ticket office and tracks are in front of you and the museum is behind. From the 1870s to the 1940s five narrow-gauge lines carrying visitors linked rural Maine communities. This particular rolling stock was preserved for many years as the Edaville Railway near Plymouth, Massachusetts, and was returned to Maine by a group of railroad enthusiasts in 1991. Includes a parlor car, locomotives, a railbus, and a Model T inspection car. A short video presents Maine's 2-footer history. A 3-mile round-trip **excursion** along Casco Bay is offered regularly May through October. It runs again during December, when the tracks are lined with thousands of lights in shapes ranging from Santa to flamingos.

&♿ **Children's Museum of Maine** (828-1234; www.childrensmuseumofme. org), 142 Free Street, Portland. Open Memorial Day through Labor Day, Monday through Saturday 10–5, Sunday noon–5; otherwise, closed Monday and Tuesday. $5 per person; first Friday night of each month free, 5–8. Next door to the Portland Museum of Art, three levels of interactive hands-on exhibits are designed to help the young and old learn together. Permanent exhibits include *Main Street USA* (with cave, farm, supermarket, bank, and fire department), a space shuttle, a news center, and a computer room. There's a science center, a toddler area, and a black-box room that's a walk-in camera obscura. Inquire about frequent storytelling and many other special programs.

Portland Harbor Museum (799-6337) on Fort Road, marked from Route 77 in South Portland. Open Memorial Day weekend through October, Thursday through Sunday 1–4; $2 adults, $1 children. Sited in a brick repair shop that was part of Fort Preble and is now part of Southern Maine Technical College, it mounts changing exhibits on local maritime history and features an ongoing restoration of the pieces of the *Snow Squall*, an 1850s Portland clipper ship wrecked in the Falkland Islands. **Spring Point Lighthouse,** at the end of a breakwater, is another good vantage point on the harbor.

Also see *Selective Shopping—Galleries*.

HISTORIC SITES
All listings are in Portland unless otherwise noted.

& **Portland Observatory** (774-5561), 138 Congress Street. Open Memorial Day through Columbus Day, Monday through Saturday 10–6, Sunday 1–5. $3 adults, $2 children, free 6 and under. Built in 1807, this octagonal, 86-foot-high shingled landmark atop Munjoy Hill is the last surviving 19th-century signal tower in the country. It has been recently restored, and interpretive displays have been added. Climb the 102 steps to the top, as so many captains' wives and mothers have, scanning the horizon for returning ships bringing loved ones.

Victoria Mansion, the Morse-Libby House (772-4841), 109 Danforth Street (at the corner of Park Street). Open for tours May through October, Tuesday through Saturday 10–4, Sunday 1–5 (closed July 4 and Labor Day). $7 per adult, $3 per child 6–18. Perhaps there are more elaborately gilded, frescoed, carved, and many-mirrored mansions in northern New England, but we haven't seen one. Built in 1859 as a summer home for Ruggles Sylvester Morse, a Maine native who made his fortune as a New Orleans hotelier, the Italianate brownstone palazzo features a three-story

CARA MALTBY

Children's Museum of Maine

grand hall with stained-glass windows and a flying staircase with 377 balusters hand-carved from Santo Domingo mahogany. Luckily the second owner, Joseph Libby, was a dry-goods merchant who valued the quality of the furnishings and fabrics and preserved them. It was rescued from destruction and opened to the public in 1941, and its restoration since has been steady. The gift shop sells well-chosen Victoriana. In December the house is dressed to the hilt by professional decorators.

Tate House (774-9781), 1270 Westbrook Street. Follow Congress Street (Route 22) west across the Fore River to Westbrook (it's just outside the Portland Jetport). Open July and August, Tuesday through Saturday 10–3, Sunday 1–4. $5 adults, $4 seniors, $1 children under 12. George Tate, mast agent for the Royal Navy, built this Georgian house in 1755 to reflect his important position. Both the interior and exterior are unusual, distinguished by fine windows, a gambrel roof, wood paneling, and elegant furniture. An 18th-century herb garden is part of the historic landscape. Inquire about summer garden teas and the annual Christmas program.

Neal Dow Memorial (773-7773), 714 Congress Street. Open year-round, Monday through Friday 11–4. Currently the headquarters of the Maine Women's Christian Temperance Union, this handsome Greek Revival mansion was built in 1829 by Neal Dow, the man responsible for an

1851 law that made Maine the first state to prohibit alcohol.

GUIDED TOURS

Greater Portland Landmarks (774-5561; www.portlandlandmarks.org), 156 State Street, Portland 04101. July 5 through Columbus Day, this nonprofit organization offers daily downtown walking tours beginning at 10:30, including both Congress Street and the Old Port ($8 per adult; free under age 16). For the departure point, phone or inquire at the visitors bureau (see *Guidance*). Special excursions with limited registration are also offered to less accessible (frequently private) places. Also note the organization's many excellent books and its *Discover Historic Portland on Foot* series of walking guides.

Mainely Tours and Gifts, Inc. (774-0808), 5½ Moulton Street. Mid-May through October. This narrated, 90-minute trolley tour begins on Moulton Street in the Old Port, stops at the visitors center, and includes Portland Head Light. $12 adults, $11 seniors, $6 kids 12 and under.

SCENIC DRIVES

Cape Elizabeth and Prouts Neck. From State Street in downtown Portland, head south on Route 77 across the Casco Bay Bridge to South Portland, then turn left on Broadway and right on Cottage Street, which turns into Shore Road. Enter 94-acre **Fort Williams Park** (4 miles from downtown) to see the **Museum at Portland Head Light** (see *To See*). There are also picnic tables with water views and a beach, as well as the ruins of the old fort. Many people like to come here early in the morning (the **Cookie Jar Pastry Shop,** 554 Shore Road, opens at 6 AM; try the sweet gingerbread). Follow Shore Road south to Route 77 and continue through Pond Cove, the main village in residential Cape Elizabeth, and on to **Two Lights State Park** (see *Green Space—Parks*) with its views of Casco Bay and the open Atlantic, good for fishing and picnicking (note The Lobster Shack, under *Eating Out*). **Crescent Beach State Park** (see *Green Space—Beaches*), just beyond, is a mile of inviting sand, the area's premiere beach.

Route 77 continues through **Higgins Beach,** a Victorian-era summer community of reasonable rentals and lodging with plenty of beach but limited parking. At the junction of Routes 207 and 77 continue on Black Point Road, past **Scarborough Beach State Park** (see *Green Space—Beaches*), and on to exclusive **Prouts Neck.** Unless you are staying or eating at the **Black Point Inn** (see *Lodging* and *Dining Out*), parking in-season is all but impossible here. Park back at Scarborough Beach and walk or bike to the **Cliff Path,** site of **Winslow Homer's studio** (see *Green Space—Nature Preserves*). Return by the same route (you are just 15 miles from downtown). A short and rewarding detour: At the junction of Cottage Road and Broadway, turn right on Broadway to Southern Maine Technical College. A granite breakwater leads to

The Old Port

the **Spring Point Light** overlooking Casco Bay. Look for signs for the **Spring Point Shoreway Path,** which follows the bay 3 miles to **Willard Beach** (see *Green Space—Beaches*).

🐾 **Falmouth Foreside.** From downtown Portland, take Route 1 north across the mouth of the Presumpscot River. Signs for the Governor Baxter School for the Deaf direct you down Andres Avenue and across a causeway to 100-acre **Mackworth Island.** Park and walk (dogs permitted) the 1½-mile path that circles the island. Views are off across the bay, and a small beach invites strolling. Return to Route 1 and continue north, looking for signs for **Gilsland Farm Sanctuary,** headquarters for the Maine Audubon Society (see *Green Space—Nature Preserves*). The blue sign comes up in less than a half mile; follow the dirt road to the visitors center. Falmouth Foreside itself is a Portland suburb with some fine old houses and a popular marina with a waterside restaurant.

Yarmouth. From downtown Portland, take I-295 to exit 17. Commercial and tourist-geared businesses are relegated to Route 1, leaving the inner village lined with 18th- and 19th-century homes mixed with interesting stores and antiques shops. Note North Yarmouth Academy's original Greek Revival brick buildings, the 18th-century meetinghouse, and several fine old churches. The village green retains its round railroad station, and **Royal River Park** offers recreation (the Royal River is popular with sea kayakers) in all seasons. Also check out **Lower Falls Landing,** a former sardine cannery that now houses interesting shops and the popular Cannery Restaurant (see *Dining Out*). Don't miss the DeLorme Map Store on Route 1 with "Eartha," the world's largest rotating and revolving globe. The famous **Yarmouth Clam Festival** is always the third weekend in July.

ISLAND EXCURSIONS

No one seems quite sure how many islands there are in Casco Bay. Printed descriptions range from 136 to 222. Seventeenth-century explorer John Smith dubbed them the Calendar Islands, saying there was one for every day of the year. Regardless of the actual number, there are plenty of offshore places for poking around. Regular year-round ferry service runs to six of the islands, five of which invite exploration.

For listings of summer cottages in the Casco Bay Islands, contact Casco Bay Development Association, Peaks Island 04108. Two local Realtors also offer rental listings: **Port Island Realty** (766-5966 or 775-7253) and **Ashmore Realty** (772-6992).

Peaks Island. Just 3 miles from Portland (a 20-minute ferry ride), Peaks is the most accessible island. Ferry service runs regularly, even off-season, as many of the island's approximately 1,000 year-round residents commute to the mainland for work and school. In summer the population swells to between 5,000 and 6,000, and day-trippers are common. Check out the bulletin boards at the top of Welch Street and at **Hannigan's IGA.** The 5-mile shore road around the island is great for walking or bicycling. Bicycle rentals are available on the island at **Brad's Re-Cycled Bike Shop** (766-5631); when Brad isn't there, folks fill out a form, place payment in the box, and return the bikes when they are through. **The Fifth Marine Regiment Center** (766-3330), Seashore Avenue, is a striking building erected in 1888 to house Maine's largest collection of Civil War memorabilia (local history exhibits are on the second floor). Open daily in July and August, weekends, June and September (hours vary). **Maine Island Kayak** (766-2373; also see *To Do—Sea Kayaking*) offers trips from a half day to several days, along with kayaking instruction. Food sources (some are open in summer only) include sandwiches at the **Peaks Island Mercantile** in summer and from Hannigan's IGA year-round. **Jones Landing** (766-3040), just off the ferry, serves lunch and dinner (burgers, sandwiches, fried seafood, steak) in-season, and offers live entertainment often, as well as reggae music every Sunday. **Peaks Island House** (766-4400) serves all three meals and has outside deck seating in nice weather. This is also the only place on the island that provides overnight lodging (766-4406 for reservations), unless you rent a cottage. Four rooms, decorated in floral and sea motifs, with private baths and water views. $85–120 per night. **Peaks Café** (766-2479) offers a complete range of coffee choices, as well as pastries, bagels, fruit, and juices. **Peaks Grill** has pizza, burgers, hot dogs, and the like. **Bakery on the Bay** (766-2079) is open year-round, selling breads and other bakery goods, sandwiches, and coffee.

Great Chebeague is the largest island in Casco Bay: 4½ miles long and 2 miles wide. Its population of 325 swells to eight times that in summer. A bike is the best way to explore the island. Rentals are available at the **Sunset House** (846-6568; sunsethse@aol.com), a comfortable B&B that is open year-round ($75–130).

Chebeague Island Inn (864-5155; www.chebeagueinn.com), open Memorial Day through September, is the island's classic old summer hotel. The 21 rooms are simple but comfortable, with private baths and harbor views. We love this place, from the large open-beamed living room with massive stone fireplace, books, brightly upholstered chairs, and rainy-day board games, to the sprawling grounds overlooking the ocean and golf course. Rates are $85–125 double in-season, including breakfast. The dining room serves all three meals in summer, but it is sometimes closed for private functions.

The Chebeague Orchard Inn (846-9488), open year-round, offers extensive flower and vegetable gardens, a common room with fireplace, and five antiques-furnished guest rooms, three with private baths, some with water views. Vickie and Neil Taliento are helpful hosts who keep bikes for guests and include a full breakfast (featuring their organic veggies). $75–125 in-season, $60–95 off-season.

You can pick up take-out at **Doughty's Island Market.** To relax and enjoy the scenery, head to **Chandler's Cove,** a white sand beach, or the beach near **Coleman's Cove.** Golfers will want to try the **Great Chebeague Golf Club** (846-9478), a beautiful nine-hole course founded in 1923, where nonmembers can play anytime except Monday or Thursday morning. New facilities on the island include a recreation center with an Olympic-sized heated swimming pool, indoor gym, weight room, and outdoor tennis/basketball courts. In 2001 a historical-society museum will also open its doors.

Casco Bay Lines ferries dock at the southern end of the island and **Chebeague Transportation Company** (846-3700) offers faster, more frequent service from Cousins Island in Yarmouth to the dock at Chabeague Island Inn. Call for directions and parking details.

Long Island is 3 miles long and approximately a mile wide. This island, like the others, has a thriving summer population. There's a general store and longtime popular restaurant, **The Spar** (766-3310), which serves lunch and dinner featuring fresh local seafood, lobster, steaks, and pasta. Full bar, moorings for boats, picnic lunches available. Bike rentals are also available here. In addition, there's **Maria's** (766-3300), a new pizza place, and the **Chestnut Hill Inn** (766-5272), a seven-room (four with private baths) establishment open year-round. On weekdays continental breakfast is included, and on weekends a full breakfast is served. Dinner is available by reservation, both to guests and others. The beaches, tidal pools, and remains of old schooners are fun to explore.

Great Diamond Island. A pleasant half-hour ferry ride from downtown, this 2-mile-long island is the site of Fort McKinley, built sturdily of brick in the 1890s, now restored as **Diamond Cove** (www.diamond cove.com), a resort-style development featuring 121 townhouses (weekly summer rentals are few: 776-3005); **Diamond's Edge** (786-5850) is the big attraction here, a casually elegant restaurant open May 20 through October 11 for lunch and dinner, also for Sunday brunch in high season; a popular place for weddings. Guided tours aside, the resort grounds are private.

Cliff Island is a full 1½-hour ride down the bay. It is the most rustic of the islands, with 8 miles of dirt roads and no overnight accommodations, a peaceful feel, and sandy beaches. There's a seasonal sandwich shop on the wharf and the general store sells sandwiches year-round. For **cottage rentals** check with the Greater Portland CVB (see *Guidance*).

TO DO

BALLOONING

Hot Fun (799-0193), Box 2825, South Portland. Hot-air balloons carry up to six passengers.

Balloon Rides (761-8373; 1-800-952-2076), 17 Freeman Street, Portland.

BICYCLING

Hundreds of acres of undeveloped land offer some great bicycling. Call **Portland Trails** (775-2411) for designated trails. Three new maps, available for $1 each, have been published by the **Bicycle Transportation Alliance of Portland (BTAP),** P.O. Box 4506, Portland 04112. These detail routes through historic Portland, the islands, and the lighthouse trail. Rentals and service are available at several locations around the city. **Cycle Mania** (774-2933), 59 Federal Street, Portland. Sponsors group rides. (Also see *Island Excursions*.)

BIRDING

See *Green Space—Nature Preserves*.

BOATING

For ferry information to Chebeague Island, see also *Island Excursions*. **Prince of Fundy Cruises to Nova Scotia** represents the ultimate boat excursion out of Portland. See *Getting There*.

Casco Bay Lines (774-7871), Casco Bay Ferry Terminal, 56 Commercial Street at Franklin, Portland. Founded in 1845, this business was said to be the oldest continuously operating ferry company in the country when it went bankrupt in 1980. The present, quasi-municipal Casco Bay Island Transit District looks and functions much the way the old line did. Its brightly painted ferries are still lifelines to six islands, carrying groceries and lumber as well as mail. The year-round, daily mail-boat run (3 hours) puts into all the islands in the morning and again in the afternoon. A variety of seasonal, special excursions includes a 5½-hour Bailey Island Cruise (see "Brunswick and the Harpswells"). Also year-round, frequent, daily car ferry service to Peaks Island.

Coast Watch & Guiding Light Navigation Co. Inc. (774-6498), Long Wharf, Portland. Runs Memorial Day through Columbus Day. The *Kristy K* takes you out to Eagle Island, the former home of Admiral Peary, now maintained by the state as a historic site and nature preserve (see *To Do—Boat Excursions* in "Brunswick and the Harpswells" and "Freeport"); the 49-passenger *Fish Hawk* is used for a harbor and island cruise and for seal-watching. Group charters available.

Bay View Cruises (761-0496), Fisherman's Wharf, Portland. Daily June through October, weekends from April. Narrated harbor cruises aboard the *Bay View Lady;* harbor lunch cruise (bring your own sandwich) 12:10–12:50.

Olde Port Mariner Fleet (775-0727), Long Wharf, Portland. Whale-watches daily in summer, weekends in early June and after Labor Day. Also summer sunset trips and a variety of other shorter excursions.

Maine Island Kayak Co. (766-2373; 1-800-796-2373; www.maineislandkayak. com), 70 Luther Street, Peaks Island. Late May through October. One of the state's leading kayaking outfitters, offering 1- to 10-day (camping) tours as far Down East as Machias; also weekend overnights on Jewell Island—on the outer fringe of Casco Bay—and 7-day expeditions throughout the islands of the bay. Introductory paddling sessions available. Casco Bay is a great place to learn to sea kayak, given its easy access both to a wide variety of islands and to open ocean.

Deep-Sea Fishing and Sailing. Several deep-sea-fishing boats and sailing yachts are based in Portland every summer. Check with the Convention and Visitors Bureau (772-5800) for current listings.

BREWERY TOURS

Microbreweries have popped up all over Portland, many with restaurants alongside them. Most give tours, either on a regular basis or by appointment. For information, contact individual breweries: **Allagash Brewing** (878-5385), 100 Industrial Way; **Casco Bay Brewing** (797-2020), 57 Industrial Way; **D. L. Geary Brewing** (878-2337), 38 Evergreen Drive; **Gritty McDuff's Brew Pub** (772-2739), 396 Fore Street; **Shipyard Brewing** (761-0807), 86 Newbury Street; **Stone Coast Brewing** (773-2337), 14 York Street; and **Sebago Brewing Company** (775-2337), 15 Philbrook Avenue, South Portland.

FOR FAMILIES

Smiling Hill Farm (775-4818), 781 County Road, Westbrook. Kids love this farm with a petting zoo and popular ice cream stand.

Southworth Planetarium (780-4249), University of Southern Maine, Falmouth Street, Portland. Astronomy and laser light shows throughout the year. Special shows for young children in summer and on holidays.

GOLF

There are several popular 9- and 18-hole courses in the area, notably: **Sable Oaks Golf Club** (975-6257), South Portland, considered among the most challenging and best courses in Maine (18 holes); **Riverside**

North (18 holes) and **Riverside South** (9 holes) in Portland; **Val Halla** (18 holes) in Cumberland; and **Twin Falls** (9 holes) in Westbrook.

GREEN SPACE

BEACHES
Crescent Beach State Park (8 miles from Portland on Route 77) is a mile of sand complete with changing facilities, a playground, picnic tables, and a snack bar. $2.50 adults, $.50 ages 5–11.

Kettle Cove, just down the road from Crescent (follow the road behind the ice cream shop), is small, with a grassy lawn and rocky beach. There is no admission fee, but parking is limited.

Higgins Beach, farther down Route 77 in Scarborough, is an extensive strand within walking distance of lodging—but there is no parking on the street. Private lots charge $4.

Scarborough Beach State Park, Black Point Road (Route 207), 3 miles south of Route 1 on Prouts Neck. Open Memorial Day through September ($2.50 admission), also for walking year-round. A 243-acre park with a superb beach, but only a 65-foot stretch is technically public. Get there early because parking is limited. Facilities include changing rooms, rest rooms, and picnic facilities. For the scenic route from Portland, see *Scenic Drives.*

PARKS
Deering Oaks, Portland's 51-acre city park designed by Frederick Law Olmsted, has a pond, ducks and swans, paddleboats, fountains, a playground, and a fine grove of oak trees. A farmer's market is held here every Saturday morning throughout the summer and into November. Ice skating on the pond in winter.

Two Lights State Park, Cape Elizabeth, is open April 15 through November. No swimming, but 40 acres of shore with stunning water views for picnicking and fishing. Also see **Fort Williams Park** in *Scenic Drives* and Fort Allen Park under Eastern Promenade in *Walks.*

NATURE PRESERVES
Gilsland Farm Sanctuary (781-2330; www.maineaudubon.org), 118 Route 1, Falmouth Foreside (3 miles east of Portland). The headquarters of the **Maine Audubon Society** are located here. The sanctuary is open sunrise to sunset, year-round. The nature-oriented shop is open Monday through Saturday 9–5, Sunday 2–5. Sixty acres of trails, rolling fields, river frontage, and salt marsh. A solar-heated education center has exhibits; special programs and field trips are held year-round.

Scarborough Marsh Nature Center (883-5100), Pine Point Road (also marked as Route 9 west), Scarborough (10 miles south of downtown Portland). Nature center open mid-June through Labor Day, 9:30–5:30. The state's largest salt marsh can be explored by foot or canoe. The nature center houses an aquarium and mounted birds and mammals, and sponsors walks, canoe tours, and rentals. Inquire about special programs; reservations required.

Fore River Sanctuary (781-2330), near Maine Turnpike exit 8, off Brighton Avenue, Portland. This 76-acre preserve owned by the Maine Audubon Society is hidden behind a suburban neighborhood where explorers may not think to look. The 2½ miles of hiking trails offer access to Portland's only waterfall, **Jewell Falls.** A set of railroad tracks (be careful—they are active) marks the beginning of a trail that leads you through woods and marshland.

Prouts Neck Cliff Path and Wildlife Sanctuary. Winslow Homer painted many of his seascapes in the small studio attached to the summer home here, which was—and still is—part of the exclusive community on Prouts Neck, beyond the Black Point Inn. It's not far from the inn to Winslow Homer Road, where the Cliff Path (unmarked) begins. It's a beautiful stroll along the rocks, around Eastern Point, and back almost to the inn. You can also walk through the sanctuary between Winslow Homer Road (just east of St. James Episcopal Church) and Library Lane, donated by Winslow's brother Charles. The studio itself is open July and August 10–4, marked only by a STUDIO sign on the shedlike room attached to a private house.

WALKS

Portland Trails (775-2411), an organization committed to developing hiking and biking trails in the city, offers a free map describing several city parks, and a dozen trails as well as bus routes to take you there. Pick up a copy at the visitors information center (see *Guidance*).

The Eastern Promenade. Follow Congress Street east to the Portland Observatory (see *To See*) atop Munjoy Hill and then continue the extra block to the Eastern Promenade, a park-lined street high on this same bluff with sweeping views of Casco Bay. Follow it around, back toward the harbor, to 68-acre **Fort Allen Park,** which dates from 1814, set on a blustery point above the bay. Down along the bay itself the paved **Eastern Promenade Trail** runs along the base of Munjoy Hill, good for biking, walking, and in-line skating (but beware the smoke from the railroad museum's excursion train, which runs alongside it).

The Western Promenade. It's ironic that Munjoy Hill (see above), the poorer section of town, now has the million-dollar view (one reason why that varied ethnic neighborhood is now being gentrified) while the Western Promenade now overlooks the airport and gas holding tanks. Still, this is Portland's poshest and most architecturally interesting residential neighborhood. Pick up a copy of the Portland landmarks leaflet "Guide to the Western Promenade" ($1) from the visitors bureau (see *Guidance*).

Baxter Boulevard. A popular 3½-mile path around the tidal flats of Back Cove (unfortunately, just off I-295), also part of the original Olmsted Plan, connects with the Eastern Promenade Trail. It's a popular spot for dog walking, jogging, biking. Fields also provide good kite flying.

Eastern Cemetery, Congress Street and Washington Avenue (near the Portland Observatory on Munjoy Hill). More than 4,000 souls are interred in these 9 acres, and the headstones, dating back to the mid–17th century, are embellished with angels and death's heads. Despite its derelict state, this is an utterly fascinating place.

Also see Prouts Neck Cliff Path and Wildlife Sanctuary under *Nature Preserves,* above.

LODGING

HOTELS

There are more than 2,000 hotel and motel rooms in and around Portland. The following are right downtown in Portland 04101.

   Portland Regency (774-4200; 1-800-727-3436; www.theregency.com), 20 Milk Street. An interesting 95-room hotel (including 8 suites), housed in a century-old armory in the middle of the Old Port Exchange. Rooms are decorated with reproduction antiques and equipped with TVs, phones, and honor bars. The formal dining room serves all three meals, and the attractive lounge offers cocktails and lighter fare. The health spa has a cardiovascular center, aerobics classes, a Jacuzzi, and massage available. From $99 January through April; in-season (Memorial Day weekend through October) $129–249.

   Eastland Park Hotel (775-5411; 1-888-671-8008; www.eastlandparkhotel. com), 157 High Street. A 12-story, 204-room landmark built in 1927. In the mid-1980s it fell into bankruptcy, and a series of ownership changes have followed. Recently restored to its original grandeur. A downtown convention hotel, it offers genuine pluses like elevator operators, a rooftop lounge with the best overall view in town, two restaurants, a fitness center, and a good location across from the art museum. Rooms have amenities like ironing boards and coffeemakers; 18 extended-stay suites have kitchens. Shuttle service from the Jetport is free. $157–165 in-season, from $119–125 in winter.

   Holiday Inn by the Bay (775-2311; 1-800-HOLIDAY), 88 Spring Street. An 11-story, 246-room downtown high rise jars with the city's architecture and ambience but offers great harbor views. Amenities include an indoor pool, a small fitness center, cable TV with video-game hook-ups, free parking, a laundry facility, and a nice restaurant and lounge. $142–157 in high season.

Note: Portland does have the major chains, but they are mainly located by I-95 at exit 8 in Westbrook or in South Portland.

INNS AND BED & BREAKFASTS

Pomegranate Inn (772-1006; 1-800-356-0408; www.pomegranateinn. com), 49 Neal Street, Portland 04102. Isabel Smiles, an interior designer and former antiques dealer, has turned this 1880s Western Prom-

Portland Regency Hotel

enade house into a work of art. Nothing stiff, just one surprise for the eye after another. Eight amazing rooms furnished in a mix of antiques and *objets,* most with hand-painted walls in bold, original designs. Downstairs, the walls of the wide entryway are a hand-mottled tangerine, and the mantel and four columns in the living room are marbleized. Guest rooms have phones, discreet TVs, and private baths; five have gas fireplaces. The living room is well stocked with art books. Breakfast is exquisite. Frankly, we're glad we stayed here before its fame spread, because what has since been described as the Pomegranate's "high style" came as a complete surprise. Still, repeat visits have been as good as the first. $175–225 per room in-season, $95–165 off-season, includes breakfast.

🐾 **The Danforth** (879-8755; 1-800-991-6557; www.danforthmaine.com), 163 Danforth Street, Portland 04102. Barbara Hathaway has restored this classic Federal-period (1821) brick mansion to its original glory and then some. The feel is of an elegant small hotel with common areas scattered throughout the house, from the wood-paneled billiard room in the basement to a third-floor solarium and a cupola with a star-studded ceiling, not to mention the gracious formal living room, den, sunporch, and sunny breakfast room. Guest rooms all have queen-sized beds, sitting areas, decorator fabrics, private baths, cable TVs, phones, and data ports. Eight of the 10 rooms have working fireplaces. We especially like Room 2. Rates ($135–285 in-season) include a full breakfast with a hot entrée and fresh fruit.

🏅 **The Percy Inn** (871-7638; 1-888-41-PERCY; www.percyinn.com), 15 Pine Street, P.O. Box 8187, Portland 04104. This is a find: a restored 1830 brick row house a few steps from the restaurants and galleries in Longfellow Square but facing a quiet side street. Owner Dale Northrop is a Portland native who has critiqued thousands of hotels for his work as a travel writer and definitely knows what he is doing. The five rooms vary in size and shape, but all are furnished in antiques and designer fabrics and have cedar closets, wet bars, fridges with complimentary soft drinks, phones, faxes, TVs, CD players, ceiling fans, and more. You might want to request a private study, two-person shower, skylight, or private entrance. There's a guest pantry on the third floor, second-floor breakfast room, and first-floor parlor. Rates are $89–169. Four larger "out suites" are scattered around the neighborhood. The State Street Cottage we saw was a gem—light and bright with a full kitchen, great for a family of four or two couples ($150–200).

The Inn on Carleton Street (775-1910; 1-800-639-1779; www.innoncarleton. com), Portland 04102. Sue and Phil Cox have lovingly restored this handsome 1860s town house, even the trompe l'oeil artwork in the entryway. Gradually they have furnished each of the six rooms with spectacularly heavy and high Victorian bedroom sets. Check out the Egyptian revival headboard in Room 1. We also like the contemporary artwork and the general feel of this place. Guests form a congenial group around the breakfast table. $159–199 in-season.

West End Inn (772-1377; 1-800-338-1377), 146 Pine Street, Portland 04102. This 1870s brick town house is a beauty, its natural elegance skillfully enhanced by the colors and decor Rosa Higgins (a native of the Dominican Republic) has brought to its 12-foot-high common rooms and six comfortable guest rooms. The guest rooms all have private baths, cable TV, ceiling fans, and air-conditioning, and there's a fireplace in the library. Breakfast, served in the dining room, usually includes yogurt, homemade granola, fruit, and a hot dish. $139–199 in-season, from $99 November through early May.

Inn at Park Spring (774-1059; 1-800-437-8511; www.innatparkspring. com). Nicely sited just downhill from the art museum and a short walk from the Old Port, Elinor and Lionel Berube's 1830s town house has been welcoming guests for almost 20 years. The six guest rooms are on all three floors and become increasingly contemporary (in decor) as you climb. All offer private baths and sitting areas, fresh flowers, and amenities. Breakfast is served in the formal dining room, which, like the living room, has floor-to-ceiling windows. Late May through October: $130–145; otherwise, $95–105.

🐾✒️♿**Inn at St. John** (773-6481; 1-800-636-9127; www.innatstjohn.com), 939 Congress Street. A 37-room hotel built in 1897 to accommodate railroad passengers arriving at Union Station (unfortunately long gone). Convenient for guests arriving by Vermont Transit, it's a long, sketchy walk from downtown. Innkeeper Paul Hood creates a turn-of-the-century feel. $50–165 depending on season.

Beyond Portland

&   **Black Point Inn Resort** (883-2500; 1-800-258-0003; blackpointinn.com),
510 Blackpoint Road, Prouts Neck 04074. Open year-round. This
vintage-1878 summer hotel is so much a part of its exclusive community
that guests are permitted to use the Prouts Neck Country Club's 18-hole
golf course and 14 tennis courts. Guests can also rent boats or moor their
own at the local yacht club. Public rooms are extensive and elegant, with
views of the Southern Coast on one side and of the open ocean on the
other. Facilities include two sandy beaches, indoor and outdoor pools,
two Jacuzzis, a sauna, and an elevator operator. There are 80 rooms,
poolside buffets, afternoon tea with a pianist, evening cocktails, and
dancing. No children under age 8 mid-July through late August. A
London taxi serves as a shuttle to the airport and into Portland. In high
season $345–650 for double MAP per night plus 15 percent gratuity; from
$220 off-season B&B. A noon buffet is offered. (See Prouts Neck Cliff Path
and Wildlife Sanctuary under *Green Space—Nature Preserves.*)

&/ **Inn by the Sea** (799-3134; www.innbysea.com), 40 Bowery Beach Road,
Cape Elizabeth 04107. A short (15-minute) drive from downtown
Portland, this beachside hotel replicates a turn-of-the-20th-century
seaside resort. The shingled complex has gables and plenty of elegant
detailing but all the amenities. The 43 units are all one- and two-bedroom
suites and cottages, all with a combination living and dining area, a full
kitchen and porch or deck, and a water view. All are furnished with
reproduction antiques, chintz, and down comforters. The cottages,
connected like town houses, are away from the inn. Beach house units
are generally larger, with woodstoves and full water views. Facilities
include an outdoor pool, tennis courts, and bicycles. A boardwalk leads
to the tip of Crescent Beach State Park. Summer prices range $269–549;
winter $139–249.

Higgins Beach Inn (883-6684; www.higginsbeachinn.com), Ocean Avenue, Scarborough 04074 (7 miles south of Portland). Open mid-May
through mid-October. An 1890s three-story wooden summer hotel near
sandy Higgins Beach. The pleasant dining room features seafood with a
large and varied menu (entrées $14–21). There is also a cocktail lounge,
a homey TV room, and a sunporch. Upstairs, the 24 guest rooms are basic
but clean and airy, 14 with private baths. Continental breakfast is available after Labor Day but not included in the room rates. $65–110 double.

WHERE TO EAT

Portland claims more restaurants per capita than any other city in America.
The quality of the dining is unquestionably exceptional, perhaps because almost all are locally owned.

DINING OUT
Fore Street (775-2717), 288 Fore Street. Open for dinner nightly. Reser-

vations a must. East of the Old Port in a former industrial building, this is a hugely popular local dining place. Applewood-grilled specialties range from hanger steak ($15.95) to Atlantic yellowfin tuna loin ($20.95). Turnspit roasted chicken, rabbit, pork loin, and wood-oven-roasted and simmered fish and seafood are what this place is about. The bar is a great meeting spot, and the kitchen is open. Watching (and sniffing) all the grilling and roasting is half the fun. If you know Lulu's in San Francisco, the similarities are striking.

    ᕃ **Street & Company** (775-0887), 33 Wharf Street. Open for dinner Sunday through Thursday 5:30–9:30, Friday and Saturday until 10. Year-round. Reservations recommended. The seafood restaurant you had hoped to find in Portland: small and informal, specializing in flapping fresh fish. The problem: It's very popular, and walk-ins may need to wait, even with the added outdoor seating in warm weather. Seafood comes grilled, broiled, pan-blackened, and steamed, much of it served right in the pan it's been cooked in. Specialties include lobster diavolo, mussels Provençal, and scallops in Pernod and cream. Homemade desserts. Entrées $13.95–18.95.

       Commissary (228-2057), 25 Preble Street. Open for lunch and dinner daily. Maine native Matthew Kenney, owner of four New York City restaurants, has opened the Portland Public Market's first full-service facility. Rustic in style with an open kitchen and wood-burning rotisserie ovens, the 70-seat restaurant offers a communal table and seasonal outside seating. You might dine on warm Maine goat cheese tart with fig jam and balsamic vinegar followed by grilled swordfish with a green olive tapenade and couscous. Entrées: from $14 for wood-oven-baked pasta with Fontina and prosciutto to $20 for Muscovy duck.

    ᕃ **Café Uffa** (775-3380), 190 State Street (in Longfellow Square near the Portland Museum of Art). Open for breakfast and dinner Wednesday through Saturday, Sunday 9 AM–2 PM. Hugely popular for Sunday brunch (get there early); no longer all vegetarian and seafood but still featuring entrées like applewood-grilled salmon with Korean barbecue sauce and grilled eggplant with veggies and polenta. Try the bourbon pecan tart. Bistro atmosphere, good wine list, sangria made in-house. Occasionally closed for vacation, so call ahead. Sidewalk tables in the summer. Entrées $10–18.

       Walter's Café (871-9258), 15 Exchange Street. Open for lunch and dinner daily. A very popular storefront bistro with unusual soups and salads at lunch. Creative offerings like Kowloon BBQ flank steak, or shrimp and andouille bake, or pan-fried black beans and rice cakes at dinner. A better than dependable bet. Dinner entrées $14.95–21.95.

       Katahdin (774-1740), 106 High Street. Dinner Monday through Saturday 5–10 PM. No reservations and it is often very busy, so you might want to call for the wait time before you go. Inventive New England entrées include wild mushroom ravioli, and specials might include grilled monkfish coated in Moroccan spices with ginger sauce. Entrées $10.95–14.95.

Aubergine (874-0680), 555 Congress Street. Open Tuesday through Saturday 5:30–10 PM, and 11–2 for Sunday brunch. David and Elizabeth Grant have actually moved this popular French bistro down the Maine coast from Camden. The menu changes nightly but might include crispy salmon with spinach Pernod or yellowfin tuna grilled with lemon and capers. Extensive wine list, all available by the glass. Very popular Sunday brunch. A three-course pre-early-bird theater menu is $19–21 for entrées.

Local 188 (761-7909), 188 State Street. Open for dinner and Sunday brunch. A tapas bar and gallery run by a collective of artists and known for the quality of the art as well as the Spanish food, which comes in small, tasty mix-and-match portions. Spanish wines are a specialty. Try the gazpacho. Tapas: $2.75–10.

Perfetto (828-0001), 28 Exchange Street. Open for lunch and dinner. Known for its creative northern Italian and Mediterranean menu and its lively wine bar. The filet mignon with bacon and leeks wrapped in fried spinach and the potato-wrapped haddock are recommended. Entrées $12–18.

Bella Cucina (828-4033), 653 Congress Street, Longfellow Square; open nightly for dinner. Chef Jim Leduc offers a menu that changes daily, featuring vegan, seafood, wood-grilled meats. Entrées $9.95–18.95.

DiMillo's Floating Restaurant (772-2216), Long Wharf. Open for lunch and dinner. Maine's only floating restaurant, this converted car ferry serves seafood, steaks, and Italian cuisine. Free parking at the heart of the waterfront is a definite plus. Entrées $15–24.95.

Boone's Restaurant (774-5725), 6 Custom House Wharf. Open for lunch and dinner year-round. Still in business on the wharf that it has occupied since 1898 but no longer a hot tourist spot, simply because foot traffic has shifted. Specialties include Mediterranean pasta dishes, lobster, and other fresh seafood. Seasonal patio dining overlooking the water. Dinner $10.95–27.95.

The Roma Café (773-9873), 769 Congress Street. Open for lunch and dinner on weekdays, dinner only on weekends. Elegant dining rooms in the Rines Mansion, right for a romantic dinner or a special group gathering. Begin with appetizers like chicken-stuffed artichokes or salads. Entrées include a delicious seafood linguine. Special requests (like leaving off the shrimp to create a good vegetarian pasta dish) are cheerfully accommodated when possible. $11.95–17.95.

PepperClub (772-0531), 78 Middle Street. Open for dinner nightly. A funky, fun spot. Creative menu options, which change frequently, are written on two large blackboards (as well as smaller table versions if you need one). Several vegetarian choices, perhaps portobello pie or lasagna with fresh basil and feta cheese, as well as some beef, chicken, and seafood. Entrées $10–15.

BiBo's Madd Apple Café (774-9698), 23 Forest Avenue. Open for dinner

Tuesday through Saturday at 5:30. Summer hours vary; call ahead for details. Reservations recommended. This is an intimate bistro with a menu that changes frequently, featuring seasonal and local ingredients. Smoked salmon and sweet potato cakes, swordfish *au poivre,* and steak New Orleans are a few specialties. Special desserts. $15–20.

Back Bay Grill (772-8833), 65 Portland Street. Open for dinner Monday through Saturday. Brightly painted murals add a lively feel to this place. The menu changes about eight times a year as the seasons change. Summer and early fall offer a unique five-course lobster-tasting menu. Their crème brûlée is always a hit. The wine lists are a full page each for reds, whites, dessert wines, and ports. Entrées over $20.

Beyond downtown Portland

Joe's Boathouse (741-2780), Spring Point Marina (end of Broadway). Open daily for lunch and dinner. Joe and Mark Loring, also owners of Walter's Café in the Old Port (see *Dining Out*), have created a winning combination here with spectacular views of Casco Bay (there's a seasonal patio) and a creative menu. You might dine on seared duck breast with a sweet blackberry glaze. Sunday brunch is a specialty. Dinner entrées $13.95–19.95.

  ᛞ **Black Point Inn** (883-4126), Prouts Neck. Dinner by reservation in a formal dining room with water views. The menu changes nightly from basics like Yankee pot roast and boiled lobster to Cajun-style sautéed shrimp on angelhair pasta; extravagant desserts. $40 prix fixe plus tax and gratuity.

The Audubon Room (767-0888), at the Inn by the Sea, 40 Bowery Beach Road, Cape Elizabeth. Overlooking the beach and water, a gracious dining room decorated with genuine Audubon prints, featuring seafood and rack of lamb. Entrées $18.95–27.95.

Snow Squall (799-2232; 1-800-568-3260), 18 Ocean Street, South Portland. Open daily for lunch Monday through Friday, Sunday brunch. A long-established, dependable place with a view of the South Port Marina. Lunch on smoked crabcake or a salad plate with duck, rabbit, and salmon; dine on pan-seared salmon with Israeli couscous, wild muchrooms, and pinot noir sauce, or a seafood pasta studded with scallops and shrimp. This place also has one of the better clam chowders in Maine. Dinner entrées $14–18.

The Cannery Restaurant at Lower Falls Landing (846-1226), Yarmouth. Open daily for lunch and dinner, Sunday brunch. Built in 1913 as a herring factory, then served as a sardine-packing plant from the 1920s right up until 1980. The building, now part of a complex that includes a marina and some interesting shops, makes an attractive restaurant space with a waterside terrace. $9.95–21.95.

EATING OUT

In and around the Old Port

Note: Most of the restaurants described under *Dining Out* also serve a reasonably priced lunch.

Norm's Bar-B-Q (774-6711), 43 Middle Street. Open Tuesday through Thursday noon–10, Friday and Saturday noon–11, Sunday 3–9. For a memorable pork sandwich or spareribs, or maybe the rib sampler with onion rings, this is the place. Entrées average $9; beer and wine served.

Bakehouse Café (773-2217), 205 Commercial Street (corner of Dana). Open for lunch daily, for dinner Thursday through Saturday. Great warm-weather dining with an upstairs terrace and streetside café; attractive but limited seating inside. Stellar lunch salads like crab and avocado with roasted corn, and grilled salmon salad Niçoise. Dinner entrées $10–18.

Becky's Diner (773-7070), 390 Commercial Street. Open 4 AM–9 PM Tuesday through Saturday, 4 AM–3 PM Sunday and Monday. This is a genuine local favorite, known for soups and pies. Breakfast is the specialty here, also reasonably priced lunch and dinner specials.

Gilbert's Chowder House (871-5636), 92 Commercial Street. Open for lunch and dinner. Delicious and filling chowders served in a bread bowl are the best choices here, but they also have a range of fried seafood and other reasonably priced specials. Outside dining in-season.

Dock Fore (772-8619), 336 Fore Street. Open for lunch and dinner. A sunny, casual pub (most seating is at the bar or side bar) serving hearty fare and homelike specialties. Large portions at good prices.

Village Café (772-5320), 112 Newbury Street. Open for lunch and dinner daily. This is an old family favorite that predates the Old Port renaissance (it's just east of the Old Port). The third generation of the Reali family is now welcoming patrons to the same comfortable place. A large, often crowded space with specialties like fried Maine clams, lobster, veal parmigiana, and steaks.

Anthony's Italian Kitchen (774-8668), 151 Middle Street. This great little place is always crowded at lunchtime. It smells like a real Italian kitchen, and the aromas are not misleading. Terrific pizza and pasta specialties, homemade meatballs, service that makes you feel like an old friend.

Beyond the Old Port

Portland Public Market, 25 Preble Street, open Monday through Saturday 9–7, Sunday 105 (doors open at 7 AM for coffee and whatever). Soups, sandwiches, salads, stuffed breads, are available from a couple of dozen vendors. Our favorite is Stone Soup, with its counter service for specialties like sausage and spinach-laced bean soup.

Norm's Bar & Grill (828-9944), 606 Congress Street. Open daily for lunch and dinner. Same ownership as Norm's Bar-B-Q, blackboard tapas and specials, and an eclectic menu ranging from black bean soup (a staple) and Greek salad with fried calamari to hot pastrami to lamb shish kebob. Try the buttermilk biscuits and the BBQ chicken quesadilla. Norm's is such a good value at night that even on weeknights it's advisable to slide into a booth by 5:30.

The Kitchen (775-0833), 593 Congress Street. Open for lunch and dinner with a friendly staff, terrific food, and reasonable prices. Convenient to the Portland Museum of Art and the Children's Museum. Breakfast served until closing on weekends. The delicious wraps include tofu teriyaki and Jamaican jerk chicken, and are plentiful. Other choices include soups, salads, and subs.

Sala Thai (797-0871), 1363 Washington Avenue. Not on the tourist route, but worth seeking out if you like Thai food. The menu is large and varied, with the usual choices, but the quality is a cut above many such places. Great sauces, generous portions. Note its convenient take-out branch at 921 Congress Street (819-2577).

Beyond Portland

The Lobster Shack (799-1677), Cape Elizabeth (off Route 77 at the tip of the cape, near Two Lights State Park). Open for lunch and dinner, April through mid-October. A local landmark since the 1920s, set below the lighthouse and next to the foghorn. Dine inside or out. We have had recent complaints, but locals continue to swear by the quality of this place. This is the place to pick a lobster out of the tank and watch it being boiled—then eat it "in the rough." Herb and Martha Porch are also known for their chowder and lobster stew, fried Maine shrimp, scallops, and clams, lobster, and crabmeat rolls.

The Good Table (799-4663), 526 Ocean House Road, Cape Elizabeth. Open Monday through Friday 11 AM–9 PM, Saturday 8 AM–9 PM, and Sunday 8 AM–3 PM. A bit of a drive from in-town Portland, but near Two Lights State Park and worth every mile. A cozy place offering hearty homestyle meals. Weekend brunch menu might include eggs Benedict and a variety of interesting quiches.

Spurwink Country Kitchen (799-1177), 150 Spurwink Road (near Scarborough Beach), Scarborough. Open mid-April through mid-October, 11:30–9. Part of this place's beauty is that it's here at all, right where you wouldn't expect to find a place to eat. Then you discover it's a special place, looking much the same and serving much the same food as when Hope Sargent opened it in 1955. Specials vary with the day and include soup, potato, vegetable or rolls, tea or coffee. Great homemade pies.

COFFEE BARS

An abundance of cozy cafés serving coffee and espresso drinks have sprung up in Portland. **Java Net** (1-800-528-2638) is a great spot for travelers who need to check their e-mail or conduct business via the Internet while vacationing. Hourly access rates; you can either bring your own laptop or use their computers. Bright and lively, with comfortable couches and chairs, and plenty of technical assistance if needed. **Coffee by Design** (772-5533), 620 Congress Street, is the first in this friendly local chain (now also in Monument Square and at 67 India Street), a cheerful spot with plenty of tables (sidewalk tables in summer), local art on display (and for sale), and all the usual coffee and espresso choices.

ENTERTAINMENT

Cumberland County Civic Center (775-3481, ext. 2 for 24-hour hotline), 1 Civic Center Square, Portland. A modern arena with close to 9,000 seats, the site of year-round concerts, ice skating spectaculars, winter hockey games, etc. Check the monthly calendar of events.

State Theatre (780-8265), 609 Congress Street. Hosting a variety of performances, from rock to classical. Call for a current schedule of events.

Center for Cultural Exchange (761-0591; www.artsandculture.org), 1 Longfellow Square. Cultural events include an Irish festival, an annual Greek festival, many varied events from theater and dance performances to concerts and workshops.

Top of the East (755-5411), Eastland Hotel, 157 High Street. Open 4–12 daily, until 1 Thursday through Saturday. Portland's only rooftop lounge, with a marble bar, black leather banquettes, and floor-to-ceiling windows encompassing Mount Washington and Casco Bay. Offering light fare (free 4–6) and live jazz Friday and Saturday.

MUSIC

Portland Symphony Orchestra (773-6128), City Hall Auditorium, Merrill Auditorium, 389 Congress Street, Portland. The winter series runs October through April, Tuesdays at 7:45 PM. In summertime outdoor pops concerts range from the shores of Casco Bay to Camden Harbor.

LARK Society for Chamber Music/Portland String Quartet (761-1522). This distinguished chamber group performs in varied Portland locations as well as around the state.

PCA Great Performances (773-3150). A series of orchestra, jazz, opera, and musical theater staged in fall and winter at Merrill Auditorium.

PROFESSIONAL SPORTS

The **Portland Pirates** (828-4665), a professional hockey team, play their home games at the Cumberland County Civic Center. The **Portland Sea Dogs** (874-9300; tickets, 879-9500) a double-A baseball team, play in Hadlock Stadium on Park Avenue (next to the Expo).

THEATER

Portland Stage Company (774-1043) and the **Ram Island Dance Company** (773-2562) are both based in the city's old Odd Fellows Hall (25A Forest Avenue), now an elegant, intimate, 290-seat theater. Both stage a variety of performances throughout the year.

Portland Players (799-7337), Thaxter Theater, 420 Cottage Road, South Portland. Stages productions September through June.

Portland Lyric Theater (799-1421), Cedric Thomas Playhouse, 176 Sawyer Street, South Portland. This community theater presents four musicals each winter.

St. Lawrence Arts & Community Center (775-4784), 76 Congress Street, Portland. An umbrella performance space for several local professional theater companies.

SELECTIVE SHOPPING

ANTIQUES
There are a plethora of small shops, especially in the Old Port and along Congress Street.

ART GALLERIES
Inquire about the **Art Walk** held the first Friday of every month, when galleries citywide hold open house.

Greenhut Galleries (772-2693; www.greenhutgalleries.com), 146 Middle Street. Peggy Golden Greenhut represents many of Maine's top artists and sculptors. A destination gallery for collectors from around the country.

Bayview Gallery (773-3007), 75 Market Street. A spacious gallery with fine paintings as well as an extensive collection of prints from well-known Maine artists.

Davidson and Daughters Contemporary Art (780-0766), 148 High Street (across from Eastland Park). Outstanding.

June Fitzpatrick Gallery (772-1961; www.fitzpatrickgallery.com), 112 High Street. Well established and showcasing contemporary and fine art.

Aucocisco (874-2060; www.aucocisco.com), 615A Congress Street. Andres Verzosa's small gallery is worth checking.

The Hay Gallery (773-2513; www.haygallery.com), 594 Congress Street. Housed upstairs in the small flatiron building across from the Portland Museum of Art. Specializing in Laura Fuller's contemporary stained glass and in photography.

Scott Potter (773-3772), 142A High Street. Potter's internationally acclaimed work is all decoupage, a technique involving layers of paper.

Eastland Gallery (775-2227), Eastland Hotel, 157 High Street. A new contemporary gallery with changing shows, some jewelry.

CRAFTS GALLERIES
Stein Gallery of Contemporary Glass (772-9072), 195 Middle Street. Anne and Philip Stein were pioneers in art glass media, and their gallery has expanded as the media have evolved. This newest space borders on the spectacular, with exquisite glass sculptures well displayed. There are also colorful perfume bottles, paperweights, and glass jewelry. Note the neon curtains in the windows at night.

Gallery 7 (761-7007), 49 Exchange Street. Wide variety of beautifully crafted items, from miniature stone fountains to furniture, glass, and jewelry.

Edgecomb Potters Gallery (780-6727), 35 Exchange Street. One of four in the state, a fine collection of reasonably priced, interesting pottery. Other merchandise includes glass designs, wind chimes, and jewelry.

Nancy Margolis Gallery (775-3822), 367 Fore Street. We love the papier-mâché mobiles, and the collection of glass, jewelry, and sculptures is just as interesting.

Abacus (772-4880), 44 Exchange Street. One in a chain of four Maine stores exhibiting fine glass, ceramics, jewelry, textiles, and home furnishings.

Maine Potters Market (774-1633), 376 Fore Street. Work by 14 Maine potters.

BOOKSTORES

Portland has become a mecca for book lovers. **Books Etc.** (38 Exchange Street) fills two storefronts and is a very inviting store. **Longfellow Books** (772-4045), 1 Monument Way, a former Bookland, stocks a full range of titles. **Casco Bay Books** (541-3842), 151 Middle Street, a new independent store, carries maps, new and used books, and has a café. **Books, Etc.** has also recently opened a second store in Falmouth (781-3784), 240 Route 1 (the Shops at Falmouth Village). **Borders Books and Music** (775-6110) in the Maine Mall parking lot (I-95, exit 7) has a huge selection. You can grab a book and read in its café for hours if you want.

Antiquarian-book lovers should check out **Carlson-Turner Books** (241 Congress Street); **Emerson Booksellers** (420 Fore Street); and, our favorite, **Cunningham Book**s (775-2246), 188 State Street on Longfellow Square, with a well-arranged selection of some 50,000 titles.

FOOD

Portland Public Market (772-8140; www.portlandmarket.com). Located a block north of Congress Street between Preble and Elm Streets, open Monday through Saturday 9–7, Sunday 10–5. The gift of the late Elizabeth Noyce, the soaring, two-story, open-timbered, glass-walled market reestablishes the tradition of indoor markets in downtown Portland: From 1825 until 1882 a market hall stood in neaby Monument Square. Among the 25 major vendors are **Borealis Breads** from Waldoboro, **Maine Beer & Beverage** (Maine beers and drinks ranging from Moxie to cider), **Miranda's Vineyard,** specializing in Maine wines, **Maine's Pantry** (a full line of Maine specialty products), **Valley View Orchard Pies** (great pastry), and **Game Table,** featuring Maine-raised game meats. We usually make this our last stop, positioning the car in the adjacent garage (2 hours are free with a receipt from the market), the better to bring home fresh produce and fish. Special events here are frequent. Also see *Eating Out.*

Standard Baking Co. (773-2112), 75 Commercial Street. Open Monday through Friday 7–7, weekends 7–5. Housed in a former billiard hall on the parking lot below Fore Street restaurant. Alison Pray and Matt James make artisanal French and Italian breads, rolls, baguettes, brioche, and pastries. Inquire about *canneles* (rich, fluted French pastries). Specialties also include small gingerbread cakes, croissants, and "morning buns."

Browne Trading Market (775-7560), 262 Commercial Street. Open Monday through Saturday 10–6. Formerly a fish wholesaler serving upscale restaurants throughout the county, now selling their own smoked salmon, trout, shrimp, scallops, mussels, and salmon jerky as well as a

BLACK COW

Portland Public Market

variety of fresh seafood (some flown in daily from the Mediterranean). Also offering a wide assortment of cheese and one of the largest selections of wine north of Boston.

- **Northern Sky Toyz** (828-0911), 388 Fore Street. An amazing kite shop, with a variety of other novelties and toys, including windsocks, banners, and games.

MORE SPECIAL SHOPS

Over the past 30 years the Old Port has had its ups and downs, but in recent years the trend has been to more substantial rather than tourist-geared shops, all independently owned. Clothing stores include:

Amarylis (772-4439), 41 Exchange Street. Susan Bergier has been here more than 20 years and still features several Maine designers and the kind of "unique clothing" you won't find in the malls.

Portmanteau (774-7276), 191 Middle Street. Nancy Lawrence began by stitching canvas bags but has long since established a reputataion for the distinctive tapestry handbags, totes, backpacks, luggage, and cloaks fabricated on her premises.

Joseph's (773-1274), 410 Fore Street. Joseph Redman is one of the Old Port originals. His store for both men's and women's upscale apparel has evolved; note the tailor in residence.

Siempre Mas (879-1676), 377 Fore Street. Unusual printed cotton dresses, shirts, and large wool sweaters; sale rack in the back.

Beyond Portland proper is the **Maine Mall** (exit 7 off I-95), whose immediate complex of more than 100 stores is supplemented by large shopping centers and chain stores that ring it for several miles.

SPECIAL EVENTS

First Sunday in June: **Old Port Festival,** a celebration that began in the 1970s with the revival of the Old Port; includes a parade, various performances, street vendors, and special sales.

Mid-July: **Yarmouth Clam Festival.** Arts and crafts, plenty of clams, performances, more.

August: **Cumberland Crafts Fair,** Cumberland Fairgrounds. **Sidewalk Art Festival,** Congress Street.

First weekend in November: **Maine Brewer's Festival.** Each year this event grows in size, due to the increasing number of Maine microbreweries.

Post-Thanksgiving–Christmas: **Victorian Holiday Portland** with tree lighting, arrival of Father Christmas, costumed carolers, special events through Christmas.

December 31: **Portland New Year's Celebration**—modeled after Boston's First Night, with performances and events throughout the city from afternoon through midnight.

Freeport

Think of Freeport, and you'll likely think of shopping. More specifically, what pops to mind immediately is the 24-hour, 365-days-a-year
superstore known as L. L. Bean. It's been a shopping landmark since
the famous boot was developed back in 1911, and even more so since
1951, when they "threw away the key." With the flood of outlet stores
that popped up in the early 1980s, the reputation of Freeport as a shopping mecca took hold.

Each year as many as 4.2 million visitors flock to the town, prowling
both sides of Main Street (Route 1) in search of big deals in brand-
name outlet stores. Scattered among the familiar names are several
classy local shops offering jewelry, handcrafts, and one-of-a-kind items
(see *Selective Shopping—Special Shops*). Once Freeport was *the* place
to find outlet stores—now outlets seem to be popping up elsewhere,
and the volume of foot traffic in Freeport saw a slight decline in summer 2000. However, money spent showed an increase, indicating that
the shopping frenzy is far from over.

Visitors shouldn't assume that shopping is all Freeport has to offer.
A rich and varied history dating back more than 200 years is hidden
behind the discounts and outlet stores. The first known residents of the
area were several tribes of Native Americans called the Wabanaki. Attempts by colonists to settle in the area resulted in a series of wars
throughout the 1600s and early 1700s. By 1715 settlers were not to be
discouraged any longer—and a peace treaty with the Penobscots was
signed in 1725.

Freeport was first a part of North Yarmouth but was granted a charter separating itself from the town in 1789. A long-time legend (though
there is no documented evidence of the occurrence) holds that in 1820
the papers separating Maine from Massachusetts were signed in the
historical Jameson Tavern (see *Dining Out*).

Early citizens made a living through agriculture and timber. With
the War of 1812, shipbuilding became an important industry, with one
famous ship inspiring Whittier's poem "The Dead Ship of Harpswell."
In the 1880s shoe factories sprouted up in Freeport, adding another
industry to its economy.

Transportation advances also had their effect on Freeport's history.

When an electric trolley was built to connect Portland and Yarmouth with Brunswick and Lewiston, it passed through Freeport. Just as many trolley companies built parks to encourage ridership, the developer built the Casco Castle Hotel to draw tourists to South Freeport. The hotel burned down, but a stone tower remains today (on private property), and can be best viewed from Winslow Memorial Park.

By 1980 the economy in Freeport was on a downward spiral. And then the outlets came to town. Despite the proliferation of shops, the village has retained the appearance of older days—even McDonald's has been confined to a gracious old Italianate house, with no golden arches in sight. The Freeport Historical Society operates a research library and museum in a historic house, in the midst of the retail sector. You can take a self-directed walking tour of Freeport historic sites.

Some come to the area simply to stroll wooded paths in Wolfe's Neck Woods State Park and the Maine Audubon's Mast Landing Sanctuary. Bradbury Mountain is just a short drive, and Pettengill Farm offers a look at 19th-century coastal life. The Desert of Maine is an interesting sight as well. Canoeing, boat trips, golf, and summer concerts in the new park outside L. L. Bean can round out the Freeport experience quite nicely.

GUIDANCE
The Freeport Merchants Association (865-1212; 1-800-865-1994; www.freeportusa.com), P.O. Box 452, Freeport 04032, operates a visitors center in a replica of a historic hose tower on Depot Street. Brochures, information, and rest rooms can be found here, and the association's office is upstairs. They also gladly respond to telephone and mail requests for information. Among their materials is an excellent, free visitors walking map, with a list of stores, restaurants, accommodations, and other services. Be sure to get one in advance or pick one up as soon as you arrive in town—almost all the merchants have them. Also ask for the fun brochure "101+ Things to Do within an Hour's Drive of Freeport."

The Maine Tourism Association's welcome center in Kittery stocks some Freeport brochures, and there is another state information center on Route 1 just south of Freeport, in Yarmouth, at exit 17 off I-95.

GETTING THERE
A number of **bus tour companies** also offer shopping trips to Freeport from Boston and beyond. Most people drive, which means there's often a shortage of parking spaces, especially in peak season. The best solution to this problem is to stay at an inn or B&B within walking distance and leave your car there.

MEDICAL EMERGENCY
Mid Coast Hospital (729-0181), 58 Baribeau Drive, Brunswick.

VILLAGES

South Freeport has been a fishing center from its beginning, when it was known as Strout's Port. Between 1825 and 1830 up to 12,000 barrels of mackerel were packed and shipped from here each year. Later the area specialty became lobster packing. Having a very different feel from the chaotic shopping frenzy of downtown Freeport, the harbor is still bustling with activity and offers great seafood. From here you can take a cruise to explore Eagle Island in summer.

Porter's Landing. Once the center of commercial activity, this is now a quiet residential neighborhood, amid rolling hills, woods, and streams. The village is part of the Harraseeket Historic District on the National Register of Historic Places.

TO SEE AND DO

✑ **Desert of Maine** (865-6962), Desert Road, Freeport. Open daily, early May to mid-October, 9 AM to dusk. Admission fee. Narrated tram tours and self-guided walks through 40 acres of sand that was once the Tuttle Farm. Heavily farmed, then extensively logged to feed the railroad, the topsoil eventually gave way to the glacial sand deposit beneath it, which spread . . . and spread until entire trees sank below the surface. It is an unusual sand, rich in mineral deposits that make it unsuitable for commercial use but interesting to rock hounds. Children love it, especially the gem hunt (stones have been scattered in a section of the desert for children to find). Overnight camping available.

✑& **The Maine Bear Factory** (865-0600), 294 Route 1 South, Freeport. A great place to learn how teddy bears are made: choose an unstuffed bear and watch as it's completed. Fun for kids, and adults love it too.

BOAT EXCURSIONS

Atlantic Seal/Arctic Seal (865-6112), Town Wharf, South Freeport. Memorial Day through mid-October. Daily narrated trips into Casco Bay include 3-hour cruises to Eagle Island, the former summer home of Admiral Robert E. Peary, the first person to reach the North Pole. Seal- and osprey-sighting trips and fall foliage cruises mid-September and October. Lobstering demonstrations are usually included, except Sunday, when lobstering is prohibited by Maine law.

CANOEING

The **Harraseeket River** in Freeport is particularly nice for canoeing. Start at Mast Landing, the northeastern end of the waterway; there are also launching sites at Winslow Memorial Park on Staples Point Road and at South Freeport Harbor. Phone the **Maine Audubon Society** in Falmouth (781-2330) for details about periodic, scheduled guided trips through the area. Nearby lake canoeing can be found at **Run Around**

Pond in North Pownal (the parking lot is off Lawrence Road, 1 mile north of the intersection with Fickett Road).

CROSS-COUNTRY SKIING

The areas listed under *Green Space* are good cross-country skiing spots; rent or purchase equipment from L. L. Bean, which also offers classes in cross-country skiing (see *Special Learning Programs*).

GOLF

Freeport Country Club (865-4922), Old Country Road, Freeport. Nine holes.

JEWELRY MAKING

✐ **The Beadin' Path** (865-4785), 15 Main Street, Freeport. Choose beads and findings from a wide variety, then sit at the table and create your own jewelry pieces. Prices are based on the beads you choose, so this can be a good, inexpensive rainy-day activity for kids (and adults).

MUSEUM

Harrington House, 45 Main Street, Freeport. Built of local brick and granite, this 1830 house is maintained by the Freeport Historical Society as a museum, research library, and archive.

SPECIAL LEARNING PROGRAMS

L. L. Bean Outdoor Discovery Schools (552-6878), Route 1, Freeport. An interesting series of lectures and lessons that cover everything from cross-country ski lessons (on weekends beginning in January) and golf to survival in the Maine woods, making soap, tanning hides, paddling sea kayaks, building fly-rods, cooking small game, and fishing for Atlantic salmon. Courses last from a couple of hours to weeklong trips. Call 1-888-552-3261 for a free program guide.

GREEN SPACE

✐ **Winslow Memorial Park** (865-4198), Staples Point Road, South Freeport. Open Memorial Day through September. A 90-acre municipal park with a sandy beach and large grassy picnicking area; also boating and 100-site campground. Facilities include rest rooms with showers. Admission fee.

✐ **Wolfe's Neck Woods State Park** (865-4465), Wolfe's Neck Road (take Bow Street, across from L. L. Bean), Freeport. Open Memorial Day through Labor Day. Day-use fee. A 244-acre park with shoreline hiking along Casco Bay, the Harraseeket River, and salt marshes. Guided nature walks are available; picnic tables and grills are scattered about.

Mast Landing Sanctuary (781-2330), Upper Mast Landing Road (take Bow Street south), Freeport. Maintained by the Maine Audubon Society, this 140-acre sanctuary offers trails through apple orchards, woods, and meadows and along a millstream. Several paths radiate from a 1-mile loop trail.

✐ **Bradbury Mountain State Park** (688-4712), Route 9, Hallowell Road, Pownal (just 6 miles from Freeport: From I-95, take exit 20 and follow signs). Open year-round. $2.50 adults, $.50 children ages 5–11, under age 5 free. The summit, accessible by an easy (even for young children) half-mile hike, yields a splendid view of Casco Bay and New Hampshire's White Mountains. Facilities in the 297-acre park include a small playground, a softball field, hiking trails, toilets, and a 41-site overnight camping area.

🐾 **Pettengill Farm** (865-3170), Pettengill Road, Freeport. Managed by the Freeport Historical Society and open for periodic guided tours. The public is welcome to wander the grounds anytime from sunrise to sunset, and pets are very welcome here. A saltwater farm with 140 acres of open fields and woodland that overlook the Harraseeket Estuary, with a totally unmodernized vintage-1810 saltbox house.

LODGING

All listings are in Freeport 04032 unless otherwise noted.

INN

&. **Harraseeket Inn** (865-9377; 1-800-342-6423; www.stayfreeport.com), 162 Main Street. Just two blocks north of L. L. Bean, this luxury hotel is the largest in the area, with 84 rooms, including five suites and nine town houses. It has maintained the elegant atmosphere of the 1800 Federal house next door, where this operation first began as a five-room B&B. Nancy and Paul Gray are native Mainers, but their family also owns the Inn at Mystic, Connecticut, and they definitely know the importance of attention to detail. Many of the rooms are decorated with antiques and reproductions, and feature canopy beds and Jacuzzis or steam baths; 20 have fireplaces. The inn has formal dining rooms (see *Dining Out*), conference spaces (one with outdoor terrace), and the casual **Broad Arrow Tavern** (see *Eating Out*). Other public spaces include a drawing room, library, and ballroom and an indoor pool surrounded by glass walls overlooking the gardens. Rates in-season are $150–325; full buffet breakfast and afternoon tea are included. Two-night minimum stay required on some holiday weekends. Package plans available.

BED & BREAKFASTS

Freeport Area Bed & Breakfast Association (865-1500), P.O. Box 267. Their 2000 brochure lists about a dozen members, all of whom must meet certain standards established by the association. The majority of Freeport's B&Bs have opened since the shopping craze began. Many are in the handsome, old, white-clapboard Capes, Victorian, and Federal-style houses that stand side by side flanking Main Street just north of the shopping district.

🐾✏ **The Isaac Randall House** (865-9295; www.isaacrandall.com), 5 Independence Drive. Open year-round. This handsome farmhouse became the first B&B in Freeport in 1984. Twelve air-conditioned rooms with antiques, Oriental rugs, and lovely old quilts. Two have working fireplaces. The Loft, furnished all in wicker (including the king bed), is interesting. We love the seasonal restored train caboose, a perfect place for families with children (who are welcome here). A full breakfast is served in the beam-ceilinged country kitchen; a playground out back can keep children entertained. Pets are also welcome. Just off Route 1 but within walking distance of the downtown shopping area. Doubles are $100–175, breakfast and snacks included.

White Cedar Inn (865-9099; 1-800-853-1269), 178 Main Street. Open year-round. This restored Victorian house was once the home of Arctic explorer Donald B. MacMillan, who went to the North Pole with Admiral Peary. There are seven bedrooms with private baths and simple but pretty furnishings. The cozy room up under the eaves offers a bit more privacy. A beautiful wooden spiral staircase leads to the newest room downstairs, which also has a private entrance, sitting area, and TV, and can sleep four. Full breakfast, included, is served at small tables in the sunroom, adjacent to the country kitchen. Doubles $95–130.

Captain Briggs House (865-1868), 8 Maple Avenue. A little off the main drag but close enough to walk to everything. Simple, pleasant rooms with private baths. The sitting room has cable TV, games, and books. $87–120 in-season includes breakfast.

The James Place Inn (865-4486; www.jamesplaceinn.com), 11 Holbrook Street. Darcy and Bill James have created a bright atmosphere with a happy feel. The five rooms, each with private bath, are decorated in peaceful pastel colors. All rooms have air-conditioning and cable TV; two have kitchenettes, and two have Jacuzzi baths. The deck with café tables and chairs looks like an inviting place to relax after an afternoon of shopping or sight-seeing. A full breakfast is served in the glassed-in breakfast/social room. $90–135 double in-season.

Applewood Inn (865-9858; www.applewoodusa.com), 8 Holbrook Street. The B&B has a new name, but the same interesting mix of art adorning the walls, all done by local artists and friends. The work of hostess Jennifer Kelley also hangs in one of the three guest rooms. Each room has a sleigh bed and private bath. The porch, with wicker furniture, is inviting. Well-behaved pets can be accommodated. Full breakfast is included in the $110–125 in-season rates.

Atlantic Seal B&B (865-6112), 25 Main Street, Box 146, South Freeport 04078. Open year-round. Just 5 minutes from downtown Freeport but eons from the bustle, this 1850 Cape in the village of South Freeport boasts views of the harbor from each of its three guest rooms. Owned and operated by Captain Thomas Ring, who also runs the *Atlantic Seal* and *Arctic Seal* tour boats, it is furnished with antiques and nautical collections. One room has a wood-burning fireplace. There is a resident cat. Swimming off the private dock, rowboats, and mountain bikes available for guest use. Summer rates, including "hearty sailor's breakfast," start at $95 and go to $135 (for a room with both a queen and a double bed, cable TV, refrigerator, and Jacuzzi). Guests also receive a discount on morning cruises.

  ♧ **The Bagley House Bed & Breakfast** (865-6566; 1-800-765-1772; www. bagleyhouse.com), 1290 Royalsborough Road, Durham 04222. Ten minutes from downtown Freeport in a serene country setting. This is the oldest house in town, built as a public house in 1772. The town's first worship services were held here, and it was the site of the first schoolhouse. Susan Backhouse and Suzanne O'Connor have created an easy, welcoming atmosphere. Rooms are furnished with antiques, custom-made pieces, and hand-sewn quilts. Details like fresh flowers, and cold drinks and cookies available anytime, make guests feel right at home. The cozy nook has slanted ceilings, one double and one three-quarter bed, and wall-to-wall carpeting. In the Barn there's a suite, two additional guest rooms—each with a gas fireplace—and a small conference room with a wood-burning stove. $110–145 double in-season ($95 single), including full breakfast and afternoon refreshments.

MOTELS

On Route 1, south of Freeport near the Yarmouth town line, there are a number of modern motels. Among these is the **Freeport Inn** (865-3106; 1-800-99-VALUE; www.freeportinn.com). Set on 25 acres of lawns and nature trails, all rooms have wall-to-wall carpeting, cable TV, air-conditioning, and in-room phones. Doubles are $100–120 in-season. There's a swimming pool and a playground. Canoes are available for paddling on the Cousins River. The inn's café and bakery, the Freeport Café, serves homestyle cooking all three meals (see *Eating Out*), and they also operate the Muddy Rudder (see *Eating Out*) just down the road. **The Casco Bay Inn** (865-4925; 1-800-570-4970) is a family-run inn, clean and comfortable with reasonable rates.

CAMPGROUNDS

🐾 **Cedar Haven Campground** (865-6254; reservations only, 1-800-454-3403), Baker Road, Freeport. Fifty-eight mostly wooded sites, each with fireplace and picnic table. Water and electricity hook-ups, four with sewer as well. Twelve tent sites. Store with wood, ice, and groceries. Mini-golf, playground, and swimming pond. Two miles from Route 1 and downtown Freeport. $15–25 per night.

🐾 **Desert Dunes of Maine Campground** (865-6962; www.desertofmaine.com), 95 Desert Road, Freeport. Fifty wooded and open sites adjacent to this natural glacial sand deposit (see Desert of Maine under *To See and Do*). Hook-ups, hot showers, laundry, convenience store, propane, fire rings and picnic tables, horseshoe pits, nature trails, swimming pool. Campsites are $19–28 per night.

Also see **Winslow Memorial Park** under *Green Space*.

WHERE TO EAT

All listings are in Freeport unless otherwise noted.

DINING OUT

ᕕ **Harraseeket Inn** (865-9377; 1-800-342-6423), 162 Main Street. Open year-round for breakfast, lunch, and dinner; Sunday brunch 11:30–2. Continental cuisine and elegant service in three formal dining rooms. The chef uses fresh ingredients from local gardeners and farmers in-season and creates mouthwatering entrées like tamarind-glazed duck confit or pan-roasted Maine salmon. The menu includes three dishes for two (one is châteaubriand, $57.50 for two) prepared at the table. Desserts are sure to please here, too. In addition to dinner the Harraseeket is known for its outstanding Sunday brunch, which often features such delicacies as caviar, oysters on the half shell, and even venison. $16–25. The dress code at dinner is a collared shirt, and reservations are suggested.

✐ **Jameson Tavern** (865-4196), 115 Main Street. Lunch (11:30–2:30) and dinner (5–closing) served in several inviting dining rooms in the 1779 tavern where the claim is that the papers separating Maine from Massachusetts were signed in 1820. Specialties include fresh seafood, like bacon-wrapped scallops with maple cream, and chicken Aberdine. Children's menu and outside patio. $11.95–21.95.

EATING OUT

✐ᕕ **The Broad Arrow Tavern** (865-9377), Harraseeket Inn, 162 Main Street. A ground-floor dining room overlooking the terrace. Open from 11:30 daily. Open kitchen with wood-fired oven and grill, relaxed atmosphere, cozy decor, and a large, varied menu ranging from brick-oven pizzas and sandwiches to full dinners.

✐ᕕ **Crickets Restaurant** (865-4005), Lower Main Street. Open daily for lunch and dinner; opens for breakfast Saturday and Sunday at 7:30 AM. The almost overwhelming menu offers something for just about everyone, from generous specialty sandwiches to fajitas, pasta dishes, steak, and seafood entrées. Reservations appreciated.

Tap Room (865-4196), Jameson Tavern, 115 Main Street. This informal tavern to the rear of the building serves inexpensive snacks and sandwiches from 11:30 AM until late in the evening.

ᕕ **Blue Onion** (865-9396), Lower Main Street. Open for lunch and dinner daily except Monday. A charming dining room in an old blue roadside house located south of Freeport's downtown traffic squeeze. Soups, salads, quiche for lunch; baked and broiled fish, lobster pie, and other fish, veal, and chicken dishes for supper. No liquor.

ᕕ **Gritty McDuff's** (865-4321), 187 Lower Main Street. The only brewpub in Freeport, this branch of the popular Portland pub offers outdoor dining, lobster, seafood, pizza, and pub food. Great ales.

☞♿ **Muddy Rudder** (846-3082), Route 1. Operated by the nearby Freeport Inn, this popular restaurant overlooks the water and serves a wide selection of seafood dishes plus steaks, sandwiches, and salads; you can also have a full clambake on the deck. The atmosphere is relaxed, with piano music in the evening.

☞ **Harraseeket Lunch & Lobster Co.** (865-4888), South Freeport (turn off Route 1 at the giant wooden Indian, then turn right at a stop sign a few miles down). Open May through October. In the middle of the Harraseeket boatyard; you order lobsters and clams on one side, fried food on the other, and eat at picnic tables (of which there are never enough at peak hours) overlooking a boat-filled harbor. Lobsters are fresh from the pound's boats. Homemade desserts. There is also a small inside dining room. Worth seeking out, but be aware that it is a busy place; you may have to wait a bit to eat.

☞ **The Corsican** (865-9421), 9 Mechanic Street. Lunch and dinner. Seafood, chicken, vegetarian entrées.

☞ **The Lobster Cooker** (865-4349), 39 Main Street. Steamed lobster, fresh-picked lobster and crabmeat rolls, sandwiches, chowders; dining on the outdoor patio. Beer and wine.

🎖 **The Freeport Café** (865-3106), Route 1. You might drive right by this small café, but you shouldn't. Open daily for all three meals. Extremely friendly service, great dinner specials, a cozy atmosphere, and great prices make it a spot worth finding.

SELECTIVE SHOPPING

FREEPORT FACTORY OUTLETS

🎖 As noted in the introduction to this chapter, Freeport's 125-plus factory outlets constitute what has probably become Maine's mightiest tourist magnet. *Boston Globe* writer Nathan Cobb described it well: "A shoppers' theme park spread out at the foot of L. L. Bean, the high church of country chic." Cobb quoted a local landlord: "The great American pastime now is shopping, not hiking."

Although hiking and hunting put L. L. Bean on the tourist map in the first place, tourists in Freeport are intently studying the map of shops these days. L. L. Bean has kept pace by selling fashionable, sporty clothing and an incredible range of sporting equipment, books, gourmet products, and gifts, as well as its golden boot.

L. L. Bean contends that it attracts at least 3.5 million customers annually—almost three times the population of Maine. In the early 1980s neighboring property owners began to claim a portion of this traffic. Instead of relegating the outlets to malls (see "Kittery and the Yorks"), they have deftly draped them in brick and clapboard, actually improving on the town's old looks (although longtime shopkeepers who were forced to move because of skyrocketing real estate prices might well disagree). Ample parking lots are sequestered behind the Main Street facade (it's still sometimes tough to find a space). In summer there is a festive atmosphere, with hot-dog and ice cream vendors on key corners. But it is the quality of the shops that ensures a year-round crowd. Just about any well-known clothing, accessory, and home-furnishing line has a factory store here. The following is a selected list of the more interesting outlets. Many stores claim 20 to 70 percent off suggested retail prices, and even L. L. Bean has a separate outlet store, which you should check first for bargains before heading to the main store.

L. L. Bean (1-800-221-4221 for orders; 1-800-341-4341 for customer service), 95 Main Street. Open 24 hours a day, 365 days a year. More than a store—for millions it is the gateway to Maine. Most shoppers arrive having already studied the mail-order catalog (which accounts for 85 to 91 percent of sales) and are buying purposefully. The store has been expanded several times in recent years, to the point where it's hard to find the old boot factory—built by Leon Leonwood Bean—that is at its heart. With its outdoor waterfall, indoor trout pond, bookstore and café, and thousands of square feet of retail space, the building now resembles a fancy shopping mall more than it does a single store. It was back in 1912 that Mr. Bean developed his boot, a unique combination of rubber bottom and leather top. He originally sold it by mail order but gradually began catering to the hunters and fishermen who tended to pass through his town in the middle of the night. L. L. Bean himself died in 1967, but grandson Leon Gorman continues to sell nearly a quarter of a million pairs of the family boots each year. Gorman's leadership, together with an excellent marketing staff, has seen Bean grow substantially in the last few decades. Current stock ranges from canoes to weatherproof cameras to climbing gear. There is a wide variety of clothing as well as every conceivable gadget designed to keep you warm. It is the anchor store for all the outlets in town.

L. L. Kids (1-800-341-4341), 8 Nathan Nye Street. Kids will love shopping here—there are interactive exhibits throughout the store, including a small climbing wall. Good selection of kids' apparel.

L. L. Bean Factory Store (1-800-341-4341), Depot Street (across the street and down the block from the main store). Seconds, samples, and irregular merchandise are offered here. You never know what you'll find, but it's always worth a look. Unlike the main store, the outlet is not open 24 hours a day.

Dooney & Bourke (865-1366), 52 Main Street (in back). Stylish pocketbooks, shoulder bags, belts, wallets, and portfolios in water-repellent, coarse-grained leather.

Cuddledown of Maine Factory Store (865-1713), Route 1 south. Comforters, pillows, gift items, all filled with goose down.

Maine Wreath & Flower Factory Outlet (865-3019), 13 Bow Street. Quality Maine dried flowers and wreaths at discount prices.

L. L. Bean, the nerve center of Freeport's shopping district

Buttons and Things Factory Outlet (865-4480), 24 Main Street. A warren of rooms chock-full of buttons, beads, bead books, and other findings.

Casey's Wood Products (865-3244), 15 School Street. Bins full of wood turnings, craft materials, and toys. Free catalog.

Dansk Factory Outlet (865-6125), 100 Main Street, Suite 11. Scandinavian-designed tableware, cookware, and assorted kitchen gadgets.

SPECIAL SHOPS

All listings are in Freeport unless otherwise noted.

Brown Goldsmiths (865-4126), 1 Mechanic Street. Open Monday through Saturday. Original designs in rings, earrings, and bracelets.

Bridgham & Cook, Ltd. (865-1040), 6 Bow Street (behind Polo–Ralph Lauren). Packaged British and Irish foods, toiletries, teas, gifts—a must for the Anglophile.

✐ **DeLorme's Map Store** (865-4171), Route 1 (south of downtown Freeport). The publishing company's own maps, atlases, and pamphlets; also guidebooks and maps of the United States and the world. In a glassed-in lobby stands "Eartha," the largest rotating and revolving globe in the world.

Edgecomb Potters/Hand in Hand Gallery (865-1705), 8 School Street. Fine contemporary crafts. Displays colorful porcelain, jewelry, blown glass, and iron.

Mangy Moose (865-6414), 112 Main Street. Moose, moose, and more moose. A fun store filled with gifts, books, and more, all featuring the majestic animal.

✎ **Play and Learn** (865-6434; 1-888-865-6434) 140 Main Street. A great source for educational toys and teaching resources, which are hard to find if you aren't a teacher.

20th Maine (865-4340), 49 West Street. Devoted to the Civil War—books, art, music, collectibles.

The Village Nut Shoppe (869-2929, 123 Main Street. A small shop filled with nuts. We especially like the chocolate-covered ones, available in several varieties.

BOOKS

Sherman's Book & Stationery Store (869-9000), 128 Main Street. Another branch of the Maine bookseller (also in Bar Harbor and Boothbay Harbor), featuring Maine books, cards, toys, and Maine gifts.

SPECIAL EVENTS

Summer: Frequent musical and comedy performances in the new **L. L. Bean Discovery Park.**

Labor Day weekend: **Sidewalk Sale,** with sales galore. **Fall in the Village** art exhibition.

First full weekend in December: **Sparkle Weekend** brings caroling, horse-drawn wagons, Santa arriving in a Maine yacht, musical entertainment, holiday readings, storytelling, complimentary refreshment and hot-cocoa stops, open houses at local inns, a talking Christmas tree, and, of course, plenty of holiday shopping. **Kittery Christmas Parade** and **Tree Lighting. York Festival of Lights Parade.**

December: **Christmas Open House Tours.**

III. MIDCOAST AND THE ISLANDS

KIM GRANT

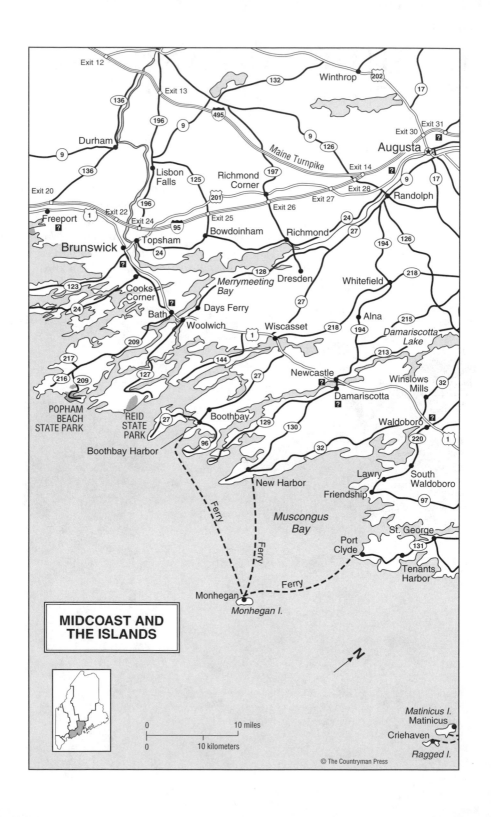

MIDCOAST AND
THE ISLANDS

0   10 miles

0   10 kilometers

© The Countryman Press

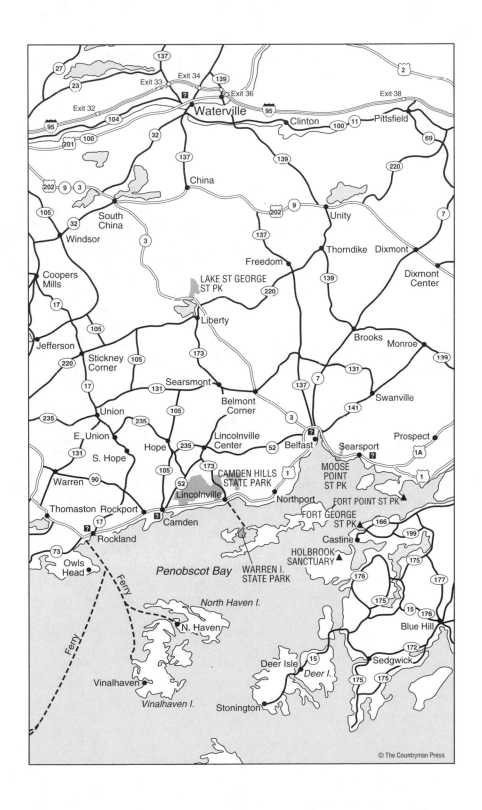

© The Countryman Press

Midcoast and the Islands

Beyond Casco Bay the shape of Maine's coast changes—it shreds. In contrast to the sandy arc of shoreline stretching from Kittery to Cape Elizabeth, the coast between Brunswick and Rockland is composed of a series of more than a dozen ragged peninsulas extending like so many fingers south from Route 1, creating myriad big and small harbors, coves, and bays. Scientists tell us that these peninsulas and the offshore islands are mountains drowned by the melting of the same glaciers that sculpted the many shallow lakes and tidal rivers in this area.

The 100 miles of Route 1 between Brunswick and Bucksport are generally equated with Maine's Midcoast, but its depth is actually far greater and more difficult to define. It extends south of Route 1 to the tips of every peninsula, from Potts Point in South Harpswell and Land's End on Bailey Island to Popham Beach on the Phippsburg Peninsula and on through the Boothbays to Pemaquid Point, Friendship, Port Clyde, and Spruce Head. Along with Rockland, Camden, Belfast, Searsport, and the islands of Monhegan, Vinalhaven, North Haven, and Islesboro, these communities have all catered to summer visitors since steamboats began off-loading them in the mid–19th century. Each peninsula differs in character from the next, but all offer their share of places to stay and eat in settings you rarely find along Route 1.

North of Route 1, this midcoastal area also extends slightly inland. Above Bath, for instance, five rivers meld to form Merrymeeting Bay, and north of Newcastle the tidal Damariscotta River widens into 13-mile-long Damariscotta Lake. This gently rolling, river- and lake-laced backcountry harbors a number of picturesque villages and reasonably priced lodging places.

We would hope that no one who reads this book simply sticks to Route 1.

Brunswick and the Harpswells

The Civil War began and ended in Brunswick, or so say local historians. A case can be made. Harriet Beecher Stowe was attending a service in Brunswick's First Church when she is said to have had a vision of the death of Uncle Tom and hurried home to begin penning the book that has been credited with starting the war. Joshua Chamberlain, a longtime parishioner in this same church was, moreover, the Union general chosen for the honor of receiving General Lee's surrender at Appomattox.

Thanks largely to the Ken Burns's PBS series *The Civil War,* Joshua Chamberlain has been rediscovered. Annual admissions to his house shot from 300 in 1993 to 5,000 in 1996 and have remained stable, fueling its restoration. A Brunswick restaurant is now named for "Joshua," and the historical society dispenses maps that pinpoint sites ranging from Chamberlain's student dorm rooms to his gravestone.

This scholar-soldier-governor is, in fact, an entirely appropriate figurehead for a town that's home to Brunswick Naval Air Station and to the current Maine governor, Angus King (who even bears an uncanny resemblance to Chamberlain), as well as to Bowdoin College, over which Chamberlain presided as president, after four terms as governor of Maine.

Brunswick began as an Indian village named Pejepscot, at the base of the Androscoggin River's Great Falls. In 1688 this site became a Massachusetts outpost named Fort Andros, and subsequently it has been occupied by a series of mills. Today, with a population of 21,500, this is Maine's largest town, a mix of Franco-Americans whose great-grandparents were recruited to work in the mills, of military and retired military families, of Bowdoin and retired Bowdoin faculty and alumni, of old seafaring families, and of an increasing number of professionals who commute the half hour to work in Portland or Augusta (Brunswick is halfway between).

Brunswick's Maine Street is the state's widest, laid out in 1717 with a grassy "mall" (a long strip of greenery that's the scene of concerts and of farmer's markets) at the upper end, near the neo-Gothic First Parish Church and the Bowdoin College campus.

A small but prestigious college, chartered in 1794, Bowdoin is surprisingly welcoming to visitors, especially in July and August, when its

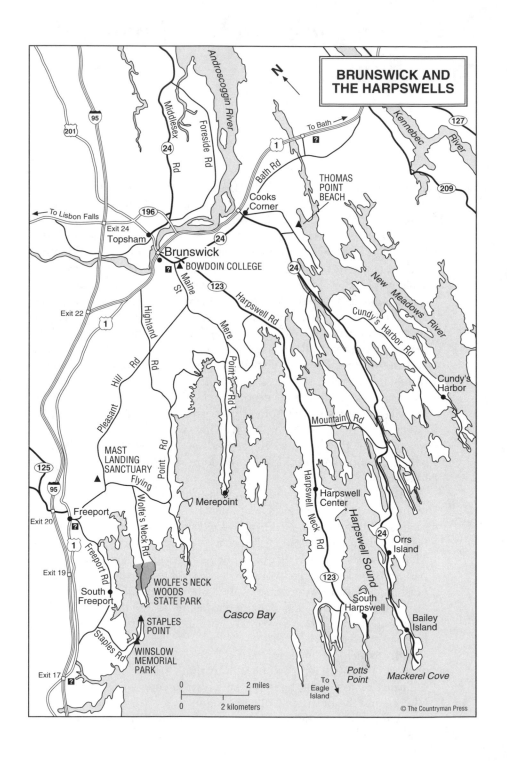

BRUNSWICK AND
THE HARPSWELLS

Androscoggin River

95
201

Middlesex Rd
Foreside Rd
24

To Bath
1

Kennebec River
127
209

THOMAS
POINT
BEACH

To Lisbon Falls
196
Exit 24
Topsham
Bath Rd

Cooks
Corner

24

Brunswick
BOWDOIN COLLEGE

New Meadows River

Cundy's Harbor Rd

Exit 22
1
123
Harpswell Rd

Highland Rd
Maine St
Mere Point Rd
Pleasant Hill Rd

Cundy's
Harbor

Mountain Rd

125
95

MAST
LANDING
SANCTUARY
Flying Point Rd

Harpswell Neck Rd

Harpswell
Center

Harpswell Sound

Merepoint

123

24
Orrs
Island

Freeport
Exit 20
1

Wolfe's Neck Rd

Exit 19
South
Freeport

WOLFE'S NECK
WOODS
STATE PARK

Casco Bay

South
Harpswell

Bailey
Island

Staples Rd

STAPLES
POINT

Exit 17

WINSLOW
MEMORIAL
PARK

0   2 miles

0   2 kilometers

To
Eagle
Island

Potts
Point

Mackerel Cove

© The Countryman Press

buildings are filled with the practicing and the performing virtuoso musicians of the Bowdoin Summer Music Festival, and when Picard Theater is the stage for the Maine State Music Theater. The Bowdoin College Museum of Art and its Peary-MacMillan Arctic Museum are well worth a stop, as are the nearby Pejepscot Museum and Chamberlain House.

Brunswick is, however, no tourist town. No kiosk proclaims the schedule of plays and concerts because most patrons know enough to read about them in the Thursday edition of the *Times Record.* Maine Street's shops, galleries, and restaurants also cater to residents, and the Eveningstar Cinema screens art films for local consumption. Grand City is still a genuine five-and-dime with a lunch counter, a basement stocked with furniture and fabrics, and a summer supply of plastic sleds, found next to the boots and gloves that clammers also need. Freeport's 125-plus outlet stores are just miles yet light-years away.

South of Brunswick three narrow land fingers and several bridge-linked islands stretch seaward, defining the eastern rim of Casco Bay. Collectively they form the town of Harpswell, better known as "the Harpswells" because it includes so many coves, points, and islands (notably Orrs and Bailey). Widely known for their seafood restaurants, these peninsulas are surprisingly sleepy, salted with crafts, galleries, and some great places to stay. They are Maine's most convenient peninsulas, yet they seem much farther Down East.

GUIDANCE

Chamber of Commerce of the Bath-Brunswick Region (725-8797; www.midcoastmaine.com), 59 Pleasant Street, Brunswick 04011. Open weekdays year-round, 8:30–5. Staff members keep tabs on vacancies and send out lodging and dining information. From Route 1 north, follow BRUNSWICK BUSINESS DISTRICT signs, which will take you up Pleasant Street; look for the chamber information center on your right.

GETTING THERE

By bus: Bus service to downtown Brunswick from Logan Airport and downtown Boston is unusually good: 2½ hours ($20–23) via **Concord Trailways.**

By car: Take I-95 to Route 1, which now doglegs around Brunswick, bypassing it entirely. Instead, continue straight ahead up Pleasant Street, which forms a T with Maine Street. Turn right for the Bowdoin College campus and the Harpswells.

MEDICAL EMERGENCY

Dial **911.**

Parkview Hospital (729-1641), 329 Main Street, Brunswick. **Mid Coast Hospital** (729-0181), 58 Baribeau Drive, Brunswick; and 1356 Washington Street, Bath (443-5524).

KIM GRANT

Bowdoin College

TO SEE

Bowdoin College (725-3100), Brunswick. Tours of the 110-acre campus with more than 50 buildings begin at the admissions office. Phone for current hours. Because Maine was part of Massachusetts when the college was founded in 1794, the school is named after a Massachusetts governor. Nathaniel Hawthorne and Henry Wadsworth Longfellow were classmates here in 1825; other notable graduates include Franklin Pierce and Robert Edwin Peary. Founded as a men's college, the school now also welcomes women among its 1,550 students. Bowdoin ranks among the nation's top colleges both in status and in cost. It isn't necessary to take a tour to see the sights.

MUSEUMS

The following museums are all in Brunswick along the head of Maine Street.

Bowdoin College Museum of Art (725-3275), Walker Art Building. Open year-round, Tuesday through Saturday 10–5, Sunday 2–5; closed Monday and holidays. Free. One of New England's outstanding art collections housed in a copper-domed building designed by McKim, Mead, and White, with murals in its rotunda by Abott Thayer, Kenyon Cox, and John La Farge. Its core collection is one of the oldest in America (James Bowdoin III was an avid collector), and displays range from Assyrian bas-reliefs and Far Eastern works through American portraits by Gilbert Charles Stuart, Robert Feke, John Singleton Copley, and Thomas Eakins; also paintings by Winslow Homer, Rockwell Kent, John Sloan, and Andrew Wyeth; special exhibits.

🖉 **Peary-MacMillan Arctic Museum** (725-3416), Hubbard Hall, Bowdoin College. Open same hours as the museum of art. A well-displayed collection of clothing, trophy walruses and seals, polar bears and caribou, and other mementos from expeditions to the North Pole by two Bowdoin alumni. Robert Edwin Peary (class of 1877) was the first person to reach the North Pole, and Donald Baxter MacMillan (class of 1898), who was Peary's chief assistant, went on to dedicate his life to exploring Arctic waters and terrain. Displays include an interactive touch screen, photo blowups, and artifacts to tell the story.

Pejepscot Historical Society Museums (729-6606). Founded in 1888 and named for an ancient Indian settlement (see the introduction to this chapter), this is one of Maine's oldest historical societies. It maintains three downtown Brunswick museums, among which the **Joshua L. Chamberlain Museum** (226 Maine Street; open June through September, Tuesday through Saturday 10–4; $4 adults, $2 children) is by far the most popular. Thanks to the PBS series *The Civil War,* the entire country now seems to know about Joshua Chamberlain (1818–1914), the college professor who became the hero of Little Round Top in the Battle of Gettysburg and went on to serve four terms as governor of Maine and to become president of Bowdoin College. His formerly forgotten, decaying home —a fanciful mansion with two top floors dating from the 1820s and a Victorian first floor from 1871—has been partially restored over the past few years. Exhibits include his bullet-dented boots and his governor's chair and desk, and a museum store sells Civil War books and souvenirs. **The Pejepscot Museum,** 159 Park Row (open weekdays year-round, 9–4:30, summer Saturdays 1–4; free), is a massive, tower-topped mansion that includes an office and archives and also displays changing exhibits on the history of Brunswick, Topsham, and Harpswell. The **Skolfield-Whittier House,** part of the same mid-19th-century Italianate double house (open for summer tours Tuesday through Saturday 10–2:30), is virtually unchanged since the 1925 death of Dr. Frank Whittier. Its high-Victorian drawing room is hung with crystal chandeliers and heavy velvet drapes, furnished in wicker and brocade, and filled with the photos, books, paintings, and clutter of three generations.

The First Parish Church (729-7331), Maine Street at Bath Road. Open for concerts and tours Tuesday, July through mid-August, 12:10–12:50, for Sunday services, and by chance. This graceful neo-Gothic building was designed in the 1840s by Richard Upjohn, architect of New York City's Trinity Church. A dramatic departure from its Puritan predecessors, it is open-beamed, mildly cruciform in shape, and has deeply colored stained-glass windows. The large sanctuary window was donated by Joshua Chamberlain, one of the first people to be married here. The Hutchings-Plastid tracker organ was installed in 1883.

Brunswick Naval Air Station (921-2000). From Route 1, take the Cooks

Corner exit just east of Brunswick, then follow Route 24 south to the entrance. Home of the navy's North Atlantic antisubmarine and general patrol squadrons, the base is now open for self-guided drive-through tours. Pick up a map and directions at the kiosk just inside the gate.

Fishway Viewing Room **Fishway Viewing Room** (795-4290), Brunswick-Topsham Hydro Station, next to Fort Andros (the former mill that's now a shopping complex), corner of Route 1 and Maine Street, Brunswick. Open during the spawning season (mid-May through June), Wednesday through Sunday 1–5. Watch salmon, smallmouth bass, and alewives climb the 40-foot-high fish ladder that leads to a holding tank beside the viewing room.

Also see **Eagle Island** under *Boat Excursions.*

SCENIC DRIVE

A tour of the Harpswells, including Orrs and Bailey Islands. Allow a day for this rewarding peninsula prowl (see map on page 172). From Brunswick, follow Route 123 south past Bowdoin College 9 miles to the picturesque village of Harpswell Center. The white-clapboard **Elijah Kellogg Church** faces the matching **Harpswell Town Meeting House** built in 1757. The church is named for a former minister who was a prominent 19th-century children's book author. Continue south through West Harpswell to **Pott's Point,** where multicolored 19th-century summer cottages cluster on the rocks like a flock of exotic birds that have wandered in among the gulls. Stop by the first crafts studio you see here and pick up a map/guide to other members of the Harpswell Craft Guild.

Retrace your way up Route 123, and 2 miles north of the church turn right onto Mountain Road, leading to busier Route 24 on Great (also known as Sebascodegan) Island. Drive south along **Orrs Island** across the only remaining **cribstone bridge** in the world. (Its granite blocks are laid in honeycomb fashion without cement to allow tidal flows.) This bridge brings you to **Bailey Island,** with its restaurants, lodging places, picturesque Mackerel Cove, and rocky **Land's End** with its statue honoring all Maine fishermen. Return up Route 24 and take Cundy's Harbor Road 4.3 miles to another picturesque fishing harbor with a couple of good little restaurants (see *Eating Out—In the Harpswells*).

TO DO

BICYCLING

The Androscoggin River Bicycle Path, a 2½ -mile, 14-foot-wide paved bicycle/pedestrian trail, begins at Lower Water Street in Brunswick and runs along the river to Grover Lane in Cooks Corner. It connects with Topsham along the way via a bicycle lane on the new Merrymeeting Bridge. **Center Street Bicycles** (729-5309) rents mountain bikes and serves as a source of local biking information.

KIM GRANT

The Cribstone Bridge to Bailey Island

BOAT EXCURSIONS
From Bailey Island, **Captain Jim Hays** (833-7825) and **Captain Charlie Abrahmson** (833-2419) both offer fishing trips, scenic cruises, and excursions of Casco Bay. **Sea Escape Charters** (833-5531) specializes in tours to **Eagle Island,** a classic one-man's island. Just 17 acres, it is the site of Admiral Robert E. Peary's shingled summer home where, on September 6, 1909, his wife received the news that her husband had become the first person to reach the North Pole. Peary positioned his house to face northeast on a rocky bluff that resembles the prow of a ship. He designed the three-sided living room hearth, made from island stones and Arctic quartz crystals, and stuffed many of the birds on the mantel. Bedrooms appear as though someone has just stepped out for a walk, and the dining room is strewn with photos of men and dogs battling ice and snow. A nature path circles the island, passing the pine trees filled with seagulls.

Casco Bay Lines (774-7871) offers a daily seasonal excursion from Cook's Lobster House on Bailey Island. It takes 1½ hours to circle around Eagle Island and through this northern end of Casco Bay.

Symbion (725-0979) is Captain Ken Brigham's 37-foot sailboat; daysails and overnight charters.

GOLF
Brunswick Golf Club (725-8224), River Road, Brunswick. Incorporated in 1888, an 18-hole course known for its beauty and challenging nature. Snack bar, lounge, and cart rentals.

SEA KAYAKING
H₂Outfitters (833-5257; 1-800-649-5257), P.O. Box 72, Orrs Island 04066.

Located just north of the cribstone bridge on Orrs Island, this is one of Maine's oldest kayaking outfitters. No rentals. Lessons for all abilities, from beginners to instructor certification; guided day trips and overnight excursions are also offered.

Seaspray Kayaking (443-3646; 1-888-349-SPRAY; www.seaspraykayaking. com), Bath. Based on the New Meadows River: guided tours, rentals, multiday expeditions.

GREEN SPACE

BEACHES AND SWIMMING HOLES

✑ **White's Beach** (729-0415), Durham Road, Brunswick. Open mid-May through mid-October. A pond in a former gravel pit (water no deeper than 9 feet). Facilities include a small slide for children. Sandy beach, lifeguards, picnic tables, grills, and a snack bar. Inquire about campsites.

✑ **Thomas Point Beach** (725-6009), off Thomas Point Road, marked from Route 24, Cooks Corner. Open Memorial Day through Labor Day, 9–sunset. The beach is part of an 80-acre private preserve on tidal water overlooking the New Meadows River. It includes groves for picnicking (more than 500 picnic tables plus snack bar, playground, and arcade), and 75 tent and RV sites. It's the scene of a series of special events, including the Maine Festival.

✑ **Coffin Pond** (725-6656), River Road, Brunswick. Open mid-June to Labor Day 10–7. $3.50 adults, $2 children. A strip of sandy beach surrounding a circular pool. Facilities include a 55-foot-long water slide, a playground, and changing rooms maintained by the town.

WALKS

Giant's Staircase, Bailey Island. Turn off Route 24 at Washington Avenue, park at the Episcopal church, and walk down to Ocean Street; follow the path along the water and follow the small sign to the well-named "stairs."

Brunswick-Topsham Land Trust (729-7694), 108 Maine Street, Brunswick. The land trust has preserved some 700 acres in the area. Pick up map/guides to the nature loops at Skofield Nature Preserve, Route 123, Brunswick (4 miles or so south of town), adjoining an ancient Indian portage between Middle Bay and Harpswell Cove and to the Bradley Pond Farm Preserve in Topsham.

LODGING

Brunswick Bed & Breakfast (729-4914; 1-800-299-4914; www.brunswick bnb.com), 165 Park Row, Brunswick 04011. Open year-round. Architect Steve Normand and quilt maker Mercie Normand have restored this mid-1800s Greek Revival home on the town green. It's within walking distance of shops, museums, and the Bowdoin College campus. The six guest rooms and two suites are furnished with antiques and a collection of both new and antique quilts, and all have private baths. A carriage house unit has a full kitchen, bath, and sleeping area. The parlor's floor-to-ceiling windows overlook the green. The breakfast (ours included perfect pancakes served with blueberries, strawberries, and melon) is included in the rate: $90–150 single or double occupancy. The Normands are eager to share the best of Brunswick with guests.

    ♿ **The Captain's Watch at Cundy's Harbor** (725-0979), 926 Cundy's Harbor Road, Harpswell 04079. Open year-round. Built during the Civil War as the Union Hotel, this classic old building with an octagonal cupola has been restored by Donna Dillman and Ken Brigham. The five guest rooms have private baths and include two with fireplaces, and the two-room Pine suite with a deck that accommodates up to four (minimum 3-day stay). The Captain's Quarters has it all: romantic, with a high queen cherry pencil-post bed, antique dressers, a large Oriental rug, water view, a fireplace in the sitting area, and access to the cupola. The Harbor View is also superb, with a view of the harbor from the king-sized bed. $125–150 includes a full breakfast. The 37-foot sloop *Symbion* is available for short sails and overnight cruises.

    Harpswell Inn (833-5509; 1-800-843-5509), 108 Lookout Point Road, Harpswell 04079. Built as the cookhouse for a boatyard, this three-story white-clapboard inn has taken in guests under a number of names but has never been as gracious. Innkeepers Susan and Bill Menz have lived in Hawaii and Texas as well as the South, collecting antiques and furnishings to fill the house—much as though it were owned by a widely traveled sea captain. A large living room has plenty of sitting space around a big hearth and windows overlooking Middle Bay. The nine guest rooms vary widely and come with and without baths (only two share), hearths, and water views, and there are three suites with kitchens. We felt pampered in The Lookout with its cathedral ceiling, sitting area, deck, gas fireplace, and Jacuzzi. Children must be over 10. No smoking. $78–135 for rooms, $155–185 for suites includes a very full breakfast (shared around the formal dining room table). Less off-season.

    Middle Bay Farm Bed & Breakfast (373-1375; www.middlebayfarm. com). Open year-round. Sited on a quiet cove, minutes from downtown Brunswick, this handsome clapboard house dates to the 1830s. In the early 1900s it was a summer boardinghouse (Helen Keller is said to have stayed here), but had stood empty for 10 years when Clark and Phyllis Truesdell bought it in 1998 and then spent almost two years renovating. Common spaces include elegant living and dining rooms and a wicker-furnished porch. The three spacious guest rooms have private full baths, water views, sitting areas, and cable TV/VCRs hidden in armoires. The downstairs room features impressive family antiques, stenciled floors, and a wood-burning fireplace obviously carved by ships' carpenters. Six more small guest rooms without water views share two large baths in the Sail Loft Cottage, which has its own living room (with fireplace) and kitchen, lending itself to group and family get-togethers. The 5 landscaped acres are on a rise above this tidal cove, with access on one side to smooth rocks from which you can fish and swim, as well as to a deepwater dock with kayaks and canoes that guests can use. Rates: $150 in-season ($135 off-season) in the house, including a full breakfast; $75 in-season ($65 off-season) in the Sail Loft Cottage, with a continental breakfast.

🐾☂🖊 **Driftwood Inn and Cottages** (833-5461), Bailey Island 04003. Open late May through Columbus Day weekend; dining room (which is open to the public) is open late June through Labor Day. Sited on a rocky point within earshot of a foghorn are three gray-shingled, traditional Maine summerhouses that contain a total of 16 doubles and eight singles (nine with half baths); there are also six housekeeping cottages. Everyone dines in the pine-walled lodge dining room. Almost all views are of the sea. There is a small saltwater swimming pool set in the rocks and plenty of room, both inside and out, to lounge. This is a rustic resort with the kind of atmosphere and value possible only under longtime (over 50 years) ownership by one family. Your hosts are Mr. and Mrs. Charles L. Conrad and their son David. $80–110 per couple, $60 single (no minimum stay, no meals). Housekeeping cottages, available by the week, are $575–650. Breakfast is $5.50; dinner, $15. No credit cards. Pets are accepted in the cottages (one pet is free, each additional is $100).

🖊 **Captain Daniel Stone Inn** (725-9898; 1-877-573-5151; www.someplaces different.com), 10 Water Street, Brunswick 04011. Thirty modern rooms and four suites are annexed to a Federal mansion. All have TV, phones, VCR, alarm clock–cassette player, and some feature whirlpool baths. Common space includes a handsome living room as well as large function rooms. Breakfast, lunch, dinner, and Sunday brunch are served in the **Narcissa Stone Restaurant.** Continental breakfast is included in the room rate. $89 off-season to $205 per room in-season; inquire about packages.

The Log Cabin, An Island Inn (833-5546; www.logcabin-maine.com), Route 24, Bailey Island 04003. Open April through October. Built decades ago as a lavish log summer home with a huge hearth (a moose head, of course, hangs above), this was for many years a popular restaurant, but in 1995 the owners refitted it to offer eight rooms, three with kitchens, several with Jacuzzis, all with private baths, fridges, coffee machines, and waterside decks. There's also a waterside heated swimming pool. Breakfast is included for $109–219 in high season, less in spring and fall. Dinner is still served, but it's no longer open to the public (figure $50 per couple).

🖊 **Bethel Point Bed and Breakfast** (725-1115; 1-888-238-8262; bethelpt@ gwi.net), 331 Bethel Point Road, Brunswick 04011. This 1830 house stands alone on a quiet cove, a good launch site for kayakers. The upstairs

Sunrise Room has two double beds, a fireplace, and three windows overlooking the ocean, while the Sunset Room has a single as well as a double bed and a view of the apple orchard and lawn. The first-floor Bay View Room can be rented separately or as part of an apartment that sleeps four with a large living room and woodstove and a kitchen ($850 per week); all have private baths. $85–140 includes a full breakfast.

Captain York House (833-6224), P.O. Box 298, Bailey Island 04003. A turn-of-the-20th-century home on a hill overlooking Harpswell Sound; guests share a den with TV and front parlor, both overlooking the water. Four guest rooms have queen-sized beds, and a small apartment with a kitchenette has a twin and a queen ($450 per week or $105 per night, 4-night minimum); $85 for rooms with shared bath, $95 with private bath; children over 12 welcome.

The Black Lantern (725-4165; 1-888-306-4165; www.blacklanternBandB. com), 6 Pleasant Street, Topsham 04086. Open year-round. Tom and Judy Connelie don't know how the words YE CANA BE BOTH GRAND AND COMFORTABLE came to be carved above their living room hearth, but they suit this circa-1810 Federal-style house and the welcome guests receive here. One block from the Androscoggin in Topsham's historic district, an easy walk from downtown Brunswick, they offer three guest rooms with private baths. Quilters are particularly welcome (try your hand on the practice piece in the parlor), and guests can borrow a bike to test the riverside bike path (also good for joggers; see *To Do—Bicycling*). No children under 10, please. $70–85 in-season, $60–75 off-season includes a full breakfast.

COTTAGES
The Chamber of Commerce of the Bath-Brunswick Region (see *Guidance*) lists weekly cottage rentals on Orrs and Bailey Islands.

MOTELS
Little Island Motel (833-2392), RD 1, Box 15, Orrs Island 04066. Open mid-May through mid-October. An attractive motel with terrific views. Eight units, each with a small refrigerator and color TV; part of a complex that also includes a gift shop (the **Gull's Nest**) and a reception area where coffee and a buffet breakfast are served each morning. The complex is set on its own mini-island with a private beach, connected to other land by a narrow neck. $96–124 per couple includes breakfast and use of boats, bicycles, and the outdoor picnic area. $10 extra for each child under 12, $20 for anyone over.

Bailey Island Motel (833-2886), Route 24, Bailey Island 04003. Open early May through late October. Located just over the cribstone bridge. A pretty, gray-shingled building on the water's edge, offering ocean views and landscaped lawns. The 11 rooms are clean and comfortable, with cable TV. No smoking. Morning coffee and muffins are included in $75–105. Guests are welcome to come by boat and tie up to the dock or a mooring.

WHERE TO EAT

DINING OUT
In Brunswick

Star Fish Grill (727-7828), 100 Pleasant Street. Dinner Tuesday through Sunday 5–9:30. Reservations suggested. In the lineup of fast-food places and gas stations along Route 1 you don't expect to find one of Maine's best restaurants, but such is the case. Dine from the Tasting Menu on mussels in lobster cream (pan-roasted in a broth of lobster-infused cream) and a Caesar salad or on grilled fish and seafood. The house specialty is lobster paella for two ($34.95). Entrées $13.95–18.95.

Richard's German/American Cuisine (729-9673), 115 Maine Street. Open for lunch and dinner Monday through Saturday. Continental fare like veal Oscar and grilled New York sirloin, but also featuring very satisfying dishes like *Gemischter salat,* Wiener schnitzel, and *Schlacht-platte.* Nightly specials include *Rindsrouladen* (thinly sliced beef rolled with onions, bacon, mustard, and pickles, braised in a brown sauce). The beer list is impressive. Dinner entrées $8–17. Lighter fare served in the pub area.

☙ **The Great Impasta** (729-5858), 42 Maine Street. Open daily for lunch and dinner. A great stop even if you are simply traveling up or down Route 1, but you might want to get there early to get a booth (plaques honor booth regulars); it's small, popular, and suffused with the aroma of garlic. Specialties include pasta dishes like seafood lasagna; try the eggplant stuffed with smoked mozzarella, mushrooms, onions, and tomatoes and topped with roasted vegetables. For lunch, try homemade soup and a half sandwich. Wine and beer served. Dinner entrées average $12.

In the Harpswells

J. Hathaway's Restaurant and Tavern (833-5305), Route 123, Harpswell Center. Open from 5 PM for dinner daily except Monday. The Hathaways labor hard to create a casual country atmosphere and delectable dishes that may include honey-mustard chicken, pan-seared salmon, or a full brace of back ribs; vegetarian dishes and chili and burgers also available. Two dinners with wine and dessert came to $42.

EATING OUT
In Brunswick

Scarlet Begonias (721-0403), 212 Maine Street. Open Monday through Thursday 11–8, Friday 11–9, Saturday noon–9, closed Sunday. In their attractive storefront "bistro," Doug and Colleen Lavallee serve some great sandwiches (we recommend the turkey spinach with mozzarella and basil mayo, grilled on sourdough bread), chunky, fresh-herbed pastas like Rose Begonia, soups, and unusual pizzas. Good crabcakes. Dinner pastas and pizzas $7.50–8.95.

Joshua's Restaurant & Tavern (725-7981), 121 Maine Street. Open 8

PM–midnight in summer, until 10 in winter. Named for General Joshua Chamberlain (see *To See—Museums*), this is a pubby, pleasant place with seasonal tables on a porch overlooking Maine Street. We can recommend the Chamberlain burger, but it's a big menu—plenty of fried and broiled fish, soups, stews, and a wide choice of beers. Dinner entrées $10.95–13.95, but you can always get a burger, bowl of stew, or salad. The brewpub is downstairs. Inquire about music.

Sea Dog Brewery (725-0162), Great Mill Island, 1 Main Street, Topsham. Open daily 11:30–1 AM. Music Thursday through Saturday. Housed in New England's most picturesque (former) paper mill, vintage 1868. A big, friendly brewpub with seasonal outdoor dining overlooking the churning Androscoggin. "Main Fare" is fairly predictable: sautéed scallops, grilled salmon, teriyaki sirloin ($15.95–17.50), and you can always get "Light Fare" like a pulled pork sandwich or a chicken Caesar wrap. The wide choice of beers includes more than a half-dozen ales brewed here or in Bangor (there are three Maine Sea Dogs).

Henry & Marty (721-9141), 61 Maine Street. Monday through Saturday 11–9, closed Sunday and January through February. Hometown atmosphere with a deli, soups, and pizza. Dinner specials like spinach linguine with mushrooms, sun-dried tomatoes, capers, and feta cheese ($10).

Bangkok Garden Restaurant (725-9708), 14 Maine Street (Fort Andros). Open daily for lunch and dinner, Sunday 4–9. This is an attractive restaurant, and reviews for classic dishes like green curry and pad Thai are good. The menu is large and includes a number of tofu and vegetable dishes.

Wild Oats Bakery and Café (725-6287), Tontine Mall, 149 Maine Street. Open Monday through Saturday 7:30–5, Sunday 8–2. Set back from Maine Street with tables on the terrace and inside. A town meeting place serving coffees and teas, from-scratch pastries and breads, healthy sandwiches, and salads.

Fat Boy Drive-In (729-9431), Old Route 1. Open for lunch and dinner, late March through mid-October. This is no 1950s reconstruct, just a real drive-in with carhops that's survived because it's so good and incredibly reasonably priced. If you own a pre-1970 car, inquire about the annual "sock hop," second Saturday in August. If you don't, you can't come.

Miss Brunswick Diner (729-5948), 101 Pleasant Street (Route 1, northbound). Open daily 5 AM–9 PM. A convenient road-food stop, a remake of a diner that originally stood in Norway (Maine) but has now been here several decades; the neon lights, booths, and jukebox are all new, but the food is what it claims to be: "home cooking at a down-home good price." We ate at an outside table, but no one needs to be that close to Route 1. Hold out for an air-conditioned booth.

In the Harpswells

The Dolphin Marina (833-6000), South Harpswell (marked from Route 123, it's 2.5 miles; also accessible by water). Open seasonally 11–8 daily.

CHRISTINA TREE

Morse Lobster

The nicest kind of small Maine restaurant—family owned, overlooking a small but busy harbor. In the morning fishermen occupy the six stools along the counter; the dining room fills for lunch and dinner (there's often a wait). Chowder, lobster stew, and homemade desserts are specialties, but there is a full dinner menu; wine and beer served.

Block & Tackle (725-5690), Cundy's Harbor Road. Open mid-May through mid-October, 6:30 AM–8 PM. A family-run and -geared restaurant, a real find. Create your own omelet for breakfast; try shrimp stew or a real crabmeat roll for lunch, homemade clam cakes or baked stuffed scallops for dinner. At $12.95 the fried seafood platter is the most expensive dinner dish.

LOBSTER

Cook's Lobster House (833-2818), Bailey Island. Open year-round, 11:30–10. A barn of a place with knotty-pine walls and booths, right on the water and adjacent to a working fishing pier. Save your leftover french fries and muffin crumbs to feed the seagulls on the dock out back. In July and August try to get there before noon, when the Casco Bay liner arrives with its load of day-trippers from Portland. $2.50–30.

Estes Lobster House (833-6340), Route 123, South Harpswell. Open mid-April through mid-October, 11–9. Another old barn of a place with red-checked oilcloth tables and a seven-masted schooner model in the center. It's on a causeway with water views and has a menu that has expanded over the years, from burgers to haddock *fromage* and crusted Atlantic salmon, but it's still about steamed and fried clams and lobster every which way (including lobster shortcake?). Wine and beer, some waterside tables. Entrées $12.95–24.95.

Morse Lobster (833-2399), off Route 123 on Allens Point, Harpswell Neck. Open 11–7 daily, weather permitting, May through September. This is a great spot overlooking Harpswell Sound. Tables are topped with umbrellas and banked in flowers, with lobster available right off the boat in all the usual ways. Also first-rate crab rolls (a "small" is plenty).

Holbrook's Lobster Wharf & Snack Bar (725-0708), Cundy's Harbor (4.5 miles off Route 24). Open in-season for lunch and dinner. Lobsters and clams are steamed outdoors. Weekend clambakes; clams, crab rolls, fish-and-chips, homemade salads, and desserts like Barbara's chocolate bread pudding with ice cream. The window boxes are filled with petunias, and you sit at picnic tables overlooking buoys and lobster boats. You can get beer and wine in the shop next door.

ENTERTAINMENT

MUSIC
Bowdoin Summer Music Festival (725-3322), Bowdoin College, Brunswick. Famed in classical music circles, this chamber music series brings together 200 talented young performers and 40 internationally acclaimed musicians, faculty members at the world's top music schools. It includes composers and choral artists as well as musicians performing original and classical pieces. The Friday-evening concerts (June through August) are staged in the new Crooker Theater at Brunswick High School. Wednesday-evening "Upbeat" concerts, free Sunday and Tuesday student concerts, and the Gamper Festival of Contemporary Music series are all held in Bowdoin campus buildings.

Also see **First Parish Church** under *To See—Museums,* and the **Maine Arts Festival** under *Special Events.*

THEATER
✐ **Maine State Music Theater** (725-8769; www.msmt.org), Bowdoin College, Brunswick. Newly renovated (and air-conditioned) Picard Hall, an 1873 memorial to the Bowdoin students who fought and died in the Civil War, ordered built, of course, by Joshua Chamberlain, is a fit stage for Maine's premier performing-arts group. This highly professional Equity company strives for a mix of classics and new scripts and frequently gets rave reviews. Summer performances at 8 PM, Tuesday through Saturday; matinees Tuesday, Thursday, and Friday. Tickets: $16–34. Also special children's shows.

Theater Project of Brunswick (729-8584), 14 School Street, Brunswick. Serious drama presented year-round in a black-box theater, Wednesday through Sunday at 8. Inquire about late-night cabarets and about Thursday-night dinner theater.

Bowdoin College (725-3000), Brunswick. Performing-arts groups from September through May. Concerts and theatrical performances.

FILM
Eveningstar Cinema (729-6796), Tontine Mall, 149 Maine Street, Brunswick. The specialty is alternative films: foreign, art, biography, documentary, and educational. Also a monthly venue for folk, jazz, and other music performances.

SELECTIVE SHOPPING

ANTIQUES
Cabot Mill Antiques (725-2855), 14 Maine Street (at Route 1; Fort Andros), Brunswick. A vast 140-dealer space with quality antiques; flea markets on summer weekends.

ARTS AND CRAFTS GALLERIES
In Brunswick

Quality galleries at the north end of Brunswick's Maine Street include **O'Farrell Gallery** (729-8228), 58 Maine Street, and **Icon Contemporary Art** (725-8157), around the corner at 19 Mason Street. Check out **Spindleworks** (725-8820), 7 Lincoln Street, an artists' cooperative for people with disabilities that produces some striking handwoven fiber clothing and hangings, quilts, accessories, paintings, prints, and more. **Wyler Gallery** (729-1321), 150 Maine Street, is a great mix of quality pottery, glassware, jewelry, clothing, fun stuff, furniture, and furnishings.

In the Harpswells

Harpswell Art & Craft Guild is an association of nine studios/galleries along Route 123 on Harpswell Neck that publishes a leaflet guide and regularly sponsors events. **Harpswell Schoolhouse Gallery** (729-8872), Route 123, Harpswell Neck, open May into December, Friday through Monday 10–5, features fine hand weavings, knitting, jewelry, and hand-painted glass ornaments with hand-painted flowers. **Widgeon Cove Studios** (833-6081), open year-round, features the handmade papers and collages of Georgeann and the gold and silver jewelry of Condon Kuhl. It's a peaceful place with gardens overlooking the water. On Route 24 (north of Mountain Road) the former Gunpoint Church now serves as a gallery for **Sebascodegan Artists** (named for the island on which it stands), a cooperative with 20 members. It's open July 4 through Labor Day, Monday through Saturday 10–5.

Hawke's Lobster (721-0472) in Cundy's Harbor is a seasonal source not only of seafood but also the work of local craftspeople.

BOOKSTORES
Gulf of Maine Books (729-5083), 134 Maine Street, Brunswick. A laid-back, full-service bookstore with a wide inventory, particularly rich in Maine titles, poetry, and "books that fall through the holes in bigger stores." Owner Gary Lawless is a founder of Blackberry Press (note the full line here), which has reissued many out-of-print Maine classics. He is also a well-known poet with an international following.

Brunswick Bookland (725-2313), Cooks Corner. Now a full-service independent bookstore.

Old Books (725-4524), 136 Maine Street, Brunswick. Closed Thursday. Upstairs from Gulf of Maine, Old Books features Clare Howell's floor-to-ceiling, well-arranged used books and a large stuffed couch, along with friendly nooks for reading.

SPECIAL STORES

Island Candy Company (833-6639), Route 24, Orrs Island. Open year-round, 11–8. Melinda Harris Richter makes everything from lollipops to truffles. Try the almond cups.

Grand City V&S (725-8964), 128 Maine Street, Brunswick. Open Monday through Saturday 9–6, Sunday 10–4. See the chapter introduction. A must-stop for anyone who misses genuine five-and-dimes.

Macbeans Music (729-6513), 141 Maine Street, Brunswick. A music store with a living room, specializing in classical, folk, jazz, and hard-to-find items.

SPECIAL EVENTS

Throughout the summer: **Farmer's market** (Tuesday and Friday, May through November) on the downtown Brunswick Mall (the town common). **Beanhole suppers** are staged during summer months by the Harpswell Neck Fire Department.

July: **Annual Lobster Luncheon,** Orrs Island United Methodist Church. **Bailey Island Fishing Tournament** (to register, phone Cook's Lobster House at 833-2818). **Great State of Maine Air Show** at the Brunswick Naval Air Station every other year.

August: **Topsham Fair** *(early in the month)*—a traditional agricultural fair complete with ox pulls, crafts and food competitions, carnival, and livestock; held at Topsham Fairgrounds, Route 24, Topsham. The **Maine Festival** (772-9012), *first weekend in the month*—a 4-day celebration of music, dance, crafts, and more, held at Thomas Point Beach and marked from Cooks Corner. **A Weekend in Harpswell** *(late in the month)*—annual art show, garden club festival in historic homes, and beanhole supper. **Annual Bluegrass Festival,** Thomas Point Beach (off Route 24 near Cooks Corner). **Maine Highland Games,** Thomas Point Beach—a daylong celebration of Scottish heritage, with piping, country dancing, sheepdog demonstrations, and Highland fling competitions. **Joshua Chamberlain Days** observed in odd-numbered years: four days of Chamberlain lectures and related events.

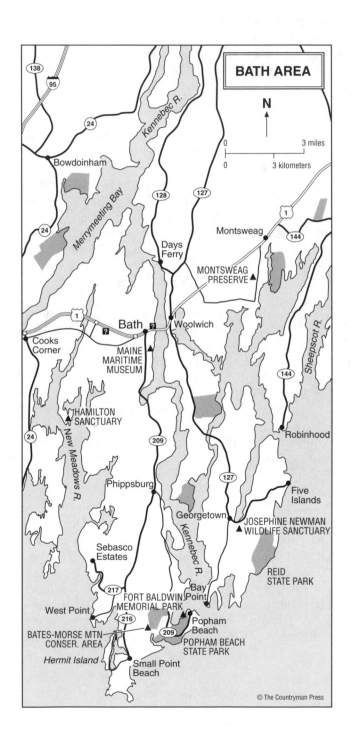

BATH AREA

N

0   3 miles

0   3 kilometers

138

95

24

Bowdoinham

Kennebec R.

Merrymeeting Bay

24

128

127

1

Montsweag

144

Days
Ferry

MONTSWEAG
PRESERVE ▲

1

Bath

Woolwich

Cooks
Corner

MAINE
MARITIME
MUSEUM ▲

144

Sheepscot R.

New Meadows R.

HAMILTON
SANCTUARY ▲

209

24

Phippsburg

Robinhood

127

Five
Islands

Georgetown

JOSEPHINE NEWMAN
WILDLIFE SANCTUARY ▲

Sebasco
Estates

Kennebec R.

REID
STATE PARK

217

Bay
Point

FORT BALDWIN
MEMORIAL PARK

West Point

216

Popham
Beach

209

POPHAM BEACH
STATE PARK

BATES-MORSE MTN
CONSER. AREA ▲

Hermit Island

Small Point
Beach

© The Countryman Press

Bath Area

Over the years some 5,000 vessels have been built in Bath. Think about it: In contrast to most communities—which retain what they build—here an entire city's worth of imposing structures have sailed away. Perhaps that's why, with a population of fewer than 10,000, Bath is a city rather than a town, and why the granite city hall, with its rounded, pillared facade and cupola (with a Paul Revere bell and a three-masted schooner for a weather vane), seems meant for a far larger city.

American shipbuilding began downriver from Bath in 1607 when the 30-ton pinnace *Virginia* was launched by Popham Colony settlers. It continues with naval vessels that regularly slide off the ways at the Bath Iron Works (BIW).

With almost 9,000 workers, BIW employs about the same number of people who worked in Bath's shipyards in the 1850s. At its entrance a sign proclaims: THROUGH THESE GATES PASS THE WORLD'S BEST SHIPBUILD- ERS. This is no idle boast, for many current employees have inherited their skills from a long line of forebears.

Obviously, this is the place for a museum about ships and ship- building, and the Maine Maritime Museum has one of the country's foremost collections of ship models, journals, logs, photographs, and other seafaring memorabilia. It even includes a 19th-century working shipyard. Both BIW and the Maine Maritime Museum are sited on a 4- mile-long reach of the Kennebec River where the banks slope at pre- cisely the right gradient for laying keels. Offshore, a 35- to 150-foot- deep channel ensures safe launching. The open Atlantic is just 18 miles downriver.

In the 1850s Bath was the fourth largest port in the United States in registered tonnage, and throughout the 19th century it consistently ranked among America's eight largest seaports. Its past prosperity is reflected in the blend of Greek Revival, Italianate, and Georgian Re- vival styles in the brick storefronts along Front Street and in the impos- ing wooden churches and mansions in similar styles along Washington, High, and Middle Streets.

Today BIW dominates the city's economy as dramatically as its red- and-white, 400-foot-high construction crane—the biggest on the East Coast—does the city's waterfront. The largest civilian employer in

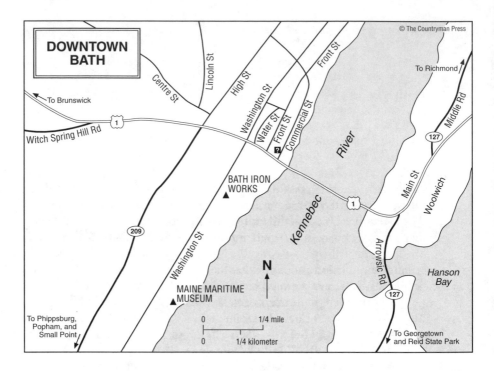

Maine, the company actually produced more destroyers during World War II than did all of Japan, and it continues to keep to its pledge to deliver naval ships ahead of schedule and under budget. In 2001 a modernization plan will be completed, updating the BIW facilities to include a land-level platform for assembly and erection of ships, and a 750-foot floating dry dock for launching and retrieval. The new facility will enable BIW to work even more efficiently, making that pledge easier to keep.

The story of BIW is one of many told in the Maine Maritime Museum—for which you should allow the better part of a day. Save another to explore the Phippsburg Peninsula south of Bath. Phippsburg's perimeter is notched with coves filled with fishing boats, and Popham Beach near its southern tip is a grand expanse of sand. Reid State Park on Georgetown Island, just across the Kennebec River, is the Midcoast's only other sandy strand. North of Bath, Merrymeeting Bay draws birders.

In the summer of 2000 the long-awaited opening of the Sagadahoc Bridge occurred. The four-lane bridge seems to have eased the traffic crunch over the Kennebec, even when BIW's shifts change.

GUIDANCE

Chamber of Commerce of the Bath-Brunswick Region (443-9751; www.midcoastmaine.com), 45 Front Street, Bath 04530. Open year-round, weekdays 8:30–5. From mid-June through mid-October, an information center on the northbound side of Route 1, at Witch Spring Hill, is one of the state's busiest. There are picnic tables and minimal rest rooms. For a lodging referral service (including weekends and evenings), phone 389-1394.

Bath Business Association (www.visitbath.com) is another helpful source of information.

GETTING THERE

By car: Route 1 passes above the city with exits from the elevated road accessing various points within the city.

By bus: **Concord Trailways** (1-800-639-3317) stops at the Coastal Plaza on Route 1.

By limo: **Mid-Coast Limo** (236-2424; 1-800-937-2424) makes runs from Portland International Jetport by reservation.

GETTING AROUND

Bath Trolley Company (443-9751) operates throughout the city, daily June through September.

MEDICAL EMERGENCY

Mid Coast Hospital (443-5524), 1356 Washington Street, Bath. There is also an addiction resource center here.

TO SEE

MUSEUMS

Maine Maritime Museum (443-1316; www.bathmaine.com), 243 Washington Street, Bath. Watch for the turnoff from Route 1. Open year-round 9:30–5 daily; closed Thanksgiving, Christmas, and New Year's Day. Admission is $7.50 adults and $4.75 children ages 6–15 (family admission is $21). Sited just south of BIW on the banks of the Kennebec River, this extensive complex includes the brick-and-glass **Maritime History Building** and the **Percy & Small Shipyard,** the country's only surviving wooden shipbuilding yard (its turn-of-the-20th-century belts for driving machinery have been restored). The size and solidity of the history building contrast with its setting and the low-slung wooden structures left from the old shipyards. Its exhibits focus, understandably, on the era beginning after the Civil War when 80 percent of this country's full-rigged ships were built in Maine, almost half of these in Bath.

The pride of Bath, you learn, were the Down Easters, a compromise between the clipper ship and the old-style freighter that plied the globe from the 1870s through the 1890s, and the big multimasted schooners designed to ferry coal and local exports like ice, granite, and lime. The museum's permanent collection of artwork, artifacts, and documents is now said to include more than a million pieces, and there is an extensive research library. Permanent exhibits range from displays on Maine's marine industries—fishing and canning as well as shipbuilding and fitting—to the story of BIW.

Did you realize that lobstering in Maine dates back to the 1820s? By the 1880s there were 23 "lobster factories" in Maine, all closed in the 1890s when a limit was imposed on the size of lobsters that could be canned. Visitors are invited to sit on the gunwale of a classic lobster boat and watch a documentary about lobstering narrated by E. B. White.

Woodworkers and wooden-boat buffs will appreciate the lofting models in the mold loft and the details of the cabinetwork in the joiners shop, as well as watching the apprentices building wooden boats. Children find hands-on exhibits scattered throughout this sprawling museum—from the World Trade Game in the main gallery to the crow's nest in the sandbox boat near the water. Visitors of all ages should take advantage of the narrated boat rides.

Historic district. In the 18th and 19th centuries Bath's successful shipbuilding and seafaring families built impressive mansions on and around upper Washington Street. Sagadahoc Preservation, Inc., offers "magical history tour" guided walks; ask for a schedule at the chamber of commerce (see *Guidance*). The historical society also produces an excellent brochure, "Architectural Tours—Self-Guided Walking and Driving Tours of the City of Bath," available from the chamber of commerce.

✎ **19th-Century Rural Life Museum,** Woolwich Historical Society Museum (443-4833; www.woolwichhistory.org), Route 1 and Nequasset Road, Woolwich. Open 10:30–2:30 daily, July through Labor Day. $2 adults, $1 children ages 6–12. An admirable small museum run by volunteers, this rambling 1910 farmhouse displays an intriguing collection of antique clothing and quilts, plus seafaring memorabilia, all gleaned from local attics.

SCENIC DRIVE

The Phippsburg Peninsula. From the Maine Maritime Museum, drive south on Route 209 (see map on page 188), down the narrow peninsula making up the town of Phippsburg, pausing at the first causeway you cross. This is **Winnegance Creek,** an ancient shortcut between Casco Bay and the Kennebec River; look closely to your left and you'll see traces of the 10 tidemills that once operated here.

Continue south on Route 209 until you come to the **Phippsburg Center Store** on your right. Turn left on Parker Head Road, into the tiny hamlet of **Phippsburg Center.** This is one of those magical places, far larger in memory than in fact—perhaps because it was once larger in fact, too. Notice the huge linden tree (planted in 1774) between the stark Congregational church (1802) and its small cemetery. Also look for the telltale stumps of piers on the shore beyond, remnants of a major shipyard. Just off Route 209, note the **Phippsburg Historical Museum** (open in summer Monday through Friday 2–4, and by appointment: 442-7606).

Continue along the peninsula's east shore on the Parker Head

Road, past a former millpond where ice was once harvested. At the junction with Route 209, turn left. The road threads a salt marsh and the area at Hoss Ketch Point, from which all traces of the ill-fated **Popham Colony** have long since disappeared. Route 209 winds around Sabino Head and ends at the parking lot for **Fort Popham,** a granite Civil War–era fort (with picnic benches) at the mouth of the Kennebec River. A wooded road, for walking only, leads to World War I and II fortifications that constitute **Fort Baldwin Memorial Park;** a six-story tower yields views up the Kennebec and out to sea.

Along the shore at **Popham Beach,** note the pilings, in this case from vanished steamboat wharves. Around the turn of the 20th century, two big hotels served the passengers who transferred here from Boston to Kennebec River steamers, or who simply stayed a spell to enjoy the town's spectacular beach. Now **Popham Beach State Park,** this immense expanse of sand remains a popular destination for fishermen, beach walkers, sunbathers, and even a few hardy swimmers. From Popham Beach, return to Route 209 and follow it west to Route 217 and out to **Sebasco Harbor Resort,** then back up to Phippsburg Center.

TO DO

BICYCLING
Bath Cycle and Ski (442-7002), Route 1, Woolwich, rents bikes and cross-country skis.
BOAT EXCURSIONS
Kennebec Jet Boat Adventure Tours (442-0092; 1-888-538-6786), 870 Washington Street, Bath. A unique choice among excursion boats. The jet boat seats 45 passengers and offers cruises of varying lengths, including historical tours, pirate adventures, wildlife cruises, and more.

Maine Maritime Museum Cruises (443-1316), 243 Washington Street, Bath. Mid-June through mid-October, the museum (see *To See*) offers periodic special-interest cruises along the Midcoast, as well as up the Kennebec River and across Merrymeeting Bay. The fireworks cruise during Bath Heritage Days offers a great vantage point and lots of fun.

M/V *Ruth*, based at Sebasco Estates (389-1161), offers a variety of coastal excursions on the New Meadows River and into Casco Bay, including pirate adventure cruises and an Eagle Island trip. **M/V *Yankee*** (389-1788) offers mid-June through Labor Day excursions from Hermit Island Campgrounds at Small Point. **Seguin Navigation Co.** (443-1677), Arrowsic, offers half- and full-day sails. **Kennebec Charters** (389-1883), Popham Beach, offers sight-seeing trips on the Kennebec, Sheepscot, Sasanoa, and New Meadows Rivers, as well as island and lighthouse tours, and fishing trips.
CANOE AND KAYAK RENTALS
Taylor Rentals (725-7400), 271 Bath Road, Brunswick, rents canoes to ex-

Bath City Hall

plore Merrymeeting Bay. **Dragonworks, Inc.** (666-8481), in Bowdoinham on Merrymeeting Bay, sells whitewater and sea kayaks and offers
instruction. **Up the Creek** (443-4845) in Phippsburg rents canoes and
kayaks. **Seaspray Kayaking** (443-3646) offers guided tours and hourly
rentals. Ask about sunset and moonlight tours.

FISHING

Surf fishing is popular at Popham Beach, and there's an annual mid-August
Bluefish Tournament in Waterfront Park. Nearly 20 boats offer fishing
on the river, and both **Kennebec Charters** (389-1883) and ***Kayla D
& Obsession* Sportfishing Charters** (442-8581 or 443-3316) offer
deep-sea-fishing charters.

GOLF

Bath Country Club (442-8411), Whiskeag Road, Bath. 18 holes, pro shop,
lessons available. **Shore Acres Golf Course** (389-9060), Sebasco Harbor Resort, Sebasco Estates. Newly renovated into an 18-hole course.
Open to the public by reservation only.

SWIMMING

If you are traveling with a dog, it is important to know that they are allowed
only in picnic areas, not on the beaches.

Charles Pond, Route 27, Georgetown (about 0.5 mile past the turnoff for
Reid State Park; 15 miles down the peninsula from the Carlton Bridge).
Often considered the best all-around swimming hole in the area, this
long and narrow pond has clear water and is surrounded by tall pines.

Pleasant Pond (582-2813), Peacock Beach State Park, Richmond. Open

Memorial Day through Labor Day. A sand-and-gravel beach with life-guards on duty. Water depth drops off gradually to about 10 feet in a 30-by-50-foot swimming area removed from boating and enclosed by colored buoys. Picnic tables and barbecue grills. Admission is $1.50 adults, $.50 ages 5–11; under 5 free.

✍ **Popham Beach State Park** (389-1335), via Route 209 south from Bath to Phippsburg and beyond. One of the best state park beaches in Maine. Three miles of sand at the mouth of the Kennebec River that never seem to be too crowded. Also a sandbar, tidal pools, and smooth rocks. It can be windy; extra layers are recommended. Day-use fees of $2 adults and $.50 children ages 5–11 (under 5 free) are charged from mid-April until mid-October.

✍ **Reid State Park** (371-2303), Route 127, Georgetown (14 miles south of Bath and Route 1). Open daily year-round. The bathhouse and snack bar overlook 1½ miles of sand in three distinct beaches that seldom become overcrowded, although the limited parking area does fill by noon on summer weekends. You can choose surf or a slightly warmer sheltered backwater, especially good for children. Entrance fees of $2 adults and $.50 children ages 5–11 (under 5 free) are charged between mid-April and mid-October.

SPECIAL LEARNING PROGRAMS

Shelter Institute (442-7938; www.shelterinstitute.com), 873 Route 1, Woolwich. A year-round resource center for people who want to build or retrofit their own energy-efficient home. Two- and 3-week daytime courses are offered May through October; Saturday-morning classes are given during the winter. Tuition varies according to course taken.

GREEN SPACE

✍ **Fort Baldwin Memorial Park,** Phippsburg. An undeveloped area with a six-story tower to climb (steep stairs, but the railing is sturdy) for a beautiful view up the Kennebec and, downriver, out to sea. There are also remnants of fortifications from World Wars I and II. At the bottom of the hill is the site where the Popham Colony struggled to weather the winter of 1607–1608, then built the pinnace *Virginia* and sailed away to Virginia.

✍ **Fort Popham Memorial Park** (389-1335 in-season) is located at one tip of Popham Beach. Picnic sites are scattered around the ruins of the 1861 fort, which overlooks the beach.

Josephine Newman Wildlife Sanctuary, Georgetown. Bounded on two sides by salt marsh; 119 acres with 2 miles of walking trails. Look for the sign on Route 127, 9.1 miles south of Route 1.

Bates–Morse Mountain Conservation Area comprises some 600 acres extending from the Sprague to the Morse River and out to Seawall Beach. Allow 2 hours for the walk to and from this unspoiled private

beach. Pack a picnic and towel, but please, no radios or beach paraphernalia: Seawall Beach is an important nesting area for piping plovers and least terns. There's a great view from the top of Morse Mountain, which is reached by an easy hike, just over a mile along a partially
paved road and through river and marsh. Parking is very limited.

Hamilton Sanctuary, West Bath. Situated on a peninsula in the New
Meadows River, offering a 1½-mile trail system and great bird-watching. Take the New Meadows exit off Route 1 in West Bath; turn left on
New Meadows Road, which turns into Foster Point Road; follow it 4
miles to the sanctuary sign.

Montsweag Preserve, Montsweag Road, Woolwich. A 1½-mile trail takes
visitors through woods, fields, and a salt marsh, and along the water.
This 45-acre preserve is owned by The Nature Conservancy (729-5181).
You will have to watch carefully for the turns (right onto Montsweag
Road about 6.5 miles from Bath on Route 1, then 1.3 miles and a left
into the preserve).

LODGING

RESORTS

Sebasco Harbor Resort (389-1161; 1-800-225-3819; www.sebasco.com),
Sebasco Estates 04565. Open May through October. This traditional
New England summer resort blends old and new well, making good use
of the property's prime ocean frontage with a dining room that overlooks
the water and a lighthouse-shaped building with a top-floor sitting area.
The 600-plus-acre complex includes a saltwater pool and an 18-hole golf
course, tennis courts, a tour boat, and a bowling alley. Other recreation
options include hiking, boating (rentals available), lobster cookouts, live
entertainment, children's programs, and special evening programs.
Choose a cottage or an inn room (115 rooms total). Rates are MAP: $169–
249 in-season per person per night, double occupancy; $299–1,499 for
cottages. EP rates available; inquire about packages.

Rock Gardens Inn (389-1339; www.rockgardensinn.com), Sebasco Estates
04565. Open mid-June through late September. Next door to Sebasco
Harbor Resort, the inn accommodates just 60 guests, providing a more
intimate atmosphere but offering access to all of Sebasco's facilities (see
above). The inn sits perched on the edge of the water, banked, as you'd
expect, by a handsome rock garden, and has its own heated swimming
pool. Guests gather in the comfortable living room, library, and old-
fashioned dining room with round tables and cornflower blue wooden
chairs. There's a Sunday cocktail party and a Friday noontime lobster
cookout. Three rooms in the inn and 10 cottages, each with living room,
fireplace, and sunporch. Most rooms have water views. $100–125 per
person MAP, plus 15 percent service charge; 5-night minimum in July
and August.

Popham Beach

BED & BREAKFASTS
In Bath 04530

🐾💰♿**The Inn at Bath** (443-4294; www.innatbath.com), 969 Washington Street. Open year-round. Nick Bayard's rambling, elegantly restored 1810 mansion features twin parlors with marble fireplaces, eight guest rooms with private baths, and a two-bedroom suite. Two sets of rooms are adjoining and can be opened to create additional suites. Five rooms have wood-burning fireplaces (two with two-person Jacuzzis overlooking the fireplaces). We especially like the River Room, an old hayloft with built-in bookshelves, window seat, and cozy nooks and crannies. All guest rooms have air-conditioning, phone, cable TV, VCR, and cassette-tape player with radio and alarm. On the grounds surrounding the house, a series of elaborate garden rooms are being developed. Rooms are $85–185 for two, including breakfast; $185–350 for suites. Children welcome and pets accepted selectively.

The Kennebec Inn (443-5202; 1-800-822-9393; www.kennebecinn.com), 1024 Washington Street. A beautifully restored Italianate mansion offering seven luxurious guest rooms year-round. The hosts, Blanche and Ron Lutz, pay close attention to detail; the rooms are warm and comfortable with private baths, phones and data ports, color cable TVs hidden inside armoires custom-made for each room, poster beds, and original light fixtures. Some rooms have gas fireplaces and Jacuzzis. Breakfast is served in the spectacular tapestried dining room, which boasts a 9-foot solid walnut table and gas fireplace. $100 and up depending on room and season.

Benjamin F. Packard House (443-6069; 1-800-516-4578; www.maine coast.com/packardhouse), 45 Pearl Street. Open year-round. A gracious 1790 Georgian home in the heart of the historic district. Once owned by Benjamin F. Packard, partner in one of the world's most successful shipbuilding companies. Three elegant guest rooms with period furnishings, one a suite with sitting room; all have private baths. Common space includes a fenced patio. $75–100 includes full breakfast.

Fairhaven Inn (443-4391; 1-888-443-4391; www.mainecoast.com/fairhaven), North Bath Road. Open year-round. Hidden away on the Kennebec River as it meanders down from Merrymeeting Bay, this 1790s house has eight pleasant guest rooms, six with private baths. Dave and Susie Reed stayed here as guests some 20 times before buying the place. The inn's 16 acres of meadow invite walking in summer and cross-country skiing in winter (the 10-acre golf course nearby makes for even more skiing). Two-night minimum stay on holidays and summer weekends. In-season rates, including a full breakfast, are $80–130.

The Galen C. Moses House (442-8771; www.galenmoses.com), 1009 Washington Street. Open year-round. You can't miss this imposing deep-pink house as you pass on the street. Built in 1874 for Galen Clapp Moses, it is listed on the National Register of Historic Homes. Hosts Jim Haught and Larry Kieft are former antiques dealers, and the interesting items they collected over the years are strategically placed throughout the house. The interior is elegantly done, from the library with built-in shelves and leather-covered seats to the formal parlors. The five guest rooms are just as impressive, all with private baths (one is in the hall—the original bath in the house), one with a white marble fireplace and bay windows. $89–129 includes gourmet breakfast.

In Phippsburg 04562

Stonehouse Manor (389-1141), HCR 32, Box 369, Route 209, Phippsburg 04563. Open year-round. Set off the road in a large field beside a small lake, this rambling old fieldstone-and-shingle house exudes the style of Maine's grand old cottages. Five large rooms, some with fireplaces and Jacuzzis, each with a lake or bay view and private bath. There is also a spectacular veranda with wicker furniture overlooking the bay and the well-groomed grounds. Jane and Tim Dennis serve a full breakfast. $100–175 per couple.

The 1774 Inn at Phippsburg (389-1774), Box 24, Parker Head Road. Open year-round. Once the home of Maine's first congressman, later owned by the area's premier shipbuilder, this house dominates the road through the center of one of the Kennebec River's most picturesque villages. Debbie and Joe Braun offer four large Federal-style guest rooms furnished in antiques. There is also a beautifully proportioned main stairway you'll want to go up and down again and again. The Congregational church is within walking distance, making this a great choice for weddings. $75–115.

Edgewater Farm Bed & Breakfast (389-1322), 71 Small Point Road. Bill and Carol Emerson continually improve upon their restored circa-1800 farmhouse set in 4 acres of beautiful gardens and fruit trees. The recently added Great Room overlooks the gardens, with picture windows and a stone fireplace with treasures they've collected (seashells, sea glass, and such) built into its facade. There is an indoor lap pool open to guests and also shared with the community, an outdoor hot tub, and a large recreation room. There are six guest rooms, including two suites, all with private baths. $95–160.

Elsewhere

Coveside Bed and Breakfast (371-2807; 1-800-232-5490; www.coveside bandb.com), Five Islands 04548. Open May through October. Ten miles down Route 127 from Route 1, beyond the turnoff for Reid State Park. Carolyn and Tom Church have created an oasis overlooking a quiet cove. This 100-year-old farmhouse has been renovated to include an atrium addition and a large deck overlooking gardens and the cove. Six guest rooms, all with private baths. In summer 2000 plans were under-way to renovate the carriage house into two deluxe rooms with private decks and fireplaces. Bicycles and canoes for guest use. $95–115 includes full breakfast.

Popham Beach Bed & Breakfast (389-2409; www.pophambeachbandb.com), 4 Riverview Avenue, Popham Beach 04562. Open year-round. Peggy Johannessen has restored this former Coast Guard station, built in 1883 right on Popham Beach, to create a B&B with as much character as the building itself. The four guest rooms all have private baths and water views. The Captain's Quarters is a suite decorated in white wicker with a lovely sitting area, a private staircase, and a large private bath. $90–165 includes a full breakfast; 2-night minimum stay.

Grey Havens (371-2616; 1-800-431-2316; www.greyhavens.com), Seguin-land Road, P.O. Box 308, Georgetown 04548. Open May through October. The donor of the land for neighboring Reid State Park also built this turreted, gray-shingled summer hotel, opened in 1904, with a huge parlor window—said to have been Maine's first picture window. The 13 rooms, all with private baths, range from small doubles to large, rounded turret rooms; half have water views and all have brass or iron beds and Victorian furniture. Call early, as it's usually booked with weddings on summer weekends. $100–220 (for an oceanfront suite with balcony); 25 percent midweek discount through June 15. "Hearty continental" breakfast; 2-night minimum on weekends and holidays.

Pleasant Cove B&B (442-0045; 1-800-949-2982; www.pleasantcovebb.com), 73 George Wright Road, Woolwich 04579. Follow the sign from Route 1, turning down a long dirt drive after leaving the highway. Set on 34 acres along Pleasant Cove, this is a quiet place with very friendly hosts, Brigit and Reinhard. A pretty, relaxing spot with bright, cheery rooms. A full breakfast, which may feature gourmet Bavarian/Austrian specials, is included in the rates. $65–80 per couple in-season.

OTHER LODGING

New Meadows Inn (443-3921), Bath Road, West Bath 04530. Open year-round, with the exception of the cottages (open late May through mid-October). A good family place, with rooms (many recently renovated) for two, cottages for more, including two log cabins. Dining room with shore dinners, traditional family fare, snacks, salad bar, and buffets; outdoor dining available. Private docking and marina facilities. Rooms start at $49 in-season; cottages start at $75 per night.

🐾 **Hermit Island** (443-2101), 42 Front Street, Bath 04530. This 255-acre almost-island at Small Point offers 275 nicely scattered camping sites, 63 on the water with fantastic views. Only tents and pop-ups are permitted. Owned since 1953 by the Sewall family, Hermit Island also has a central lodge with a recreation room and snack bar where kids can meet. Beyond the camping area are acres of private beaches and unspoiled woods and meadows perfect for hiking and quiet exploration. Wildlife is abundant. $27–38 per night; less off-season.

Cottage listings are available from the Chamber of Commerce of the Bath-Brunswick Region (see *Guidance*) and in the Maine Tourism Association's "Maine Guide to Camp and Cottage Rentals." (Also see *Cottage Rentals* in "What's Where in Maine.")

WHERE TO EAT

DINING OUT

The Robinhood Free Meetinghouse (371-2188), Robinhood Road (off Route 127), Robinhood. Open year-round. Michael Gagne, known regionally for his fresh, innovative dishes, has turned the vintage-1855 Robinhood Free Meetinghouse into an attractive dining space decorated with local art, all for sale. The second-floor chapel has a 16-foot ceiling and 10-foot windows, and is perfect for weddings or private groups. The menu is almost overwhelming in the number of choices offered and might include appetizers of grilled shrimp adobo on homemade tortillas or artichoke strudel. Fettuccine, seafood, beef, pork, and chicken are all among the entrées (over 30 of them) offered. The dessert menu is just as extensive—and selection just as difficult, with choices like Obsession in Three Chocolates and hazelnut soufflé.

The Osprey (371-2530), at Robinhood Marina, Robinhood (just off Route 127, near Reid State Park). Open spring through fall for lunch and dinner, Sunday brunch; fewer days off-season. Reservations appreciated and a must on summer weekends. Overlooks a boatyard and, yes, there is an osprey nest on the day marker; you can see it from the window. Owned by the folks who own J. R. Maxwell's (see below), with similar fare; we've heard mixed reviews.

🐾 **Kristina's** (442-8577), corner of High and Center Streets, Bath. Closed on Mondays and for all of January. Open weekdays for all three meals (and café menu 2:30–5), brunch and dinner on Saturday, and brunch-only on Sunday. Attractive dining rooms, plus outdoor dining on the tree-shaded deck in summer. You'll still find the same great quiche, cheesecake, and other incredible breads and pastries (which you can buy to go at the bakery counter) for which it was first known (inquire about the bread of the day), plus such entrées as Maine crabcakes with red pepper tartar sauce, or summer-vegetable lasagna with fresh herbs and mascarpone cheese. Entrées $11–19.

✐ **J. R. Maxwell's** (443-4461), 122 Front Street, Bath. Open year-round for lunch and dinner daily. Located in the middle of the shopping district, in a renovated 1840s building that was originally a hotel. Predictable burgers, salads, crêpes, and seafood sandwiches; also dinner steaks, prime rib, chicken, fresh seafood, and Sunday brunch. Children's menu. Exposed old brick walls, hanging plants. Downstairs is the **Boat Builder's Pub,** with live bands on weekends. Entrées $6.95–17.95.

EATING OUT

✐ **Beale Street Barbeque & Grill** (442-9514), 215 Water Street, Bath. Open for lunch and dinner. Brothers Mark, Mike, and Patrick Quigg have built their slow-cooking pits and are delivering the real Tennessee (where Mark lived for six years) goods: pulled pork, ribs, sausage, a big Reuben; also nightly specials (frequently fish) to round out the menu. This place is well worth finding, but you almost have to know it's there, in a renovated old BIW building behind Reny's (see *Selective Shopping—Special Shops*).

Kennebec Tavern and Marina (442-9636), 119 Commercial Street, Bath. Open for lunch and dinner daily. Brunch on Sunday 11–2. On the banks of the Kennebec River, overlooking the new Sagadahoc Bridge, this pleasant dining room offers seafood, chicken, steak, and combos. Outdoor dining in summer.

✪ **Starlight Café** (443-3005), 15 Lambard Street, Bath. Open for breakfast and lunch weekdays, breakfast only on Saturday. This bright, funky place is a real find. Large, filling sandwiches (create your own by picking bread, meat, cheese, and veggies) and daily specials. Crowded at lunchtime, but worth the wait.

✐ **Front Street Deli/1840 Lounge** (443-9815), 128 Front Street, Bath. Open year-round 8 AM–11 PM. A storefront with inviting booths and standard breakfast and lunch fare, soup of the day, good pies. Downstairs is the lounge with comfy mismatched sofas and couches; same menu.

✐ **Spinney's Restaurant and Guesthouse** (389-1122), at the end of Route 209, Popham Beach. Open weekends in April and daily May through October for lunch and dinner. Our kind of beach restaurant: counter and tables, pleasant atmosphere with basic chowder-and-a-sandwich menu. Pete and Jean Hart specialize in fried fish and seafood, but they also serve it steamed and broiled; good lobster and crabmeat rolls. Beer, wine, and cocktails.

✐⛄ **Lobster House** (389-1596), 395 Small Point Road (follow Route 1 to Route 209, then Route 209 to Route 216). Open summer season only, Tuesday through Saturday 5–9 PM, Sunday noon–8:30 PM. Mrs. Pye's is a classic lobster place specializing in seafood dinners and homemade pastry; it's down near Small Point, surrounded by salt marsh. Beer and wine are served.

Five Islands Lobster and Grill (371-2950), 13 miles south of Route 1 on Route 127 at the Five Islands wharf in Georgetown. Run by the Georgetown Fisherman's Co-op. Open seasonally, specializing in steamed lobsters and clams, lobster rolls, fried seafood, and their "somewhat famous" crabcake sandwich. No credit cards.

Lisa's Lobstah House & Grill (371-2722), Moore's Turnpike Road, Five Islands. A small take-out place accessible by car or boat. Seafood, homemade onion rings, and sandwiches. Open daily in summer. Locals say they love this place.

ENTERTAINMENT

Chocolate Church Arts Center (442-8455), 804 Washington Street, Bath. Year-round presentations include plays, concerts, and a wide variety of guest artists. Special children's plays and other entertainment are included on the schedule. The handsome church has been completely restored inside. There is also a very nice gallery in a separate building beside the Chocolate Church (so called because of the chocolate color of this Greek Revival building).

SELECTIVE SHOPPING

ANTIQUES

Along **Front Street** there are a number of interesting shops carrying a wide array of merchandise for the antiques lover. Allow plenty of time for browsing. We especially enjoy **Brick Store Antiques** (443-2790), 143 Front Street, and **Front Street Antiques and Books** (443-8098), 190–192 Front Street.

ART AND ARTISANS

The Greater Bath Cultural Resource Center (442-8455; www.gbcr.org) is a good source of information on the arts in the Bath region.

Georgetown Pottery, Route 127, Georgetown (some 9 miles south of the Carlton Bridge). Jeff Peters produces an extensive selection of dishes, mugs, and other practical pottery pieces, including hummingbird feeders and soap dishes.

BOOKSTORE

Bath Book Shop (443-9338), 96 Front Street, Bath. Finally, there is a great independent bookstore located in Bath's downtown district.

FLEA MARKET

Montsweag Flea Market (443-2809), Route 1, Woolwich. A field filled with tables weighted down by every sort of collectible and curiosity you could

KIM GRANT

Montsweag Flea Market

imagine. It is a beehive of activity, open on Wednesday and weekends.

SPECIAL SHOPS

Bath's **Front Street** is lined with mid-19th-century redbrick buildings. Among the gift shops, don't overlook **Reny's** (46 Front Street), one in a small chain of Maine department stores that are good for genuine bargains. **Yankee Artisan** (56 Front Street) offers a wide selection of Maine crafts and gifts. **Springer's Jewelers** (76 Front Street) is a vintage emporium with mosaic floors, chandeliers, and ornate glass sales cases.

Woodbutcher Tools (442-7938), 873 Route 1, Woolwich. The Shelter Institute (see *To Do—Special Learning Programs*) maintains this woodworker's discovery, specializing in hard-to-find woodworking tools.

Kennebec Angler (442-8239), 97 Commercial Street, Bath. A fisherman's dream, filled with tackle and gear. Demo rods are available for full-day trials before purchasing.

Dronmore Bay Farm (443-4228), Route 209, Phippsburg. Spread along the ridge above Cutting Creek, this cheerful spot offers a formal garden stroll and a wide variety of herbs, wildflowers, fruits, and vegetables. The shop is a nice mix of antiques, seasonal gifts crafted by local artisans, and Millie Clifford's arrangements of dried flowers.

SPECIAL EVENTS

✎ *Three days surrounding the Fourth of July:* **Bath Heritage Days,** a grand celebration with an old-time parade of antique cars, marching bands, clowns, guided tours of the historic district, crafts sales, art shows, musical entertainment in two parks, a triathlon, strawberry shortcake festival, carnival, train, and Fireman's Follies featuring bed races, bucket relays, and demonstrations of equipment and fire-fighting techniques. Fireworks over the Kennebec.

Second Saturday in July: **Popham Circle Fair** at the Popham Chapel features the sale of bird feeders (shaped like the chapel) that residents make all year; profits keep the chapel going.

July and August: Wednesday-evening concerts by the **Bath Municipal Band,** Library Park. In August Bath holds an annual **Bluefish Tournament** in Waterfront Park.

December: **Old-Fashioned Christmas** *(all month)*, with competitions and special events.

Wiscasset

Wiscasset bills itself as "the prettiest village in Maine," and we aren't inclined to argue. After toiling past clusters of commercial activity and crowded downtowns along Route 1, here finally is a bit of the Maine you've imagined. Sea captains' mansions and mid-19th-century shops line the road in this historic village, listed on the National Register of Historic Places since 1973, as it slopes toward the Sheepscot River.

Still the shire town of Lincoln County, Wiscasset is only half as populous as it was in its shipping heyday, which—as the abundance of clapboard mansions attests—came after the American Revolution but before the Civil War. The harbor today is home to local fishermen and recreational boaters.

Several historic buildings in or near the center of town are open to the public, and many more house shops, galleries, and restaurants. Though traffic on Route 1 can be extremely heavy, the village itself is a peaceful place to explore even in the height of summer. Parking spaces can always be found, and the village is small enough to be a pleasant walk from one end to the other.

In recent years there's been an explosion of antiques shops in Wiscasset. On Main Street alone we counted close to a dozen shops, and there are several more scattered down side streets. Many have specialties, but there's a little bit of everything to be found in town.

For 66 years the weathered remains of two early-19th-century four-masted schooners, the *Hesper* and the *Luther Little*, were picturesquely positioned just offshore and often photographed. In May 1998 they were removed and salvaged by the town.

GUIDANCE

The **Wiscasset Regional Business Association,** P.O. Box 150, Wiscasset 04578 (www.wiscassetmaine.com), offers a listing of members and useful local information. **Wiscasset Hardware and General Store** (882-6622), on Water Street (to your left just before you cross the bridge from Wiscasset to Edgecomb), is also a good source of information. Ask for a street map. Park at the Water Street entrance and walk up through the appliances; built in 1797 as a chandlery, this hospitable establishment also offers an upper deck on which to get your bearings with a cup of coffee and a river view.

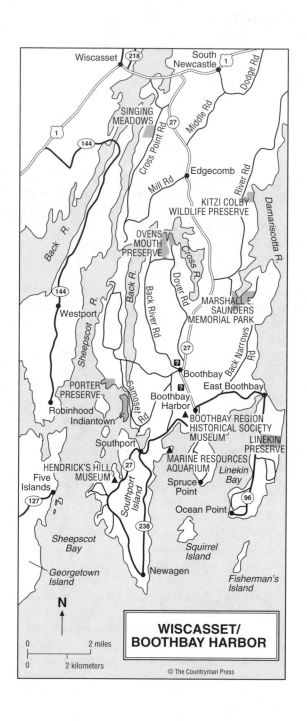

N

0 ——— 2 miles

0 ——— 2 kilometers

**WISCASSET/
BOOTHBAY HARBOR**

© The Countryman Press

GETTING THERE
Concord Trailways (1-800-639-3317) stops here en route from Portland to Bangor. **Downeast Flying Service** (882-6752) offers air charters year-round. **Wiscasset Taxi** (758-1679) serves a 60-mile radius of town, including the airports in Portland, Damariscotta, and Boothbay Harbor.

PARKING
Parking is not a problem here. If you can't find a slot along Main Street, you can always find one in the parking lot or elsewhere along Water Street.

MEDICAL EMERGENCY
Mid Coast Hospital (443-5524), 1356 Washington Street, Bath.

VILLAGES

Sheepscot Village. Go north on Route 218 from Wiscasset; look for the sign in about 4 miles. An unusually picturesque gathering of 19th-century buildings.

Head Tide Village. Eight miles up Route 218 (follow sign), an early-19th-century village that was the birthplace of the poet Edward Arlington Robinson; note the Old Head Tide Church (1838), open Saturday 2–4. Watch for the swimming hole beneath the old milldam.

TO SEE

HISTORIC HOMES
Musical Wonder House (882-7163), 18 High Street. Open daily late May through October, 10–5. An intriguing collection covering two centuries of musical history. Music boxes, reed organs, pump organs, Victrolas, and other musical machines displayed in a fine 1852 sea captain's mansion. Tours of just the ground floor are $10 per person (discounts for children and senior citizens); tours of the entire house are by reservation only. They take about 3 hours and are $30 per person. The gift shop at the Musical Wonder House is open 10–6 every day that the museum is open (no admission charge).

Nickels-Sortwell House (882-6218), corner of Main and Federal Streets. Open June 1 through October 15 , Wednesday through Sunday noon–5 (last tour begins at 4). $4 adults, $3.50 seniors, $2 children 12 and under. This classic Federal-era mansion in the middle of town was built by a shipowner and trader. After he lost his fortune, the house became a hotel for many years. In 1895 a Cambridge, Massachusetts, mayor purchased the property; some of the furnishings date from that time. It is now one of six historic house museums in Maine operated by the Society for the Preservation of New England Antiquities. The elliptical staircase is outstanding.

Castle Tucker (603-436-3205), Lee and High Streets. Open June 1 through

October 15, Tuesday through Saturday 11–4; you're also welcome to walk around the grounds when the house is closed. Admission $4. Castle Tucker was built in 1807 by Judge Silas Lee, who overextended his resources to present his wife with this romantic house. After his death it fell into the hands of his neighbors, to whom it had been heavily mortgaged, and passed through several owners until it was acquired in 1858 by Captain Richard Holbrook Tucker. Captain Tucker, whose descendants owned the house until 1997, added the elegant portico. Castle Tucker is said to be named after a grand house in Scotland. Highlights include a freestanding elliptical staircase, Victorian furnishings, and original wallpapers. This house is also among the six in Maine operated by the Society for the Preservation of New England Antiquities.

HISTORIC SITES

Lincoln County Old Jail and Museum (882-6817), Federal Street (Route 218), Wiscasset. Open July through Labor Day, Tuesday through Saturday 10–4, Sunday 12–4. In June and September open Saturday 10–4 and Sunday 10–2. $3 adults, $2 ages 7–17. The museum comprises a chilling 1811 jail (in use until 1930) with damp, thick granite walls (some bearing interesting 19th-century graffiti), window bars, and heavy metal doors. The jailer's house (in use until 1953) display tools and changing exhibits. Includes an antiques show in August.

Pownalborough Court House (882-6817), Route 128 (off Route 27), Dresden (8 miles north of Wiscasset). Open July through Labor Day, Tuesday through Saturday 10–4, Sunday 12–4. In June and September open Saturday 10–4 and Sunday 10–2. $3 adults, $2 ages 7–17. Worth the drive. The only surviving pre–Revolutionary War courthouse in Maine, it is maintained as a museum by the Lincoln County Historical Association. The three-story building, which includes living quarters for the judge upstairs, gives a sense of this countryside along the Kennebec in 1761, when it was built to serve as an outpost tavern as well as a courtroom. This site is still isolated, standing by a Revolutionary War–era cemetery and a picnic area; there are nature trails along the river. Special events include a mustering of the militia and wreath-laying ceremonies on Memorial Day and a cider pressing in October.

Lincoln County Courthouse. Open during business hours throughout the year. Built in 1824, this handsome redbrick building overlooking the town common is the oldest functioning courthouse in New England.

Fort Edgecomb State Memorial (882-7777), Edgecomb (off Route 1; the turnoff is just across the Sheepscot River's Davey Bridge from Wiscasset, next to the Sheepscot River Inn and restaurant). The fort is open May 30 through Labor Day, daily 9–6. $1; pay in the box. This 27-foot, two-story octagonal blockhouse (built in 1809) overlooks a narrow passage of the Sheepscot River. For the same reasons that it was an ideal site for a fort, it is today an ideal picnic site. Tables are provided on the grassy grounds.

Wiscasset, Waterville, & Farmington Railway Museum (882-6897; www.wwfry.org), Sheepscot Station, Alna (about 5 miles north of Wiscasset, just off Route 218). Open Saturdays year-round 9–5, Sundays from Memorial Day through Columbus Day weekend. An eager group of volunteers help this nonprofit organization preserve the history of the 2-foot narrow-gauge railroads. The museum includes an engine house/shop, replicas of the original Sheepscot station and Weeks Mills freight house, an original flatcar, and the oldest 2-footer locomotive in the United States. Track has been laid, and both steam- and diesel-engine rides are offered. Check for special events.

OTHER SITES

Sunken Garden, Main Street, Wiscasset. Down a few steps, easy to miss, but a wonderful little garden surrounded by a stone wall. Planted by the Sortwell family in the foundation of an old inn, the property was donated to the town in 1959. Quiet and peaceful, with the exception of passing Route 1 traffic sounds, this is a pretty place to take a break from browsing.

✍ **Morris Farm** (882-4080), Route 27, Wiscassset. A community working farm, open to the public during daylight hours for walking, hiking, and picnicking. It offers rolling pastures, forest trails, a pond, a waterfall, and streams. Also includes an education center offering a day camp for children, farm tours, various workshops throughout the year, and special events. Farmer's market Saturday mornings from Memorial Day through Labor Day.

TO DO

Downeast Flying Service (882-6752), Wiscasset, offers year-round sightseeing and fall foliage flights; $50 for up to three passengers.

✍ **Maine Coast Railroad** (882-8000; 1-800-795-5404), at the Wiscasset Town Landing (Water Street, next to Le Garage restaurant). Memorial Day through mid-October. Excursions through the coastal countryside to Bath or Damariscotta/Newcastle (depending on the day of the week) and back aboard a bright red, restored 1920s train; $10 adults, $5 children ages 5–12, family packages. Ask about special events, fall foliage tours, and rail/sail packages.

Ledgewood Riding Stables (882-6346), Bradford Road, Wiscasset. Trail rides Monday through Saturday beginning at 10 AM, Sunday by appointment only.

The Trading Post (882-9645), Route 1, Wiscasset, rents canoes and kayaks, and stocks a large line of canoe and kayak equipment for sale.

LODGING

All listings are in Wiscasset 04578 unless otherwise noted.

INNS

Squire Tarbox Inn (882-7693; www.squiretarboxinn.com), 1181 Westport Island Road (Route 144; turn off Route 1 onto Route 144 just south of Wiscasset), Westport 04578. Open mid-May through late October. The inn, located 8.5 miles down a winding country road from Route 1, is one of the quietest country locations we have found on the coast. The handsome Federal-style farmhouse (begun in 1763, completed in 1825) offers 11 inviting guest rooms and an atmosphere that's a mix of elegance (in the common rooms and dining room) and working goat farm. Guests are invited out to the barn to visit the goats and see how innkeepers Bill and Karen Mitman make their cheeses (Tellicherry pepper, herb and garlic, and jalapeño as well as plain). They can also take advantage of the swing hanging from the barn rafters. Other animals on the farm include a horse, two donkeys, and laying hens. A path leads through the woods to a saltwater inlet where a screened area is equipped with binoculars and a birding book, and where a rowboat awaits your pleasure. Four large, formally furnished guest rooms are in the original house, while seven more country-style rooms are in the 1820s converted barn. All have private baths and either king or queen beds. A five-course, candlelit dinner (see *Dining Out*) is served at 7. Doubles $152–241 MAP; $90–179 includes breakfast only; add 12 percent service charge.

BED & BREAKFASTS

Marston House (882-6010; 1-800-852-4157), Main Street, P.O. Box 517. Open May through October. The front of the house is a shop featuring American antiques. In the carriage house behind this building—well away from the Route 1 traffic noise—are two exceptional rooms, each with private entrance, working fireplace, and private bath. They adjoin each other and can become a two-bedroom suite perfect for families. Breakfast is served in the beautiful gardens or in your room and features fresh fruit, yogurt, home-baked muffins, and fresh orange juice. $90 double, $75 single. No smoking.

Snow Squall (882-6892; 1-800-775-7245; www.maine.com/snowsquall), corner of Bradford Road and Route 1. Open year-round. Anne and Steve Kornacki offer elegant accommodations in this 1850s house named for a clipper ship that was wrecked in the Falkland Islands. The six rooms, each named after a clipper ship built in Maine, offer private baths and king or queen beds. Two guest rooms have fireplaces, as does the library. Doubles are $85–140; carriage-house suites accommodating two to four people are $125–195. Full breakfast included. Rates reduced by 20 percent beginning November 1.

Anniversary Farm Bed and Breakfast (586-5590; 1-877-781-0455; www.anniversaryfarm.com), 2282 Alna Road, Alna 04535. Open year-round. A farmhouse on beautiful grounds overlooking a small pond. Hiking, nearby canoeing, and garden on the premises. Two guest rooms, which can be combined to create a two-room suite. Queen beds and shared bath. There is also a rustic cottage. $85–95 includes breakfast; dinner is available by prior arrangement. Two-night minimum stay.

Cod Cove Farm B&B (882-4299; www.gwi.net/~codcovbb), P.O. Box 94, Edgecomb 04556. Route 27 south. Open most of the year—closed

Squire Tarbox Inn

Thanksgiving to New Year's Day. Four simple but well-thought-out rooms, each decorated around a theme. Our favorites are Moon and Stars, with its willow canopy bed, and Adirondack, with twig furniture and a bed made of birch. $85–105 includes full breakfast.

OTHER LODGING

🐾🛏 **Sheepscot River Inn & Restaurant** (882-6343; 1-800-437-5503; www. sheepscotriverinn.com), 306 Eddy Road (off Route 1, across the bridge from Wiscasset), Edgecomb 04556. Open all year. Commands a fine view of Wiscasset; 25 rooms (including efficiency suites in the lodge) and 15 cottages. Tennis courts on the premises. Next door, the restaurant serves lunch and dinner daily (see *Eating Out*). Pets are accepted. Doubles $79–130 in-season, including continental breakfast buffet.

WHERE TO EAT

DINING OUT

Squire Tarbox Inn (882-7693), 1181 Westport Island Road (Route 144), Westport (also see *Inns*). Open mid-May through late October, by reservation only. A candlelit five-course dinner is served in an 18th-century former barn with a large fireplace reflecting off ceiling beams that were once ship's timbers. Dinner is preceded by a cocktail hour (6 PM) featuring a complimentary selection of savory goat cheeses (made here by innkeepers Karen and Bill Mitman), served in the living room, in the less formal game room, by the player piano, or out on the deck, where bird-watching is exceptional. Dinner begins at 7. The menu changes frequently but might include appetizers like chanterelle mushroom and

Red's Eats

leek bisque, and entrées from roasted rack of lamb in a rosemary Dijon crust to grilled halibut with bouillabaisse sauce. Leave room for dessert, perhaps baked Alaska or frozen white chocolate raspberry mousse torte. Guests are invited to visit the barn to pat the friendly Nubian goats as they line up for milking. The prix fixe is $36 per person (plus 15 percent service charge).

🐐♿ **Le Garage** (882-5409), Water Street, Wiscasset. Open daily in summer for lunch and dinner (additional brunch features on Sunday). Closed for all of January, and Mondays off-season. A 1920s-era garage, now an exceptional restaurant with a glassed-in porch overlooking the Sheepscot River (when you make reservations, request a table on the porch). At dinner many large wrought-iron candelabra provide the illumination. The menu features plenty of seafood choices, steaks, and vegetarian meals. Specialties include traditional finnan haddie, charbroiled native lamb, and seafood Newburg. Entrées are $7.25–18.25. "Light suppers" are also available for $7.25–8.95, giving you the option of smaller portions of many menu selections. The lunch menu features omelets and crêpes, soups and salads, as well as sandwiches. Lunch is $5.95–9.95.

EATING OUT

✑ **Red's Eats,** Water Street, just before the bridge, Wiscasset. Open April through September until 2 AM on Friday and Saturday, until 11 PM weeknights, and noon–6 on Sunday. Al Gagnon has operated this classic hot-dog stand since 1977. Tables on the sidewalk and behind, overlooking the river. A Route 1 landmark for the past 60 years, good for a quick crab roll or pita pocket as well as a hot dog. Special children's meals.

✑ **Sarah's Pizza and Café** (882-7504), Main Street, Wiscasset. Open Monday through Friday 11–9, Saturday and Sunday 6:30 AM–9 PM. A popular spot with an outdoor deck for summer dining. Everything is prepared from scratch, and the extensive menu includes exceptionally good pizza (try the Greek pizza with extra garlic), sandwiches in pita pockets or baked in dough, vegetarian dishes, Mexican fare, and lobster 12 different ways. Well known for their soup and bread bar. Fabulous desserts. Wine and a wide choice of beers, including Maine microbrews, are also served.

✑& **Sheepscot River Inn and Restaurant** (882-7748), Route 1, North Edge-comb (across the bridge from Wiscasset). Open year-round 11–11 daily. Riverside dining room, deck, Sunday jazz brunch. Appetizers might include grilled strawberry spinach salad. Entrées like fried seafood, grilled swordfish, or even châteaubriand for two.

& **The Sea Basket** (882-6581; 1-800-658-1883), Route 1, south of Wiscasset. Open 11–8; closed Tuesdays. Call for hours. The Belanger family has owned and operated this cheerful diner for 20 years. "Famous" lobster stew, which is also sold frozen and shipped all over the country. Other seafood choices include lobster rolls and sea scallops. Bring your own beer or wine.

SELECTIVE SHOPPING

ANTIQUES SHOPS
Antiques are everywhere in Wiscasset. On and just off Water Street, in or attached to attractive old homes, we counted more than 20 shops. Pick up a map (available in most shops) and browse the day away; many specialize in nautical pieces and country primitives.

ART GALLERIES
Maine Art Gallery (882-7511), Warren Street (in the old 1807 academy), Wiscasset. A historic schoolhouse with upper and lower galleries that house exhibits of Maine artists, including Andrew Wyeth, William Zorach, Dahlov Ipcar, and others.

Wiscasset Bay Gallery (882-7682), Water Street. Changing exhibits in attractive spacious exhibit rooms. Specializes in 19th- and 20th-century Maine and New England marine and landscape paintings.

ARTISANS
Sheepscot River Pottery (pastel, floral designs), Route 1 just north of Wiscasset in Edgecomb. **Sirus Graphics,** Wiscasset; mostly made-in-Maine crafts, original-design T-shirts. **Feed the Birds,** Port Wiscasset Building, Water Street; birdhouses, feeders, accessories. **The Butterstamp Workshop,** 55 Middle Street, features exquisite hand-crafted folk art from antique chocolate and butter molds.

SPECIAL EVENTS

June: **Strawberry Festival and County Fair** features strawberries galore, crafts, and an auction.

Early July: **Morris Farm Fair**—animal exhibits, farm tours, crafts, games, and food.

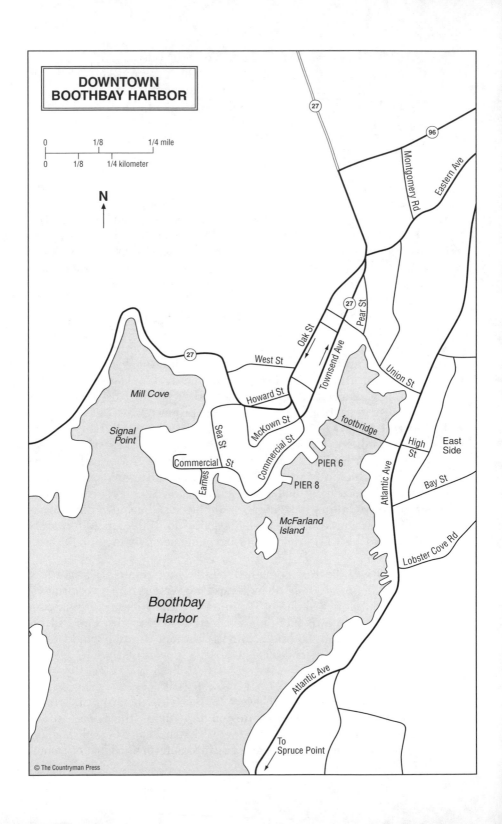

DOWNTOWN
BOOTHBAY HARBOR

0   1/8   1/4 mile
0   1/8   1/4 kilometer

N

Mill Cove

Signal
Point

27

West St

Oak St

Townsend Ave

Pear St

27

Montgomery Rd

Eastern Ave

96

Union St

Howard St

McKown St

footbridge

High
St

East
Side

Sea St

Commercial   St

Commercial St

PIER 6

Atlantic Ave

Bay St

Eames

PIER 8

McFarland
Island

Lobster Cove Rd

Boothbay
Harbor

Atlantic Ave

To
Spruce Point

© The Countryman Press

Boothbay Harbor Region

The water surrounding the village of Boothbay Harbor brings with it more than just a view. You must cross it—via a footbridge—to get from one side of town to the other, and you can explore it on a wide choice of excursion boats and in sea kayaks. It is obvious from the very lay of this old fishing village that its people have always gotten around on foot or in boats. Though parking has increased in recent years, cars don't have room to pass each other, and still feel like an obvious intrusion. The peninsula's other coastal villages, Southport and East Boothbay, also do not lend themselves to exploration by car. Roads are walled by pines, permitting only occasional glimpses of water.

Boats are what all three of the Boothbays have traditionally been about. Boats are built, repaired, and sold here, and sailing and fishing vessels fill the harbors. Excursions range from an hour-long sail around the outer harbor to a 90-minute crossing (each way) to Monhegan Island. Fishermen can pursue giant tuna, stripers, and blues, and nature lovers can cruise out to see seals, whales, and puffins.

In the middle of summer Boothbay Harbor resembles a perpetual carnival, a place everyone plays tourist: licking ice cream cones, chewing freshly made taffy and fudge, browsing in shops and looking into art galleries, listening to band concerts on the library lawn, and, of course, eating lobster. You get the feeling it's been like this every summer since the 1870s.

Boothbay Harbor is just a dozen miles south of Route 1 as the road (Route 27) runs, down the middle of the peninsula. The coastline is, however, a different story, measuring 100 miles as it wanders down the Sheepscot, around Southport Island and up into Boothbay Harbor, out around Spruce Head, around Linekin Bay, out Ocean Point, and back up along the Damariscotta River.

Thanks to the fervor of developers from the 1870s on, this entire coastline is distinguished by the quantity of its summer cottages, many of which can be rented by the week for much less than you might think. Still, thanks to the Boothbay Region Land Trust, there are now also easily accessible waterside preserves with many miles of trail meandering through hundreds of acres of spruce and pines, down to smooth rocks and tidal pools.

It was precisely this landscape that inspired Rachel Carson, who first summered on the peninsula in 1946 and built a cottage on the Sheepscot River in 1953, to write much of *The Edge of the Sea* (1955) and then *Silent Spring,* the book that, when it was published in 1962, changed global thinking about human beings' relation to basic laws of nature.

GUIDANCE

Boothbay Harbor Region Chamber of Commerce (633-2353; www.boothbayharbor.com), P.O. Box 356, Boothbay Harbor 04538. Open year-round. Look for a satellite information booth at the **Bay View Inn** (882-5539), junction of Routes 1 and 12, open mid-May through October, weekends in fringe times, daily in high season. The chamber publishes an annual guide and maintains a Route 27 office stocked with brochures.

The Boothbay Information Center (633-4743), Route 27, Boothbay, (open daily Memorial Day through Columbus Day), is an unusually friendly walk-in center that does its best to help people without reservations find places to stay. It keeps an illustrated scrapbook of options, also a cottage rental list.

Note: You can use the above numbers to find out who has current vacancies.

GETTING THERE

By air or bus: Private planes can fly into the **Wiscasset Airport.** If you fly into the **Portland International Jetport, Boothbay Stage Line** (633-7380) offers 24-hour daily service. They will also pick you up at the nearest **Concord Trailways** bus stop (in Wiscasset, 14 miles away), and from anywhere else within reason.

By car: Take I-95 from Portland, getting off at exit 22 (Brunswick) or exit 24 (Topsham). We prefer the Topsham exit, as you miss the commercial stretch of Route 1 that leads into Brunswick. Follow signs to Route 1 north and connect just beyond Brunswick. Follow Route 1 through Bath and Wiscasset, turning onto Route 27 into Boothbay and Boothbay Harbor.

GETTING AROUND

A **trolley-on-wheels** circulates between the Rocktide Motor Inn on the east side of the harbor and the shops on the west. Runs daily July and August, every 30 minutes, 7–11 AM (check current schedule).

Harbor Scooters (633-3003), Route 27, Boothbay Harbor, is one of the newest ways to get around in summer. Rent a scooter made for two for a half day, a full day, or a week.

PARKING

In-town parking has been substantially increased in the past few years. We had no trouble in August. Stop on your way into town at one of the information centers (see *Guidance*) and pick up a detailed map to downtown. The biggest public lot is at the municipal building.

MEDICAL EMERGENCY

St. Andrew's Hospital (633-2121), Hospital Point, Mill Cove, Route 27 south, Boothbay Harbor. A well respected shoreside hospital, St. Andrew's serves the community by land and by water (the hospital has a pier).

TO SEE

Boothbay Region Historical Society Museum (633-3666), 70 Oak Street, Boothbay Harbor. Open July and August, Wednesday, Friday, and Saturday 10–4; off-season, Saturday 10–2 and by appointment (633-3462). This is a friendly museum filled with photos of hotels and cottage colonies.

Hendricks Hill Museum (633-2370), Route 27, Southport Island. Open July and August, Tuesday, Thursday, Saturday 11–3. An old boarding-house displays pictures of Southport's old boardinghouses and hotels as well as other village memorabilia, wooden boats, and farm implements. Try to time your visit to coincide with the open hours at the **Southport Memorial Library** (Tuesday, Thursday, and Saturday 1–4), which has an impressive butterfly collection. Southport happens to be in the narrow heart of the migratory route of the monarch butterfly.

FOR FAMILIES

✍ **Boothbay Railway Village** (633-4727), Route 27 (1 mile north of Boothbay Harbor). Open daily 9:30–5, mid-June through Columbus Day; weekends beginning Memorial Day. The 2-foot narrow-gauge railway wends its way through a re-created miniature turn-of-the-20th-century village made up of several restored buildings, including vintage railroad stations, the Boothbay Town Hall (1847), and the Spruce Point chapel (1923). Displays include a general store and a doll museum. More than 50 antique autos (1907–1949) are also on display. Admission is $6 adults and $3 children. Many special events, including a large weekend antique auto meet (more than 250 cars) in the latter part of July.

✍ **Marine Resources Aquarium** (633- 9559), McKown Point Road, West Boothbay Harbor. Open 10–5 daily from Memorial Day weekend through September. $3 adults; $2.50 ages 5–18 and over 60; 4 and under free. An octagonal waterside aquarium that's been expanded in recent years. We find it fascinating because, in contrast to the bright tropical fish you usually see in aquariums, here are fish you know by name because you are accustomed to eating them. We were fascinated with silver-and-black striped bass, the prettily dappled cod, and the silver alewife. The stars of the show are, of course, the sharks and skates in the large touch tank. Presentations several times a day in July and August. All the exhibits are the kind that the more you look at them, the more you see. The grounds, overlooking the harbor, are set up for picnicking.

✍ **The By-Way.** Don't miss Boothbay Harbor's old-fashioned harborside boardwalk area. See *To Do—Bowling* and *Where to Eat—Snacks*. Walk from the By-Way down to the footbridge across the harbor.

TO DO

ART STUDIO

∅ **Mackerel Sky Studio** (633-7686), 18 Todd Avenue, Boothbay Harbor. A unique public art studio where you can rent by the hour and do fabric painting, silk painting, floor mats, or paper projects. They frequently offer workshops and special events. Also a retail art-supply store.

BICYCLING

Tidal Transit Co. (633-7140), by the footbridge, Boothbay Harbor, rents mountain bikes. Our favorite bike route begins at Boothbay Village and follows relatively lightly trafficked Barter's Island Road, past Knicker-bocker Lake and Knickerkane Island Park (see *Green Space—Nature Preserves*) to Hogdon Island and on to Barter's Island and the Porter Preserve (again, see *Green Space*).

BOAT EXCURSIONS

∅ **Balmy Days Cruises** (633-2284; 1-800-298-2284), Pier 8, Boothbay Harbor. *Balmy Days II* offers supper cruises and sails to Monhegan every morning from early June through late September and weekends in shoulder seasons (see "Monhegan"); the crossing is 90 minutes each way, and you have close to 4 hours on the island. A half-hour boat ride around the island is sometimes offered. Bring a picnic and hit the trail. *Novelty* offers 1-hour harbor tours all day.

∅ **Boothbay Whale Watch** (633-3500; 1-888-942-5363), Fisherman's Wharf, Boothbay Harbor, offers whale-watches (guaranteed—if you don't see a whale, your next trip is free) and sunset nature cruises daily, guided by naturalists; full bar and galley.

∅ **Cap'n Fish Boat Cruises** (633-3244; 1-800-636-3244), Pier 1 (red ticket booth), Boothbay Harbor. Operates mid-May through mid-October, 7 days a week. A variety of cruises, including whale-watches, puffin nature cruises, Pemaquid Point lighthouse trips, seal-watches, and sunset sails. Friday is senior citizens' day on 2-hour trips. Coffee, snacks, soft drinks, beer, wine, and cocktails are available on board (don't bring your own). Children under 12 are half price.

∅ *Miss Boothbay* (633-6445), Pier 6, Boothbay Harbor, is a lobster boat offering Tuesday-through-Sunday lobster-hauling cruises.

BOAT RENTALS

Midcoast Boat Rentals (633-4188), Pier 8, Boothbay Harbor, rents power-boats on a weekly basis only.

BOWLING

∅ **Romar Bowling Lanes** (633-5721), at the By-Way, Boothbay Harbor. Open summer months only. In business since 1929, under the same ownership since 1946, this log-sided pleasure hall with its sandwich bar,

Boothbay Harbor

pool tables, and video games is a genuine throwback. A great rainy-day haven.

FISHING

Several deep-sea-fishing charters are based in Boothbay Harbor. Check with the chamber of commerce (see *Guidance*) The catch is mackerel, tuna, shark, bluefish, and stripers. Also see *Boat Rentals.*

The Tackle Shop at the White Anchor (633-3788), RR 1, Box 438 (Route 27), Boothbay, is one of the largest tackle shops on the Maine coast.

GOLF

Boothbay Region Country Club (633-6085), Country Club Drive (off Route 27), Boothbay. Open spring through late autumn. Nine holes, restaurant and lounge, carts, clubs for rent.

Dolphin Mini-Golf (633-4828), off Route 27 (turn at the lighthouse), Boothbay; 18 holes.

HORSEBACK RIDING

Ledgewood Riding Stables (882-6346) in Wiscasset has horses and trails for all levels of expertise. Hourly rates.

RECREATIONAL FACILITY

Boothbay Region YMCA (633-2855), Route 27 (on your left as you come down the stretch that leads to town). An exceptional facility open to nonmembers (use-fee charged) in July and August, with special swimming and other programs for children. Worth checking out if you will be in the area for a week or more. A wide variety of programs for all ages: tennis, racquetball, gymnastics, aerobics, soccer, and swimming; the new field house has a three-lane track.

SAILING

Several traditional sailing yachts offer to take passengers out for an hour or two, a half day, or a day. These include *Eastwind* (633-6598) and the *Sylvaina W. Beal* (633-1109), a restored 84-foot schooner built in 1911 in East Boothbay Harbor. *Tribute* (882-1020), a racing yacht, sails from Ocean Point.

SEA KAYAKING

Tidal Transit Co. (633-7140), Boothbay Harbor, in the "Chowder House" building by the footbridge, offers guided tours as well as hourly, half-, and full-day rentals (basic instruction included). Tours include a light-house tour with picnic lunch, 2- to 2½-hour wildlife tours, and sunset tours.

TENNIS

Public tennis courts are located across Route 27 from the YMCA.

GREEN SPACE

BEACHES

Beaches are all private, but visitors are permitted in a number of spots. Here are four: (1) Follow Route 27 toward Southport, across the Townsend Gut Bridge to a circle (white church on your left, monument in the center, general store on your right); turn right and follow Beach Road to the beach, which offers roadside parking and calm, shallow water. (2) Right across from the **Boothbay Harbor Yacht Club** (Route 27 south), just beyond the post office and at the far end of the parking lot, is a property owned by the yacht club, which puts out a float by July. There are ropes to swing from on the far side of the inlet, a grassy area in which to sun, and a small sandy area beside the water, but the water is too deep for small children. (3) **Barrett Park,** Lobster Cove (turn at the Catholic church, east side of the harbor), is a place to picnic and get wet. (4) **Grimes Cove** has a little beach with rocks to climb at the very tip of Ocean Point, East Boothbay. (Also see **Knickerkane Island Park** under *Nature Preserves.*)

GARDEN

Coastal Maine Botanical Gardens (633-4333), P.O. Box 234, Boothbay. Accessible from Barter's Island Road. At the moment, there isn't much there but the land and a dream, but the goal for the 128 acres over the next few years is to create a garden that will protect, preserve, and en-hance the botanical heritage of coastal Maine.

NATURE PRESERVES

Boothbay Region Land Trust (633-4818), 1 Oak Street, Boothbay Har-bor. Open Monday through Friday, 9–4. Pick up a brochure and map to the eight easily accessible properties here, or at the chamber of com-merce (see *Guidance*). Inquire about guided walks. We walked down to the Sheepscot River in the **Porter Preserve** (19 wooded acres, includ-ing a beach) on Barter's Island, accessible by bridge. An osprey peered from its nest atop a marker along a ledge just offshore, and another ledge was so thick with seals that we assumed they were some kind of brown growth—until a dog barked and the entire ledge seemed to heave and rise, then flop and splash off in different directions. We also explored the **Ovens Mouth Preserve,** a narrow passage between the Sheepscot and Back Rivers and a tidal basin. In the mid-1700s this area was settled by families from Dover, New Hampshire. They built ships and cleared pastures—still suggested by the white pines that obviously needed open space to grow so tall, and an occasional apple tree. Separating the two peninsulas that constitute this preserve is Ice House Cove, and across it are the remnants of the 1880s dam that once turned it into a freshwater pond. It's fascinating to think of schooners mooring just outside the dam and sailing for the Caribbean with their cargoes of ice. The former pond has reverted to salt marsh and teems with wildlife. The trust's other properties open for visits are **Linekin Preserve** (a 94½-acre parcel with 2½ miles of hiking trails) on Route 96 south of East Boothbay; **Marshall E. Saunders Memorial Park** (22½ acres) and **Kitzi Colby Wildlife Preserve** (12 acres), both on the Damariscotta River; **Singing Meadows,** a 16-acre former saltwater farm in Edgecomb; **Mill Pond Overlook,** an East Boothbay view that the residents loved enough to raise $90,000 in 90 days to protect; and **Adams Mill Preserve,** the 1⅔-acre site of a 1700s mill.

Knickerkane Island Park, Barter's Island Road, Boothbay. Paths lead from the parking lot onto a small island with picnic tables and swimming.

LODGING

The chamber of commerce lists more than 100 lodging places in its 2000 booklet, from resorts to B&Bs to campgrounds and cottages. Families should explore the possibilities of the area's many rental cottages. Because the chamber of commerce is open year-round, it's possible to contact the people there in time to reserve well in advance. See *Guidance* for the numbers you can call to check current vacancies in the area.

RESORTS

Spruce Point Inn (633-4152; 1-800-553-0289; www.sprucepointinn.com), P.O. Box 237, Boothbay Harbor 04538. Open Memorial Day through late October. A full-service resort at the end of a 100-acre wooded peninsula jutting into Boothbay Harbor. Nine guest rooms are in the main inn, with a private porch and terrific views. Twelve lodge rooms, some with cathedral ceilings and hardwood floors; 40 suites in condo-style structures featuring unusually large bedrooms and baths (with whirlpool soaking tubs), TVs, woodstoves, and balconies with water views; and seven cottages, two oceanfront, perfect for families. Facilities include a large living room, a TV room and study, both formal and informal dining rooms, and a recreation room (geared to kids) beside a freshwater pool; also a saltwater pool and whirlpool on the ocean, clay tennis courts, lawn games, and a private pier. Organized children's programs are available in July and August. $155–505 (for oceanfront cottage); many packages are available; children free under age 4. A service charge is added.

&⟨ **Newagen Seaside Inn** (633-5242; 1-800-654-5242; www.newagenseaside inn.com), Route 27, Southport Island, Cape Newagen 04576. Open mid-May through September. A boxy 1940s building (the original hotel was destroyed by fire) that Peter and Heidi Larsen rejuvenated. It stands at the seaward tip of Southport Island, just 6 miles "out to sea" from Boothbay Harbor, but feels worlds away. Secluded among the pines, the inn's lawn sweeps down to a mile of bold coastline. Don't miss the monument to Rachel Carson on the shore where her ashes were spread. There are 23 rooms and three suites in the main inn, all with private baths. The four first-floor rooms all have private decks. Heated freshwa-ter pool, large saltwater pool, two tennis courts, many lawn games, and rowboats are all included in the rates. Meals are served in the screened dining area. Breakfast is included; lunch and dinner are also available. Doubles are $120–200, depending on room and season. Children are just $10–15 extra. The three cottages begin at $950 per week.

Ocean Point Inn (633-4200; 1-800-552-5554; www.oceanpointinn.com), P.O. Box 409, East Boothbay 04544. Open Memorial Day through Co-lumbus Day. Only 10 minutes from Boothbay Harbor but so tranquil and quiet it feels much farther. Set on 12 acres at the tip of a peninsula, this cluster of traditional white-clapboard buildings is adorned with flower boxes filled with red geraniums. There are a total of 61 rooms, suites, cottages, and apartments, most with ocean views and porches. All rooms and cottages have private baths, cable TV, mini-refrigerators, phones; some have fireplaces; some have air-conditioning. There is a heated pool with a hot tub alongside it, and guests can relax in Adiron-dack chairs on the seawall overlooking the ocean. The inn also offers an oceanfront dining room (see *Dining Out*). $105–175 in-season.

INNS AND BED & BREAKFASTS

Five Gables Inn (633-4551; 1-800-451-5048), Murray Hill Road (off Route 96), P.O. Box 335, East Boothbay 04544. Open mid-May through Octo-ber. Built around 1890, this rambling building is a luxurious B&B with a historic feel. Mike and De Kennedy offer guests 15 comfortable rooms, all with ocean views and private baths; most have queen-sized beds (many with handmade quilts), and 5 have working fireplaces. A few of the rooms have spectacular murals created by a local artist. You have to see them to truly appreciate the atmosphere they create. Mike has crafted some great built-in touches, ranging from beds to bookshelves. Almost all the guests are couples, and the atmosphere is low-key and romantic. There are rocking chairs on the wraparound veranda and a welcoming fireplace in the common room; an extensive buffet break-fast, prepared by Mike, a Culinary Institute of America graduate, is included in $110–175 double. Afternoon tea is also offered.

Hodgdon Island Inn (633-7474; www.hodgdonislandinn.com), Barter's Island Road, Boothbay (mailing address: Box 492, Boothbay 04571). Open year-round. On a quiet road overlooking a cove. New owners Peter Wilson and Peter Moran offer eight rooms with water views in a restored sea captain's house. All have private baths and ceiling fans, and two of the rooms share a porch. The heated swimming pool is set in a landscaped garden, and the living room has a gas fireplace, TV, VCR, books, and games. A large front porch with white wicker furniture is another space to relax, as are benches on the waterfront. $105–135 includes full breakfast.

Welch House (633-3431; 1-800-279-7313; www.welchhouse.com), 56 McKown Street, Boothbay Harbor 04538. Open April through early December. A view of the harbor and islands beyond can be enjoyed from most of the 16 individually decorated rooms. A new common area with paneled walls, hardwood floor, fireplace, and leather couches is a wonderful gathering spot. The views from a third-floor observation deck, main deck, and glass-enclosed breakfast room are definitely hard to beat, especially combined with a downtown location. $85–165 off-season includes a full breakfast.

🐾 **Lawnmeer Inn** (633-2544; 1-800-633-7645; www.lawnmeer.com), Box 505, West Boothbay Harbor 04575 (on Route 27 on Southport Island, 2 miles from downtown Boothbay Harbor). Open mid-May through mid-October. The location is difficult to beat, with broad lawns sloping to the water's edge. Most of the 13 comfortably decorated rooms in the main inn, and the 18 rooms (with decks) in the motel wing, have water views; there's also a small cottage. The Lawnmeer, built as a summer hotel in the 1890s, has a small, personal feel with lots of attractive common space. There is also a popular restaurant (see *Dining Out*). Small pets are accepted in a few of the motel wing rooms. $95–145 in summer; less off-season. Two-night minimum weekends in July and August.

🎖 **Lion d'Or** (633-7367; 1-800-887-7367; www.gwi.net/liondor), 106 Townsend Avenue, Boothbay Harbor 04538. Fern Robichaud redecorated this 1857 Victorian home, lightening the interior with pretty pastel colors. She welcomes guests in five bedrooms, each with private bath and cable TV. Breakfast, which is included in her reasonable rates, features homemade granola, fruit, breads or muffins, and a gourmet entrée. $75–105; less off-season.

Linekin Bay Bed & Breakfast (633-9900; www.linekinbaybb.com), HC 65, Box 771, East Boothbay 04544. Open year-round. Quiet and peaceful, but just minutes away from the activity in the harbor. A nicely decorated 1878 home overlooking Linekin Bay. Three of the four attractive rooms have strategically placed beds to maximize the water views; two have fireplaces. $105–175 includes full breakfast; less off-season.

1830 Admiral's Quarters Inn (633-2474; www.admiralsquartersinn.com),

71 Commercial Street, Boothbay Harbor 04538. Open most of the year. Les and Deb Hallstrom have done a great job renovating this big old sea captain's house. The six tidy, bright (frill-free) rooms, most two-room suites, have private baths, phones, cable TV, air conditioning, fireplaces, and decks, with a seagull's-eye view of the waterfront. The sitting room is a solarium with that same great view. The gardens are gorgeous, the sliding swing inviting. $135–165 in high season includes breakfast.

🐾🍷 **Topside** (633-5404; 1-877-486-7466; www.gwi.net/topside), 60 McKown Street, Boothbay Harbor 04538. Open May through October. This combination inn and motel has a lot going for it: its location at the top of McKown Hill with views over the harbor; its comfortable rooms with private baths, both in the 1876 house and the two 2-story motel-style annexes; and its reasonable rates: $67–155 (for two-bedroom units with kitchens), continental breakfast included; from $45 off-season.

Atlantic Ark Inn (633-5690 ; www.atlanticarkinn.com), 62 Atlantic Avenue, Boothbay Harbor 04538. Open late May through October. Simply furnished with antiques and Oriental rugs, this pleasant B&B is removed (but accessible by footbridge) from the bustle of the harbor. Six rooms; all have private baths; some have harbor views and private balconies. One of the third-floor rooms has a cathedral ceiling, an oak floor, a Jacuzzi, a panaroamic view of the harbor through 17 windows, and French doors opening onto a balcony. This room can be combined with the other third-floor room to form a suite with private entrance. Full breakfast might include entrées like zucchini crescent pie or old-fashioned bread pudding with strawberries. Iced tea, iced coffee, or springwater are served in the afternoon on the wraparound porch. $99–175. Two-night stays on weekends.

COTTAGES

Note: Contact the chambers of commerce (see *Guidance*) for lists of rental cottages; quality is traditionally high and prices are affordable in the Boothbays. In addition, the locally based **Cottage Connection of Maine** (663-6545; 1-800-823-9501; www.cottageconnection.com) represents dozens of properties.

🐾🍷 **Ship Ahoy Motel** (633-5222; www.shipahoymotel.com), Route 238, Southport (mailing address: Box 235, Boothbay Harbor 04538). Open late May through mid-October. We are embarrassed that it took us so long to discover this fabulous find (and we never would have, had it not been for an English friend): a family-owned motel with 54 tidy units, all with TV and air-conditioning, many with private balconies right on the water, also a pool and a coffee shop on a total ¾ mile of waterfront. $39–69 per couple in high season; $29–49 off-season.

🐾🐾🍷 **Hillside Acres Cabins and Motel** (633-3411; hillside@clinic.net), Adams Pond Road (just off Route 27), P.O. Box 300, Boothbay 04537. Open year-round. Seven comfortable cabins, including three efficiency units, and a motel building with four apartments and two B&B rooms. Electric heat, showers, color TVs. Swimming pool. Complimentary muffins, coffee cake, and coffee are served late June through Labor Day. $40–70; weekly rates.

Boothbay Harbor has a number of inviting motels, many of them expansive and on the water, but we defer to the Mobil and AAA guides.

WHERE TO EAT

DINING OUT

Lawnmeer Inn (633-2544; 1-800-633-7645), Route 27, Southport Island (just across the bridge). Open for breakfast and dinner daily in-season. Off-season hours vary; call ahead. Reservations appreciated. Large windows in this pleasant dining room overlook the water. The menu changes frequently but might include Maine lobster in Thai green curry, or roast duckling breast with blueberry chutney. Some people come just for dessert. Entrées $15–27.

✎ **Andrew's Harborside Restaurant** (633-4074), Boothbay Harbor (downtown, next to the municipal parking lot and footbridge). Open daily May through October, for breakfast, lunch, and dinner. The chef-owner specializes in creative seafood and traditional New England dishes. Wonderful cinnamon rolls at breakfast, the usual crab rolls and burgers at lunch, Round Top ice cream at the window, and seafood entrées at dinner, which ranges from fish-and-chips to lobster pie; also pasta, steak, salads, and a great, informal waterside atmosphere.

✎ **Lobsterman's Wharf** (633-3443), Route 96, East Boothbay (adjacent to a boatyard). Open mid-May through Columbus Day, serving until midnight. Perhaps it's because we had a waterside table, but this big old restaurant, decorated with lobster buoys, backlit stained glass, snowshoes, and ship models (for starters), rates high on our list. Just far enough off the beaten track to escape crowds, it's popular with locals. The large menu includes all the usual seafood, also pastas and pizzas. We dined well on lobster stew, crabcakes, spinach salad, and a decent house wine. Entrées from $4.50 for a burger to $18.25 for a mixed seafood grill, not counting lobster (market price).

Spruce Point Inn (633-4152), east side of outer harbor at Spruce Point. Open mid-June through mid-September; reservations advised. A gracious, old-fashioned inn with a sophisticated menu to match its decor. Entrées might include marinated breast of chicken with tropical salsa, North Atlantic salmon grilled or pan-roasted in a dill sauce, or cioppino. $14.75–24.50.

♿ **Newagen Seaside Inn** (633-5242; 1-800-654-5242), Route 27, Southport Island, Cape Newagen. Open for breakfast, lunch, and dinner seasonally; closed for dinner on Tuesday. A pleasant, old-fashioned dining room with ocean and sunset views, and splendid grounds to walk off the entrées. Chef Eric Botka delights diners with entrées like Poulet Provençal and seared pork medallions. Desserts are wonderful.

✑& **Ocean Point Inn Restaurant** (633-4200; 1-800-552-5554), East Boothbay. Open mid-June through Columbus Day weekend. Serving full breakfast buffet in summer, continental breakfast off-season, and dinner nightly. Reservations suggested. Over 100 years of tradition in these three informal dining rooms with ocean views. Choices might include roast beef, fresh Maine salmon (prepared four ways), and Black Angus steaks. Children's menu. $12.95–23.95.

EATING OUT

✑ **Ebb Tide** (633-5692), Commercial Street, Boothbay Harbor. Open year-round, 6:30 AM–8 PM; till 8:30 PM on Friday and Saturday. Great breakfasts are served all day, plus lobster rolls, club sandwiches, fisherman's platters, and reasonably priced specials. Homemade desserts like peach shortcake are wonderful. Old-fashioned, with knotty-pine walls, booths; look for the red-striped awning.

✑ **Chowder House Restaurant** (633-5761), Granary Way, Boothbay Harbor (beside the municipal parking lot and footbridge). Serves lunch and dinner daily mid-June through Labor Day. A restored old building that also houses several small shops. Seating is around an open kitchen and on a waterside deck. There is also an outdoor boat bar. Chowders, lobster stew, salads, homemade breads, seafood, and full dinners. Homemade pies. Children's menu.

MacNab's (633-7222; 1-800-884-7222), Back River Road (first driveway on your left), Boothbay. Open Tuesday through Saturday 10–5. A Scottish-style tearoom serving cock-a-leekie soup, scone sandwiches, and Highland pie as well as tea and scones; afternoon tea and high tea by reservation.

✹ **Everybody's** (633-6113), Route 27, Boothbay Harbor. Open year-round for breakfast, lunch, and dinner. A casual, inexpensive place that's popular with locals. Salad entrées plus light suppers and dinners. Sandwiches at lunchtime.

J. H. Hawk Ltd. (633-5589), Boothbay Harbor (right on the dock in the middle of town, upstairs). Liberally decorated with nautical artifacts, a large menu ranging from basic burgers to pastas and steaks, pan-blackened fish, and Louisiana Cajun–style meat dishes. Ask about live entertainment.

Carriage House (633-6025), Ocean Point Road, East Boothbay. Open year-round, daily 11–10. Entrées range from a fried fisherman's platter and charbroiled beef to pastas and sandwiches. Daily specials always include an all-you-can-eat haddock fry.

✑ **Brud's Hotdogs,** in the middle of the village and on the east side of the harbor. Keep an eye out for Brud's orange motorized cart—he has been selling juicy dogs around town for more than 50 summers.

Dunton's Doghouse, Signal Point Marina, Boothbay Harbor. Open May through September, 11–8. Good, reasonably priced take-out food, including a decent $4.25 crabmeat roll.

LOBSTER POUNDS

🦞 **Robinson's Wharf** (633-3830), Route 27, Southport Island (just across Townsend Gut from West Boothbay Harbor). Open mid-June through Labor Day; lunch and dinner daily. Children's menu. Sit on the dock at picnic tables and watch the boats unload their catch. Pick out your lobster before it's cooked, or buy some live lobsters to prepare at home. Seafood rolls (fresh-picked lobster meat in the lobster rolls), fried shrimp, clams, scallops, fish chowder, lobster stew, sandwiches, and homemade desserts. Take-out available.

Boothbay Region Lobstermen's Co-op (633-4900), Atlantic Avenue (east side of the harbor), Boothbay Harbor. Open mid-May through mid-October, 11:30–8. Boiled lobsters and steamed clams to be eaten at picnic tables on an outside deck, on the water or indoors. Corn on the cob, fried seafood dinners, desserts.

🦞 **Clambake at Cabbage Island** (633-7200). The *Argo* departs Pier 6 at Fisherman's Wharf daily in summer, twice on Saturday and Sunday, carrying passengers to 6-acre Cabbage Island for a clambake (including steamed lobsters), served on picnic tables. An old lodge, built in 1900, seats up to 100 people by a huge fireplace.

The Lobster Dock (633-7120), Boothbay Harbor, at the east end of the footbridge. Open seasonally noon–8:30. When downtown Boothbay restaurants are packed, you can walk across the footbridge to this relatively peaceful little place, offering both inside and outside lunches and dinners. Featuring lobster and shore dinners, steamed clams, mussels, steaks, prime rib, and more.

SNACKS

🍦 **Greater Boothbay Ice Cream Factory** (633-2816), the By-Way, Boothbay Harbor. Homemade ice cream and make-your-own sundae buffet; all sorts of toppings, including real hot fudge.

🍦 **Daffy Taffy and Fudge Factory** (633-5187), the By-Way, Boothbay Harbor. Watch taffy being pulled, designed, and wrapped—then chew! The fudge is made with fresh cream and butter.

Cream teas are served at **MacNabs;** see *Eating Out.*

ENTERTAINMENT

🎭 **Carousel Music Theatre** (633-5297), Route 27, near Boothbay Harbor. Performances mid-May through late October. Doors open at 6:30 PM; show begins at 7. Closed Sundays. Light meals (sandwich baskets and such) and cocktails are served by the cast before they hop onto the stage to sing Broadway tunes cabaret-style and then to present a fully costumed and staged revue of a Broadway play.

Thursday-evening concerts by the Hallowell Band on the library lawn,

Boothbay Harbor. July 4 through Labor Day, 8 PM.

Lincoln Arts Festival (633-4676). Concerts throughout the summer in varied locations.

SELECTIVE SHOPPING

ART GALLERIES

Gleason Fine Art (633-6849), 7 Oak Street, Boothbay Harbor. Tuesday through Saturday 10–5. Museum-quality paintings by Farfield Porter and James Fitzgerald, as well as sculpture and paintings by some of Maine's best contemporary artists.

ARTISANS

"The Lincoln County Cultural Guide" is a great starting point for finding artisans in the area. Categorical listings make finding what you want quite simple. The guide is available at the chamber.

Boothbay Harbor Artisans (633-1152), 11 Granary Way, Boothbay Harbor. A cooperative crafts market featuring a wide variety of gifts, including interesting stained glass, pottery, and gourmet food items.

Boothbay Region Art Foundation (633-2703), 7 Townsend Avenue, Boothbay Harbor. Open daily 11–5 weekdays and Saturday noon–5 on Sunday. Three juried shows are held each season in the 1807 Old Brick House. Works are selected from submissions by artists of the Boothbay region and Monhegan Island.

Andersen Studio (633-4397), Route 96 at Andersen Road, East Boothbay. Acclaimed stoneware animal sculptures of museum quality.

Nathaniel S. Wilson (633-5071), East Boothbay. A sailmaker who also fashions distinctive tote bags from canvas. Call for directions.

Hasenfus Glass Shop (633-6228), Commercial Street, Boothbay Harbor. It's called glassblowing, but it's really the heating and bending of glass tubes into all sorts of imaginative ornaments, from sailing ships to tiny animals.

A Silver Lining, 21 Townsend Avenue, Boothbay Harbor. Working metal-smiths. Original sculpture and jewelry in brass, sterling, and gold; an exceptional store.

Edgecomb Potters, Route 27, Edgecomb. Open year-round. Also a seasonal shop on McKown Street in Boothbay Harbor. Maine's largest, most famous pottery store (with branches in Portland and Freeport). A two-tiered gallery filled with deeply colored pots, vases, and table settings, lamps, bowls, cookware, and jewelry. There's also a sculpture garden and a small seconds corner.

Abacus Gallery, 12 McKown Street, Boothbay Harbor. Contemporary crafts, fine furniture, whimsical pieces. Worth a look.

Gold/Smith Gallery, 41 Commercial Street, Boothbay Harbor. Contemporary art and an unusual selection of jewelry in gold and silver.

SPECIAL SHOPS

The Palabra Shop, 85 Commercial Street, Boothbay Harbor, across from

Hasenfus Glass. A warren of more than a dozen rooms offering everything from kitschy souvenirs to valuable antiques. Upstairs (open by request) is a Poland Spring Museum with an impressive collection of the Moses bottles this natural springwater used to come in, plus other memorabilia from the heyday of the resort at Poland Spring.

Sherman's Book & Stationery Store, 7 Commercial Street, Boothbay Harbor. A two-story emporium filled with souvenirs, kitchenware, and games, as well as a full stock of books; specializing in nautical titles.

SPECIAL EVENTS

April: **Fishermen's Festival**—contests for fishermen and lobstermen, cabaret ball, crowning of the Shrimp Princess, tall-tale contest, boat parade, and blessing of the fleet.

Late June–early July: **Windjammer Days**—parade of windjammers into the harbor, fireworks, band concert, street dance, church suppers, parade of floats, bands, and beauty queens up Main Street. The big event of the summer.

July: **Friendship Sloop Days**—parade and race of traditional fishing sloops built nearby in Friendship. **Antique Auto Days,** Boothbay Railway Village, Route 27. **Harbor Jazz Weekend.**

October: **Fall Foliage Festival**—boat cruises to view foliage, as well as food booths, craft sales, live entertainment, antique auto museum, steam train rides.

Early December: **Harbor Lights Festival**—parade, crafts, holiday shopping.

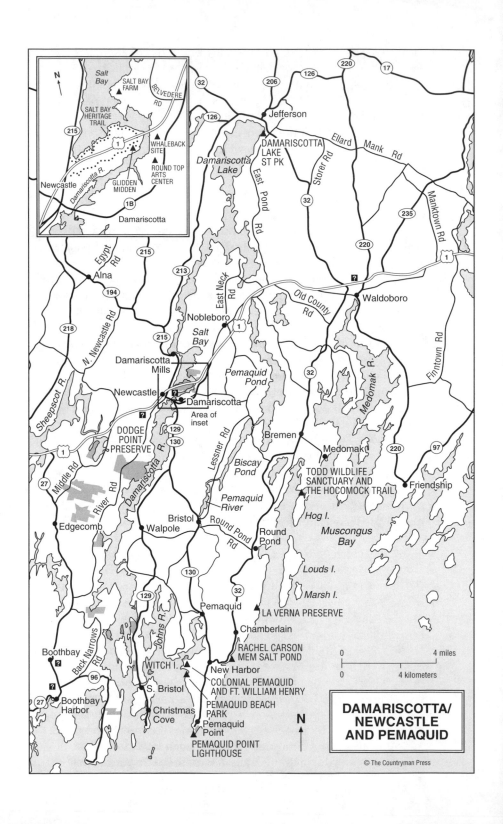

DAMARISCOTTA/
NEWCASTLE
AND PEMAQUID

© The Countryman Press

Damariscotta/Newcastle and Pemaquid Area

Damariscotta is a small region of large, quiet lakes, long tidal rivers, and almost 100 miles of meandering coastline, all within easy striking distance of Route 1. It encompasses the Pemaquid Peninsula communities of Bristol, Pemaquid, New Harbor, and Round Pond as well as communities around Lake Damariscotta, the exceptional twin villages of Damariscotta and Newcastle, and neighboring Waldoboro.

Damariscotta's musical name means "meeting place of the alewives," and in spring spawning alewives can indeed be seen climbing more than 40 feet up a newly restored fish ladder, from Great Salt Bay to the fresh water in Damariscotta Lake.

The area's first residents must also have found an abundance of oysters here, judging from the shells they heaped over the course of 1,500 years, on opposite banks of the river just below Salt Bay. Native Americans also had a name for the peninsula jutting 10 miles seaward from this spot: Pemaquid, meaning "long finger."

Pemaquid loomed large on 16th- and 17th-century maps because its protected inner harbor was the nearest mainland haven for Monhegan, a busy fishing area for European fishermen. It was from these fishermen that the Pemaquid Native American Samoset learned the English with which he welcomed the Pilgrims at Plymouth in 1621. It was also from these fishermen that Plimoth Plantation, the following winter, secured supplies enough to see it through to spring. Pemaquid, however, lacked a Governor William Bradford. Although it is occasionally referred to as this country's first permanent settlement, its historical role remains murky.

The site of Maine's "Lost City" is a mini-peninsula bordered by the Pemaquid River and Johns Bay (named for Captain John Smith, who explored here in 1614). At one tip stands a round stone fort. In recent years more than 40,000 artifacts have been unearthed in the adjacent meadow, many of them now on display in a small state-run museum. An old cemetery full of crooked slate headstones completes the scene.

Since the 19th-century steamboats began bringing guests, this region has supported an abundance of summer inns and cottages. It is especially appealing to families with young children since it offers warm-water lakes, including 15-mile-long Damariscotta, which has the kind of clarity and largely wooded shore that you expect to find much farther inland.

Pemaquid Light is pictured in countless calendars and books because it not only looks just like a lighthouse should but stands atop dramatic but clamber-friendly rocks, composed of varied seams of granite schist and softer volcanic rock, ridged in ways that invite climbing, and pocked with tidal pools that demand stopping.

While there is plenty to see and to do (and to eat), it's all scattered just widely enough to disperse tourist traffic. The villages are small. Damariscotta, just a few streets built of mellow old local brick, is the region's compact shopping, dining, and entertainment hub.

GUIDANCE

Damariscotta Region Chamber of Commerce (563-8340; www. drcc.org), P.O. Box 13, Damariscotta 04543. The chamber office, open year-round, weekdays 9–5, fronts on the parking lot just off Main Street beside the Salt Bay Café. Inquire about cottage rentals.

GETTING THERE

By bus: **Concord Trailways** (1-800-639-8080) stops in Damariscotta and Waldoboro en route from Portland to Bangor.

By air: **Mid Coast Limo** (1-800-834-5500 within Maine; 1-800-937-2424 outside the state) runs to and from the Portland International Jetport. Most inns on the peninsula will pick up guests in Damariscotta, but basically this is the kind of place where you will want to have a car—or a boat—to get around. **Wiscasset Taxi** (758-1679) also serves the Damariscotta area.

By car: The obvious way is up Route 1, but if you are stuck in the summer traffic backed up in Wiscasset Village, you might want to avoid the worst of the crunch by heading up Route 28 for 4.5 miles to Sheepscot Road, cross the river into Sheepscot Village, and continue until it meets Route 1.

PARKING

Parking in Damariscotta is much better than it first looks. Large lots are sequestered behind buildings on both sides of Main Street.

MEDICAL EMERGENCY

Miles Memorial Hospital (563-1234), Bristol Road, Damariscotta.

VILLAGES

Damariscotta/Newscastle. The twin villages of Newcastle and Damariscotta (connected by a bridge) form the commercial center of the region. The main street is flanked by fine brick commercial buildings built after the fire of 1845. Shops and restaurants are tucked down alleyways. Note the towns' two exceptional churches and check the program of concerts and festivals at the Round Top Center for the Arts on Upper

Main Street (see *Entertainment*). Damariscotta Mills, a short drive up Route 215 from Newcastle, has some elegant houses and a great picnic spot on Lake Damariscotta.

Waldoboro. An inscription in the cemetery of the Old German Church (see *To See—Historic Churches*) relates the deceptive way in which landholder General Samuel Waldo lured the town's first German settlers here. The church and much of the town overlook the tidal Medomak (pronounced with the emphasis on "Med") River. Bypassed by Route 1, this village on the Medomak includes some architecturally interesting buildings, one of the country's oldest continuously operating five-and-dimes, and a theater presenting films, concerts, and live performances. The **Waldoborough Historical Society Museum,** Route 220, just south of Route 1 (open daily 1–4:30 in summer months) includes a restored school, a barn and hall housing plenty of colorful local memorabilia, also a town pound. Free.

Round Pond. The name was obviously inspired by the village's almost circular harbor, said to have been a pirate base. It was once a major shipbuilding spot, and still is a working fishing and lobstering harbor. (Also see *Where to Eat—Lobster Pounds.*)

New Harbor. As picturesque a working harbor as any in Maine. Take South Side Road to Back Cove and walk out on the wooden pedestrian bridge for a great harbor view. Note the Samoset Memorial, honoring the Native American who greeted the Pilgrims at Plymouth and also sold land here, creating the first deed executed in New England. The village itself is far bigger than it looks at first. **Hanna's Garage,** for instance, looks like a Mobil station but inside is a serious hardware and marine-supply store with an upstairs (past the huge moosehead) stocked with clothing ranging from T-shirts and Woolrich jackets to clamming gear, and **E. E. Reilly & Son** (established 1828) offers far more than most supermarkets.

South Bristol. Find a parking space as near as you can to the cluster of charming houses and shops around a busy drawbridge.

Jefferson, the village at the head of Damariscotta Lake, also at the junction of Routes 126, 32, and 206. Old farmhouses, a general store, and summer homes along the river now form the core of the village, and Damariscotta Lake State Beach is on the fringe. Be sure to drive west a couple of miles on Route 213 to Bunker Hill with its old church commanding a superb panorama down the lake.

TO SEE

HISTORIC SITES
🖋 **Colonial Pemaquid State Historic Site** (677-2423), Pemaquid (off Route 130). Maintained by the state Bureau of Parks and Lands and open daily Memorial Day through Labor Day, 9:30–5. Admission, $1 adults, also

Pemaquid Light

gains you entry to Fort William Henry and Old Fort House; free rest rooms. In the early 19th century local farmers filled in the cellar holes of the 17th-century settlement that once stood here. Archaeologists have uncovered the foundations of early-17th-century homes, a customs house, a tavern, and the jail. The museum displays dioramas of the original 1620s settlement and period tools and pottery, Spanish oil jars, and wampum— all found in the cellar holes just outside. Nearby, the old burial ground, dating from 1695, overlooks the quiet inner harbor. Inquire about evening lectures sponsored by the Friends of Colonial Pemaquid.

Fort William Henry, off Route 130, Pemaquid Harbor. Open daily Memorial Day through Labor Day, 9:30–5. (For admission, see above.) This round, crenellated stone fort, built in 1907, is one of New England's very few reminders of the French and Indian Wars. It replicates 1692 Fort William Henry, the third fort on this spot, built to be "the most expensive and strongest fortification that has ever been built on American soil," but destroyed by the French a year later. Fort Frederick, built in 1729, was never attacked, but during the American Revolution locals tore it down lest it fall into the hands of the British. The present building contains exhibits on the early explorations of Maine and enshrines the "Rock of Pemaquid," obviously meant as a rival Plymouth Rock, suggesting that settlers alighted on it long before the Pilgrims ever got to Plymouth. Both the proven and possible history of this place are fascinating: The stockade built on this spot in 1630 is said to have been sacked and burned by pirate Dixie Bull. In 1677 Governor Andros built a wooden redoubt fortified by 50 men, but this was captured by Baron Castine and his Native allies (see "Castine"). The striking 1790 captain's house adjacent to the fort is also slated to be open to the public. Picnic tables on the grounds command water views.

✐ **Pemaquid Point Lighthouse** (677-2494/2726), Route 130 (at the end), Pemaquid Point. The point is owned by the town, which charges an entrance fee during the summer. The lighthouse, built in 1824 and automated in 1934, is a beauty, looking even more impressive from the rocks below than from up in the parking lot. These rocks offer a wonderfully varied example of geological upheaval, with tilted strata and igneous intrusions. The tidal pools can occupy children and adults alike for an entire day, but take care not to get too close to the water; the waves can be dangerous. The rocks stretch for a half mile to Kresge Point. The **Fishermen's Museum,** housed in the former lighthouse keeper's home, is open Memorial Day through Columbus Day, Monday through Saturday 10–5 and Sunday 11–5. It contains photographs, ship models, and other artifacts related to the Maine fishing industry, as well as a description of the coast's lighthouses. Voluntary donations. The complex also includes the **Pemaquid Art Gallery,** picnic tables, and public toilets.

Thompson Ice House (644-8551 in summer; 729-1956 in winter), Route 129 in South Bristol, 12 miles south of Damariscotta. Open July and August, Wednesday, Friday, and Saturday 1–4. One of the few surviving commercial icehouses in New England, this 150-year-old family business uses traditional tools for cutting ice from an adjacent pond. In summer a slide and video presentation shows how the ice is harvested (in February); tools are also on display.

✐ **Old Rock Schoolhouse,** Bristol (follow signs from Route 130 to Route 132). Open during summer months, Tuesday and Friday 2–4. Dank and haunting, this 1827 rural stone schoolhouse stands at a long-overgrown crossroads in the woods.

Shell heaps. These ancient heaps of oyster shells, left by generations of Native Americans at their summer encampments in what are now the villages of Newcastle and Damariscotta, have become incorporated into the hillsides along the riverbank. The heaps—or middens, as they are called—are accessible via the **Great Salt Bay Preserve Heritage Trail** (see *Green Space—Nature Preserves*).

Chapman-Hall House, corner of Main and Church Streets, Damariscotta. Open mid-June through mid-September daily, except Monday, 1–5. Built in 1754, this is the oldest homestead in the region. The house has been restored with its original kitchen, and an herb garden with 18th-century rosebushes.

HISTORIC CHURCHES

This particular part of the Maine coast possesses an unusual number of fine old meetinghouses and churches, all of which are open to the public.

Old German Church (832-5100), Route 32, Waldoboro. Open daily during July and August, 1–4. Built in 1772 with square-benched pews and a wineglass pulpit; note the inscription in the cemetery: "This town was settled in 1748 by Germans who immigrated to this place with the promise and expectation of finding a prosperous city, instead of which they found nothing but wilderness." Bostonian Samuel Waldo—owner of a large tract of land in this area—had not been straight with the 40 German families he brought to settle it. This was the first Lutheran church in Maine; it's maintained by the German Protestant Society. You may recognize this as the setting of one of Andrew Wyeth's most famous Helga paintings.

St. Patrick's Catholic Church (563-6038), Academy Road, Newcastle (Route 215 north of Damariscotta Mills). Open daily year-round, to sunset. This is the oldest surviving Catholic church (1808) in New England. It is an unusual building: brick construction, very narrow, and graced with a Paul Revere bell. The pews and stained glass date from 1896, and there is an old graveyard out back. Mass is frequently said in Latin.

St. Andrew's Episcopal Church (563-3533), Glidden Street, Newcastle. A charming half-timbered building on the bank of the Damariscotta River. Set among gardens and trees, it was the first commission in this country for Henry Vaughan, the English architect who went on to design the National Cathedral in Washington, D.C.

Old Walpole Meeting House (563-5318), Route 129, South Bristol. Open during July and August, Sunday for 3 PM services, and by appointment. A 1772 meetinghouse with box pews and a pulpit with a sounding board.

Harrington Meeting House, Route 130, Pemaquid. Open during July and August, Monday, Wednesday, Friday, and Saturday 2–4:30. Donations accepted. The 1772 building has been restored and serves as a museum of Old Bristol. A nondenominational service is held here once a year, usually on the third Sunday in August.

SCENIC DRIVES

From Newcastle, Route 215 winds along **Damariscotta Lake** to Damariscotta Mills (see map on page 230); continue along the lake and through farm country on Route 213 (note the scenic pullout across from the Bunker Hill Church, with a view down the lake) to Jefferson for a swim at **Damariscotta Lake State Park.**

Pemaquid Peninsula. Follow Route 129 south from Damariscotta, across the **South Bristol Bridge** to **Christmas Cove.** Backtrack and cross the peninsula via **Harrington Meeting House Road** to **Colonial Pemaquid** and **Pemaquid Beach** (this corner of the world is particularly beautiful at sunset). Turn south on Route 130 to **Pemaquid Point** and return via Route 32 and **Round Pond;** take Biscay Road back to Damariscotta or continue on Route 32 into Waldoboro.

TO DO

BIRDING

National Audubon Ecology Camp, Hog Island (a quarter mile offshore at the head of Muscongus Bay). June through August. One-week programs including family and adult camps and a 10-day Youth Camp (for 10- to

14-year-olds) focusing on the island's wildlife; also boat trips to see the puffins that were reintroduced to nearby Eastern Egg Rock by the Audubon-related Puffin Project. There are 5 miles of spruce trails, wildflower and herb gardens, and mudflats surrounding rustic bungalows and a dining room in a restored 19th-century farmhouse. For details, call 203-869-2017 or write to the National Audubon Society Ecology Camps and Workshops, 613 Riverville Road, Greenwich, CT 06831.

Also see *Green Space.*

BOAT EXCURSIONS

Hardy Boat Cruises (Stacie Davidson and Captain Al Crocetti: 677-2026; 1-800-278-3346), Shaw's Wharf, New Harbor. May through October the sleek 60-foot Maine-built *Hardy III* offers daily service to **Monhegan** (for a detailed description, see "Midcoast Islands"). Pick a calm day. It doesn't matter if it's foggy, but the passage is more than an hour and no fun if it's rough. A cruise also circles **Eastern Egg Rock,** one of only five Maine islands on which puffins breed; the tours are narrated by an Audubon naturalist (inquire about other special puffin-watching and birding trips). There are also sunset cruises to Pemaquid Point. Parking is free but roughly a quarter mile back up the road. The crew do everything they can to make the trip interesting, like the seal-watching detour on the way back from Monhegan.

Muscongus Bay Cruises (529-4474), Bremen. April through November Captain Chris Butler offers a variety of nature and pleasure cruises; inquire about rentals ranging from a classic "lobster yacht" to a 25-foot Hunter sloop.

BOAT RENTALS

Damariscotta Lake Farm (549-7953) in Jefferson rents boats and motors for use on 13-mile-long Damariscotta Lake. **Lake Pemaquid Camping** (563-5202), Egypt Road, Damariscotta, rents canoes. **Pemaquid River Canoe Rental** (563-5721), Route 130, Bristol (5 miles south of Damariscotta), has canoe sales and rentals at the Bristol Dam, from which you can paddle up along the river and across Biscay into Pemaquid Pond. **Just for the Fun of It** (586-6752 or 563-1280), Biscay Road in Damariscotta, offers canoe rentals and shuttle service. **Sea Spirit Adventures** (529-4732), Round Pond Village, offers sea kayak rentals and tours.

FISHING

Damariscotta Lake is a source of bass, landlocked salmon, and trout.

GOLF

Wawenock Country Club (563-3938), Route 129 (7 miles south of Damariscotta). Open May through November. Nine holes.

HORSEBACK RIDING

Hill-n-Dale Riding Stables (273-2511) in Warren offers trail rides.

SWIMMING

On the peninsula there is public swimming at **Biscay Pond,** off Route 32,

Damariscotta Lake State Park

and at **Bristol Dam** on Route 130, 5 miles south of Damariscotta (also
see *Green Space—Beaches*).

GREEN SPACE

BEACHES

Pemaquid Beach Park (677-2754), Route 130, Pemaquid. A town-owned
area open Memorial Day through Labor Day, 9–5. Admission is $1
adults, under 12 free. Bathhouse, rest rooms, refreshment stand, and
picnic tables. Pleasant, but it can be windy, in which case try the more
pebbly but more sheltered (and free) beach down the road. This is also
a great place to walk and watch the sunset in the evening.

Damariscotta Lake State Park, Route 32, Jefferson. A fine sandy beach
with changing facilities, picnic tables, and grills at the northern end of
the lake. Nominal admission.

Also see **Dodge Point Preserve** under *Nature Preserves*, below.

NATURE PRESERVES

Rachel Carson Memorial Salt Pond, at the side of Route 32, just north
of New Harbor. The Salt Pond is on the opposite side of the road from
the parking lot. There's a beautiful view of the open ocean from here,
and at low tide the tidal pools are filled with tiny sea creatures. Look for
blue mussels, hermit crabs, starfish, and green sea urchins. Here Rachel
Carson researched part of her book *The Edge of the Sea.* Inland from
the pond, the preserve includes fields and forest.

La Verna Preserve, Route 32, 3 miles north of New Harbor. Walk the half
mile down a gravel road to the preserve, which includes 3,600 feet on

Muscongus Bay, maintained by the Maine Chapter of The Nature Conservancy.

* **Todd Wildlife Sanctuary and the Hocomock Trail,** Medomak (take Keene Neck Road off Route 32). A visitors center (529-5148) is open daily June through August, 1–4. The nature trail leads down to the beach. This is a great family picnic spot, accessible with short legs.

Damariscotta River Association (563-1393), based at 100-acre Heritage Center Farm (P.O. Box 333, Belvedere Road, Damariscotta 04543), publishes a free map/guide to the properties that it maintains, frequently in conjunction with other landowners. These total more than 1,000 acres in more than a dozen easily accessible places. They include **Great Salt Bay Preserve Heritage Trail** (see *To See—Shell heaps*), which loops around Glidden Point, first hugging the shore of Great Salt Bay (look for horseshoe crabs, great blue herons, and eagles) and then tunnels right under Route 1 and leads down to the "Glidden Midden" of oyster shells that's now on the National Register and said to date back 2,400 years. The trail begins beside the Newcastle post office.

Dodge Point Preserve is a 506-acre property on Newcastle's River Road (2.6 miles south of Route 1). It includes a sand beach as well as a freshwater pond, a beaver bog, and trails.

Witch Island, South Bristol. An 18-acre wooded island lies a quarter mile offshore at the east end of the Gut, the narrow channel that serves as South Bristol's harbor. A trail around the island threads through oaks and pines, and there are two sheltered beaches.

LODGING

INNS

The Newcastle Inn (563-5685; 1-800-832-8669; www.newcastleinn.com), River Road, Newcastle 04553. Open year-round. Howard and Rebecca Levitan offer 14 tasteful and comfortable rooms, all with private baths, several with canopy beds, 8 with fireplaces, and 2 with Jacuzzis. Common spaces include a sunporch with a woodstove and French doors opening on a deck with water views. Howard has schooled himself in culinary arts in Paris, the better to prepare four-course dinners (see *Dining Out*) that are the centerpiece of a stay here. Rates are $95–240 double, including a three-course breakfast. Inquire about special wine-tasting and holiday weekends. No smoking.

* **Gosnold Arms** (677-3727; www.gosnold.com), 146 Route 32, New Harbor 04554. Open mid-May through mid-October. Just across the road from the water (and from the Hardy boat offering day trips to Monhegan and puffin cruises around Egg Rock), this friendly family-owned and -run inn has been welcoming summer guests since 1925. Nothing fancy; it's a rambling, white-clapboard farmhouse with scattered cottages, some right on the picturesque harbor. Eleven guest rooms (all with private

baths) with unstained pine walls, pleasant furnishings, and firm beds have been fitted into the barn, above a gathering room with a huge fireplace. There are 14 cottages, some with kitchenettes and fireplaces. The Pilot doesn't have a hearth, but it's still our favorite. You are lulled asleep by the bell buoy, and it's hard to tear yourself away from the view. Guests breakfast on the enclosed porch overlooking the water. All rates include breakfast. $89–110 double B&B in the inn, $75–154 for cottages; less off-season.

  ♿ **Bradley Inn** (677-2105; 1-800-942-5560; www.bradleyinn.com), 3063 Pemaquid Point, New Harbor 04554. Open year-round. Warren and Beth Busteed are energetic innkeepers who have established a culinary reputation for this turn-of-the-century inn (see *Dining Out*). The 16 guest rooms are divided among the main house, the carriage house, and a cottage, all nicely furnished (private baths), all set in landscaped grounds. Request one of the third-floor rooms with a view of Johns Bay. The entry area also serves two dining rooms, but there is a living room with a fireplace, wing chairs, and a library of nautical books for guests. Old clunker bicycles are free, and the inn is less than a mile from Pemaquid Lighthouse and Kresge Point. From $95 off-season to $195 in-season; inquire about special birding weekends.

  Coveside Inn (644-8282), Christmas Cove, South Bristol 04568. Motel units are open late May through mid-October; the restaurant and inn rooms, from early June through Labor Day. As many guests probably sail as drive to this holly-berry red Victorian inn. It offers five old-fashioned guest rooms (all have private baths but some are across the hall), a big living room with a woodstove and plenty of books, shared with guests in the 10 shorefront motel units (private decks, pine paneling, and cathedral ceilings with skylights). The complex also includes a restaurant, serving all three meals, and a yacht brokerage. $80–105 includes continental breakfast.

  ♿ **The Hotel Pemaquid** (677-2312), Pemaquid 04554. Open mid-May through mid-October. A century-old summer hotel just a short walk from Pemaquid Point but without water views. The 25 rooms are neat and tidy, divided among the main house and new annexes. The decor is high Victorian, the living room has a big stone fireplace, and the long porch is lined with wicker. Rooms in the inn itself come with and without private baths, but all others have private baths, and several are reserved for smokers. Coffee is set out at 6:30 AM, and the nearby **Sea Gull Shop** (see *Eating Out*) overlooks the ocean. From $64 off-season with shared bath to $185 for a three-bedroom suite in August; a four-bedroom housekeeping cottage is $650–695 per week. Inquire about art workshops.

BED & BREAKFASTS

  ℗ **Mill Pond Inn** (563-8014; www.millpondinn.com), Route 215, Damariscotta Mills (mailing address: 50 Main Street, Nobleboro 04555). Open year-round. A quiet spot with a wide terrace overlooking a pond. Damariscotta Lake is just across the road. You can canoe or kayak out from the pond into the lake, where you might well see a resident bald eagle. Temptations not to budge, however, include two-person hammocks under the willow trees, a beach, and (relatively) warm water. The 1780 gray-clapboard house with a red door offers six double rooms (all with private baths), all so different from each other that you might want to ask for descriptions, but all cost $95. Request a pond view. Breakfast might be an omelet with crabmeat and vegetables from the inn's garden. In winter pack a picnic lunch and skate across the lake to an island. In summer ask for a ride in the 16-foot restored antique motorboat. You can also explore the rolling countryside on one of the inn's mountain bikes. Owner Bobby Whear, a Registered Maine Guide, also will arrange fishing trips. $95.

Brannon-Bunker Inn (563-5941), 349 State Route 129, Walpole 04573. Open March through December. This 1820s Cape was a barn that was a Prohibition-era dance hall before it became a B&B. The upstairs sitting-area walls are hung with memorabilia from World War I, and there are plenty of antiques and collectibles around (the adjoining antiques shop is open May through October). Your hosts are the Hovance family, and children are welcome. There are seven rooms, five with private baths ($75) and two that share ($65); a suite with a kitchen, living room, and bathroom is $85–125. A path leads to the river and a kitchen is available for guests' use.

Barnswallow B&B (563-8568), 362 Bristol Road (Route 129/130), Damariscotta 04543. Open year-round. Rachael Sherill's classic 1830s Cape is well up and back from the road, and you can feel its welcome the moment you walk through the side door. The three guest rooms all have private baths and charm; we favor the one in back with the canopy bed. It's a snug house with five fireplaces—the largest in the formal dining room, where breakfast is served, and two more in the two parlors, one with a TV. $70–80 includes breakfast.

The Flying Cloud (563-2484; www.theflyingcloud.com), River Road, Newcastle 04553. Open most of the year. An 1840s sea captain's home expanding on a 1790s Cape with five spacious guest rooms, all with private baths, four with water views. All are named for ports of call made by clipper ship *Flying Cloud*. Our favorite is third-floor Melbourne with its skylight and view of both the river and harbor. Ron and Betty Howe are your hosts. $85–105 includes a full breakfast; less off-season.

Broad Bay Inn & Gallery (832-6668; 1-800-736-6769; www.broadbayinn.com), 1014 Main Street, Waldoboro 04572. Closed January through March. Within walking distance of village restaurants, shops, and performances at the Waldo Theatre, this is a pleasant 1830s home with Victorian furnishings and canopy beds. The five guest rooms share three baths. Afternoon tea and sherry are served on the sundeck in summer and by the fire in winter. The art gallery in the barn exhibits works by Maine artists, and limited-edition prints. Inquire about workshops. Rates include a full breakfast (host Libby Hopkins studied at the Cordon Bleu); guests can arrange Saturday-evening candlelight dinners in advance. Two-night minimum stay required in July and August. $70–75 double.

Oak Gables (563-1476), P.O. Box 276, Pleasant Street, Damariscotta 04543. Open year-round. Set on its own 13 acres overlooking the Damariscotta River, minutes from village shopping and dining, Martha Scudder's gracious house has four second-floor rooms that share a bath and a first-floor room (private bath). There are also three cottages, one three-bedroom and two studios, all available by the week: $550–750. The grounds include a heated swimming pool and a boathouse on the river. Rooms are $75–110 with breakfast.

Glidden House (563-1859), 24 Glidden Street, Newcastle 04553. Open most of the year. This Victorian house on a quiet street lined with elegant old homes is a convenient walk to shops. Doris Miller offers three guest rooms with private baths and a three-room apartment. Breakfast is served in the dining room or on the porch. $70 per couple, $65 single; $80 for the apartment.

The Harbor View Inn at Newcastle (563-2900; www.theharborview.com), P.O. Box 791, Newcastle 04553. Set above Main Street in Newcastle this luxurious B&B has a large beamed living room with windows overlooking the harbor; two upstairs guest rooms have fireplaces, river views, and private decks. Breakfast is a production. $110–150.

The Bristol Inn (563-1125; www.bristolinn.com), 28 Upper Round Pond Road, Bristol 04539. Open year-round. Beth and Nathan Moss have brought new life to this early-1900s farmhouse, squarely, solidly built and set in fields with five guest rooms, all with private baths. A large first-floor room has a fireplace. Children are welcome and breakfasts are full. $85–100 per couple, $20 for each additional guest.

The Roaring Lion (832-4038), 995 Main Street, Waldoboro 04572. Open year-round. A 1905 home with tin ceilings, fireplaces, and a big screened porch. The kitchen can cater to special, vegetarian, and macrobiotic diets. One room with private bath; three with shared bath. $70–80 double, $10 less for single occupancy. No smoking.

Inland

The Jefferson House (549-5768), Route 126, Jefferson 04348. Jim and Barbara O'Halloron's comfortable 1835 farmhouse feels like home the moment you walk in. The large, bright kitchen with its big old cookstove is the center of the house, or you can breakfast on the deck overlooking the village and millpond. Guests can use the canoe on the river. Rooms are homey and comfortable; shared baths. $60 double, $50 single; $75 for room with private bath.

Snow Drift Farm B&B (845-2476; snodrift@midcoast.com), 117 Fitch

Boats in New Harbor

Road, Washington 04574. Open year-round. George and Arlene Van-Deventer's restored mid 1800s farmhouse is set in the country with a garden, a deck, fields, nature trails, a trout stream, and a pond (skating in winter). A professional massage therapist is available. From $50 with shared bath to $60 with private bath includes a full country or lighter breakfast. Four-course dinners are available ($18–22 per person).

Hidden Acres Llama Farm (549-5774), 84 Old County Road, Jefferson 04348. Sited near the northern tip of Damariscotta Lake, Philippa and Terry Beal's llama farm includes a fully equipped one-bedroom apartment. Guests are invited to take llamas along on treks over the farm's trails, and welcome to participate in farm activities and to use the hot tub. In-season rates range from $250 for a weekend to $650 for a full week. Ingredients are supplied for a hearty breakfast.

COTTAGES

Many rental properties are listed with the Damariscotta area chamber (see *Guidance*); for cottages and apartments down on the peninsula, also request a copy of the current "Map & Guide" published by the Pemaquid Area Association (Chamberlain 04541).

The Thompson House and Cottages (677-2317), New Harbor 04554. Open May through November with 21 cottages, many with ocean views and facing New Harbor or Back Cove; they run $850–1,100 a week; less off-season. The house itself offers two guest rooms with private baths, and there are four apartments ($450–550 per week) on the property.

MOTEL

The Oyster Shell Motel (563-3747; 1-800-874-3747). Open all year. A condo-style motel complex on Business Route 1, north of Damariscotta

Village. No view but clean and comfortable; good for a family for a night or two. One-bedroom or two-bedroom suites with cooking facilities. From $89 off-season to $139 in-season.

CAMPING

🖉& **Lake Pemaquid Camping** (563-5202), Box 967, Damariscotta 04543. Off Biscay Road. Many tent and RV sites are right on 7-mile Lake Pemaquid, and canoe and boat rentals are available. Facilities also include tennis, a pool, swimming, a playground, a game room, laundry facilities, a sauna, and a store.

WHERE TO EAT

DINING OUT

The Newcastle Inn (563-5685), River Road, Newcastle. Open nightly June through October; Friday and Saturday off-season. Chef-owner Howard Levitan recently studied culinary arts in Paris to sharpen his cooking skills. Candlelight and the flowery dining rooms with their fine china are the setting for a dinner that might begin with local mussels steamed in a broth of cream, garlic, saffron, and ouzo. Entrées might include grilled boneless duck breast served with a raspberry cassis glaze. The four-course prix fixe dinner includes appetizer or soup, salad, entrée, dessert, and coffee. $39.50 plus 15 percent gratuity. The wine list is extensive.

Bradley Inn (677-2105; 1-800-942-5560), Pemaquid Point Road, New Harbor. Open for dinner year-round; nightly in-season, Thursday through Sunday November through March. There's live jazz or folk music on Friday and Saturday nights, frequently piano music other nights. Fine dining is what these two attractive dining rooms are about. The rooms are decorated in nautical antiques and soothing greens, and tables are well spaced and candlelit. The à la carte menu might include carrot-orange soup and crisp fried calamari for starters, and entrées like oven-roasted whole game hen and potato-crusted Scottish salmon. Entrées $21–29.

🖉 **Anchor Inn** (529-5584), Round Pond. Open daily for lunch and dinner, mid-May through Labor Day, then open except Monday and Tuesday until Columbus Day. A real find. Jean and Rick Hirch offer a tiered dining room overlooking the harbor in this small fishing village. Try the native crabcakes for either lunch or dinner. The Italian seafood stew is loaded with fish, shrimp, scallops, and mussels. Daily specials. Children's menu. Dinner entrées $12.67–21.75. Most seafood dishes are under $14.

Coveside Waterfront Restaurant (644-8282), Christmas Cove, South Bristol. Open June through Labor Day; three meals daily. This is a large waterside dining room; accessible by boat. Dinner entrées range from Mike's Pasta ($14.95) to seafood Alfredo (shrimps, scallops, and lobster on spinach pasta, $28).

Backstreet Restaurant (563-5666), Elm Street Plaza, Damariscotta. Open daily year-round for lunch (11:30–2:30) and dinner (from 5). In back of Main Street, overlooking the Damariscotta River, this very pleasant, low-key restaurant and gathering place has good, dependable food. Lunch options include freshly made soups and a long sandwich board as well as quiche. Dinner entrées range from pasta to coquille Saint-Jacques as well as Jake's BBQ ribs combo. $12.96–19.95.

ℰ **Salt Bay Café** (563-1666), Main Street, Damariscotta. Open year-round for lunch and dinner. A pleasant, chef-owned, and locally liked restaurant with booths and a fireplace. Lunch features salads and soup and sandwich combos. The dinner menu ranges from crabcakes and fried oysters to filet mignon, with vegetarian options. Dinner entrées $10.95–18.95.

EATING OUT

On or just off Route 1

ℰ **King Eider's Pub** (563-6008), 2 Elm Street, Damariscotta. Open year-round 11–11. A family-run favorite among locals and visitors alike. The downstairs pub is the perfect foggy-evening spot for light grub and a boutique brew. The pleasant upstairs restaurant, with a moderately priced menu, features local produce and seafood. Try Damariscotta River oysters on the half shell. Sandwiches available at dinner along with entrées from $9.50 for fish-and-chips to a lobster and scallops combo for $21.95.

ℰ **S. Fernald's/Waldoboro 5+10** (832-4624), 17 Friendship Street, Waldoboro. Still billed as the oldest five-and-ten in the country (established 1927), this friendly old establishment is now owned by Sumner Richards; it looks like his former place (S. Fernald's Country Store in Damariscotta) and offers the same menu: Deli-style sandwiches, fresh soups and chilis, specials, and baked goods are available at the old-style soda fountain. Cards and toys, stationery, sewing supplies, and much more are still sold too.

ℰ& **Moody's Diner** (832-7785), Route 1, Waldoboro. Open Monday through Friday 4 AM–11:30 PM, Saturday 5 AM–11:30 PM, Sunday 6 AM–11:30 PM. A clean and warm, classic '30s diner run by several generations of the Moody family along with other employees who have been there so long they have become part of the family. Renovated and expanded, it still retains all the old atmosphere and specialties like cream pies and family-style food—corned beef hash, meat loaf, and stews—at digestible prices. You can now buy T-shirts and other Moody's paraphernalia, but you can also still get chicken croquettes at prices that haven't soared with fame. Couples and groups may have to wait, but singles can usually find a seat at the counter.

Pine Cone Café (832-6337), 13 Friendship Street, Waldoboro. Open year-round except Monday for breakfast, lunch, and dinner. Laura Cabot's attractive restaurant has evolved from a small café/bakery to a 135-seat restaurant with a bar (wine and beer). Stained-glass insets in the booths and paintings on the brick walls are by noted North Haven artist Eric

Hopkins, and a back deck overlooks the Medomak River. Peasant breads, salads, soups, and sandwiches; full menu at dinner.

Pemaquid area

Rosario's (677-6363), Southside Road, New Harbor. Open daily in July and August, most days in spring and fall, then some days until Christmas. Middle of the village, Rosario Vitanza's pizzas are light and crispy, the best we've found in Maine. The proscuitto bianco blew us away, and we can't wait to get back to try the *melazane e funghi* or Rosario's cannoli. Tables inside by the espresso bar, also outside on the deck. Italian breads also made and sold.

Samoset Restaurant (677-2142), Route 10, New Harbor. Open daily year-round 11–9. No view but great on a foggy or rainy day or evening. Geared to locals with homemade specials, good chowder, and fresh seafood. Live entertainment on weekends and other selected nights.

Sea Gull Shop (677-2374), next to the Pemaquid Lighthouse at Pemaquid Point. Open daily in-season, 8–8, serving all three meals. The shop's Monhegan Room has water views. Standard menu. BYOB.

✍ **Bridge House Café,** Route 129 south of "the Gut," South Bristol. Seasonal. In summer few cars get across the swing bridge at this narrow but busy channel on the first try. Which is a good thing because it's one of the most scenic spots on the coast. The café offers a harborside seat, squeeze-your-own lemonade, and a daily changing blackboard menu. Owner Diane Haas says she found this spot through this book.

✍ **Osier's Wharf** (644-8101), Route 129 north of "the Gut" in South Bristol. Open 8–8. Another classic spot from which to watch passing lobster boats. This is a general store and fish market, and the dining deck is upstairs overlooking the water; a place for a morning "clucker muffin," a crabmeat or lobster roll at lunch, or fresh-dough pizza all day; also deli sandwiches.

✍ **Bullwinkle's Family Steakhouse** (832-6272), Route 1, Waldoboro. Locally loved and a good bet for road food. Steaks are the specialty along with baby back ribs, seafood baskets, and subs.

LOBSTER POUNDS

Note: Muscongus Bay is a particularly prime lobster source, and genuine lobster pounds are plentiful around the harbors of the Pemaquid Peninsula.

✍ **Shaw's Wharf** (677-2200), New Harbor (next to the New Harbor Co-op). Open late May through mid-October, daily for lunch and supper. You can't get nearer to a working harbor than this popular dockside spot. In addition to lobster and steamed clams, the menu ranges from meat loaf to scallops, and sandwiches. Liquor is also served. Choose to sit at a picnic table either outside or in.

At the picture-perfect harbor in **Round Pond,** two competing companies share the town wharf, resulting in satisfying prices. **Muscongus Bay Lobster Company** (529-5528) and **Round Pond Lobster** (529-5725) both have great views and offer no-frills (no toilets) facilities.

Pemaquid Fisherman's Co-op (677-2801), Pemaquid Harbor. Open Saturday and Sunday 11–6. Lobster, steamed clams and mussels, and shrimp to be enjoyed at outdoor tables over the harbor.

ICE CREAM

Round Top Ice Cream (563-5307), Business Route 1, Damariscotta. Open Memorial Day through Columbus Day. Rest rooms. You'll find delicious Round Top ice cream offered at restaurants throughout the region, but this is the original shop just up the road from the farm where it all began in 1924 (that property is now Round Top Center for the Arts; see *Entertainment*). The ice cream comes in 36 flavors, including fresh blueberry. A deck overlooks a sloping meadow.

ENTERTAINMENT

Round Top Center for the Arts (563-1507), Upper Main Street, Damariscotta. On the grounds of the old Round Top Farm, this nonprofit organization offers an ambitious schedule of concerts, exhibitions, classes, and festivals. Summer concerts can be anything from the Portland Symphony Orchestra to rousing ethnic music by Mama Tongue. Bring a blanket and a picnic.

Lincoln Theater (563-3424), entrance off Main Street, Damariscotta. The biggest hall east of Boston in 1875, later boasting the largest motion-picture screen in the state. Recently restored by the Lincoln County Community Theater, which stages its own productions here in winter and spring. First-run films and special programs.

Waldo Theatre (832-6060), Main Street, Waldoboro. March through December, a schedule of films, concerts, and live performances. Inquire about outlets for advance sales of concert tickets in Damariscotta, Rockland, and Thomaston.

SELECTIVE SHOPPING

ANTIQUES

"Antiquing in the Newcastle, Damariscotta, Pemaquid Region," a free pamphlet guide, lists more than 30 dealers in this small area. Check local papers for auctions or call **Robert Foster** (563-8110), based at his auction gallery on Route 1, Newcastle. **Kaja Veilleux Antiques** (563-1002; 1-800-924-1032) is the area dean in quality art and antiques; also organizes occasional auctions.

ART AND CRAFT GALLERIES AND STUDIOS

The Firehouse Gallery (563-7299), corner of Main Street and Route 130, Damariscotta. Open May through October, Monday through Saturday 10–5. A fine art and craft gallery.

Victorian Stable Gallery (563-3548), Water Street, Damariscotta. Open

June through October, 10–5. Handsome stalls in this carriage house behind a Victorian mansion display Maine craftswork at its best: original designs in natural materials—clay, straw, slate, and wood. Barbara Briggs seems to know all the possibilities from which she can pick and choose. Handblown glass, colorful enamels, silver, iron, porcelain, rugs, and some original furniture.

David Margonelli (633-3326), 780 River Road, Edgecomb. Open year-round 10–5 weekdays, 10–3 Saturday. Exquisite, completely handmade furniture with a classic influence.

Damariscotta Pottery (563-8843), around back of Weatherbird, Damariscotta. Majolica ware, decorated in floral designs. You won't see this advertised. It doesn't have to be. Watch it being shaped and painted.

Sheepscot Pottery (882-9410; 1-800-659-4794). The big shop is on Route 1 in Edgecomb, but this shop stocks a range of distinctive hand-painted dinnerware, plates, and ovenware as well as lamps and tiles.

River Gallery (563-6330), Main Street, Damariscotta. Open in-season Monday through Saturday 10–3; features 19th- and early-20th-century landscapes.

SPECIAL SHOPS

Reny's (563-3177), Main Street, Damariscotta. First opened in Camden in 1949, Reny's has since become a small-town Maine institution from Biddeford to Fort Kent. The stores sell quality items—ranging from TVs to sheets and towels and whatever "the boys" happen to have found to stock this week. The headquarters for the 15-store chain are in Damariscotta's former grade school; on Main Street look for Reny's and the recently expanded **Reny's Underground.**

Maine Coast Book Shop (563-3207), Main Street, Damariscotta. One of Maine's best bookstores, with knowledgeable staff members who delight in making suggestions and helping customers shop for others.

Weatherbird, Northey Square, Damariscotta. Open Monday through Saturday 8:30–5:30. A combination café and gift shop with mouthwatering pastries and specialty foods, wines, home accessories, clothing, gifts, toys, and cards.

Granite Hall Store (529-5864), Route 32, Round Pond. Open Tuesday through Sunday 10–5. There's penny candy up front, but this is no general store. It's filled with Scottish-, Irish-, and Maine-made woolens, a few antiques and baskets, toys, books, and a good selection of greeting cards. There's also homemade fudge, and, at an outdoor window, ice cream.

Jean Gillespie Books (529-5555), Route 32 south of the village of Round Pond. Open daily in summer. An exceptional antiquarian bookstore, since 1961. Some 15,000 titles line shelves in a barnlike annex to the house. We recently found here a 19th-century Maine guidebook that we had been hunting high and low for, reasonably priced.

Old Post Office Shop, New Harbor center. Open May through December; good selection of gifts and local crafts.

The Roserie at Bayfields (832-6330; 1-800-933-4508), Route 32, just 1.7 miles south of the light on Route 1 in Waldoboro. Open daily April 19 until late July, then Tuesday through Saturday through the growing season. Rose lovers across the country are aware of this unusual nursery, specializing in hundreds of varieties of "practical roses for hard places."

SPECIAL EVENTS

July: Annual **July 4th sale/outdoor lobster bake and fireworks.**
Early August: **Olde Bristol Days,** Old Fort Grounds, Pemaquid Beach— parade, fish fry, chicken barbecue, bands, bagpipers, concerts, pancake breakfast, road race, boat race, firemen's muster, crafts, and the annual **Bristol Footlighters Show** (which has been going on for more than 40 years).

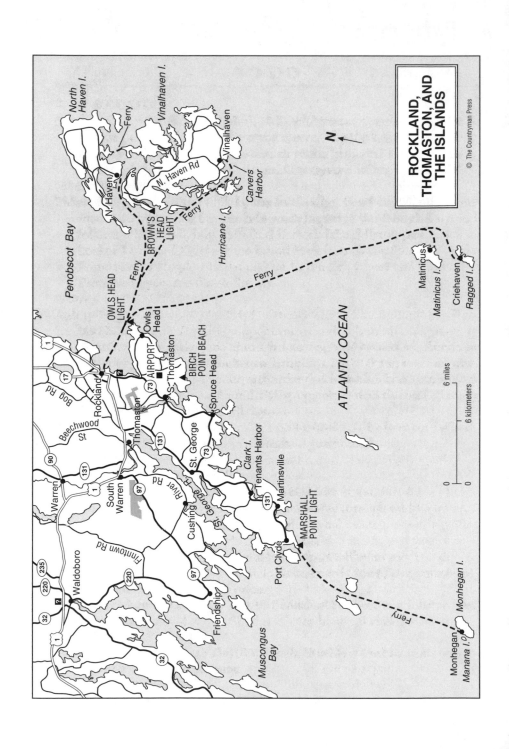

ROCKLAND,
THOMASTON, AND
THE ISLANDS

© The Countryman Press

Rockland/Thomaston Area

The shire town of Knox County, Rockland (population around 8,000) is the commercial center for a wide scattering of towns and islands. The departure point for ferries to the islands of Vinalhaven, North Haven, and Matinicus (see "Midcoast Islands"), it is also now home port for the majority of Maine's windjammers, as well as for several daysailers and an ever-increasing number of private yachts. Long billed as the "Lobster Capital of the World," it is now better known as home of the Farnsworth Museum, with its exceptional collection of Maine-based paintings, including works by three generations of Wyeths, housed in a middle-of-downtown, five-building campus.

Little more than a decade ago Rockland was far from the obvious Maine art venue. Camden-bound visitors avoided the place if they knew how to. Odors from the SeaPro fish-rendering plant were famous. A popular jingle ran: "Camden by Sea, Rockland by Smell." This gritty, sagging brick burg was not the Maine tourists came to see.

SeaPro has since gone the way of the city's two sardine-packing and other fish-processing plants, and the huge harbor, protected by a nearly mile-long granite (walkable) breakwater, is now sparkling clean and equipped to accommodate pleasure boats. The wave of change is, moreover, washing down Main Street, bringing galleries, restaurants, and specialty shops. Along the waterfront, west of the already visitor-geared Public Landing, old industrial sheds have disappeared, replaced by office space. The harborside walking trail is lengthening.

Rockland, however, still prides itself on its grit. The city's industrial base still includes FMC Bio-Polymer (processing carrageenan from seaweed) and homegrown Fisher Snowplow, and the harbor, Maine's second largest after Portland, remains home to 700 vessels, including a sizable fishing and lobstering fleet, tugs, and U.S. Coast Guard and commercial vessels.

Rockland has remade itself several times over the centuries. Initially known for its shipbuilding, the city became synonymous in the late 19th century with the limestone it quarried, burned, and shipped off to be made into plaster. When wallboard replaced plaster, Rockland quickly switched to catching and processing fish. Now with fishing on the decline, city entrepreneurs are once more widening their base.

A century ago summer people heading for Bar Harbor as well as the islands took the train as far as Rockland, switching here to steamboats. Today a similar summer crowd rides the bus to the ferry terminal or flies into Knox County Regional Airport on Owls Head, just south of town, here transferring to rental cars, air taxis, or windjammers, to charter boats as well as ferries. The old train terminal is, moreover, still on Union Street, and now passenger rail service from Boston to Rockland is planned with passengers transferring here to a high-speed ferry to Bar Harbor.

Southwest of Rockland, two peninsulas separate Muscongus Bay from Penobscot Bay. One is the fat arm of land on which the villages of Friendship and Cushing doze. The other is the skinnier St. George Peninsula with Port Clyde at its tip, the departure point for the year-round mail boat to Monhegan Island (again, see "Midcoast Islands").

The peninsulas are divided by the 10-mile-long St. George River, on which past residents of Thomaston launched their share of wooden ships. Although its Main Street mansions stand today in white-clapboard testimony to the shipbuilders' success, and Thomaston is a beautiful town, it's best known as the site of the state prison—and its popular prison shop.

GUIDANCE

Rockland-Thomaston Chamber of Commerce (596-0376; 1-800-562-2529; www.midcoast.com/~rtacc), Public Landing, Rockland (write P.O. Box 508, Rockland 04841). Open daily Memorial Day through Labor Day 9–5 weekdays, and 9–4 Saturday and Sunday until Columbus Day, then just weekdays. The chamber's large, comfortable information center in Harbor Park serves the entire Rockland area, which includes Owls Head, Thomaston, the peninsula villages, and the islands. It has cottage and vacation rental listings.

GETTING THERE

By air: **Knox County Regional Airport** (594-4131), at Owls Head, just south of Rockland. Daily service via **U.S. Airways Express** (operated by Colgan Air: 1-800-428-4322) to Boston, Bar Harbor, Augusta, and New York. Inquire about charter services to the islands. **Telford Aviation** (596-5557; 1-800-780-6071) and **Downeast Air** (594-2171; 1-888-594-2171) offer charter service. Rental cars are available at the airport. Also see taxi service under *Getting Around;* all offer service to **Portland International Jetport** (see "Portland Area").

By bus: **Concord Trailways** (1-800-639-3317) offers service to Rockland with a stop at the ferry terminal.

By boat: The city has 20 moorings, and there are many more at commercial marinas. Contact the **Harbormaster** (594-0312) and chamber of commerce (see above).

GETTING AROUND

By taxi: **Schooner Bay Limo** (594-5000) and **Hit the Road Driver Ser-**

KIM GRANT

Farnsworth Museum

vice (230-0095; beeper, 851-5506) will get you there. **The Maine State Ferry Service Terminal** (596-2022) adjoins the bus stop (see above).

MEDICAL EMERGENCY

Penobscot Bay Medical Center (596-8000), 6 Glen Cove Drive (off Route 1), Rockport.

VILLAGES AND ISLANDS

Friendship. Best known as the birthplace of the classic Friendship sloop, first built by local lobstermen to haul their traps (originals and reproductions of this sturdy vessel hold races here every summer). Friendship remains a quiet fishing village with a museum in a former schoolhouse on Martin's Point (it's open July through Labor Day).

Tenants Harbor has a good little library and, beyond, rock cliffs, tidal pools, old cemeteries, and the kind of countryside described by Sarah Orne Jewett in *The Country of the Pointed Firs.* Jewett lived just a few bends down Route 131 in Martinville while she wrote the book.

Port Clyde welcomes visitors at the tip of the St. George Peninsula (the end of Route 131) with a wharfside general store (sandwiches and outside tables), a small eatery, a hospitable inn, and good art gallery. More services and the Marshall Point Light (see *To See—Lighthouses*) is well worth finding.

Union is a short ride from the coast but surrounded by gentle hills and farm country (the Union Fair and the State of Maine Wild Blueberry Festival are big; see *Special Events*). This place is also a good spot to swim, eat, and explore the unusually interesting Matthews Museum of Maine

Heritage at the fairgrounds (open July 1 through Labor Day, daily except Monday, noon–5).

Islands. An overnight or longer stay on an island is far preferable to a day trip. From Rockland you can take a Maine State (car) Ferry to **Vinalhaven** and **North Haven.** Together these form the Fox Islands, with just a narrow passage between them. Yet the islands are very different. On Vinalhaven summer homes are hidden away along the shore, and what visitors see is the old fishing village of Carver's Harbor. On North Haven most of the clapboard homes (mainly owned by wealthy summer people) are set in open fields. **Matinicus,** also accessible from Rockland, is the most remote Maine island and quietly beautiful. Tiny **Monhegan,** accessible from Port Clyde, offers the most dramatic cliff scenery and the most hospitable welcome to visitors. For details, see the descriptions of each island in the next chapter.

TO SEE

MUSEUMS AND HISTORIC HOMES

Farnsworth Art Museum (596-6457; www.farnsworth@midcoast.com), 352 Main Street, Rockland. Open year-round, daily Memorial Day through Columbus Day 9–5, otherwise Tuesday through Saturday 10–5, Sunday 1–5. Admission to the museum and Farnsworth Homestead (see next entry) is $9 adults, $8 senior citizens, $5 students over 18; no charge under 18. This exceptional art museum was established by Lucy Farnsworth, an eccentric spinster who lived frugally in just three rooms of her family mansion. When she died in 1935 at age 96, neighbors were amazed to find that she had left $1.3 million to preserve her house and build a library with a small art gallery next door. As luck would have it, however, the city acquired a public Carnegie Library soon after Lucy's death, and so the focus shifted to art. From the beginning the collection included paintings of Maine by Winslow Homer, George Bellows, and a (then) little-known local summer resident, Andrew Wyeth.

"People come to a museum like this to see what makes Maine unique," observes Chris Crosman, the Farnsworth director credited with catapulting the museum from a way stop to a destination for art lovers. It attracts twice as many visitors as it did just five years ago.

The museum's expansion, now housed in five buildings, has been steady and Maine focused. A permanent exhibit, *Maine in America,* traces the evolution of Maine landscape paintings. The museum features Hudson River School artists like Thomas Cole, and 19th-century marine artist Fitz Hugh Lane; American impressionists Frank Benson, Willard Metcalf, Childe Hassam, and Maurice Prendergast; early-20th-century greats like Rockwell Kent and Charles Woodbury; and such "modernists" as John Marin and Marsden Hartley. Rockland-raised painter and sculptor Louise Nevelson is also well represented.

The Farnsworth Museum Center for the Wyeth Family in Maine, a two-story exhibit space in a former church, displays works by America's most prominent artistic dynasty: N. C. Wyeth (1882–1945), Andrew Wyeth (born 1917), and Jamie Wyeth (born 1946). Exhibits vary. The Jamien Morehouse Wing, housing four new galleries, was added in 2000 (shaped from a former five-and-dime) to house changing exhibits.

The Farnsworth's original Georgian Revival library houses an extensive collection of reference materials and serves as the site for regularly scheduled lectures and concerts. A sculpture garden connects the main museum with the Wyeth Center. Note Robert Indiana's *Love* sculpture near the museum entrance.

Farnsworth Homestead (596-6457), Elm Street, Rockland. Open Memorial Day through Columbus Day during main museum hours, and weekends in December (when it's decorated for Christmas and free). Included in museum admission. The Farnsworth Homestead was built in 1850 by Miss Lucy's father, a tycoon who was very successful in the lime industry and who also owned a fleet of ships. Brimming with lavish, colorful Victorian furnishings (all original), it remains—according to a stipulation in Miss Lucy's will—just as it was when she died at the age of 96. Curious details of the decor include draperies so long that they drag on the floor, to indicate that the family could afford to buy more fabric than was required. Nevertheless, the walls are hung with inexpensive copies of oil paintings known as chromolithographs, a fireplace mantel is glass painted to resemble marble, and doors are not made of fine wood grains but, rather, have been painted to imitate them.

The Olson House (596-6457), Hawthorn Point Road, Cushing. Open Memorial Day through Columbus Day, daily 11–4. $4 over age 18; free under. Administered by the Farnsworth Art Museum, this house served as a backdrop for many works by Andrew Wyeth, including *Christina's World.*

✐ **Montpelier** (354-6854), High Street, Thomaston. Open June through early October, Tuesday through Saturday 10–4, Sunday 1–4. Admission $5 adults, $4 seniors, $3 children ages 5–11. A 1926 re-creation of the grand mansion (financed by *Saturday Evening Post* publisher and Camden summer resident Cyrus Curtis) built on this spot in 1794 by General Henry Knox, the portly (5-foot-6-inch, 300-pound) Boston bookseller who became a Revolutionary War hero, then our first secretary of war. He married a granddaughter of Samuel Waldo, the Boston developer who owned all of this area (and for whom the county is named). Inquire about concerts, lectures, and special events.

✐ **Owls Head Transportation Museum** (594-4418; www.ohtm.org), adjacent to the Knox County Regional Airport off Route 73, Owls Head (just south of Rockland). Open daily year-round. April through October, 10–5; November through March, 10–4. Regular admission is $6 adults, $4 under 12, under 5 free, $5 seniors; $16 family admission, more for the frequent special weekend events staged spring through fall. One of the country's outstanding collections of antique planes and automobiles, and unique because everything works. On weekends there are special demonstrations of such magnificent machines as a 1901 Oldsmobile and a 1918 "Jenny" airplane; sometimes rides are offered in a spiffy Model T. In the exhibition hall you can take a 100-year journey through the evolution of transportation, from horse-drawn carriages to World War I fighter planes; from a 16-cylinder Cadillac to a Rolls Royce; from the Red Baron's Fokker triplane to a Ford trimotor. There are also wagons, motorcycles, and bikes. All vehicles have been donated or lent to the museum.

✎ **Shore Village Museum** (594-0311), 104 Limerock Street, Rockland. Open June 1 through October 15, 10–4 daily; by appointment the rest of the year. Free but donations welcome. A large and fascinating collection of historic artifacts of the U.S. Coast Guard, including one of the most extensive collections of lighthouse materials (working foghorns, flashing lights, search-and-rescue gear, buoys, bells, and boats), plus Civil War memorabilia and changing exhibits.

Island Institute (594-9202; www.islandinstitute.org), 386 Main Street, Rockland. A nonprofit organization founded in 1983 to focus on the human dimension of Maine's 14 surviving year-round island communities (a century ago there were 300). The idea initially was to get residents of different islands talking to each other. The monthly *Working Waterfront* newspaper as well as the glossy *Island Journal* focus on shared concerns ranging from fisheries to schools to mapping. These handsome new quarters in the city's former department store include space for changing exhibits.

LIGHTHOUSES

✎ Maine has more lighthouses (63) than any other state, and Penobscot Bay boasts the largest number of lighthouses of all. Three in the Rockland area are accessible by land. One is the **Rockland Breakwater Light,** at the end of the almost mile-long granite breakwater (turn off Route 1 onto Waldo Avenue just north of Rockland, then right onto Samoset Road to the end); the breakwater is a good spot for a picnic. The second lighthouse is the **Owls Head Light,** built in 1825 atop sheer cliffs, but with safe trails down one side to the rocks below—good for scrambling and picnicking. From Rockland or the Owls Head Transportation Museum, take Route 73 to North Shore Drive. After about 2 miles you come to a small post office at an intersection. Turn left onto Main Street and after a quarter mile make a left onto Lighthouse Drive. Just north of the village of Port Clyde (turn off Route 131 onto Marshall Point Road) is the **Marshall Point Lighthouse Museum** (372-6450), open June through September, Sunday through Friday 1–5 and Saturday 10–5; also weekends in May and October, 1–5. Built in 1885, deactivated in 1971, this is a small light on a scenic point; part of the former lighthouse keeper's home is now a lively museum dedicated to the history of the town of St. George in general and the light station (established in 1832) in particular. Even if the lighthouse isn't open, this is a great spot to sit, walk, and picnic.

Lighthouse buffs should also be sure to visit the **Shore Village Museum** (see *Museums and Historic Homes*).

Rockland Breakwater. Be sure to walk out on this pleasant nearly mile-long promontory, the ideal vantage point for watching the windjammers sail in and out.

TO DO

BICYCLING
"Georges River Bikeways" is the name of a free map/guide tracing routes along the river and in its watershed area from Thomaston north into Liberty. Check with the **Georges River Land Trust** (594-5166), 328 Main Street, Studio 206, Rockland. See *To Do—Bicycling* under "Camden/Rockport Area" for the nearest bike rentals.

BOAT EXCURSIONS
Check with the chamber of commerce (see *Guidance*) for current excursions. Also see the **Maine State Ferry Service** described above (under *Getting Around*). Ferry passage to North Haven and Vinalhaven is cheap and takes you the distance. **Monhegan Boat Line** (372-8848) offers a variety of cruises from Port Clyde. **Friendship sloop Surprise** (372-6366; 1-800-241-VIEW) from the East Wind Inn in Tenants Harbor.

BOAT RENTALS
Midcoast Boat Rentals (633-4188 or 882-6445), Rockland, rents power-boats. **Bay Island Yacht Charters & Sailing School** (596-7550; 1-800-421-2492), 117 Tilson Avenue, Rockland, rents sailboats.

SEA KAYAKING
Breakwater Kayak (596-6895; www.breakwaterkayak.com), Buoy Park/ Middle Pier, next to Rockland Public Landing. Two-hour to multiday guided kayaking tours.

WINDJAMMERS
Note: All these vessels are members of the **Maine Windjammer Association** (1-800-807-WIND; www.sailmainecoast.com). Also see *Windjammers* in "What's Where in Maine" and *To Do—Windjammers* in "Camden/Rockport Area." In 3 days aboard a windjammer you can explore islands and remote mainland harbors that would take hundreds of miles of driving and several ferries to reach. Three- and 6-day cruises range from $335 to $750 (slightly less early and late in the season). All the vessels are inspected and certified each year by the Coast Guard.

American Eagle (594-8007; 1-800-648-4544; www.midcoast.com/~schooner), North End Shipyard, Rockland. One of the last classic Gloucester

GREGG CRANNA

Schooner American Eagle, *a national historic landmark*

fishing schooners to be launched (in 1930), this 92-foot vessel continued to fish (minus its original stern and masts, plus a pilothouse) off Gloucester until 1983, when Captain John Foss brought her to Rockland's North End Shipyard and spent the next two years restoring and refitting her. The *Eagle* was built with an engine (so she still has one) as well as sails, and she offers some comfortable belowdecks spaces, well stocked with the captain's favorite books about Maine. The *Eagle* sails farther out to sea (to see whales and seabirds) than other windjammers and also offers a 10-day July cruise to New Brunswick and a Labor Day sail to Gloucester (Massachusetts) to participate in a race that she won in both 1997 and 1998. She offers 3- and 6-day cruises, accommodating 26 guests in 14 double cabins.

Heritage (594-8007; 1-800-648-4544; www.midcoast.com/~schooner), North End Shipyard, Rockland. Captain Doug Lee likes to describe his graceful, 95-foot, 33-passenger vessel as "the next generation of coasting schooner rather than a replica." He notes that schooners were modified over the years to suit whatever cargo they carried. Here headroom in the cabins and the top of companionways was raised to accommodate upright cargo, and the main cabin is an unusually airy, bright space in which to gather. Captain Lee is a marine historian who, with his wife and co-captain, Linda, designed and built the *Heritage* in Rockland's North End Shipyard. Their two daughters, Clara and Rachel, have always summered aboard ship and now sail as crew. Both captains are unusually warm hosts.

J&E Riggin (594-1875; 1-800-869-0604; www.riggin.com) was built in 1927 for the oyster-dredging trade. A speedy 90-footer, she was extensively rebuilt in the 1970s before joining the windjammer trade. Captain Jon Finger and Ann Mahle take 26 passengers in 10 double, 2 triple cabins; no children under 16.

Stephen Taber (236-3520; 1-800-999-7352; www.stephentaber.com), Windjammer Wharf (at the State Ferry Landing), Box 1050, Rockland, was launched in 1871 and is the oldest documented U.S. sailing vessel in continuous use. She is 68 feet long and accommodates 22 passengers. She has a handheld hot-water shower on deck. Ken and Ellen Barnes, both licensed captains, bought, restored, and continue to sail the *Taber* after careers as (among other things) drama professors. Their enthusiastic following proves that they approach each cruise as a new production, throwing their (considerable) all into each sail. This tends to be the most music-filled cruise.

Victory Chimes (594-0755; 1-800-745-5651; www.victorychimes.com), P.O. Box 1401, Rockland. "There was nothing special about this boat in 1900 when she was built," Captain Kip Files is fond of telling his passengers at their first breakfast aboard. "But now she's the only three-masted American-built schooner left. And she's the largest commercial sailing vessel in the United States." The *Chimes* is 170 feet long, accommodating 44 passengers in a variety of cabins (4 singles, 2 quads, 1 triple, 12 doubles).

Nathaniel Bowditch (273-4062; 1-800-288-4098; natbow@midcoast. com), Box 459, Warren 04864, comes by her speed honestly: She was built in East Boothbay as a racing yacht in 1922. Eighty-two feet long, she took special honors in the 1923 Bermuda Race and served in the Coast Guard during World War II. She was rebuilt in the early 1970s. A Maine guide from Rangeley, Captain Gib Philbrick came to the coast to sail aboard a windjammer in 1966 and has been at it ever since. He and his wife, Terry, met aboard the *Bowditch* (she was a passenger). They remain a great team. Twenty-four passengers in 11 double-bunked cabins, two single "Pullmans"; in-cabin sinks. Children ages 10 and up; 3-, 4-, and 6-day cruises, some geared to whale-watching.

Isaac H. Evans (238-1325; www.midcoast.com/~evans), P.O. Box 791, Rockland 04841. A trim 22-passenger schooner dating (in part) from 1886, built for oystering in Delaware Bay, now back in service with owner/captain Brenda G. Walker. It has 11 double berths, some side-by-side as well as upper-lower bunks. Three- and 4-day and weeklong cruises are offered.

OTHER SCHOONER CRUISES

Wendameen (594-1751; www.midcoast.com/wendameen) is a classic 67-foot schooner, her wood and brass beautifully restored by owner-captain Neal Parker, who takes passengers on overnight cruises from Rockland. Board at 1 PM to sail and spend the night in a quiet cove. $170 per person includes dinner and breakfast. Fourteen passengers maximum.

Summertime (563-1605; 1-800-562-8290 outside Maine), 115 South Street, Rockland, is a 53-foot pinky schooner offering 3- and 6-day cruises for up to six passengers throughout the summer. In spring and autumn Captain Bill Brown offers daysails.

Kathryn B (1-800-500-6077), a 105-foot, three-masted, steel-hulled schooner. A luxury version of the traditional windjammer, launched in 1996, accommodating just 10 passengers in five luxurious cabins. Sailing only May through September. Staterooms have private or shared (just two on a head) baths, Victorian detailing and furnishings, and working portholes; the saloon (with fireplace) and dining area (where five-course gourmet meals are served by candlelight) are topside. Three to 6-day cruises $750–1,425.

GOLF

Rockland Golf Club (594-9322), 606 Old County Road, Rockland. Open April through October. This 18-hole public course gets high marks from pros; complete with a modern clubhouse serving meals from 7 AM.

For the local resort specializing in golf, see **Samoset Golf Course** under *To Do—Golf* in "Camden/Rockport Area."

SPECIAL LEARNING PROGRAMS

Hurricane Island Outward Bound School (594-5548), 75 Mechanic Street, Rockland 04841. Outward Bound challenges participants to do things they never thought they could and then push themselves just a little farther. Founded in 1964, this is the largest of the five Outward Bound Schools and two Outward Bound Urban Centers in this country. Courses run May through October, 5 to 26 days on Hurricane Island (near Vinalhaven). Tailored to age and sex, the courses focus on sailing, rock climbing, and outdoor problem solving.

Merle Donovan's Maine Coast Art Workshops (594-2300), 2 Park Street, Suite 501, Rockland 04841. June through Labor Day. A well-established program of weeklong landscape workshops (both oil and watercolor) taught by a series of prominent artists from throughout the country. Lodging is at the Tradewinds motel in downtown Rockland.

GREEN SPACE

BEACHES

⚲ **Johnson Memorial Park,** Chickawaukee Lake, Route 17 (toward Augusta).

⚲ **Birch Point State Park,** also known as Lucia Beach, off Ash Point Road in Owls Head. Sandy, with smooth boulders for sunning, wooded walking trails, and picnic benches. Marked from Route 73.

Drift Inn Beach in Port Clyde, down Drift Inn Road by the Harpoon Restaurant, just off Route 31; a small beach in a great spot.

BIRDING

Waldo Tyler Wildlife Sanctuary, Buttermilk Lane (off Route 73), South Thomaston, is a birding spot on the Weskeag River.

HIKING
The Georges River Land Trust (594-5166), 328 Main Street, Studio 206, Rockland, publishes a map/guide to the Georges Highland Path, a foot trail through the hills of the Georges River watershed. Maps are available at the chamber of commerce (see *Guidance*).

PICNICKING
There's a Route 1 picnic area overlooking Glen Cove, between the towns of Rockland and Rockport.

LODGING

INNS
Craignair Inn (594-7644; 1-800-320-9997; www.craignair.com), Clark Island, Spruce Head 04859. Open year-round. Steve and Neva Joseph have breathed new life into this old inn, an unusual building that was originally erected for workers at a nearby granite quarry. Sited on 4 shorefront acres, it offers 21 guest rooms, divided between the main house (4 with private baths; the rest shared) and more luxurious units (private baths) in the Vestry, set in gardens in the rear. In the main house, bedrooms are small but pleasing, with phones, furnished with antiques, some with water views. We like Room 8 with its paisley green spread, braided rug and rocker, oak dresser, and view of Clark Island. The dining room overlooks the water and is open to the public for dinner (see *Dining Out*). Walk across the causeway and the path to Clark Island's quarry. There's good bird-watching along the way and swimming in the quarry. From $88 per couple, $62 single (less off-season), including a buffet breakfast. Two-night minimum stay on holiday weekends. Weekly rates are available. $8.50 extra for a pet.

Ocean House (372-6691; 1-800-269-6691), P.O. Box 66, Port Clyde 04855. Open May through mid-October. The logical place to spend the night before boarding the morning ferry to Monhegan, a friendly old village inn run by former islander Bud Murdock. Eight of the 10 upstairs guest rooms in this building have private baths (two share) and several have water views (also available from the upstairs porch); every year a couple get redone. This is a good place for a single traveler, thanks to the pleasant single rooms and rates and the ease with which you can dine with others. A reasonably priced family-style dinner is by reservation (BYOB), and breakfast is served to both guests and the public, 7–noon. Rooms are $84 double, less single and off-season.

East Wind Inn (372-6366; 1-800-241-VIEW; www.eastwindinn.com), P.O. Box 149, Tenants Harbor 04860. Open April through November; for special functions the remainder of the year. Under the longtime ownership of Tim Watts, this is a very tidy and rather formal waterside inn. The parlor is large, with a piano that guests are welcome to play, but the best seats in the house are on the wraparound porch overlooking Tenants

Harbor. Rooms vary from singles with shared baths ($75) and standard double with private bath ($90) to suites ($162) and apartments in the waterside Meeting House ($188) and Wheeler Cottage with three luxurious units ($180–275). All rates include a $6 breakfast allowance and are less off-season. The dining room serves breakfast and dinner in-season (see *Dining Out*). A number of guests sail in. The **Chandlery** on the wharf offers light food as well as marine supplies.

In "Camden/Rockport Area," also see the **Samoset Resort,** which over-looks Rockland Harbor.

BED & BREAKFASTS
In and around Rockland

 ♿ **The Captain Lindsey House** (596-7950; 1-800-523-2145; www.rockland maine.com), 5 Lindsey Street, Rockland 04841. Built in 1837 as one of Rockland's first inns, this sturdy brick building just off Main Street was eventually converted into offices and labs by the Camden-Rockland Water Company. By the 1990s it took real imagination to envision its original use. Ken and Ellen Barnes, who have also restored the windjammer *Stephen Taber*, have created a gem of a small hotel with richly paneled public rooms and nine spacious guest rooms (one handicapped accessible). All have air-conditioning, phones, and TVs. Rates are $100–170, including continental breakfast. Ask about discounts for windjammer passengers.

✎ **Weskeag Inn** (596-6676; 1-800-596-5576), Route 73, P.O. Box 213, South Thomaston 04858. Open year-round (weekends-only in winter). Convenient to the Owls Head Transportation Museum and the Knox County Regional Airport (where they'll gladly pick you up, perhaps in an antique car). A hospitable 1830s home overlooking the Weskeag estuary, within walking distance of shops in the village of South Thomaston, and handy to a public boat landing. Six guest rooms have private baths; two share. Request a water view. There's a comfortable living room, but guests are drawn to the sunny sitting room/dining area off the kitchen where Lynn Smith usually presides, dispensing advice on the best local dining, shopping, swimming, and birding spots. Gray Smith is an antique-car enthusiast. $85–120, less off-season, includes a full breakfast.

♿ **Old Granite Inn** (594-9036; 1-800-386-9036; www.oldgraniteinn.com), Main Street, Rockland 04841. An 1840s mansion built of local granite, attached to a 1790 house, set in a flower and sculpture garden, right across from the Maine State Ferry Terminal (also the Concord Trailways stop). The obvious place to stay before boarding a ferry to Vinalhaven, North Haven, or Matinicus (see "Midcoast Islands"). Innkeepers Ragan and John Cary have lived and worked in the area many years, and this is a welcoming B&B. The living room and dining room feature rich woodwork, and the 11 guest rooms (9 with private baths) are hung with art and furnished with antiques. Five rooms are on the ground floor (all are wheelchair accessible), six are on the second floor (the two with harbor views are the largest and most expensive), and one third-floor room has a queen bed, private bath, and harbor view. $100–150 per night in high season, $55–85 in low; includes a full breakfast.

LimeRock Inn (594-2257; 1-800-LIME-ROC), 96 Limerock Street, Rockland 04841. An 1890s Queen Anne–style mansion on a quiet residential street, the inn has been thoroughly restored, its eight guest rooms (all with private baths) furnished with splendid reproduction antiques (the innkeepers own a furniture store in Intervale, New Hampshire). Rates range from $100 for a small room decorated in floral prints to $185 for a large room with a mahogany four-poster and whirlpool bath or for a turret room with a "wedding canopy" bed. They include a very full breakfast and afternoon tea.

Beech Street Guest House (596-7280; www.midcoast.com/~beechstr), 41 Beech Street, P.O. Box 71, Rockland 04861. We like the feel of this unpretentious house on a quiet side street. Hosts Charles Grey (a piano tuner) and Gina Fry (a massage therapist) offer just two guest rooms, both with private baths. They also offer sails in their classic 42-foot wooden Zivio yawl and full breakfasts featuring local produce. $50–80.

Berry Manor Inn (596-0376; 1-800-562-2529; www.berrymanorinn.com), 81 Talbot Avenue, P.O. Box 1117, Rockland 04841. An expansive 19th-century mansion with eight guest rooms decorated in real and reproduction antiques; offers whirlpool tubs and some fireplaces. $95–195 per night includes a full breakfast; less off-season.

The St. George Peninsula and Friendship

✐ **The Outsiders' Inn** (832-5197), corner of Routes 97 and 220, 4 Main Street, Friendship 04547. Open year-round, except for a few weeks in midwinter. Comfortable atmosphere in an 1830 house. Guests can take advantage of Bill Michaud's kayaking expertise; eight kayaks are available for rent and guided expeditions in nearby Muscongus Bay. Pleasant doubles with private baths are $70; $55 with shared bath. A small cottage in the garden is $350 per week. Facilities include a sauna.

🐾 **Harbor Hill** (832-6646), P.O. Box 35, 5 Harbor Hill Lane, Friendship 04547. Open May through November 1, also winter weekends by arrangement. Liga and Len Jahnke's 1800s farmhouse is set on a hillside sloping to the sea, with views of the islands in Muscongus Bay. The three suites all have water views and private baths; $90–95 includes a Scandinavian-style breakfast. A two-bedroom cottage is $550 per week.

Friendship Harbor House Bed & Breakfast (832-7447; friendship@midcoast.com), P.O. Box 226, Friendship 04547. This B&B offers four guest rooms and an apartment. Facilities include a beach, dock, and kayak rental. $95–125; cottage also available.

MOTEL

Navigator Motor Inn (594-2131), 520 Main Street, Rockland 04841. Open all year. Geared to families bound for the islands of Vinalhaven, North Haven, and Matinicus. The Maine State Ferry Terminal is across the street so you can park your car in line for the early-morning ferry and walk back to your room. This is a five-story 80-room motel with cable TV and a restaurant that serves from 6:30 AM.

COTTAGES AND EFFICIENCIES

A list of cottages, primarily in the Owls Head and Spruce Head areas, is available from the Rockland-Thomaston Chamber of Commerce (see *Guidance*).

WHERE TO EAT

DINING OUT

Primo (596-0770; www.primorestaurant.com), 2 South Main Street (Route 73), Rockland. Open Thursday through Monday, 5:30–9:30. Reservations a must. Melissa Kelly, winner of the coveted Best Chef in the Northeast award from the James Beard Foundation, and pastry chef Price Kusher have created a very special place. The big old house that used to house Jessica's restaurant is now five intimate dining rooms, and an upstairs bar. The menu features local organic ingredients with a distinct Italian accent. You might begin with a crisp crêpe of montasio cheese with eggplant caponata and arugula salad ($8.50) and dine splendidly on grilled leg of lamb with a fava, fiddlehead fern, tomato, and olive fondue ($26). Entrées $12–26. The wine list is extensive.

Amalfi (596-0012), 421 Main Street, Rockland. Open year-round for dinner, chef David Cooke's cheerful restaurant gets rave reviews for specialties drawn from all sides of the Mediterranean. Begin with a bowl of minestrone or grilled quail glazed with a Turkish mulberry sauce and dine on Spanish paella, chicken Piccata, or roasted salmon with tomato jam, lentil, and couscous pilaf. Entrées $12.95–16.95.

Café Miranda (594-2034), 15 Oak Street, Rockland. Open year-round 5:30–9:30. Be sure to reserve for dinner because chef Kerry Altiero's small, bright dining room—in an array of southwestern colors and flavors—is usually filled. The open kitchen features a brick oven and seafood grill, and the menu, fresh pastas and herbs. Our pink-pottery platter of curried mussels and shrimp (both in the shell) was served on polenta with sweet peppers and onions, mopped up with flatbread and olive oil. Wine and beer are served. The handwritten menu changes daily. Entrées $11.50–17.

Craignair Inn (594-7644), Clark Island, Spruce Head (off Route 73). Open for dinner May through November. This attractive water-view dining room has a locally respected chef. Dinner entrées might include a bouillabaisse of local mussels, shrimp, and fish ($17.95) and the house lobster Newburg (priced daily). Entrées from $15.95.

The Harpoon (372-6304), corner of Drift Inn and Marshall Point Roads, Port Clyde. Open May through mid-October. In July and August open for lunch and dinner every day. Spring and fall, dinner only, Wednesday through Sunday. This engaging little seafood restaurant in the seaside village of Port Clyde (just off Route 131, around the corner from the harbor) specializes in the local catch. Try the Cajun seafood, lazy lobster, fried combo plate, or prime rib. Full bar.

East Wind Inn (372-6366), Tenants Harbor. Open for dinner and Sunday brunch. Reservations suggested. A dining room overlooking the working harbor with a porch on which cocktails are served in summer. The menu features local seafood and produce. Dinners might include roasted Atlantic salmon with a walnut-pesto crust, served with a roasted pepper coulis ($15.95), or char-grilled sirloin ($16.95).

Harbor View Restaurant (354-8173), Thomas Harbor Point, Thomaston. Open year-round for lunch and dinner. Chef-owner Bernard Davodet's restaurant in a former boathouse is a local standby, hidden down on the harbor. In-season there's dining on the deck. Fish fried and broiled is the specialty, and there is a wide choice of "light fare" like crab salad or steamers. Entrées $8.95–16.95; more for boiled lobster. Nightly specials. Full license.

Also see **Thomaston Café and Bakery,** under *Eating Out,* and **Marcel's** at the Samoset Resort, under *Dining Out,* in "Camden/Rockport Area."

EATING OUT

In Rockland

𝒮 **The Water Works** (596-2753), Lindsey Street. Serving lunch and dinner daily, late light fare. The Barnes family have converted a former eight-bay garage for the Camden-Rockland Water Company into an attractive meeting spot with two distinct atmospheres: a dining area with a striking fountain sculpture (by Captain Ken Barnes) at one end and a congenial pub at the other. Former windjammer chef Susan Barnes is the hand behind the large and satisfying menu. Staples include lentil and walnut steak as well as London broil, broiled fish of the day, and lobster stew; the blackboard dinner menu changes nightly. The brew list is extensive. Children's menu.

Market on Main (594-0015), 315 Main Street. Open daily for lunch, dinner, and Sunday brunch. An attractive and popular new storefront café and deli geared to the museum crowd; good for salads and sandwiches. Serving wine, beer, and espresso.

𝒮 **The Brown Bag** (596-6372), 606 Main Street (north of downtown). Open Monday through Saturday 6:30 AM–4 PM. This expanded storefront restaurant offers an extensive breakfast and sandwich menu. Make your selection at the counter and carry it to your table when it's ready.

Second Read Books & Coffee (594-4123), 328 Main Street. Open 8–5:30, much later on music nights, noon–4 on Sunday. Patrick Reilley and Susanne Ward's café seems to serve as a living room for the city's sizable creative community, serving cappuccino and croissants. Also see *Entertainment*.

The Landings Restaurant & Pub (596-6563), 1 Commercial Street. Open year-round. On the harbor with outside as well as inside seating, serves 11–9:30 from a menu that ranges from a hot dog to steak, lobster, and a full-scale clambake. Fried clams, fish-and-chips, and a good selection of sandwiches. Entrées $5–16.

🖉 **Rockland Café** (596-7556), 411 Main Street. Open daily 6 AM–9 PM. This is a reliable family eatery, good for fish-and-chips, soups, salad, clam rolls, and daily specials. Warning: The crabcakes are more like crab pancakes. Look for the green-and-white-striped awning.

Kate's Seafood (594-2626), Route 1, south of Rockland. April through October. A local favorite for fried, boiled, and steamed seafood, chowder, and lobster rolls. For dinner, try the seafood primavera or seafood sauté with scallops, Maine shrimp, lobster, and mussels. Beer and wine served.

🖉 **Dave's Restaurant** (594-5424), Route 1, between Thomaston and Rockland. Seafood dinners and the area's only smorgasbord, with old-fashioned classics such as macaroni and cheese and beans and franks. Breakfast and lunch buffets, plus a large salad bar. Breakfast is served all day; sandwiches, pizza, seafood dinner, too.

🖉 **Wasses Wagon,** 2 North Main Street. A local institution for hot dogs.

In Thomaston

Thomaston Café and Bakery (354-8589), 88 Main Street. Open 7–2, also for dinner Friday and Saturday and for Sunday brunch. Homemade soups, great sandwiches, specials like fish cakes with homefries, salads, and a wicked quesadilla with Maine shrimp, goat cheese, and salad. The dinner menu ranges from wild mushroom hash to fresh fettuccine with brandied lobster meat. Dinner entrées $13.25–17.50.

Elsewhere

Dip Net Coffee Shop, Port Clyde. Seasonal. Offers counter service and table seating, good food, and access to the harborside deck, but it seems to be closed more than it is open. The neighboring **Port Clyde General Store** makes good sandwiches and has picnic benches on the deck, and the **Ocean House,** just up the road, serves breakfast, a real convenience if you have driven from a distance to catch the Monhegan ferry.

Hannibal's Café on the Common (785-3663), Union. Open year-round from 10 AM Tuesday through Friday, from 7 AM Saturday, Sunday brunch 8–2. Good lunch and dinner; specializing in "classical, ethnic, and vegetarian cuisine," now in an 1839 farmhouse with views of Seven Tree Pond.

LOBSTER POUNDS

Cod End (372-6782), on the Wharf, Tenants Harbor. Open Memorial Day through late September, daily 7 AM–9 PM; spring and fall, 8–6. Hidden down a lane, a combination fish shop and informal wharfside eatery (tables inside and out) right on Tenants Harbor with a separate cook house: breakfast muffins and eggs, lunch chowders and lobster rolls, dinner lobsters and clams. BYOB.

Miller's Lobster Company (594-7406), Wheeler's Bay, Route 73, Spruce Head. Open 10–7, Memorial Day through Labor Day. On a working harbor, old-fashioned, family owned and operated, with a loyal following. Tables are on the wharf; lobsters and clams are cooked in seawater.

Waterman's Beach Lobsters (594-2489), off Route 73, South Thomaston. Open daily 11–7 in summertime. Oceanfront feasting on the deck: lobster and clam dinners, seafood rolls, homemade pies.

ENTERTAINMENT

The Farnsworth Museum (596-6457) stages a year-round series of Sunday concerts, free with museum admission; reservations advised.

Second Read Books & Coffee (594-4123), 328 Main Street, Rockland, has live music, usually jazz or folksinging, on many Friday and Saturday evenings; also poetry readings.

Live bands can usually be found on summer weekends at the **Time Out Pub** (593-9336), 275 Main Street in Rockland, and at **The Water Works** (see *Eating Out*).

Strand Cinema (594-7266), Main Street, Rockland. A classic '20s vaudeville theater turned movie house showing first-run films at a reasonable price. We hope it weathers the competition from the **Flagship Cinemas** (594-2100) with its seven screens on Route 1 at the Rockland-Thomaston line.

Down East Singers (354-2262), Thomaston. The Midcoast's largest community chorus performs throughout the year. Inquire about their new stage in the evolving Lincoln Street Center for the Arts, Rockland.

SELECTIVE SHOPPING

Rockland's mile-long **Main Street** recalls 19th-century prosperity in florid brick. Since the opening of the **Farnsworth Museum Store** (corner of Main and Elm Streets), boutique-style stores as well as galleries have proliferated around it. Note especially: **Archipelago** (#386), formerly Islands of Maine Gallery, now in expanded quarters at the new Island Institute quarters, representing roughly 100 craftspeople and artists on "hinged" as well as real islands. **Huston Tuttle & Gallery One** (#365) is a serious art store with a gallery upstairs; **The Store** (#435), featuring a wide selection of cooking supplies; **The Grasshopper Shop** (#400), a major link in a small Maine chain; **Meander** (#373), a mix of things you have never thought of needing; **G. F. MacGregor** (#338), a blend of tasteful furniture and furnishings obviously catering to museumgoers. More shops worth noting: **Trillium Soaps** (#436), all-natural soaps (like essential oil of pine with comfrey leaf and alfalfa juice) made by Peter and Nancy Digirolamo in nearby Jefferson; **Sea Street Graphics Outlet Store** (#475), with silk-screened designs on T-shirts and clothing

KIM GRANT

You can admire the work of local artists in many Rockland galleries.

(made here, widely distributed); the **Black Parrot** (#328) specializes in its colorful fleece-lined reversible garments but carries a mix of clothing, toys, cards, and more; **Caravans** (#429) sells clothing with its own label too, as well as much more; and we never pass up **Ravishing Recalls** (#389), a useful trove of secondhand clothing.

ART AND CRAFT GALLERIES

So many galleries have opened around the Farnsworth area that an "Arts in Rockland" map is available at most. They include the prestigious **Caldbeck Gallery** (12 Elm Street across from the museum; here since 1982); goldsmith Thomas O'Donovan's **Harbor Square Gallery,** filling a former bank building (374 Main Street) with art but also featuring fine jewelry; **337 Main** shows top Maine artists; and the **Anne Kilham Gallery** (28 Elm Street), recently relocated from Rockport, displays work, prints, and cards. Maine's most popular graphic artist. **Deborah Beckwith Winship**'s bright, primitive-style graphics are also familiar to Maine visitors, and her studio at 53 Fulton Street is an excuse to explore Rockland's quickly changing South End. Wyeth fans should check out **OP Limited** (www.wyetharchives.com) in Thomaston, an upstairs gallery at 103 Main Street selling out-of-print and limited-edition works on paper from the Wyeth Archive.

Along Route 131 to Port Clyde

Check out **St. George Pottery** (4.5 miles off Route 1), George Pearlman's combination studio and contemporary ceramics gallery; **Noble Clay** in Tenants Harbor is open year-round and displays Trish and Steve Barnes's functional white-and-blue-glazed porcelain pottery with whimsical and botanical designs. Also in Tenants Harbor: **Harbor Frame Shop & Gallery** (372-8274) on Barter's Point Road (look for the totem pole out front), displaying both established and upcoming artists; **Port Clyde Arts & Crafts Society Gallery,** also off Route 31 in Tenants Harbor, showcases works by its members. **Gallery-by-the Sea** in the village of Port Clyde (open daily June through October) is a standout: Sally MacVane knows her Maine artists and carries the best.

In South Thomaston

At **Keag River Pottery** (Westbrook Street, marked from Route 73), Toni Oliveri shapes unusual but functional creations like the glazed vase we bought and love: Its inner ribbons of pottery make it easier to artistically display flowers. **Old Post Office Gallery & Art of the Sea** on Route 73 displays nearly 100 museum-quality full-rigged ship models; also half models and nautical paintings.

BOOKSTORES

The Reading Corner (596-6651), 408 Main Street, Rockland, is a full-service bookstore with an unusual interior filling two storefronts.

✎ **The Personal Book Shop** (354-8056), 78 Main Street, Thomaston. Open year-round 10–6. Marti Reed's shop is more like a book-lined living room than your ordinary bookstore: plenty of places to sit and read but also a large selection of titles; many Maine authors, including out-of-print John Gould and Elisabeth Ogilvie books and a well-stocked children's room. Special orders and out-of-print searches.

Dooryard Books, 436 Main Street, Rockland (open Memorial Day through Columbus Day). A good general stock of hardcover and paperback used books.

Lobster Lane Book Shop (594-7520), Spruce Head. Marked from the Off-Island Store. Open June through September, Thursday through Sunday and weekends through October, 12:30–5. Vivian York's stock of 50,000 titles is well known in bookish circles. Specialties include fiction and Maine.

Also see **Second Read Books & Coffee** under *Eating Out* and *Entertainment*.

SPECIAL SHOPS

Prison Shop at the Maine State Prison in Thomaston, Main Street (Route 1), at the southern end of town. A variety of wooden furniture—coffee tables, stools, lamps, and trays—and small souvenirs, all carved by inmates. Prices are reasonable and profits go to the craftsmen.

Local Talents of Maine (354-0013), 119 Main Street, Thomaston. A consignment shop for 160 local craftspeople with the stress on variety: jams, dried flowers, quilts, and more.

SPECIAL EVENTS

June: **Warren Day**—a pancake breakfast, parade, art and quilt shows, chicken barbecue, and auction.

July: **Fourth of July** celebrations in most towns, with parades. Thomaston's festivities include a big parade, foot races, live entertainment, a craft fair, barbecue, and fireworks. **Schooner Days** and the **North Atlantic**

KIM GRANT

The Maine State Prison shop in Rockport features handmade ship models.

Blues Festival, Harbor Park, Rockland *(Friday, Saturday, and Sunday after July 4)*—see the wonderful windjammers vie for first place in a spectacular race that recalls bygone days. The best vantage point is the Rockland breakwater. **Friendship Sloop Days,** Rockland. **Full Circle Summer Fair,** at the Union Fairgrounds, sponsored by WERU-FM—the emphasis is on everything natural and on crafts.

August: **Maine Lobster Festival,** Harbor Park, Rockland *(first weekend, plus the preceding Wednesday and Thursday).* This is probably the world's biggest lobster feed, prepared in the world's largest lobster boiler. Patrons queue up on the public landing to heap their plates with lobsters, clams, corn, and all the fixings. King Neptune and the Maine Sea Goddess reign over the event, which includes a parade down Main Street, concerts, an art exhibit, contests such as clam shucking and sardine packing, and a race across a string of lobster crates floating in the harbor. The **Annual North Atlantic Folk Festival** in Rockland's Harbor Park is midmonth, followed by the **Annual Transportation Spectacular and Aerobatic Show** at the Owls Head Transportation Museum. **Union Fair** and **State of Maine Wild Blueberry Festival** *(third week)*—a real agricultural fair with tractor- and ox-pulling contests, livestock and food shows, a midway, the crowning of the Blueberry Queen, and, on one day during the week, free mini–blueberry pies for all comers.

October: **Farnsworth Festival of Scarecrows,** Farnsworth Museum. Rockland community scarecrow contest, dance, related events.

November–December: **Rockland Festival of Lights** begins on Thanksgiving; parade, Santa's Village, sleigh rides.

Midcoast Islands

Monhegan; The Fox Islands: Vinalhaven and North Haven; Matinicus

MONHEGAN

Eleven miles at sea and barely a mile square, Monhegan is a microcosm of Maine landscapes, everything from 150-foot sheer headlands to Cathedral Woods, from inland meadows filled with deer to the smooth, low rocks along Lobster Cove. "Beached like a whale" is the way one mariner in 1590 described the island's shape: headlands sloping down to Lobster Cove, a low and quiet tail.

Monhegan is known for the quality (also quantity) of its artists and the grit of its fishermen—who lobster only from January through June. The island's first recorded artist arrived in 1858, and by the 1890s a mansard-roofed hotel and several boardinghouses were filled with summer guests, many of them artists. In 1903 Robert Henri, a founder of New York's Ashcan School and a well-known art teacher, discovered Monhegan and soon introduced it to his students, among them George Bellows and Rockwell Kent. Monhegan remains a genuine art colony. Jamie Wyeth owns a house built by Rockwell Kent. Some 20 artists open their studios to visitors (hours are posted on "The Barn" and printed in handouts) during summer weeks.

The island continues to draw artists in good part because its beauty not only survives but also remains accessible to all. Prospect Hill, the only attempted development, foundered around 1900. It was Theodore Edison, son of the inventor, who amassed property enough to erase its traces and keep the island's cottages (which still number just 130) bunched along the sheltered Eastern Harbor, the rest preserved as common space and laced with 17 miles of footpaths.

In 1954 Edison helped organize Monhegan Associates, a nonprofit corporation dedicated to preserving the "natural, wild beauty" of the island. Ironically, this is one of the country's few communities to shun electricity until relatively recently. A number of homes and one inn still use kerosene lamps. Vehicles are limited to a few trucks to haul lobstering gear and visitors' luggage to and from the dock.

Monhegan has three inns, several B&Bs, and a number of rental

Coming ashore on Monhegan Island

cottages; it is also a summer day's destination for day-trippers from Boothbay Harbor and New Harbor as well as Port Clyde—obviously a heavy tide of tourists for such a small, fragile island. Luckily the fog and frequently rough passage discourage casual visitors. The island's year-round population of around 70 swells to a little more than 400 (not counting day-trippers) in summer; visitors come to walk, to paint, and to reflect. An unusual number come alone.

GETTING THERE

Monhegan-Thomaston Boat Line operates both the sleek *Elizabeth Ann* and the beloved old *Laura B* from Port Clyde (reservations are advisable: P.O. Box 238, Port Clyde 04855; or call 372-8848; www. monheganboat.com). Service is three times daily in-season, less frequent in spring and fall, and only Monday, Wednesday, and Friday in winter. It's a 60-minute trip. For details about the *Balmy Days II,* see *To Do—Boat Excursions* in "Boothbay Harbor Region," and for the *Hardy III,* see *To Do—Boat Excursions* in "Damariscotta/Newcastle and Pemaquid Area."

EQUIPMENT AND RULES

Come properly shod for the precipitous paths, and bring sweaters and windbreakers. Wading or swimming from any of the tempting coves on the back side of the island can be lethal. Flashlights, heavy rubber boots, and rain gear are also good ideas. There is no bank or ATM on the island. Public phones are few. Camping is prohibited. Do not bring bicycles or dogs (which must be leashed at all times). No smoking outside the village, and please don't pick the flowers.

PUBLIC REST ROOM

Up a lane behind the Monhegan House, this facility is central; please use it and pay the requested $.50. This is a small price to pay for visiting such a beautiful but fragile island.

GETTING AROUND

Several trucks meet each boat as it arrives and provide baggage service. Otherwise visitors have no access to motorized transport; you need none because distances are all walkable and there are no paved roads.

MEDICAL EMERGENCY

Dial **911** (most private homes as well as island businesses now have phones). Unfortunately, the island's Emergency Rescue Squad gets plenty of practice; they are a highly skilled group.

TO SEE

Monhegan Island Light, built in 1850 and automated in 1959, caps a hill that's well worth climbing for the view alone. The former keeper's cottage is now the **Monhegan Museum** (open daily July through mid-September, 11:30–3:30; 12:30–2:30 in September), a spellbinding display of island art, artifacts, flora, fauna, some geology, lobstering, and an artistic history of the island, including documents dating back to the 16th century. A separate art museum preserves the invaluable paintings that have accrued to the museum and offers space for special exhibits like that of 2001, acknowledged as the opening year, on James Fitzgerald.

Manana Island (across the harbor from Monhegan) is the site of a famous runic stone with inscriptions purported to be Norse or Phoenician. At Fish Beach on Monhegan, you may be able to find someone willing to take you over in a skiff.

TO DO

BIRDING

Mid- through late September, it's difficult to find a room on the island because Monhegan is well known among birders as one of the best birding places on the East Coast. Your local Audubon Society may have a trip going.

HIKING

Pick up a trail map to the island's 17-mile network before setting out. Day-trippers should take the Burnt Head Trail and loop back by the village via Lobster Cove rather than trying a longer circuit; allow at least 5 hours (bring a picnic) to go around the island. Our favorite hike is Burnt Head to White Head along high bluffs, with a pause to explore the unusual rocks in Gull Cove, and back through Cathedral Woods. On another day head for Blackhead and Pulpit Rock, then back along the shore to Green Point and Pebble Beach.

LODGING

INNS
All listings are on Monhegan Island 04852.

🐾✐ **Island Inn** (596-0371; fax, 594-5517; www.islandinnMonhegan.com). Open late May through mid-October. Owners Howard Weilbacker and Philip Truelove continue to steadily upgrade this vintage wooden hotel. In the two small living rooms (part of the original circa-1850 house that is the nucleus of the 1906 inn), note the hand-painted murals. The large, old-fashioned dining room serves three meals a day to the public as well as to overnight guests. The 30 rooms and four suites are small, typically old-fashioned summer hotel rooms with a sink, simply furnished; 15 now have private baths. Opt for a water view. $105–210 double (the low end is for shared bath, "meadow" view), $250 for a one-bedroom suite, $75–110 single, including a full breakfast.

✐ **The Trailing Yew** (596-0440; 1-800-592-2520), Monhegan Island 04852. Open mid-May through mid-October. In 1996 Josephine Day died, having operated the Yew since 1926. At present it is run as a trust to preserve the spirit as well as physical shape of this quirky, affordable institution, New England's last genuine 19th-century-style "summer boardinghouse." It's been spiffed up considerably, however, in the past few years. The 35 rooms are divided among the main house and adjacent annexes and cottages on the grounds and up the road. Baths are shared but spotless and equipped with electricity. Guest rooms are comfortable, lit with kerosene lamps. Before meals, guests gather around the flagpole outside the main building to pitch horseshoes and compare notes; dining at shared tables features lots of conversation, making this a great place for solo travelers. It's also a favorite with artists. Request a room in Seagull. $60 per person per day includes breakfast and dinner and all taxes and tips; under age 10, $15–35. No credit cards.

Monhegan House (594-7983; 1-800-599-7983), Box 345, Monhegan 04852. At this writing, open Memorial Day through Columbus Day. An 1888 summer inn with 33 rooms. No closets, shared baths, but clean, comfortable, and bright; rooms are furnished with antique oak pieces, and many have water views. The downstairs lobby is often warmed by a glowing fireplace and has ample seating for foggy mornings; on sunny days guests tend to opt for the rockers along the porch, a vantage point from which you can watch the comings and goings of just about every-one on the island. Singles are $60; doubles $95; $115 for three people. Also see *Where to Eat.*

BED & BREAKFASTS
🐾 **Shining Sails Guesthouse** (596-0041; fax, 596-7611; www.shiningsails.-com), Box 346, Monhegan Island 04852. Open year-round. John and Winnie Murdock maintain this charming old Monhegan home on the

edge of the village and water. There are two rooms, one with views of the meadow and one of the ocean (our favorite guest room on the entire island); also five efficiencies, four with ocean views and private decks. All rooms are tastefully decorated, as is the common room, which has a water view and Franklin stove. An ample continental breakfast is served May through Columbus Day. John Murdock is an island lobsterman and the couple are helpful hosts. Rooms are $80–105 per night, $540–680 per week; apartments are $85–135 per night, $575–885 per week.

Hitchcock House (594-8137), Horn's Hill, Monhegan Island 04852. Open year-round. Hidden away on top of Horn's Hill with a pleasant garden and deck. Barbara Hitchcock offers several rooms and efficiencies with views of the meadows. The studio, a separate cabin, has a kitchen and bedroom. Two rooms sharing one bath are $60 per night, $385 per week; efficiencies are $90 per night, $580 per week.

COTTAGES AND EFFICIENCIES

Cooking facilities come in handy here: You can buy lobster and good fresh and smoked fish (bring meat and staples) and a limited line of vegetables. **Shining Sails Real Estate** (596-0041; fax, 596-7166; www.shiningsails.com) manages two dozen or so rental cottages, available by the weekend as well as by the week. Demand is so high, however, that it's wise to get in your bid in early January for the summer.

WHERE TO EAT

Monhegan House Café at the Monhegan House is an attractive and informal place to eat. The long, many-windowed dining room is in the back of the inn, overlooking the village and meadow. Homemade breads and omelets for breakfast; luncheon sandwiches like cheese, lettuce, tomato, and avocado on homemade bread; fresh-ground peanut butter; or "the ultimate burger." Dinner entrées include vegetarian choices as well as seafood and steak ($14–18). BYOB.

The Island Inn (mid-June through mid-September). Open to the public for all three meals. The traditional hotel dining room offers a large à la carte dinner menu; entrées might include spinach and caramelized onion lasagna or jumbo lobster and spinach ravioli. Entrées $16–24.

The Trailing Yew (mid-May through mid-October). Open to the public by reservation: $17 for fruit cup, entrée, salad, and dessert—whatever is being served that night. Ask when you reserve. The big attraction here is the conversation around communal tables. BYOB.

The Periwinkle, open seasonally, serves breakfast, lunch, and dinner. A two-floor restaurant with water views, varied menu, BYOB. Outside seating at lunch. Dinner entrées $14.95–29.95.

North End Market (594-5546), open year-round 9–7 for lunch and dinner. Soups, sandwiches, and rice dishes as well as pizza; also selling grocery staples at this writing because the general store is closed and up for sale.

SELECTIVE SHOPPING

ART GALLERIES

The Lupine Gallery (594-8131). Bill Boynton and Jackie Bogel offer original works by 60 artists who paint regularly on the island. This is a very special gallery, showcasing the work of many professional artists within walking distance. You can pick out work that you like and then check the artist's hours on the island's "open-studio" list at "The Barn."

Open studios: Many resident artists welcome visitors to their studios; pick up a schedule, check "The Barn," or look for shingles hung outside listing the hours they're open. To see works by James Fitzgerald, contact his longtime patron, Anne Hubert. In addition, some of the island's most prestigious artists do not post hours but still welcome visitors by appointment. Several give occasional workshops.

SPECIAL SHOPS

Carina. The spiritual successor of the old Island Spa, with booths, books, quality crafted items, wines, and fresh-baked goods and vegetables.

Winter's Work. Open Memorial Day through Labor Day, by the ferry dock. A former fish house filled with work produced by the island's 20 craftspeople: a surprising variety and quality of knitted goods, jewelry, Christmas decorations, and more.

Black Duck. Open Memorial Day through Columbus Day, a gift store hidden on Fish Beach, selling imaginative T-shirts and the like.

THE FOX ISLANDS: VINALHAVEN AND NORTH HAVEN

The Fox Islands Thoroughfare is a rowable stretch of yacht-filled water that separates Vinalhaven and North Haven, two islands that differ deeply.

Vinalhaven is heavily wooded and marked by granite quarries that include two public swimming holes. Life eddies around the village of Carver's Harbor, home to Maine's largest lobster fleet. In 1880, when granite was being cut on Vinalhaven to build Boston's Customs House, 2,855 people were living here on the island, a number now reduced to about 1,200—a mix of descendants of 18th-century settlers and the stonecutters who came here from Sweden, Norway, Finland, and Scotland. In recent years the island has also attracted a number of artists, including Robert Indiana. Summer visitors far outnumber year-round residents, but there is no yacht club or golf course. This is Maine's largest year-round working island community. It's not an island resort.

By contrast, North Haven is half as big, with just 325 year-round residents. It's rolling and open, spotted with idyllic farmhouses, summer homes for some of the country's wealthiest and most influential families. Pastimes include wagon rides and golf. Many children sail in the same distinctive dinghies their grandparents sailed.

It was British explorer Martin Pring who named the Fox Islands in 1603, ostensibly for the silver foxes he saw on both islands. A dozen miles out in Penobscot Bay, these islands are still understandably protective of their considerable beauty, especially in view of their unusual— by Maine island standards—accessibility by Maine State Ferry.

Be it said that there is just one B&B on North Haven and only 30 or so beds on Vinalhaven for visitors in August. Neither is there an excursion boat, and bringing your car isn't always easy.

Still, for the kind of tourist who loves islands, especially less crowded islands with ample places to walk, Vinalhaven is a real find. And contrary to rumor, it's very possible to cross the Thoroughfare (see *Getting Around*) to spend the day on North Haven, but you may have to wait a little while. These islands dictate their own terms.

Vinalhaven makes sense as a day-trip destination only if it's a nice day and if you take the early boat. Pick up the first map you find and don't be discouraged by the walk into Carver's Harbor, along the island's ugliest quarter mile. Don't miss the Historical Society Museum, and walk or bike out to Lane's Island. This is a great place to be on the Fourth of July.

GUIDANCE

Town offices on **North Haven** (867-4433) and **Vinalhaven** (863-4471/ 4393) field most questions. The chamber of commerce web site is www. foxislands.net/~vhcc; fax, 863-4866; vhcc@foxislands.net. The chamber phone (863-4826) rings in The Paper Store (see *Selective Shopping*), so don't be surprised if you are put on hold while Carlene Michael takes care of a customer.

GETTING THERE

The Maine State Ferry Service (in Rockland: 596-2202). Ferries are frequent and day-trippers never have a problem walking on; the bike fee is nominal. Each ferry takes a set number of cars, and only a handful of these spaces can be reserved; otherwise, cars are taken in order of their position in line. For the morning boats, it's wise to be in line the night before. During the summer season, getting off the island can be more complicated. It doesn't make sense to bring a car unless you plan to stay a while. *Note:* **Concord Trailways** stops daily at the **Rockland Ferry Terminal**.

Telford Aviation (596-5557; 1-800-780-6071) will fly you in from Portland or Boston as well as Rockland to either Vinalhaven or North Haven. **Downeast Air** (594-2171; 1-888-594-2171) also offers service.

GETTING AROUND

By boat: **Fox Islands Thoroughfare Water Taxi** (867-4621/4894). Shuttle service between North Haven and Vinalhaven is possible in summer months. In North Haven contact the J. O. Brown Boatyard. In

Vinalhaven try the phone at the Thoroughfare boat landing.

By bicycle: Given the lack of public transport and rental multigear bikes, many visitors bring their own. Be advised, however, that islanders frown on visiting bicyclists because they frequently are oblivious to local traffic and to the lobster trucks that are as much king of these island roads as lumber trucks are in the North Woods.

By car: Rental cars are available from the **Tidewater Motel** (see *Lodging—On Vinalhaven*).

Note: **Day-trippers** to North Haven will find shopping and food within walking distance of the ferry dock, but on Vinalhaven the distances from the ferry to Carver's Harbor and from there to quarries and nature preserves is a bit far on foot. The **Tidewater Motel** (see *Lodging*) rents clunker bikes.

MEDICAL EMERGENCY

Islands Community Medical Services (863-4341) is based on Atlantic Avenue in Carver's Harbor, Vinalhaven. For the **ambulance,** call 594-5656.

TO SEE

On Vinalhaven

The Victorian-style town of **Carver's Harbor** is picturesque and interesting, its downtown a single street straddling a causeway and narrow land strip between the harbor and Carver's Pond. A boomtown dating from the 1880s when Vinalhaven was synonymous with granite, the village is built almost entirely of wood, the reason why many of the best of its golden-era buildings are missing. The strikingly Victorian Star of Hope Lodge, owned by artist Robert Indiana, is the sole survivor of three such amazing buildings that once marked the center of town.

The Vinalhaven Historical Society Museum (863-4410/4318; www.midcoast.com/~vhhissoc), top of High Street. Open mid-June though early September, daily 11–3. Volunteer staffers Esther Bissell and Roy Heisler maintain one of Maine's most welcoming and extensive community museums. It's housed in the former town hall, which has also served as a theater and skating rink, built in 1838 in Rockland as a Universalist church, brought over in 1878. Displays, including striking photographs, feature the island's granite industry. The first order for Vinalhaven granite, you learn, was shipped to Boston in 1826 to build a jail, but production really skyrocketed after the Civil War, when granite was the preferred building material for the country's building boom. On an island map, 40 red pins mark the sites of major quarries, but there are also countless "motions," or backyard pits. Museum displays also depict island life and other industries, like fishing (the Lane-Libby Fisheries Co. was once one of Maine's largest fish-processing companies) and lobstering (in the 1880s the Basin, a large saltwater lake here, was used as a giant holding tank, penning as many as 150,000 lobsters until prices peaked). Knitting horse nets (to keep off flies) in intricate designs was yet another island industry. Check out the nearby **Carver Cemetery.** At the opposite end of town note the **Galamander,** a huge wagon such as those used to carry stone from island quarries to schooners, which stands in the small park at the top of the hill (junction of Main, Chestnut, Carver, and School Streets and Atlantic Avenue).

Brown's Head Lighthouse, now automated, commands the entrance to the thoroughfare from the northern end of Vinalhaven, more than 8 miles from Carver's Harbor.

On North Haven

North Haven Village is of most interest to visitors. While it has no museum or sight-to-see as such, the village itself is charming and several shops, notably North Haven Gift Shop and the Eric Hopkins Gallery (see *Selective Shopping—In North Haven Village*) are destinations in their own right. **Pulpit Harbor** is the island's other community, a low-key cluster of homes with a general store and the **North Island Historical Museum,** theoretically open Tuesdays in summer months, 9:30–11:30.

TO DO

BICYCLING

See *Getting There* and *Getting Around* on the logistics of bringing/renting/ riding bikes. The truth is that if you take care to keep to the roadside, both North Haven and Vinalhaven are suited to bicycling. On Vinalhaven we recommend the Granite Island Road out along the Basin or following Main Street the other direction out to Geary's Beach (see *Green Space*). The North Haven Road is an 8-mile slog up the middle of Vinalhaven but the rewards are great: Browns Head Light, the Perry Creek Preserve, and views of North Haven.

GOLF

North Haven Golf Club (867-2061), Waterman Cove, North Haven, is open to the public, accessible by foot from North Haven Village, and surprisingly visitor friendly (nine holes). Call before coming.

SEA KAYAKING

Sea Escape Kayak (863-9343; SeaEscapekayak@worldnet.att.net). Kurke Lynch has all the right credentials for guiding novices. Paddlers should meet at his shop at the east end of Main Street, 9 AM.

SWIMMING

Lawson's Quarry. From the middle of Carver's Harbor, turn (uphill) at the Bank Building and continue up and up High Street, past the historical society, and then turn right on the North Haven road for 0.5 mile. We prefer this public swimming hole to the Booth Quarry. **Booth Quarry.** Continue east (uphill) on Main Street 1.5 miles past the Union Church to the Booth Brothers granite quarry. A town park and swimming hole.

GREEN SPACE

On Vinalhaven

The Vinalhaven Land Trust (863-2543) maintains most of the preserves mapped on island handouts. These include:

Lane's Island Preserve, on the southern side of Carver's Harbor (cross the Indian Creek Bridge and look for the sign on your left). It includes 45 acres of fields, marsh, moor, and beach. This is a great spot to picnic or to come in the evening. Stroll out along the beach and up into the meadows facing open ocean and filled with wild roses and beach peas.

Armbrust Hill is on the way to Lane's Island, hidden behind the medical center. The first place in which the island's granite was commercially quarried, it remained one of the most active sites on the island for many decades. Notice the many small pits ("motions") as well as four major quarries. The main path winds up the hill for a splendid view.

Grimes Park, just west of the ferry terminal, is a 2-acre point of rocky land with two small beaches. Note the rough granite watering trough once used by horses and oxen.

Geary's Beach. Turn right off Main Street a bit farther than the Booth Quarry (see *To Do—Swimming*), just after the Coke Statue of Liberty (you'll see), and bear left for this stony beach, its trails, and picnic table. The view is off to Isle au Haut, Brimstone, and Matinicus.

Note: This list is just a sampling.

LODGING

On Vinalhaven 04863

Fox Island Inn (863-2122; gailrei@juno.com), P.O. Box 451, Carver Street. Open June through mid-September. A restored century-old town house near the library, just a 10-minute walk from the ferry landing, through the village and up the hill. Gail Reinertsen, a competitive long-distance runner, is a warm and helpful host, knowledgeable about the island and beauty spots. Several bikes are available to guests. Rooms are nicely decorated, and the living room is well stocked with books. Guests are welcome to use the kitchen to prepare light meals. Two single and four double guest rooms share (immaculate) baths; two rooms can be one suite (private bath). Doubles are $45–85; the suite is $105; rates include breakfast. To reserve off-season, call Gail at 850-425-5095.

✐ **Tidewater Motel** (863-4618; tidewater@foxislands.net), Carver's Harbor. Open year-round. Phil and Elaine Crossman's outstanding little motel is located right on the harbor in the heart of the village. There are 11 units and one apartment; some have waterside decks, others kitchens, some both. June 15 through Labor Day: $79 single, $89 double; $95–102 for waterfront units with kitchens; $55–69 off-season. The Tidewater also

Booth Quarry

rents bicycles. Pickup service from the ferry is available.

Libby House (863-4696; winter, 516-369-9172), Water Street. Open July and August. Built in 1869, this handsome, rambling home is furnished with Victorian pieces, including heavily carved beds. The comfortable common rooms are often filled with music; innkeeper Philip Roberts is a music teacher. It's a short walk from here to Lane's Island Preserve (see *Green Space*). Breakfast is included; $52–100.

Payne Homestead at the Moses Webster House (863-9963; 1-888-863-9963; payne@foxislands.net), Atlantic Avenue. Open May through October, a high-Victorian mansion with five guest rooms; $75–100 in-season, less off. Two-night minimum.

On North Haven 04853

Our Place Inn and Cottages (867-4998), Crab Tree Point Road. Open year-round. A guest house under many names over the years, this snug, attractive old house near Pulpit Harbor, now owned by Marnelle Bubar, offers two rooms ($75–95) when it isn't rented by the week ($1,500). There are also efficiency cottages ($125 per night).

COTTAGES

Vinalhaven Rentals (863-2241) specializes in summer rentals. **The Island Group** (863-2554) offers both sales and rentals for both islands.

WHERE TO EAT

On Vinalhaven

The Haven Restaurant (863-4969), Main Street. Open year-round. In summer open for dinner Tuesday through Saturday; call for days and hours off-season. Two dining rooms—an open-beamed room overlooking the water and a smaller streetside café—flank a kitchen. Dinner in the waterside room is elegant and by reservation for seatings at 6 and 8:15; lighter meals are served in the pub-style streetside room. Occasional live music. Liquor served. No smoking. Entrées $11–16.

Candlepin Lodge (863-2730), Roberts Cemetery Road. Open from 5 PM daily except Monday, dinner 6–9, Sunday noon–10. Rusty Warren's rustic cedar lodge is the island's real community center. There are booths near the soda fountain and a grill within earshot of the jukebox and sight of the pool tables, and tables in the more formal (still informal) dining room, where the specialty is reasonably priced seafood, including freshly dug steamers. The attached candlepin bowling alley is another great family amenity.

The Islander (863-2028), East Main Street. Open daily for breakfast, Monday through Saturday 4:30–10:30 and Sunday 6–10:30; lunch, Monday through Saturday; dinner, Wednesday through Saturday. An attractive restaurant in a former pharmacy, retaining the ornate woodwork and tin ceilings. Dinner entrées might range from fettuccine ($13.95) to Delmonico steak or boiled lobster ($16.95).

The Harbor Gawker (863-9365), Main Street, middle of the village. Open daily, early and late, great chowder, crabmeat rolls, and baskets of just about anything. Take-out but you can take it a couple doors down to tables in the **Mill Race** (same ownership), a former full-service restaurant that serves coffees and pastries with a view of Carver's Pond.

Surfside (863-2767), Harbor Wharf, West Main Street. Donna Webster opens at 4 AM for the lobstermen and technically closes at 10:30 AM. A great harborside breakfast spot with tables on the deck, and specials like a zucchini and cream cheese omelet with homefries.

On North Haven

Cooper's Landing, North Haven Village across from the ferry landing. Open seasonally for light fare and ice cream, 11–7. Truly great burgers.

Coal Wharf Restaurant (867-4739), down on the water next to Brown's Boatshop. Open for dinner daily in July and August, weekends in spring and fall. Call. No credit cards. Good food. Reservations advised.

SELECTIVE SHOPPING

In Carver's Harbor on Vinalhaven

The Paper Store (863-4826) is the nerve center of the island, the place everyone drops by at least once a day. Carlene Michael is as generous about dispensing directions to visitors as she is news to residents. This is also the place to check for current happenings like plays and concerts.

The Fog Gallery, at Harbor Wharf, features the work of Fox Islands artists.

The Island Gift Shop, West Main Street. Open June until Christmas. Amy Durant's shop, in the front room of her house, is the oldest gift shop on the island: clothespins bags, STOP PUFFIN signs, buoy key chains, assorted gifts. Amy enjoys people, even if you just stop by to talk.

In North Haven Village

Eric Hopkins Gallery (867-2229/4401). Open June through Labor Day, Monday through Saturday 10–6, Sunday 11–4; otherwise by appointment. This gallery is the reason many people come to North Haven. One of Maine's best-known artists, Hopkins is the son of a North Haven fisherman and a graduate of prestigious art schools. The waterside gallery is hung with bold, distinctive paintings ranging from large canvases to small watercolors. Most Hopkins paintings are of clouds, deep blue water, and spiky green islands, all seemingly in motion.

North Haven Gift Shop (876-4444). Open Memorial Day through mid-September, but closed Sunday. Since 1954 June Hopkins (mother of Eric) has run this shop with rooms that meander on and on, filled with pottery, books, accessories, jewelry, and much more.

Calderwood Hall Gallery (867-2265). Open Memorial Day through Columbus Day in a weathered building that has served as movie theater and dance hall, featuring paintings by owner Herbert Parsons; also offering an interesting mix of clothing and gifts.

SPECIAL EVENTS

Warm-weather months: **Saturday Flea Market,** 10 AM in the field next to the Galamander, Carver's Harbor, Vinalhaven. **Union Church Baked Bean Supper** (*every other Thursday*), Vinalhaven.

Year-round: **North Haven Community School Dramatic Presentations** are exceptional. For details, phone 867-2237. For details about **Fox Island Concerts** and other regular occurrences on both islands, consult *The Wind*, a weekly newsletter published on Vinalhaven.

MATINICUS

Home to less than 70 hardy souls in winter, most of whom make their living lobstering, Matinicus's population grows to about 200 in summer. A very quiet, unspoiled island, it lies 23 miles at sea on the outer edge of Penobscot Bay. Walking trails thread the meadows and shore, and there are two sand beaches—one at each end of the 750-acre island. Matinicus Rock is offshore, a protected nesting site for puffins, a lure for birders in June and July.

GETTING THERE

The Maine State Ferry (see "The Fox Islands," above; 624-777) takes 2 hours and 15 minutes to ply between Matinicus and Rockland, several times a month, May through October; once a month the rest of the year. The flying time via **Telford Aviation** (596-5557; 1-800-780-6071) from Owls

Head is 12 minutes, but flights may be canceled because of weather. Check with **Tuckanuck Lodge** (see *Lodging*) about the island-based water taxi.

LODGING

☀☞ **Tuckanuck Lodge** (366-3830), Box 217, Shag Hollow Road, Matinicus 04851. Open year-round. Pets and well-behaved children welcome. Nantucket islander Bill Hoadley offers five rooms (two shared baths), some with a view of Old Cove and the ocean. $45–80 double, $40–55 single, including breakfast; half rate for children. Lunch and supper are available at the **Pirates Galley** when it's open; when it's not, guests have kitchen privileges for lunch (bring your own fixings); the lodge offers supper ($12–15, BYOB).

For **cottage rentals:** Write or call the Harriet Williams at the Matinicus Chamber of Commerce (366-3868), Box 212, Matinicus 04851.

Note: With the store closed and the one restaurant iffy, visitors must bring groceries. Islanders fax their order to the supermarkets in Rockland and it's delivered by **Telford Aviation** (weather permitting; 596-5557; 1-800-780-6071); $6 charge.

Camden/Rockport Area

Islesboro

All I could see from where I stood
Was three long mountains and a wood;
I turned and looked another way,
And saw three islands in a bay.

—Edna St. Vincent Millay

These opening lines from "Renascence" suggest the view from the top of Mount Battie. Millay's hometown—Camden—lies below the mountain on a narrow, curving shelf between the hills and bay.

Smack on Route 1, Camden is the most popular way station between Kennebunkport or Boothbay Harbor and Bar Harbor. Seemingly half its 19th-century captains' homes are now B&Bs. Shops and restaurants line a photogenic harbor filled with private sailing and motor yachts. It's also a poor man's yacht haven.

Here, in 1935, artist Frank Swift refitted a few former fishing and cargo schooners to carry passengers around the islands in Penobscot Bay. He called the boats windjammers. A half-dozen members of Maine's current windjammer fleet are still based here (the rest are in neighboring ports), and several schooners offer daysails. You can also get out on the water in an excursion boat or a sea kayak.

From the water you can see two aspects of Camden that you can't see from land. The first is the size and extent of the Camden Hills. The second is the size and number of the palatial old waterside "cottages" along Beauchamp Point, the rocky promontory separating Camden from Rockport. Here, as in Bar Harbor, summer residents were wise and powerful enough to preserve the local mountains, seeding the creation of the present 6,500-acre Camden Hills State Park, one of Maine's more spectacular places to hike.

Camden's first resort era coincided with those colorful decades during which steam and sail overlapped. As a stop on the Boston–Bangor steamboat line, Camden acquired a couple of big (now-vanished) hotels. In 1900, when Bean's boatyard launched the world's first six-masted schooner, onlookers crowded the neighboring ornate steamboat wharf to watch.

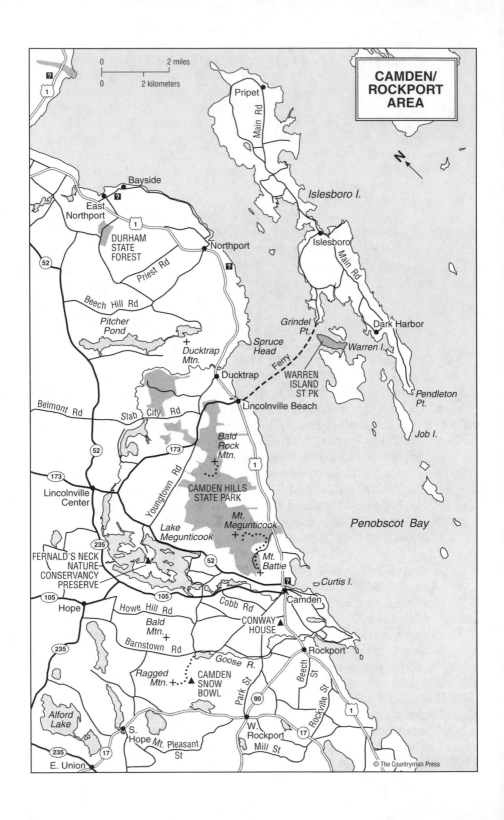

CAMDEN/
ROCKPORT
AREA

0   2 miles
0   2 kilometers

N

1

Pripet

Main Rd

Islesboro I.

Bayside

East
Northport

1

DURHAM
STATE
FOREST

52

Priest Rd

Northport

Islesboro

Main Rd

Dark Harbor

Beech Hill Rd

Pitcher
Pond

Ducktrap
Mtn.

Spruce
Head

Grindel
Pt.

Warren I.

Ferry

Ducktrap

WARREN
ISLAND
ST PK

Pendleton
Pt.

Belmont Rd

Slab City Rd

Lincolnville Beach

Job I.

52

173

Bald
Rock
Mtn.

1

173

Lincolnville
Center

Youngtown Rd

CAMDEN HILLS
STATE PARK

Penobscot Bay

235

Lake
Megunticook

Mt.
Megunticook

FERNALD'S NECK
NATURE
CONSERVANCY
PRESERVE

52

Mt.
Battie

Curtis I.

105

Hope

Howe Hill Rd

Cobb Rd

Camden

235

Bald
Mtn.

Barnstown Rd

CONWAY
HOUSE

Goose R.

Rockport

Beech St

Ragged
Mtn.

CAMDEN
SNOW
BOWL

Park St

90

Rockville St

Alford
Lake

S.
Hope

Mt. Pleasant
St

W.
Rockport

Mill St

17

1

235

17

E. Union

© The Countryman Press

In contrast to Boothbay and Bar Harbor, Camden has always been a year-round town that's never been overdependent on tourism. Camden's early business was, of course, building and sailing ships. By the mid-1800s a half-dozen mills lined the series of falls on the Megunticook River, just a block or two from the waterfront. The vast wooden Knox Woolen Company—the "Harrington Mill" portrayed in the movie *Peyton Place*—made the felts used by Maine's paper mills to absorb water from paper stock. It operated until 1988, and the complex is now the New England headquarters for a major credit-card company, the most recent among dozens of companies to locate in Camden.

Culturally enriched by its sophisticated populace—workaday residents, retirees, and summer people alike—Camden (along with Rockport) offers a bonanza of music, art, and theatrical productions surprising in quality. There are also programs in filmmaking, computer science, and photography, as well as the long-acclaimed summertime Salzedo Harp Colony.

Ironically, only a small fraction of the thousands of tourists who stream through Camden every summer take the time to discover the extent of its beauty. The tourist tide eddies around the harborside restaurants, shops, and galleries and continues to flow on up Route 1 toward Bar Harbor. Even in August you are likely to find yourself alone atop Mount Battie (accessible by car as well as on foot) or Mount Megunticook (highest point in the Camden Hills), or in the open-sided Vesper Hill Children's Chapel, with its flowers and sea view. Few visitors see, let alone swim in, Megunticook Lake or set foot on the nearby island of Islesboro.

A dozen years ago you could count on your fingers the number of places to stay here, but Camden has since become synonymous with B&Bs, which, at last count, totaled close to 30, including those in the surrounding area. A total of some 1,000 rooms can now be found in hotels, motels, inns, and cottages as well as the B&Bs between Camden and neighboring Lincolnville and Rockport.

GUIDANCE

Camden-Rockport-Lincolnville Chamber of Commerce (236-4404; 1-800-223-5459; www.visitcamden.com), P.O. Box 919, Public Landing, Camden 04843. Open year-round, Monday through Friday 9–5 and Saturday 10–5; also open Sunday noon–4, mid-May through mid-October. You'll find all sorts of helpful brochures here, plus maps of Camden, Rockport, and Lincolnville, along with knowledgeable people to send you in the right direction. The chamber keeps tabs on vacancies during the high season, as well as on what is open off-season and cottages available to rent (a list is ready for requests each year by January). Be sure to secure their booklet "The Jewel of the Maine Coast," as well as the Camden-Rockport Historical Society's "A Visitor's Tour," which outlines tours of historic districts in Camden and Rockport.

KIM GRANT

Rockport Harbor

GETTING THERE

By air: **Knox County Regional Airport,** at Owls Head, about 10 miles from Camden (see "Rockland/Thomaston Area"), offers daily flights to and from Boston. **Bangor International Airport** (see "Bangor Area") and **Portland International Jetport** (see "Portland Area") offer connections to all parts of the country.

By bus: **Concord Trailways** stops on Route 1 south of Camden en route from Bangor to Portland and Boston and vice versa.

By limo: **Mid Coast Limo** (236-2424; 1-800-937-2424) makes runs from Portland International Jetport by reservation.

By car: Our preferred route, to bypass Route 1 traffic, is to take I-95 to Gardiner, then follow signs to Route 226. When this road ends, take a right onto Route 17, which winds through pretty countryside to Route 90, which then intersects with Route 1 leading into Camden.

PARKING

Parking is a problem in July and August. In-town parking has a stringently enforced 2-hour limit (just 15 minutes in a few spots, so be sure to read the signs). There are a few lots outside the center of town (try the Camden Marketplace and a lot on Mechanic Street). There's an advantage here to finding lodging within walking distance of the village.

MEDICAL EMERGENCY

Penobscot Bay Medical Center (596-8000), 6 Glen Cove Drive (off Route 1), Rockport.

VILLAGES

Rockport's harbor is as picturesque as Camden's, and the small village is set high above it. Steps (you have to look closely for them) lead down to

Marine Park, a departure point in 1816 for 300 casks of lime shipped to Washington, D.C., to help construct the capitol building. In the small park you'll see the restored remains of a triple kiln, a saddleback steam locomotive, and a granite sculpture of Andre the Seal, the legendary performer who drew crowds every summer in the early and mid-1980s. The village (part of Camden until 1891) includes the restored Rockport Opera House, site of the Bay Chamber Concerts, the noted Maine Coast Artists Gallery, the Maine Photographic Workshops program, and a salting of restaurants and shops.

Lincolnville is larger than it looks as you drive through. The village's landmarks—the Lobster Pound Restaurant and Maine State Ferry to Islesboro (see *Getting There* under "Islesboro")—serve as centerpieces for proliferating shops, restaurants, and B&Bs.

TO SEE

LIGHTHOUSE

Curtis Island Light. Walk down to where Bayview Street connects with Beacon to find the lookout spot, with views of this 26-foot stone tower on Curtis Island.

MUSEUMS

✐& **Old Conway House Complex** (236-2257; www.mint.net/~chmuseum), Conway Road (off Route 1 just south of Camden). Open July and August, Tuesday through Friday 10–4; admission $2 for adults, $1 for students, $.50 for children over 6. Administered by the Camden-Rockport Historical Society, this restored early-18th-century farmhouse has been furnished to represent several periods. The barn holds collections of carriages, sleighs, and early farm tools, and there is a Victorian privy, a blacksmith shop, and an 1820 maple sugar house where sugaring demonstrations are held each spring. **The Cramer Museum** displays local memorabilia and changing exhibits.

Knox Mill Museum, MBNA offices, Mechanic Street, Camden. Open weekdays 9–5. A sophisticated little museum dramatizes the 125 years of operation of the Knox Woolen Mill. Exhibits include a video, many photographs, and some machinery. The mill was the prime supplier of felts for the endless belts used in paper manufacturing.

Schoolhouse Museum (789-5445), P.O. Box 211, Lincolnville. Open noon–3 PM on Monday, Wednesday, Friday, and Sunday. A small museum detailing the history of Lincolnville, with exhibits that change often.

SCENIC DRIVE

Drive or, better yet, bicycle (see *To Do—Bicycling*) around **Beauchamp Point.** Begin on Chestnut Street in Camden and follow this peaceful road by the lily pond and on by the herd of belted Galloway cows (black on both ends and white in the middle). Take Calderwood Lane through the woods and by the **Vesper Hill Children's Chapel,** built on the site of a former hotel and banked with flowers, a great spot to get married or simply to sit. Continue along Beauchamp Avenue to Rockport Village to lunch or picnic by the harbor, and return via Union Street to Camden.

OTHER SITES

Kelmscott Farm (763-4088; www.kelmscott.org), RR 2, Box 365, Lincolnville. Open Tuesday through Sunday 10–5 from May through October, 10–3 November through April. Adults $5, children $3, under 4 free. A delightful farm dedicated to the conservation of rare livestock breeds. Wander through the farm buildings at your leisure, stopping to read the informative signs about the various breeds on stalls and fences. A peaceful, interesting place worth the short drive. Tours, special events and learning programs, gift shop, and exhibits.

Cellardoor Winery (763-4478), 4150 Youngtown Road, Lincolnville. A 5-acre vineyard with 18 varieties of grapes. Open for wine tastings in the 18th-century barn tasting room Friday through Sunday 1–5. They also have two rooms available for a B&B farm stay.

TO DO

BICYCLING

Camden Hills State Park, Route 1, Camden, has a 10-mile (round-trip) ride through the woods on a snowmobile trail. Bikes are not allowed on hiking trails. The **Camden Snow Bowl** also offers a number of rides through woods and swamps, as well as riding on ski trails. It's a hearty ride, but the views from the top are terrific. You can bring your own or rent from area outfitters.

Georges River Bikeways. The Georges River Land Trust offers a pamphlet that plots out several good biking routes, with light traffic and many scenic spots within the Georges River watershed.

Brown Dog Bikes (236-6664), 53 Chestnut Street, Camden, across from the YMCA, rents a variety of mountain and road bikes, Kiddie Kart trailers, and accessories, and delivers them to inns and B&Bs. Ask about evening group rides. They also have rental locations in Rockport at the Samoset Resort and at Lincolnville Beach.

Mainely Mountain Bike Tours (785-2703), Union, offers 2- and 3-hour guided mountain bike tours.

Maine Sport Outfitters (236-7120; 1-888-236-8797) rents Specialized Crossroads and Specialized Rockhoppers, as well as bike trailers and car racks for a day or extended periods. Rentals include helmet, lock, and cable.

BOAT EXCURSIONS

(See also *Windjammers.*)

Yacht charters are offered spring to autumn along the Maine coast. Most charters run for a week, although sometimes it is possible to charter a boat just for a long weekend, with or without crew. For more information, contact **Johanson Boatworks** (236-7021; 1-877-JOHANS). **Bay Island Yacht Charters** (236-2776; 1-800-421-2492) has yachts available for bare-boat skippered or crewed charters out of Rockland as well as other ports the length of Maine's coast. **Wildwood Water Taxi & Charter** (236-6951) offers charters in a 30-foot powerboat by the hour.

It would be a shame to be in Camden and not spend some time on the water. The **2-hour sailing excursions** are a wonderful way to get a taste of what the harbor has to offer if your time is limited. Remember to bring a jacket, as the air can get chilly once you are offshore, even on a sunny day. Wander down the wooden boardwalk and check the offerings, which include:

Appledore (236-8353), an 86-foot schooner (the largest of the daysailing fleet), has sailed around the world and now offers several trips daily, including sunset cruises.

Surprise (236-4687), a traditional, historic, 57-foot schooner, offers entertaining, informative 2-hour sails. Captain Jack and wife, Barbara Moore, spent seven years cruising between Maine and the Caribbean, educating their four children on board in the process.

Olad and *Northwind* (236-2323), 55 and 75-foot schooners, respectively, offer 2-hour sails.

Shantih II (236-8605; 1-800-599-8605) offers full-day, half-day, and sunset sails out of Rockport for a maximum of six passengers.

Betselma (236-4446), a motor launch, provides 1- and 2-hour sight-seeing trips (owner Les Bex was a longtime windjammer captain) around the harbor and nearby coast.

Lively Lady and *Lively Lady Too* (236-6672), traditional lobster boats, take passengers on 2- and 3-hour cruises that can include watching lobster traps being hauled or an island lobster bake and sunset cruise.

Maine State Ferry from Lincolnville Beach to Islesboro (789-5611). At $4.50 round-trip per passenger and $4 per bicycle, this is the bargain of the local boating scene; see *Getting Around* under "Islesboro."

GOLF

Goose River Golf Club (236-8488), Simonton Road, Rockport. Nine holes, but you can play through twice using different starting tees. Cart rentals. Clubhouse. Tee times recommended for weekends and holidays.

Samoset Resort Golf Course (594-1431, clubhouse), Rockport, has 18 holes with 7 oceanside holes, and ocean views from 14 holes. The clubhouse has a pro shop, locker rooms, video golf simulator, and the **Clubhouse Grille.** Carts are available.

HIKING

The Camden Hills are far less recognized than Acadia National Park as a hiking haven, but for the average hiker, they offer ample challenge and some spectacular views. **Mount Battie,** accessible by a moderate and sometimes steep half-mile trail just off Route 52, is the only peak also accessible by car. The 1-mile **Maiden Cliff Trail** (park off Route 52, 2.9 miles from Route 1) is favored by locals for its views from the top of 800-foot sheer cliffs overlooking Lake Megunticook; it connects with the 2½-mile **Ridge Trail** to the summit of **Mount Megunticook** (1,380 feet). A complete trail map is available from most B&Bs and at Camden Hills State Park (see *Green Space*).

Bald Rock Mountain. This 1,100-foot mountain in Lincolnville once had a ski area at the top. Great views of Penobscot Bay and the Camden Hills. You'll find the trailhead 1¼ miles down a dirt road from the gate on Ski Lodge Road (off Youngtown Road). The climb is about a half mile long and moderate. Ask about overnight camping at the Camden Hills State Park headquarters on Route 1 in Camden.

Georges Highland Path is a trail network maintained by the Georges River Land Trust (594-5166). The project is constantly expanding, with plans to take the path through the wild Oyster River Bog and link to the existing path in the Thomaston Town Forest section. A map put out by the trust details distances and hiking times, and a map shows where the trails are.

Riverdance Outfitters (see *Sea Kayaking*) offers guided hiking tours.

HORSEBACK RIDING

Lily Hill Farm, (236-2504), West Street Extension, Rockport. Offers trail rides for all levels, at 10 AM. Lesson available before the ride.

SEA KAYAKING

Ducktrap Sea Kayak Tours (236-8608), Lincolnville Beach, offers 2-hour and half-day guided tours in Penobscot Bay. No experience is necessary; in fact, most patrons are first-time kayakers. Group and family tours, rentals, and lessons are also available.

Maine Sport Outfitters (236-8797; 1-800-722-0826), on Route 1 just south of Rockport, is a phenomenon rather than merely an outfitter. Be sure to stop. They offer courses in kayaking and canoeing, guided excursions around Camden Harbor and out into Penobscot Bay, and island-based workshops. They also rent kayaks and canoes. Contact them for their catalog of activities (also see *Special Learning Programs*).

Mt. Pleasant Canoe and Kayak (785-4309), West Rockport, offers a 2-hour sunset trip on Megunticook Lake as well as full- and half-day guided coastal tours.

Riverdance Outfitters (230-0033). The Belmont's new innkeeper, Joshua Perry, is also a Registered Maine Guide. He offers half-day and 2-hour sunset canoeing and kayaking tours.

SKIING

Camden Snow Bowl (236-3438), Hosmer's Pond Road, Camden. With a 950-foot vertical drop, nine runs for beginner through expert, and night skiing, this is a comfortably sized area where everyone seems to know everyone else. Facilities include a base lodge, a rental and repair shop, a ski school, and a cafeteria. There is also a toboggan chute ($1 ride) and tube sliding ($3 per hour).

Camden Hills State Park marks and maintains some trails for cross-country skiing, and there's a ski hut on Mount Battie (see *Green Space*).

Tanglewood 4-H Camp (789-5868), off Route 1 near Lincolnville Beach. Ungroomed, scenic cross-country trails. Map and description of trails available at the chamber (see *Guidance*).

SPECIAL LEARNING PROGRAMS

Camden Yacht Club Sailing Program (236-3014), Bayview Street, Camden, provides sailing classes for children and adults, boat owners and non–boat owners, during July and August; among them is an excellent weeklong course just for women. There is also a lecture series open to the public.

Bay Island Sailing School (236-2776; 1-800-421-2492), headquartered in Camden but based at Journey's End Marina in Rockland, an American Sailing Associate–certified sailing school offering beginner, coastal cruising, and bare-boat certification programs ranging from intensive weekend workshops to 5-day hands-on cruises. $395–995.

Maine Photographic Workshops (236-8581), Rockport. A nationally respected year-round school that offers a choice of 200 programs that vary in length from 1 week to 3 months for every level of skill in photography, cinematography, television production, and related fields. Teachers are established, recognized professionals who come from across the country, as do the students. There is also a gallery with changing exhibitions open to the public. The school provides housing for most of its students and helps arrange accommodations for others.

Maine Sport Outfitters (236-8797), P.O. Box 956, Rockport. This Route 1 complex is worth a stop whether you are up for adventure sports or not. The place is more than simply a store or kayaking, canoeing, mountain biking center; it has evolved over the years from a fly-fishing and canvas shop into a multitiered store that's a home base for adventure tours. Inquire about a wide variety of local kayaking tours and multiday kayaking workshops geared to all levels of ability, based at its facilities on Gay Island.

Center for Furniture Craftsmanship (594-5611), 25 Mill Street, Rockport. June through October. Hands-on 1- and 2-week workshops for novice, intermediate, and advanced woodworkers. Twelve-week intensive courses also offered a couple of times a year.

SWIMMING

Saltwater swimming from Camden's **Laite Memorial Park and Beach,** Upper Bayview Street; at **Lincolnville Beach,** Route 1 north of Camden; and in Rockport at **Walker Park,** across the road from Marine Park. Freshwater swimming at Megunticook Lake, Lincolnville (**Barret Cove Memorial Park and Beach;** turn left off Route 52 northwest of Camden), where you will also find picnic grounds and a parking area;

Shirttail Beach, Camden (Route 105); and at the **Willis Hodson Park** on the Megunticook River, Camden (Molyneaux Road). At the **Camden YMCA** (236-3375), Chestnut Street, visitors can pay a day-use fee that entitles them to swim in the Olympic-sized pool (check hours for family swimming, lap swimming, and other programs), use the weight rooms, and play basketball in the gym.

TENNIS

There are two public tennis courts at the **Camden Snow Bowl** on Hosmer's Pond Road. In addition, **Samoset Resort** (594-2511), Rockport, has outdoor courts, as do the **Whitehall Inn** and the **Rockport Recreation Park.**

WALKING TOUR

The **Camden-Rockport Historical Society** has prepared a brochure (available at the chamber of commerce) with a 2½-mile walk past historic buildings. The brochure includes historical details and a sketch map. An expanded tour by bicycle or car is also included.

WINDJAMMERS

Windjammer cruises are offered mid-June through mid-October. A half-dozen schooners and a ketch sail from Camden and Rockport on 3- to 6-day cruises throughout Penobscot Bay. For brochures and sailing schedules, contact the **Maine Windjammers Association** (374-2952; 1-800-807-WIND). (See also *To Do—Windjammers* in "Rockland/ Thomaston Area" and *Windjammers* under "What's Where in Maine.")

Angelique (236-8873; 1-800-282-9989; www.angelique.com), P.O. Box 736, Camden, is a 95-foot ketch that was built expressly for the windjammer trade in 1980. Patterned after 19th-century English fishing vessels, she offers a pleasant deck-level salon and belowdecks showers.

Timberwind (236-0801; 1-800-759-9250; www.schoonertimberwind.com), P.O. Box 247, Rockport, was built in Portland in 1931 as a pilot schooner. This pretty 75-foot vessel was converted to a passenger vessel in 1969. She has an enclosed handheld shower on deck. The *Timberwind* is the only windjammer sailing out of Rockport Harbor.

Roseway (236-4449; 1-800-255-4449), Yankee Schooner Cruises, P.O. Box 696, Camden, was built in 1925 as a fishing schooner and later spent 32 years as a pilot vessel escorting ships in and out of Boston Harbor. She was the last pilot schooner active in the United States. *Roseway* has been a passenger vessel sailing out of Camden since 1975. There are enclosed, hot, freshwater showers on deck.

Lewis R. French (236-9411; 1-800-469-4635; www.midcoast.com/~windjam), P.O. Box 992 CC, Camden, was launched on the Damariscotta River in 1871. Before becoming a passenger vessel, she carried cargo along the coast. She had three major rebuilds, the most recent in 1976 when she was brought into passenger service. Sixty-five feet long, she accommodates 23 passengers. Hot, freshwater shower on board. Native Maine Captain Dan Pease met his wife, Kathy, when she came aboard for a vacation. Now their sons, Joe and Bill, come along every chance they get. No smoking.

Mary Day (1-800-992-2218; www.schoonermaryday.com), Box 798, Camden, was the first schooner built specifically for carrying passengers. She's among the swiftest; Captains Barry King and Jen Martin have extensive sailing experience. Features include a fireplace and parlor organ and hot, freshwater showers on the deck.

Grace Bailey, Mercantile, and ***Mistress*** (236-2938; 1-800-736-7981; www.mainewindjammercruises.com), Maine Windjammer Cruises, P.O. Box 617, Camden. For years known as the *Mattie, Grace Bailey* took back her original name following a thorough restoration in 1990. Built in 1882 in New York, she once carried cargo along the Atlantic coast and to the West Indies. She has belowdecks showers. *Mercantile* was built in Maine in 1916 as a shallow-draft coasting schooner; 78 feet long, she has been in the windjammer trade since its beginning in 1942. Each cabin has its own private head, and there are belowdecks showers nearby. *Mistress*, the smallest of the fleet, carries just six passengers. A topsail schooner built along the lines of the old coasting schooners, she is also available for private charter. All three cabins have private heads, but there is no shower on board.

GREEN SPACE

Camden Hills State Park (236-3109), Route 1, Camden. In addition to Mount Battie, this 6,500-acre park includes Mount Megunticook, one of the highest points on the Atlantic seaboard, and a shoreside picnic site. You can drive to the top of Mount Battie on the road that starts at the park entrance, just north of town. Admission through the gate is $2 adults; $.50 ages 6–12; 5 and under free. At the entrance pick up a "Camden Hills State Park" brochure, which outlines 19 trails, with distance and difficulty level. For highlights of this 25-mile network, see *To Do— Hiking.* In winter many of the trails are suitable for cross-country skiing, given snow. There are 112 campsites here.

Warren Island State Park, also administered by Camden Hills State Park, is just a stone's throw off the island of Islesboro. There are picnic tables, trails, and tent sites here. Accessibility is the problem: You can arrange to have a private boat carry you over from the mainland, rent your own boat in Camden, or paddle out in a sea kayak (see *To Do—Sea Kayaking*). Because of this, the island is seldom used and always peaceful.

Marine Park, off Russell Avenue (just after you cross the bridge), Rockport. A nicely landscaped waterside area with sheltered picnic tables. Restored lime kilns and a train caboose are reminders of the era when the town's chief industry was processing and exporting lime (see *Villages*). You're likely to see several painters capturing the picturesque harbor on canvas while you are there.

Merryspring Horticultural Nature Park and Learning Center (236-2239), Camden. Open year-round during daylight hours. A 66-acre preserve with walking trails, an herb garden, a lily garden, a rose garden, raised beds, a demonstration garden, and an arboretum. The preserve is bisected by the Goose River and is accessible by way of Conway Road from Route 1 in Camden. Weekly talks in summer.

Fernald's Neck Nature Conservancy Preserve (729-5181). Near the junction of Route 52 and the Youngtown Road, Lincolnville. The preserve's 315 acres cover most of a heavily wooded peninsula that juts into Lake Megunticook. A brochure of walking trails is available at the registration box near the entrance. One trail leads to 60-foot cliffs. Trails can be boggy: Wear boots or old shoes.

Camden Amphitheatre, Atlantic Avenue, Camden. A magical setting for summertime plays and concerts, and a good place to sit, think, and read anytime. Tucked behind the library and across the street from the harbor park—a gentle, manicured slope down to the water.

Curtis Island, in the outer harbor. A small island with a lighthouse that marks the entrance to Camden. It is a public picnic spot and a popular sea kayaking destination.

LODGING

All listings are Camden 04843 unless otherwise indicated. Rates are for high season; most have off-season rates as well. *Note:* If you choose one of the many B&Bs in historic houses on Elm, Main, or High Street (all are Route 1), you might want to ask what pains have been taken to muffle the sound of passing traffic.

Camden Accommodations (1-800-344-4830; www.camdenac.com), 43 Elm Street, is a reservations service representing most places to stay in the Camden area. It also coordinates rentals for some six dozen cottages and condos.

Camden Bed & Breakfast Association (www.camdeninns.com), P.O. Box 553. The brochure lists 14 members with descriptions of each, and contact information.

RESORT

✒️♿ **Samoset Resort** (594-2511; 1-800-341-1650; www.samoset.com), 220 Warrenton Street, Rockport 04856. Open year-round, a full-service resort set on 230 oceanfront acres, with 178 rooms, including one- and two-bedroom suites. Many have ocean views, all have balconies or patios, private baths, color TVs, and climate-controlled air-conditioning and heat; time-share units and the two-bedroom Flume Cottage, perched on a rocky outcropping above the water are also available (cottage weekly in season). A scenic, peaceful spot with many amenities, including an outstanding 18-hole golf course, indoor golf center, outdoor tennis courts, a Nautilus-equipped fitness club, racquetball courts, and indoor and outdoor pools. A children's program is offered during the summer months and other school holiday periods. This is a popular meeting and convention site. The dining room, **Marcel's** (see *Dining Out*), is generally rated among the best on the Midcoast. The adjacent **Breakwater Café** has a large fireplace and floor-to-ceiling windows overlooking the water. Rooms are $129–329 in summer. Suites are $339 in the height of the season. Ask about packages.

INNS

The Belmont (236-8053; 1-800-238-8053; www.thebelmontinn.com), 6 ⟨140⟩ Belmont Avenue. Open mid-May through October. An 1890s Edwardian house with a wraparound veranda. Though ownership has changed, not much on the inside of the inn has. Six guest rooms, some very large, have private baths and are attentively furnished with careful details. Three have gas fireplaces. In the living room, accented by Oriental rugs on shining wood floors, guests are invited to relax in comfortable wing chairs and chat about the day's adventures or enjoy a cocktail from the bar. $75–115 double per night.

✒️&. **Whitehall Inn** (236-3391; 1-800-789-6565; www.whitehall-inn.com), 52 High Street (Route 1). Open Memorial Day through Columbus Day weekend. There's an air of easy elegance and comfort to this rambling inn on Route 1, east of the village. The inn has been in operation for 100 years, with the Dewing family at the helm for almost 30 of those. The large, low-beamed lobby and adjoining parlors are fitted with Oriental rugs and sofas, games, and puzzles. The Millay Room, with its vintage 1904 Steinway, looks much the way it did on the summer evening in 1909 when a local girl, Edna St. Vincent Millay, read a poem, "Renascence," to assembled guests, one of whom was so impressed that she undertook to educate the young woman at Vassar. The inn offers 40 guest rooms in the main inn, 5 more in both the Maine House and the Wicker House across Route 1. These rooms are simpler than most to be found in neighboring B&Bs, but each has its appeal. Most have private baths. All have the kind of heavy old phones your children have never seen. There is a tennis court and shuffleboard, and it's just a short walk to the Salzedo Harp Colony (summer concerts) and a "sneaker" beach (wear shoes because of the rocks) on Camden's outer harbor. Families are welcome but asked to dine early. Doubles are $135–175 MAP, $105–150 B&B ⟨135–165⟩ July through mid-October; off-season rates Memorial Day through June. Add 15 percent service for MAP, 10 percent for B&B.

🏅 **The Blue Harbor House** (236-3196; 1-800-248-3196; www.blueharbor house.com), 67 Elm Street. Open mid-May through November. This place is friendly and warm, and they serve dinner to guests (by reservation) as well as breakfast on the spacious sunporch. We haven't sampled the multicourse dinners ($35 per person), but guests have raved about entrées like beef Wellington, stuffed rack of lamb, or the ever-popular Down East lobster dinner. Breakfast is just as delectable, and might be

Dutch babies (custard-type pancakes with fresh fruit, Maine maple syrup, almonds, and powdered sugar) or blueberry pancakes with blueberry butter. Recent renovations have created a two-room suite with gas fireplace and claw-foot tub, and a soft blue room in the back, again with claw-foot tub and fireplace. All seven rooms are pleasantly decorated with country antiques, stenciling, and handmade quilts; all have private baths, telephones, and air-conditioning. A few have TVs with VCRs. Suites are warm and cozy, some with whirlpool tubs, some with gas fireplaces. Hosts Jody Schmoll and Dennis Hayden are warm, fun to talk to, and eager to help. Doubles $95–165.

Hartstone Inn (236-4259; 1-800-788-4823; www.hartstoneinn.com), 41 Elm Street. Open year-round. Mary Jo and Michael Salmon each worked in the hotel industry for more than 10 years before buying this inn. Their experience shows in the attention to detail, both in the decor of the inn and the quality of the dinner offered to guests (and the public, by reservation only; one entrée offered per night). The 10 guest rooms include 2 suites, all with private baths. They are dainty and pretty, some with fireplaces and lace canopy beds. The porch is a perfect spot for dinner, an elegant affair served by candlelight. The presentation of your food and the friendly conversation from the hosts will leave you feeling spoiled and content. $100–160 double with full breakfast and afternoon tea and cookies. Dinner is $38.50 prix fixe per person.

Youngtown Inn (763-4290; 1-800-291-8438; www.youngtowninn.com), Route 52 and Youngtown Road, Lincolnville 04849. This 1810 farmhouse is 4 miles from Camden Harbor at the end of Megunticook Lake, near Lincolnville Center. Five rooms plus a suite are furnished in a simple, dainty country style. All rooms have private decks and air-conditioning. The larger upstairs rooms also offer TVs with VCRs. The suite has a bedroom and a sitting area with a fireplace. The dining room (see *Dining Out*) is open to the public. $110–150 double occupancy in summer includes a full country breakfast. Ask about packages.

BED & BREAKFASTS

The Maine Stay (236-9636; www.mainestay.com), 22 High Street (Route 1). Open year-round. This Greek Revival house is one of the oldest in Camden's High Street Historic District, and innkeepers Peter Smith, his wife, Donny, and her twin sister, Diana Robson, are constantly working to improve it. There are now four standard rooms and four suites. The lower-level carriage-house room is especially appealing, with well-stocked, built-in bookshelves, a woodstove, and French doors opening onto a private patio with lawn and woods beyond (the 2-acre property includes an extensive, well-tended wildflower garden with benches scattered throughout). The two parlors (with fireplaces), the TV den, and the dining room are all salted with interesting furnishings and curiosities collected during Peter's wide-ranging naval career. The innkeepers are warm and unusually helpful, offering a personalized area map to

The Maine Stay B&B

each guest, as well as computer printouts of things to do, day trips, and more. Breakfast is served at the formal dining room table or on the sunporch, overlooking the gardens; afternoon tea and sweets are included in the $100–150 (suites) double room rate. Needlepointers should inquire about the March Stitch-Inn weekend.

The Hawthorn (236-8842; www.camdeninn.com), 9 High Street (Route 1). Open year-round. Nick and Patty Wharton strive to operate an elegant, comfortable inn, and they are doing a beautiful job. Their attention to detail is evident, from the proper cup of English tea to the hand-painted napkin rings at breakfast. Two elegant parlors available for quiet relaxation. Each of the 10 guest rooms has a theme to its decor; some have views of the harbor. The four carriage-house rooms are more modern, with Jacuzzis, TVs and VCRs, fireplaces, and private decks. $100–205 includes a delicious full breakfast, served on the porch overlooking the harbor in nice weather.

Norumbega (236-4646; 1-877-363-4646; www.norumbega.com), 61 High Street (Route 1). Open year-round. With one of the most imposing facades of any B&B anywhere, this turreted stone "castle" has long been a landmark just north of Camden. Inside, the ornate staircase with fireplace and love seat on the landing, formal parlor with fireplace, and dining room capture all the opulence of the Victorian era. Eleven guest rooms and two suites with king or queen beds, private baths, and are decorated with antiques, art, and period pieces. Some have water views, fireplaces, and balconies. Rooms are located both upstairs and downstairs, the latter with private terrace entrances. We are intrigued by the Library Suite, two rooms with a loft balcony full of books, which was the original castle library. There is a billiard room open to guests until 9 PM. Doubles are $160–475 (penthouse) in high season, including full breakfast. Dinner is offered to guests, with five entrée selections each night, in the elegant dining room. Two-night minimum on weekends.

Windward House (236-9656; 1-877-492-9656; bnb@windwardhouse. com), 6 High Street (Route 1). Open year-round. In 1999 Del and Charlotte Lawrence bought this handsome Greek Revival clapboard home surrounded by lawn and gardens. They promptly soundproofed the house and renovated the eight guest rooms, which all have private baths, air-conditioning, color cable TV, clock radios with CD players, and telephones with data ports. Their signature Mount Battie room has a king bed, cathedral ceilings, skylights, gas fireplace, TV/VCR, a Jacuzzi, and a private second-floor balcony with views of Mount Battie. The common rooms and back porch are comfortable and inviting. A full breakfast is served, and guests have their choice of several entrées each day, as well as juice, coffee or tea, muffins, and more. $155–225; $89–149 in quiet season.

A Little Dream (236-8742), 66 High Street (Route 1). Open year-round except March. This place has a casually elegant feel, with seven guest rooms, including a carriage-house suite they call the Isle Watch, as it overlooks Curtis Island. It has a gas fireplace, king canopy bed, and covered porch. A multicourse breakfast is served on the side porch. $129–250 double, includes breakfast. Two-night minimum on holiday weekends.

The Blackberry Inn (236-6060; 1-800-388-6000; www.blackberryinn.com), 82 Elm Street. Open year-round. Cindy and Jim Ostrowski have made extensive renovations to the property, including creating comfortable common rooms that invite curling up with a book or sitting down for a game of Scrabble on the unique pedestal board with golden tiles. Rooms have been redone, and include small touches like quilts and window treatments made by Cindy and her daughter, a hand-painted sink, and gas fireplaces. All rooms have private baths; some are air-conditioned and others feature king-sized beds, whirlpool baths, TVs, fireplaces, and ceiling fans. Children are welcome in the carriage house. The garden rooms are private and cozy, with fireplaces and whirlpool baths. Rates are $95–165 in high season, with a full breakfast served in the dining room or alfresco in the courtyard included.

Inn at Ocean's Edge (236-0945; www.innatoceansedge.com), P.O. Box 704, Lincolnville 04849. Open year-round. Ray and Marie Donner fell in love with this property, sold their former B&B, the Victorian, and built this literally ocean's-edge B&B from scratch. In 2000 they were at it again, building an additional 12 rooms. From the outside it resembles a shingled Maine summer mansion. Inside, the elegant common space has plenty of windows overlooking the water. With the soft music that plays in the background, these areas are a perfect spot to relax and enjoy the view. When the new section is completed, there will be 27 guest rooms, equipped with all the bells and whistles (Jacuzzi, gas fireplace, TV, VCR, stereo, and more). Facilities include an exercise room. Steps lead down to a private "shingle" beach. The property is 7 landscaped acres in all, accessible via a private drive off Route 1, a couple of miles north of the Camden line in Lincolnville. Mid-June through mid-October, $220–250 includes a full breakfast; off-season $150.

The Inn at Sunrise Point (236-7716; 1-800-435-6278; www.sunrisepoint. com), P.O. Box 1344, Lincolnville 04849. Open May through October. Set on a 4-acre waterfront estate just over the town line in Lincolnville, this small, luxurious B&B is owned by Jerry Levitin, author of the *Country Inns and Back Roads* guidebooks. Levitin tends to be on the road in summer, but an affable innkeeper is on hand to welcome guests. The location is a definite asset here. Four cottages have large picture windows with an incredible view, fireplaces, and Jacuzzis. The three rooms in the main house have fireplaces and water views. All accommodations have queen- or king-sized beds, phones, and color TVs with VCRs. Common rooms include a glass conservatory that lets the sun shine in, plus a snug, wood-paneled library with fireplace that's just right for cooler days. Rooms are $195–375, with full breakfast included.

The Victorian by the Sea (236-3785; 1-800-382-9817; www.victorianbythe sea.com), Lincolnville Beach 04849. Open year-round. Ginny and Greg Ciraldo own this quiet, romantic spot overlooking the water, away from the bustle of Route 1. As the name suggests, decor is Victorian but subtle. Seven guest rooms, all with queen beds and private baths; most have fireplaces. The third-floor suite has a bathroom sink set into an antique library table, a claw-foot tub, a sitting area, and a loft with twin beds. We especially like the pretty first-floor room with canopy bed. The $145–215 rate includes full breakfast and afternoon sweets. The Ciraldos also recently purchased the motel at the top of the road and are renovating the 13 units.

OTHER LODGING

High Tide Inn (236-3724; 1-800-778-7068 outside Maine; www.hightide inn.com), Route 1. Open May through October. Set far enough back from Route 1 to preclude traffic noise, this friendly complex appeals to singles and couples (who tend to choose one of the five rooms in the inn) and families, who opt for a cottage or motel unit (some with connecting, separate sleeping rooms). Most of the 30 rooms have views. The complex is set on 7 quiet acres—formerly a private estate—of landscaped grounds and meadow that slope to the water, where there's more than 250 feet of private ocean beach. Continental breakfast, including just-baked popovers and muffins, is served on the glass-enclosed porch; the living room also has ample windows with views of the bay. Pets are allowed in three of the rooms. The porch, living room, and bar all have working fireplaces. Rates: $65–175 in-season; less May through late June. Two-night minimum weekends in July and August and over holidays.

✐ **Lord Camden Inn** (236-4325; 1-800-336-4325), 24 Main Street. Open year-round. In a restored 1893 brick Masonic hall, the "inn" occupies several floors above a row of Main Street shops. Restored antique furnishings blend with modern amenities: color cable TV, private baths, in-room telephones, and elevator service. Most rooms have two double beds, and balconies overlooking the town and harbor or the river and hills beyond; there are also three luxury suites on the first floor. Rates include a full breakfast. $158–208 , depending on the view, in summer; $88–118 off-season. Children 16 and younger stay free.

Cedarholm (236-3886; www.tiac.net/users/jobson), Route 1, Lincolnville Beach 04849. This family-run cluster of cottages is set on 16 acres of beautifully landscaped property. Four upper cottages with private baths (one with kitchenette) are clean and comfortable looking. The two luxury cottages set down a quarter mile of wooded access road are hidden gems overlooking the water, with fireplaces, Jacuzzis, queen beds, kitchenettes, and private decks. Two more will be completed for the 2001 season. Continental breakfast includes muffins baked with berries grown right on the property, fresh fruit, cereal, coffee, and tea. Upper units begin at $85 per night. Luxury cottages $250–275 per night.

CAMPING

🐾✐ **Megunticook by the Sea** (594-2428), P.O. Box 375, Rockport 04856. Open May through Columbus Day. Wooded campground with 80 sites and a tenting area. Facilities include a store, a recreation hall, swimming, fishing, and a pool.

WHERE TO EAT

DINING OUT

✐& **Marcel's** (594-0774), Rockport (at the Samoset Resort). Open every day year-round for breakfast, dinner, and Sunday brunch. The fare merits the formality it receives; the wait staff wear tuxedos, and jackets are suggested for gentlemen at dinner. Specialties include tableside service of Caesar salad, steak Diane, and rack of lamb or châteaubriand for two. Extensive selection of beer and wine. The children's menu ($5.25–6) features fish-and-chips and fettuccine Alfredo prepared tableside among its choices. There's piano music at dinner and entertainment in the adjacent **Breakwater Café.** $14.50–28. Reservations suggested.

✐ **The Sail Loft** (236-2330), P.O. Box 203, Rockport 04856. Open year-round for lunch and dinner daily, and Sunday brunch. The Sail Loft overlooks Rockport Harbor and the activities of the boatyard below. The focus is on seafood. At dinner there's a variety of options, from smaller, lighter meals to the shore dinner with chowder, steamed mussels or clams, and a 2-pound lobster. Lighter meals begin at $8.95, but the average range is $17–30. The shore dinner is $46.

Youngtown Inn (763-4290; 1-800-298-8438), corner of Route 52 and Youngtown Road, Lincolnville. Open for dinner Tuesday through Sunday 6–9 PM. Four miles from Camden, this inn's (see *Lodging—Inns*) dining rooms are warmed by fireplaces on cool evenings. The French chef and owner, Manuel Mercier, serves up a five-course menu that changes weekly and might include rack of lamb, smoked salmon terrine, or lobster ravioli. He uses fresh local ingredients. $40 per person. There is also a small, cozy lounge.

Chez Michel (789-5600), Lincolnville Beach (across the road from the beach). Open for dinner Tuesday through Saturday, lunch and dinner on Sunday. This pleasant restaurant serves exceptional food with a French flair. Moderately priced entrées include bouillabaisse, beef bourguignon, and lamb kebobs. Outside dining in-season. A well-kept secret among loyal regulars. Dinner entrées run $8.75–14.95.

Frogwater Café (236-8998), 31 Elm Street, Camden. Open for dinner at 5 PM daily June through September; closed Sunday the rest of the year. Highly recommended by local innkeepers, this restaurant features creative appetizers and entrées, fresh breads and desserts. Children's entrées are $5, including drink and dessert. $10–18.

Peter Ott's (236-4032), 16 Bavview Street, Camden. Open year-round for dinner, with a large, varied menu. Entrées are served with the salad bar, unless you choose a lighter entrée (we did, and we still couldn't eat it all). Seafood, steaks, chicken. $7–19.

Rathbone's (236-3272), 21 Bayview Street. Open Tuesday through Sunday 11 AM 10 PM (bar stays open until 1 AM). This location has seen a number of restaurants in recent years, but this one has remained for two years now and is a favorite of local innkeepers. Menu choices in this elegant setting include fresh seafood and beef. $9–16.

Cork Restaurant (230-0533), 51 Bayview Street, Camden. This unique restaurant evolved from a wine and espresso café into a gourmet dining spot serving dinner Tuesday through Saturday 5–9 (call for off-season hours). The menu changes every night, with specialties like château-briand with béarnaise sauce, and ostrich fillet with bordelaise sauce. Dozens of wines are offered by the glass, even more by the bottle—they've been awarded a *Wine Spectator* award two years running. Chef Brian's desserts might include crème brûlée and chocolate molten cake. $16–35.

The Marquis at the Belmont (236-1226), 6 Belmont Avenue, Camden. Scott Marquis and Rebecca Brown lease the restaruant space at the Belmont and have created a lovely fine-dining experience. Entrées might include sesame grilled yellowfin tuna with wasabi aioli, and other seafood choices. $10–24.

EATING OUT

In Camden

🦞 **Cappy's Chowder House** (236-2254), Main Street. Open year-round. Lunch and dinner daily in summer; call for winter hours. An extremely popular pub—they claim that "sooner or later, everyone shows up at Cappy's," and it's true. Good food with reasonable price tags: treats from the on-premises bakery for breakfast; croissant sandwiches, burgers, full meals for lunch; seafood entrées, special pasta dishes, meat dishes for dinner. Upstairs in the **Crow's Nest** (open in summertime only) you will find a quieter setting, a harbor view, and the same menu. Kids get their own "giggle meals" served in a souvenir carrying box. This is also a good bet if you're in a hurry and just want a chowder and beer at the bar. Bakery, coffeehouse, and company store downstairs.

The Waterfront (236-3747), Bayview Street. Open for lunch and dinner. Terrific waterfront dining where you can watch the activity in the harbor. It fills up fast, and they don't take reservations, so be prepared to wait. Entrées include fisherman's stew and seafood Newburg.

🦞 **Sea Dog Brewing Co.** (236-6863), 43 Mechanic Street. Housed in the former Knox mill with views of the waterfall; a large, cheerful, family-run brewpub decorated with windjammer and other nautical paraphernalia, featuring a large, moderately priced menu and generous portions. Though there are many choices, your best bet here is the pub food: fish-and-chips, burgers, and the like. The specialty brews are lagers and ales with a half-dozen staples and several monthly specials.

🦞♿ **Village Restaurant** (236-3232), Main Street. Open year-round for lunch and dinner, daily from July through October; closed Tuesday the rest of the year. Family owned for more than 40 years, this is a longtime favorite with locals. Emphasis on broiled and sautéed seafood, home-baked desserts. Children's menu. The two dining rooms overlook Camden Harbor.

🦞 **Gilbert's Public House** (236-4320), Bayview Street. Tucked underneath the shops along Bayview Street (you enter through a side door just off the road), this is a good place for a beer and a sandwich, snacks or light meals for the kids, or a simple supper before the evening's activities. There's an international flavor to the "pub food" offered: Mediterranean shrimp salad, wurst platter, egg rolls, and nachos are among the favorites. There's also a frozen drink machine here, plus frothy and colorful daiquiris, margaritas, and the like. Live music for dancing in the evening.

🦞♿ **Fitzpatrick's Café** (236-6011), Bayview Landing, Bayview Street. Open year-round for breakfast, lunch, and dinner. Fitzi's is easy to miss as you walk to the public landing. But it's a find: a wide variety of sandwiches and salads plus daily specials. You order at the counter, and they call you by name when it's time to pick up your food. Popular with locals. Outside patio for summertime dining.

🦞♿ **Camden Deli** (236-8343), 37 Main Street. All three meals served daily. Over 35 sandwich choices, combining all of the regular deli meats and cheeses, as well as some less expected choices, like chicken broccoli salad or hummus. Large selection of homemade soups, salads, and desserts also. The back dining room overlooks the waterfall in downtown Camden.

In Rockport

♪ **The Helm** (236-4337), Route 1 (1.5 miles south of Camden). Open for lunch and dinner April through late October; closed Monday. There's a French accent to the menu, with such dishes as coquilles Saint-Jacques and bouillabaisse, plus Maine shore dinners. The menu offers about 50 entrées. One dining room overlooks the Goose River. Children's menu. At the take-out window you can order real onion soup and fresh rabbit pâté, plus delicious crabmeat rolls and sandwiches on French bread.

🐾& **Rockport Corner Shop** (236-8361). Open daily year-round for breakfast and lunch. Regulars greet each other warmly at this spot in the heart of the village, but newcomers are made to feel welcome, too. An exceptional find with almost no decor but plenty of atmosphere. Fresh coffee cakes are baked each morning; all salads are made with garden-grown vegetables. Breakfast specialties include eggs Benedict and Swedish pancakes; lunch offers pocket sandwiches, lobster and crabmeat rolls, and daily specials. No liquor. Very reasonable prices.

LOBSTER POUNDS

🐾 **Lobster Pound Restaurant** (789-5550), Route 1, Lincolnville Beach. Open every day for lunch and dinner, the first Sunday in May through Columbus Day. This is a mecca for lobster lovers—some people plan their trips around a meal here. Features lobster, boiled or baked, also clams, other fresh seafood, roast turkey, ham, steaks, and chicken. A family-style restaurant that seats 260 inside and has an outside patio near a sandy beach. Take-out and picnic tables offered across the beach. Always popular (always crowded).

Captain Andy's (236-2312), 156 Washington Street, Route 105, Camden. Call and order your lobsters with all the fixings, and they'll be delivered right to you at the harbor park or town landing for a delicious picnic.

SNACKS

Rockport Chocolates (230-0512), Route 1, Rockport. Handmade chocolates, nuts, and a variety of other confections as well as coffee, tea, and cappuccino.

TAKE-OUT

The Market Basket (236-4371), Routes 1 and 90, Rockport. Open Monday through Friday 7:30 AM–6:30 PM; Saturday 8 AM–6:30 PM. This specialty food store offers a wide variety of creative salads, delicious French bread, soups, entrées, sandwich specials for take-out, more than 500 wines from around the world, and more than 75 varieties of cheese.

Scott's Place (236-8751), Elm Street, Camden. For 27 years, this tiny building in the parking lot of a small shopping center has served hundreds of toasted crabmeat and lobster rolls, chicken sandwiches, burgers, veggie burgers, hot dogs, and chips. Prices are among the best around: $1.10

for a hot dog, under $6 for a lobster roll. This is one of several small take-out buildings around town, but it's the only one open year-round.

Also see **The Helm** under *Eating Out* and **Captain Andy's** under *Lobster Pounds.*

ENTERTAINMENT

Bay Chamber Concerts (236-2823), Rockport Opera House, Rockport. Thursday- and Friday-evening concerts during July and August (some concerts off-season also) in this beautifully restored opera house with its gilded interior. Outstanding chamber music presented for more than 30 years. Summer concerts are preceded by free lectures; there are postconcert receptions at the Maine Coast Artists Gallery on Thursdays, and the Opera House on Fridays.

Camden Civic Theatre (236-2281), Camden Opera House, P.O. Box 362, Main Street, Camden. A variety of theatrical performances are presented in the restored Camden Opera House, a second-floor theater with plum seats and cream-and-gold walls. Tickets are reasonably priced.

Camerata Singers (Sandra Jerome, director: 236-8704). This award-winning, 15-member, a cappella singing group presents a summer series in July and a Twelfth Night Concert in January. Performances are given in Camden, Belfast, and Waldoboro.

Maine Coast Artists (236-2875; see *Art Galleries*) sponsors a series of lectures and live performances June through September.

Bayview Street Cinema (236-8722), 10 Bayview Street, Camden. Showings daily. A mixed bag of old favorites, foreign and art films, and current movies.

SELECTIVE SHOPPING

ANTIQUES
At the chamber of commerce (see *Guidance*), pick up the leaflet guide to antiques shops scattered among Camden, Rockport, and Lincolnville.

ART GALLERIES
Maine Coast Artists Gallery (236-2875), 162 Russell Avenue, Rockport. Major exhibitions June through September; open Tuesday through Saturday 10–5, Sunday noon–5. Ongoing special exhibits off-season; call for details. $2 admission. A late-19th-century livery stable, then a firehouse, then the town hall, and, since 1968, one of Maine's outstanding art centers. Showcasing contemporary Maine art, the gallery sponsors several shows each season, an art auction, a crafts show, gallery talks, and an evening lecture series.

Maine's Massachusetts House Galleries (789-5705), Route 1, Lincolnville (2 miles north of Lincolnville Beach). Open year-round Monday through Saturday 9–5; Sunday in summer and fall, noon–5. A large barn

Shopping in Camden

gallery that's been a landmark since 1949, exhibiting works by Maine artists: oils, watercolors, and sculpture.

Art of the Sea (236-3939), 12 Bayview Street, Camden. Full- and half-rigged ship models, prints, scrimshaw, nautical jewelery, and more.

Bay View Gallery (236-4534), 33 Bayview Street, Camden. One of the largest galleries in the Midcoast area. Original paintings and sculptures by contemporary Maine artists plus several thousand posters and prints. Expert custom framing, too.

A Small Wonder Gallery (236-6005), Commercial Street (across from the Camden Chamber of Commerce), Camden. A small gallery with well-chosen limited-edition graphics, watercolors, hand-painted tiles, porcelain, and original sculpture.

ARTISANS

Windsor Chairmakers (789-5188), Route 1, Lincolnville Beach. Filling two floors of an old farmhouse, the inviting display encompasses not only Windsor chairs but also tables, highboys, and four-poster beds, all offered in a selection of finishes, including "distressed" (instant antique). The owner welcomes commissions—he's always ready to make a few sketches as you describe your ideas—and enjoys chatting with visitors and showing them around the workshop.

Brass Foundry (236-3200), Park Street, West Rockport (diagonally across from Mystic Woodworks). Custom metal castings in bronze and aluminum. Also handblown glass vases, bowls, and goblets.

James Lea (236-3632), 9 West Street, Rockport. Showroom is open by appointment Monday through Friday. Jim Lea is a third-generation craftsman fashioning museum-quality furniture reproductions using antique tools as well as more modern devices; all work is done on commission.

BOOKSTORES

ABCD Books (236-3903), 23 Bayview Street, Camden. Open daily except Sunday from July 4 through Labor Day; also closed Monday April through December; closed January through March. A Camden literary landmark: an unusually extensive and organized collection of rare and used books featuring maritime, art, New England, and history titles.

Down East (594-9544), Route 1, Rockport. The headquarters for Down East Enterprises (publishers of *Down East, Fly Rod & Reel, Fly Tackle Dealer,* and *Shooting Sportsman* magazines, as well as a line of New England books) is a fine old mansion that includes a book and gift shop.

✍&. **The Owl and Turtle Bookshop,** Bayview Street, Camden. One of Maine's best bookstores, much larger than it appears at first glance. Six rooms full of books, including special ones devoted to arts and crafts, boats, sports, and young adults and children. Special orders and searches for out-of-print books. Great for browsing.

SPECIAL SHOPS

All shops are in Camden and open year-round unless otherwise noted.

✍ **Camden 5 & 10.** The Camden Store. A huge old five-and-dime on Mechanic Street, just off Main. They have a little bit of everything, and a wall dedicated to crafts as well.

Unique 1, Bayview Street. Woolen items made from Maine wool, designed and hand-loomed locally. Also some pottery.

Once a Tree, Bayview Street. Wooden crafts, including beautiful clocks, kitchen utensils, desk sets; a large game and toy section.

✍ **The Smiling Cow,** Main Street. Seasonal. Three generations ago, a mother and five children converted this stable into a classic gift shop, one with unusual warmth and scope. Customers help themselves to coffee on the back porch overlooking a waterfall and the harbor.

Ducktrap Bay Trading Company, Bayview Street. Decoys and wildlife art. Many of these really special pieces have earned awards for their creators. There are also some less expensive carvings, plus jewelry.

Etienne Fine Jewelry, Main Street. Gallery of designer jewelry in 14- and 18-carat gold; contemporary and unusual pieces made on the premises.

L. E. Leonard, 67 Pascal Avenue, Rockport. An old general store with a fine selection of antique and contemporary furnishings from Indonesia and India; pieces range from jewelry to carved beds.

Danica Candleworks (236-3060), Route 90, West Rockport. In a striking building of Scandinavian design, a candle factory and shop.

SPECIAL EVENTS

Late June: **Down East Jazz Festival,** Camden Opera House.
Late July: **Annual Open House and Garden Day,** sponsored by the

Camden Garden Club. Very popular tour of homes and gardens in Camden and Rockport held every year for five decades. **Arts and Crafts Show,** Camden Amphitheatre *(third Saturday and Sunday in July).*

Early August: **Maine Coast Artists Annual Art Auction.** Maine's largest exhibit and auction of quality contemporary Maine art.

Late August: **Union Fair and Blueberry Festival,** Union Fairgrounds (see "Rockland/Thomaston Area").

Labor Day weekend: **Windjammer Weekend,** Camden Harbor. A celebration of the windjammer industry, featuring a parade of boats, music, nautical history, fireworks, and the **Schooner Bum Talent Contest.**

First weekend in October: **Fall Festival of Arts and Crafts,** Camden Amphitheatre—75 artisans displaying work for sale.

First weekend in December: **Christmas by the Sea**—tree lighting, Santa's arrival, caroling, holiday house tour, refreshments in shops, **Christmas Tree Jubilee** at the Samoset Resort.

ISLESBORO

A 14-mile-long, string-bean-shaped island just 3 miles off Lincolnville Beach (a 20-minute ferry ride), Islesboro is a private kind of place. There are three distinct communities on the island. The town of Islesboro with the necessary services (town office, post office, health center, and fire department) sits in the center between Dark Harbor and Pripet. Dark Harbor (described by Sidney Sheldon in his best-seller *Master of the Game* as the "jealously guarded colony of the super-rich") has long been a summer resort village, where huge "cottages" peek from behind the trees along the road to Pendleton Point. Pripet is a thriving year-round neighborhood of boatbuilders and fishermen.

GETTING THERE

The car-carrying **Maine State Ferry** (789-5611; 734-6935; $4.50 per passenger, $13.50 per car with driver, $4 per bicycle) from Lincolnville Beach lands midisland, at Grindle Point. The crossing is a 3-mile, 20-minute ride. The schedule varies depending on season. If you are there for a day trip only, pay close attention to when the last ferry leaves the island, to avoid being stranded At the landing there is a clean ferry terminal with public rest rooms.

GUIDANCE

The **Islesboro town office** (734-2253) is a great source of information. When you board the Maine State Ferry, ask for a map and schedule. The island map is detailed and informative, showing locations of businesses, a full map of the island, ferry schedule, brief description of the island, and historical-society events calendar.

RICK WEBB

The lighthouse at Grindle Point, Islesboro

TO SEE AND DO

The old lighthouse on **Grindle Point** (built in 1850, now automated) and keeper's cottage is now the seasonal **Sailors' Memorial Museum** (734-2253), open 9–4:30 Tuesday through Sunday, July through Labor Day. There are summer musical and theatrical performances at the **Free Will Baptist Church.** Check out the **Up Island Church,** a fine old structure with beautiful wall stencils and fascinating old headstones in the adjacent graveyard.

The layout of the island makes at least a bicycle necessary to get a real feel for the place. The roads are narrow, winding, and have no shoulder. Bicyclists should use great caution. Even so, after both driving and biking the island, we prefer biking. The relaxed pace allows you to see what you are passing rather than simply moving from one point to another. A drive from one end of the island to the other is a nice way to spend a couple of hours. On bicycles, it'll take you most of a day. In **Dark Harbor** you'll see huge "cottages" and impressive architecture. In summer you'll also find shops for browsing, including **Island Books** (734-6610), a great source for used books at good prices; **Isleboro Trader** (734-9788), a varied selection of merchandise from clothing to knickknacks; and the **Dark Harbor Shop** (734-8878), with souvenirs, gifts, ice cream, and a deli. A picnic area and town beach at **Pendleton Point** have spectacular water views. The trip down the other side of the island will take you past the **Islesboro Historical Society** (734-6733) in the former town hall, which houses rotating exhibits on the first floor and a permanent collection upstairs. The historical society also presents a variety of programs throughout the summer season, including a talent show, art shows, dancing, and music. Check their calendar for event dates. Also on this end of the island you'll find **Isleboro Artisans** (734-6944), a summer gift shop and gallery, and a small B&B.

LODGING

The **Islesboro town office** (734-2253) is a friendly source of information and can refer you to local real estate agents who handle cottage rentals.

Dark Harbor House (734-6669; www.darkharborhouse.com), Box 185, Main Road, Dark Harbor, Islesboro 04848. Open mid-May through mid-October. Built on a hilltop at the turn of the 20th century as a summer cottage for the president of the First National Bank of Philadelphia, this imposing, yellow-clapboard inn offers elegance from a past era. The gardens and landscaping are outstanding. Inside you'll find a summery living room with glass French doors opening onto a porch and a cozier library with a fireplace just right for crisp autumn afternoons. The double staircases to the second floor are wonderful. Jerry Ames and Chris Dickman have placed many antiques throughout the inn, creating an unusual and eclectic decor. All 12 guest rooms have private baths, and some feature balconies. An à la carte dining and full wine service is offered to guests and to the public by reservation, upon availability. Entrées might be *paupiettes* of sole with native crabmeat, chicken roulades with leek, Gruyère, and prosciutto. Dessert might be lemon mousse, raspberry-blueberry crisp, or chocolate caramel walnut torte. Picnic baskets can be prepared for day trips. Doubles are $115–275, including a full four-course breakfast. Dinner entrées $17.95–26.95.

Dark Harbor B&B (734-9772; www.IsleboroMaine.com), 119 Derby Road, Islesboro 04848. Open year-round. Amy and Bob McMullen purchased this 1890s farmhouse from the town (it was the physician's assistant's residence until the island got two PAs—Bob is one of them) and renovated it into a cozy B&B with four guest rooms (all private baths). Amy has plenty of experience in both hospitality and island living. Originally from Monhegan Island, she co-owned and managed Shining Sails for 15 years. The rooms are comfortable, with beautiful hardwood floors, pretty quilts, and interesting furnishings. There's also a living room, "maid's kitchen" where guests can prepare simple meals, Internet access, and a laundry facility for those on extended stays. Breakfast, included in the room rate, is served in the dining room with fireplace. $125 per couple late May through early September. Rates decrease $10 per night for 2–6 nights. $750 weekly. Off-season rates $75 per night ($65 for 2–6 nights); $425 weekly.

Aunt Laura's B&B (734-8286; lbebb@aol.com), 812 Main Road, Islesboro

04848. On the other side of the island, Louanne Bebb offers two guest rooms and a living room for guests in the wing attached to her 1855 Cape.

WHERE TO EAT

You can pick up a snack (breakfast specials, burgers, lobster rolls, and such for lunch and dinner) at the **Islander** (734-2270), a take-out stand at the far end of the ferry terminal parking lot; open 7–5 Monday through Friday, until 7 PM Friday and Saturday. The luncheonette in the **Dark Harbor Shop** is the local gathering place. **Durkee's General Store** (734-2201) and **The Island Market** (734-6672) both sell sandwiches, pizza, and provisions for picnics. The **Dark Harbor House** (see *Lodging*) offers dinner by reservation upon availability. **Latitude 44** (734-6543), 107 Derby Road, in Dark Harbor offers fine dining in a casual atmosphere. Reservations are recommended. They are open 5 PM–midnight, Wednesday through Sunday, from April through October. November through March they serve on Friday and Saturday nights only. **Longitude 69** is the pub, open Wednesday through Sunday 5 PM–midnight year-round. There's a pool table, darts, big-screen TV, jukebox, and the usual pub fare.

Belfast, Searsport, and Stockton Springs

Belfast has a history of unusual commercial diversification, including a highly successful sarsaparilla company, a rum distillery, and a city-owned railroad, not to mention poultry and shoe enterprises as well as shipyards. The city's present big employer, MBNA (credit cards), is squirreled away on a landscaped campus north of town. A sense of the sea once more prevails, in the fine old captains' houses up on the hill, then down along the length of Main Street in its plunge to the bay.

East of Belfast, Route 1 shadows the shore of Penobscot Bay as it narrows and seems more like a mighty river. With its sheltered harbors, this area was once prime shipbuilding country. In Searsport's Penobscot Marine Museum you learn that more than 3,000 different vessels have been built in and around Penobscot Bay since 1770. Searsport alone launched eight brigs and six schooners in one year (1845) and for many years boasted more sea captains than any other town its size, explaining the dozens of 19th-century mansions lining Route 1 in Searsport.

Quite a few of the many captains' mansions between Belfast and Stockton Springs (just north of Searsport) are now B&Bs, which work not only as way stops but also as hubs from which to explore the entire region, from Camden to Bar Harbor.

This part of Waldo County also has more than its share of inland villages that are a real pleasure to explore. If you have the time, take the scenic route to this region from Augusta, poking through the communities of Unity, Thorndike, and Brooks, detouring to Liberty then down to Belfast (see *To See—Scenic Drive*).

GUIDANCE

Belfast Area Chamber of Commerce (338-5900; www.belfastmaine. org), P.O. Box 58, Belfast 04915, maintains a seasonal information booth on Main Street down near the waterfront; open seasonally 10–6.

Waldo County Regional Chamber of Commerce (948-5050), P.O. Box 577, Unity 04988. Publishes a guide covering county communities.

GETTING THERE

By air: For commercial service, see *Getting There* in "Rockland/Thomaston Area," "Bangor Area," and "Portland Area."

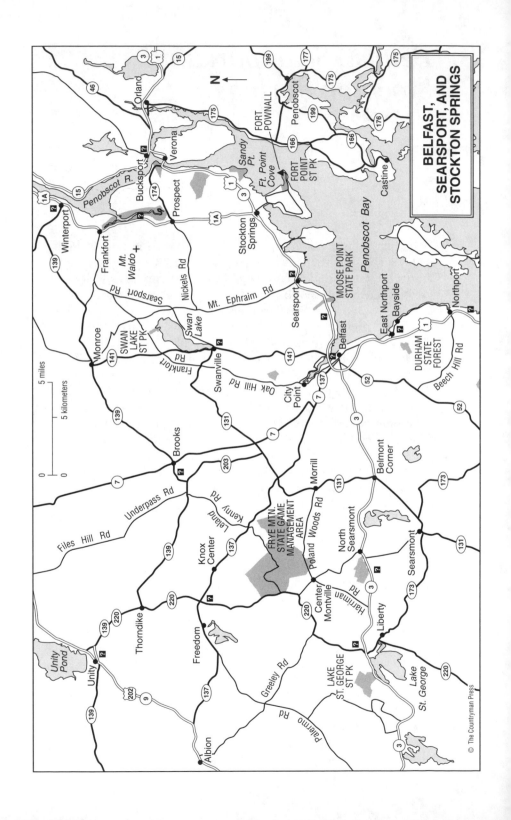

BELFAST,
SEARSPORT, AND
STOCKTON SPRINGS

N

Penobscot Bay

Penobscot R.

Orland
Verona
Bucksport
Winterport
Frankfort
Prospect
Stockton Springs
Sandy Pt.
Ft. Point Cove
FORT POWNALL
FORT POINT ST PK
Penobscot
Castine
Mt. Waldo
Searsport Rd
Nickels Rd
Mt. Ephraim Rd
Swan Lake
SWAN LAKE ST PK
Monroe
Swanville
Searsport
MOOSE POINT STATE PARK
Belfast
East Northport
Bayside
Northport
DURHAM STATE FOREST
Beech Hill Rd
City Point
Frankfort Rd
Oak Hill Rd
Brooks
Underpass Rd
Files Hill Rd
Leland Rd
Kenny Rd
Knox Center
FRYE MTN. STATE GAME MANAGEMENT AREA
Poland Woods Rd
Morrill
Belmont Corner
North Searsmont
Searsmont
Thorndike
Freedom
Center Montville
Harriman Rd
Liberty
LAKE ST. GEORGE ST PK
Lake St. George
Greeley Rd
Palermo Rd
Unity
Unity Pond
Albion

5 miles
5 kilometers
0

© The Countryman Press

Penobscot Marine Museum

By car: The most direct route to this region from points south and west is via I-95, exiting in Augusta and taking Route 3 to Belfast.

By bus: **Concord Trailways** (1-800-639-3317) stops in Searsport and Belfast seasonally.

MEDICAL EMERGENCY

Waldo County General Hospital (338-2500; 1-800-649-2536), 118 Northport Avenue, Belfast.

VILLAGES

Brooks. In the center of this quiet county, surrounded by hills, this town has the most scenic golf course around, and a summer theater group.

Liberty is home to Lake St. George State Park, and the Liberty Tool Company on Main Street, with its bizarre mix of antiques and items found in an old-fashioned hardware store. The octagonal post office houses the historical society (open weekends in summer) and is itself a museum with all of its original equipment.

Northport. A deceptively sleepy-looking little town has a yacht club, a golf club, pretty gingerbread cottages lining the bay, a popular Saturday-night dance club, and a well-known Mexican restaurant.

Unity. Home to the headquarters of the Belfast & Moosehead Lake Railroad, a rural college, a raceway, and the new fairgrounds for the popular Common Ground Fair.

Stockton Springs. Route 1 now bypasses this former shipbuilding town. The home of the biggest shipbuilder is now the Hichborn Inn, and one of the few surviving shops is now Birdworks of Maine (see *Selective*

Shopping—Special Shops). Follow East Street down to Fort Point (see *Green Space*).

TO SEE

MUSEUMS

Penobscot Marine Museum (548-2529; www.penobscotmarinemuseum. org), Route 1, Searsport. Open Memorial Day through mid-October, Monday through Saturday 10–5 and Sunday noon–5; year-round by appointment. Adults $6, children 7–15, $2. Family rate $14. (The library is open weekdays year-round, except closed on Mondays, December through March.) The 13 buildings include 8 on the National Register of Historic Places. The museum shop is at the entrance to the complex, which is more extensive than it looks from Route 1. Displays in the 1845 town hall trace the evolution of sailing vessels from 17th-century mast ships to the Down Easters of the 1870s and 1880s—graceful square-rigged vessels that were both fast and sturdy cargo carriers. In other buildings there are fine marine paintings, scrimshaw, a variety of lacquerware, Chinese imports, and more. You learn that Searsport didn't just build ships; townspeople owned the ships they built and sailed off in them to the far reaches of the compass, taking their families along. In 1889 Searsport boasted 77 deep-sea captains, 33 of whom piloted full-rigged Cape Horners. There are pictures of Searsport families meeting in distant ports, and, of course, there is the exotica they brought home— much of which is still being sold in local antiques shops. The **Fowler-True-Ross House** tells the story of two prominent captains' families. Not everyone led the life of a sea captain, however, and a museum exhibit, *Working the Bay: The Ports and People of Penobscot Bay*, focuses on the working-class people who made their living here in the granite, lime, ice, fishing, and lobstering industries. The galleries in the **Captain Jeremiah Merithew House** have been refurbished and now hold a collection of paintings by father and son marine artists Thomas and James Buttersworth. Inquire about lecture, film, and concert series.

Belfast Museum (338-2078), 6 Market Street, Belfast. Open Thursday and Sunday in summer 1–4, and by appointment year-round. A small but interesting museum featuring local artifacts, paintings, scrapbooks full of newspaper clippings about the area, and other displays.

Harbor Church, Route 1, Searsport. Phone 548-6663 or pick up the key at the Harbor House across the street and check out the fabulous stained-glass windows in this church, built in 1815.

Bryant Museum (568-3665), Rich Road (junction of Routes 220 and 129), Thorndike. Open year-round, Monday through Saturday 8–4:30. What began as a stove shop has evolved into a fascinating museum, chock-full of things to look at. The front is crammed with restored woodstoves. Walk through these to the doll circus, with its array of mechanical, musical dolls from Barbie to Disney characters and everything in between. The back room houses a collection of player pianos, nickelodeons, and vintage automobiles. Worth the drive.

SCENIC DRIVE

Route 3, past Lake St. George and Sheepscot Pond, through the China Lakes region, is the most direct path between Belfast and Augusta, but take time to detour down Route 173 to **Liberty** to see the octagonal post office and the **Liberty Tool Company.** For a leisurely tour of the villages between Belfast and Augusta, head north from East Belfast on Route 141 to Monroe. Ask for directions to **Stone Soup Farm** to see their gardens, then check out **Monroe Falls,** just off Route 139, and maybe have a picnic. Head out on Route 139, through Brooks, and then on toward Thorndike, where you will want to be sure to stop at the **Bryant Museum** (see *To See—Museums*). Continue on Route 139 to Unity, where you will pass the new home of the Common Ground Fair and the pretty station for the **Belfast & Moosehead Lake Railroad** (see *To Do—Train Excursion*). Follow Route 139 into Kennebec County to Fairfield to meet up with I-95, or detour yet again onto Route 202, which will bring you through the China Lakes region to Augusta.

TO DO

BERRY PICKING

Staples Homestead Blueberries (567-3393/3703), County Road, Stockton Springs. Turn at the ball field on Route 1/3, then drive 3 miles to the T at County Road; turn right. Or ask directions in Stockton Springs village. Open 8–5 daily while berries are in-season (mid-August). Friendly owners Basil and Mary Staples will instruct you in the mysteries of blueberry raking then let you go to it, or you can pick by hand.

GOLF

Country View Golf Course (722-3161) in Brooks is the most scenic in the area: nine holes, par 36, cart rental, club rentals, lessons, clubhouse.

SWIMMING

Lake St. George State Park (589-4255), Route 3, Liberty. Open May 15 through October 15. A great way station for travelers going to or from Down East. A deep, clear lake with a small beach, lifeguard, bathhouse, parking facilities, 31 campsites, and a boat launch. **Swan Lake State Park,** Route 141, Swanville (north of town; follow signs). This beach has picnicking facilities on Swan Lake. **Belfast City Park,** Route 1, Belfast (south of town). Swimming pool, tennis courts, picnicking facilities, and a gravel beach. **Sandy Point Beach,** off Route 1 north of Stockton Springs (it's posted HERSEY RETREAT; turn toward the water directly across from the Rocky Ridge Motel).

TRAIN EXCURSION

Belfast & Moosehead Lake Railroad Co. (338-2330; 1-800-392-5500),

May through October. Operates 1½-hour excursions from the Belfast waterfront along the Passagassawakeag River to the inland village of Waldo and back. Inquire about Rail & Sail combos. The Unity station, at 1 Depot Square, is painted bright red with green and white trim, hardly what you expect to see as you drive down the quiet roads of this area. There is a gift shop, rest rooms, snack bar, and waiting area with a stuffed black bear, plenty of cushioned seats, and historical photos on the walls. A Swedish steam engine carries passengers on a 1½-hour narrated journey from Unity to Burnham Junction. Pre-ride demonstration as the engine is turned on the old Armstrong turntable. $14 adults, $7 children. Several special events and packages throughout. Inquire about excursion boat rides.

GREEN SPACE

Also see *To Do—Swimming.*

Moose Point State Park, Route 1, south of Searsport. Open May 30 through October 15. A good spot for picnicking; cookout facilities are in an evergreen grove and an open field overlooking Penobscot Bay. Also check out **Mossman Park** in downtown Searsport; take Steamboat Avenue from Route 1 to the harbor with its picnic benches by tidal pools and the public landing.

Fort Pownall and **Fort Point State Park,** Stockton Springs (marked from Route 1; accessible via a 3.5-mile access road). The 1759 fort built to defend the British claim to Maine (the Penobscot River was the actual boundary between the English and French territories) was burned twice to prevent its being taken; only earthworks remain. The adjacent park, on the tip of a peninsula jutting into Penobscot Bay, is a fine fishing and picnic spot. A pier accommodates visitors who arrive by boat. The lighthouse is another great spot. Views from the point are back down to the Camden Hills.

LODGING

INNS AND BED & BREAKFASTS
In Belfast 04915

Harbor View House (338-3811; 1-877-393-3811; www.harborviewhouse. com), 213 High Street. This vintage-1807 Federal mansion turned B&B seems to have it all: Federal-era grace, all the comforts, and a sweeping view of Penobscot Bay from its perch above downtown Belfast. All six rooms have private baths with tub showers, working fireplaces, and TV/VCR (there's a film library); five have water views. Our favorites are the second-floor Joshua Chamberlain Room ($125) with a queen bed and rocker by the fireplace, and the Harbormaster Room ($135) with an equally stunning view from a window seat. Common space includes a

KIM GRANT

Downtown Belfast

deck as well as living room, and rates (from $95) include a full breakfast served in the dining room.

The Alden House (338-2151; 1-877-337-8151; www.TheAldenHouse. com), 63 Church Street. Bruce and Sue Madara are your hosts in this gracious 1840 mansion, which has been totally renovated and tastefully furnished. Architectual details include Italian marble mantels and sinks and a circular staircase. There are seven guest rooms, one on the ground floor, five with private baths. In the Hiram Alden room two antique chairs face a working fireplace, and fires also grace the library and South Parlor. The North Parlor features a grand player piano. A porch overlooks the lawns, where guests can play croquet. $86–120 includes a full breakfast, served at separate tables.

The Jeweled Turret Inn (338-2304; 1-800-696-2304), 40 Pearl Street. Open year-round. A handsome gabled and turreted house built ornately inside and out in the 1890s. The fireplace in the den is said to be made of stones from every state in the Union at that time, from the collection of the original owner. Each of the seven guest rooms has a private bath, is decorated in shades reminiscent of the gem it is named for, and is furnished with antiques and plenty of knickknacks. The Amethyst Room is in the turret; the Opal Room features a marble bath with a whirlpool tub. Carl and Cathy Heffentrager serve a full breakfast and tea and take time to visit with guests, perhaps on one of two verandas that overlook the historic district. $85–135 double includes breakfast and afternoon refreshments.

Thomas Pitcher House (338-6454; 1-888-338-6454; www.thomaspitcher house.com), 19 Franklin Street. Open year-round. Set just off the main drag, this is a comfortable, friendly place. Fran and Ron Kresge are warm hosts, eager to help guests enjoy the area. Each of the four guest rooms has a private bath and a speaker (which guests control) for the music that is piped throughout the house. We especially like the Thomas Pitcher Room with its four-poster bed, bay-window reading area, and claw-foot tub in the bathroom. Downstairs is a cozy common room with a TV and VCR. $75–95 includes breakfast served family-style in the dining room.

In Searsport 04974

Watchtide (548-6575; 1-800-698-6575; www.watchtide.com), Route 1. This is a bright house with a 60-foot-long, 19-windowed, wicker- and flower-filled sunporch with a periwinkle blue floor, overlooking fields stretching to the bay. Nancy-Linn Nellis and Jack Elliott are warm, welcoming hosts. Nancy-Linn also operates **Angels to Antiques**—a gift store (specializing in angels) in the adjacent barn. The four guest rooms with private baths are furnished with antiques, and attention is paid to small details. Eleanor Roosevelt slept here several times when this was the College Club Inn (opened in 1917). One ocean-view room now has a Jacuzzi. Staying here is like staying with old friends, and the chocolate-covered dried cranberries in guest rooms are addictive. $85–175 includes a breakfast that might begin with strawberries and nectarines, move on hot popovers, and then a crabmeat soufflé with Jarlsberg and pecorino cheeses. Inquire about off-season specials.

Homeport Inn (548-2259; 1-800-742-5814), Route 1. Open year-round. An 1861 captain's mansion complete with widow's walk overlooking the bay. Dr. and Mrs. George Johnson were the first Searsport B&B hosts. Rooms in front are old-fashioned—three of the four have shared baths—but the six downstairs rooms in the back are modern and elegantly decorated, with private baths and bay views. Also offered are two 2-bedroom cottages. The landscaped grounds, with lovely flower gardens, slope to the water. A full breakfast is included in the rates, which range from $35 (single with shared bath) to $90 (double with private bath); lower rates November through April. The cottages are $600–750 per week.

Captain Green Pendleton B&B (548-6523; 1-800-949-4403), Route 1. Open year-round. Another fine old captain's home with 80 acres set well back from Route 1. The three bedrooms, one downstairs (with private bath) and two upstairs, are comfortably furnished, and the spacious common rooms have a welcoming feel. All guest rooms have working fireplaces, and there's a Franklin fireplace in the parlor. A path circles the meadow, a cross-country ski trail goes through the woods, and there's a large spring-fed trout pond. The Greiners are warm and helpful hosts. $75 per night downstairs, $65 upstairs, includes tax as well as a full breakfast; less off-season. "Reasonable-sized dogs" are accommodated in the barn for $15 extra.

🐾👤 **The Captain Butman Homestead** (548-2506; 1-877-33-HOSTEL; www. NewEnglandHostel.com), Route 1. A classic 1830s farmhouse on 5½ acres. Open mid-April through October. This was home for generations of Searsport's deepwater captains, and there's a right-of-way down to Penobscot Bay. The four guest rooms share 1½ baths. A full breakfast is included in $60 double. A spotless, spacious International Youth Hostel is attached: five dorm-style beds each for men and women, a large sitting and kitchen area, and three private rooms, including one that's fully handicapped accessible. A bargain at $15 for members, $18 for non-members ($20–25 per person for a private room).

In Stockton Springs 04981

The Hichborn Inn (567-4183; 1-800-346-1522; www.HichbornInn.com), Church Street, P.O. Box 115. Open year-round except Christmas. This stately Victorian Italianate mansion complete with widow's walk is up a side street in an old shipbuilding village that's now bypassed by Route 1. Built by a prolific shipbuilder (N. G. Hichborn launched 42 vessels) and prominent politician, it remained in the family, preserved by his daughters (there's a tale!) until 1939. For Nancy and Bruce Suppes, restoring this house has meant deep involvement in its story—and its friendly ghosts. Bruce, an engineer on supertankers, has done much of the exceptional restoration work himself. There's a comfortable "gent's parlor," where evening fires burn; also a music room and an elegant library. Elaborate breakfasts are served either in the dining room or on the sunporch. There are four rooms, two with private baths; niceties include books and magazines by all the beds, a pitcher of ice water on the dresser, and chocolates on the nightstand. Your hosts will pick you up at the dock in Searsport or Belfast and provide transport to dinner or for supplies. Nancy and Bruce are a font of local tips. $65–95 per night; $55–81 off-season.

WHERE TO EAT

DINING OUT

Nickerson Tavern (phone not available at press time), Route 1, Searsport. This handsome 1830s sea captain's house has been a dining landmark for decades and never more so now that it's under the new ownership of Searsport native Matthew Kenney, who owns several New York City restaurants as well as the new Commissary Restaurant in Portland. The main dining room features two fireplaces, yellow-pine floors, wainscoting, linens, and flowers. Plans call for the 11-acre grounds to include a greenhouse and apiary as well as gardens. The menu is seasonally driven and features local products; the aim is to be clean and elegant, not fussy.

Rhumb Line (548-2600), 200 East Main Street (Route 1), Searsport. Fine dining in a relaxed atmosphere. Owners Charles and Diana Evans ran a successful restaurant on Martha's Vineyard before coming to Searsport.

Dinner guests are invited into the parlor for drinks before heading to tables. The menu changes daily, but usually includes roast rack of lamb or horseradish-crusted salmon. Dessert choices may include French bread pudding or chocolate temptation (a flourless cake filled with raspberry hazelnut ganache). Entrées $16–24.

EATING OUT

Anglers (548-2405), Route 1, Searsport. Open daily 11–8. Buddy Hale's roadside (Maine-style) diner styles itself "Maine's Family Seafood Restaurant," and the seafood ranges from every kind of chowder and seafood stew through fried and broiled fish dinners, including lobster every which way. "Land Lovers" get a token chicken parmigiana or broiled sirloin, and the Minnow Menu is for "the smaller appetite" (you don't have to be small).

Darby's Restaurant and Pub (338-2339), 155 High Street, Belfast. Open daily for lunch and dinner. A storefront café with tin ceilings and local artwork. Salads, burgers, and upscale lunch sandwiches. A reasonably priced dinner find: Entrées might include pad Thai or Moroccan lamb. Soups, salads, and sandwiches are served all day.

Bay Wrap (338-9757), 20 Beaver Street (just off Main), Belfast. Open daily for lunch and dinner. A great choice of fillings in flatbread wraps. Try the samurai salmon with nori, sprouts, cucumber, sesame seeds, avocado, scallions, and jasmine rice with soy-wasabi vinaigrette living harmoniously in a spinach tortilla.

Bell the Cat (338-2084), Reny's Plaza, Route 3, Belfast. Open 9–9 except Sunday, when it's 9–6. Relocated from downtown to a spacious up-front corner of Mr. Paperback, the local favorite for designer sandwiches and suggested choices ranging from the PB&J ($2.50) to dill Havarti or a fat Reuben. Also good for salads and soups. Coffees and teas.

NTWH Bakery/Café (338-9177), 70–72 Main Street, Belfast. Open Monday through Saturday 9–5, Sunday noon–5 in season. A gallery adjoins this aromatic oasis with its shiny espresso machine and tempting pastries. Proceeds benefit the National Theater Workshop of the Handicapped uptown.

LOBSTER POUND

Young's Lobster Pound (338-1160), Mitchell Avenue (posted from Route 1 just across the bridge from Belfast), East Belfast. Open in-season 7–6:30. A pound with as many as 30,000 lobsters, and seating (indoor and outdoor) to accommodate 500. Order, and enjoy the view of Belfast across the Passagassawakeag River while you wait.

ENTERTAINMENT

The Belfast Maskers (338-9668). A year-round community theater that puts on several shows each season at the Railroad Theater on the waterfront. Schedule available at the theater. They also offer acting workshops and classes for adults and children.

✐ **The Playhouse** (338-5777), Church Street, Belfast. A cozy 36-seat theater offering shows by the Assembled Players company. Founder Mary Weaver also offers after-school and Saturday workshops for actors of all ages.

The Colonial Theater (338-1930), Belfast. The new home of the outsized carved elephants from a Belfast landmark, Perry's Nut House; three screens with nightly showings in a restored theater in downtown Belfast.

SELECTIVE SHOPPING

ANTIQUES SHOPS

Searsport claims to be the "Antiques Capital of Maine." After counting 29 shops on Route 1, we may be inclined to agree: The **Searsport Antique Mall,** open daily year-round, is a cooperative of 74 dealers. Everything from 18th-century furniture to 1960s collectibles is spread over two floors. Next door, **Hickson's Flea Market** has both indoor shops (most have specialties) rented for the season and outdoor tables where anyone can set up. The **Pumpkin Patch,** we're told by an experienced dealer, is one of the best shops in the state. They've been in business close to 20 years and have 26 dealers represented. Mary Harriman ran a truck stop until 1989. When it closed, she opened the **Hobby Horse,** which has since grown to house 20 shops, 30 tables, and a lunch wagon. The **Searsport Flea Market,** held weekends in-season, is also big. Antiques at **Hillman's** (Route 1 across from the Nickerson Tavern): good linens, china, glassware.

BOOKSTORES

Fertile Mind Bookshop (338-2498), 13 Main Street, Belfast. An outstanding browsing and buying place featuring Maine and regional books and guides, maps, records, and cards. **Victorian House/Book Barn** (567-3351), East Street, Stockton Springs. Open April through December, 8–6; otherwise, by chance or appointment. A landmark collection of 20,000 antiquarian books, and a special find for mystery-book buffs.

SPECIAL SHOPS

In Belfast

Coyote Moon (338-5659), 54 Main Street, Belfast. A nifty, reasonably priced women's clothing and gift store. **All About Games** (338-9984), 171 High Street, Belfast, is a great place to buy and play traditional board games, as well as some more unusual nonautomated games. **Colburn Shoe Store** (338-1934), 79 Main Street, Belfast, bills itself as the oldest shoe store in America. **Reny's** (338-4588), Reny's Plaza, Route 3 just north of the junction with Route 1. One in Maine's chain of distinctive outlet stores. Always worth a stop (good for everything from TVs to socks).

North along Route 1

Perry's Nut House (338-1630), Route 1 just north of the Belfast Bridge.

Reopened but not what it used to be. **Monroe Saltworks** (338-3460), Route 1, Belfast. This distinctive pottery, which originated in nearby Monroe, now has a wide following around the country. There are seconds and unusual pieces both here and in the Ellsworth outlets. **Mainely Pottery** (338-1108), features the work of owner Jamie Oates and carries varied work by 24 other potters.

In Searsport and Stockton Springs

Silkweeds (548-6501), Route 1, Searsport. Specializes in "country gifts": tinware, cotton afghans, rugs, wreaths. **The Talisman** (548-6279), Navy Street, Searsport. Open year-round except Sunday and Monday. Handcrafted gold and silver jewelry. **Birdworks of Maine** (567-3030), School Street (just off Route 1), Stockton Springs. Open weekdays 9–5. Decorative pottery bird feeders, nesting roosts, suet keepers, and much more, all made on the premises. **Waldo County Co-op,** Route 1, Searsport Harbor. Open June through October, daily 9–5. A showcase for the local extension service. Dolls, needlework, wooden crafts, quilts, pillows, jams, and ceramics—and lots of them.

SPECIAL EVENTS

July and August: **Free Thursday-night street concerts** in downtown Belfast.

July 4: **Parade, fairs, and fireworks** in Searsport.

Mid-July: **Belfast Bay Festival**—a week of events, including a giant chicken barbecue, midway, races, and parade.

August: **Searsport Lobster Boat Races** and related events.

September: **Common Ground Fair** in Unity—organic farm products, demonstrations, children's activities, sheepdog round-up, crafts, entertainment. The Belfast & Moosehead Lake Railroad runs to the fairgrounds.

Columbus Day weekend: **Fling to Fall** celebration—parade, bonfire, church suppers.

Second weekend in December: **Searsport Victorian Christmas**—open houses at museum, homes, and B&Bs.

IV. DOWN EAST

East Penobscot Bay Region
Acadia Area
Washington County and the Quoddy Loop

KIM GRANT

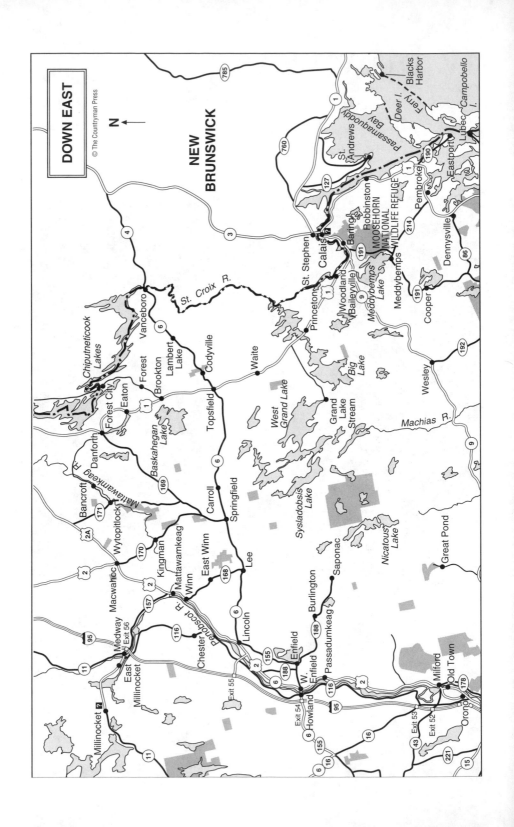

DOWN EAST

© The Countryman Press

N

NEW BRUNSWICK

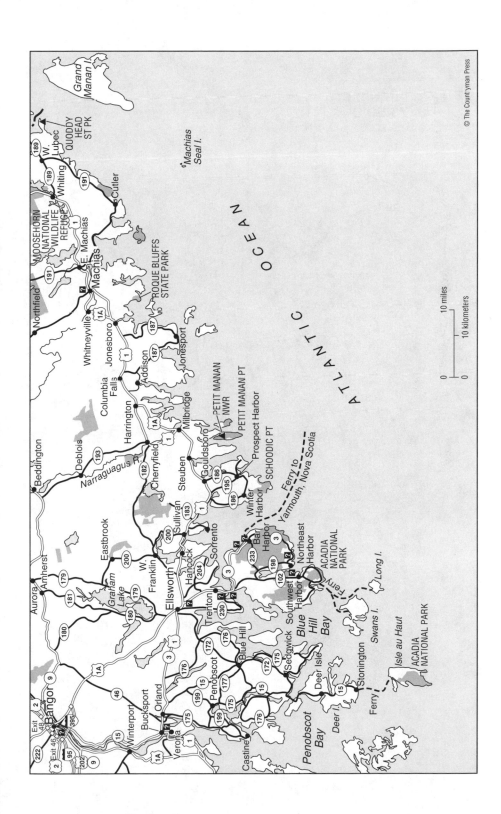

Grand Manan I.

W. Lubec
QUODDY HEAD ST PK
189

189 Whiting
Cutler
191

MOOSEHORN NATIONAL WILDLIFE REFUGE
1
191 Northfield
E. Machias
Whitneyville
Machias
ROQUE BLUFFS STATE PARK
1A
Jonesboro
187
Addison
187
Jonesport
1
Milbridge

Machias Seal I.

Columbia Falls
Harrington
1A
Cherryfield
1
Gouldsboro
PETIT MANAN NWR
PETIT MANAN PT
Prospect Harbor
SCHOODIC PT
182
193
Steuben
Narraguagus R.
186
195
186
Winter Harbor
Ferry to Yarmouth, Nova Scotia

Beddington
Deblois

ATLANTIC OCEAN

Eastbrook
183
Sullivan
200
Sorrento
Hancock
204
2
233
Bar Harbor
3
198
Northeast Harbor
2
ACADIA NATIONAL PARK
102
Southwest Harbor

W. Franklin
Graham Lake
200
Ellsworth
Trenton
230
2
3
Ferry

Amherst
179
179
Aurora
181
180
180
3
1
Blue Hill
Sedgwick
Deer Isle
Blue Hill Bay
Long I.

1A
Bangor
9
Winterport
46
Bucksport
Orland
Penobscot
176
172
177
175
172
Deer I.
Stonington
15
Ferry
Swans I.
Isle au Haut
ACADIA NATIONAL PARK

222
Exit 2
Exit 46B
395
95
202
9
15
Verona
1
1A
Castine
175
199
15
199
176
Penobscot Bay

10 miles
10 kilometers
0
0

© The Countryman Press

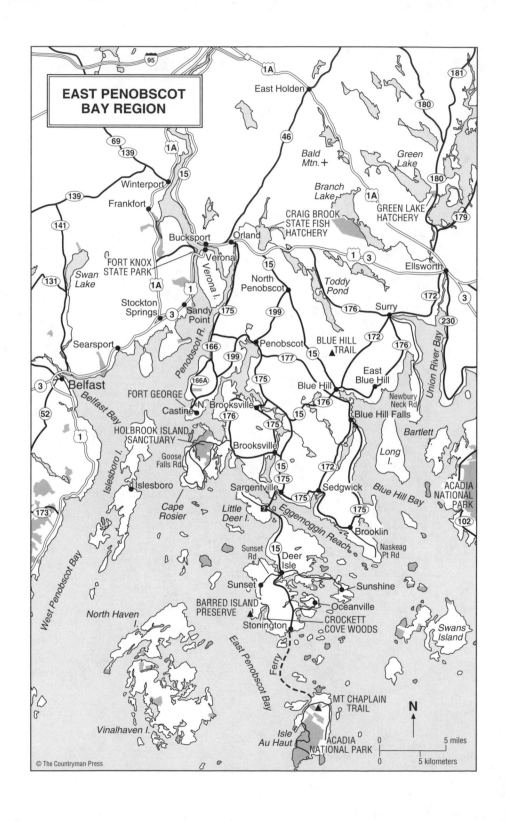

EAST PENOBSCOT BAY REGION

95

1A

East Holden

181

180

69
139

46

Bald
Mtn. +

Green
Lake

1A

15

Winterport

180

Branch
Lake

1A

GREEN LAKE
HATCHERY

139

Frankfort

141

CRAIG BROOK
STATE FISH
HATCHERY

179

Bucksport

Orland

1   3

Ellsworth

Verona

3

131

Swan
Lake

FORT KNOX
STATE PARK

15

North
Penobscot

Toddy
Pond

176

Surry

172

3

230

Stockton
Springs

1A

1

175

199

15

Searsport

3

Sandy
Point

166

199

Penobscot

177

15

BLUE HILL
TRAIL ▲

172

176

Belfast

3

166A

175

Blue Hill

East
Blue Hill

52

FORT GEORGE

Castine

N. Brooksville

176

176

15

Newbury
Neck Rd

1

Bartlett

Blue Hill Falls

HOLBROOK ISLAND
SANCTUARY

175

Brooksville

175

Long
I.

Goose
Falls Rd

Islesboro I.

Islesboro

Cape
Rosier

Sargentville

15

172

Sedgwick

Blue Hill Bay

ACADIA
NATIONAL
PARK

175

175

Little
Deer I.

?

175

Eggemoggin Reach

175

102

Brooklin

173

Sunset
Rd

15

Deer
Isle

Naskeag
Pt Rd

West Penobscot Bay

Sunset

Sunshine

North Haven
I.

BARRED ISLAND
PRESERVE ▲

Oceanville

CROCKETT
COVE WOODS

Swans
Island

Stonington

East Penobscot Bay

Ferry

MT CHAPLAIN
TRAIL ▲

N

Vinalhaven I.

Isle
Au Haut

ACADIA
NATIONAL PARK

0   5 miles

0   5 kilometers

© The Countryman Press

Union River Bay

East Penobscot Bay Region

Bucksport; Blue Hill Area; Castine; Deer Isle, Stonington, and Isle au Haut

BUCKSPORT

Gateway is a much overused touring term, but crossing the high, narrow Waldo–Hancock County suspension bridge (vintage 1931) above the confluence of the Penobscot River and Bay, you can't escape the sense of turning a corner in the coast. Beyond is Bucksport, a workaday river and paper-mill town with a couple of very good places to eat and a 1916 movie theater/museum showcasing New England films dating back to the turn of the 20th century.

Bucksport began as a major shipping port in 1764, the reason it was burned by the British in 1799 and was again occupied by the British during the War of 1812. In the 1820s it was the largest town in eastern Maine. Note the Jed Prouty Tavern in the middle of Main Street, now elderly housing but once a dining stop for a half-dozen presidents down through the years. Bucksport overlooks New England's biggest fort, a memorial to its smallest war.

GUIDANCE

Bucksport Bay Area Chamber of Commerce (469-6818; bbac@ mint.net), P.O. Box 1880, Bucksport 04416. The information office, next to the town offices on Main Street, is open 24 hours for browsing; live assistance is available part time. It publishes a "SourceBook" that includes Orland and Verona Islands. Public rest rooms are at the town dock. Also see www.penobscotbay.com.

TO SEE AND DO

✐ **Fort Knox State Park** (469-7719), Route 174 (off Route 1), Prospect (just across the Penobscot from Bucksport). Open daily May 1 through November 1, 9 AM–sunset. $2 adults, $.50 children ages 5–11. Built in 1844 of granite cut from nearby Mount Waldo, it includes barracks, storehouses, a labyrinth of passageways, and even a granite spiral staircase. There are also picnic facilities. The fort was to be a defense against Canada during the boundary dispute, called the Aroostook War, with New Brunswick. The dispute was ignored in Washington, and so in 1839 the new, lumber-rich state took matters into its own hands by arming its northern forts. Daniel Webster represented Maine in the 1842 treaty that formally ended the war, but Maine built this fort two years later, just in case. It was never entirely completed and never saw battle. Troops were, however, stationed here during the Civil War and again during the Spanish-American War. Check out the interpretive center and gift shop. Inquire about reenactmens and other special events.

Northeast Historic Film/The Alamo Theatre (469-0924; www.alamo theatre.org), 379 Main Street, Bucksport. Open year-round Monday through Friday 9–4 and for performances. Housed in the vintage-1916 Alamo Theatre (closed in '56 and recently restored), this is New England's only "moving-image" archive—source of silent Maine-made films with thousands of viewing tapes dating back to 1901 (www.oldfilm. org). Current as well as vintage films are shown regularly in the 125-seat theater, and there are occasional live performances. Stop at least to see the displays in the lobby. The gift shop features videos and classic posters.

Bucksport Historical Society Museum (469-2464), Main Street, Bucksport. Open July and August, Wednesday through Friday 1–4, and other announced times. Admission $1. Housed in the former Maine Central Railroad Station; local memorabilia.

At **Buck Cemetery,** near the Verona Bridge (across from the Shop 'n Save), a granite obelisk marks the grave of Colonel Jonathan Buck, founder of Bucksport. The outline of a leg on the stone has spurred many legends, the most popular being that a woman whom Judge Buck sentenced to death for witchcraft is carrying through a promise to dance on his grave. Attempts to remove the imprint have failed, and it is still there.

Craig Brook National Fish Hatchery (469-2803), on Alamoosook Lake in East Orland (marked from Route 1). First opened in 1871, this is the country's oldest salmon hatchery. New in summer of 2001: a large visitors center (open daily, year-round, 8–3) with films and interactive displays on Maine rivers, watersheds, and salmon. A small **Atlantic Salmon Museum** is open daily 12–3 in summer. The facility also includes a boat launch on Alamoosook Lake, a picnic area on Craig Pond, and hiking/ski trails.

SPECIAL LEARNING PROGRAMS

Verna Cox (469-6402; fax, 469-6243), on Verona Island, offers multiday rug-braiding and rug-hooking classes; also inquire about spinning, weaving, crewel, cross-stitching, tatting, and wool-felting workshops.

LODGING

Jed Prouty Motor Inn (469-3113; 1-800-528-1234), Main Street, Bucksport 04416. Open year-round. Built as a modern annex to the old Jed Prouty Inn, now a Best Western offering 40 motel-style rooms with two double beds and great views of the mouth of the Penobscot River and Fort Knox. $69–99 per couple depending on the season; $59–89 single.

WHERE TO EAT

MacLeods (469-3963), Main Street, Bucksport. Open weekdays 11:30–9, weekends for dinner only. A pubby atmosphere with booths. Dependable dining. Good lunch specials. Dinner entrées might include barbecued ribs or broiled fresh scallops. Entrées $8.95–15.95.

L'Ermitage (469-3361), 219 Main Street, Bucksport. Open for dinner by reservation, Tuesday through Sunday. Traditional French fare in the dining rooms of a Victorian house. Entrées from $12.95.

Sail Inn, Route 1 in Prospect just before the bridge. The name always makes us laugh since there is no way you could sail into this classic family-owned diner, perched as it is atop a high bluff. Blackboard specials supplement a menu featuring fried chicken and fish, seafood chowders, and stews.

Riverview (469-7600), Main Street, Bucksport. Open for all three meals. Adjacent to the public landing, overlooking the Penobscot and Fort Knox. Good road food; casual lounge.

SELECTIVE SHOPPING

Mayari (469-0868; www.mayari.com), Route 1, Verona Island. Ariadne Donnell keeps a herd of rare San Clemente goats in the rear of her store, source of the goat's-milk lotions, soaps, and creams that she makes here and sells primarily by mail order.

Book Stacks (469-8992; 1-888-295-0123), 333 Main Street, Bucksport. Open Monday through Saturday 9–8, Sunday 9–5. An inviting full-service bookstore.

SPECIAL EVENTS

Late July: **Fort Knox Bay Festival.** Encampments, parade, events on the river; at the fort and along the Bucksport waterfront.

BLUE HILL AREA

In Maine, Blue Hill refers to a specific hill, a village, a town, a peninsula—and also to an unusual gathering of artists, musicians, and craftspeople.

Blue Hill is a shade off the beaten path, one peninsula west of Mount Desert and nowhere near a beach, but it always has had its own following—especially among creative people. Over the entrance of the Bagaduce (sheet music) Lending Library a mural depicts Blue Hill Village as the center of concentric creative circles, radiating out over the peninsula. Helen and Scott Nearing, searching for a new place to live "the Good Life" in the 1950s (when a ski area encroached on their seclusion in southern Vermont), swung a dowsing pendulum over a map of coastal Maine. It came to rest on Cape Rosier. For many decades the tiny town of Brooklin was a familiar byline in *The New Yorker* thanks to E. B. White, the same decades during which millions of children were reading about Blueberry Hill in Robert McCloskey's *Blueberries for Sal* and about Condon's Garage (still a South Brooksville family-owned landmark) in the 1940s classic *One Morning in Maine*.

Energy lines or not, this peninsula's intermingling of land and water—along lakes and tidal rivers as well as bays—creates a landscape that's exceptional, even in coastal Maine. Pause at the turnout on Caterpillar Hill, the height-of-land on Route 15/175 (just north of the Deer Isle Bridge), to appreciate the extent of this phenomenon. Then plunge down the hill to that improbably narrow, soaring suspension bridge.

Across the bridge, Deer Isle is a chapter in its own right (see "Deer Isle, Stonington, and Isle au Haut"); it is both physically and otherwise distinct from the Blue Hill peninsula, but both are distinguished by their number of narrow roads threading numerous land fingers, leading to studios of local craftspeople and artists. What you remember afterward is the beauty of clouds over fields of wildflowers; quiet coves; the loveliness of things woven, painted, and blown; and conversations with the people who made them.

The 1939 bridge spans Eggemoggin Reach, a 10-mile-long passage dividing the Blue Hill peninsula from Deer Isle but linking Penobscot and Jericho Bays. A century ago this was a busy thoroughfare, a shortcut from Rockland to points Down East for freight-carrying schooners and passenger steamboats. It remains a popular route for windjammers, yachts, and, increasingly, for sea kayakers. Route 175 hugs "the Reach" on its way through Sedgwick to Brooklin.

Castine, the tip of an arm of the Blue Hill peninsula with its own history and feel, has its own chapter too. Once positioned in the thick of traffic—the pivotal point at the mouth of the Penobscot River and head of Penobscot Bay—it's still the home of the Maine Maritime Academy.

GUIDANCE
The Blue Hill Chamber of Commerce publishes a map/guide available locally and at: www.penobscotbay.com. Also pick up the current free copies of the "Browser's Trail" and the "Gallery Guide."

GETTING THERE
By car: The obvious way is Route 1 to Route 15 to Blue Hill, but there are many shortcuts through the confusing web of roads on this peninsula; ask directions to your lodging place.

MEDICAL EMERGENCY
Blue Hill Memorial Hospital (374-2836), Water Street, Blue Hill. The largest facility in the area, it has a 24-hour emergency room. **Ambulance:** 374-9900 and 911.

TO SEE

Parson Fisher House (374-2459), 0.5 mile south of Blue Hill Village on Route 15/176. Open July through mid-September, Monday through Saturday 2–5. A house built in 1814 by Blue Hill's first pastor, a Harvard graduate who augmented his meager salary with a varied line of crafts and by teaching (he founded Blue Hill Academy), farming, and writing. His furniture, paintings, books, journals, and woodcuts are exhibited. $3 admission.

Holt House (326-8250), Water Street, Blue Hill. Open during July and August, Tuesday and Friday 1–4, Saturday 9–12. Donation. The Blue Hill Historical Society collection is housed in this restored 1815 Federal mansion near the harbor and is noted for its stenciled walls.

Blue Hill Library (374-5515), Main Street, Blue Hill. Open daily except Sunday. A handsome WPA-project building with periodicals and ample reading space; changing art shows in summer.

Bagaduce Lending Library (374-5454), Route 15, Blue Hill. Open Tuesday, Wednesday, and Friday 10–3. This Blue Hill phenomenon features roughly 625,000 volumes of sheet music, some more than a century old and most of it special for one reason or another—all available for borrowing. The collection includes 1,400 pieces about Maine, by Maine composers, or published in Maine. Stop by just to see the mural over the entrance, depicting Blue Hill at the center of concentric, creative circles.

Forest Farm: The Good Life Center (326-8211), on the loop road, facing Orr's Cove (opposite side of the road), Harborside, on Cape Rosier. Open June through September, Thursday through Tuesday 1–5; closed Tuesday and Wednesday off-season. The stone home built in 1953 by Helen and Scott Nearing, coauthors of *Living the Good Life* and seven other books based on their simple, purposeful lifestyle, is now maintained by a nonprofit trust. Through a stewardship program a couple maintains the property year-round. Inquire about weekly programs in summer and periodic workshops. The grounds include an intensively cultivated organic garden, a greenhouse, and a yurt.

Eggemoggin Reach Bridge

🦀 **MERI Resource Center** (359-8078; www.meriresearch.org), Route 175, Brooklin. Open daily May through August. The nonprofit Marine Environmental Research Institute, based in a storefront in the middle of Brooklin Village, offers frequent family-geared cruises as well as weeklong programs for youngsters to tune them in to shore and sea life. The center has a small aquarium and a "sea library."

Brooksville Historical Society Museum (362-8022), 150 Coastal Road, Brooksville. Open July and August, Wednesday and Sunday 1–4. Artifacts describe life in Brooksville from the 18th to the early 20th centuries.

Reverend Daniel Merrill House (359-4447), Route 172, Sedgwick. Open July and August, Sunday 2–4. This complex includes the town's original parsonage, a restored schoolhouse, and an 1820s cattle pound. It is part of the Sedgwick Historic District and includes an 18th-century town house. Check out the large old **Rural Cemetery.**

Also see *Selective Shopping—Art Galleries.*

SCENIC DRIVES

To come as far as Blue Hill Village and go no farther would be like walking up to a door and not opening it. The beauty of the peninsula lies beyond—via roads that wander west to **Brooksville** (see map on page 328) by taking Route 15 south to Route 176/175 north to Route 176 (yes, that's right) and across the **Bagaduce River** and south on Route 176 (never mind). Turn off at the sign for **Cape Rosier** to see **Holbrook Island Sanctuary** (see *Green Space—Conservation Area*) and **Forest Farm** (see above). Return to Route 176 and continue into the village of South Brooksville (be sure not to miss **Buck's Harbor**). Route 176 rejoins Route 175 and then Route 15; turn south and follow Route 15 south over **Caterpillar Hill** (be sure to pull out for the view) and then head down to **Eggemoggin Reach.** The alternate scenic route is 175 south to **Brooklin** and back along the Reach through Sedgwick. These two routes meet at the **Little Deer Isle Bridge.** Be sure to cross the bridge (see "Deer Isle, Stonington, and Isle au Haut").

TO DO

SAILING
Buck's Harbor Marine (326-8839), South Brooksville, is the place from which daysail charters leave.

Summertime (359-2067; 1-800-562-8290 outside the state), a 53-foot pinky schooner, offers daysails and longer cruises from several ports around Penobscot Bay.

SEA KAYAKING
See *To Do—Sea Kayking and Canoeing* in "Deer Isle, Stonington, and Isle au Haut."

SPECIAL LEARNING PROGRAMS
WoodenBoat School (359-4651; www.woodenboat.com), off Naskeag Point Road, south of the village of Brooklin. A spinoff from *WoodenBoat* magazine more than 14 years ago, this seafaring institute of national fame offers summer courses that range from building your own sailboat, canoe, or kayak to navigation and drawing and painting. Facilities are a former estate on Eggemoggin Reach, and visitors are encouraged. For a course catalog, write: WoodenBoat School, P.O. Box 78, Brooklin 04616. Accommodations available.

Also see "Deer Isle, Stonington, and Isle au Haut."

GREEN SPACE

Blue Hill. Our friends at the Blue Hill Bookstore tell us that this was not the setting for the children's classic *Blueberries for Sal,* by Robert McCloskey—a longtime summer resident of the area. But we choose to disbelieve them. It looks just like the hill in the book and has its share of in-season blueberries. The big attraction, however, is the view of the Mount Desert mountains. To find the mile-long trail to the top, drive north from Blue Hill Village on Route 172 and take a left across from the Blue Hill Fairgrounds; after 0.8 mile, a sign on your right marks the start of the path.

Blue Hill Town Park. Follow Water Street to this pleasant park with picnic tables and great rocks for kids to clamber.

CONSERVATION AREA
Holbrook Island Sanctuary (326-4012), Route 176 in West Brooksville (on Cape Rosier), is a state wildlife sanctuary of 1,350 acres, including 2⅓ miles of shore and 115-acre Holbrook Island. No camping is permitted, but a lovely picnic area adjoins a pebble beach. A network of

old roads, paths, and animal trails leads along the shore and through marshes and forest. It's the creation as well as the gift of Anita Harris, who died in 1985 at age 92, the sole resident of Holbrook Island. Her will stipulated that her mansion and all the other buildings on the island be demolished. She was also responsible for destroying all homes within the sanctuary. Wildlife is plentiful and birding is exceptional, especially during spring and fall migrations. Great blue herons nest around the pond and the estuary. Bald eagles and peregrine falcons and an eagle's nest may also be seen. Inquire about guided nature walks on Tuesday and Thursday in July and August.

LODGING

RUSTIC RESORTS

Oakland House Seaside Resort (359-8521; 1-800-359-RELAX; www. oaklandhouse.com), 435 Herrick Road, Brooksville 04617. Most cottages open May through October; Lone Pine and Boathouse Cottages are open year-round. The picturesque old mansard-roofed hotel opened by Jim Littlefield's forebears in 1889 now houses only the dining rooms and serves as a centerpiece for this extensive property, with a half mile of frontage on Eggemoggin Reach, and lake as well as saltwater beaches. Sixteen cottages (each different, most with living rooms and fireplaces) are scattered throughout the woods and along the shore, each accommodating two to nine people. Some accept smokers. There are no TVs (with the exception of Lone Pine), and firewood is free. Families feel particularly welcome. Facilities include a dock, rowboats, badminton, croquet, a recreation hall full of games, and hiking trails. Breakfast and dinner are served in the old-fashioned dining rooms, one reserved for families, the other adults-only. After a century of "plain Maine cooking," the menu is now on a par with the best old Acadia hotels (see *Dining Out*); wine and beer are served. Thursday is lobster picnic night. Cottages rent by the week: $455–1,010 MAP adults in-season (children's rates slide) and $415–995 per week (housekeeping) in shoulder seasons. This is a great spot for a wedding or family reunion. (Also see **Shore Oaks Seaside Inn** under *Inns and Bed & Breakfasts*.

Hiram Blake Camp (326-4951), Cape Rosier, Harborside 04642. Open mid-May through mid-October. Well off the beaten track, operated by the same family since 1916, this is the kind of place you come to stay put. All cottages are within 200 feet of the shore, with views of Penobscot Bay. There are 6 one-bedroom cottages, 5 cottages with two bedrooms, and 3 with three bedrooms; each has a living room with a wood-burning stove; some have a fireplace as well. Each has a kitchen, a shower, and a porch. Guests with housekeeping cottages cook for themselves in the shoulder months, but in July and August everyone eats in the dining room, which doubles as a library because thousands of books are ingeniously filed away by category in the ceiling. There are rowboats at the dock, a playground, and a recreation room with table tennis and board games; also trails. From $425 per week MAP for the one-room Acorn Cottage to $1,775 for a three-bedroom cottage (up to five guests). Additional guests are each $225 per week. Rates drop during "house-keeping months" to $200–600 per week.

Maine Coast Experience & Resort (359-5057; 1-888-559-5057; www.mainecoastexperience.com), HC 64, Box 380, Brooklin 04616. Not a resort in the traditional sense, the idea is to get guests off having active "adventures": excursions aboard a lobster boat, sea kayaking, biking, and whale-watching. Rooms are fairly basic, but the central lodge (dining, bar, and common space) is attractive, overlooking Eggemoggin Reach. $110–190 per day includes breakfasts with "daily adventures" $30–50 each; weekly packages with meals and activities are $1,850 per couple; $1,250 single; $500 per youth under 17.

INNS AND BED & BREAKFASTS
In Blue Hill 04614

   Blue Hill Inn (374-2844; 1-800-826-7415; www.bluehill.com), near the junction of Main Street and Route 177. Open mid-May through Thanksgiving. A classic 1830s inn on a quiet, elm-lined street in the village. Don and Mary Hartley offer 11 guest rooms, some with sitting rooms and/or working fireplaces. All are carefully furnished with antiques and equipped with private baths. A pine-floored suite with kitchen, sitting areas, deck, fireplace, and handicapped-access bath is next door in the Cape House. Common rooms are ample and tasteful. In good weather guests gather for cocktails in the garden. A full breakfast, afternoon tea and hors d'oeuvres are included in $118–245 double.

First Light Bed & Breakfast (374-5879; www.acadia.net/firstlight), 176 Curtis Cove Road, East Blue Hill 04629. A coveside home with a tower built to look like a lighthouse. Its dining room and living room have large windows overlooking the harbor and, on clear days, beyond to Mount Desert Island. Two bedrooms on the second floor share a bath, but the Lighthouse Suite is the real star: a round bedroom, with bird's-eye maple dressers built into the curve of the wall and rockers with views, plus a dressing room overlooking the cove (full bath). Narrow stairs lead to the ersatz lighthouse level with its 360-degree views. $95–125.

Blue Hill Farm (374-5126), Box 437. Open year-round. A former barn has been reworked as an open-beamed combination breakfast room/dining and living room with plenty of light and space to read quietly alone or mingle with other guests. Upstairs are seven small guest rooms, each with a private bath. The attached farmhouse offers seven more guest rooms with shared baths (including one appealing single) and more common rooms, one with a woodstove. $80–95 double, $70–80 single (less off-season), includes a continental breakfast. A set dinner menu, frequently with live music, is also offered some nights.

Elsewhere on the Blue Hill peninsula

Eggemoggin Reach Bed & Breakfast (359-5073; 1-888-625-8866; www.eggreachbb.com), RR 1, Box 33A, Herrick Road, Brooksville 04673. Open Memorial through Columbus Day. Susie and Mike Canon built themselves a retirement home with a view across Penobscot Bay to the Camden Hills, then decided to share their retreat. They built a cottage in the pines, divided into two attractive "studio" units, each with stove, cathedral ceiling, sitting area, and private screened porch over-looking Deadman's Cove. Then they added Bay Lodge with six more pine-walled units with efficiency kitchens, and porches or decks. In-quire about Tuckaway Cottage, also waterfront. A dock with rowboat and canoe await. Children must be 16. $135–145 per couple includes continental breakfast the first day. Three-night minimum stay.

Shore Oaks Seaside Inn (359-8521; 1-800-359-RELAX; www.oakland house.com), on the Oakland House property (see *Rustic Resorts*) and one of the best-kept secrets of the region. Built at the turn of the 20th century as a private "cottage," it eventually became absorbed into the resort complex—where it dozed until Sally, a trained designer, married Jim (Littlefield) and focused her considerable energy on this 10-bed-room stone-and-shingle building, renovating it totally but preserving the old simple feel of summer life centered on the water (the porch with rocking chairs and a gazebo right on the water command sweeping views of the entrance to Eggemoggin Reach) and the big stone hearth. Guests have full use of all Oakland House facilities and can breakfast as well as dine in the hotel dining room, but this is a place apart. Coffee and tea are available from early morning in the dining room (where breakfast is also frequently served), and the living room and library are delightful. Rooms have bedtime reading lights and the deep old tubs. Our favorites are Number 7, a corner room overlooking the water, with no less than six windows and a working fireplace, mission oak furniture, and a sense of space and comfort; and Number 6, with its white wicker and working fireplace. $99–239 per room MAP in-season; B&B rates available; less in shoulder seasons. The entire house can be rented for family reunions and weddings.

Seaside Bed and Breakfast (359-2792; seaside@altavista.net), RR 1, Box 6800, Sedgwick 04676. Open May through September. Wally and Darcy Campbell built their classic Cape on Eggemoggin Reach in 1982 when the Maine couple returned from Saudi Arabia. With their daughter now launched on her own career, the Campbells offer three rooms, two upstairs (each with a bath), and a basement-level garden apartment with a canopy double bed, a full kitchen, and living and dining areas. All rooms have water views, and the common rooms are attractive. Well sited for kayakers (within walking distance of the boat landing on the Benjamin River). Worth noting: Darcy and Wally spend the winters on the road—in a vintage-1958 Greyhound bus that they have fitted out as a vehicle for

Shore Oaks

touring "blue highways" in North America and Mexico. From $85 double to $170 for five in the two upstairs rooms.

Breezemere Farm Inn (326-8628; 1-888-223-FARM), 71 Breezemere Road, Brooksville 04617. Open year-round. An 1850s farmhouse overlooking Orcutt's Harbor that's been taking in guests since 1917 and was revitalized by innkeepers Laura Johns and Carolyn Heller. There are seven guest rooms in the house itself (five share baths) and six cottages (sleeping two to six). Resident animals include sheep, goats, and chickens. Buffet breakfast included in the rates: $55–95 per night, $475 per week for "studio cottages," $575–800 for housekeeping cottages.

☀ **The Brooklin Inn** (359-2777; www.brooklininn.com), P.O. Box 175, Route 175, Brooklin 04616. A casual, friendly old inn on the edge of the village. Chip (a former tugboat captain) and Gail Angell are the new innkeepers. The five upstairs bedrooms share two baths. $65–95 per couple.

The Maples (359-8309), Route 175, Brooklin 04616. Open year-round. We like the hospitable feel of this old-fashioned guest house with its four resident cats. Dorothy Jordan offers three upstairs rooms sharing two baths. $55 per room includes coffee but no breakfast. (The Brooklin Inn is across the road.)

Brass Fox Bed and Breakfast (326-0575), Southern Bay Road, Route 175, Penobscot 04476. This 1803 farmhouse is filled with antiques. Common space includes two dining rooms (with original tin ceilings), a small library (with phone jack for Internet connection), and parlor. All of the second-floor guest rooms (each with bath) share views off across fields and woods. A full breakfast includes fresh-squeezed orange juice, an entrée, and homemade pastries; the Bagaduce Lunch (see *Eating Out*) is handy. Gerry and Dawn Freeman are helpful hosts. $75–105 ($10 less for 2 nights or more).

WHERE TO EAT

DINING OUT

Arborvine (374-2119), Main Street, Blue Hill. Open 5–8 for dinner. Reservations a must. Chef-owner John Hikade is well known, the founder of the town's long-lived (former) Firepond restaurant and a local caterer for 20 years. Just south of the village on Route 172, Arborvine is housed in a 200-year-old building and consists of several simple but elegant, open-beamed dining rooms with fireplaces. The mouthwatering entrées might include crispy roast duckling with amaretto glaze, or medallions of lamb with wild mushrooms and fresh basil. $16–21.

Toscana (374-3899), Main Street, middle of Blue Hill Village. The former Firepond, a pleasant setting by a stream, now features a Tuscan menu: antipasti, pastas, and *secundi* such as venison carpaccio. It's all the work of Jonathan Chase, former owner of Jonathan's (see below), which he still helps manage. Entrées $19–25.

Jonathan's (374-5226), Main Street, Blue Hill. Open daily year-round for lunch and dinner. Now owned by the same New York restaurateur who owns Toscana, still a dependably good bet for seafood prepared imaginatively and well. Entrées $16.95–18.95.

Surry Inn (667-5091), Route 172, Contention Cove, Surry. Open nightly for dinner. This pleasant dining room overlooking a cove is well known locally for reasonably priced fine dining. The menu changes often but always includes interesting soups—maybe Hungarian mushroom or lentil vegetable—and a wide entrée selection that might include veal tarragon, medallions of pork sautéed with herbs and red wine vinegar, spicy garlic frogs' legs, and scallops with pesto and cream. Entrées $14–17.

The Lookout (359-2188), Flye Point (2 miles off Route 175), North Brooklin. Memorial Day through Columbus Day. Dinner 5:30–8:30; Sunday brunch. Reserve a table on the porch for the view of Herrick's Bay. This 1890s summer hotel is still in the family that built the house. The menu varies with what's available, but specialties include crabcakes, baked crab and artichokes, and seared venison with port and boysenberries. Entrées $19–21. We actually made a meal of appetizers: crabcakes ($9) and grilled portobello mushrooms with wild greens ($8). Full bar and wine list.

Oakland House (359-8521), off Herrick Road, Brooksville. Open mid-June through September for dinner 6–8 and a Sunday brunch buffet. Reservations requested. This old-fashioned dining room is a hidden gem because, while it has been here more than a century, its fare has changed radically and wine and beer have been added within the past few years. Chef Woody Clark uses local, seasonal ingredients featuring organic herbs and edible flowers to create a five-course menu that changes daily. Outside, guests can order à la carte from a choice of four entrées—perhaps prime rib ($17.95), charbroiled swordfish with Mediterranean salsa ($15.95), or shiitake and button mushroom strudel. Entrées include soup or salad as well as starch and vegetable. In spring and fall dinner is served in the smaller dining room at Shore Oaks Seaside Inn (see *Lodging*).

The Brooklin Inn (359-2777), Route 175, Brooklin Village. Under new ownership but offering the same casual old intimate dining rooms. Specializing in local ingredients and a varied menu, including plenty of seafood: from $13 for baked haddock to $28 for lobster sautéed with scallops and mussels. The pub is small but lively.

Also see *Dining Out* in "Deer Isle, Stonington, and Isle au Haut."

LUNCHING OUT

Jean-Paul's Bistro (374-5852), Main Street, Blue Hill Village. Open except Sundays in July and August, 11–3 for lunch and then for tea. Fitting neither into "dining out" or simply "eating out," this bistro is a category in its own right. The view of Blue Hill Bay is unbeatable, and the food is summer light, with a French accent as thick and authentic as Jean-Paul's. "Les Sandwiches" include *croque monsieur*, a walnut tarragon chicken salad with watercress on whole-grain bread, and "quiche du jour." A prix fixe lunch—soup, Caesar salad, and chicken with tea or lemonade—is $13.95. Of course there are also profiteroles. The preferred seats are outside under umbrellas or, better yet, in one of the Adirondack chairs on the lawn overlooking the water. Wine is served.

EATING OUT

Café-Out-Back at the Buck's Harbor Market (326-8683), center of Brooksville Village, Route 176. The market has a lunch counter, and the fully licensed café is a very attractive space, open year-round for breakfast, lunch, and dinner; hours vary. Check. All baking is done here, and the stuffed croissants and breads are exceptional (great picnic fare). The menu ranges from pizzas to full seafood dinners.

Captain Isaac Merrill Inn & Café (374-2555), Blue Hill Center. Daytime chowders, baguette sandwiches, soda fountain, moderately priced evening meals like roast Maine turkey and local haddock broiled in herb lemon butter; also Portuguese seafood stew.

Bagaduce Lunch, Route 176, North Brooksville (at the Reversing Falls). Seasonal. A great spot for seafood baskets and burgers, with picnic tables by the river.

Morning Moon Café (359-2373), Route 175, Brooklin. Open daily 7 AM–2 PM, except Monday; also for dinner Thursday through Sunday 5–8. A tiny oasis in the middle of Brooklin Village. Fresh-dough pizza, full menu includes a really good BLT and fine fish-and-chips.

PICNIC FIXINGS

Don't waste a nice day by eating inside! For picnic sites, see *Green Space*.

Moveable Feasts (374-2119), Main Street, Blue Hill. The daytime deli side of Arborvine (see *Dining Out*). Good for a roasted red pepper and herb cheese sandwich with veggies or curried chicken salad on fresh-baked whole-wheat breads. There are benches in the garden.

Merrill & Hinckley (374-2821), Union Street, middle of Blue Hill. A great old-fashioned general store and a source of picnic fixings.

Also see *Eating Out* in "Deer Isle, Stonington, and Isle au Haut."

ENTERTAINMENT

MUSIC

✒ **Kneisel Hall Chamber Music School and Festival** (374-2811; www. kneisel.org), Pleasant Street, Route 15, Blue Hill. One of the oldest chamber music festivals in the country (dating back to 1924). Faculty and students present string and ensemble music in a series of Sunday-afternoon and Friday-evening concerts, June through August.

WERU (469-6600), a nonprofit community radio station in East Orland (89.9 FM) known for folk and Celtic music, jazz, and reggae.

Bagaduce Chorale (326-8532), Blue Hill. A community chorus staging several concerts yearly, ranging from Bach to show tunes.

Surry Opera Company (667-2629), Morgan Bay Road, Surry. Zen master Walter Nowick founded this company in 1984 and mounts fairly spectacular productions most (but not all) summers.

Flash in the Pan Steel Band, Brooksville. A community steel-drum band that performs Monday nights in summer months in South Brooksville.

Also see **Blue Hill Farm** under *Dining Out*.

SELECTIVE SHOPPING

ART GALLERIES

In Blue Hill

Leighton Gallery (374-5001), Parker Point Road. Open June through mid-October. One of Maine's most prominent contemporary art galleries, with exhibits in the three-floor gallery changing every few weeks. There are some striking staples, however, including carvings by local patriarch Eliot Sweet, Judith Leighton's own oils, and the wonderful variety of sculpted shapes in the garden out back.

Jud Hartman Gallery and Sculpture Studio (374-9917), Main Street. Open mid-June through mid-September daily. Now in newly expanded quarters with a water view, Hartman exhibits his realistic bronze sculptures of northeastern Native Americans.

Randy Eckard (374-2510), 4 Pleasant Street. Open late June through September, Tuesday through Saturday. Limited-edition prints of the artist's precise, luminous landscapes.

Liros Gallery (374-5370), Parker Point Road, specializes in fine paintings, old prints, and Russian icons.

S. L. Kinney Gallery at Standing Bear Center for Shamanic Studies (667-4472), Route 176, Surrey. Several years ago Scarlet Kinney moved the gallery, which shows her own work (paintings feature animals and landscapes), to a wooded setting and expanded its focus to include Shamanic workshops.

The Gallery at Caterpillar Hill (359-6577). Positioned right next to the scenic pullout (Route 15/17), it offers changing works featuring local landscapes.

Also see *Selective Shopping—Art Galleries and Artisans* in "Deer Isle, Stonington, and Isle au Haut."

ARTISANS

Rowantrees Pottery (374-5535), Union Street, Blue Hill. Open year-round, daily in summer (8:30–5), Sunday (from noon) and weekdays in winter (7–3:30). Find your way back behind the friendly white house into the large studio. It was a conversation with Mahatma Gandhi in India that got Adelaide Pearson going on the idea of creating pottery in Blue Hill by using glazes gathered from the town's abandoned copper mines, quarries, and bogs. Watch tableware being hand-thrown and browse through the upstairs showroom filled with plates, cups, vases, and jam pots. Note the prints and original work by a longtime Blue Hill summer resident, artist Frank Hamabe.

Rackliffe Pottery (374-2297), Route 172, Blue Hill. Open Monday through Saturday 9–5; also Sunday afternoon. Phyllis and Phil Rackliffe worked at Rowantrees for 22 years before establishing their own business. They also use local glazes, and their emphasis is on individual small pieces rather than on sets. Visitors are welcome to watch.

Handworks Gallery (374-5613), Main Street, Blue Hill. Open Memorial Day through late December, Monday through Saturday 10–5. A middle-of-town space filled with unusual handwoven clothing, jewelry, furniture, rugs, and blown glass.

North Country Textiles, Route 175, South Penobscot (326-4131); and Main Street, Blue Hill (374-2715). Open May through December in Blue Hill, summer months on Route 175. A partnership of three designer/weavers: Sheila Denny-Brown, Carole Ann Larson, and Ron King. The shop displays jackets and tops, mohair throws, guest towels, and coasters, all in bright colors and irresistible textures.

Scott Goldberg Pottery, Route 176, Brooksville. Open daily May through October. Wheel-thrown pots, bowls, cups, plates, and vases plus other functional pieces with rich, subdued glazes.

Peninsula Weavers (374-2760), Route 172, Blue Hill. Open Monday through Saturday. Weavers share a studio in the Bagaduce Library complex, using Swedish looms and techniques. Woven rugs, scarves, weaving supplies. Inquire about weaving classes.

Jutta Graf (348-7751) of Brooksville weaves stunning one-of-a-kind contemporary rugs usually on view in local galleries; also at her studio by appointment.

BOOKSTORES

Blue Hill Books (374-5632), 2 Pleasant Street (two doors up from the post office), Blue Hill. A long-established, full-service, family-run bookstore.

North Light Books (374-5422), Main Street, Blue Hill. The village's other full-service, family-run bookstore.

Wayward Books (359-2397), Route 15, Sargentville. Open mid-May through December weekdays 10–5, Saturday noon–5. A good used-book store.

SPECIAL SHOPS

Blue Hill Wine Shop (374-2161), Main Street, Blue Hill. Open Monday through Saturday 10–5:30. A long-established shop with a new name, dedicated to the perfect cup of tea or coffee, a well-chosen wine, and the right blend of tobacco.

Blue Hill Yarn Shop (374-5631), Route 172 north of Blue Hill Village. Open Monday through Saturday 10–4. A mecca for knitters in search of a variety of wools and needles. Lessons and original hand knits.

H.O.M.E. Co-op (469-7961), Route 1, Orland. Open daily in-season 9–5. A remarkable complex that includes a crafts village (visitors can watch pottery making, weaving, leatherwork, woodworking); a museum of old handicrafts and farm implements; a large crafts shop featuring handmade coverlets, toys, and clothing; a market stand with fresh vegetables, herbs, and other garden produce. There is a story behind this nonprofit enterprise, which has filled an amazing variety of local needs.

Blue Poppy Garden (359-2739), Route 175, Sedgwick. A crisp white barn has been transformed into an unusual garden shop/gallery featuring gardening books and furniture. High tea is served daily in-season, 2:30–5:30 in the rear garden.

SPECIAL EVENTS

Last weekend in July: **Blue Hill Days**—arts and crafts fair, parade, farmer's market, antique-car rally, shore dinner, boat races.

August: **St. Francis Annual Summer Fair, Downeast Antiques Fair,** Blue Hill.

Labor Day weekend: **Blue Hill Fair,** at the fairgrounds—harness racing, a midway, livestock competitions; one of the most colorful old-style fairs in New England.

December: A weekend of Christmas celebrations.

CASTINE

Sited at the tip of a finger of the Blue Hill peninsula, Castine is one of Maine's most photogenic coastal villages, the kind writers describe as "perfectly preserved." Even the trees that arch high above Main Street's clapboard homes and shops have managed to escape the blight that has felled elms elsewhere, and Castine's post office is said to be the oldest operating post office in the country.

Situated on a peninsula at the confluence of the Penobscot and Bagaduce Rivers, the town still looms larger on nautical charts than on road maps. Yacht clubs from Portland to New York visit annually. Castine has always had a sense of its own importance. According to the historical markers that pepper its tranquil streets, it has been claimed by four different countries since its early-17th-century founding as Fort Pentagoet. It was an early trading post for the Pilgrims but fell into the hands of Baron de Saint Castine, a young French nobleman who married a Penobscot Indian princess and reigned as a combination feudal lord and Indian chief over Maine's eastern coast for many decades.

Since no two accounts agree, we won't attempt to describe the outpost's constantly shifting fortunes—even the Dutch owned it briefly. Nobody denies that in 1779 residents (mostly Tories who fled here from Boston and Portland) welcomed the invading British. The commonwealth of Massachusetts retaliated by mounting a fleet of 18 armed vessels and 24 transports with 1,000 troops and 400 marines aboard. This small navy disgraced itself absurdly when it sailed into town in 1779. The British Fort George was barely in the making, fortified by 750 soldiers with the backup of two sloops, but the American privateers refused to attack and hung around in the bay long enough for several British men-of-war to come along and destroy them. The surviving pa-

KIM GRANT

Castine Harbor

triots had to walk back to Boston, and many of their officers, Paul Revere included, were court-martialed for their part in the disgrace. The
town was occupied by the British again in 1814.

Perhaps it was to spur young men on to avenge this affair that
Castine was picked (150 years later) as the home of the Maine Maritime Academy, which occupies the actual site of the British barracks
and keeps a training ship anchored at the town dock, incongruously
huge beside the graceful, white-clapboard buildings of a very different
maritime era.

In the mid–19th century, thanks to shipbuilding, Castine claimed to
be the second wealthiest town per capita in the United States. Its genteel

qualities were recognized by summer visitors, who later came by steamboat to stay in the eight hotels. Many built their own seasonal mansions.

Only two of the hotels survive. But the town dock is an unusually welcoming one, complete with picnic tables, parking, and rest rooms. It remains the heart of this walking town, where you can amble uphill past shops or down along Perkins Street to the Wilson Museum. Like many of New England's most beautiful villages, Castine's danger seems to lie in the perfect preservation of its beauty, a shell unconnected to the lives that built it. Few visitors complain, however. Castine is exquisite.

GUIDANCE

Castine Merchants Association (326-4884), P.O. Box 329, Castine 04421. Request the helpful map/guide, available by mail or around town. The obvious place to begin exploring is the Castine Historical Society on the common. Also check www.penobscotbay.com.

GETTING THERE

By air: See *Getting There* in "Bar Harbor and Ellsworth" and "Portland Area" for air service.

By car: The quickest route is the Maine Turnpike to Augusta, then Route 3 to Belfast, then Route 1 to Orland, then 15 miles down Route 175.

MEDICAL EMERGENCY

Blue Hill Memorial Hospital (374-2836), Water Street, Blue Hill, the largest facility in the area, has a 24-hour emergency room. **Castine Community Health Services** (326-4348), Court Street, Castine, has a doctor on call.

TO SEE

MUSEUMS

Wilson Museum (326-8545), Perkins Street. Open May 27 through September 30, Tuesday through Sunday 2–5; free. Housed in a fine waterside building donated by anthropologist J. Howard Wilson, a summer resident who amassed many of the displayed Native American artifacts. There are also changing art exhibits, collections of minerals, old tools and farm equipment, an 1805 kitchen, and a Victorian parlor. **Hearse House** and a blacksmith shop are open Wednesday and Sunday afternoons in July and August, 2–5. The complex also includes the **John Perkins House,** open only during July and August, Wednesday and Sunday 2–5 ($4 admission): a pre–Revolutionary War home, restored and furnished in period style. Guided tours and crafts.

Castine Historical Society (326-4118), Abbott School Building, Castine town common. July through Labor Day 10–4; from 1 on Sunday; closed Monday. The former high school, converted to a historical society and welcome center. Note the stunning quilted mural stitched by more than 50 townspeople and the ornate chair, said to be carved from the wood of a sunken English warship.

HISTORIC SITES

Fort George. Open May 30 through Labor Day, daylight hours. The sorry tale of its capture by the British during the American Revolution (see chapter introduction, above) and again during the War of 1812, when redcoats occupied the town for eight months, is told on panels at the fort—an earthworks complex of grassy walls (great to roll down) and a flat interior where you may find Maine Maritime Academy cadets being put through their paces.

State of Maine (326-4311). The current training vessel for Maine Maritime Academy cadets, a 498-foot former U.S. Navy hydrographic survey ship, is open to visitors weekdays in July and August; 30-minute tours are conducted by midshipmen.

TO DO

BIKING

Mountain Bike Rentals (326-9045) available at Dennett's Wharf.

BOATING

Castine Steamboat Company (326-9045; www.castinesteamboat.com), Dennett's Wharf. The steam launch *Laurie Ellen*, billed as the only wood-fired steam passenger boat in the country, is a jaunty 18-passenger launch built specifically to tour Castine's harbor. Captain Randy Flood, a Maine Maritime Academy graduate and former officer on commercial tankers, offers five cruises a day. Inquire about picnic cruises to **Holbrook Island** (also see *Green Space—Conservation Area* in "Blue Hill Area").

GOLF AND TENNIS

Castine Golf Club (326-4311), Brattle Avenue. Offers nine holes and four clay courts.

SEA KAYAKING

Guided Sea Kayak Tours (326-9045; www.castinekayak.com), Dennett's Wharf. Half- and full-day, sunset, and moonlight guided tours are offered.

SWIMMING

British Canal, Backshore Road. During the War of 1812 the British dug a canal across the narrow neck of land above town, thus turning Castine into an island. Much of the canal is still visible. **Maine Maritime Academy** (326-4311) offers, for a nominal fee, gymnasium facilities to local inn guests. This includes the pool, weight room, and squash and racquetball courts.

GREEN SPACE

Witherle Woods is an extensive wooded area webbed with paths at the western end of town. The ledges below **Dyce's Head Light,** also at the western end of town, are great for clambering. The **Castine Conser-**

vation Commission sponsors nature walks occasionally in July and August. Check local bulletin boards.

LODGING

All listings are for Castine 04421.

- **Castine Inn** (326-4365; www.castineinn.com), P.O. Box 41, Main Street. Open May through mid-December. A genuine 1890s summer hotel that's been lovingly and deftly restored, right down to the frieze beneath its roof. It offers 19 light and airy, but unfrilly guest rooms, all with private baths and many with harbor views. Guests enter a wide, welcoming hallway and find a pleasant sitting room and a pub, both with frequently lit fireplaces. A mural of Castine by the previous innkeeper covers all four walls of the dining room—a delightful room with French doors leading out to a broad veranda overlooking the inn's terraced formal gardens (a popular place for weddings) and the town sloping to the harbor beyond. Children over 8 welcome. Innkeeper-chef Tom Gutow maintains the inn's long-established culinary fame (see *Dining Out*). $85–210 (more for two-room suites if occupied by four) includes a full breakfast; less off-season. Minimum 2-day stay in July and August.
- **The Manor Inn** (326-4861; www.manor-inn.com), P.O. Box 873, Brattle Avenue. An expansive 1890s stone-and-shingle summer mansion set in 5 acres bordering conservation land. New innkeepers Tom Ehman and Nancy Watson have renovated throughout, bringing new beds and new life to all 12 rooms. The size of guest rooms varies but so do prices, from $110 for twin-bedded "Dices Head" to $195 for spacious Pine Tree with its king canopy bed, fireplace, and sitting porch, fit for the governor and his wife (who were checking in as we stopped by). There is a spacious library/common room, and a restaurant and pub (see *Dining Out*). Rates drop in spring and fall.
- **Pentagoet Inn** (326-8616; 1-800-845-1701; www.pentagoet.com), P.O. Box 4, Main Street. Open May through October. The main inn is a very Victorian summer hotel with a turret, gables, and a wraparound porch. The rooms are unusually shaped and nicely furnished; one room in neighboring **Ten Perkins Street** (a 200-year-old home that's an annex) has a working fireplace. In all there are 16 guest rooms, each with private bath. Common space includes sitting rooms, a breakfast room, and the **Passports Pub.** New owners Jack Burke and Julie VandeGraaf had just taken over when we stopped by. $80–150 includes a full breakfast.

WHERE TO EAT

DINING OUT
- **Castine Inn** (326-4365), Main Street. Open daily in-season (May through October) for breakfast and dinner. The ambience, quality, and value of

this dining room are well known locally, filling it most nights. Crabmeat cakes in mustard sauce and chicken and leek potpie have been the house specialty for so long that current chef-owner Tom Gutow has had to continue the tradition or face mutiny. However, Gutow has established his own reputation for dishes like roasted beef carpaccio for starters ($7), entrées like warm oil-poached salmon with red cabbage and snow pea slaw and hot and sour broth ($22), and grilled beef tenderloin with spiced vegetables and a port reduction ($30). Save room for the lavender crème brûlée. The wine list is well priced and balanced.

The Manor Inn (326-4861), Brattle Avenue. Open year-round (but check). Dinner is served 8–8:30 on an enclosed porch overlooking the sweeping front lawn and gardens and, when it gets too cool, in the adjacent library. Starters might include crab bisque ($8) or escargots ($6); entrées, ginger tuna with mango relish ($16) and Boston club sirloin ($22). Entrées come with a salad as well as a starch and vegetable. Full liquor license.

EATING OUT

Dennett's Wharf (326-9045), Sea Street (off the town dock). Open daily spring through fall for lunch and dinner. An open-framed, harborside structure said to have been built as a bowling alley after the Civil War. Seafood, smoked fish, seafood pasta salads, and a wide choice of microbrews, including Dennett's Wharf's own Wharf Rat Ale.

Bah's Bake House (326-9510), Water Street. Open 7 AM–9 PM daily, until 8 PM on Sunday. A few tables and a great deli counter featuring sandwiches on baguette bread, daily-made soups, salads, and baked goods.

The Breeze (326-9034), town dock. Seasonal. When the summer sun shines, this is the best place in town to eat: fried clams, hot dogs, onion rings, and soft ice cream. The public facilities are next door and, with luck, you can dine at the picnic tables on the dock.

The Pub at the Manor Inn (326-4861). A paneled, cozy corner of this grand old mansion, open from 5 PM for burgers, chili, and more.

Also see **Compass Rose Bookstore & Café** under *Selective Shopping*.

SELECTIVE SHOPPING

Leila Day Antiques (326-8786), Main Street. An outstanding selection of early-American furniture, also paintings, quilts, and Maine-made Shard Pottery. The shop is in the historic Parson Mason House, and the approach is through a formal garden.

McGrath-Dunham Gallery (326-9175), 9 Main Street. Open May through mid-October, 10–5 except Sunday. A long-established gallery featuring sculpture and pottery as well as paintings and original prints.

✐ **Compass Rose Bookstore & Café** (326-9366; 1-800-698-9366), 3 Main Street. Under new ownership. Open late (in summer until 7 most nights, 6 on Sunday), this local institution has moved down the street and expanded, still featuring children's titles, summer reading, nautical and regional books, now also including a pleasant café serving coffee, tea, smoothies, and snacks.

Water Witch (326-4884), Main Street. Jean de Raat sells original designs made from Dutch Java batiks, English paisley prints, and Maine-made woolens. This is a totally standout store, worth the trip in itself.

SPECIAL EVENTS

June–October: **Windjammers** usually in port on Tuesdays.

Third weekend in June: **Summer Festival**—craft show, ethnic food, children's activities.

July: **Sea Kayaking Symposium** sponsored by L. L. Bean.

DEER ISLE, STONINGTON, AND ISLE AU HAUT

The narrow suspension bridge across Eggemoggin Reach connects the Blue Hill peninsula with a series of wandering land fingers linked by causeways and bridges. These are known collectively as Deer Isle and include the towns of Deer Isle and Stonington, the villages of Sunset and Sunshine, and the campus of the nationally respected Haystack Mountain School of Crafts. Many prominent artisans have come here to teach or study—and stayed. Galleries in the village of Deer Isle display outstanding work by dozens of artists and craftspeople who live, or at least summer, in town.

Stonington, a full 40 miles south of Route 1, remains a working fishing harbor, but it too now has its share of galleries. Most buildings, which are scattered on smooth rocks around the harbor, date from the 1880s to the World War I boom years, during which Deer Isle's pink granite was shipped off to face buildings from Rockefeller Center to Boston's Museum of Fine Arts. At the height of the granite boom Stonington's population was 5,000, compared to 1,200 today.

In Stonington life still eddies around Bartlett's Supermarket, Billings Diesel and Marine, and the Commercial Pier, home base for one of Maine's largest fishing/lobstering fleets. But the tourist tide is obviously rising again as it did in the 1880s (when tourists arrived by steamer). Galleries and seasonal, visitor-geared galleries and shops are multiplying along Main Street; and the Opera House, now restored, is the scene of frequent films, live performances, and readings.

Why not? Deer Isle offers the kind of coves and lupine-fringed inlets usually equated with "the real Maine," and Isle au Haut, a mountainous island 8 miles off Stonington, is accessible by mail boat. It's a glorious place to walk trails maintained by the National Park Service.

GUIDANCE

Deer Isle–Stonington Chamber of Commerce (348-6124; www.

Stonington

deerislemaine.com) maintains a booth on Route 15 at Little Deer Isle, south of the bridge. Open 10–4 mid-June through Labor Day, sporadically after that for a few weeks. Also check www.penobscotbay.com.

GETTING THERE
Follow directions under *Getting There* in "Blue Hill Area"; continue down Route 15 to Deer Isle.

MEDICAL EMERGENCY
Island Medical Center (367-2311), Airport Road, Stonington. **Ambulance:** 348-2300. (Also see *Medical Emergency* in "Blue Hill Area.")

TO SEE

🕊️&️ **Deer Isle Granite Museum** (367-6331), Main Street, Stonington. Open Memorial Day through Labor Day, Monday through Saturday 10–5, Sunday 1–5. Housed in the former pharmacy, this beautifully conceived and executed small museum features an 8-by-15-foot working model of quarrying operations on Crotch Island and the town of Stonington in 1900. Derricks move and trains carry granite to waiting ships. Photo blowups and a video also dramatize the story of the quarryman's life during the height of the boom (see chapter introduction, above).

Salome Sellers House (348-2897), Route 15A, Sunset. Open late June through late September, Wednesday and Friday 1–4. This is the home of the Deer Isle–Stonington Historical Society, an 1830 house displaying ship models, Native American artifacts, and old photos; interesting and friendly.

Lighthouses. Pick up a copy of the "Deer Isle Lighthouse Trail" at the chamber booth on Little Deer Isle or at the Island Heritage Trust office in Deer Isle Village. **Pumpkin Island Light,** near enough to the old ferry landing for a good photo (it's 3 miles from the chamber booth, down Eggemoggin Road), is now a private home. **Eagle Island Light** can be viewed from Sylvester Cove in Sunset or, better yet, from the Eagle Island mail boat (see *To Do—Boat Excursions*), from which you can also see the **Heron Neck, Brown's Head,** and **Goose Rocks Lights.** From Goose Cove Lodge in Sunset you can see and hear the now-automated **Mark Island Light** (its old bronze bell sits on the resort's lawn); the **Saddleback Ledge Light** is also visible on the horizon. (For details about reaching the **Isle au Haut Light,** see *To Do— Boat Excursions.*)

Haystack Mountain School of Crafts (348-2306; www.haystack-mtn.org), Deer Isle (south of Deer Isle Village; turn left off Route 15 at the Mobil station and follow signs 7 miles). Visitors are welcome to join campus tours offered Wednesday at 1 PM, June through August, and to shop at the school store, the campus source of art supplies and craft books. Phone to check when visitors are also welcome to view student shows and to attend lectures and concerts. Celebrating its 50th anniversary in 2001, this is one of the country's outstanding crafts schools. The building itself is a work of art: a series of small, spare buildings clinging to a steep, wooded hillside above Jericho Bay.

TO DO

BICYCLE RENTALS
Finest Kind Restaurant and **Old Quarry Charters** (see *Sea Kayaking and Canoeing*) both offer rental bikes.

BOAT EXCURSIONS
🐾🦈 **Isle-au-Haut Company** (367-5193; www.isleauhaut.com) links Stonington with the island at least twice daily except Sunday year-round (one Sunday round-trip in summer). See *Green Space* for a description of the island; note that the island's famous hiking trails cluster around Duck Harbor, a mail-boat stop only on selected seasonal runs; a ranger usually meets the morning boat to orient passengers to the seven hiking trails, the picnic area, and drinking-water sources (otherwise, a pamphlet guide serves this purpose). The boat tends to fill up in July and August, so reserve with a credit card or aim for an early boat. The ferry takes kayaks and canoes for a fee, but not to Duck Harbor. $13 adults, $6 children, $4 pets.

A **Penobscot Bay cruise** aboard the *Miss Lizzie* is also offered daily in-season by Isle-au-Haut Company (see above).

Eagle Island mail boat. Operated by the Sunset Bay Company (348-9316), the *Katherine* leaves Sylvester's Cove in Sunset from mid-June through mid-September, Monday through Saturday, at 9 AM. A half mile off Sunset, Eagle Island is roughly a mile long with rocky ledges, a sandy beach, and an abandoned lighthouse. Inquire about island rentals. Kayaks are carried.

Jericho Bay Charters (348-6114), Sunshine. Captain Dave Zinn offers 4-hour cruises for up to six people aboard the sleek deep-sea-fishing boat *Lady Michele*—a good way to explore Jericho Bay with its many islands, including little-visited Frenchboro.

Old Quarry Ocean Adventures (367-8977; www.oldquarry.com) offers charter fishing, sight-seeing cruises, also sailing charters and lessons, accommodations.

SeaBorne Ventures (479-7220; www.mainevacation-sail.com) offers daysails on a 49-foot trimaran from Eggemoggin Landing Marina, Deer Isle. Inquire about sailing lessons.

Powerboat rentals are available from **Eggemoggin Landing** (348-6115), Little Deer Isle, just south of the bridge.

SEA KAYAKING AND CANOEING

Note: The waters off Stonington, with their many islands—known as Merchant's Row—are among the most popular along the coast with kayakers, but it's imperative, especially for novices, to explore these waters with a guide.

Granite Island Guide Service (348-2668; www.graniteislandguide.com), Deer Isle. Dana Douglas, a Registered Maine Guide, a former whitewater canoe racer, and a Congregational minister who has biked around the world, and his wife, Anne, a veteran schoolteacher, offer guided kayaking and canoeing ranging from a half day to 2 days with overnight island camping. Full-day and 3-day expeditions also offered. Inquire about canoeing trips in northern Maine. If you are not an ace kayaker familiar with local currents, it's far safer and more enjoyable to take a guided tour.

Kayak rentals are available from **Finest Kind Restaurant** (348-7714) at Joyce's Crossroad (off Routes 15 and 15A); from **Eggemoggin Landing** (348-6115), Route 15, Little Deer Isle; and from **Old Quarry Charters** (367-8977), east of Stonington. Guided tours are offered, along with a kayak practice pond. Also caters to kayakers with campsites, a B&B, and a launch site.

GOLF AND TENNIS

Island Country Club (348-2379), Deer Isle, welcomes guests mid-June through Labor Day; nine holes.

✎ **Finest Kind Restaurant** (348-7714) operates an 18-hole mini-golf course.

SPECIAL LEARNING PROGRAMS

Haystack Mountain School of Crafts (348-2306), Deer Isle. Offers 2- and 3-week sessions June through Labor Day, attracting some of the country's top artisans in a variety of crafts. See directions and details under *To See.*

The Stonington Painter's Workshop (367-2368 mid-June through September; otherwise, 617-776-3102). Nationally prominent artist and art teacher Jon Imber coordinates and is one of several instructors at this July series of weeklong landscape workshops. The current fee is $500 per week plus lodging.

SWIMMING

Lily Pond, off Route 15 north of Deer Isle Village. The island's freshwater swimming hole at which mothers congregate with small children.

GREEN SPACE

Island Heritage Trust (348-2455), P.O. Box 42, Deer Isle 04627. Write ahead or stop by the trust's office in Deer Isle Village for detailed maps to walking trails, which include Settlement Quarry and several offshore islands.

Ames Pond, east of town on Indian Point Road, is full of pink-and-white water lilies in bloom from June through early September.

Holt Mill Pond Preserve. A walk through unspoiled woodland and marsh. The entrance is on Stonington Cross Road (Airport Road)—look for a sign several hundred feet beyond the medical center. Park on the shoulder and walk the dirt road to the beginning of the trail, then follow the yellow signs.

Isle au Haut (pronounced *eye-la-ho*) is 6 miles long and 3 miles wide; all of it is private except for the 2,800 acres of national park that are wooded and webbed with hiking trails. More than half the island is preserved as part of Acadia National Park (see "Acadia Area"). Camping is forbidden everywhere except in the five Adirondack-style shelters at Duck Harbor (each accommodating six people), which are available by reservation only. For a reservation form, phone 288-3338 or write to Acadia National Park, P.O. Box 177, Bar Harbor 04609; the form must be sent on or as soon after April 1 as possible. Camping is permitted mid-May through mid-October, but in the shoulder season you have to walk 5 miles from the town landing to Duck Harbor. In summer months the mail boat arrives at Duck Harbor at 11 AM, allowing plenty of time to hike the island's dramatic Western Head and Cliff Trails before returning on the 5:30 boat. Longer trips, such as that to the summit of Mount Champlain near the northern end of the island, are also possible. Trails are pine carpeted and shaded, with water views. For more about day trips to the island, see *Boat Excursions.*

Crockett Cove Woods Preserve (a Maine Nature Conservancy property) comprises 100 acres along the water, with a nature trail. Take Route 15 to Deer Isle, then Sunset Road; 2.5 miles beyond the post office, bear right onto Whitman Road; a right turn at the end of the road brings you to the entrance, marked by a small sign and registration box. From Stonington, take Sunset Road through the village of Burnt Cove and turn left onto Whitman Road.

Settlement Quarry, Stonington. A quarter-mile walk from the parking area follows an old road to the top of this former working quarry for a view off across Webb Cove and west to the Camden Hills. Side trails mender off through woods. The parking area is on Oceanville Road, 0.9 mile off Route 15.

Barred Island Preserve is a 2-acre island just off Stinson Point, accessible by a wide sandbar; request permission for access from Goose Cove Lodge (see *Lodging—Rustic Resort*).

LODGING

RUSTIC RESORT

&⚭ **Goose Cove Lodge** (348-2508; 1-800-728-2508; www.goosecovelodge. com), Sunset 04683. Open mid-May through mid-October. Sited on a secluded cove, this many-windowed lodge with its fine library and dining, attractive common space and cabins, and waterside/island trails is a real standout. Joanne and Dom Paris have retained the rustic feel but brightened the lodge, suites, and cottages (sleeping four to eight) with well-chosen art, quilts, hooked rugs, and attractive fabrics. Not far from Stonington, Goose Cove is set in a 21-acre preserve with trails along the shore and low-tide passage to Barred Island, a Nature Conservancy property well known to birders. In-season, children dine early and enjoy an evening program in Toad Hall. Food is a point of pride (see *Dining Out*). Widely scattered, most cottages have water views. Two suites are attached to the lodge, and there are nine annex rooms with shared sundecks and four units in nearby "duplex cabins"; the remaining nine cabins are so secluded that you will need a flashlight to walk there from the main lodge after dinner. From late June through August a week's reservation is requested, but shorter stays are frequently available due to cancellations. $70–150 per person B&B in high season; $120–$207 per couple B&B, low season. For MAP add $40 per night; children's rates slide from $20 (under 1 year) to 60 percent of the adult rate in high season, $30–45 in low.

INNS

In Stonington 04681

The Inn on the Harbor (367-2420; 1-800-942-2420; innontheharbor.com), P.O. Box 69. Open year-round. Each of the 14 comfortable rooms (private baths, phones, cable TV), is named for a different windjammer (the passenger schooners usually visit Stonington in the course of a summer week). While the inn is smack on Main Street, rooms face the ample deck and working harbor, one of Maine's most photographed views. Request this view, if possible, from a second-floor room like the Heritage (with a working hearth made of local granite) or the American Eagle (with a full kitchen and private deck). The Stephen Taber is a freestanding room retaining its tin walls and ceiling (it used to be a barber shop), and the Shipps House is a two-bedroom suite in the proprietor's own vintage-1850 house. Innkeeper Christina Shipps also now owns the town's waterside restaurant, the Café Atlantic (see *Dining Out*). Rates are $100–125 with continental breakfast.

*   **Pres du Port** (367-5007), Box 319, West Main and Highland Avenue. Open June through October—a find. A cheery, comfortable B&B with three imaginatively furnished guest rooms. One in back has a cathedral ceiling and loft, kitchenette, deck access, and private bath; the other two share two baths (each room also has its own sink) and have screened and glassed-in porches with harbor views, plus there's an outdoor hot tub overlooking the water. Charlotte Casgrain is a warm, knowledgeable hostess who enjoys speaking French. $80–85 double with a generous buffet breakfast, perhaps featuring crustless crabmeat and Parmesan quiche. Guests breakfast on the sunporch, watching birds and boats. $80–85 per couple; less for a single; price includes tax.

In Deer Isle 04627-0595

*   **The Inn at Ferry Landing** (348-7760; www.ferrylanding.com), Old Ferry Road, RR 1, Box 163. Overlooking Eggemoggin Reach is this 1840s seaside farmhouse with magnificent water views, spacious rooms, patchwork quilts, and a great common room with huge windows and two grand pianos that innkeeper-musician Gerald Wheeler plays and uses for summer recitals and spontaneous music sessions. The six guest rooms include a huge master suite with a woodstove and skylights; $95–100 for double rooms, $150 for the suite; less off-season. The Mooring, a two-story, two-bedroom, fully equipped housekeeping cottage, perfect for families, is $1,100 per week. Room rates include a full breakfast; minimum of 2 nights in high season.

*   **Pilgrim's Inn** (348-6615; www.pilgriminn.com). Open mid-May through mid-October. Squire Ignatius Haskell built this house in 1793 for his wife, who came from Newburyport, Massachusetts, and demanded an elegant home. Of the 15 guest rooms, 12 have private baths, and 3 on the top floor share one. All rooms have water views, and many have fireplaces. There are four common rooms, and a dining room is in the old barn, known for its fine fare (see *Dining Out*). Eighteenth-century colors predominate, and the inn is furnished throughout with carefully chosen antiques and local art; $165–190 per couple, plus 15 percent service charge includes breakfast, dinner, and evening hors d'oeuvres. The 2 one-bedroom units in the cottage next door are $150 EP. Weekly rates.

*   **The Haskell House** (348-2496), P.O. Box 595, Route 15. Open year-round. Margaret Haskell Logue is a pleasant host who genuinely welcomes guests to the gracious house a seafaring forebear built in 1899. Two attractive guest rooms, one up and one downstairs, share a bath; $60–65 includes a full breakfast.

On Isle au Haut

The Keeper's House (367-2261), P.O. Box 26. Open mid-May through October. This turn-of-the-century lighthouse keeper's house sits back in firs behind its small lighthouse on a point surrounded on three sides by water. Guests arrive on the mail boat from Stonington just in time for a glass of sparkling cider before dinner (BYOB for anything stronger). Dinner is by candlelight, and guests tend to sit together, four to a table, and after dinner wander down to the smooth rocks to gaze at the pinpoints of light from other lighthouses and communities in Penobscot Bay. There are four guest rooms in the main house and a self-contained room in the tiny Oil House. It's a hike to the island's most scenic trails in Duck Harbor on the southeastern end of the island. $280–319 per room includes all meals and use of bikes; add round-trip for the ferry plus $4 parking.

MOTEL

🐾♪ **Eggemoggin Landing** (348-6115), Little Deer Isle 04650. Open mid-May through mid-October. A nicely sited motel just beyond the Deer Isle suspension bridge, overlooking Eggemoggin Reach. The 20 rooms are clean; the **Sisters Restaurant** next door (same owners) serves breakfast, lunch, and dinner; and moorings and a marina are part of the complex. This is a great place for children, with plenty of room to run and a play area. $59–75 per unit. Pets accepted in the off-season with permission.

COTTAGE RENTALS

Reasonably priced rentals are available on both Deer Isle and Isle au Haut. Check with **Island Vacation Rentals** (367-5095) in Stonington.

CAMPGROUND

Sunshine Campground (348-6681), RR 1, Box 521D, Deer Isle 04627. Open Memorial Day weekend through mid-October. Long established and the only campground in the area; wooded RV and tent sites.

WHERE TO EAT

DINING OUT

Pilgrim's Inn (348-6615), Main Street, Deer Isle Village. Open mid-May through late October. Dinner is by reservation only. The five-course set meal includes soup, salad, and an entrée that varies with the night, such as herbed seafood stew, pan-roasted chicken from Deer Isle, or a polenta with portobello and Shiitake mushrooms; breads and desserts are baked daily. The dining room is a converted goat barn; tables are covered with checked cloths and lighted by candles. Wine is served. Prix fixe $32.50.

Goose Cove Lodge (348-2508; 1-800-728-1963), Route 15A, Sunset. Open May through mid-October for lunch at the **Outdoor Café** on the deck (weather permitting), dinner, and Sunday brunch. Water views and fine food are the draw here. Outside guests should reserve for dinner and brunch. The à la carte menu offers a choice of a half-dozen entrées: seared tofu with broccoli rabe, roasted Shiitakes, baby corn, and vegan pesto ($18) or lobster in a saffron-ginger cream sauce ($28).

The Café Atlantic (367-2420), Main Street, Stonington. Open seasonally for lunch and dinner. An offshoot of the Inn on the Harbor, this middle-of-town restaurant features a big harborside deck as well as an attractive dining room serving staples like baked haddock with native crab stuffing ($14.95) and grilled Black Angus steak ($15.95). Lobster several ways ($18.95–21.95) is a specialty.

Eaton's Lobster Pool Restaurant (348-2383), Deer Isle. Seasonal. Monday through Saturday 5–9, Sunday noon–9. This is a barn of a place with a great view. For the best value, be sure to order lobster à la carte and by the pound instead of the higher-priced "lobster dinner." The restaurant is still in the family that settled the spot, and it is the area's premier lobster pound. BYOB. We've received both rave reviews and complaints from readers.

EATING OUT

Lily's Café (397-5936), Route 15, Stonington. Open in summer 8–8, in winter Tuesday through Thursday 10–7, Friday until 8, Saturday 5–8. A Route 15 house with a series of dining rooms upstairs and down. The table we lunched on was a sheet of glass over a collection of shells. The dinner specials vary widely, so call after 2 PM to check: from penne with shiitake mushrooms to roast beef ($4.95–9.95). BYOB.

✍ **Sisters Restaurant** (348-6115), Little Deer Isle. Open May 15 through October 15 for breakfast, lunch, and dinner. Sisters Robin Rosenquist and Patty Show now operate this restaurant just on the Little Deer Isle side of Eggemoggin Reach. Lunch inside or take out to the picnic benches by the water, but dinner is an inside affair (unless you want your steamed lobster by the water). The menu is interesting, ranging from chicken sauté with penne pasta ($9.95) to salmon on puff pastry with caramelized onions and Maine blueberries ($14.95). Sail-in guests welcome; the 15-acre complex includes room for kids to run and the Eggemoggin Landing Marina. Full liquor license.

Harbor Café, Stonington. Open year-round, Monday through Saturday 5 AM–8 PM, Sunday 7–2. Spanking clean and friendly; dependable food at counter and booths. Friday night it's a good idea to reserve for the all-you-can-eat seafood fries ($6.95–9.95).

Penobscot Bay Provisions (367-5177), West Main Street, Stonington. Open Wednesday through Saturday 8–3, Sunday 8–2. Stonington's waterfront offers plenty of places to enjoy the exceptional sandwiches you can pick up here. We highly recommend the Seal Cove chèvre with olive tapenade and roasted red and green peppers. See *Green Space* for picnic venues.

✍ **Finest Kind** (348-7714), marked from Route 15 between Stonington and Deer Isle Village. Open April through November, lunch and dinner; Sunday breakfast from 8 AM. Neat as a pin, a log cabin with counter and booths. Dinner from $6.25 for chopped steak to $12.95 for prime rib. Pizzas, fried seafood, salad bar, calzones, draft and imported beers. The mini-golf course, part of this scene, makes this a favorite with families.

Fisherman's Friend Restaurant (367-2442), School Street, Stonington (just up the hill from the harbor). Open daily 11–9, BYOB. Simple decor, reasonably priced food, great pies.

ENTERTAINMENT

Stonington Opera House (367-2788; www.operahousearts.org), School Street, Stonington. Open June through August. This striking wooden building, vintage 1912, served as the town's theater and movie house until 1992, when it was closed. It was reopened in 2000 by a group of dedicated women. The inaugural season included music and other live performances as well as films.

SELECTIVE SHOPPING

ART GALLERIES AND ARTISANS

In Deer Isle

Deer Isle Artists Association (348-2330), 6 Dow Road, Deer Isle Village. Open June through Labor Day. A 150-member cooperative gallery with exhibits changing every 2 weeks.

Turtle Gallery (348-9977), Route 15, north of Deer Isle Village. Open daily June through September. Housed in the Old Centennial House Barn, filling two levels with paintings, photographs, prints, sculpture, and outstanding craftswork.

The Blue Heron (348-6051), Route 15, Deer Isle (near the center of the village). Open daily June through Columbus Day. An old barn attached to Mary Nyburg's pottery studio is filled with fine contemporary crafts and featuring work by Haystack Mountain School's faculty (see *To See*).

Terrell S. Lester Photography (348-2676), 4 Main Street, Deer Isle Village. Open in-season Monday through Saturday 10–5, also mid-October until Christmas, same days 1–5.

Dockside Quilt Gallery (348-2531), Church Street, Deer Isle Village. Open July through September. Tacked by hand, finished by machine; stunning quilts.

Mainstreet Studio & Gallery (348-5667), Deer Isle Village. Open mid-June through mid-September, a working jewelry studio and standout gallery representing upward of 100 artists in a variety of media.

Pearson's Jewelry (348-2535), Old Ferry Road (off Route 15), Deer Isle. Ron Pearson has an international reputation for creative designs in gold and silver jewelry as well as delicately wrought tabletop sculpture in other metals.

Also see **Haystack Mountain School of Crafts** under *To See*.

In Stonington

Hoy Gallery (367-2368), East Main Street, Stonington. Open daily July through September. A big white barn set back from the street, filled with Jill Hoy's bold, bright Maine landscapes.

Turtle Gallery

Eastern Bay Gallery (367-6368), West Main Street, Stonington. Open daily mid-May through mid-October. Janet Chaytor owns this fine crafts gallery, featuring fine clothing, jewelry, pottery, and such, most made within 40 miles of Stonington.

G. Watson Gallery (367-0983), Main Street (above the Grasshopper Shop), Stonington. Open daily June through October. Ron Watson shows contemporary painting and sculpture featuring New England artists.

Firebird Gallery (367-0955), West Main Street, Stonington. Open daily June through Columbus Day. Ginny Lee's mix of contemporary crafts: jewelry, ceramics, prints, and metal sculpture.

SPECIAL SHOPS

Old Deer Isle Parish House (348-9964), Route 15, Deer Isle Village. Open daily June through October. Mother and daughter Genevieve Bakala and Janice Glenn operate a combination antiques, crafts, and whatever shop that's a phenomenon in its own right: handmade quilts, used books, rag rugs, whatever. Browser's heaven.

Dockside Books and Gifts (367-2652), West Main Street, Stonington. Seasonal. Al Webber's waterside bookstore has an exceptional selection of Maine and marine books, also gifts, sweaters by local knitters, and a great harbor view from the balcony.

✏ **Nervous Nellie's Jams and Jellies and Mountainville Café** (348-6182; 1-800-777-6845), Sunshine Road, halfway between Deer Isle and Sunshine. Open daily mid-June through mid-October, 10–5; café open July and August. Sculptor Peter Beerits displays his whimsical life-sized sculptures, sells his jams and jellies (wild blueberry preserves, blackberry peach conserve, hot tomato chutney), and serves tea, coffee, and scones. Children of all ages love the sculptures, like the big red lobster playing checkers as a 7-foot alligator looks on. Follow directions for Haystack (see *To See*).

The Dry Dock (367-5528), Main Street, Stonington. Open daily mid-May through Christmas. A varied trove of craftswork and mostly New England–made products.

The Clown (367-6348), Main Street, Stonington. Ultimate proof of Stonington's resortification: high-ticket European antiques, ceramics, fine wine, and art.

The Periwinkle, Deer Isle. Open June through mid-October, a tiny shop with a vintage-1910 cash register, crammed with books and carefully selected gifts.

The Grasshopper Shop (367-5070), Main Street, Stonington. A Maine chain with a mix of clothing, gifts, and gadgets that you usually don't get away from without buying something.

SPECIAL EVENTS

May: **Memorial Day parade.**
July: **Independence Day** parade, fish fry, and fireworks in Deer Isle Village.
August: Lobster-boat races and **Stonington Fisherman's Festival.**

Acadia Area

Mount Desert Island; Acadia National Park; Bar Harbor and Ellsworth;
The Quiet Side of Mount Desert; East Hancock County

MOUNT DESERT ISLAND

Mount Desert (pronounced "dessert") is New England's second largest island, one conveniently linked to the mainland. Two-fifths of its 108 square miles are maintained as Acadia National Park, laced with roads ideally suited for touring by car, 45 miles of "carriage roads" specifically for biking and skiing, and 120 miles of hiking trails.

The beauty of "MDI" (as it is locally known), cannot be overstated. Seventeen mountains rise abruptly from the sea and from the shores of four large lakes. There are also countless ponds and streams, an unusual variety of flora, and more than 300 species of birds.

Native Americans first populated the area, using it as hunting and fishing grounds. Samuel de Champlain named it L'Isle de Monts Deserts in 1604. Although it was settled in the 18th century, this remained a peaceful, out-of-the-way island even after a bridge was built in 1836 connecting it to the mainland. In the 1840s, however, landscape painters Thomas Cole and Frederic Church began summering here, and their images of the rugged shore were widely circulated. Summer visitors began arriving by steamboat, and they were soon joined by travelers taking express trains from Philadelphia and New York to Hancock Point, bringing guests enough to fill more than a dozen huge hotels that mushroomed in Bar Harbor. By the 1880s many of these hotel patrons had already built their own mansion-sized "cottages" in and around Bar Harbor. These grandiose summer mansions numbered more than 200 by the time the stock market crashed. Many are now inns.

Mount Desert Island seems far larger than it is because it is almost bisected by Somes Sound, the only natural fjord on the East Coast, and because its communities vary so in atmosphere. Bar Harbor lost 67 of its 220 summer mansions and five hotels in the devastating fire of 1947, which also destroyed 17,000 acres of woodland, but both the forest and Bar Harbor have recouped, and then some, in recent decades.

Northeast Harbor, Southwest Harbor, and the remaining villages on the island—which also enjoy easy access to hiking, swimming, and

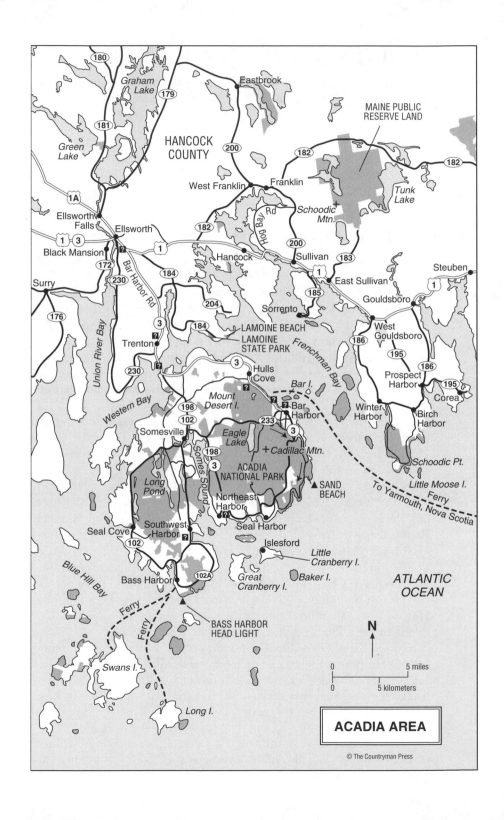

ACADIA AREA

© The Countryman Press

boating within the park—are relatively quiet, even in July and August, and the several accessible offshore islands are quieter still.

Mount Desert's mountains with "their gray coats and rounded backs look like a herd of elephants, marching majestically across the island," travel writer Samuel Adams Drake wrote in 1891, describing the first impression visitors then received of the island. They were, of course, arriving by steamboat instead of traveling down the unimpressive commercial strip that's Route 3. Today it's a shade harder to get beyond the clutter and crowds but still not that hard. The memorable march of rounded mountains is still what you see from excursion boats and from Little Cranberry Island, as well as from the eastern shore of French-man Bay, the area described in this chapter as "East Hancock County."

ACADIA NATIONAL PARK

The legacy of Bar Harbor's wealthy "rusticators" is Acadia National Park. A cadre of influential citizens, which included Harvard University's President Charles W. Eliot, began to assemble parcels of land for public use in 1901, thus protecting the forests from the portable sawmill. Boston textile heir George Dorr devoted his fortune and energy to amassing a total of 11,000 acres and persuading the federal government to accept it. In 1919 Acadia became the first national park east of the Mississippi. It is now a 40,000-acre preserve, encompassing almost half of Mount Desert Island.

Almost two-thirds of the park's 3 million annual visitors actually get out of their cars and hike the park's trails. They usually begin by viewing the introductory film in the visitors center and then drive the 27-mile Park Loop Road, stopping to see the obvious sites and noting what they want to explore more fully (see below). The park has much more to offer, from simple hikes to rock climbing, horse-drawn carriage rides to swimming, bicycling, canoeing, and kayaking.

Within the park are 45 miles of carriage roads donated by John D. Rockefeller Jr. These incredible broken-stone roads take bikers, hikers, joggers, and cross-country skiers through woods, up mountains, past lakes and streams. The paths also lead over and under 17 spectacular stone bridges. In recent years volunteers have rallied to refurbish and improve this truly spectacular network.

Isle au Haut (see "Deer Isle, Stonington, and Isle au Haut") and the Schoodic Peninsula (see "East Hancock County") are also part of Acadia National Park, but they are not located on Mount Desert Island and are much quieter, less traveled areas.

FEES

The entrance fee for vehicles is $10 for a weekly pass. For individuals on foot or bicycle, the fee is $5 for a weekly pass.

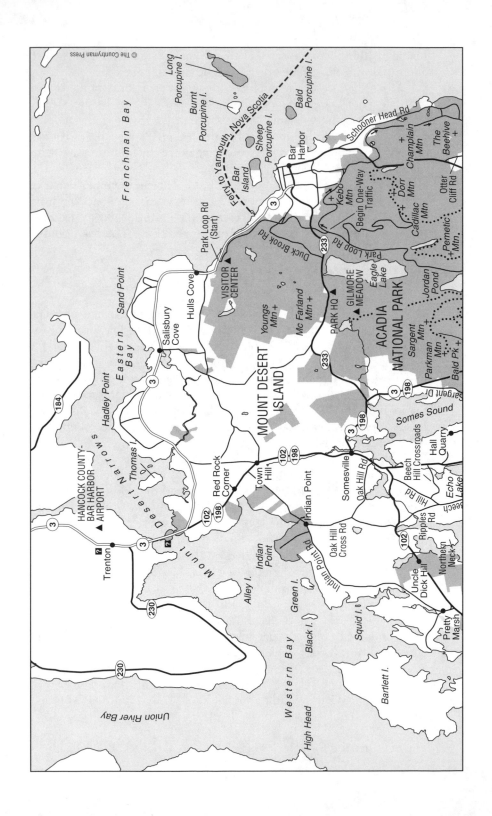

© The Countryman Press

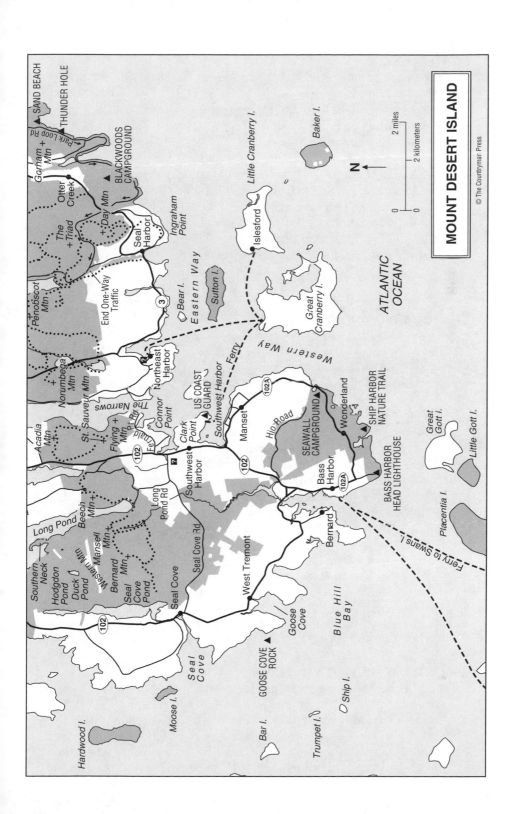

MOUNT DESERT ISLAND

N

2 miles

2 kilometers

© The Countryman Press

GUIDANCE

The park maintains its own visitors center (288-3338; www.nps.gov/acad) at Hulls Cove, open mid-April through October. From mid-June through August 31, 8–6 daily; during shoulder seasons, 8–4:30. The park headquarters at Eagle Lake on Route 233 (288-3338) is open daily throughout the winter 8–4:30. The glass-and-stone visitors center, set atop 50 steps, shows a 15-minute introductory film and sells books, guides, and postcards. Pick up a free map and a copy of the current "Acadia's Beaver Log" (a listing of all naturalist activities), and sign up for the various programs scheduled June through September, at the amphitheaters in Blackwoods and Seawall Campgrounds (see *To Do—Camping*). Children of all ages are eligible to join the park's Junior Ranger Program; inquire at the visitors center.

TO SEE

PARK LOOP ROAD

The 27-mile Loop Road is the prime tourist route within the park. There is a weekly fee of $10 per car on the road.

The Loop Road officially begins at the visitors center but may be entered at many points along the way. Most of the road is one-way, so be alert to how traffic is flowing. Places of interest along the Loop Road include **Sieur de Monts Spring,** a stop that could include the Wild Gardens of Acadia, the Abbe Museum, and Park Nature Center (see Museum and Gardens) as well as the covered spring itself; **Sand Beach,** which is actually made up of ground shells and sand and is a great beach to walk down and from which to take a dip, if you don't mind 50-degree water (there are changing rooms and lifeguards); **Thunder Hole,** where the water rushes in and out of a small cave, which you can view from behind a railing; **Jordan Pond House** (see *Where to Eat—Snacks*), popular for afternoon tea and popovers; and **Cadillac Mountain.** From Cadillac's smooth summit (accessible by car), you look north across Frenchman Bay dotted with the Porcupine Islands, which look like giant stepping-stones, and way beyond Down East. To the west, Jericho and Blue Hill Bays are directly below, and beyond the Blue Hill peninsula you see Penobscot Bay and the Camden Hills. Many visitors come at sunrise, but sunset can be far more spectacular, a sight not to be missed.

MUSEUM AND GARDENS

Robert Abbe Museum at **Sieur de Monts Spring** (288-3519), posted from both Route 3 (south of Jackson Laboratory) and the Park Loop Road. Open May through October, 9–5 daily during July and August; otherwise, 10–4. Don't miss this exceptional collection of New England Native American artifacts: sweetgrass baskets, jewelry, moccasins, a birch-bark canoe, dioramas of Native American life during all seasons,

Bicycling on the carriage roads of Acadia National Park

an authentic wigwam. Changing exhibits teach about early life on Mount Desert Island, recent archaeological excavations, culture and traditions, and more. $2 adults, $.50 children. The museum overlooks the **Park Nature Center** and the **Wild Gardens of Acadia,** a pleasant walk where more than 300 species of native plants are on display with labels. *Note:* See *To See* in "Bar Harbor and Ellsworth" for the Abbe's new downtown museum.

TO DO

BIKING
The 45 miles of broken-stone carriage roads make for good mountain biking. Several outfitters in Bar Harbor (see *To Do—Bicycling* in "Bar Harbor and Ellsworth") rent equipment and can help you find good trails.

CAMPING
The two campgrounds within the park are both in woods and close to ocean. One vehicle, up to six people, and two tents are allowed on each site. Neither campground has utility hook-ups. Facilities include comfort stations, cold running water, a dump station, picnic tables, and fire rings. Showers and a camping store are within a half mile of each. There are also five group campsites at each campground, which can be used by educational organizations and other formally organized groups. These must be reserved through the park, by writing to the superintendent after January 1 for a park reservation form (P.O. Box 177, Bar Harbor 04609). The two campgrounds within Acadia National Park are:

Blackwoods (288-3274), open all year. Reservations can be made for the period between June 15 and September 15 through the National Park Reservation Service (1-800-365-2267). Cost of sites is $18 per night during the reservation period, $14 per night in shoulder seasons; varying fees off-season.

Seawall (244-3600), near Southwest Harbor, open late May through late September. Sites at Seawall are meted out on a first-come, first-served basis. Get there early because a line forms; as campers check out, others are checked in. Cost is $18 with a vehicle, $12 if you walk in.

HIKING

The park is a mecca for hikers. Several detailed maps are sold at the visitors center, which is also the source of an information sheet that profiles two dozen trails within the park. These range in difficulty from the **Jordan Pond Loop Trail** (a 3⅓-mile path around the pond) to the rugged **Precipice Trail** (1½ miles, very steep, with iron rungs as ladders). There are 17 trails to mountain summits on Mount Desert. **Acadia Mountain** on the island's west side (2 miles round-trip) commands the best view of Somes Sound and the islands. **The Ship Harbor** on Route 102A (near Bass Harbor) offers a nature trail that winds along the shore and into the woods; it is also a great birding spot.

HORSE-DRAWN CARRIAGE TOURS

& **Carriages in the Park** (276-3622), Wildwood Stables. Two-hour horse-drawn tours in multiple-seat carriages are offered six times a day.

RANGER PROGRAMS

A wide variety of programs—from guided nature walks and hikes to birding talks, sea cruises, and evening lectures—are offered throughout the season. Ask at the visitors center for a current schedule.

ROCK CLIMBING

Acadia National Park is the most popular place to climb in Maine; famous climbs include the Precipice, Goat Head, and Otter Cliffs. See *To Do— Rock Climbing* in "Bar Harbor and Ellsworth" for guide services.

SWIMMING

Within Acadia there is supervised swimming at **Sand Beach,** 4 miles south of Bar Harbor, and at **Echo Lake,** a warmer, quieter option, 11 miles west (see *To Do—Swimming* in "The Quiet Side of Mount Desert").

WINTER SPORTS

More than 40 miles of carriage roads at Acadia National Park are maintained as ski touring and snowshoeing trails. Request the "Winter Activities" leaflet from the park headquarters (write to Superintendent, Acadia National Park, P.O. Box 177, Bar Harbor 04609).

BAR HARBOR AND ELLSWORTH

Bar Harbor is the island's big town, one of New England's largest clusters of hotels, motels, inns, B&Bs, restaurants, and shops—all within easy reach of the park visitors center and main entrance on the one hand, and to an array of water excursions and the ferries to Nova Scotia on the other.

Ellsworth is the shire town and shopping hub of Hancock County, a place with a split personality: the old brick downtown blocks along and around the Union River and its falls, and the strip of malls and outlets along the mile between the junction of Routes 1A and 1 and Routes 1 and 3. If you are coming down Route 1A from Bangor you miss the old part of town entirely, and it's well worth backtracking. Downtown Ellsworth offers the restored art-deco Grand Theater, several good restaurants, and rewarding shopping, as well a sense of the lumbering-boom era in which the Colonel Black Mansion, arguably the most elegant in Maine, was built.

The 6 miles of Route 3 between Ellsworth and Bar Harbor are lined with a mix of commercial attractions (some of which are vacation savers if you are here with children in fog or rain), 1920s motor courts and 1960s motels, newer motor inns and hotels.

In Bar Harbor itself shops and restaurants line Cottage, Mount Desert, West, and Main Streets, which slope to the Town Pier and to the Shore Path, a mile walk between mansions and the bay. During July and August Bar Harbor is expensive and crowded. Between Labor Day and Columbus Day it is cheaper and less crowded, and Mount Desert is still beautiful. On sunny days most visitors tend to be out in the park or on the water, so it's in the evening that the downtown really hums. Most shops stay open until 9 PM.

GUIDANCE

Bar Harbor Chamber of Commerce (year-round, 288-5103; 1-800-288-5103; www.barharbormaine.com), P.O. Box 158, 93 Cottage Street, Bar Harbor 04609, maintains seasonal information booths.

Mount Desert Island Regional Visitors Center (288-3411) is open daily May through mid-October (9–8 during high season) on Thompson Island, just after Route 3 crosses the bridge. This is the island's most helpful walk-in center. It offers rest rooms, national park information, and help with lodging reservations on all parts of the island.

Ellsworth Chamber of Commerce (667-5584/2617; www.ellsworth.com), 163 High Street, Ellsworth 04605, maintains an information center in the Ellsworth Shopping Center on the Route 1/3 strip; look for Burger King.

Also see "Acadia National Park."

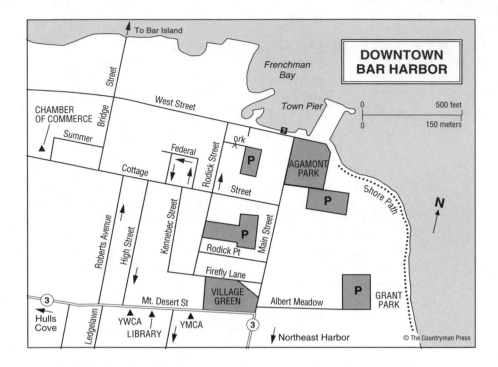

DOWNTOWN BAR HARBOR

To Bar Island

Frenchman Bay

West Street

CHAMBER OF COMMERCE

Summer

Bridge Street

Cottage

Federal

Rodick Street

York

Street

Town Pier

Shore Path

AGAMONT PARK

P

P

P

Roberts Avenue

High Street

Kennebec Street

Rodick Pt

Firefly Lane

Main Street

VILLAGE GREEN

Albert Meadow

P

GRANT PARK

3

Hulls Cove

Ledgelawn

Mt. Desert St

YWCA

LIBRARY

YMCA

3

Northeast Harbor

500 feet

150 meters

N

© The Countryman Press

GETTING THERE

By air: **Colgan Air** has been absorbed by U.S. Airways but still serves the Hancock County–Bar Harbor Airport in Trenton (between Ellsworth and Bar Harbor) from Boston and Rockland. Rental cars are available at the airport. **Bangor International Airport** (947-0384; www.flybangor.com), 26 miles north of Ellsworth, offers connections with most American cities.

By boat: **"The Cat"** (288-3395; 1-888-249-7245). With this high-speed ferry the trip to Nova Scotia now takes just 2½ hours (the old Bluenose ferry took 6 hours), and the boat departs both Bar Harbor and Yarmouth twice daily, making a day trip feasible (though rather pricey). One-way summer fares are $55 for adults, $50 seniors, $25 children ages 5–16. Vehicles cost $80–105 depending on size/height.

By private boat: For details about moorings, contact the Bar Harbor harbormaster at 288-5571.

By bus: **Concord Trailways** (1-800-639-3317) offers unbeatable year-round service from Boston's Logan Airport and South Station (4 hours, 40 minutes) to Bangor, with seasonal shuttle service from Bangor to Bar Harbor. **Vermont Transit** (1-800-451-3292) serves Bar Harbor May through October.

By car: From Brunswick and points south (including Boston and New York), the shortest route is I-95 to Bangor to I-395 to Route 1A south to Ellsworth. A slightly slower route that includes some coastal views is I-95 to Augusta, then Route 3 east to Belfast (stop for a swim at Lake St. George State Park), and north on Route 1 to Ellsworth.

GETTING AROUND

Acadia Shuttle buses operated by **Downeast Transportation** (667-5796) are big, free, clean, and propane powered. They circulate through the park and the island's towns on seven different routes. Hikers take note: You can get off at one trailhead and be picked up at another. Bus schedules are timed to coincide with ferry departures to Nova Scotia, Swans Island, and the Cranberry Isles.

PARKING

In high season, parking here is a pain. Note the lots on our Downtown Bar Harbor map (see page 372). Much of the lodging is downtown (with parking) and the village is compact. Park and walk.

MEDICAL EMERGENCY

Maine Coast Memorial Hospital (667-4520), Ellsworth. **Mount Desert Island Hospital** (288-5081), Bar Harbor, provides 24-hour emergency care.

TO SEE

In Bar Harbor

✎ **Abbe Museum** (288-3519; www.abbemuseum.org), 26 Mount Desert Street, Bar Harbor. Due to open late in 2001, this new, year-round facility showcases the museum's 50,000-object collection representing 10,000 years of Native American life in Maine. Also see the seasonal Abbe Museum under *To See* in "Acadia National Park."

✎ **College of the Atlantic** (COA; 288-5015), Route 3, Bar Harbor. Housed in the original Acadia National Park headquarters, which has been moved to the COA campus and expanded in 2000, the **Natural History Museum** here is a worthwhile stop (mid-June through Labor Day 10–5 daily; otherwise, Thursday and Friday 1–4, Saturday 10–4, Sunday 1–4). $3.50 adults, $2.50 seniors and teens, $1 children ages 3 and older. Exhibits include the skeleton of a rare true-beaked whale and dioramas of plants and animals of coastal Maine. Inquire about **Summer Field Studies** programs for children. **The Ethel H. Blum Gallery,** open Monday through Saturday 9–5, with changing exhibits, is also worth checking. Founded in 1969, COA is a liberal-arts college specializing in ecological studies. Its waterside acres, an amalgam of four large summer estates, are now a handsome campus for 230 students. Inquire about summer workshops.

Bar Harbor Historical Society (288-0000), 33 Ledgelawn Avenue, Bar Harbor. Open mid-June through September, Monday through Saturday 1–4. Free. In winter, open by appointment. Well worth finding. A fascinating collection of early photographs of local hotels, steamers, cottages, the cog railroad, paintings, gilded-age clothing, books by local

Downtown Bar Harbor

authors and about Bar Harbor and the story of the big fire of 1947. Microfilm collection of area newspapers.

Shore Path. This mile-long path runs from Agamont Park near the Bar Harbor Town Pier and along the bay. It's also accessible from Grant Park, off Albert Meadow at the corner of Main and Mount Desert Streets.

In Ellsworth

Colonel Black Mansion (Woodlawn) (667-8460), West Main Street (Route 172). Open June through mid-October, Monday through Saturday 10–4:30. $5 adults, $2 children. An outstanding Georgian mansion built as a wedding present in 1862 by John Black, who had just married the daughter of the local agent for a Philadelphia land developer, owner of this region. Supposedly, the bricks were brought by sea from Philadelphia, and it took Boston workmen three years to complete it. It is now open to the public, furnished just as it was when the Black family used it (three generations lived here). Besides the fine period furniture and spiral staircase, there is a lovely garden and a carriage house full of old carriages and sleighs.

Birdsacre Wildlife Sanctuary (667-8460), Route 3. Old homestead and gift shop open daily May through October, 10–4; sanctuary open year-round. Token admission. Don't miss this exceptional place: a 160-acre nature preserve that is a memorial to Cordelia Stanwood (1865–1958), a pioneer ornithologist, nature photographer, and writer. The old homestead (1850) contains family furnishings and a collection of Stanwood's photos. There are gardens, a picnic area, and a gift shop.

New England Museum of Telephony (667-9491), 166 Winkumpaugh Road, marked from Route 1A north of Ellsworth. Open July through September, Wednesday and Sunday 2–5. The evolution of telephone service, from 1876 to 1983 (when the museum opened), is the subject of this quirky museum and its varied equipment.

FOR FAMILIES

* **Route 3 attractions** include waterslides, mini-golf, and go-carts, as well as:
* **Mount Desert Oceanarium** (288-5005). Open 9–5 daily, except Sunday, mid-May through late October. $6.95 adults, $4.95 children ages 4–12. Tour the lobster hatchery (for an additional fee) and the seal exhibit; also visit the **Thomas Bay Marsh Walk.**
* **Acadia Zoological Park** (667-3244), Route 3, Trenton. Open spring through Christmas. $6 adults, $5 children. Fifteen acres house native and exotic animals, as well as a rain forest display.
* **The Maine Lumberjack Show** (667-0067), Route 3, Trenton. Late June through September, nightly at 7. The 1¼ -hour nightly show includes ax throwing, log rolling, speed climbing, and more.

TO DO

AIRPLANE RIDES

Acadia Air (667-5534), Route 3, Hancock County Airport, Trenton. Flight instruction, aircraft rentals, and sight-seeing flights.

Island Soaring Glider Rides (667-SOAR), also at the airport, offers motorless soaring flights.

BICYCLING

The network of gravel carriage roads (see "Acadia National Park") constructed by John D. Rockefeller Jr. in 1915 lends itself particularly well to mountain biking. In Bar Harbor, **Bar Harbor Bicycle Shop** (288-3886; www.barharborbike.com), 141 Cottage Street, is the oldest bike outfitter in town and still rents only bikes: mountain, tandem, and everything that goes with them. **Acadia Bike & Canoe Company** (288-9605), 48 Cottage Street, also rents every kind of bike and support item. Companies offering sunrise rides from the top of Cadillac Mountain seem to vary each season.

BIRDING

Downeast Nature Tours (288-8128; www.mainebirding.net) offers excellent 4-hour guided bird tours daily. For special programs led by park naturalists, consult "Acadia's Beaver Log," available at the park visitors center (see *Guidance* in "Acadia National Park").

BOAT EXCURSIONS

A number of cruises are available daily in summer; **Frenchman Bay Nature Cruise** (288-3322) is narrated by a naturalist from Acadia National Park. **Bar Harbor Ferry Co.** (288-2984) cruises from the Bar Harbor Inn Pier 1 hour across Frenchman Bay to Winter Harbor. ***The***

Katherine (288-3322), Municipal Pier, Bar Harbor. This 42-foot lobster/passenger boat combines lobstering and seal-watching.

BOAT RENTALS
In Bar Harbor, **Harbor Boat Rentals** (288-3757) rents powerboats and sailboats.

BREWERY TOURS
Atlantic Brewing Company (288-BEER; www.antlanticbrewing.com), in Town Hill (across from the Town Hill Market), has re-created an indoor/outdoor European brewery/pub. Daily tours and tastings 1–5.

Bar Harbor Brewing Co. and Sodaworks (288-4592), Otter Creek Road, 1 mile north of Blackwoods Campground, also offers tours.

CANOEING AND SEA KAYAKING
Most ponds on Mount Desert offer easy access. Long Pond, the largest lake on the island, has three access points. Boats can be launched at Echo Lake from Ike's Point, just off Route 102. Seal Cove Pond is less used and accessible from fire roads north of Seal Cove. Bass Harbor Marsh is another possibility at high tide. Canoe rental sources offer suggestions and directions. **National Park Canoe Rentals** (244-5854) on Long Pond near Somesville offers tours as well as rentals, including kayaks.

Kayaking is a booming sport, and a half-dozen companies now offer guided tours and rentals. If you are not an experienced kayaker, be sure to take a guided tour. We went out with **Coastal Kayaking Tours** (288-9605), 48 Cottage Street, Bar Harbor, and discovered that guides discussed the day's wind and weather and then decided where to paddle. Our tour began in Seal Cove on the opposite side of the island. Bar Harbor outiftters include **Island Adventures** (288-3886), 137 Cottage Street; **National Park Sea Kayak Tours** (288-0342), 38 Cottage Street; and **Acadia Outfitters** (288-8118), 106 Cottage Street. **Loon Bay Kayak** (288-0099) in Trenton also offers tours, rents kayaks, and will deliver to your location for a minimal fee.

GOLF
Kebo Valley Club (288-3000), Route 233, Bar Harbor. Open daily May through October. Eighteen holes. "Oldest golf grounds in America," since 1892. **Bar Harbor Golf Course** (667-7505), Routes 3 and 204, Trenton. Eighteen holes.

HIKING
See *To Do—Hiking* in "Acadia National Park."

ROCK CLIMBING
Acadia Mountain Guides (288-8186) and **Atlantic Climbing** (288-2521) offer instruction and guiding for beginner through advanced climbers. (Also see *To Do—Rock Climbing* in "Acadia National Park.")

SAILING
The *Margaret Todd* (288-4585) sails from the Bar Harbor pier from late June through early October. This new 151-foot four-masted schooner

Kebo Valley Club, Bar Harbor

offers 2-hour cruises through Frenchman Bay several times a day in high season, less frequently in slower weeks.

SWIMMING

🏊 **Lake Wood** near Hull's Cove is a pleasant freshwater beach, ideal for children. Also see **Molasses Pond** under *To Do—Swimming* in "East Hancock County."

Also see *To Do—Swimming* in "Acadia National Park."

WHALE-WATCHING

Whale-watching is offered by a number of Bar Harbor–based companies, including **Acadian Whale Watcher Co.** (288-9794), **Bar Harbor Whale Watch Co.** (288-2386), **Sea Bird Watcher Company** (288-5033). Bring a jacket, sunblock, binoculars, and a camera. If it matters, either philosophically or physically, inquire about the size and speed of the whale-watch boat. Ask how long it takes to get out to the whales and note weather—and sea—conditions on the day you book.

LODGING

Many of Bar Harbor's nearly 3,000 beds, ranging from 1920s motor courts to large chain hotels and motels, are strung along Route 3, north of the walk-around town—where a few dozen surviving summer mansions are now B&Bs commanding top dollar. Be warned: Never come to Bar Harbor in July or August without a reservation. You will find a room, but it may well cost more than $300. We cannot claim to have inspected every room in town, but we have checked out the most appealing options.

WATER-VIEW BED & BREAKFASTS
All listings are in Bar Harbor 04609.

Ullikana Bed & Breakfast (288-9552; www.ullikana.com), 16 The Field. Open May through October. This is our top pick in downtown Bar Harbor, steps from both Main Street and the Shore Path, yet with an away-from-it-all feel. Innkeeper Helene Harton combines a rare flair for decorating with a genuine warmth that sets guests at ease. Helene and her husband (and genial co-innkeeper), Roy Kasindorf, bought Ullikana, a vintage 1885 Tudor-style summer mansion, in 1990 and transformed it into such an attractive inn that the owners of the neighboring Yellow House, another classic Bar Harbor "cottage," actually asked if they would like to buy that too. Breakfast (maybe poached pears and light pancakes stuffed with fresh berries) is served on the terrace overlooking the water or in Ullikana's attractive dining room. Both "cottages" have ample common rooms, and the artwork throughout is exceptional. The 10 guest rooms—all with private baths, 3 with fireplaces—in Ullikana itself are each decorated with imagination and taste (Audrey's Room simply sings), but we also like the airy old-style feel of the Yellow House (the 6 spacious rooms retain most of their original furnishings) and the rockers on its wraparound porch. $135–235 varies with room size and view.

Nannau Seaside B&B (288-5575; www.nannau.com), Box 710, 396 Main Street. Open June through October. Sited on peaceful Compass Harbor a mile from downtown Bar Harbor and abutting the national park, this vintage-1904, shingled, 20-room "cottage" offers four guest rooms ranging from a third-floor double to one with a fireplace and a large bay window on the ocean. There is also a two-bedroom suite for four with ocean views. A large breakfast is served, and Vikki and Ron Evers invite guests to make themselves at home in the parlor and living room. The property includes an organic vegetable garden, a young orchard, and perennial flower beds. A path leads down to a granite seat facing the ocean. No smoking. $135–185 (for a suite).

Inn at Canoe Point (288-9511; www.innatcanoepoint.com), Box 216. Open year-round. Two miles north of Bar Harbor near the entrance to the Acadia National Park visitors center. Tom and Nancy Cervelli have refurbished this lovely inn overlooking the bay, separated from Route 3 by a small pine forest. The five guest rooms have water views and private baths. The master suite, with its fireplace and French doors onto a deck, is ideal for a romantic getaway. The garret suite occupies the third floor; the garden room exudes the charm of a traditional Bar Harbor cottage guest room. Guests gather in the Ocean Room for breakfast to enjoy the fireplace, grand piano, and 180-degree view. $170–285 in-season.

Sunset on West (288-4242; 1-877-406-4242; sunsetonwest.com), 115 West Street. Nancy and Mel Johnson have the furniture ("we've been collecting it for years") and flair to turn this vintage-1910 shingled "cottage" into a singular B&B. Three of the four guest rooms overlook

Frenchman Bay, and two of these are suites: Sunset has a deck, fireplace, and Jacuzzi tub. Common rooms include an inviting living room with a baby grand piano and great art. $150–275 includes afternoon wine and cheese, and a large and exotic breakfast.

The Tides (288-4968), 119 West Street. Open year-round. In summer 2000 this gracious 1887 mansion was in the throes of a total makeover by its new owners, Ray and Loretta Harris. Staple features include two-room suites with sitting rooms, queen or king four-poster beds, fireplaces, cable TV, and window seats with water views. The veranda, with its wicker chairs and fireplace, overlooks the gardens and water. $195–375 includes a full breakfast.

OTHER DOWNTOWN B&BS

Manor House Inn (288-3759; 1-800-437-0088; www.barharbormanor house.com), 106 West Street. Open in part year-round. No real water views, but 17 comfortable rooms with private baths, some in the vintage-1887 "cottage" with its rich woodwork. The full acre of landscaped grounds also include the Chauffeur's Cottage with its guest room and two suites and the two cottages (with gas fireplaces). A new annex at the rear of the garden offers additional rooms and its own living room. $85–175 per room (less off-season) includes full breakfast and afternoon tea.

Mira Monte Inn and Suites (288-4263; 1-800-553-5109), 69 Mount Desert Street. Open May through mid-October. Marian Burns offers comfortable guest rooms in her gracious 1865 mansion. Thirteen rooms, many with private balconies overlooking the deep, peaceful lawn in back or the formal gardens on the side; plus two suites with kitchenettes, whirlpool tubs, and private decks; and a four-room housekeeping apartment. A native of Bar Harbor, Marian is an avid hiker who likes to steer her guests off the park's beaten paths. Thirteen units have fireplaces, private baths, phones, clock radios, and TVs. Guests share the inviting library and sitting room with fireplaces. Rates include a full breakfast and afternoon refreshments. $145–225, less off-season.

The Maples Inn (288-3443; www.maplesinn.com), 16 Roberts Avenue. Open year-round. Innkeepers Tom and Sue Palumbo get rave reviews for the hospitality that they offer in this pleasant 1903 house on a quiet side street within walking distance of shops and restaurants. The six rooms (all with private baths) are crisply decorated, furnished with queen-sized beds, down comforters, and reading lamps. Red Oak, under the eaves, has its own small deck, and the two-room White Birch Suite includes a sitting room (with sofa bed) and fireplace. Breakfasts are an event. $90–150 per couple; $60–95 off-season.

Seacroft Inn (288-4669; 1-800-824-9694), 18 Albert Meadow. Open year-round. Bunny and Dave Brown's gracious, many-gabled old "cottage" is sequestered on a quiet street, steps from the Shore Path. Extended stays are the norm; of the five rooms has a fridge and a microwave. $79–109 in-season, $39–59 off; a two-bedroom apartment, sleeping six, is

$1,150 per week. Guests plan their days over morning coffee.

Primrose Inn (288-4031; 1-877-TIME-4-BH; www.primroseinn.com), 73 Mount Desert Street. This 1878 stick-style "painted lady" Victorian summer cottage has recently received a thorough spiffing. Guest rooms are bright with floral wallpaper, and several have gas fireplaces, whirlpool tubs, and private balconies. Children are welcome in the one- and two-bedroom apartments with kitchenettes and separate living/dining areas. $90–175, less off-season.

Anne's White Columns Inn (288-5357; 1-800-321-6379; www.anneswhite columns.com), 57 Mount Desert Street. Built in the 1930s as a Christian Science church, hence the columns. The 10 rooms have private baths, air-conditioning, and cable TV. Innkeeper Anne Bahr delights in helping guests explore the park and area. $90–135 in July and August; otherwise, $80–120, including continental breakfast.

Canterbury Cottage (288-2112), 12 Roberts Avenue. Open year-round. Armando and Maria Ribeiro have pleasantly renovated this architecturally interesting Victorian house (its original owner was the B&M stationmaster, and its architect specialized in railroad stations). Rooms are comfortably decorated, each with private bath. One has a small balcony. $90–110 double in-season includes breakfast served in the pretty, formal dining room.

Ivy Manor Inn (288-2138; ivymanor@acadia.net), 194 Main Street. Robert and Judith Stanley have transformed a Tudor-style insurance building into an elegant inn and restaurant. Judy designed the layout, with its mahogany-paneled lobby, imported European tile, antique sconces, and antique tubs. There are eight rooms, all with air-conditioning, cable TV, and gas fireplaces. $175–325 includes a breakfast buffet. Also see **Michelle's Fine Dining Bistro** under *Dining Out*.

Bass Cottage in the Field (288-3705), The Field. Open late May through mid-October. This grand old home, just off Main Street but in a quiet byway, has been in Anna Jean Turner's family since 1929. Her niece now assists her in running this old-style guest house. The large enclosed porch is stacked with local menus and furnished with wicker. Nine rooms with high ceilings and one suite that's simply, traditionally furnished; six have private baths. Morning coffee and tea served on the porch. $65–100 double; the $45 single (in-season) is a real find.

HOTELS AND MOTELS

Bar Harbor Inn (288-3351; 1-800-248-3351; www.barharborinn.com), Newport Drive, Bar Harbor 04609. Open March through November. With 153 units, this landmark hotel get its share of groups, but its downtown waterside location is unbeatable. It's also a genuinely gracious hotel, with a 24-hour front desk, bellhops, a restaurant, and room service. The hotel-sized lobby with its formal check-in desk and seating near the fire is quite grand, the venue for complementary lemonade and cookies in summer, hot cider in fall. The **Reading Room Restaurant,** begun as an elite men's social club in 1887, offers fine dining with water views. The 51 guest rooms in the Main Inn were the first new hotel rooms available in town after the 1947 fire. Of these, 43 were completely rebuilt in 1998; balconies, jetted tubs, and fireplaces were added. The grounds also include a 64-unit Oceanfront Lodge with private balconies on the bay, and the Newport Building—38 equally comfortable rooms without views. All rooms have phone, cable TV, and access to the pool, Jacuzzi, fitness room, and 7 acres of manicured lawns on the water. Summer rates: $139–329, continental breakfast included. Children 15 and under are free; 2- to 5-night packages bring the rack rates down.

✍ **Wonder View Inn** (288-3358; 1-888-439-8439; wonderviewinn.com), P.O. Box 25, 50 Eden Street, Bar Harbor 04609. Open mid-May through mid-October. Children are welcome in the 79-unit motel built on 14 acres, the site of an estate once owned by Mary Roberts Rinehart, author of popular mystery stories. Near both the ferry terminal and downtown Bar Harbor, the motel overlooks Frenchman Bay. Extensive grounds are nicely landscaped, include a swimming pool and the Rinehart Dining Pavilion, which serves breakfast and dinner. $98–142.

COTTAGES

✍ "Maine Guide to Camp & Cottage Rentals," available free from the Maine Tourism Association (623-0363), lists many great rental cottages within easy striking distance of Mount Desert.

✍ **Emery's Cottages on the Shore** (288-3432; 1-888-240-3432; www.emerys cottages.com), Sand Point Road, Bar Harbor 04609. Open May through late October. Twenty-two cottages on Frenchman Bay (14 with kitchens), electric heat, showers, cable TV. Linens, dishes, and cooking utensils provided. Private pebble beach. Telephone available for local calls. No pets. $470–960 per week late June through late August; $435–690 and daily rates available before and after.

PUBLIC CAMPGROUNDS

Lamoine State Park, Route 184, Lamoine. Open mid-May through mid-October. Actually just minutes from busy Route 3 (between Ellsworth and Bar Harbor), this 55-acre waterside park offers a boat launch and 61 campsites (no hook-ups, no hot showers, 2-night minimum); $17 per night for nonresidents. Neighboring Lamoine Beach is great for skipping stones. *Note:* There are frequently vacancies here in July and August when Acadia National Park campsites are full. (For reservations, phone 287-3824.)

Also see *To Do—Camping* in "Acadia National Park." There are more than a dozen commercial campgrounds in this area; check local listings.

OTHER LODGING

✪ **Bar Harbor Youth Hostel** (288-5587; 1-800-444-6111), 41 Mount Desert Street (behind St. Savior's Episcopal Church), P.O. Box 32, Bar Harbor 04609. Open mid-June through August. Conveniently located right downtown. Two dorms with a total of 20 cheery red-and-white bunks in

Tea and popovers at the Jordan Pond House

a clean, cozy building; kitchen facilities. $15 per person for nonmembers; $12 per person for members. Great for solo travelers.

WHERE TO EAT

DINING OUT

All listings are in Bar Harbor unless otherwise noted.

Jordan Pond House (276-3316), Park Loop Road, Seal Harbor. Open mid-May through mid-October for lunch 11:30–2:30, for tea on the lawn 2:30–5:30, and for dinner 5:30–9. First opened in the 1870s, this landmark was beautifully rebuilt after a 1979 fire, with dining rooms overlooking the pond and mountains. It's best known for popovers and outdoor tea (see *Afternoon Tea*), but is pleasant and least crowded at dinner (jackets suggested). Specialties include prime rib, and crabmeat and Havarti quiche. Children's menu and half portions available. $14–18.

Maggie's Restaurant (288-9007), 6 Summer Street, off Cottage (corner of Bridge). Open June through October, Monday through Saturday, 5–9:30. Maggie O'Neil began her career on commercial draggers and later sold fish to local restaurants before opening her own place back in 1987. While it lacks a view, the pleasant dining room (formerly Maggie's Classic Scales) is well known to locals who value the freshness of the fish and the sensitivity with which it's prepared. Most vegetables and herbs are grown on her own farm. Desserts are another point of pride. You might begin with clams and mussels steamed in wine and garlic sauce ($7.25), followed by seared salmon over spinach ($17.95), or a shiitake mushroom ragout with tofu over wheat berries ($14.94).

Café This Way (288-4483), 14½ Mount Desert Street. Open seasonally for breakfast and dinner. Tucked back off the street, just off the village green, this newcomer is a winner, dedicated to "quality without high prices." Start with a plate of Asiago cheese, roasted red peppers and garlic, and an olive tapenade with homemade bread ($6), followed by Maine crabcakes pan-fried and served with a tequila-lime sauce. Entrées $14–19. Full liquor license.

George's Restaurant (288-4505), 7 Stephen's Lane (just off Main Street behind the First National Bank). Open mid-June through October. Dinner 5:30–10. Creative, fresh, vaguely Greek cuisine in a summery house with organdy curtains. Extensive choice of appetizers, grazers, and entrées. You might dine on lamb in a phyllo shell and lobster strudel. All entrées are $25, and the prix fixe for a three-course meal is $37 or $40 depending on appetizer choice. You can also just go with appetizers, choosing three and a desert for $40.

The Burning Tree (288-9331), Route 3, Otter Creek. Open June through Columbus Day 5–10; closed Tuesday, also Mondays after Labor Day. Admired for its fresh fish and organically grown produce, imaginatively prepared. Dine inside or on a lattice-enclosed porch on a wide choice of seafood, chicken, and vegetable entrées. The menu might include Cajun crab and lobster ($21.50), and lavender-roasted free-range chicken with red potatoes, baby carrots, asparagus, and beet greens ($18.75).

Havana (288-CUBA), 318 Main Street. Open from 5:30 nightly; reservations suggested. The menu changes nightly, the accent is Caribbean but wide ranging, and the reviews have been good. Entrées ($12–28) might range from a veggie paella to ale-roasted leg of lamb.

Galyn's Galley (288-9706), 17 Main Street. Easy to miss among the shops near the bottom of Main Street, this is one of the best bets in town for seafood at either lunch or dinner. Try the Frenchman Bay stew. The large menu actually ranges from Pasta Galyn to filet mignon. There is lighter fare in the **Galley Lounge,** featuring weekend jazz until 11 PM. Entrées $14–18.95.

The Porcupine Grill (288-3884), 123 Cottage Street. Open most of the year for dinner, daily from 6 PM. Reservations recommended. Well-chosen antiques, photos of the Porcupine Islands, and fresh flowers complement dishes that might range from marinated portobellos in phyllo to roasted lobster. Extensive wine list, cocktails a specialty.

Café Bluefish (288-3696), 122 Cottage Street. Dark wood, books, cloth napkins patterned with varying designs, and mismatched antique china create a pleasant atmosphere. Chef-owner Bobbie Lynn Hutchins, a fourth-generation Bar Harbor native, specializes in chicken, vegetarian, and seafood entrées, plus dinner strudels. $14.95–20.95.

The Reading Room (288-3351), Bar Harbor Inn, Newport Drive. Opened in 1887 as an elite men's club, the horseshoe-shaped formal dining room commands a splendid harbor view; frequent piano music at dinner. Open for all three meals, specializing in daily lobster bakes on the outdoor terrace. Dinner entrées range from herbed veal saltimbocca to steak-and-lobster pie (market price). $16.95–23.95. A Sunday champagne brunch buffet is served 11:30–2:30 ($19.95 adults, $10.95 children).

124 Cottage Street (288-4383). Pleasant, flowery atmosphere, a large vegetarian salad bar (included in all meals), and genuine early-bird specials (5–6 PM): a three-course dinner for $12.95. The extensive menu includes a broiled seafood sampler and steaks. $13.95–23.95.

🏵 **Poor Boy's Gourmet** (288-4148), 300 Main Street. Open from 4:30 for dinner nightly. Chef-owner Kathleen Field provides a decent dining experience at reasonable prices. Choices range from lobster to vegetarian entrées. $9.95–14.95. Early-bird specials. Wine and beer.

✎ **Testa's at Bayside Landing** (288-3327), 53 Main Street. Open 7 AM–midnight, June 15 through September, when the family moves to its Palm Beach restaurant. In Bar Harbor since 1934, serving three daily meals. Extensive menu, including Italian and seafood specialties. Entrées $11.95–20.95. Children's menu.

Michelle's Fine Dining Bistro (288-2138), 194 Main Street. This intimate, elegant dining room in the Ivy Manor Inn is open for dinner, with an à la carte menu featuring such entrées as scallops *l'ermitage* and châteaubriand for two. Entrées $22–34.

LOBSTER POUNDS

Lobster pounds are the best places to eat lobster. The easiest to find are the clutch around the Trenton Bridge on Route 3. The **Trenton Bridge Lobster Pound** (667-2977), open in-season 8:30–8, has been in George Gascon's family a long time, and the view is great. (Also see *Where to Eat—Lobster Pounds* in "The Quiet Side of Mount Desert" for lobster-pound options.)

♿ **Bar Harbor Lobster Bakes** (288-5031), Route 3, Hulls Cove, is a twist on the traditional lobster pound. One seating nightly. Reservations are a must. Choices are lobster or steak. Watch the lobsters being steamed with your potatoes and corn in the large steel cookers. $23 per person.

Also see **Union River Lobster Pot** under *Eating Out—In Ellsworth.*

EATING OUT: BREAKFAST

Café This Way (288-4483), 14½ Mount Desert Street, Bar Harbor. Open for breakfast 7–11. Rave reviews.

Jordan's Restaurant, 80 Cottage Street, Bar Harbor. Open 5 AM–2 PM. Under David Paine's ownership (since 1976) this remains an old-style diner: breakfast all day, specializing in blueberry pancakes and muffins. The place to fuel up after watching the sunrise from Cadillac Mountain.

EATING OUT: LUNCH AND DINNER

In Bar Harbor

Anthony's Cucina Italiana (288-3377), 191 Main Street. Highly recommended by local innkeepers: pizza to pasta and other Italian specialties.

✎ **Fisherman's Landing** (288-4632), 47 West Street. Open in-season 11:30–

8. Right on the dock. Boiled lobster dinner, steamed clams, hamburgers, hot dogs, and fried foods; liquor license.

Lompoc Café & Brew Pub (288-9392), 34 Rodick Street. Open daily 11:30 AM–3 PM and 5–9:30 PM. Billed as the original home of Bar Harbor Real Ale (the Atlantic Brewing Company itself has outgrown its birthplace; see under *To Do—Brewery Tours*), this is a congenial oasis with an open knotty-pine dining room, plus porch and terrace tables by a boccie court. Entrée choices might include chicken breast baked with sun-dried tomato sauce and an olive oil and feta marinade ($12.95) or a thin, crisp pizza ($10.95); live jazz on weekends.

Nakorn Thai Restaurant (288-4060), 30 Rodick Street. Open weekdays at 11:30 AM, weekends at 4:40 PM. Locally liked, reasonably priced. Try the crispy duck or pork spareribs with fried spring roll and fried rice.

✍ **Rosalie's Pizza** (288-5666), 46 Cottage Street. Locals head for a booth at Rosalie's when they want pizza. Calzones, salads, and baked subs are also served, and an eggplant dinner is just $6.50.

✍ **Epi Sub & Pizza** (288-5853), 8 Cottage Street. Open 7 AM–11 PM. Tops for food and value but zero atmosphere. Cafeteria-style salads, freshly baked calzones, pizza, quiche, and pasta, and crabmeat rolls. Clean and friendly; game machines in back.

Bubba's (288-5871), 30 Cottage Street. Open 11:30 AM–1 AM but serving food to 8:30 PM only. Steam-bent oak and mahogany in art-deco style creates a comfortable atmosphere. Soup and sandwiches; full bar.

✍ **Island Chowder House** (288-4905), 38 Cottage Street. Open 11–11. A toy train circles just below the ceiling, and the atmosphere is bright; good service, homemade soups, thick chowder, seafood, pasta, and chicken. Bar. Early-bird dinners (4–6): $7.99.

EATING OUT: DINNER ONLY

In Bar Harbor

Elaine's Starlight Oasis (288-3287), 78 West Street. Open daily for dinner from 5 PM. A truly vegetarian restaurant with several creative choices; fantastic desserts.

Miguel's Mexican Restaurant (288-5117), 51 Rodick Street. Open 5–10 nightly. Best Mexican food Down East: fajitas, blue-corn crabcakes with roasted red pepper sauce. A crab and avacado salad with Mexican beer hit the spot late one evening. Lively but pleasant; friendly to solo diners.

In Hulls Cove

Chart Room (288-9740), Route 3. Open for breakfast, lunch, and dinner. A dependable, family-geared, waterside restaurant with seafood specialties.

In Ellsworth

🎖 **Union River Lobster Pot** (667-5077), behind Rooster Brothers at the western edge of Ellsworth. Open daily June through October, 11:30–9. Brian Langley established his reputation as operator of the Oak Point Lobster Pound (which we can no longer recommend). This pleasant riverside restaurant serves a full menu, including St. Louis–style ribs, but the specialty is seafood. Try the Mess of Mussels. Leave room for pie. Beer and wine.

The Mex (667-4494), 185 Main Street. Open daily for lunch and dinner. Tiled booths in front; the inner dining room has white stucco walls, beaded curtains, and heavy wooden chairs and tables. The Mex serves standard Mexican food—we always order too much. (The bean soup is a meal in itself.) Sangria, margaritas, and Mexican beer.

Riverside Café (667-7220), 151 Main Street. Open 5:30 AM–3 PM weekdays, 7–2 weekends for breakfast and lunch in expanded, bright, spacious new quarters. Good food and coffees.

AFTERNOON TEA

Jordan Pond House (276-3316), Park Loop Road. Tea on the lawn at the Jordan Pond House (served 2:30–5:30) has been de rigueur for island visitors since 1895. The tea comes with freshly baked popovers and homemade ice cream. Reservations suggested.

SNACKS

J. H. Butterfield Co. (288-3386), 152 Main Street, Bar Harbor. FANCY FOODS SINCE 1887, the sign says, and John Butterfield preserves the atmosphere of the grocery that once delivered to Bar Harbor's summer mansions. Now featuring Maine specialty foods. Carry sandwiches to a bench on the village green, or to Grant Park overlooking the water.

Rooster Brothers (667-8675), Route 1, Ellsworth. Just south of the bridge. Gourmet groceries, cheese, fresh-roasted coffee blends, take-out.

ENTERTAINMENT

MUSIC

Bar Harbor Music Festival (288-5744), the Rodick Building, 59 Cottage Street, Bar Harbor. Mid-July through mid-August. For more than 30 years, this annual series has brought top performers to the island. The 8:30 PM concerts are staged at a variety of sites around town.

Arcady Music Festival (288-3151/2141). Late July through August. A relative newcomer (this is its 14th season) on the Mount Desert music scene. A series of concerts held at the College of the Atlantic (each concert performed in Bangor and Dover-Foxcroft as well).

Also see *Theater,* below; and *Entertainment* in "The Quiet Side of Mount Desert."

Also see **Galyn's Galley** under *Dining Out.*

FILM

Criterion Theater (288-3441), Cottage Street, Bar Harbor. A vintage-1932, art-deco, 891-seat theater. Gorgeous but musty (asthmatics, beware); first-run and art films nightly. Rainy-day matinees.

Reel Pizza Cinema (288-3828), 22 Kennebec Place, Bar Harbor. Pizza and art, foreign, and independent films in a funky setting (beanbag chairs and big sofas). Films at 6 and 8:30 nightly, year-round.

The Grand Theater (667-9500), Main Street, Ellsworth. A classic old the-

ater. Live performances, first-run and art films are shown.
Ellsworth Cinemas (667-3251), Maine Coast Mall, Route 1A, Ellsworth. First-run films.

THEATER

See **Acadia Repertory Theatre** in "The Quiet Side of Mount Desert."

The Grand Theater (667-9500), Main Street, Ellsworth. Live performances by singers, comedians, and theatrical groups.

Also see **The Maine Lumberjack Show** under *To See—For Families*.

SELECTIVE SHOPPING

ART AND FINE CRAFTS GALLERIES

Eclipse Gallery (288-9048), 12 Mount Desert Street, Bar Harbor. Seasonal. A quality gallery specializing in contemporary handblown American glass, ceramics, and fine furniture; also showing metal sculpture, fine jewelry, and art photography.

Island Artisans (288-4214), 99 Main Street, Bar Harbor. A cooperative run by 75 Maine artists and craftspeople.

Alone Moose Fine Crafts (288-4229), 78 West Street, Bar Harbor. A long-established collection of "made in Maine" craftswork, specializing in wildlife sculpture in bronze and wood.

Birdsnest Gallery (288-4054), 12 Mount Desert Street, Bar Harbor. Open mid-May through October: original oils, watercolors, and pastels.

Spruce Grove Gallery (288-2002), 29 Cottage Street, Bar Harbor. Work by a group of Maine artists, including **Salt Marsh Pottery.**

BOOKSTORES

Sherman's Bookstore and Stationery (288-3161), Main Street, Bar Harbor. A great browsing emporium; really a combination five-and-dime, stationery store, gift shop, and well-stocked bookshop.

Big Chicken Barn Books and Antiques (667-7308), Route 1/3 south of Ellsworth. Open daily year-round, generally 10–5. Maine's largest used-book store fills the vast innards of a former chicken house. Annegret Cukierski has 90,000 books in stock: hardbacks, paperbacks, magazines, and comics; also used furniture and collectibles.

Also see **Port in a Storm Bookstore** under *Selective Shopping—In Somesville* in "The Quiet Side of Mount Desert."

OUTLET STORE

L. L. Bean Outlet, High Street, Ellsworth. Clothing, sporting equipment, and a wide variety of discounted items from Maine's most famous store.

SPECIAL EVENTS

Memorial Day weekend: **Celebrate Bar Harbor.**
Throughout the summer: **Band concerts**—Bar Harbor village green (check current listings).
June: **Antique Auto Rally, Lobster Races,** Bar Harbor.

July: **Independence Day**—midnight square dance with breakfast for dancers, followed by sunrise dance on top of Cadillac Mountain, street parade, and seafood festival. **Art Show**—Bar Harbor's Agamont Park *(later in the month).* **Dulcimer and Harp Festival,** Bar Harbor. **Ellsworth Craft Show** *(end of the month).*
August: **Crafts Show** and **Art Show,** Bar Harbor.
September: **Marathon road race, bicycle race,** Bar Harbor.

THE QUIET SIDE OF MOUNT DESERT

A Southwest Harbor innkeeper claims to have coined the term Quiet Side for the longer, thinner arm of land that's divided by Somes Sound from the part of Mount Desert on which Bar Harbor and the busier part of Acadia National Park (including its visitors center and Park Loop Road) are found. The name has stuck and generally also applies to Northeast Harbor.

"Northeast" is the island's yachting center, with a large marina geared to visiting yacht owners and summer residents. Beyond a brief lineup of boutiques and art galleries, summer mansions trail off along Somes Sound. The village also offers splendid public gardens and a wide choice of ways onto the water. Try to get to Islesford (Little Cranberry Island) and be sure to follow Sargent Drive (rather than Route 3/ 198) along the Sound. The Mount Desert Historical Society in Somesville is well worth a stop. Some of Acadia's best hiking, as well as its best public swimming beach (at Echo Lake) and canoeing (on Long Pond) are found west of Somes Sound.

Southwest Harbor is still a boatbuilding center, home of The Hinckley Company, the Rolls Royce of yacht builders. Nearby Bass Harbor is the island's fishing village, departure point for Swans and several other islands that were once far busier.

Ironically, back in the 1840s Mount Desert's first summer visitors—artists in search of solitude—headed for the Bar Harbor area precisely because it was then far less peopled than the boatbuilding and fishing villages on this western side of the island. Much as the Route 1 town of Ellsworth is today, Southwest Harbor back then marked the crossroads of Down East Maine, and several island harbors were as busy as any on the mainland.

GUIDANCE
Mount Desert Chamber of Commerce (276-5040), Sea Street, Northeast Harbor. A walk-in cottage (with showers), geared to visitors arriving by water, is open daily mid-June through mid-October at the town dock. Pick up a copy of the current "Mount Desert Guide & Northeast Harbor Port Directory."
Southwest Harbor/Tremont Chamber of Commerce (244-9264;

1-800-423-9264; www.acadia.net/swhtrcoc), 204 Main Street, Southwest Harbor 04679. The visitors center is on Route 102, on the northern edge of the village.

GETTING THERE

By air and bus: See *Getting There* in "Bar Harbor and Ellsworth."

Note: **Airport & Harbor Taxi** (667-5995) meets planes, buses, and boats; serves the entire area.

By boat: Contact the harbormasters in **Northeast Harbor** (276-5737) and **Southwest Harbor** (244-7913) about transient moorings.

By car: **From Ellsworth:** Fork right off Route 3 as soon as it crosses the Mount Desert narrows; follow Route 102/198 to Somesville and Route 198 to Northeast Harbor, or Route 102 to Southwest Harbor. **From Bar Harbor:** Follow Route 3 south to Northeast Harbor and on along Somes Sound on Sargent Drive to Somesville, back down along Echo Lake on Route 102 to Bass Harbor, and back up through Pretty Marsh to Route 3.

GETTING AROUND

This is one place in Maine where water transport is still as important as land. **MDI Water Taxi** (244-7312) supplements the services out of Northeast and Southwest Harbors listed under *Boat Excursions* (see *To Do*), and the **Maine State Ferry Service** (244-4353; 1-800-491-4883) services Swans Island and Frenchboro. **Airport and Harbor Taxi** (667-5995; 1-888-814-5995) meets boats, planes, and buses. Also see Acadia Shuttle under *Getting Around* in "Bar Harbor and Ellsworth."

MEDICAL EMERGENCY

Maine Coast Memorial Hospital (667-4520), 50 Union Street, Ellsworth. **Mount Desert Island Hospital** (288-5081), 10 Wayman Lane, Bar Harbor, provides 24-hour emergency care. **Ambulance** in Southwest Harbor (244-5233); Northeast Harbor (276-5111).

TO SEE

In Northeast Harbor

Asticou Terraces, Thuya Garden, and **Thuya Lodge** (276-5130). Parking for the Asticou Terraces (open July through Labor Day, 7–7; $2 donation) is marked on Route 3, just east of the junction with Route 198. The exquisite 215-acre garden, begun by landscape artist Joseph Henry Curtis around 1900, features a system of paths and shelters on Asticou Hill. It's now open to the public along with his home, Thuya Lodge (open late June through Labor Day, 10–5), which houses an important collection of botanical books and floral paintings. Thuya Garden behind the lodge was designed by the landscaper and artist Charles Savage; it's semiformal, with perennial beds and a reflecting pool. The gardens descend in terraces, then through wooded paths to the harbor's edge.

Asticou Azalea Gardens, Route 3 (near the junction of Route 198). Open April through October. Also designed by Charles Savage. Stroll down winding paths and over ornamental bridges. Azaleas (in bloom mid-May until mid-June), rhododendrons, laurel, and Japanese-style plantings.

Petite Plaisance (276-3940), South Shore Road. Open mid-June through August by appointment. The former home of French author Marguerite Yourcenar has long been a pilgrimage destination for her fans. English translations of her books are available in local bookstores.

Great Harbor Maritime Museum (276-5262), the Old Firehouse, Main Street. Open June through Columbus Day, Monday through Saturday 10–5. $1 per person, $2 per family. A collection of model shops, small boats, and historical artifacts ranging from an early fire engine to a parlor room, clothing, sleighs, and a player piano; demonstrations.

From Northeast (and Southwest) Harbor

Little Cranberry Island. Also known as Islesford, this 400-acre island, 20 minutes offshore, is exceptionally appealing, both naturally and in the ways visitors can interact with the people who live and summer here. The official "sight-to-see" is the incongruously brick and formal **Islesford Historical Museum** (244-9224; open daily mid-June through September, 10:45–4:30), built in 1928 with funds raised by Bangor-born, MIT-educated summer resident William Otis Sawtelle, to house his fascinating local historical collection. Acadia National Park now maintains the museum, one reason why the island enjoys such good boat service from both Northeast and Southwest Harbors (see To Do—Boat Excursions). **Islesford Market** (244-7667) is the island's living room. Chairs and counter stools are within easy reach of coffeepots. Pizza and light lunches are served year-round, and island-bred postmistress Joy Sprague dispenses cream puffs (every 25th Express Mail customer receives a dozen) as well as stamps. Frequently Islesford sells more stamps per year than any other post office in Maine, despite the fact that it has just 80 year-round and some 400 summer residents. Requests for Sprague's "Stamps by Mail" come from as far as Fiji, Iceland, and Istanbul—perhaps because with each order she encloses one of her fine island photos and a monthly newsletter (her address is USPO, Islesford 04646). Ask directions in the market to the home studio of nationally known artist and folklorist **Ashley Bryan,** and to lobsterman-artist Danny Furnald's **Islesford Artists Gallery,** exhibiting some of Maine's top artists. Be sure to lunch or dine at **Islesford Dock** (see Dining Out), and at the dock also check out Marian Baker's **Islesford Pottery** (244-5686). Consider spending the night on Little Cranberry at Frances Bartlett's **Braided Rug Inn** (244-5943): three attractive guest rooms; $65 with shared bath, $70 with private. Rooms are hung with extraordinary turn-of-the-century photos taken by Bartlett's grandfather Fred Morse (published in 1998 as *Maine Island* by the Maine Folklife Center).

Asticou Azalea Gardens, Northeast Harbor

In Somesville

This tiny white wooden village at the head of Somes Sound is a National Historic District; be sure to check out **Brookside Cemetery** and the **Mount Desert Historical Society** (244-5043), Route 102. Open June through October, Tuesday through Saturday 10–5 ($1 adults), the historical society maintains a lively museum: two tidy buildings, one dating back to 1780, connected by a moon bridge, house many artifacts and photographs of the island's vanished hotels and the shipyards for which this village was once widely known. Inquire about special programs. The society also has restored the one-room 19th-century **Sound School House** on Route 198, housing changing exhibits.

In Southwest Harbor

⚲ **Oceanarium** (244-7330), Clark Point Road. Open mid-May through mid-October, 9–5 daily except Sunday. A large old waterside building filled with exhibits, including 20 tanks displaying sea life, whale songs, a "lobster room," and a touch tank. $6.95 adults, $4.95 children.

Wendell Gilley Museum (244-7555), Route 102. Open May through December, 10–4 (10–5 July and August), daily except Monday; Friday through Sunday only in May, November, and December. A collection of more than 200 bird carvings by the late woodcarver and painter Wendell Gilley. $3 adults, $1 children under age 12.

Also see the **Ship Harbor Nature Trail** under *To Do—Hiking* in "Acadia National Park."

⚲ **Seal Cove Auto Museum** (244-9242), Pretty Marsh Road (off Route 102), between Bass Harbor and Somesville. Open daily June through September, 10–5. Squirreled away in an unpromising-looking warehouse in the foggiest, least-trafficked corner of the island, this collection is a real find: over 100 gleaming antique cars and 30 motorcycles, including the country's largest assemblage of pre-1915 cars—the life's work of a private collector; $5 adults, $2 children.

Indian Point Blagden Preserve, a 110-acre Nature Conservancy preserve in the northwestern corner of the island, includes 1,000 feet of shorefront and paths that wander through the woods. It offers a view of Blue Hill Bay and is a tried-and-true seal-watching spot. From Route 198 north of Somesville, turn right on Indian Point Road, bear right at the fork, and look for the entrance; sign in and pick up a map at the caretaker's house.

From Bass Harbor

Swans Island. At the mouth of Blue Hill Bay, 6 miles out of Bass Harbor, with frequent car ferry service (see *Getting Around*), this is a large lobstering and fishing island with a year-round population of 350, a library, a general store (no alcohol), three seasonal restaurants, **Quarry Pond** to swim in, and **Fine Sand Beach** to walk. With a bike it's a possible day trip, but be forewarned: The ferry docks 5 hilly miles from **Burnt Coat Harbor,** the picturesque island center with **Hockamock Light** (built in 1872) at its entrance. **Swans Island Educational Society** (526-4350), a historic complex that includes a store, school, old tools, and photographs, is less than a mile from the dock. Swans, however, works better as an overnight. Jeannie Joyce offers three rooms (**Jeannie's Place,** 526-4116), open year-round at Burnt Coat Harbor ($45 double, $35 single). **Harbor Watch Motel** (526-4563; 1-800-532-7926; www.swansisland.com), Minturn Road at the head of Burnt Coat Harbor (next to the general store), offers four year-round units, two full kitchens, and will pick you up at the ferry; $60–75. This is also the island's source of kayak and bicycle rentals. September through May, Maili Bailey coordinates roughly 20 property rentals: cottages, houses, and apartments (**Swans Island Vacations,** 526-4350; off-season, 474-7370; www.wtvl.net/maili). The big annual event is the **Sweet Chariot Festival** (526-4443), usually the first weekend in August. Folksingers gather from throughout the East.

Frenchboro is accessible via **Island Cruises** (244-5785), which offers a lunch cruise daily in-season (weather permitting) that includes an island walking tour. **Frenchboro Historical Society** (334-2929), open seasonally, displays old tools, furniture, and local memorabilia. A good excuse to explore this very private island 8 miles offshore. Bring a bike. *Note:* One day a year (early in August) the island welcomes visitors with a lobster feed, plenty of chicken salad, and pies. Ferry service: 244-3254.

SCENIC DRIVES

Sargent Drive (see map on page 366), obviously built for carriages, runs from Northeast Harbor north a half-dozen miles right along Somes Sound.

Route 102A loop. This isn't the quickest way between Southwest and Bass Harbors but it's beautiful, threading national park shoreline at the **Sea Wall** with its oceanside picnic tables and the **Ship Harbor Nature Trail** down to gorgeous, flat pink rocks (see *To Do—Hiking* in "Acadia National Park"). Be sure to turn onto Lighthouse Road to see **Bass Harbor Light** and continue on into Bass Harbor and Bernard (see *Where to Eat* and *Selective Shopping*).

TO DO

✐ **Acadia Ranger Programs.** Pick up a copy of "Acadia's Beaver Log" at Seawall Campground (Route 102A) if you cannot find it in local chambers (see *Guidance* in "Acadia National Park") or shops. The free handout "Acadia Weekly" also lists programs ranging from guided walks and cruises to evening programs.

BICYCLING
The 45-mile network of gravel carriage roads (see *To Do—Biking* in "Acadia National Park") constructed by John D. Rockefeller Jr. in 1915 lends itself particularly well to mountain biking. (Also see **Swans Island** under *To See—From Bass Harbor.*) **Northeast Harbor Bike Shop** (276-5480), Main Street, Northeast Harbor, offers rentals. **Southwest Cycle** (244-5856; 1-800-649-5856) in Southwest Harbor rents mountain and touring bicycles, children's bikes, baby seats, car racks, and jog strollers.

BIRDING
For special programs led by park naturalists, consult "Acadia's Beaver Log" (see *Guidance* in "Acadia National Park"); also see the **Wendell Gilley Museum** under *To See—In Southwest Harbor* and *To Do* in "Bar Harbor and Ellsworth."

BOAT EXCURSIONS
See **Little Cranberry Island, Swans Island,** and **Frenchboro** under *To See.*

From Bass Harbor: The car-carrying **Maine State Ferry** (244-3254) runs to Swans Island several times a day, twice weekly to Frenchboro.

Island Cruises (244-5785), Little Island Marine, Bass Harbor. Eric and Kim Strauss offer daily (weather-dependent) lunch cruises to Frenchboro and around Placentia and Black Islands as well as Great and Little Gott Islands, all depicted in novels by Great Gott native Ruth Moore (1903–1989). In *The Weir, Speak to the Winds,* and *Spoonhandle,* Moore describes the poignant ebb of life from these islands in the 1930s and 1940s.

Bass Harbor Cruise (244-5365) offers nature cruises and a cruise with dinner served on Swans Island (see *To See*).

From Northeast Harbor: **Beal & Bunker** (244-3575) offers year-round mail-boat and ferry service aboard *Island Queen* to the Cranberries (see *To See*) and Sutton Island. The excursion boat *Islesford Ferry* (276-3717) offers a lunch cruise to Little Cranberry, and a park-naturalist-led nature cruise to Baker Island. *Sea Princess* (276-5352) offers a dinner cruise to Little Cranberry. The *Delight* (244-5724), an old-style launch, offers water taxi service. See **Little Cranberry Island** under *To See,* and **Islesford Dock** under *Dining Out.*

From Southwest Harbor: **Cranberry Cove Boating** (244-5882) offers frequent service to the Cranberries and Sutton Island. The *Elizabeth T* (244-9160), a 34-foot wood lobster boat, offers water taxi service and also daily, seasonal nature cruises. The old-style launch *Water Lilly* (244-7927) offers 2-hour cruises from the Claremont Hotel.

BOAT RENTALS
In Southwest Harbor both **Manset Yacht Service** (244-4040) and **Mansell Boat Co., Inc.** (244-5625), rent power- and sailboats.

CANOEING AND KAYAKING
Long Pond, the largest lake on any Maine island, has three access points. Boats can be launched at Echo Lake on Ike's Point, just off Route 102. **Seal Cove Pond** is less used and accessible from fire roads north of Seal Cove. **Bass Harbor Marsh** is another possibility at high tide. Canoe rental sources offer suggestions and directions. **National Park Canoe & Kayak Rentals** (244-5854), on Long Pond near Somesville, offers guided paddles and instruction. Guided half- and full-day paddles are offered by **Maine State Sea Kayak** (244-9500; www.mainestate kayak.com), 244 Main Street, Southwest Harbor; **Yak Man Adventures** (244-3333; www.yakmanadventures.com), based in Bernard, rents kayaks and offers tours. **Loon Bay Kayak** (266-8888; 1-888-786-0676), Route 102 near Manset Town Dock, offers guided tours and rentals (will deliver).

GOLF
Causeway Golf Club (244-3780), Fernald Point Road, Southwest Harbor. Nine-hole course, clubhouse and pull carts, pro shop.

FISHING
Deep-sea fishing is offered aboard the party boat *Mosako Queen* (667-1912), departing Beal's Lobster Pier in Southwest Harbor June through September.

HIKING
The highest mountains on the western side of Somes Sound are Bernard and Mansett, but both summits are wooded. The more popular hikes are up **Acadia Mountain** (3½ miles round-trip, off Route 102) with an east–west summit trail commanding a spectacular view of the sound and islands. Admittedly we have only climbed **Flying Mountain,** a quick hit with a great view too. The trail begins at the Fernald Cove parking area. Don't miss **Asticou Terraces** and the **Indian Point Blagden Preserve,** described under *To See.*

SAILING
Mansell Boat Company (244-5625), Route 102A, Manset (near Southwest Harbor), offers sailing lessons; also rents small sailboats. For sail-

boat charters, contact **Classic Charters** (244-7312), Northeast Harbor; **Hinckley Yacht Charters** (244-5008), Southwest Harbor; or **Manset Yacht Service** (244-4040). Schooner *Rachel B. Jackson* (244-7813) sails out of Southwest Harbor.

SWIMMING

Echo Lake offers a beach with a lifeguard, rest rooms, and parking; Route 102 between Somesville and Southwest Harbor.

LODGING

GRAND OLD RESORTS

🏊 **The Claremont** (244-5036; 1-800-244-5036), Claremont Road, Southwest Harbor 04679. Open May through mid-October. Mount Desert's oldest hotel, first opened in 1884; it has the grace and dignity but not the size of a grand hotel and the best views on the island. Never attempting to compete in size and glitz with all those Bar Harbor hotels that burned in the fire of 1947, the Claremont has remained low-key and gracious but not stuffy. It's been lucky in its owners, just three couples, who have preserved its appeal for families. Current owner Gertrude McQue's family has been summering on Mount Desert since 1871. Her grandfather was among the island's elite who met in 1901 to first discuss the idea of preserving "points of interest on the Island for the perpetual use of the public." "We didn't expect to make money, just to keep it going and to improve it" is the way McQue explains how she and her late husband, Allen, happened to buy the hotel in 1968. All 24 guest rooms have new plumbing, wiring, and phones, and each is carefully furnished in cottage furniture and wicker. Wildflowers brighten bureaus, wood floors gleam around Oriental carpets in sitting rooms, the wraparound porch is lined with rockers, and every table in the dining room has a view. Visitors are welcome to dine (or to lunch) in the boathouse and to attend Thursday-evening lectures. There are large suites in Phillips and Clark Houses, also 13 cottages, each with living room and fireplace, one with a kitchenette. Recreation options include tennis on clay courts, croquet, badminton, and water sports; rowboats are available. The Croquet Classic in August is the social high point of the season. A room in the hotel is $200–225 double MAP in-season; $150–155 B&B; before July 15 and after Labor Day rates drop to $130–190 MAP, $89–115 B&B; children's rates. Weekly rates. A 15 percent gratuity is added.

Asticou Inn (276-3344; 258-3373; www.asticou.com), Route 3, Northeast Harbor 04662. Mid-May through mid-October. The elegant Asticou Inn offers superb food, simply furnished rooms with water views, luxurious public rooms with Oriental rugs and wing chairs by the hearth, and a vast porch overlooking formal gardens. In all there are 46 rooms and suites, all with private baths, divided among the main house and annexes, which include Cranberry Lodge across the road and the

Adirondack chairs at the Claremont Hotel overlook Southwest Harbor.

Topsider suites in modern water-view cottages. In recent years the mood has lightened here: Bellhops are now in shirtsleeves so as not to intimidate guests, and nonguests in shorts feel far more welcome at lunch, served on the deck overlooking the harbor; see *Dining Out*. Facilities include a cocktail lounge, tennis courts, and a heated swimming pool. Music many summer nights. $264–364 double MAP in July and August, $55–325 EP; from $117 per couple EP off-season.

INNS AND BED & BREAKFASTS

In Northeast Harbor 04662

Harbourside Inn (276-3272; www.harborsideinn.com). Open June through September. An 1880s shingle-style inn set in 4 wooded acres, with 11 guest rooms and three suites (two with kitchenettes) on three floors, all with private baths; some kitchens. There are also working fireplaces in all the first- and second-floor rooms. All are large with interesting antiques and fine rugs. This is a very special place, as only an inn with long-term family management and a returning clientele can be. Flowers from the garden brighten every guest room. Guests mingle over breakfast muffins served on the wicker-furnished sunporch. There is also a comfortable living room, but most guests spend their days in adjacent Acadia National Park. The Asticou Azalea Gardens, shops, and the town landing with its water excursions are all within walking distance. Your hosts, the Sweet family, are longtime island residents. $125–135 for a room to $175–195 for a suite.

✎ **The Maison Suisse Inn** (276-5223; 1-800-624-7668; www.masionsuisse. com), Main Street at Kimball Lane, P.O. Box 1090. Open late May through late October. A gracious 19th-century Acadia summer mansion, right in the middle of Northeast Harbor's shops and restaurants but set back behind its large garden and backing, in turn, onto its own small forest of firs. Beth and David White offer six spacious antiques-furnished rooms with private baths and four suites, one with a private entrance and tiled breakfast area with a microwave, small sink, and fridge; good for families. All rooms have phones and are equipped for cable TV (if wanted). Three large adjoining common rooms are sparely, elegantly furnished, hung with Audubon prints, and warmed with fireplaces. In the study is a big bay window filled with flowers. High-season rates: $135–195 for rooms ($205–255 for two-room suites) includes breakfast at a bakery/café across the street. Inquire about the new annex with five rooms on the mansion's rear acre.

In Southwest Harbor 04679

Penury Hall (244-7102; www.acadia.net/penury-n), Box 68, Main Street. Open year-round. An attractive village house with three guest rooms (private baths), all nicely decorated with interesting art and tempting reading material. This was the first B&B on the island. Toby and Gretchen Strong take their job as hosts seriously. Breakfast includes a choice of eggs Benedict, blueberry pancakes, or a "penurious omelet." $95 May through October also includes modest use of the fridge and laundry facilities, library and music, games (they play backgammon for blood); also a canoe and sauna. Guests receive feline welcomes from Widget and Patches.

The Birches (244-5182; www.acadia.net/birches), Fernald Point Road, P.O. Box 178. Open year-round. "Great-Grandma bought these 8 acres for $50 and for another $50 she could have had 20 more," Dick Homer quips. The Homer home, built in 1916, commands a water view from its spacious paneled living room and ample grounds (which include a croquet court). The guest rooms are furnished in family antiques (private baths), and you feel like a guest in a gracious but informal home. $105–115 includes a full breakfast.

The Island House (244-5180), Box 1006. Open all year. Across from the harbor, this large 1850s house was part of a vanished hotel (ask to see the scrapbook). Ann and Charlie Bradford offer four double rooms with two shared baths, also an attractive efficiency apartment with a loft in the carriage house, large enough for a family of four. $95–145 double in high season includes a breakfast that might be fresh fruit crêpes or eggs Florentine; 2-night minimum in July and August; less off-season.

The Inn at Southwest (244-3835; www.innatsouthwest.com), P.O. Box 593, Main Street. Open May through October. Built in 1884 as a high-Victorian-style annex to a now-vanished hotel. A carved fireplace with couches grouped around it is the heart of the house. Of the nine guest rooms, all with private baths and named for lighthouses, we particularly like Moose Peak, decorated in deep rose with a chapel-style window and a window seat. Innkeeper Jill Lewis obviously enjoys preparing breakfasts, such as crab potato bake with poached pears; $95–145 per couple in high season; from $65 in shoulder seasons.

Lindenwood Inn (244-5335; 1-800-307-5335; www.lindenwoodinn.com), 118 Clark Point Road, Box 1328. Open all year. A turn-of-the-20th-century sea captain's home set by the harbor among stately linden trees, this is a pleasing fusion of old and new. Australian-born owner Jim Kind has a sure decorating touch, reflected in the rich colors of rooms and intriguing artwork. Many of the nine rooms (all private baths) have water views, as do the six housekeeping units with balconies and fireplaces in the annex. There are three cottages, one at water's edge. The heated pool and hot tub are appreciated after hiking or biking. A full breakfast is served in the paneled dining room, where the fire is lit most mornings. $95–255 double in-season; $75–195 in low; $20 per extra person.

The Kingsleigh Inn (244-5302; www.kingsleighinn.com), 373 Main Street. Open year-round. The check-in desk is the counter of a country kitchen, the living room has a wood-burning fireplace; wicker chairs fill the wraparound porch. We would opt Room 5 or Room 3, both with balconies overlooking the harbor. A three-room suite on the third floor has a fireplace and a telescope, positioned in a turret window. Hosts Ken and Cyd Collins are both hikers who enjoy sharing their knowledge of Acadia trails. They serve a candlelit breakfast: homemade granola, freshly baked pastries, plus the day's specials, which might include ricotta-filled crêpes or lemon French toast with warm Maine blueberry sauce. In-season $95–125; $210 for the suite.

Heron House (244-0221; www.acadia.net/heronhouse), 1 Fernald Point Road. Open year-round. Sue and Bob Bonkowski offer three pleasant guest rooms with private baths. Guests are welcome to use the living room and den and to enjoy the large greenhouse off the kitchen; the grounds include a flower garden and small pond, resident ducks and geese, and a pet seagull named Mo. $95–105 depending on season ($15 per extra person), includes a full breakfast served family-style. Sue's reputation as a chef is celebrated locally, and Saturday-night dinner is served (open to the public; see *Dining Out*).

In Bass Harbor 04653

Pointy Head Inn and Antiques (244-7261), HC 33, Box 2A. Open late May through late fall. This 1780 sea captain's home on Route 102A overlooks the harbor. Doris and Warren Townsend offer six guest rooms, some with views of water, mountains, or both, two with private baths, the rest sharing baths. "Mature" children only. An antiques shop with wood carvings by Warren is on the premises. $50–120 per room includes a full breakfast; $20 per extra person.

The Willows at Bass Harbor (244-0512; www.acadia.net/willows), P.O. Box 393. Built recently as a B&B, this attractive house and guest rooms have private baths, phones, and cable TV/VCRs, some with gas fireplaces. A full breakfast is served on the hand-hewn dining room table by the fireplace or on the porch. The 3-acre property has water views and a full-sized championship croquet lawn. $85–165 per night; a two-bedroom rental cottage is $750–1,385.

Bass Harbor Inn (244-5157), P.O. Box 326. Open May through October. In an 1860 house with harbor views, within walking distance of village restaurants, Barbara and Alan Graff offer eight rooms ranging from doubles with shared baths to a top-floor studio with kitchenette. One room with half bath has a fireplace. $65–110 in-season, $45–90 off-season; includes breakfast.

✒ **Bass Harbor Cottages and Country Inn** (244-3460), Route 102A, P.O. Box 40. Open year-round. This is a family find. The inn itself is a friendly, informal old house, and guest rooms have private baths and fridges; one has a full kitchen. The cottages vary in size but all have water views, kitchens, and decks; the carriage house accommodates six. Guest rooms and cottages start at $85 in high season; cottages are available by the day when not rented. $700–1,400 weekly (the high end is for six people) in high season; in winter from $500, depending on cottage and week. In winter the room rates start at $50, and the inn caters to cross-country skiers.

Elsewhere

✒ **West of Eden** (244-9695; www.acadia.net/westofeden.net), P.O. Box 65, Route 102 and Kelleytown Road, Seal Cove 04695. Open May through mid-October. The only place to stay in the quietest corner of the "Quiet Side." The 1872 farmhouse is right on Route 102, but it's surrounded by gardens. The three upstairs rooms are light and airy; Room 3 is especially large and inviting, with a queen-sized bed, a private bath, a skylight, and a sleeping loft with futons—good for a family. Regina Ploucquet and George Urbanneck keep a vegetarian kitchen; breakfasts include home-made granola and sweet potato pancakes. $55–75 single, $70–90 double, $10 per extra child, $20 per extra adult.

MOTEL

🐾😺✒**Harbor View Motel & Cottages** (244-5031; 800-538-6463), P.O. Box 701, Southwest Harbor 04679. Open mid-May through mid-October. Lorraine and Joe Saunders have owned this pleasant 20-unit motel for 34 years. It's hidden down by the harbor. In July and August the nine rooms with decks right on the water are $90–98, while others are $63–75; in September rooms are $70–77 on the water, $48–60 otherwise, less for solo travelers and by the week. A third-floor apartment and seven cottages are available by the week ($375–895, depending on the size and week). A continental breakfast is served in the cheerful lobby, and the landscaped grounds overlook the harbor.

OTHER LODGING

✒ **Appalachian Mountain Club's Echo Lake Camp** (244-3747), AMC/Echo Lake Camp, Mount Desert 04660. Open late June through August. Accommodations are platform tents; family-style meals are served in a central hall. There is a rustic library and reading room, and an indoor game room. The focus, however, is outdoors: There are boats for use on the lake, daily hikes, and evening activities. Reservations should be made on April 1. Rates for the minimum 1-week stay (Saturday to Saturday) are inexpensive per person but add up for a family. All meals included. For a brochure, contact the AMC, 5 Joy Street, Boston, MA 02108.

COTTAGES AND EFFICIENCIES
Both chambers of commerce listed under *Guidance* keep and publish lists.

WHERE TO EAT

DINING OUT
Seaweed Café (244-0572), 146 Seawall Road, Southwest Harbor. Open most of the year, nightly in-season; otherwise, Tuesday through Saturday. Reservations a must. A winner. Well-known local chef Bill Morrison uses natural local ingredients to prepare vegetarian and Oriental dishes. You might begin with a seaweed salad with miso dressing or mussels in sake, Thai curry with cilantro and lime, or a variety of sushi rolls. Entrées range from a noodle dish ($12.40) to a seared five-spice duck breast served with black currant sauce and Thai black rice ($21). BYOB.

Fiddlers' Green (244-9416), 411 Main Street, Southwest Harbor. Reservations recommended. Open for dinner nightly May through October. Chef-owner Derek Wilbur changes the menu frequently, but a staple is "Fiddlers' Own Trio": three oversized free-form raviolis, variously stuffed, in a ginger-curry-coconut sauce ($21.75).

Redfield's (276-5283), Main Street, Northeast Harbor. Open most of the year, for dinner daily in summer, weekends in the off-season. Reservations a must. Chef Scott Redfield's trendy café (seating just 25 at a time) is *the* place to dine in Northeast Harbor. You might begin with sautéed lobster meat with cream sauce in pastry followed by grilled veal rib chop with wild mushroom glaze. Entrées $22–28.

XYZ Restaurant & Gallery (244-5221), Shore Road, Manset. Open May through Columbus Day nightly in summer for dinner; Friday and Saturday off-season. Reservations suggested. Billed as "classical food from the Mexican interior," the fare is authentic and good. Entrées change constantly but always include pork and chicken dishes, and are all $16. Across the road from the water, decorated in the colors of the Mexican flag and hung with folk art.

The Preble Grill (244-3034), 14 Clark Point Road, Southwest Harbor. Open 5–10. Reservations suggested. Billed as regional cuisine with a Mediterranean touch, the à la carte menu usually includes entrées ranging from manicotti filled with spinach, caramelized onions, and much more ($13.95) to rack of (Australian) lamb ($17.95).

Islesford Dock (244-7494), Little Cranberry Island. Open mid-June through Labor Day. Destination dining. Cynthia and Dan Lief's restaurant, sited right at the island dock, serves lunch (11–3) but it's really the place to watch the sun set behind the entire line of Mount Desert's mountains. The Liefs grow their herbs and tomatoes, and secure most of their seafood and produce within a boat ride of their dock. Specialties include nicely seasoned steamed mahogany quahogs, clams, or mussels, also tuna and salmon. Crabcakes are the big seller, and the menu also includes hamburgers and pasta. A Summer Night's Dream is a cold plate of lobster tail, crab claws, locally smoked salmon, and salmon tartare ($21). For lunch, try the lobster club sandwich with homemade carrot chips (that's what Mrs. Astor was having on our last visit). Sunday brunch is also special, and we can vouch for this venue as magical for a wedding reception. See *Boat Excursions* under *To Do* and **Little Cranberry** under *To See*.

The Claremont (244-5036), Clark Point Road, Southwest Harbor. Open for dinner late June through Columbus Day; lunch at **The Boathouse** (see *Eating Out*), mid-July through August. Also the place for a drink before dinner, with a view that's as spectacular as any on the island. In the handsome dining room, recently redone in deep rose, most tables have some water view, and both food and service are traditional (jacket and tie are required). Dinner entrées might range from fresh lemon fettuccine tossed with grape tomatoes, chanterelle mushrooms, baby broccoli, and Swiss chard to seafood paella with lobster, scallops, mussels, squid, and shrimp with saffron rice cake. Entrées $16–23.

Asticou Inn (276-3344), Route 3, Northeast Harbor. Open mid-May through mid-October for breakfast, lunch, and dinner. The Thursday-night buffet and dance is an island tradition. Grand old hotel atmosphere with a waterside formal dining room (window seats, however, are reserved for longtime guests). The kitchen is staffed by chefs and students of the Vermont-based New England Culinary Institute. Dinner entrées might include roasted rack of lamb and barley risotto with mushroom and artichoke compote ($16–27). Reservations required.

Chef Marc (244-4344), 326 Main Street, Southwest Harbor. An informal, colorful café atmosphere with a wide-ranging menu, from pasta to roasted duckling, boneless lamb loin, and a brace of quail stuffed with lobster. Beer and wine served. Entrées $13.95–23.50.

Heron House (244-0221), 1 Fernald Point Road, Southwest Harbor. Open July through Labor Day weekend for Saturday-night dinner only. Reservations required. Sue Bonkowski is well known locally for these dinners, served in the greenhouse attached to her B&B (see *Lodging*). The menu changes nightly but might include haddock and mussels in bell pepper confetti and saffron broth with a basmati-lentil pilaf and sautéed spaghetti squash ($16.50). BYOB.

Also see **The Burning Tree** under *Dining Out* in "Bar Harbor and Ellsworth."

LOBSTER POUNDS

Thurston's Lobster Pound (244-7600), Steamboat Wharf Road, Bernard.

CHRISTINA TREE

Thurston's Lobster Pound

Open Memorial Day through September daily 11–8:30. Our favorite. Weatherproofed, on a working wharf overlooking Bass Harbor. Fresh and tender as lobster can be, plus corn and pie, also seafood stew, sandwiches, chowder. Wine and beer.

Beal's Lobster Pier (244-7178; 244-3202), Clark Point Road, Southwest Harbor. Dock dining (also a weatherproofed area). Crabmeat rolls, chowder, fresh fish specialties, and lobster. Hopefully Beal's will stop charging for butter; that seems a bit much. (Both pounds pack and ship.)

EATING OUT

The Boathouse at the Claremont Hotel (244-3512), Clark Point Road, Southwest Harbor. Open July and August; serving lunch until 2 PM. Location, location! The view from this informal dockside facility on the grounds of the island's oldest hotel arguably offers the island's best view, east across the mouth of Somes Sound with Acadia's mountains rising beyond. Sandwiches, salads, and burgers; also good for drinks at sunset.

Little Notch Café (244-3357), 340 Main Street, Southwest Harbor. Open year-round 11–8 except Sundays in October, closed weekends off-season. Specializing in freshly made soups and sandwiches like grilled tuna salad with cheddar on wheat. Cheese, fresh-roasted coffee blends. Limited seating; take-out.

Docksider (276-3965), Sea Street, Northeast Harbor. Open 11–9. Bigger than it looks, with a no-frills, knotty-pine interior, amazingly efficient, friendly waitresses, and great chowder and Maine crabcakes; also salads, burgers, clam rolls, and a shore dinner. Wine and beer; lunch menu all day; early-bird specials 4:30–6. This little landmark, owned since 1979 by sisters Brenda and Gail Webber, never lets you down.

Seafood Ketch (244-7463), on Bass Harbor. Open mid-May through mid-

October, 11 AM–9:30 PM daily. Lisa, Stuart, and Ed Branch work hard to make this place special. Known for homemade breads and desserts, and fresh, fresh seafood. Dinner specialties include baked lobster-seafood casserole and baked halibut with lobster sauce; luncheon fare includes burgers, BLTs, and crabmeat rolls. Dinner entrées $12.95–16.95.

✎ **DuMuro's Top of the Hill Restaurant** (244-0033), Route 102 north of Southwest Harbor. Open seasonally. We have had only good reports about this family-run and -geared place with a very reasonably priced menu ranging from fried chicken and salad plates to mussels marinara over linguine. Early-bird specials.

🐾✎ **The Deacon Seat** (244-9229), Clark Point Road, Southwest Harbor. Open daily 5 AM–4:30 PM except Sunday. Good for breakfast, and the village gathering spot. A choice of 22 sandwiches for picnics.

Eat-a-Pita (244-4344), 326 Main Street, Southwest Harbor. Open Monday through Saturday for breakfast (at 7), and lunch; at dinner this becomes **Chef Marc** (see *Dining Out*). A lively, bright café with soups, salads and pastas, specialty coffees, and pastries.

🐾✎ **Keenan's Restaurant** (244-3403), junction of Route 102 and Route 102A. Open for dinner year-round, in summer Tuesday through Sunday, in winter Thursday through Sunday. Funky exterior, casual hideaway atmosphere but up for sale at this writing, so who knows if the legendary seafood gumbo and barbecued back ribs will be there when you read this. Worth checking.

ENTERTAINMENT

The Claremont Hotel Thursday Evening Lecture Series (244-5036), Claremont Road, Southwest Harbor. July and August. An impressive array of authorities speak on a variety of topics. The millennium season began with a slide lecture on "American Artists at the Seaside"; subsequent subjects included jazz, mountain climbing, and Mount Desert history. All lectures are at 8:30, the hour also of the **Tuesday Evening Music Series** (August only).

MUSIC

Mount Desert Festival of Chamber Music (276-3988), Neighborhood House, Main Street, Northeast Harbor. A series of six concerts presented for more than 35 seasons mid-July through mid-August.

THEATER

Acadia Repertory Theatre (244-7260), Route 102, Somesville. Performances during July and August, Tuesday through Sunday at 8:15 PM; Sunday matinees at 2. A regional repertory theater group performs in the Somesville Masonic Hall, usually presenting a half-dozen popular plays in the course of the season.

Deck House Cabaret Theatre (244-5044), Great Harbor Marina, Southwest Harbor. July and August. A dining/entertainment landmark for

Wicker is the specialty at E. L. Higgins Antiques.

almost 30 years, now housed in a refurbished sardine-canning factory, a
great spot with an excellent view and menu; nightly cabaret theater by
the serving staff, beginning at 8:30 PM. Entertainment cover. Full bar.
Reservations are a must.

SELECTIVE SHOPPING

In Somesville
Port in a Storm Bookstore (244-4114), Route 102. Open year-round,
   Monday through Saturday 9:30–5:30 and Sunday 1–5. A 19th-century
   general-store building with water views, two floors of books, disks and
   cassettes, soft music, reading nooks, coffee. Linda Lewis and Marilyn
   Mays have created a real oasis for book lovers.
Along Main Street in Northeast Harbor
The quality of the artwork showcased in this small yachting haven is amazing. **The Wingspread Gallery** (276-3910) has changing exhibits in the
   main gallery and a selection by well-established artists like Rockwell
   Kent (for a mere $40,000). **Redfield Artisans Gallery** (276-3609) of-
   fers a mix of high-end and affordable works, and **A. J. Buechee Fine
   Art** (244-5353) shows 19th- and 20th-century paintings by established
   artists. **Shaw Contemporary Jewelry** (276-5000), 100 Main Street,
   open year-round, is an outstanding shop featuring Sam Shaw's own
   work; check out the exquisite beach-stone jewelry.
In Southwest Harbor
Aylen & Son Jewelry, 320 Main Street. Open year-round. Peter Aylen
   fashions gold, silver, and Maine gemstone jewelry, and Judy Aylen's

hand-carved bead necklaces are distinctive.

Hot Flash Anny's (244-7323), 4 Clark Point Road. A stained-glass studio featuring one-of-a-kind pieces.

Sandcastle (244-4118), 360 Main Street. Ocean and nature gifts.

Carroll Drug Store (244-5588), just off Main Street at the north end of the village. A supermarket-sized store with a genuine general-store feel.

In Bernard

E. L. Higgins (244-3983) Bernard Road (the way to Thurston's), mid-April through mid-October, 10–5 or by appointment; an 1890s schoolhouse filled with Maine's largest stock of antique wicker (ask to see the coffin basket); also antique furniture, glassware, and Ruth Moore titles.

Nancy Neale Typecraft (244-5192), Steamboat Wharf Road (just beyond Thurston's on the harbor). Open June through October by chance or appointment. This is a mini-museum of printing memorabilia and offers authentic, antique wood printing type.

The Islands

Swans Island Blankets. Carolyn and John Grace, both former Boston lawyers, raise sheep and dye and weave their wool to make blankets that sell (priced from $525) as fast as they can produce them. Available at www.atlanticblanket.com as well as at their island showroom.

Also see **Little Cranberry Island** under *To See* for galleries and studios.

SPECIAL EVENTS

July: **Southwest Harbor Days**—crafts show, parade, sidewalk sales.

Early August: **Sweet Chariot Festival** on Swans Island. **Frenchboro Days** in Frenchboro.

Columbus Day weekend: **Octoberfest Food Festival,** Southwest Harbor.

EAST HANCOCK COUNTY

At the junction of Routes 3 and 1 in Ellsworth it's Route 3 that continues straight ahead and Route 1 that angles off abruptly, obviously the road less taken. Within a few miles you notice the absence of commercial clutter. Nowhere in Maine does the coast change as abruptly as along this rim of Frenchman Bay.

On the western side is Mount Desert Island with busy Bar Harbor, magnet for everyone from everywhere. The northern and eastern shores are, however, a quiet, curving stretch of coves, tidal bays, and peninsulas, all with spectacular views of Acadia's high, rounded mountains. This is actually an old, now-quiet resort area with its own high mountains, hidden lakes, fishing villages, fine inns, and a rich cultural life.

In 1889 the Maine Central's Boston & Mount Desert Limited carried passengers in less than 8 hours from Boston's North Station to

Mount Desert Ferry, the name of the terminal in Hancock. Briefly billed as the fastest train in New England, it connected with ferries to several points on this far side of Frenchman Bay, as well as Bar Harbor. That era's huge old summer hotels are long gone, and only the surviving summer colonies (in Sorrento, Grindstone Neck, and Hancock Point) evince steamboats and railroads.

The 29 miles along Frenchman Bay that begin on Route 1 at the Hancock/Sullivan bridge and loop around the Schoodic Peninsula to Prospect Harbor are a National Scenic Byway.

A new bridge spans the tidal Taunton River. Beyond it Route 1 shadows the curve of Frenchman Bay, offering spectacular views. Be sure to stop at the scenic turnout (the site of a former inn) just before Dunbar's Store.

It's said that on a clear day you can see Katahdin as well as the Acadia peaks from the top of Schoodic Mountain, some 20 miles inland, back up between Sullivan and Franklin and handy to swimming at Donnell Pond. Most travelers who come this far are, however, bound for the Schoodic Point loop, actually a part of Acadia National Park.

Schoodic is the name that has come to apply to the entire peninsula that forms the eastern side of Frenchman Bay. It's also known as the Gouldsboro Peninsula. In her 1958 book titled simply *The Peninsula*, Louise Dickinson Rich describes the area as "thirty thousand acres of granite, heath and shallow topsoil."

Positioned at the entrance to the park, Winter Harbor serves the old summer colony on adjacent Grindstone Neck. Prospect Harbor, at the eastern end of the park, is more of a fishing village, the site of one of Maine's last sardine-processing plants (Stinson Seafood) and of red-flashing Prospect Harbor Light. Corea, beyond on Sand Cove, is another much painted and photographed fishing village. The tiny village of Gouldsboro itself is just off Route 1.

Too many visitors simply day-trip to this area. Given the choice of attractive places to stay and to eat, to shop, and to hike—not to mention the kayaking and mountain biking and distinctive beauty of this area— East Hancock County should be viewed as a destination in its own right.

GUIDANCE

Schoodic Peninsula Chamber of Commerce (963-7658; 1-800-231-3008; www.acadia-schoodic.org), P.O. Box 381, Winter Harbor 04693; request the helpful pamphlet guide.

GETTING THERE

For a shortcut to Hancock from Bar Harbor, take Route 3 north to Route 204, posted for Lamoine State Park. Turn left onto Route 184 and then immediately right at the Marlboro Meeting House on Pleasant Creek Road and then left at the sign for Route 1 (Mud Creek Road). From points south, see *Getting There* in "Bar Harbor and Ellsworth."

TO SEE

SCENIC DRIVE
Acadia National Park: Schoodic Peninsula. Allow 2 to 3 hours. The park's 7.2-mile one-way shore drive begins beyond Winter Harbor (see map on page 364). **Frazer Point Picnic Area** (comfort station) is a good first stop, a place to unload bikes if you want to tour on two wheels. It's said to have been an Indian campsite for thousands of years.

A little more than 2.5 miles farther along, look for the unmarked, unpaved road on your left that leads up to **Schoodic Head,** where a short trail leads to a rocky summit, just 400 feet high but with long views.

The drive continues along Frenchman Bay and then bursts onto **Schoodic Point,** where the smooth rocks thrust into the Atlantic. On sunny days tidal pools invite clambering, but on stormy days surf and spray can shoot as high as 40 feet. It's a popular spectacle, but beware of the surf, which can be deadly.

Bear right along the drive to the **Blueberry Hill Parking Area** (about a mile beyond Schoodic Point) with its views of Moose and Schoodic Islands. Note the trail to the top of a 180-foot promontory, **The Anvil.** Continue along the drive 2 more miles to Route 186 in the village of Birch Harbor.

TO DO

BIKING, SEA KAYAKING, AND FISHING
Moose Look Guide Service (963-7720), South Gouldsboro, offers guided fishing trips as well as rental canoes and kayaks. Danny Mitchell is as comfortable on as off the water and familiar with all the best places to both paddle and fish. Rental bikes, canoes and kayaks, also rowboats and pedal boats. We can vouch for Danny's guided sunset tour on Frenchman Bay. Inquire about overnight fishing and kayak-camping trips.

BOAT EXCURSION
Lobster boat *Lulu* (963-2341) offers sight-seeing/storytelling rides on Frenchman Bay from Hancock Marine at Hancock Point.

GOLF
Grindstone Neck Golf Course (963-7760), Gerrishville. A nine-hole course; open to the public.

HIKING
Schoodic Mountain, off Route 183 north of Sullivan, provides one of eastern Maine's most spectacular hikes, with 360-degree views (see introduction to East Hancock County). The Bureau of Parks and Lands (287-5936) has improved the parking area and trail system here. Take the first left (it's unpaved) after crossing the railroad tracks on Route 183;

bear left at the Y and in 0.8 mile bear right to the parking lot. The hike to the top of Schoodic Mountain (1,069 feet) should take around 45 minutes; a marked trail from the summit leads down to sandy Schoodic Beach at the southern end of **Donnell Pond** (good swimming and a half-dozen primitive campsites); return to the parking lot on the old road that's now a footpath (a half mile). From the same parking lot, you can also follow a dirt path down to Donnell Pond or hike to the bluffs on Black Mountain, a mesmerizingly beautiful hike with summit views north to Tunk Lake and east across Washington Country. Another trail descends to Schoodic Beach. This is now part of 14,000 acres known as Donnell Pond Public Preserved Land, which also includes Tunk and Spring River Lakes and primitive campsites.

SWIMMING
The clearest water and softest sand we have found in the area are at **Molasses Pond** in Eastbrook. Also see **Donnell Pond** under *Hiking*.

LODGING

🐾 **Le Domaine** (422-3395/3916; 1-800-554-8498; www.ledomaine.com), HC 77, Box 496, Hancock 04640. Best known for its dining room (see *Dining Out*), this elegant little French Provençal–style inn has recently reduced its rooms to create three luxurious rooms and three exceptional suites. All face the gardens and lawns that stretch back 80 acres, with paths through the woods leading to a tranquil trout pond. Chef-owner Nicole Purslow grew up in this house, helping her mother—who had fled France during World War II—in the kitchen of Maine's first genuine French restaurant, for which she eventually assumed responsibility, creating upstairs guest rooms. Until recently, however, the rooms remained an afterthought. No longer. Provençal antiques, fabrics, original paintings, and small niceties (like bowls of lavender) create real charm and a high comfort level. Bathrooms have porcelain soaking tubs and separate showers as well as heated towel racks, lighted vanity mirrors, and fluffy towels; the suites have gas fireplaces and cathedral ceilings, and all rooms have phones, bed lights, and access to the balconies on which you can enjoy the flakiest of croissants with home-made honey and jam and French roast coffee. An atttractive new sitting area for guests, with a gas fireplace and French windows on the garden, has also been added. Pets are accepted for an additional charge. Rates: $180 per room B&B, $265 per couple MAP (good value given the price of two dinners); suites are $365 B&B, $350 MAP per couple.

✎ **Crocker House Country Inn** (422-6806; www.acadia.net/crocker), Hancock Point 04640. Open daily mid-April through Columbus Day, weekends (Thursday through Sunday) mid-November to New Year's Eve. The three-story, gray-shingled 1880s inn has 11 guest rooms, 9 in the inn itself and 2 on the second floor of the carriage house, including a big room

Acadia Mountains from across Frenchman Bay

that's good for families. All rooms have private baths (new and nicely done with natural woods) and country antiques, quilts, and stenciling. Richard and Elizabeth Malaby have been the innkeepers since 1980, and there is an easy, unpretentious air to this inn. The common rooms are spacious, and there's more lounging space on the ground floor of the carriage barn near the hot tub. The second smallest post office in the United States sits across the road next to the tennis courts, and the octagonal library is a short walk. The nearby dock is maintained by the Hancock Improvement Association. Breakfast and dinner are served in the dining room, which is open to the public (see *Dining Out*). $110–145 in August, includes a full breakfast; less in late June and July, still less before June 15 and after October 15. Moorings are available and a few touring bikes are kept for guests.

Island View Inn (422-3031; www.maineus.com/islandview), HCR 32, Box 24, Sullivan Harbor 04664. Open Memorial Day through mid-October. This is a spacious, gracious, turn-of-the-20th-century summer "cottage" set well back from Route 1 with splendid views of Frenchman Bay and the mountains on Mount Desert. Evelyn and Sarah Joost offer seven guest rooms, all with private baths and four with water views. All are nicely decorated, and there is ample and comfortable common space; a full breakfast is included. $90–125 in-season, $85–110 in shoulder seasons; $15 per extra person. An 18-foot sailboat is available for guests to rent, and a canoe and rowboat are available at no charge.

Sullivan Harbor Farm (422-3735; 1-800-422-4014), Route 1, Sullivan Harbor 04664. Built in 1820 by Captain James Urann, who launched his vessels from the shingle beach across the road. The house, overlooking Frenchman Bay, is cheerfully, tastefully decorated and includes a library and an enclosed porch on which breakfast is served. The three guest rooms with double beds are simply, sparely furnished with exquisite taste and sense of color; private baths ($95). Cupcake, a particularly bright year-round cottage with working fireplaces, also has water views and can sleep six ($850 per week, less off-season). Another cottage, Milo, sleeps four ($650 per week). A canoe is available, and hosts Joel Frantzman and Leslie Harlow delight in tuning guests in to local hiking, kayaking, biking, and paddling possibilities. They also smoke salmon on the premises (see *Selective Shopping—Special Shops*).

🖉♿ **Oceanside Meadows Inn** (963-5557; www.oceaninn.com), P.O. Box 90, Prospect Harbor 04669. Open May through October, off-season by special arrangement. This 200-acre property/nature preserve includes an 1860s sea captain's home and neighboring 1830 farmhouse overlooking well-named Sand Cove. Sonja Sundaram and Ben Walter (who met at an environmental research center in Bermuda) have spiffed up the guest rooms (there are seven in each building, including several suites good for small families) and gracious common rooms. The farmhouse, in particular, lends itself to rental as a whole; ideal for family reunions. The meadows and woods are webbed with trails leading to a salt marsh and a rehabbed open-timbered barn used as a theater, conference, or wedding reception center. $115–145 during July and August, includes a three-course breakfast. See *Entertainment* for details about the Oceanside Meadows Institute for the Arts and Sciences.

The Black Duck (963-2689; www.blackduck.com), P.O. Box 39, Corea 04624. Overlooking picturesque Corea Harbor. Barry Canner and Robert Travers offer four guest rooms, comfortably furnished with antiques, contemporary art, and Oriental rugs. Common areas display collections of antique toys and lamps, and the living room has a cozy fireplace. Twelve acres of land and waterfront property invite hiking, photography, artistic pursuits, and quiet relaxation. Two dogs, two cats, and Dolly the potbellied pig will welcome you, so please leave your pets at home. Two waterfront cottages are also available. $80–155.

Sunset House Bed & Breakfast (963-7156; 1-800-233-7156; www.sunset housebnb.com), Route 186, West Gouldsboro 04607. Open year-round. Carl and Kathy Johnson's Victorian farmhouse offers six attractive guest rooms, four with private baths. The views are of Flanders Bay on one side and of Jones Pond, good for swimming, fishing, and canoeing, on the other. Common space includes a double parlor and sunporch as well as a dining room, where ample breakfasts are served. $79–99, less in winter.

Bluff House Inn (963-7805; www.bluffinn.com), Route 186, South Gouldsboro 04607. This is a modern lodge with a dining room (open to the public in summer) featuring floor-to-ceiling windows overlooking the water and a comfortable sitting area/lobby behind it. The eight guest rooms line the upstairs hall; only the two at the end have water views. It's set off by itself, above the pink granite shore from which you can launch a kayak onto Frenchman Bay. The availability of dinner is a real plus, and guests tell us the food is good. $59.50–86.50 includes breakfast; dinner is $15, BYOB.

Main Stay Inn & Cottages (963-2601; www.awa-web.com/stayinn), Main and Newman Streets, Winter Harbor 04693. Open all year in downtown Winter Harbor. Three clean and comfortable rooms with private baths (showers) and several housekeeping units ranging from a two-bedroom suite on the second floor and a ground-level unit with a fireplace and its own entrance. $50 double per room, $60–79 for suites and other units. Inquire about the cottage on Molasses Pond (see *To Do—Swimming*).

COTTAGES
Albee's Shoreline Cottages (963-2336; 1-800-963-2336; www.theshore house.com), Route 186, Prospect Harbor 04669. Open Memorial Day through mid-October. The 10 waterside cottages are classic old Maine motor-court vintage, but each has been painstakingly rehabbed and all but 4 are right on the water; all have woodstoves or fireplaces. Larry Caldwell and Richard Rieth enjoy orienting guests to the best of what's around. $55–82 per night, $357–546 per week.

Black Duck Properties (963-7495) in Corea handles local seasonal rentals. "Maine Guide to Camp & Cottage Rentals," free from the **Maine Tourism Association** (623-0363), lists rentals in this area.

CAMPGROUND
Ocean Woods Campground (963-7194), P.O. Box 111, Birch Harbor 04613. Open early May through late October. Wooded, mostly oceanside campsites, some with hook-ups, some wilderness; hot showers.

WHERE TO EAT

DINING OUT
Le Domaine (422-3395), Route 1, Hancock (9 miles east of Ellsworth). Open early June through Thanksgiving, Tuesday through Saturday 6–9 PM. Reservations recommended. Nicole Purslow, *propriétaire et chef,* prepares highly rated French cuisine. Nicole's mother, French chef Marianne Purslow-Dumas, established the restaurant in the 1940s, near the conducting school founded by a relative, Pierre Monteux (see *Entertainment*). Most summer residents on MDI know the shortcut to Le Domaine (see *Getting There*). Just 14 tables are nicely spaced in the softly lit dining rooms, decorated in Provençal prints with fresh flowers

from the cutting garden and frequently a glowing fire, reflected in gleaming wood and copper. The meal might begin with the legendery pâté de foie maison or mussels lightly sautéed with butter, garlic, herbs, and almonds. The choice of entrées might include French-cut hanger steaks pan-seared and served with a green peppercorn demiglaze sauce and two quail roasted with juniper berries and whole garlic. Even the bread pudding is spectacular: bread, eggs, rum-soaked currants, and cream, baked in a mold and surrounded by caramel. The wine list numbers 5,000 bottles. The menu is à la carte with appetizers around $8 and entrées $22–28.

Crocker House Country Inn (422-6806), Hancock Point. Open nightly for dinner, 5:30–9. A pleasant country-inn atmosphere and varied menu; the specialty is Crocker House scallops, sautéed with mushrooms, scallions, garlic, and tomatoes with lemon and wine sauce ($18.95). In summer request the sunporch. All entrées come with homemade bread, salad, vegetables, and a choice of rice pilaf or potatoes dauphinois. Sunday brunch is big here, as are desserts. Entrées $17.50–23.25.

Chippers (422-8238), Route 1, Hancock. Open for dinner Tuesday through Saturday 5–10, Sunday 4–8. Country casual but highly rated, with entrées ranging from lemon haddock ($13.95) to rack of lamb ($21.95).

Fisherman's Inn Restaurant (963-5585), 7 Newman Street, Winter Harbor. Open April to October, then weekends most of the year, dinner only; 4:30–9. The new chef-owner is Carl Johnson, previously at the Bar Harbor Inn. Seafood is the specialty, with entrées like fresh haddock with crabmeat dressing and local cod wrapped in smoked salmon slices, oven-broiled. Salad, vegetable, and starch are included in the entrée prices ($13.95–18.95). Early-bird specials 4:30–5:30.

Also see **Kitchen Garden Restaurant** under *Dining Out* in "The Atlantic Coast: Steuben to Campobello" (it's just over the county line in Steuben).

LOBSTER POUNDS

Tidal Falls Lobster Pound (422-6818), 0.5 mile off Route 1 (take East Side Road), Hancock. For sale at this writing, but hopefully it will still be open June through Labor Day 5–9. Sited by the reversing falls. Bring your own wine, salad, and dessert and feast on steamers, lobster, mussels, crabs, and the view. There's a weatherproofed pavilion.

West Bay Lobsters in the Rough (963-7021), Route 186, north of Prospect Harbor. Look for the greenhouses. Seasonal. Joan and Vince Smirz let you pick your own lobster, then they serve it up with steamers and local corn, slaw, and beans that are baked daily.

EATING OUT

Chase's Restaurant (963-7171), 193 Main Street, Winter Harbor. Open all year for all three meals. A convenient, no-nonsense eatery on Route 186 near the entrance to the park. Booths, salad bar, fried lobsters and clams, good chowder; will pack a picnic.

J. M. Gerrish (963-5575), 352 Main Street, Winter Harbor. Open May through October for breakfast, lunch, and ice cream. An old-fashioned ice cream parlor with a marble counter and scattering of tables. A social center for the summer community, also selling books and Maine gifts, cards, and penny candy.

Downeast Deli (963-2700), corner Routes 186 and 195, Prospect Harbor. Open 8–8:30. Huge New York deli sandwiches, along with pizza and garden salads. Inquire about picnic spots.

ENTERTAINMENT

Pierre Monteux Memorial Concert Hall (546-4495), Hancock, is the setting for a series of June and July chamber music concerts, presented by faculty and students at the respected Pierre Monteux School for Conductors.

Oceanside Meadows Institute for the Arts and Sciences (963-5557; www.oceaninn.org), staged in a renovated, open-beamed barn behind the Oceanside Meadows Inn, Route 195, Corea. May through September: a series of lectures and concerts and other performances, from gospel music and light opera to jazz and chamber music.

✎ **Farmstead Barn** (422-3615), Tuesdays in July and August. Phone for performance times. Free live shows for children.

SELECTIVE SHOPPING

ART AND FINE CRAFTS GALLERIES

Barter Family Gallery and Shop (422-3190), Franklin. Open mid-May through December, Monday through Saturday 9–5, or by appointment. Posted from Route 1 at Sullivan's common (it's 2.5 miles). "We never get busy here," Priscilla Barter will tell you. Never mind that her husband's paintings hang in museums and fetch big money in the best galleries. This gallery, attached to the small house that Barter built and in which the couple raised seven children, is easily the most colorful in Maine, and still remote enough to keep browsers and buyers to a trickle. Any one of Barter's primitive, bold paintings could brighten a large, empty room; but here, added to dozens of distinctive Barter mountains, houses, and harbors are off-the-wall pieces, wood sculptures, and Barter-made furniture. Barter himself is probably out back in the sculpting (as opposed to sculpture) garden. The gallery also features Priscilla's braided rugs.

Hog Bay Pottery (565-2282), 4 miles north of Route 1 on Route 200, Franklin. Susanne Grosjean's award-winning rugs and the distinctive table and ovenware by Charles Grosjean.

Spring Woods Gallery (442-3007), Route 200 (off Route 1), Sullivan. Open daily 10–5 except Sunday. This gallery represents five members of the Breeden family. It features fine arts, jewelry, and sculpture.

Gull Rock Pottery (422-3990), Eastside Road (1.5 miles off Route 1), Hancock. Open year-round, Monday through Saturday. Torj and Kurt Wray wheel-throw functional blue-and-white stoneware with hand-brushed designs. The gallery setting is beautiful, right on the bay.

Lunaform (422-0923), marked from Route 1 at the Sullivan common. Open year-round, Monday through Friday 9:30–4:30. Striking hand-made, steel-reinforced concrete garden urns (some are huge) as well as pots and planters are made in this former granite quarry.

U.S. Bells (963-7184), Route 186, Prospect Harbor. Open daily in summer, by appointment off-season. Richard Fisher creates (designs and casts) bells that form musical sculptures.

Lee Art Glass Studio (963-7004), Main Street, Winter Harbor. It's diffi-cult to describe this fused-glass tableware, which incorporates ground enamels and crochet doilies or stencils. It works.

SPECIAL SHOPS

✎ **Hattie's Shed at Darthia Farm** (963-7771), 520 West Bay Road (marked from Route 1), Gouldsboro. Open June through September. A 133-acre organic farm with resident sheep, Scottish Highland cattle, turkeys, sheep, chickens, and bees. In July and August farm tours are offered Tuesday and Thursday at 2. The farm stand featues produce, justly famed for its vinegars, jams, salsas, and cheeses (there's even crème fraîche); **Hattie's Shed,** a weaving shop also at the farm, features coats, jackets, scarves, and shawls. It also sells owner Cynthia Thayer's newest novel, *A Certain Slant of Light* (St. Martin's Press).

Sullivan Harbor Salmon (422-3735), Route 1, Sullivan Harbor. The salmon is local, and visitors are welcome to tour the smokehouse in which the fish are cured in a blend of salt and brown sugar, then cold-smoked in the traditional Scottish way, using hickory and applewood.

Bartlett Maine Estate Winery (546-2408), off Route 1, Gouldsboro. Open June through mid-October, Monday through Saturday 10–5; other times by appointment. Maine's first winery and its most presti-gious, specializing in blueberry, apple, and pear wines; also limited rasp-berry, strawberry, and honey dessert wines. An attractive complex in the pines, just off Route 1. Guided tours, tasting rooms, and gift packs. Call for tour times.

SPECIAL EVENTS

May: **Annual Trade Day and Benefit Auction**—peninsula-wide yard sales climaxed by an auction at the Winter Harbor Grammar School.

August: **Schoodic Arts Festival** (*first week*) features dozens of nominally priced workshops in a wide variety of arts and many performances at venues scattered throughout the Schoodic Peninsula. **Winter Harbor Lobster Festival** (*second Saturday*), Winter Harbor—includes road race, lobster feed, and lobster-boat races.

Washington County and the Quoddy Loop

The Atlantic Coast: Steuben to Campobello; Eastport and Cobscook Bay; Calais and the St. Croix Valley; St. Andrews and Grand Manan, New Brunswick

As Down East as you can get in this country, Washington County is a ruggedly beautiful and lonely land unto itself. Its 700-mile coast harbors some of the most dramatic cliffs and deepest coves—certainly the highest tides—on the eastern seaboard, but relatively few tourists. Lobster boats and trawlers still outnumber pleasure craft.

Created in 1789 by order of the General Court of Massachusetts, Washington County is as large as the states of Delaware and Rhode Island combined. Yet it is home to just 35,000 people, widely scattered among fishing villages, canning towns, logging outposts, Native American reservations, and saltwater farms. Many people (not just some) survive here by raking blueberries in August, making balsam wreaths in winter, and lobstering, clamming, digging sea worms, and diving for sea urchins the remainder of the year. Washington County supplies more than 80 percent of the country's wild blueberries.

Less than 10 percent of the visitors who get as far as Bar Harbor come this much farther. The only "groups" you see are scouting for American bald eagles or ospreys in the Moosehorn National Wildlife Refuge; for puffins, auks, and arctic terns on Machias Seal Island; or for whales in the Bay of Fundy. You may also see fishermen angling for landlocked salmon and smallmouth bass in the lakes.

Happily, word has begun to spread that you don't drop off the end of the world beyond Eastport or Campobello, even though since 1842—when a boundary was drawn across the face of Passamaquoddy Bay—New England maps have included only the Maine shore and Campobello Island (linked to Lubec, Maine, by a bridge), and Canadian maps have detailed only New Brunswick. In summer when the ferries are running, the crossing from either Eastport or Campobello to the resort town of St. Andrews, New Brunswick, is among the most scenic in the East. This circuit, which is best done driving one way and taking ferries the other, has come to be known as the Quoddy Loop. The drive is up along the St. Croix River to Calais, and the ferry trip involves transfer-

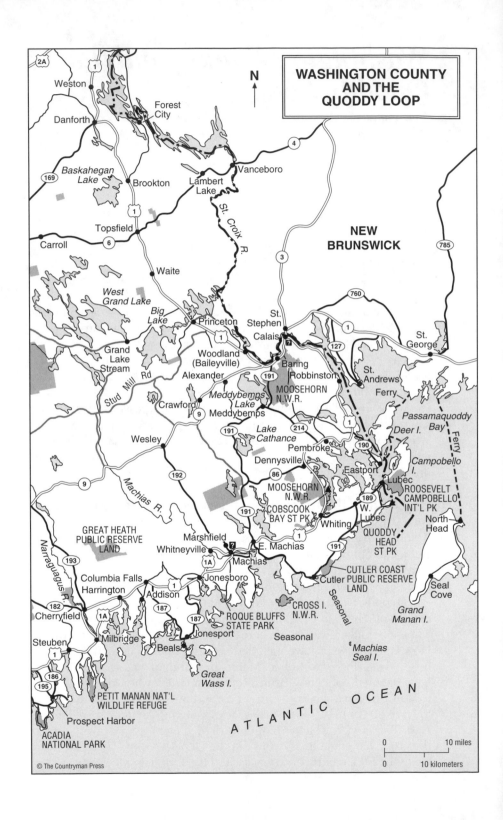

N

WASHINGTON COUNTY
AND THE
QUODDY LOOP

2A
Weston
Forest
City
Danforth
Brookton
169
Baskahegan
Lake
Vanceboro
4
1
Lambert
Lake
St. Croix R.
NEW
BRUNSWICK
785
Topsfield
6
Carroll
Waite
3
760
West
Grand Lake
Big
Lake
Princeton
St.
Stephen
Calais
1
St.
George
1
127
Grand
Lake
Stream
Woodland
(Baileyville)
Baring
Robbinston
St.
Andrews
Ferry
Stud Mill Rd
Alexander
191
MOOSEHORN
N.W.R.
Crawford
Meddybemps
Lake
Passamaquoddy
Bay
9
Meddybemps
Deer I.
Wesley
191
Lake
Cathance
214
190
Campobello
I.
192
Pembroke
Dennysville
86
Eastport
Ferry
9
MOOSEHORN
N.W.R.
Lubec
ROOSEVELT
CAMPOBELLO
INT'L PK
189
GREAT HEATH
PUBLIC RESERVE
LAND
191
COBSCOOK
BAY ST PK
Whiting
W.
Lubec
North
Head
Machias R.
1
QUODDY
HEAD
ST PK
Marshfield
Narraguagus R.
Whitneyville
1A
191
193
E. Machias
Machias
CUTLER COAST
PUBLIC RESERVE
LAND
Seal
Cove
Columbia Falls
Harrington
Addison
1
Jonesboro
Cutler
Seasonal
182
187
CROSS I.
N.W.R.
Grand
Manan I.
Cherryfield
1A
187
ROQUE BLUFFS
STATE PARK
Milbridge
Jonesport
Seasonal
Steuben
1
Beals
Machias
Seal I.
186
195
Great
Wass I.
ATLANTIC OCEAN
PETIT MANAN NAT'L
WILDLIFE REFUGE
Prospect Harbor
ACADIA
NATIONAL PARK
© The Countryman Press

0   10 miles

0   10 kilometers

ring from a small to a larger (free) Canadian ferry on Deer Island in the middle of Passamaquoddy Bay. Because St. Andrews itself probably offers a greater number and variety of "rooms" and dining than all Washington County combined and because the exchange rate (at this writing) favors Americans, it is a logical place to spend the night. We also include the magnificent island of Grand Manan, which lies off Maine's Bold Coast but is also part of New Brunswick, accessible from Blacks Harbour not far from St. Andrews.

For exploring purposes, Washington County is divided into four distinct regions: (1) the 60-mile stretch of Route 1 between Steuben and Lubec (with roughly 10 times as many miles of wandering coastline), an area for which Machias is the shopping, dining, and information center; (2) Eastport and Cobscook Bay, the area of the highest tides and an end-of-the-world feel (by water, Lubec and Eastport—both of which claim to be the country's easternmost community—are just 3 miles apart, but separated by 40 land miles); (3) Calais and the St. Croix Valley, including the lake-splotched backwoods and the fishermen's havens at Grand Lake Stream; and (4) St. Andrews and Grand Manan, New Brunswick.

Wherever you explore in Washington County—from the old sardine-canning towns of Eastport and Lubec to the coastal fishing villages of Jonesport and Cutler, and the even smaller villages on the immense inland lakes—you find a Maine you thought had disappeared decades ago. You are surprised by the beauty of old buildings such as the 18th-century Burnham Tavern in Machias and Ruggles House in Columbia Falls. You learn that the first naval battle of the Revolution was won by Machias men; that some local 18th-century women were buried in rum casks (because they were shipped home that way from the Caribbean); and that pirate Captain Richard Bellamy's loot is believed to be buried around Machias.

And if any proof were needed that this has always been one isolated piece of coast, there is Bailey's Mistake. Captain Bailey, it seems, wrecked his four-masted schooner one foggy night in a fine little bay 7 miles south of Lubec (where he should have put in). Considering the beauty of the spot and how far he was from the Boston shipowner, Bailey and his crew unpacked their cargo of lumber and settled right down on the shore. That was in 1830, and many of their descendants have had the sense to stay put.

Local historians will also tell you why Deer Island and Campobello now belong to Canada rather than to the United States. Daniel Webster, the story goes, drank a few too many toasts the night Lord Ashburton sailed him out to check the boundaries.

GUIDANCE

Washington County Promotions Board (255-3656; 1-800-377-9748), P.O. Box 679, Machias 04654; call for printed information. Click onto www.quoddyloop.com/sunrise.htm for natural and historical sights, and suggestions for hiking, kayaking, fishing. Copies of "Maine's Washington County," a free 60-page-plus guide to the entire county, are available locally or by request from Jay Hinson, P.O. Box 38, Robbinston 04671. There is no Washington County–wide information booth, but at the New Brunswick border in Calais the **Maine Tourism Association** maintains a full-service center (454-311) at 7 Union Street; open daily year-round. Also note chambers listed under *Guidance* in the areas they promote within the county.

GETTING THERE

By air: See *Getting There* in "Bar Harbor and Ellsworth," and "Bangor Area" under "The North Woods," for scheduled airline service. **Quoddy Air** (853-0997), based in Eastport, will pick up in any northeastern city and fly anywhere in Maine on demand (five passengers). Charter service is also available to the following airports: **Eastport Municipal** (853-2951), **Machias Valley** (255-8709), **Lubec Municipal** (733-5532), and **Princeton Municipal** (796-2744).

By bus: **Concord Trailways** (1-800-639-3317) and **Vermont Transit** (1-800-451-3292) both serve Bangor year-round; some summers Vermont Transit comes as close as Ellsworth.

By car: The fastest way is via I-95 to Bangor, then Route 1A north to Ellsworth, then Route 1. For coastal points east of Harrington, you save 9 miles by cutting inland on Route 182 from Hancock to Cherryfield. For eastern Washington County, take I-95 to Bangor, then the Airline Highway (Route 9) for 100 miles straight through the blueberry barrens and woods to Calais. The state maintains camping and picnic sites at intervals along this stretch, and food and lodging can be found in Beddington, Wesley, Alexander, and Baring.

GETTING AROUND

East Coast Ferries Ltd. (506-747-2159), based on Deer Island, serves both Campobello (45 minutes) and Eastport (30 minutes). Generally these run every hour from around 9 AM to around 7 PM, mid-June through mid-September, but call Stan Lord to check. The Campobello ferry takes 15 cars, and the Eastport ferry takes 12 but gets fewer passengers. It's $10 per car and driver, motorcycles $6, $2 per extra passenger, no charge for children 12 and under; $15 maximum. Deer Island itself is more than a mere stepping-stone in the bay. Roughly 9 miles long and more than 3 miles wide, it's popular with bicyclists and bird watchers. It boasts the world's three largest lobster pounds, the original salmon aquaculture site, a staffed lighthouse, and several B&Bs.

The free 18-car **Deer Island–L'Etete (New Brunswick mainland) Ferry** (506-453-2600) crossing takes 20 minutes, departing April through September every hour, 7–7, but call to confirm. This ride across Cobscook Bay is exceptional. (See also **East Coast Ferries** under *To Do—Boat Excursions and Puffin-Watching*).

MEDICAL EMERGENCY

Calais Regional Hospital (454-7531); **Down East Community Hospital** (255-3356), Machias. In case of emergency—fire or human or wildlife injury—call the **State Police** (1-800-432-7381).

FILLING UP

This is the part of coastal Maine in which you may have to drive a ways to an ATM or gas station. Both can be found in Milbridge, Columbia Four Corners Mall on Route 1, Machias, Lubec, Pembroke, Eastport, and Calais.

THE ATLANTIC COAST: STEUBEN TO CAMPOBELLO

GUIDANCE

Downeast Coastal Chamber of Commerce (483-2131; www.down eastcoastalchamber.org), P.O. Box 331, Harrington 04643. A brochure and web site cover the first eight coastal towns heading east, from Steuben to Jonesport/Beals Island.

The **Machias Bay Area Chamber of Commerce** (255-4402), P.O. Box 606, Machias 04654; www.nemaine.com/mbacc. A seasonal, weekday, walk-in information center on Route 1 south of town, next to Moore's Takeout, serves the coastal and lake area extending from Jonesboro to Cutler and Whiting. The chamber publishes a useful list of summer rental cottages.

Lubec Chamber of Commerce (733-4522; www.nemaine.com/ lubec_cc), P.O. Box 123, Lubec 04652. Look for the volunteer-run, seasonal information center in the **Lubec Historical Society,** a former general store, as you enter town on Route 189.

The **Campobello Tourist Bureau** (506-752-7018 or 752-7043), at the entrance to the island, is open daily May through Columbus Day. New Brunswick tourist information is available from 1-800-561-0123; www.tourismnbcanada.com.

TO SEE

Entries are listed geographically, traveling east.

Steuben, the first town in Washington County, is known as the site of the 6,000-acre **Petit Manan National Wildlife Refuge** (546-2124). The preserve includes two coastal peninsulas and 24 offshore islands. (For details, see *To Do—Hiking.*)

Milbridge, a Route 1 town with a wandering coastline, is the administrative home of one of the oldest wild blueberry processors (Jasper Wyman and Sons). The town also supports one of Maine's surviving sardine canneries, a Christmas wreath factory, and a great little movie theater.

The Ruggles House in Columbia Falls

McClellan Park, overlooking Narraguagus (pronounced *"Nair-a-gway-gus"*) Bay, offers picnic tables, fireplaces, campsites, rest rooms, and drinking water (see *To Do—Picnicking* and *Lodging—Camp-grounds*). The **Milbridge Society and Museum** (546-4471), open late May through September, Saturday and Sunday 1–4; also Tuesday 1–4 in July and August and by appointment. This is a delightful window into this spirited community, with ambitious changing exhibits and displays on past shipyards, canneries, and 19th-century life. **Milbridge Days** (late July) has attracted national coverage in recent years; the highlight is a greased-cod contest (see *Special Events*).

Cherryfield. A few miles up the Narraguagus River, Cherryfield boasts stately houses and a fine Atlantic salmon pool. The **Cherryfield-Narraguagus Historical Society** (546-7979), Main Street (just off Route 1), is open July and August, Wednesday and Friday 1–4; by appointment May through October. **Stewart Park** on Main Street and **Forest Mill Dam Park** on River Road are good places for a swim. Cherryfield (why isn't it called *Berryfield?*) bills itself Blueberry Capital of Maine; there are two processing plants in town.

Columbia Falls is an unusually picturesque village with one of Maine's most notable houses at its center. The **Ruggles House** (483-4637; ruggles@midmaine.com; 0.25 mile off Route 1; open June through mid-October, Monday through Saturday 9:30–4:30, Sunday 11–4:30; suggested donation is $3.50 adults, $1.50 children) is a Federal-style mansion built by wealthy lumber dealer Thomas Ruggles in 1818. It is a beauty, with a graceful flying staircase, a fine Palladian window, and superb woodwork. Legend has it that a wood-carver was imprisoned in the house for three years with a penknife. There is an unmistakably tragic feel to the place. Mr. Ruggles died soon after its completion. The house had fallen into disrepair by the 1920s, and major museums were eyeing its exquisite flying staircase when local pharmacist Mary Chandler, a Ruggles descendant, galvanized local and summer people to save and restore the old place.

Jonesport and **Beals Island.** Jonesport and Beals are both lobstering and fishing villages, separated by Moosabec Reach and linked by a bridge— a popular viewing spot on July 4 for the lobster-boat races. Beals is the home of the **Beals Island Regional Shellfish Hatchery** (497-5769), open to the public May through November, daily 9–4, where up to 10 million clams are annually seeded for distribution to local clam flats, and old photos depict the history of local clamming. Beals Island, still populated largely by Allens and Beals, is known for the design of its lobster boats, and it's not hard to find one under construction. Beals is connected to **Great Wass Island,** one of the county's most popular places to walk (see *To Do—Hiking*). Jonesport is the kind of village that seems small the first time you drive through but grows in dimensions as you slow down. Look closely and you will find a colorful marina, several restaurants, grocery stores, antiques shops, B&Bs, chandleries, a hardware/clothing store, an art gallery, and more. Railroad buffs should stop in to see Buz and Helen Beal's **Maine Central Model Railroad** (call ahead: 497-2255), where 380 cars traverse 3,000 feet of tracks that wind through hand-built miniature replicas of local towns and scenery. The Tiffany-style stained-glass windows in the Congregational church are point of local pride. Together Jonesport and Beals are home for eastern Maine's largest lobstering fleet.

Jonesboro is represented on Route 1 by a general store (closed at present), a church, a post office, and (larger than any of these) the popular **White House Restaurant.** The beauty of this town, however, is in its shoreline, which wanders in and out of points and coves along the tidal Chandler River and Chandler Bay on the way to **Roque Bluffs State Park** (see *To Do—Swimming*), 6 miles south of Route 1. A public boat launch with picnic tables is 5 minutes south of Route 1; take the Roque Bluffs Road but turn right onto Evergreen Point Road.

Machias is the county seat, an interesting old commercial center with the Machias River running through town and over the Bad Little Falls. **The Burnham Tavern** (255-4432), Main Street (up and around the corner from Route 1), is open early June through mid-September, Monday through Friday 9–5 and by appointment. A 1770s gambrel-roofed tavern, it's filled with period furnishings and tells the story of British man-of-war *Margaretta,* captured on June 12, 1775, by townspeople in the small sloop *Unity.* This was the first naval battle of the American Revolution. Unfortunately, the British retaliated by burning Portland.

The **University of Maine at Machias** maintains an interesting art gallery featuring paintings by John Marin and sponsors weeklong (live-in) summer workshops for birders. There is summer theater and music, including concerts in the graceful 1836 **Congregational church** (centerpiece of the annual Wild Blueberry Festival). Also note the picnic tables and suspension bridge at the falls and the many headstones worth pondering in neighboring **O'Brien Cemetery.**

Early in the 19th century Machias was second only to Bangor among Maine lumber ports. In 1912 the town boasted an opera house, two newspapers, three hotels, and a trotting park. Today Machias retains its share of fine houses and is home to the **Maine Wild Blueberry Company** and the annual **Wild Blueberry Festival,** held the third weekend in August.

Machiasport. Turn down Route 92 at Bad Little Falls Park in Machias. This picturesque village includes the **Gates House** (255-8461, open mid-June through early September, Tuesday through Saturday 12:30–4:30), a Federal-style home with maritime exhibits and period rooms. **Fort O'Brien** is an earthwork mound used as an ammunitions magazine during the American Revolution and the War of 1812. We recommend that you continue on down this road to the fishing village of Bucks Harbor and on to **Jasper Beach,** so named for the wave-tumbled and polished pebbles of jasper and rhyolite that give it its distinctive color. The road ends with great views and a beach to walk in **Starboard.**

Cutler. From East Machias, follow Route 191 south to this small fishing village that's happily shielded from a view of the Cutler navy communications station—said to be the world's most powerful radio station. Its 26 antenna towers (800 to 980 feet tall) light up red at night and can be seen from much of the county's coast. Cutler is the departure point for Captain Andy Patterson's excursions to see the puffins on **Machias Seal Island** (see *To Do—Boat Excursions and Puffin-Watching*) and the home of the **Marine Lobster Hatchery** (259-3693), open to visitors June through September. Beyond Cutler, Route 191 follows the shoreline through moorlike blueberry and cranberry country, with disappointingly few views. Much of this land is now publicly owned, and the high bluffs can be accessed via the **Bold Coast Trail** (see *To Do—Hiking*). In South Trescott bear right onto the unmarked road instead of continuing north on Route 191 and follow the coast through **Bailey's Mistake** (see introduction to "Washington County and the Quoddy Loop") to West Quoddy Light.

West Quoddy Light State Park, South Lubec Road, Lubec. Open mid-April through October, sunrise to sunset. Marking the easternmost tip of the United States, the red-and-white-striped lighthouse dates back to 1858. The park, adjacent to the lighthouse, offers benches from which you are invited to be the first person in the United States to see the sunrise. There is also a fine view of Grand Manan Island, a pleasant picnic area, and a 2-mile hiking trail along the cliffs to Carrying Place Cove. Between the cove and the bay, roughly a mile back down the road from the light, is an unusual coastal, raised-plateau bog with dense sphagnum moss and heath.

Lubec. Visitors pass through this "easternmost town" on their way over the FDR Memorial Bridge to Campobello Island. The **Lubec Historical Society Museum** (733-4696), open summer months, Tuesday through Thursday and Saturday, 9–3, fills an old storefront on the edge of town and doubles as an information center. Once there were 20 sardine-canning plants in Lubec, an era evoked in the **Old Sardine Village Museum** (open in summer Tuesday through Friday 1–5 and Saturday 1–4; $5 adults, $4 children). Barney and Becky Rier have spent many years building, assembling, and interpreting this collection of sardine-industry and related memorabilia. Check out the new full-service municipal **Lubec Marina** and the old town landing with its public boat launch, breakwater, and a view of the Sparkplug, as the distinctive little Lubec channel light is known. One longtime sardine cannery has switched to processing the salmon that are farmed offshore in Cobscook Bay: **R. J. Peacock Canning Company** (733-5556), 72 Water Street, offers summer tours. Inquire about the free concerts presented Wednesday evenings (see Mary Potterton Memorial Piano Concerts under *Entertainment*).

✐ **Roosevelt Campobello International Park** (506-752-2922; www.fdr.net), Welshpool, Campobello Island, New Brunswick, Canada (for a brochure, write Box 121, Lubec 04652). Open daily Memorial Day weekend through mid-October, 9–5 eastern daylight time (10–6 Canadian Atlantic daylight time). Although technically in New Brunswick, this manicured 2,800-acre park with a visitors center and shingled "cottages" is the number-one sight to see east of Bar Harbor. You turn down a side street in Lubec, and there is the bridge (built in 1962) and Canadian customs. The house in which Franklin Delano Roosevelt summered as a boy has disappeared, but the airy 34-room **Roosevelt Cottage,** a wedding gift to Franklin and Eleanor, is sensitively maintained just as the family left it, charged with the spirit of the dynamic man who contracted polio here on August 25, 1921. It's filled with many poignant objects like the toy boat FDR carved for his children. During his subsequent stints as governor of New York and then as president of the United States, FDR returned only three times. Neighboring **Hubbard Cottage,** with its oval picture window, gives another slant on this turn-of-the-20th-century resort. There's a visitors center here with an excellent historical exhibit and a 15-minute introductory film. Beyond stretch more than 8 miles of trails to the shore and then inland through woods to lakes and ponds. There are also 15.4 miles of park drives, modified from the network of carriage drives that the wealthy "cottagers" maintained on the island. Beyond the park is **East Quoddy Head Lighthouse,** accessible at low tide, a popular whale-watching station but a real adventure to get

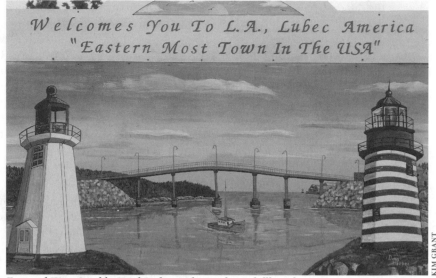

East and West Quoddy Head Lights as depicted on a billboard

to (attempt only if you are physically fit). Note the small car ferry to Deer Island that runs during July and August (see *Getting Around*) and the description of the Owen House under *Inns and Bed & Breakfasts*. Campobello Park was granted to Captain William Owen in the 1760s and remained in the family until 1881, when it was sold to Boston developers, who built large (long-gone) hotels. Another major real estate development failed in the 1990s, and the land amassed for that venture is presently being lumbered.

TO DO

BOAT EXCURSIONS AND PUFFIN-WATCHING

Note: Birders and naturalists should be aware that the area's many wildlife-rich offshore islands, such as **Cross, Petit Manan, Bois Bubert, Seal, and Pond Islands,** as well as **Machias Seal Island,** are the focus of the following excursions; inquire about exploring the islands themselves.

Machias Seal Island is a prime nesting spot for puffins in June and July; it is also a place to see razor-billed auks and arctic terns in August and September. Although just 9 miles off Cutler, the island is maintained by Canada as a lighthouse station and wildlife refuge. But **Captain Barna Norton** (497-5933; 1-888-889-3222) of Jonesport, who has been offering bird-watching cruises to Machias Seal since the 1940s, refuses to concede the island. Since it was never mentioned in the 1842 Webster-Ashburton Treaty, he insists that it was claimed by his grandfather in 1865. Thus he continues to offer puffin-watching and other birding trips to the island, ably assisted by his son John, emphasizing his views by

shading himself with an umbrella displaying an American flag on top.
Captain Andrew Patterson's **Bold Coast Charter Company** (259-4484;
www.boldcoast.com) is based in Cutler, just 9 miles from Machias Seal
Island, to which he offers frequent bird-watching trips from May
through August. Captain Patterson also uses his 40-foot passenger vessel *Barbara Frost* to cruise the Bold Coast (as the stretch of high, rocky
bluffs east of Cutler is known), to visit the **Cross Island Wildlife Refuge** (hiking trails thread a dense spruce forest, and there are many
mosses, wildflowers, and berries, as well as good birding) at the mouth
of Machias Bay, and, on special request, to go all the way out to **Grand
Manan Island.**
Machias Bay Boat Tours (259-3338; www.machiasbay.com), Route 191,
East Machias. Captain Martha Jordan offers tours aboard the six-pas-
senger, 34-foot, fiberglass, diesel-powered *Martha Ann.* Destinations
include **Cross Island** for bird- and seal-watching. She also offers fishing trips and lobstering trips, and guides visitors to several **ancient Indian petroglyph sites** (see also Machias Bay Sea Kayaking, below).
Captain Laura Fish (497-3064/2445), Kelley Point Road, Jonesport. From
mid-June through mid-September (weather permitting), the 23-foot
Aaron Thomas, named for Jonesport's first settler—from whom the captain and first mate are descended—offers 3-hour cruises around the
islands, lighthouses, beaches, and salmon farms; also a walk around
Mistake Island, site of 72-foot-high Moose Peak Light.
East Coast Ferries Ltd. See *Getting Around.* Departing from Eastport
every hour, and from Campobello every 90 minutes, this is the bargain
cruise of the eastern seaboard: a small car ferry that sails out into
Cobscook Bay, past **Old Sow**—billed as the world's second largest
whirlpool. Drive across Deer Island and take the free Canadian ferry
from Lord's Cove to the **New Brunswick mainland** or simply explore
Deer Island (see *Getting Around*) and come back.
CANOEING AND KAYAKING
The **Machias River,** fed by the five Machias Lakes, drops through the backwoods with technically demanding rapids and takes 3 to 6 days to run.
The Narraguagus and East Machias Rivers are also good for trips of 2 to
4 days. For rentals and guided tours, see **Sunrise County Canoe and
Kayak** (454-7708) under *To Do* in "Calais and the St. Croix Valley."
Machias Bay Sea Kayaking (259-3338; www.machiasbay.com). Registered guides Martha and Rick Jordan (see Machias Bay Boat Tours under *Boat Excursions and Puffin-Watching*) offer year-round guided
kayaking tours, with an emphasis on trips to the **Machias Bay petroglyphs** near their base at Holmes Bay (Route 191). On our expedition
Martha pointed out a number of petroglyphs that state archaeologists
say were carved between 1,500 and 3,000 years ago. The artists were
Etchimins, seafaring Indians for whom Machias Bay seems to have been
a central congregating point. This year the Jordans discovered a carving

(which has been authenticated) of a European-style ship, several hundred years old. We are told it is the only known carving portraying the arrival of Europeans on the North American continent.

FISHING

Atlantic salmon, long the draw for fishermen to the Narraguagus and Machias Rivers, are currently illegal to catch and will be until stocks have been replenished. Landlocked salmon are, however, still fair game and can be found in **Schoodic Lake** (8 miles north of Cherryfield), **Bog Lake** in Northfield on Route 192 (10 miles north of Machias), **Gardner Lake** in East Machias (look for the new boat ramp and parking area), and **Cathance Lake** on Route 191 (some 18 miles north of East Machias with a nice boat landing). Trolling lures, streamer flies, or bait from a boat is the most popular way to catch landlocked salmon.

Brook trout can be caught in May and June in local rivers and streams, but in warm weather they move to deeper water like **Six Mile Lake** in Marshfield (6 miles north of Machias on Route 192), **Indian Lake** along Route 1 in Whiting, and **Lily Lake** in Trescott. **Brown trout** are found in **Simpson Pond** in Roque Bluffs (park in Roque Bluffs State Park), as well as in the lakes listed above. **Gregg Burr** (255-4210) is an experienced local fishing guide.

Saltwater and tidewater fishing is usually for striped bass or mackerel. For information about licenses, guides, and fish, check with the regional headquarters of the **Inland Fisheries and Wildlife Department** in Jonesboro.

GOLF

Great Cove Golf Course (434-2981), Jonesboro Road, Roque Bluffs, offers nine holes, water views, a clubhouse, rental clubs, and carts.

Herring Cove Golf Course (506-752-2449), in the Herring Cove Provincial Park (open mid-May through mid-November), has nine holes, a clubhouse restaurant, and rentals.

HIKING

Listed from west to east.

Pigeon Hill, Steuben. The turnoff for the Petit Manan National Wildlife Area is not marked on Route 1; look for Pigeon Hill Road. After something more than 5 miles, look for a small graveyard on your left. Stop. The well-trod path up Pigeon Hill begins across the road. The climb is fairly steep in places. It's a pleasant 20-minute hike, and the view from the summit reveals the series of island-filled bays that stretch away to the east, as well as mountains inland.

Petit Manan Point, Steuben. Continue another mile or so (see above) down Pigeon Hill Road and past the sign announcing that you have entered a 2,166-acre preserve with over 10 miles of shoreline, part of the 6,000-acre **Petit Manan National Wildlife Refuge.** There are two loop trails, and you can drive to the parking lot for the second. This is a varied area with pine stands, cedar swamps, blueberry barrens, marshes, and great birding (more than 250 species have been identified here). Maps are posted at the parking lots. A half-mile shore path hugs the woods and coastline. For details about the entire refuge, contact Refuge Headquarters, Main Street, Millbridge (546-2124).

Great Wass Island. The Maine Chapter of The Nature Conservancy owns this 1,579-acre tract at the southern tip of the Jonesport-Addison peninsula. Trail maps are posted at the parking lot (simply follow the main road to its logical end). The interior of the island supports one of Maine's largest stands of jack pine and has coastal peatlands. We prefer the 2-mile trek along the shore to Little Cape Point, where children can clamber on the smooth rocks. Wear rubber-soled shoes and bring a picnic.

Western Head, off Route 191, 11 miles south of East Machias, is maintained by the Maine Coast Heritage Trust, Brunswick (276-5156). Take the first right after the Baptist church onto Destiny Bay Road and follow it to the sign. The loop trail is through mixed-growth woods and spruce to the shore, with views of the entrance to Cutler Harbor and high ledges with crashing surf, large expanses of open ocean, as well as the high, sheer ledges of Grand Manan to the northeast, and Machias Seal Island to the southeast. The loop takes a good hiker 35 minutes.

Bold Coast Trail. Look for the trailhead some 4 miles east of Cutler Harbor. Maine's Bureau of Parks and Lands (287-4920) has constructed inner and outer loop trails from Route 191 to the rugged cliffs and along the shore overlooking Grand Manan Channel. It's a 5½-mile loop. The Coastal Trail begins in spruce-fir forest, bridges a cedar swamp, and climbs to a promontory, continuing along the cliffs to Black Point Cove, a cobble beach. *Note:* The cliffs are high and sheer, not good for children or shaky adults. Bring a picnic and allow at least 4 hours. The trail continues from Black Point Cove to Fairy Head, site of three primitive campsites.

For the hiking guide "Cobscook Trails," which includes the Bold Coast, contact the **Quoddy Regional Land Trust** (733-5509), P.O. Box 49, Whiting 04691. It details hikes in Lubec to **Horan Head** (6 miles round-trip), to the **Boot Head Preserve** (less than 2 miles round-trip), along the **South Lubec Sand Bar,** and to **Commissary Point in Trescott.**

Roosevelt Campobello International Park. At the tourist information center, pick up a trail map. We recommend the trail from Southern Head to the Duck Ponds. Seals frequently sun on the ledges off Lower Duck Pond, and loons are often seen off Liberty Point. Along this dramatic shoreline at the southern end of the island, also look for whales from July through September.

Also see **East Quoddy Head Lighthouse** within the description for Roosevelt Campobello International Park under *To See*.

PICNICKING

McClellan Park, in Milbridge, 5 miles south of town at Baldwin's Head, which overlooks the Atlantic and Narraguagus Bay (from Route 1, follow Wyman Road to the park gates). A town park on 10½ acres donated in 1926 by George McClellan, a onetime mayor of New York City. There's no charge for walking or picnicking. (Also see *To See—Milbridge* and *Lodging—Campgrounds.*)

SPECIAL LEARNING PROGRAMS (ADULT)

SummerKeys (733-2316; winter, 201-451-2338), 6 Bayview Street, Lubec. July through mid-August. New York piano teacher Bruce Potterton offers programs for a variety of instruments, including piano. Beginners to advanced students are welcome. Lodging is at local B&Bs.

SWIMMING

Roque Bluffs State Park, Roque Bluffs (6 miles off Route 1). The pebble beach on the ocean is frequently windy, but a sheltered sand beach on a freshwater pond is good for children. But the water is *cold*. Tables, grills, changing areas with vault toilets, and a playground.

Sandy River Beach in Jonesport (off Route 187) is a rare white sand beach marked by a small sign.

Gardner Lake, Chases Mills Road, East Machias, offers freshwater swimming, a picnic area, and a boat launch. **Six Mile Lake,** Route 192, in Marshfield (north of Machias), is also good for a dip. On Beals Island the **Backfield Area,** Alley's Bay, offers saltwater swimming.

WHALE-WATCHING

The unusually high tides in the Bay of Fundy seem to foster ideal feeding grounds for right, minke, and humpback whales and for porpoises and dolphins. East Quoddy Head on Campobello and West Quoddy Head in Lubec are favored viewing spots. *The Captain's Lady* (733-2805), based in Lubec, a 33-passenger boat, cruises Passamaquoddy Bay and the Bay of Fundy in search of wildlife.

LODGING

INNS AND BED & BREAKFASTS

Entries are listed geographically, heading east.

Ricker House (546-2780; rickerhouse@mymailstation.com), Cherryfield 04622. Open May through November. A classic Federal house built in 1803 (it's on the National Register) with a double parlor and furnished comfortably with plenty of books and an inviting country kitchen. There are three guest rooms, two with river views. All are nicely furnished with antiques and old quilts, and all share one bath. A path leads to a picnic table by the river, and the tennis courts across the road are free. Lawn games include horseshoes and croquet. Jean and Bill Conway are delighted to help guests explore the area, especially on foot, or by bicycle or canoe (both are available to guests). Many guests, however, see no reason to explore farther than the screened-in pine porch. $65 per couple ($10 per extra person), $55 single, includes breakfast.

Dream Catcher B&B (483-0937), Route 1, Columbia Falls 04623; www. nemaine.com/dreamcatcher). Set back from Route 1, this attractive, mansard-roofed B&B offers rooms with private baths, one with a canopy bed and fireplace. $80 per night includes breakfast.

🐾✔ **Pleasant Bay Bed & Breakfast** (483-4490; www.pleasantbay@nemaine. com), P.O. Box 222, West Side Road, Addison 04606. Open year-round. After raising six children and a number of llamas in New Hampshire, Leon and Joan Eaton returned to Joan's girlhood turf, cleared this land, and built this gracious house with many windows and a deck and porch overlooking the Pleasant River. Opening onto the deck is a large, sunny room (with couches, a piano, and a fireplace), and an adjoining open kitchen and dining room, all with water views. A more formal living room is well stocked with puzzles and books for foggy days. This is a 110-acre working llama farm, and guests are invited to meander the wooded trails down to the bay with or without llamas. The three upstairs guest rooms with views include one family-sized room with private bath. There are moorings for guests arriving by water. $45–70 per couple ($10 per child) includes a splendid breakfast of fresh fruit and, if you're lucky, Joan's popover/pancake. Evening meals are available by prior arrangement off-season.

Harbor House on Sawyer Cove (497-5417; fax, 497-3211; www.harborhs. com), P.O. Box 468, Sawyer Square, Jonesport 04649. Open year-round. Maureen and Gene Hart have transformed an 1880s building that housed the telegraph office, general store, and ship's chandlery into an antiques store downstairs and two large, attractive guest rooms upstairs. One has a king-sized bed and windows overlooking the marina and harbor; the other has a queen-sized featherbed and in-room binoculars to focus in on the water view. Both have sitting areas, cable TV, and private baths. Guests can request a lobster dinner, served on the harborside porch. $110 in-season, $85 off, weekly rates. Breakfast is included.

🐾🐾 **Tootsie's Bed and Breakfast** (497-5414; fax, 483-4653), RFD 1, RRO, Box 252, Jonesport 04649. This was the first B&B in Washington County, and it is still one of the nicest. Charlotte Beal (Tootsie, as her grandchildren call her) offers two rooms—nothing fancy, but homey and spanking clean—and routinely makes a 6 AM breakfast for guests who need to leave at 6:45 to catch Barna Norton's boat (see Machias Seal Island under *To Do*). The Beals raised eight children in their shipshape house, which sits in a cluster of lobstermen's homes on the fringe of this fishing village, handy to Great Wass Island. $30 single, $50 double includes a full breakfast. Children over age 5 are $10 extra. Small and well behaved pets possible.

Raspberry Shores B&B (497-2463; skitech@midmaine.com, Route 187, Jonesport 04649. Nan and Timothy Ellis moved here from Alaska and settled right into this Victorian house in the middle of the village, with water views out the back. The three guest rooms are pleasant, all with water views. When we visited more baths were planned. Barna Norton (see *To See*) is next door. $75 per couple.

Jonesport by the Sea (497-2590; 1-888-475-2590; www.jonesportbythe sea.bigstep.com), P.O. Box 541, Jonesport 04649. Lobsterman Joe McDonald has spiffed up this B&B in the middle of the village. Some water views. Guests enter through a cheery country kitchen and a small living room. The four guest rooms are upstairs, one with two double beds and a private bath ($75 double), the others each with a double and sharing a bath ($60).

Moose-A-Bec Manor (497-2121), P.O. Box 557, Old House Point, Jonesport 04659. Open year-round for weekly rentals. Charlie and Abby Alley have renovated an 1875 waterside house that's been in Abby's family for generations, turning it into two large waterside apartments, each with two bedrooms plus a sleep sofa and full kitchen, including dishwasher, washer/dryer, and cable TV. Views are of Mooseabec Reach. $850 per week includes linens.

✿ **Micmac Farm Guesthouses** (255-3008; www.micmacfarm.com), P.O. Box 336, Route 336, Machiasport 04655. Open July through September. After almost 20 years Micmac Farm no longer offers fine dining, but this house, built by Ebenezer Gardner beside the Machias River in 1776, happily remains a place to stay. In the Gardner house itself is a large downstairs guest room with a deck and a whirlpool tub. The housekeeping cabins on the property, each with two double beds, also overlook the river. $55–65 daily per unit; $325–375 per week.

✿ **Riverside Inn & Restaurant** (255-4134; www.riversideinn-maine.com), Route 1, East Machias 04630. Open year-round. Built originally in 1805 and Victorianized in the 1890s, including the fan lights (white glass was replaced with red) and the tin ceilings. Tom and Carol Paul have authentically restored this home, from its ornate detailing in the two upstairs guest rooms and parlors to the antique linens and the woodwork in the common rooms, all deftly restored or installed by Tom. The house is on Route 1, but terraced gardens overlook the river, and two suites (one with two bedrooms, the other with a living room, bedroom, and kitchen facilities) in the carriage house have balconies with river views. $69–95 includes a full breakfast; the specialty is blueberry-stuffed French toast. Carol is well known in the area for the quality of her dinners (see *Dining Out*).

✿✿ **Downeast Farm House** (733-2496), Route 189, Trescott (mailing address: RR 1, Box 3860, Lubec 04652). Open year-round. Priscilla and Henry Merrill's 1810 Cape is set way back from Route 189 and includes a spacious suite with a living room furnished with well-chosen art and antiques as well as a bedroom facing the meadow and bath. Avid sailors, the owners are knowledgeable about local boating and birding; they also maintain a small antiques shop. $70 includes a full country breakfast.

Whiting Bay Bed & Breakfast (phone/fax: 733-2463; dsbrad@acadia.net),

Route 1, HCR 74, Box 5000, Whiting 04651. This is a new B&B on the Whiting-Edmunds line, a few miles from Cobscook Bay State Park. The two units both overlook Whiting Bay and have private baths, king-sized beds, and cable TV. The second floor "Lighthouse" has a private deck and kitchenette. $75–85 includes a light breakfast.

    Peacock House (733-2403; fax, 733-2403; www.peacockhouse.com), 27 Summer Street, Lubec 04652. Open May 15 through October 15. An 1860s house on a quiet side street, home to four generations of the Peacock family (owners of the major local cannery). The two guest rooms and three suites (all with private baths), like the formal common rooms, are immaculate and furnished with souvenirs from the far-flung places where Chet and Veda Childs previously lived; one of two ground-floor suites is handicapped accessible. Afternoon tea as well as a full breakfast are included. $60–90 per couple. No children under 7 please.

    Lubecker Gast Haus (733-4385), 31 Main Street, Lubec 04652. Open June through September. A rear deck overlooks the garden and bay. Robert and Irmgard Swiecicki hail originally from Lubec, Germany, and have furnished their four guest rooms (shared baths) with flair. $80 ($70 single) includes a full breakfast and tax.

    Betsy Ross House (733-8942; www.atlantichouse.net), 61 Water Street, Lubec 04652. Open most of the year. The style replicates that of the Betsy Ross House in Philadelphia, but this brand-new shingled building fits into the eclectic lineup on this funky old street. Bill and Dianna Meehan have completed two pleasant rooms with private baths. $95 includes a credit for breakfast at the **Atlantic House** across the street (see *Eating Out*). Inquire about the fairly spectacular unit that this family has created in the former brick bank building down the street. It sleeps five, with one bedroom (with fireplace) in the old office and another in the vault, a spiffy open kitchen, and plenty of space that really works: $700 per week.

    The Owen House (506-752-2977; www.campnet.nb.ca/~owen/), Welsh-pool, Campobello, New Brunswick, Canada E5E 1G3. Open late May through mid-October. This delightful inn is reason enough to come to Campobello. Built in 1835 by Admiral William Fitzwilliam Owen, son of the British captain to whom the island was granted in 1769, this is probably the most historic house on the island, and it's a beauty, set on a headland overlooking Passamaquoddy Bay. Joyce Morrell, an artist who maintains a gallery here, has furnished the nine guest rooms (five with private baths) with friendly antiques, handmade quilts, and good art. With the help of co-owner Janice Meiners, the place has, more-over, been recently, thoroughly refurbished. One room (#1) is really a suite with a single bed in the adjoining room. The four rooms without private baths are the former servants' quarters on the third floor, all with water views. Guests gather at a formal dining room table for breakfast and around one of several fireplaces in the evening. Paths lead through the 10-acre property to the water, and the Deer Island ferry leaves from the adjoining beach (see *Getting Around*). From $62 for the fourth-floor rooms to $95 for the suite; private-bath rooms range from $69–86 plus the 15 percent tax for which non-Canadians can get a refund.

COTTAGES

Check with the **Machias Bay Area Chamber of Commerce** (see *Guidance*) and in "Maine Guide to Camp & Cottage Rentals," available from the **Maine Tourism Association** (see *Information* in "What's Where in Maine"). Summer rentals in this area still begin at around $300 per week. Also see **Hearts of Maine Waterfront Rental Properties** (255-4210; www.boldcoast.com/mainecottages).

MOTELS

Blueberry Patch Motel and Cabins (434-5411), Route 1, Jonesboro 04648. This spic-and-span 19-unit motel is next door to **The White House** restaurant (see *Eating Out*). Each unit has a refrigerator, air-conditioning, a phone, TV, and coffee. There is a pool and sundeck surrounded by berries. The '30s tourist cabins way in back are surprisingly roomy and comfortable (two double beds), and there are three efficiencies. $35–58 in-season.

Machias Motor Inn (255-4861), Route 1 next to Helen's Restaurant, Machias 04654. Bob and Joan Carter maintain a two-story, 35-unit motel; most rooms are standard units, each with two double, extra-long beds, cable TV, and a phone. Rooms feature decks overlooking the Machias River. There are six efficiency units, and **Helen's Restaurant,** serving all three meals, is part of the complex. An indoor pool is a welcome plus if you are traveling this foggy coast with kids. Pets are an extra $5. $50–65 double, $85 for efficiencies, less off-season.

Eastland Motel (733-5501), Route 189, Lubec 04652. Open year-round. A good bet if you are taking the kids to Campobello and want a clean, comfortable room with TV; $54–64 double mid-April through mid-October, $42–52 single, less off-season. Higher prices are for rooms in the newer section. Owner Lee Aragon helps guests plan their days.

CAMPGROUNDS

McClellan Park, marked from Route 1, Milbridge. Open Memorial Day through Columbus Day. See *To Do—Picnicking* for more on this dramatically sited, town-owned park. Free for day use plus a nominal charge for tenting and full campsites; 18 campsites and water are available, but no showers. For details, call the town hall at 546-2422.

Henry Point Campground (497-9633), Kelly Point Road, Jonesport. Open April through November. Surrounded on three sides by water, this is another great town-owned campground that's usually got space (its crunch weekend is July 4). Neither showers nor water is available, but you can shower and use the coin-operated laundry at the Jonesport Shipyard across the cove. Good water is also available from an outside faucet at the town hall. This is a put-in place for sea kayaks. Turn off Route 187 at the purple house.

Herring Cove Provincial Park (506-752-2396), Campobello Island. Adjoining the Roosevelt Campobello International Park is this campground offering 87 campsites; there's a beach, a golf course, and extensive hiking trails.

Also see **Cobscook Bay State Park** under *Lodging—Campground* in "Eastport and Cobscook Bay."

WHERE TO EAT

DINING OUT
Entries are listed geographically, heading east.

Kitchen Garden Restaurant (546-2708), 335 Village Road (just off Route 1), Steuben. Open most of the year for dinner 6–8; weekends-only off-season. Reservations recommended. Dining rooms fill the first floor of an 1860s Cape decorated with local art. Everything is organic and delicious. Entrées might include Alva's Jamaican jerk chicken (broiled free-range chicken marinated and served with rice and peas) and tender goat marinated in allspice and Jamaican curry powder, simmered in coconut milk. From $27 per person.

Seafarer's Wife (497-2365), 9 miles down Route 187 from Route 1 (after the high school, look for a small sign on the left), or 3 miles north of Jonesport. The **Ol' Salt Café** is open for lunch and dinner, the **Down East** dining room is open 5:30–8:30; reservations required. Entrées range from a vegetarian plate and stuffed baked chicken to Fisherman's Bounty, a baked medley of shrimp, lobster, halibut, scallops, and more. The entrée price ($14.95–19.95) includes hors d'oeuvres, soup, salad, and dessert. Faye Carver is the owner-chef. BYOB.

Artist's Café (255-8900), 3 Hill Street, Machias. Open Monday through Saturday, 11–2 for lunch; dinner 5–8. Reservations accepted. This delightful restaurant is tucked away off Route 1 south of the bridge. Light, bright rooms are hung with local art. Lunch on crab salad served on organic greens, or sandwiches with artistic names like The Impressionist (natural chicken breast sautéed and sliced on a French baguette with basil pesto mayonnaise). Dinner entrées might range from vegetable and tofu curry to rack of veal braised in white wine. Wine and beer. Dinner entrées $12–22.

Riverside Inn & Restaurant (255-4134), Route 1, East Machias. Dinner Friday, and Saturday by reservation. Tables line the sunporch overlooking the East Machias River and fill a lacy, flowery dining room. Innkeeper Carol Paul's reputation as a chef is well deserved. The four-course meals feature a choice of five entrées: always a fish dish and a beef dish, perhaps pork tenderloin marinated in orange wine sauce. $14.95–17.95. BYOB.

EATING OUT

Entries are listed geographically, heading east.

Joshy's Place, Route 1, Milbridge. Good seasonal take-out. Having researched crab rolls up and down the coast, we think Joshy's rates an 8 on a scale of 1–10. Gifford's ice cream.

✐ **The Red Barn** (546-7721), Main Street (junction of Routes 1 and 1A), Milbridge. Open daily year-round, 6 AM–9 PM in summer. The main, pine-paneled dining room offers a counter and booths. The menu is large: pastas, burgers, steak, seafood, fried chicken, and an extensive salad bar. Fully licensed. Children's menu; great cream pies.

The Blue Beary (546-2052), Route 1, Cherryfield. Open 11–9, a friendly dining room; also a picnic area featuring fresh-dough pizza (try the garlic and cheese), homemade soups, and pies.

Perry's Seafood, Route 1, Columbia. Open daily 11–9. Easy to pass without noticing and favored by locals for dinner as well as other meals; try the clam pizza, homemade soups and onion rings, or the special of the day.

Tall Barney, Main Street, Jonesport. Open daily 5 AM–7 PM. Don't be put off by the exterior of this local gathering spot, set back behind its parking lot across from the access to the big bridge. Particularly welcoming for breakfast on a foggy morning (papers are stacked on the counter). *Note:* The long table down the middle of the front room is reserved for the local lobstermen, who drift in one by one.

The White House (434-2792), Route 1, Jonesboro. Open 5 AM–9 PM. Finally this old brown-shingled landmark will be painted white (we're promised). Inside are cheery blue booths, a counter, and friendly service. The new owners are Buck and Lorraine Proctor, who first met here when she waited on him and he left her a $5 tip. Memorable breakfasts, outstanding fish chowder (better than the lobster); specialties include fried seafood platters and delectable pies.

Melanie's Chowder House, Dublin Street, Machias. Open for lunch (11–2) and dinner (5–8). Approaching Machias from the south on Route 1, it's easy to miss this small restaurant, housed in the former fish market across from Napa Auto Parts. Melanie Colbeth frequently alters the blackboard menu. It might include salmon chowder and carrot cashew soup, mini–crab and lobster quiches, and shepherd's pie. Homemade breads come with soups like 15-bean (bread and soup is under $3). The cheery decor features plants, flowered tablecloths made by Melanie's mother, and two booths allegedly from a 1920s Machias speakeasy. Everything's cheaper off-season.

✐ **Helen's Restaurant** (255-6506), 32 Main Street, Machias (north of town on the water). Open 6 AM–8 PM. Geared to bus groups en route from Campobello to Bar Harbor, but there's plenty of room for everybody. Generous servings: a wide choice of seafood, meat entrées, salads, fish stews, and sandwiches. "Whipped" pies are a specialty: strawberry, blueberry, and a dozen more. Children's plates.

Blue Bird Ranch (255-3351), Lower Main Street (Route 1), Machias. Open year-round for all three meals. A diner atmosphere for breakfast and lunch, but the dining room features lobster, fried seafood, salad bar, homemade pies, specials like baby ribs or beans and franks; fully licensed. This is high on our family dining list.

Joyce's Lobster House, Route 1, Machias (north of town). Open daily April through September for lunch and dinner. The menu is fairly varied and the fish chowder is good; pleasant atmosphere.

Phinney's Seaview (733-0941), Route 189, Lubec. Open year-round, 6:30 AM–9 PM in summer, 7 AM–8 PM the remainder of the year. An outside deck overlooks Johnson's Bay. A full menu but specializing in seafood dishes (a fish market is part of the complex); good chowder, but service can be slow.

Down East (733-4440), Route 189, Lubec. Open daily year-round, 6 AM–8 PM. A find: a great little restaurant in a roadside house with homemade soups, biscuits and desserts, turkey dishes (a turkey is roasted daily), specials.

Atlantic House (733-0906), 52 Water Street, Lubec. Open year-round, Monday through Saturday 6 AM–9 PM, Sunday 7–7. A welcome addition to this reawakening street: pastries, pizza. stromboli, calzones, and sandwiches. Dianna Meehan does it all. Note the back deck on the water.

The Café Kontinental (733-4385), 31 Main Street, Lubec. Seasonal; call beforehand. German pastries, sandwiches, soups, beer, and wine served in a room and on a deck overlooking the bay.

Lupine Lodge (506-752-2555), Campobello. Open noon–9. This former log "cottage" features a great hearth and has some charm. The dinner menu ranges from $9.95 for vegetarian pasta to $16.95 for a fried seafood platter. Full liquor license.

Herring Cove Restaurant (506-752-2467), Herring Cove Provincial Park Golf Course, Campobello. A café specializing in fish-and-chips; vague views of the water.

ENTERTAINMENT

Milbridge Theater (546-2038), Main Street, Milbridge. Open nightly May through November, 7:30 show time; Saturday and Sunday matinees for children's films; all seats $3.75. A very special theater: a refurbished movie house featuring first-run and art films with truly affordable prices. Fresh popcorn; ice cream parlor.

University of Maine, Machias (255-3313, ext. 284), offers both a winter and summer series of plays, performances, and concerts.

Downriver Theater Productions (255-4997) stages plays June through August at Liberty Hall in Machiasport. Community theater productions—a mix of safe musicals and original plays. We saw *Barefoot in the*

Park and were impressed. Tickets are very affordable.

Machias Bay Chamber Concerts (255-3889), Center Street Congregational Church, Machias. A series of six chamber music concerts, July through early August, Tuesday at 8 PM. Top groups such as the Kneisel Hall Chamber Players and the Vermeer Quartet are featured.

Mary Potterton Memorial Piano Concerts, Sacred Heart Church Parish Hall, Lubec. Wednesday evenings (7:30 PM) all summer. Free. Featuring SummerKeys faculty (see *To Do*) and guest artists.

SELECTIVE SHOPPING

Entries are listed geographically, heading east.

Tunk River Gardens (546-2269), Steuben Center. Peter and Jane Weil offer a first-rate gallery and sculpture garden.

Sea-Witch (546-7495), Route 1, Milbridge. Describing itself as "the biggest little gift shop in Washington County," this is a trove of trinkets and treasures: collector dolls, spatterware, and local specialty foods.

The Dusty Rose Antiques (546-8997), Route 182, Cherryfield. Mary Weston has a good mix of antiques and interesting old stuff.

Narraguagus Trading Company (546-2143). Housed in the Knights of Phythias Building, Routes 1 and 193, Cherryfield. Closed Monday. A group shop with a mix of antiques, collectibles, and crafts.

Columbia Falls Pottery (483-4075; 1-800-235-2512), Main Street, Columbia Falls. Open year-round. Striking, bright, sophisticated creations by April Adams: mugs, platters, kitchenware, lamps, wind chimes, and more, featuring lupine and sunflower designs; catalog.

Crossroads Vegetables (497-2641), posted from Route 187 (off Route 1), Jonesport. Open daily except Saturday 9–5:30 in-season. Bonnie and Arnold Pearlman built their house, windmill, sauna, and barn and have reclaimed acres of productive vegetable garden from the surrounding woods. In addition to their outstanding vegetables (salad lovers get their greens picked to order; Bonnie adds edible flowers like nasturtiums), they also sell the hand-hollowed wooden bowls that Arnold carves all winter and the dried-flower wreaths that Bonnie makes.

Jonesport Antiques (497-5655; www.nauticalantiques.com), Cogswell and Main Streets, Jonesport Village. Open late June through October. Nautical antiques and reproductions are the specialty.

Harbor House on Sawyer Cove (497-5417), Sawyer Square, Jonesport Village. Art, antique furnishings, and linens.

Nelson Decoys Gallery and Gifts (497-3488), School Street, Jonesport. Bob is the carver and Charlene Nelson paints the prizewinning decoys sold here in the former Cross Cove Elementary School. Other local art and Maine-made gifts also sold.

Woodwind Gallery (255-3737), 62½ Dublin Street (Route 1 south of the bridge), Machias. Open year-round, Tuesday through Sunday in July and August; closed Sunday off-season. Holly Garner-Jackson's combination framery and gallery shows some 40 local artists and sculptors. Work includes glass, pottery, photography, and metal.

McKinney Books (255-0075), 50 Main Street, Machias. New and used books and other interesting and useful items.

The Sow's Ear (255-4066), 7 Water Street, Machias. A mix of cards, jewelry, toys, clothing, and things "from away."

Machias Hardware Co. (255-6581; 1-800-543-2250), 26 Main Street, Machias. An unexpected source of reasonably priced herbs and spices in 2-ounce and 1-pound packages. Also local products like those by A. M. Look Canning (see below).

A. M. Look Canning Co. (259-3341; 1-800-962-6258), Route 191, East Machias. Retail shop open weekdays 8–4. A former sardine-processing plant now processes Atlantic and Bar Harbor brand seafoods. Also offers New England specialty foods like Indian pudding.

Connie's Clay of Fundy (255-4574), Route 1, East Machias. Open year-round. Connie Harter-Bagley's combination studio/shop is filled with her distinctive glazed earthenware in deep colors. Bowls, pie plates, platters, lamps, and small essentials like garlic jars and ring boxes.

Maine-ly Smoked Salmon Company (1-888-733-0807; www.rier.com), Route 189, Lubec. Maria and Frank Rier offer samples of their delicious smoked salmon (using both hot and cold methods). Stop by 9–5 any day except Sunday.

Cottage Garden (733-2902), North Lubec Road, Lubec. Open in-season Wednesday through Sunday 10–5; 4.5 miles from Lubec. Gretchen Mead welcomes visitors to her steadily expanding perennial gardens. A short trail through woods leads to a picnic meadow, and a deck behind the shop (herbs, flower wreaths, toys, Christmas ornaments, birdhouses) overlooks the garden and a small pond.

CHRISTMAS WREATHS

Wreath making is a major industry in this area. You can order in fall and take delivery of a freshly made wreath right before Christmas. Prices quoted include delivery. Sources are **Cape Split Wreaths** (483-2983), Box 447, Route 1, Addison 04606; **Simplicity Wreath** (483-2780), Sunset Point, Harrington 04643; **The Wreath Shoppe** (483-4598), Box 358, Oak Point Road, Harrington 04643 (wreaths decorated with cones, berries, and reindeer moss); and **Maine Coast Balsam** (255-3301), Box 458, Machias 04654 (decorations include cones, red berries, and bow).

SPECIAL EVENTS

July: **Independence Day** celebrations in **Jonesport/Beals Island** (lobster-boat races, easily viewed from the bridge); **Cherryfield** (parade and fireworks); and **Steuben** (firemen's lobster picnic and parade); **Lubec** goes all out with a grand parade, contests, and fireworks; **Cut-**

ler and **Machias** also celebrate. **Campobello** celebrates **Canada Day**
with a parade and other events.

Last weekend in July: **Milbridge Days** (546-2406) include a parade, a
dance, a lobster dinner, and the famous **greased-codfish relay race.**

August: **Wild Blueberry Festival** and **Machias Craft Festival** (*third
weekend*) in downtown Machias, sponsored by Penobscot Valley Crafts
and Center Street Congregational Church: concerts, food, major crafts
fair, and live entertainment.

EASTPORT AND COBSCOOK BAY

Eastport is just 3 miles north of Lubec by boat but 40 miles by land
around Cobscook Bay. Cobscook is said to mean "boiling water" in the
Passamaquoddy tongue, and tremendous tides—over 26 feet—rush in
through this passage and slosh up deep inlets divided by ragged land
fingers along the north and south shores. One gap between the opposite shores is just 300 yards wide and the tides funnel through it at 6 to 8
knots, alternately filling and draining the smaller bays beyond. For several hours, the incoming tide actually roars through these "Cobscook
Reversing Falls."

The force of the tides in Passamaquoddy Bay—the wider water
that Eastport faces—is so powerful that in the 1930s President Roosevelt backed a proposal to harness this power to electrify much of the
Northeast Coast, including Boston.

The ecological considerations stacked against this "Quoddy Dam"
project are, it turns out, huge. Thanks to the extreme tides and currents, marine life is more varied than in other places. Nutrients that
elsewhere settle to the bottom, shoot here to the surface and nourish
some forms of life that exist nowhere else. The fact that you can see
only a few inches down into the water around Eastport is due not to
pollution but to this rich nutrient life. It's no coincidence that Maine's
first salmon farms were in Cobscook Bay, where this aquaculture industry continues to thrive.

The sardine-canning process in America was invented in Eastport
in 1875 and a boom era quickly followed, but today the population is
down to 2000, far less than half what it was at the turn of the 20th
century. Still, Eastport remains a working deepwater port. Large
freighters regularly dock at the new shipping pier near Estes Head to
take on woodland products, a reminder (as is the surviving Federal and
Greek Revival architecture) that by the War of 1812 this was already an
important enough port for the British to go capture and occupy it.

Today there are many gaps in the old waterfront, now riprapped in
pink granite to form a seawall. With its flat, haunting light, Eastport has
an end-of-the-world feel and suggests an Edward Hopper painting. It's

a landscape that draws many artists, and galleries line Water Street.

Eastport consists entirely of islands, principally Moose Island, which is connected to Route 1 by Route 190—via a series of causeways linking other islands. It's a departure point for the small car ferry and excursion boats that ply Passamaquoddy Bay. Old Sow, a whirlpool between Eastport and Deer Island said to be 230 feet in diameter, is reportedly the largest in the Western Hemisphere.

Route 190 runs through the center of the Pleasant Point Indian Reservation, home to some 550 members of the Passamaquoddy Indian tribe. The Waponahki Museum is dedicated to telling the story of the tribe, and several shops sell finely crafted baskets. The 3-day Indian Ceremonial Days in early August fully celebrate Passamaquoddy culture.

Unfortunately, the 20 miles of Route 1 between Whiting (turnoff for Lubec) and Perry (turnoff for Eastport) offer few glimpses of Cobscook Bay. Be sure to take the short detour into Cobscook Bay State Park (see *Green Space—Walks*) and into the ghostlike village of Pembroke, with its empty commercial buildings—including a trapezoidal movie hall and general store, dating from the village's 1870s prime, when its ironworks and shipyards prospered. Today Pembroke is best known for Reversing Falls Park (see *To See*).

GUIDANCE

Cobscook Bay Area Chamber of Commerce (726-9529; www.cobscookbay.com), P.O. Box 1, Route 68, Dennysville 04628. Good for information about the area between Lubec and Eastport.

Eastport Chamber of Commerce (853-4644; www.eastport.net), P.O. Box 254, Eastport 04631. **The Quoddy Maritime Museum** (853-4297), corner of Water and Boynton Streets, features a 14-by-16-foot concrete model of the Passamaquoddy Tidal Power Project (see chapter introduction) and is open Memorial Day through September, daily except Sunday. It triples as a museum, crafts cooperative, and **information center.**

Island Tours (853-831), 37 Washington Street, Eastport. Jim Blankman (also see Wood, Wheels, and Wings under *Selective Shopping*) offers lively, reasonably priced picnic tours of the Eastport area in a classic 1947 wood-paneled Dodge station wagon.

A "Quoddy Loop Tour Guide" and an excellent map, bridging the Canadian and Maine sides of Passamaquoddy Bay, is available from Old Sow Publishing (phone/fax: 853-6036; www.quoddyloop.com), P.O. Box 222, Moose Island, Eastport 04631.

TO SEE

Waponahki Museum & Resource Center (853-4001), Route 190, Pleasant Point. Open weekdays 8:30–11 and noon–4. Easy to miss, a small red building adjacent to the large VFW bingo hall. Passamaquoddy elder Joseph Nicholas has created an outstanding museum with photos, tools, baskets, and crafts that tell the story of the Passamaquoddy tribe.

Barracks Museum (853-4674/6630), 74 Washington Street, Eastport. Open July and August, Tuesday through Saturday 1–4. Originally part of Fort Sullivan and occupied by the British during the War of 1812, this house has been restored to its 1820s appearance as an officers' quarters and displays old photos and memorabilia about Eastport.

Reversing Falls Park. Turn off Route 1 at Route 214 into the village of Pembroke; follow the slight jog in the road then Leighton Neck for 3.4 miles, and turn right (the sign may or may not be there) then left at the T. The road degenerates before it ends at a parking area. A short trail leads to picnic tables and the water. Try to time your visit to coincide with the couple of hours at the height of the incoming tide, which funnels furiously through the gap between Mahar's Point and Falls Island. As the salt water flows along at 6 to 8 or more knots, it strikes a series of rocks, resulting in rapids. At low water this is a great place to hunt for fossils. **Tidal Trails** on Leighton Neck (see *To Do*) offers tours at midtide in a motorized inflatable raft.

Old Sow. What's billed as the largest whirlpool in the Western Hemisphere, and one of five significant whirlpools in the world, is sited between the tips of Moose Island and Deer Island. It's said to be produced by 70 billion cubic feet of water rushing into Passamaquoddy Bay, much of which finds its way around the tip of Deer Island and an underwater mountain at this narrow point in the bay. The area's smaller whirlpools are called Piglets. See *To Do—Boat Excursions* for viewing. Old Sow is visible from the ferry crossing, and we once saw a small cruise ship heel over dramatically when it came too close to the vortex. Small craft beware.

TO DO

BIRDING

Birding is what **Moosehorn National Wildlife Refuge** is about. Vast tidal flats in Eastport are good places to watch migrating plovers, sandpipers, and other shorebirds. American bald eagles are frequently seen around Cobscook Bay. See *Green Space—Walks.*

BOAT EXCURSIONS

Whale-watching (853-4303), out of Eastport. Captain George Harris and his son Butch offer 3-hour cruises of Passamaquoddy Bay.

Tidal Trails Eco-tours and Fishing Trips (726-4799). The 36-foot lobster boat *Copepod* offers 3-hour fishing tours and sight-seeing excursions, and the 18-foot motorized Zodiac raft *Sea Flea* is used for early-morning shoreline excursions.

Eastport Charter Company (853-2869) offers half-day and full-day sailing excursions out of Eastport on the 25-foot *Guillemot.*

Ferry to Deer Island, New Brunswick, with connections to Campobello

COURTESY QUODDY TIDES

Deer Island Ferry and landing at Eastport

and the New Brunswick mainland. For details about **East Coast Fer-ries Ltd.** (506-747-2159), see *Getting Around* in the introduction to "Washington County and the Quoddy Loop." Late June through early September the ferry departs every hour from the beach beside Eastport Lobster and Fish House. Be sure to take it at least to Deer Island. We strongly suggest you go the whole way around the Quoddy Loop (see the introduction to "Washington County and the Quoddy Loop").

SEA KAYAKING, CANOEING, AND BICYCLING

Tidal Trails (726-4079; www.nemaine.com/tidaltrails). From their base on Leighton Neck in Pembroke, Amy and Tim Sheehan offer a variety of ways to explore Cobscook Bay—which Tim points out is "really a net-work of bays"—specializing in guided kayak and canoe trips and rent-als. A biology teacher, Sheehan enthuses about the many forms of life in and around the waters he paddles. The Sheehans also rent mountain bikes and suggest a series of loop tours, including one to nearby Revers-ing Falls. Or take a tour through the falls in their Zodiac, at midtide.

GREEN SPACE

The **Quoddy Regional Land Trust** (733-5509), P.O. Box 49, Whiting 04691, with the help of the Maine Coast Heritage Trust, publishes a thick, ever-expanding booklet titled "Cobscook Trails: A Guide to Walk-ing Opportunities around Cobscook Bay and the Bold Coast." See *To Do—Hiking* in "The Atlantic Coast: Steuben to Campobello."

WALKS

Shackford Head State Park (posted from Route 190 south of Eastport) is a 90-acre peninsula with a trail (roughly two-thirds of a mile) from the parking lot to a half-mile trail to a 173-foot high headland overlooking Campobello and Lubec in one direction and Cobscook Bay in the other. Another quarter-mile-long trail leads down the headland and permits access to the shore. Views are of the bay with its floating salmon pens. Look for fossils at low water.

Moosehorn National Wildlife Refuge, Unit 2, Edmunds (off Route 1 between Dennysville and Whiting). Some 7,200 acres bounded by Whiting and Dennys Bays and the mouth of the Dennys River. North Trail Road is 2.5 miles long and leads to a parking area from which canoes can be launched into Hobart Stream. South Trail Road covers 0.9 mile and leads to a parking area for a 10-mile unmaintained trail network. Trails in the Baring section (Unit 1) of the refuge (see *Green Space* in "Calais and the St. Croix Valley") are maintained.

Cobscook Bay State Park (726-4412), off Route 1 between Dennysville and Whiting, has 888 acres that include a 2-mile nature trail with water views and a half-mile Shore Trail. Wildlife and birds are plentiful.

Gleason Point, Perry. Take the road next to the Quoddy Wigwam Gift Shop on Route 1 and follow signs to the beach and boat landing.

LODGING

Also see **Brewer House** under *Lodging—Bed & Breafast* in "Calais and the St. Croix Valley."

INNS AND BED & BREAKFASTS

Weston House (853-2907; 1-800-853-2907), 26 Boynton Street, Eastport 04631. Open year-round. An elegant Federal-style house built in 1810 with two large guest rooms sharing a full bath. One of these has a working fireplace and a tall four-poster, views of the bay and gardens, and antiques, but it was in the other—equally spacious and gracious—room that John James Audubon slept on his way to Labrador in 1833. A small room, tucked into the back of the ell, is perfect for solo travelers. Jett and John Peterson continue to add "rooms"—a bricked terrace here and a rose garden there—to the ever-expanding grounds. Rates are $50–80 double, including a sumptuous breakfast in the formal dining room: maybe Eastport salmon and eggs Benedict. Jett's four-course dinner ($35) or a picnic lunch can be arranged. The common rooms are furnished with Oriental rugs and wing chairs, but if you want to put your feet up, there is a very comfortable back room with books and a TV.

Todd House (853-2328), Todd's Head, Eastport 04631. Open year-round. A restored 1775 Cape with great water views. Breakfast is served in the common room in front of the huge old fireplace. In 1801 men met here to charter a Masonic Order, and in 1861 the house became a temporary barracks. The four large double rooms (shared baths) vary in feel, view, and access to baths. Our favorites are the ground-floor Cornerstone Room (but its bath is across from the common room) and the Masonic Room, both with working fireplaces ($55). There are also two efficiency suites ($70–85), both with water views. Guests are welcome to use the deck and barbecue. Innkeeper Ruth McInnis welcomes well-behaved children and pets; her own pets include a Maine coon cat, two cockatiels, and a pet seagull that keeps his eye on the goldfish in the ornamental pond.

The Milliken House (853-2955), 29 Washington Street, Eastport 04631. This 1840s house retains Victorian charm with a large double parlor, ornate detailing, and some original furniture. Artist-innkeeper Joyce Weber maintains a large studio that guests are welcome to use. There are three guest rooms with private baths, two that share. Rates ($50–65, $10 per extra guest) include a sumptuous breakfast.

Kilby House Inn (853-0889; 1-800-435-4529), 122 Water Street, Eastport 04631. A spotless Victorian house on the waterfront with an attractive double parlor and formal dining room, five pleasant upstairs guest rooms decorated with antiques and family heirlooms, private baths. $55–75. Owner Greg Noyes also sells antiques in the carriage house.

MOTEL

The Motel East (853-4747), 23A Water Street, Eastport 04631. This two-story motel has 14 units, some handicapped accessible, all with water views, some with balconies. Amenities include direct-dial phones, cable TV, 10 kitchenettes. $80 per night, $95 for a suite, $125 for five people.

COTTAGES AND MORE

Cinqueterre Farm Cottage (726-4766), RR 1, Box 1264, Ox Cove Road, Pembroke 04666. Les Prickett and Gloria Christie, two of the area's outstanding chefs, offer a jewel of a waterside, two-bedroom cottage with a living room and full kitchen on 600 acres. Your choice of catered or cook-your-own meals. $400–500 per week.

Yellow Birch Farm (726-5807; yellowbirchfarm@acadia.net), Young's Cove Road, Pembroke 04666. May through September. Bunny Richards and Gretchen Gordon maintain a 200-year-old working farm near the reversing falls and rent out a two-room cottage with a fully equipped kitchen, outdoor hot shower, outhouse, woodstove, and small deck ($350 per week, $50 per extra guest or child). Farm animals include pigs, lambs, and a flock of hens. Extras: croquet and horseshoes; both organic veggies and eggs are sold.

Tide Mill Farm (733-2110; tidemill@nemaine.com), Tide Mill Road, Dennysville 04628. This 200-year-old working farm on Whiting Bay and Crane Mill Stream has been in the Bell family since it was built and is set in the family's 1,600 acres, with 6 miles of shorefront. The century-old farmhouse has five bedrooms sharing 1½ baths, a complete kitchen, and large dining and living rooms. $800 per week and $25 extra for every person over age 5.

CAMPGROUND

Cobscook Bay State Park (726-4412), South Edmunds Road just off Route 1, between Dennysville and Whiting. Open mid-May through mid-October. Offers 150 camping sites, most of them for tents and many with water views. There are even showers (unusual in Maine state campgrounds). The 880-acre park also offers a boat-launch area, picnic benches, and a hiking and cross-country ski trail.

WHERE TO EAT

Waco Diner, Water Street (853-4046), Eastport. Open year-round, Monday through Saturday 6 AM–7 PM, until midnight for bar/restaurant. Begun as a pushcart in 1924, the Waco has recently expanded to include a waterside Schooner Room. The old section with booths and a long shiny counter survives, and specials are posted. You can get a full roast turkey dinner; also beer, chowder, and great french fries.

Eastport Cannery Restaurant (formerly Eastport Lobster and Fish House; 853-9669), 167 Water Street, Eastport. Open seasonally, daily 11:30–9. A good location, on the site of the country's first fish and sardine cannery. The menu in the upper dining rooms runs from sandwiches to bouillabaisse. The downstairs pub on Cannery Wharf is informal, and it's possible to get take-out (thus park in line) for the ferry that departs from the adjacent beach.

La Sardina Loca (853-2739), 28 Water Street, Eastport. Open daily 4–10 in-season, Thursday through Sunday off-season. "The crazy sardine" is so flashy, cheerful, and out of character with the rest of Water Street that you figure it's a mirage, or at best somebody's one-season stand. But it's been there for years in the former A&P with its Christmas lights, patio furniture, and posters, and a menu that's technically Mexican, including "la Sardina Loca" chili with hot chiles and sour cream. Where else can you get fresh crabmeat enchiladas? Fully licensed.

Crossroads Restaurant (726-5053), Route 1, "at the Waterfall," Pembroke. Open 11–9 daily. Bigger than it looks from outside, a great road-food stop, serving lobster rolls and deep-fried seafood pies; liquor served.

The New Friendly Restaurant (853-6610), Route 1, Perry. Good road food. Known for the most lobster in a lobster sandwich.

Rosie's Hot Dog Stand at the Breakwater in Eastport. Open seasonally for over 25 years.

ENTERTAINMENT

Stage East (726-4670), a 100-seat theater in the 1887 Masonic Hall at the corner of Water and Dana Streets; summer-season performances.

SELECTIVE SHOPPING

Along Route 190 and in Eastport

Skicin Arts & Crafts (853-2840), on Route 190 at the Pleasant Point Reservation, is attached to the home of Passamaquoddy patriarch Joseph Nicholas and features Passamaquoddy-made baskets and handmade jewelry.

Raye's Mustard Mill (853-4451; 1-800-853-1903), Route 190 (Washington Street), Eastport. Open daily 9–5 in summer; winter hours vary. In business since 1903, this company is billed as the country's last remaining stone-ground-mustard mill. This is the mustard in which Washington County's sardines were once packed, and it's sensational. Try the samples in **The Pantry** gift store; tours in July and August.

Wood, Wheels, and Wings (853-4831), corner of Water and Sullivan Streets, Eastport. Jim Blankman, a consummate craftsman with wood, is presently devoting his considerable imagination and energy to creating adult-sized scooters, even "scooters for two." His colorful shop with its potbellied stove also features beautifully crafted skateboards and plain pine "woody-motif" coffins. Blankman prides himself on his vintage 1947 wood-paneled Dodge nine-passenger station wagon (see *Guidance*), for which he also makes teardrop-shaped made-to-order trailers.

Earth Forms Pottery, corner of Water and Dana Streets, Eastport. Open daily in-season. Nationally known potter Donald Sutherland specializes in large garden and patio pots, also in free-form sculptures and in smaller functional but striking pieces like our fruit bowl.

The Eastport Gallery (853-4166), 69 Water Street, Eastport. Open daily in summer. A cooperative gallery representing more than 20 local artists. Note the upstairs back balcony over the harbor.

Crow Tracks (853-2336; www.crowtracks.com), 11 Water Street, Eastport. Open year-round. R. J. LaVallee carves a variety of birds, from decoys to Christmas ornaments.

Quoddy Crafts. See *Guidance*. Sharing space with the Quoddy Maritime Museum and the town information center, this juried crafts outlet is well worth checking out.

S. L. Wadsworth & Sons (853-4343), 42 Water Street, Eastport. Billed as the country's oldest ship chandlery and Maine's oldest business (no one really noticed until the present generation took over), this marine-geared store has recently added "nautical gifts" to hardware. There's no question that it was founded in 1818 by Samuel Wadsworth, son of General Peleg Wadsworth and uncle of poet Henry Wadsworth Longfellow.

Fountain Books, Water Street, Eastport. A funky former pharmacy filled with books, retaining the old soda fountain, adding cappuccino.

Along Route 1, heading north from Whiting

Cinqueterre Farm Bakery (726-4766), Ox Cove Road (off Route 1), Pembroke. Open May through October Monday through Saturday. Les Prickett and Gloria Christie, both locally respected chefs, operate a bakery specializing in 5-grain breads, pizza, and rolls; soups and eggs, honey, jams, and pickles also available along with a selection of wines.

Quoddy Wigwam Gift Shop (853-4812), Route 1, Perry. Open daily 9–6. This is a prime retail outlet for Penobscot and Passamaquoddy baskets, pottery, and quill jewelry, also for **Quoddy Trail Moccasins** made next door (853-2488; quoddytrail@nemaine.com). Hand-sewn and produced here just since 1997, these items are acquiring a fine reputation.

45th Parallel (854-9500; www.fortyfifthparallel.com), "halfway between the Equator and the North Pole" on Route 1, Perry. Open late May through October. Self-described as "an eclectic mix of new home furnishings, exotic antiques, architectural elements and accessories from around the Globe," this is something you might expect to find in Bar Harbor or Portland, certainly not at the 45th parallel in the former Perry Elementary School. Chicago designers Britani Holloway-Pascarella and Philip Pascarella have filled this space—from floor to 12-foot-high ceilings—with stained glass and antique beds, drawer pulls and lamps, jewelry and bird feeders. A clue to how Britani comes by her eye for both decorating and antiques can be found up Route 1 at the **Brewer House,** Washington County's most fancifully furnished B&B (see *Lodging* in "Calais and the St. Croix Valley").

Katie's on the Cove (454-8446; www.katieschocolates.com), Route 1, Mill Cove, Robbinston. All handmade and hand-dipped chocolates. Favorites, the luscious truffles aside, include Passamaquoddy Crunch, Maine Potato Candy, and Maine Black Bear Paws.

SPECIAL EVENTS

July: **Independence Day** is celebrated in **Pembroke** (parade, canoe races) and for a week in **Eastport,** with parades, a military flyover, and fireworks. Eastport's is the first flag in the United States to be raised on July 4 itself (at dawn). **Cannery Wharf Boat Race** *(last weekend).*

Mid-August: **Annual Indian Ceremonial Days,** Pleasant Point Reservation—a celebration of Passamaquoddy culture climaxing with dances in full regalia.

September: **Paint Eastport Day** *(Saturday after Labor Day)*—Artists of all ages are invited to come paint their favorite scene of the island city. At the end of the day artists return to the gallery for a silent auction. **Eastport Salmon Festival** *(Sunday after Labor Day)*—a celebration of Eastport's salmon industry; salmon, trout, and Maine potatoes are grilled dockside, and free tours of fish farms in the bay are offered, along with live entertainment, games, an art show, an antiques auction, and a fishing derby.

CALAIS AND THE ST. CROIX VALLEY

Calais (pronounced "Cal-us"), the largest city in Washington County, is the sixth busiest point of entry into the United States from Canada. It's also a shopping center for those on both sides of the international border. Its present population is 4,000, roughly 2,000 less than it was in the 1870s, the decade in which its fleet of sailing vessels numbered 176. The downtown area is small, but there are a few interesting shops and a new waterfront walkway along the river. Late summer, during the International Festival, is a great time to visit.

GUIDANCE
Calais Information Center (454-2211), 7 Union Street, Calais. Open year-round, daily 8–6, July through October 15; otherwise, 9–5. This center, operated by the **Maine Tourism Association,** is a source of brochures for all of Maine as well as the local area. The staff is friendly and eager to help, and there are public rest rooms.

Though it's not set up as a walk-in information center, the **Calais Regional Chamber of Commerce** (454-2308; www.visitcalais.com) is also helpful. Call or e-mail and they will send you information on the area before you visit.

Grand Lake Stream Chamber of Commerce, P.O. Box 124, Grand Lake Stream 04637. Request the brochure listing local accommodations and outfitters, and get a map showing hiking and mountain biking trails.

GETTING THERE
By car: The direct route to Calais from points west of Washington County is Route 9, the Airline Highway. From the Machias area, take Route 191.

MEDICAL EMERGENCY
Calais Regional Hospital (454-7521), 50 Franklin Street, Calais.

VILLAGES

Grand Lake Stream. A remote but famous resort community on West Grand Lake, with access to the Grand Lake chain. Grand Lake Stream claims to have been the world's biggest tannery town for some decades before 1874. Fishing is the big lure now: landlocked salmon, lake trout, smallmouth bass, also pickerel and white perch. Some of the state's outstanding fishing lodges and camps are clustered here, and there are many good and affordable lakeside rental camps, a find for families. Local innkeepers can get you into the **historical museum,** a trove of Native American artifacts, cannery-era photos, and canoe molding. Inquire about hiking and biking trails and guided kayaking.

TO SEE

St. Croix Island overlook, Route 1, Red Beach (8 miles south of Calais). The view is of the island on which Samuel de Champlain and Sieur de Monts established the first white settlement in North America north of Florida. That was in 1604. Using the island as a base, Champlain explored and mapped the coast of New England as far south as Cape Cod. The rest area here is a beauty, a great spot for a picnic.

Whitlock Mill Lighthouse, off Route 1 (3 miles south of Calais). The pleasant rest stop is another good place for a picnic. We were expecting a trail that would get us closer, but it isn't there. You can look at the lighthouse, however, built in 1893 originally and rebuilt in 1910. The lighthouse was a necessity when Calais was a big shipping port, and it's still a working lighthouse today.

MUSEUMS

St. Stephen's Chocolate Museum (506-466-7848). An interesting museum that tells the story of the Ganong Bros. Ltd. Company. Displays of old candy boxes, hand-dipping demonstrations, videos, a game to test your packing speed, and free samples. Out front in the same building is the chocolatier, where you can purchase the tempting goodies.

The Holmes Cottage, 237 Main Street. The oldest exisiting house in Calais, built in 1804. Open in summer and maintained by the local historical society. A good restoration of the house, to what it probably looked like when Dr. Holmes lived here.

The architecture of some of the houses, notably the "gingerbread houses" on South Main Street, is also interesting.

GREEN SPACE

Moosehorn National Wildlife Refuge (454-7161), RR 1, Box 202, Suite 1, Baring. Established in 1937, this area is the northeast end of a chain of wildlife and migratory bird refuges extending from Florida to Maine and managed by the U.S. Fish and Wildlife Service. The refuge has two sections, some 20 miles apart. The larger, 17,200-acre area is in Baring, 5 miles north of Calais on Route 1. Look for eagles, which seem to nest each spring at the intersection of Charlotte Road and Route 1. The Edmunds division is found heading south on Route 1 from Calais, between Dennysville and Whiting (see *Green Space* in "Eastport and Cobscook Bay"). This 7,200-acre area lies on the border of the tidal waters of Cobscook Bay. Ask about special programs—guided hikes, bike and van tours—which sometimes take you down roads you wouldn't be able to explore on your own—offered late June through August. Also inquire about fishing in the lakes and streams within the refuge.

TO DO

CANOEING

Sunrise County Canoe and Kayak (454-7708), Cathance Lake, Grove Post Office 04638. March through October. Offers advice, canoe and kayak rentals, and guided trips down the Grand Lake chain of lakes and the St. Croix River along the Maine–New Brunswick border; good for a 3- to 6-day run spring through fall. We did this trip with Sunrise (putting in at Vanceboro) and highly recommend it. In business more than 20 years, Sunrise is headed by photographer and naturalist Martin Brown; expeditions to the Arctic and Rio Grande are offered as well as to the Machias, St. John, and St. Croix Rivers.

FISHING

Grand Lake Stream is the focal point for dozens of lakes, ponds, and streams known for smallmouth bass and landlocked salmon (May through mid-June). There are also chain pickerel, lake trout, and brook trout. Fishing licenses, available for 3 days to a full season, are also necessary for ice fishing. For information on fishing guides, lodges, and rules, write to the Regional Headquarters of the Inland Fisheries and Wildlife Department, Machias 04653. Several lakes and streams in the **Moosehorn National Wildlife Refuge** (see *Green Space*) are open to fishing.

GOLF

St. Croix Country Club (454-8875), River Road, Calais. A tricky nine-hole course on the banks of the St. Croix River.

SWIMMING

Reynolds Beach on Meddybemps Lake by the town pier in Meddybemps (Route 191) is open daily 9 AM–sunset. Meddybemps is a very small, white, wooden village with a church, general store, and pier; a good spot for a picnic and a swim. **Red Beach** on the St. Croix River is named for the sand on these strands, which is deep red due to the red granite in the area. There is also swimming in dozens of crystal-clear lakes. Inquire about access at local lodges and general stores.

LODGING

BED & BREAKFAST

✿✍ **Brewer House** (454-2385; 1-800-821-2028; www.brewerhouse.com), Route 1, P.O. Box 94, Robbinston 04671. Open year-round on Route 1, 12 miles south of Calais, a striking 1828 mansion with graceful Ionic pillars. The interior, filled with treasures amassed in over 30 years of antiques dealing by David and Estelle Holloway, is very Victorian, a mix of fun and formality. A life-sized saint stands in the deep-blue living room, next to a marble fireplace. Each of the five bedrooms is named for one of David and Estelle's children and each is different, most featuring massive antique beds and fanciful baths, with views of Passamaquoddy Bay across the road. The Servants Quarters, a small apartment with cottage furniture (two beds, a TV and VCR, an efficiency kitchen) has an outside entrance; suited to families. $60–95 in summer includes a very full breakfast (with dessert!) served with silver and crystal in the sunny breakfast room. Estelle sells antiques next door at **The Landing.**

SPORTING LODGES

*   **Weatherby's** (796-5558, winter 237-2911; www.weatherbys.com), P.O. Box 69, Grand Lake Stream 04637. Open early May through October 1. A rambling, white 1870s lodge set in roses and birches by Grand Lake Stream, the small river that connects West Grand Lake with Big Lake. Ken and Charlene Sassi have been welcoming guests for more than 27 years, and their experience shows. There is a big sitting room—with piano and hearth—in the lodge; also a homey dining room with a tin ceiling and better than down-home cooking (served by the owner-chef). Each of the 16 cottages is unique, but most are log-style with screened porches, bath, and a Franklin stove or fireplace. Fishing is what this place is about, and it's a great place for children. $102 per person double occupancy, $125 single; children under 14 are $55 MAP (family rates available); motorboats are $42 per day, and a guide, $150; 15 percent gratuity added. Inquire about the L. L. Bean Introduction to Fly-Fishing Schools.

    Leen's Lodge (796-5575; 1-800-995-3367; www.leenslodge.com), Box 40, Grand Lake Stream 04637. November 1 through April 30 write to P.O. Box 92, Newport 04953 or call 368-5699. A peaceful cluster of cottages on the shore of West Grand Lake. Dick and E. J. Beaulieu offer 10 cabins, nicely scattered through the woods. Ranging in size from one to eight bedrooms, each has a full bath, fireplace or Franklin stove (with gas heat as a backup), and fridge. The spacious dining room overlooks the water. The Tannery, a pine-paneled gathering space with a picture window, is equipped with games, books, and a TV—a good spot to relax before dinner (BYOB). $90 per person per day MAP. Family rates available in nonpeak periods; 15 percent gratuity; lunch, boat rentals, and guide service are extra.

*   **Indian Rocks Camps** (796-2822; 1-800-498-2821), Grand Lake Stream 04637. Open year-round. The Canells offer five century-old log cabins and a central lodge. It's a friendly compound that caters to families and fishermen in summer, cross-country skiers, snowmobilers, and ice fishermen in winter. Amenities include miniature golf and a store on the premises. $62 per person includes all meals; $25 per person (no meals) in the housekeeping cabins. Summer rates in cabins: $375 per week. Inquire about fly-fishing school and guide service.

    Lakeside Inn and Cabins (796-2324), 2 Park Street, Princeton 04668. Open year-round; cabins May through November. A handsome old inn with twin chimneys and seven guest rooms; five basic housekeeping cabins on Lewy Lake (the outlet to Big Lake, also a source for the St. Croix River). Rooms in the inn are simple and nicely furnished; each has a sink. Although baths are shared, there are plenty. Common areas are inviting, especially the front porch and the sporting room with a pool table. Rooms in the inn are $31 per day for two; camps are $44–58 per night; meals are available at additional cost. They also offer guide service, boat rentals, and nonresident hunting/fishing licenses.

✎ **Shoreline Camps** (796-5539), P.O. Box 127, Grand Lake Stream 04637. Open ice-out until mid-October. A very attractive set of camps on the banks of Big Lake. Peaceful and remote, offering hiking, swimming, boating, and fishing. Ten cabins range from one to three bedrooms, each with bath and private deck. Boat rental, guides, fishing licenses available. Facilities also include a coin-operated laundry and the **Last Cast Lounge** (open to the public). $30 per person per day with a $60–85 minimum, depending on the cottage. Children under 12 are half price; under 3, free.

CAMPING
See **Cobscook Bay State Park** under *Lodging—Campground* in "Eastport and Cobscook Bay."

WHERE TO EAT

DINING OUT
The Chandler House (454-7922), 20 Chandler Street, Calais. Open 4–11 daily except Monday. Chef owned. Specializing in seafood like blackened whitefish and known for the best prime rib around. Entrées $9–18.95.

Bernardini's (454-2237), 89 Main Street, Calais. Open year-round except Sunday for lunch and dinner. An attractive storefront trattoria; traditional Italian entrées, pasta specials, and desserts. Entrées $11–15.

The Townhouse Restaurant (454-8021), 84 Main Street, Calais. Open mid-April through mid-October daily (except Sunday) 11–9. Seafood specialties include haddock with lobster sauce ($12.95) and prime rib.

Redclyffe Dining Room (454-3270), Route 1, Robbinston. Open 5–9 for dinner. The view overlooking Passamaquoddy Bay and the St. Croix River is superb through the solarium windows. The vast menu offers pasta, steaks, chicken, and seafood; specialties include baked haddock with lobster sauce, and "mariner's haul." Entrées $8.95–18.50. Reservations suggested.

Heslin's (454-3762), Route 1, Calais (south of the village). Open May through October, 5–9. A popular local dining room specializing in steak and seafood entrées; homemade desserts. Moderately priced.

EATING OUT
Wickachee (454-3400), 282 Main Street, Calais. Open year-round 6 AM–10

PM. Steak and seafood with a big salad bar are the dinner specialties; even dinner entrées start at just $7. Spacious, clean, and friendly, but the rest rooms are tiny.

SELECTIVE SHOPPING

Knock on Wood (1-800-336-7136), Route 1 west of Calais. Larger than it looks from the outside, a gift shop with a wide variety of crafts, candles, and more.

Marden's (454-1421), 61 Main Street. A new addition to the chain of Maine discount centers, which has been doing business in the state since 1964. Big-time bargains can be found here, from furniture to fabrics, housewares to clothing.

Pine Tree Store (796-5027), Water Street, Grand Lake Stream. Open daily year-round. A general store that also carries many sportsmen's essentials.

Pandora's Box (454-3604), 5 Lowell Street, Calais. Open 10–4. Seven rooms of a former boardinghouse are filled with an unpredictable assortment of clothing, furniture, jewelry, books—whatever Nellie Walton finds at auctions and estate sales. Special orders are happily filled.

SPECIAL EVENTS

July: **Indian Festival** at **Indian Township,** near Princeton. **Grand Lake Stream Folk Art Festival** *(last weekend)*—bluegrass and folk music, woodsmen's skills demonstrations featuring canoe building, crafts, dinner cooked by Maine guides.

August: **International Festival,** Calais and St. Stephen, New Brunswick. A week of events on both sides of the border, including pageants, a parade, entertainment, and more.

ST. ANDREWS AND GRAND MANAN, NEW BRUNSWICK

Beyond Eastport and Calais, you don't drop off the end of the world. Instead you cross the Canadian border—either via Route 1 at Calais or via ferry across Passamaquoddy Bay—into coastal New Brunswick. Suddenly it's an hour earlier, distance is measured in kilometers, signs are in French as well as English, gas is priced by the liter, and—for Americans—everything is cheaper. Most tourists here are, of course, Canadian.

Historically and geographically, in this corner Maine and Canada are intrinsically linked. Both St. Andrews (New Brunswick's liveliest resort town) and the island of Grand Manan (a haven for whale-watchers, birders, and hikers) were settled by loyalists during the Revolution, and Grand Manan, which lies just 9 miles off West Quoddy Light, is geographically closer to Maine than to Canada.

GUIDANCE

Complete lodging listings for both St. Andrews and Grand Manan are detailed in the "New Brunswick Travel Planner," available toll-free in Canada and the United States (1-800-561-0123; www.tourismnbcanada.com), or by writing to Economic Development & Tourism, P.O. Box 12345, Woodstock, New Brunswick E7M 5C3, Canada. A large **Provincial Visitors Information Center** (506-466-7390), 5 King Street, St. Stephen, stands a few blocks beyond the border crossing, surrounded by banks at which you can exchange American for Canadian dollars.

GETTING THERE

In good weather the ride across Passamaquoddy Bay from Eastport or Campobello via Deer Island is a delight, certainly the way to go at least one way to St. Andrews (see *Getting Around* in the introduction to "Washington County and the Quoddy Loop"). If you are heading directly to Grand Manan, however, it makes more sense to drive to Blacks Harbour to board that island's ferry. From the Calais–St. Stephens border, it's 19 miles to St. Andrews and 35 miles to Blacks Harbour. See *Getting There* in "Grand Manan" for details about the ferry.

TIME

Note that New Brunswick's Atlantic time is 1 hour ahead of Maine.

TAXES

The Canadian Harmonized Sales Tax (HST) is 15 percent on food, lodging, and just about everything else in Canada. Visitors who spend more than $100 (Canadian) on goods and short-term accommodations will get most of it back by mailing in a Revenue Canada application and appending all receipts.

ST. ANDREWS

St. Andrews is much like Bar Harbor, but with the genteel charm and big hotels that have vanished in Bar Harbor. The crowds aren't as big, even in summer months. The result is a pleasant resort town with plenty of choices for lodging, several decent restaurants, a range of activities from historical tours to day adventures, and a handful of ever-changing but upscale gift shops.

The big hotel in St. Andrews is the Algonquin, a 200-room, many-gabled, neo-Tudor resort dating from 1915. The Algonquin sits enthroned like a queen mother above this tidy town with loyalist street names like Queen, King, and Princess Royal. St. Andrews was founded in 1783 by British Empire loyalists, American colonists who so strongly opposed breaking away from the mother country that they had to leave

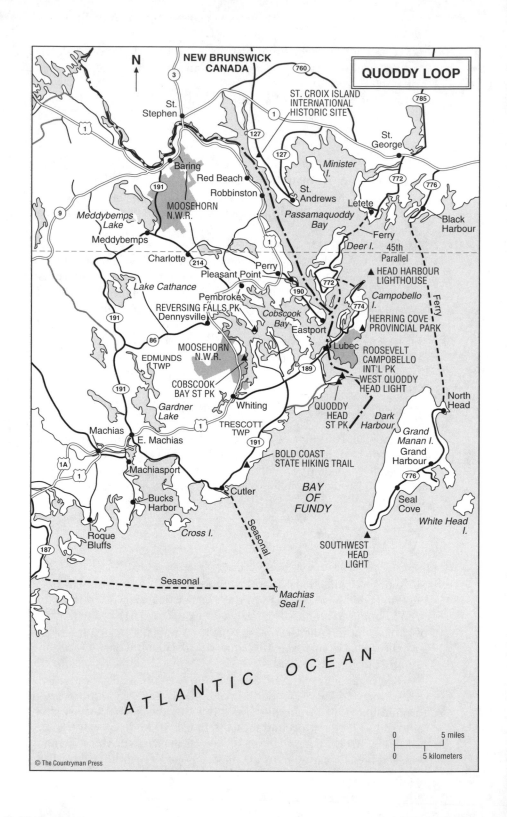

N

NEW BRUNSWICK
CANADA

QUODDY LOOP

760

3

1

785

St.
Stephen

ST. CROIX ISLAND
INTERNATIONAL
HISTORIC SITE

St.
George

127

127

772

Baring

191

Red Beach

Robbinston

*Minister
I.*

776

MOOSEHORN
N.W.R.

St.
Andrews

Letete

Black
Harbour

9

*Meddybemps
Lake*

*Passamaquoddy
Bay*

Meddybemps

1

Ferry

Deer I.

45th
Parallel

Charlotte

214

Perry

772

▲ HEAD HARBOUR
LIGHTHOUSE

Pleasant Point

190

*Campobello
I.*

Lake Cathance

Pembroke

774

HERRING COVE
PROVINCIAL PARK

191

REVERSING FALLS PK.
Dennysville

*Cobscook
Bay*

Eastport

86

Lubec

ROOSEVELT
CAMPOBELLO
INT'L PK

Ferry

MOOSEHORN
N.W.R.

EDMUNDS
TWP

WEST QUODDY
HEAD LIGHT

North
Head

191

COBSCOOK
BAY ST PK

189

*Gardner
Lake*

Whiting

QUODDY
HEAD
ST PK

*Dark
Harbour*

Machias

1

TRESCOTT
TWP

*Grand
Manan I.*

1A

E. Machias

191

Grand
Harbour

1

Machiasport

BOLD COAST
STATE HIKING TRAIL ▲

776

Bucks
Harbor

Cutler

*BAY
OF
FUNDY*

Seal
Cove

187

*Roque
Bluffs*

Cross I.

Seasonal

*White Head
I.*

▲
SOUTHWEST
HEAD
LIGHT

Seasonal

*Machias
Seal I.*

ATLANTIC   OCEAN

0   5 miles

0   5 kilometers

© The Countryman Press

the new United States after independence was won. Most came from what is now Castine, many of them unpegging their houses and bringing them along in the 1780s. Impressed by this display of loyalty, the British government made the founding of St. Andrews as painless as possible, granting the settlers a superb site. British army engineers dug wells, built a dock, constructed a fort, and laid out the town on its present grid. Each loyalist family was also given a house lot twice the usual size. The result is an unusually gracious, largely 19th-century town, hauntingly reminiscent of Castine. The focal point remains Market Wharf, where the first settlers stepped ashore—now the cluster point for outfitters offering whale-watching, sailing, and kayaking tours—and Water Street, lined with shops.

GUIDANCE

St. Andrews Chamber of Commerce (506-529-3555), Reed Avenue, St. Andrews, New Brunswick EOG 2XO, Canada. The office is open year-round; the information center, May through October.

Complete lodging listings for both St. Andrews and Grand Manan are detailed in "Welcome to New Brunswick." Request a copy by calling (toll-free in Canada and the United States) 1-800-561-0123.

GETTING THERE

By car: Route 1 via Calais. From the border crossing at Calais, it's just 19 miles to St. Andrews.

By car ferry: See *Getting Around* in the introduction to "Washington County and the Quoddy Loop"; also see *To Do—Boat Excursions* in the first two chapters under "Washington County and the Quoddy Loop." The ferry docks in L'Etete, and the road curves up the peninsula through the town of St. George, where you pick up Canadian Route 1, following it 13 unremarkable miles to the turnoff (Route 127) for St. Andrews.

TO SEE

Ross Memorial Museum (506-529-1824), corner of King and Montague Streets, St. Andrews. Open Monday through Saturday mid-June through Labor Day 10–4:30, then closed Mondays until mid-October. An 1824 mansion displaying the fine decorative art collection of the Reverend and Mrs. Henry Phipps Ross of Ohio, world travelers and collectors who fell in love with the area while on a picnic on Chamook Mountain. They purchased the 1824 house and donated it, along with their collections, to the town.

Sheriff Andrews House Historic Site, 63 King Street, St. Andrews. Open June through early September, Monday through Saturday 9:30–4:30, Sunday 1–4:30. An 1820 house that belonged to Elisha Andrews, high sheriff of Charlotte County; fine detailing. Costumed guides offer tours and demonstrate open-hearth cooking techniques and traditional do-

CHRISTINA TREE

St. Andrews

mestic handiwork, such as quilting.

Ministers Island Historic Site (506-529-5081), Chamcook. Open June through mid-October. One of the grandest estates, built around 1890 on an island connected by a "tidal road" (accessible only at low tide) to St. Andrews, **Covenhoven** is a 50-room mansion with 17 bedrooms, a vast drawing room, a bathhouse, and a gigantic and ornate livestock barn. The builder was Sir William Van Horne, the driving force in construction of the Canadian Pacific Railway. Pre-set 2-hour guided tours only. Phone before coming.

Huntsman Aquarium Museum Marine Science Centre (506-529-1202; www.unb.ca/huntsman), Brandy Cove Road (off Route 127), St. Andrews. Open daily. A nonprofit aquaculture research center sponsoring educational programs and cruises; the aquarium-museum features hundreds of living plants and animals found in the Quoddy region, including resident harbor seals, fun to watch at feeding times (11 AM and 4 PM). The touch pool is popular with kids. Other exhibits include information on the Fundy tides, aquaculture, and marine science research. A small fee is charged.

Atlantic Salmon Conservation Centre (506-529-4581; www.asf.ca), Chamcook, 5 miles east of St. Andrews on Route 127. The complex, opened in 1998, is made up of four post-and-beam buildings connected by porches and boardwalks. The Atlantic Salmon International Hall of Fame looks like an old river lodge, complete with great room. Salar's World is the primary display area, with a waterfall, a giant map of where Atlantic salmon live, and Chamcook Stream flowing right through the room, with salmon of all sizes (best seen in the special viewing chamber). The complex also features a multimedia room, a room for special events and workshops, an adventure walk on the grounds along Chamcook Stream, and picnic areas.

Kingsbrae Horticultural Garden (506-529-3335), 220 King Street, St. Andrews. Twenty-seven acres of elaborately formal gardens with walking paths, a café, an art gallery, and a gift shop. Built on the grounds of several long-gone estates, the garden uses mature cedar hedges, flower beds, and old-growth forest in the new design. Specialized areas include display gardens with rare and exotic plants, demonstration gardens, a woodland trail through the old-growth forest, a therapy garden, and bird and butterfly gardens.

TO DO

DAY ADVENTURES
An organized network of activities that can be done in a day, from whale-watching to museum tours, candle making to cooking classes. Twenty-five **Day Adventure Outlets,** with consultants to help you plan, are located throughout New Brunswick, as are over 600 **Adventure Stations,** where tickets can be purchased in advance. Look for the special symbol designating Day Adventures, or pick up a copy of "Welcome to New Brunswick," which lists more than 100 adventures.

BOAT EXCURSIONS
In addition to the whale-watching tours and sailing cruise listed in this section, **Fundy Guardian Boat Tours Inc.** (506-529-8838) offers marine wildlife tours, aquaculture tours, and diving charters on their 25-foot Boston whaler.

GOLF
Algonquin Signature Golf Course (see *Lodging—Resort*). The resort's golf course was completely redesigned in 2000. Thomas McBroom, an award-winning architect, laid out the 18-hole course. From oceanfront to forest holes, the natural flow of the course and the scenic views make this an unforgettable golfing experience. Hole 17 is adjacent to the old clubhouse, now a museum highlighting the Algonquin's golf history. Clubhouse, pro shop.

SAILING
S/V *Cory* (506-529-8116), St. Andrews Wharf, a 72-foot gaff- and square-rigged cutter built by her captain in New Zealand, offers 3-hour sails in Passamaquoddy Bay and up the St. Croix River, where you might see whales, dolphins, and other wildlife. Passengers are welcome to take the helm or help hoist sails.

SEA KAYAKING AND CANOEING
In St. Andrews **Seascape** (506-529-4012), 12 King Street, offers half- and full-day guided tours as well as longer expeditions. They also have several skills courses, including introduction to sea kayaking and sea kayak

safety. **Eastern Outdoors** (1-800-56-KAYAK), 165 Water Street, also offers guided half- and full-day tours; beginners welcome.

SWIMMING
Katy's Cove, Acadia Road, St. Andrews, has (relatively) warm water, a sandy beach, and a clubhouse; nominal admission.

WHALE-WATCHING
In St. Andrews along King Street and the adjacent waterfront you can comparison shop: **Cline Marine** (506-526-4188) is the local pioneer in bird- and whale-watching tours; **Fundy Tide Runners** (506-529-4481) features fast, 24-foot, rigid-hulled Zodiac Hurricane boats, and clients wear flashy orange, full-length flotation suits; **Quoddy Link Marine** (506-529-2600) offers Whale Search and Island Cruises aboard two larger, slower vessels with enclosed, heated viewing areas as well as outdoor decks. **Island Quest Marine Adventures** (506-529-9885) offers a 3-hour tour on a custom-built 38-foot tour boat.

TOURS
HMS Transportation (529-4443) offers narrated tours of St. Andrews by-the-Sea, including visits to the Charlotte County Court House, the Greenoch Presbyterian Church, and the War of 1812 Blockhouse. Tours leave from the Algonquin (see *Lodging—Resort*) daily in summer. They also offer walking tours, and private and group tours.

LODGING

RESORT
The Algonquin (506-529-8823; in the U.S., 1-800-441-1414), 184 Adolphus Street, St. Andrews, New Brunswick, Canada E5B 1T7. Open year-round. The last of the truly grand coastal resorts in northeastern America: a 250-room, Tudor-style hotel with formal common and dining rooms, as well as banquet space geared to the many groups that keep it in business. The resort was built in 1889, with the castle facade, but only 80 rooms. Ownership began with the St. Andrews Land Company, passed to the Canadian Pacific Railway Company, and in the 1970s was leased (and later purchased) by the province of New Brunswick. The golf course has undergone extensive renovations in recent years, and there are five dining options, a spa and fitness center, fitness classes year-round, a heated outdoor pool, tennis courts, shuffleboard, and a daily activity program for children in summer. The rack rate averages $119–369 (Canadian) per couple, but look for special packages; children are free.

INNS
Kingsbrae Arms (506-529-1897), 219 King Street, St. Andrews, New Brunswick, Canada E5B 1Y1. Canada's first five-star inn (decreed by Canada Select) opened in 1997 by Harry Chancey Jr. and David Oxford, owners of the deluxe Centennial House in East Hampton. We were impressed with the elegance of the softly colored drawing room

with its grand piano and gardens beyond; there is also a comfortable beamed study and a formal dining room. The guest rooms exude a similar sense of luxury, with king or queen beds, fireplaces, telephones, marble bathrooms, and water or garden views. Suites are expansive and have private balconies. Many rooms have Jacuzzis. We were assured that a guest's every need is met and anonymity preserved. Rates in 2001 were $560 (Canadian) for rooms, $720 for suites, including a full breakfast and a four-course dinner.

The Hiram Walker Estate (506-529-4210; 1-800-470-4088; www.walker estate.com), 109 Reed Avenue, St. Andrews, New Brunswick, Canada E5B 2J6. Built in the grand manner in 1912 as a summer retreat and set in 11 wooded acres for the Walker (as in Hiram Walker Canadian Club whiskey) family, the châteaulike mansion became Canada's second five-star inn in 1997. The formal drawing room, library, music room, dining room, and upstairs suites are opulent by today's standards (seven with king-sized beds and whirlpool tubs). This is a distinctly romantic inn, ideal for honeymoons and anniversaries. Breakfast is served with crystal, silver, and candlelight, and English tea is laid midafternoon. Dinner is by reservation. There's also a cozy bar area. Innkeeper Elisabeth Cooney, who was born in St. Andrews, prepares the meals. U.S. $175–295. Facilities include an outdoor heated pool and outside hot tub.

The Windsor House of St. Andrews (506-529-3330; 1-888-890-9463), 132 Water Street, St. Andrews, New Brunswick, Canada E5B 1A8. This six-room hotel in the center of town is a gem, furnished in antiques and artwork from the private collection of American owners Jay Remer (who has worked at Sotheby's) and Greg Cohane. The building dates to 1798 and includes a (public) dining room and a billiard room (the table is from a Newport mansion). Guest rooms all have phones and concealed TV/VCRs. $125–300 (Canadian) includes a full breakfast.

BED & BREAKFASTS

Check with the chamber of commerce (see *Guidance*) for other reasonably priced B&Bs, many of which seem to change each season.

Pansy Patch (506-529-3834; 1-888-726-7972; www.pansypatch.com), 59 Carleton Street, St. Andrews, New Brunswick E5B 1M8. Open mid-May through mid-October. Built fancifully in 1912 to resemble a Norman cottage, right across from the Algonquin. Michael O'Connor offers five guest rooms with private baths, water views, and antiques in the house itself (an attic suite has a kitchenette), and four more in the adjacent Cory Cottage. Breakfast, served in the sunroom, is included in $150–230 (Canadian) per couple. An art gallery and tea garden are also on the premises, and guests have access to an outdoor pool, tennis, and other resort facilities at the **Algonquin.** Lunch and dinner are open to the public in their fully licensed dining room (see *Dining Out*).

❦   **Treadwell Inn** (506-529-1011; 1-888-529-1011; www.townsearch.com/ treadwell), 129 Water Street, St. Andrews, New Brunswick, Canada

E5B 1A7. Open practically year-round. A real find, with four spacious guest rooms furnished in antiques; private baths. Two rooms have balconies overlooking the water (35 feet away). Two third-floor efficiency suites have sitting areas and whirlpool baths with private waterside balconies. At $95–165 (Canadian; $75–125 off-season), including breakfast, this is great value.

It's the Cat's Meow (506-529-4086), 62 Water Street, Box 206, St. Andrews, New Brunswick E0G 2X0. Bonnie Nelson and her family offer four spacious rooms, decorated in a pretty, simple style; private baths. The garden solarium is a great place to read (they have a library of books to choose from), watch TV, or chat with other guests. There is always a rug-hooking project going—it's Bonnie's hobby, and she can explain how it works to interested guests. The cats live in the Nelsons' quarters but are brought out for visits upon request. Smoke-free environment. $95 (Canadian) includes a full breakfast served family-style in the dining room.

MOTEL
St. Andrews Motor Inn (506-529-4571), 111 Water Street, St. Andrews, NB, E5B 1A3. A three-story motel with 33 units and a heated indoor swimming pool. All rooms have two queen-sized beds and color TVs, some have kitchenettes, and all have private balconies overlooking Passamaquoddy Bay. $100 (Canadian) plus tax includes coffee and doughnuts.

CAMPING
Passamaquoddy Park Campground (506-529-3439), Indian Point Road. Maintained by the Kiwanis Club of St. Andrews, this is a beautifully sited campground with full hook-ups as well as tent sites.

WHERE TO EAT

All listings are in St. Andrews unless otherwise noted.
DINING OUT
L'Europe Dining Room and Lounge (506-529-3818), 63 King Street. Open for dinner daily except Monday in-season. Ownership has changed, and we are told it's even better than before. Fine dining in a fully licensed dining room.

The Passamaquoddy Dining Room at the Algonquin (506-529-8823), 184 Adolphus Street. The dining room is huge and its most pleasant corner is in the Veranda, with windows overlooking formal gardens. The menu is large, featuring local salmon and lobster. Entrées $19.95–29.95 (Canadian) plus tax. The hugely popular Sunday buffet is $29.95 (Canadian).

The Gables (506-529-3440), 143 Water Street. Open 11–10. Reasonably priced, good food, and a tiered, shaded deck with a water view. Specialties include fresh fish ranging from fried haddock and chips to a seafood platter. We recommend the mussels. Fully licensed; wine by the glass and a wide selection of beers. Entrées $9.50–17.95 (Canadian).

The Pansy Patch (506-529-3834; 1-888-726-7972), 59 Carleton Street. Fully licensed dining room open for lunch and dinner. At lunch there's an assortment of soups, salads, and sandwiches as well as lighter portions of some dinner entrées. Dinner includes appetizers like escargots and jumbo shrimp brochette; entrées include seafood paella and lamb chops. $19.95–22.95 (Canadian).

EATING OUT

Historic Chef's Café (529-8888). Billing itself as "Canada's Oldest Restaurant," this is a fun, nostalgic place. Decorated in 1950s style, with plenty of memorabilia to look at while you wait. Huge menu features burgers and specialty sandwiches, seafood, steak, and chicken.

Lighthouse Restaurant (506-529-3082), Lower Patrick Street. Open for lunch and dinner May through October. The best weatherproof view of the bay is from this restaurant serving mostly seafood, but also beef and chicken.

SELECTIVE SHOPPING

Cottage Craft Ltd., Town Square, St. Andrews. Open year-round, Monday through Saturday. Dating back to the 1940s, Cottage Craft showcases yarns, tweeds, and finished jackets, sweaters, and skirts; also distinctive handwoven throws made in homes throughout Charlotte County. Skirt and sweater kits as well as the finished products are the specialties.

Boutique La Baleine, 173 Water Street, St. Andrews. A large, well-stocked gift shop with books of local interest, music, and a variety of interesting items.

The China Chest Ltd., 234 Water Street, St. Andrews. This store has been offering china and crystal since 1928. Also featuring candles, handcrafts, miniature tea sets, pewter miniatures, thimbles, and more.

Serendipin' Art (529-3327). A large selection of handmade New Brunswick crafts, including jewelry, handblown glass objects, pottery, handpainted silks, and more.

SPECIAL EVENTS

December: **Candlelight tours**—historic homes are open to the public with decorations and refreshments.

GRAND MANAN

Little more than 15 miles long and less than 7 miles wide, Grand Manan is Canada's southernmost island, far enough at sea to be very much its own place, a rugged outpost at the mouth of the Bay of Fundy.

Right whales are what draw many visitors. These are the largest, liveliest, and rarest of whales. Just 320 are known to exist worldwide, and they all seem to be here in summer months, feeding on krill and other nutrients in the tide-churned waters. Birds are another draw: 240 species frequent the island. Machias Seal Island, the prime viewing place for puffins, is as easily accessible from Grand Manan as from Maine. Hiking trails are another plus, hugging cliffs that vary from 100 to almost 400 feet.

Fishing boats line the wharves the way they used to in New England. While fish are fewer than they once were here too, fishing is more profitable than ever. Connors Brothers sardine factory at Seal Cove remains the island's largest employer, and salmon farming is big, along with lobster and clams, periwinkles, and that Grand Manan delicacy: dulse. The hundreds of herring smokehouses for which the island was once known are, however, all gone, the last one preserved as an unusual museum.

Grand Manan's population has hovered around 2,700 since the late 19th century, clustered in the sheltered harbors and coves along its gentle Bay of Fundy shore, which is protected by many small islands. In contrast the northern and southern "heads" of the island are soaring cliffs, as is almost the entire western shore. It's a mirror image of Maine's Bold Coast, notched only by well-named Dark Harbor.

In many ways Grand Manan remains as out of the way and unspoiled as it was during the 20 summers (1922–1942) that Willa Cather spent here, working on some of her most famous novels, including *Death Comes for the Archbishop*. Her cottage on Whale Cove is one among the island's many summer rentals.

GUIDANCE

Grand Manan Tourism Association, P.O. Box 193, North Head, Grand Manan, New Brunswick EOG 2MO, Canada. The seasonal **Tourist Information Center** (506-662-3442) is at the Grand Manan Museum (see *To See*). The association publishes several handy, nominally priced booklet guides.

GETTING THERE

By car: 19 miles to St. Andrews and 35 miles to Blacks Harbour.

By ferry: **Coastal Transportation** (506-662-3724) operates ferries on the 20-mile, 90-minute sail between Blacks Harbour on the mainland (35 miles from the Calais–St. Stephen border) and North Head on the island. During high season (June 29 through Labor Day), ferries run six times a day, every 2 hours beginning at 7:30 AM. Service from the mainland is first come, first served. Things we wish we had known: (1) The ferry terminal is a couple of miles beyond the village of Blacks Harbour, so you may want to stock up on food and drink before you get in line. (2) Call to check which ferry runs when. Avoid the *MV Grand Manan*, the smaller seasonal ferry, which takes just around 20 cars or, as on our run, 15 cars (we were car 16) and a few big trucks; the *MS Grand Manan V* is capable of swallowing many more vehicles. For the return trip, everyone reserves. Food is available on both ferries. Cars are $26.20 (Canadian) round-trip, motorcycles $8.75, and bicycles $2.75. Passenger fares are $8.75 adults, $4.40 children ages 5–12. Pedestrians and bicyclists have no problem getting on. Parking is ample and free in Blacks Harbour, and whale-watching, sea kayaking tours, and rental bikes are also within walking distance of the ferry terminal.

TO SEE

✐ **The Grand Manan Museum** (506-662-3524), 1141 Route 776, Grand Harbor, across from the school. Open May through September, 10–4. The *Allan Moses Bird Collection,* an exhibit of more than 300 mounted birds, documents the island's bird life, and the history of the island's smoked-herring industry is dramatized in paintings, photographs, and memorabilia. Novelist Willa Cather's typewriter and manuscript table are also here. Inquire about evening slide shows and rainy-day programs.

Dark Harbor. The only road across the width of the island ends abruptly at the harbor (it's a tight turnaround at high tide), the one nick in what is otherwise a wall of cliffs that run the length of the western shore. This is a prime dulse-harvesting spot, but there are no commercial enterprises, just seasonal cottages that are inaccessible except by boat at low tide.

Southwest Head. Your first instinct is to drive the length of the island on the one north–south road, grandiosely numbered 776. It ends at Southwest Head Lighthouse, and a path leads along spectacular cliffs.

Hole in the Wall. The view of this much-photographed natural arch near the northern end of the island is most easily accessed via a fairly steep path, from a parking area that lies within Hole-in-the-Wall Park, a former airport that's now a commercial campground.

Sardine Museum and Herring Hall of Fame (506-662-9913), Seal Cove, Grand Manan. Open seasonally, most days. The island's herring smokehouses once numbered 300. Herring were hung on racks above smoldering fires until they turned the color of burnished gold, and lines of women gutted and deboned fish with the speed and skill of surgeons. This was the last smokehouse to close. A token rack of fish still hangs in one window, and the tables are there, thanks to New York architect Michael Zimmer, who couldn't resist the FOR SALE sign on this picturesque collection of long wooden sheds. One building is now Zimmer's

summer home, and the others house art installations or historic memorabilia or both. An aluminum boat in the shape of a sardine can (the top
is rolled back, complete with giant key) is moored to the wharf. "People
wander around here smiling," Zimmer observes. "Slowly they see that
this isn't the kind of museum in which you have to read labels." It's free.

TO DO

BIRDING
The island is visited annually by 240 species of birds and many, many more
bird-watchers. **Castalia Marsh,** accessible via a nature trail in Castalia
Provincial Park, is a favorite spot at dawn and dusk. One of the first
visitors was John James Audubon, who came in 1831 to check out the
unlikely-but-true story that island seagulls nest in trees. From mid-June
through early August **Sea Watch Tours** (506-662-8332; www.angelfire.
com/biz/seawatch) offers trips from Seal Cove to **Machias Seal Island**
to see puffins, arctic terns, and razor-billed auks. (Landing on the island
involves transfer from a 42-foot boat into a 16-foot dory and then walking across seaweed-covered rocks.)

BOAT EXCURSIONS
Sea View Adventures (506-662-3211; 1-800-586-1922). Departs from North
Head at Fisherman's Wharf. These 3½-hour tours aboard a sleek new
26-foot excursion boat feature underwater views on a console, projected
via a live underwater diver. Salmon pens, herring seines, bird life, and
seals are staples of the tour. Also see Whale-Watching.

HIKING
Some 45 miles of marked hiking trails cover a variety of terrain along the
shore. Pick up a copy of "Heritage Trails and Footpaths" (available in
most island stores) and a picnic and you're set.

KAYAKING AND BIKE RENTALS
Adventure High (506-662-3563; 1-800-732-5492; www.adventurehigh.
com), 83 Route 776. Guided tours range from a 2-hour moonlight trip
to 6-hour explorations and include Seal Watch Tours and a Kayak Tour
& Dinner on the Beach. Mountain and hybrid bikes are also rented.
Inquire about the solar-heated rental cottage on a remote cove.

WHALE-WATCHING
Whales-n-Sails Adventures (506-662-1999; 1-888-994-4044; www.
whales-n-sails.com), North Head, Fisherman's Wharf, offers two daily
trips, weather permitting, June through mid-September. Sailing and
whale-watching are a great combination. The 56-foot, 47-passenger
ketch *Elsie Menota* supplements sail with power to reach the deeps in
the Bay of Fundy (12 miles northeast of Grand Manan), where Atlantic
right whales feed and play, but then it's quiet and pleasant to tack and
jibe among these huge creatures. Owner Allan McDonald points out
bird and sea life en route.

Island Coast Boat Tours (506-662-8181) uses a 40-foot, 25-passenger excursion boat for whale-watches (same times, same place as the above).
Also offers a coastal sight-seeing tour.

Sea-Land Adventures (506-662-8997; www.angelfire.com/biz2/sealand),
North Head, Fisherman's Wharf. Mid-June through October. The gaff-
rigged schooner *D'Sonoqua* offers full-day (10–5) sails to see the whales.
Captain James Bates and his vessel have followed whales around much
of the world, and marine biologist Laurie Murison, who offers com-
mentary, has studied the bay and its inhabitants since 1982. Lunch and
snacks are included.

Sea Watch Tours (see *Birding*) also offers whale-watch cruises.

LODGING

Note: The choice of lodgings and cottages is large, and there are several
campgrounds (see *Guidance* in "The Quoddy Loop: St. Andrews and
Grand Manan"). The following represent the best of the inns and B&Bs
we checked.

The Inn at Whale Cove Cottages (506-662-3181; www.holidayjunction.
com), 25 Whale Cove Cottage Road, Grand Manan NB 356 2B5. The
gray-shingled Main House dates back to 1816, overlooking a quiet cove
with a large fish weir, backed by rugged Fish Head. It was here in
picturesque Orchardside cottage that Willa Cather first came to write in
1922, eventually building a replica of it a ways down the shore (also
available for rent). The inn and cottages are owned and operated by
Laura Buckley and her mother, Kathleen, who remembers waiting on
Cather in the dining room, three times a day. Even without the Cather
connection this would be a very special place. The Main House parlor has
changed little since it began welcoming "rusticators" in 1910. The
fireplace is large and usually glowing, and the walls are lined with books,
also a feature in the cottages. Orchardside has four bedrooms as well as
a kitchen living room and dining room ($500 per week); Coopershop
features a huge fireplace and two upstairs bedrooms as well as a living
room and kitchen/dining area ($500 per week). There are also the one-
bedroom Bungalow ($85 per night) and three delightful rooms in the
Main House ($75 per night). An expansive lawn with children's play
equipment overlooks the cove, and a path leads down to the beach. Rates
are in Canadian dollars and include a very full breakfast. Dinner is also
served (see *Where to Eat*).

Compass Rose (506-662-8570; off-season: 613-692-1781; www.angelfire.
com/biz/compassrose), North Head, Grand Manan, NB, EOG 2M0.
Open May through October. Within walking distance of the ferry terminal and handy to water excursions and bike rentals, this is a gem of an
inn, overlooking the busy harbor of North Head. Owner Nora Parker
has recently renovated the entire inn. Each of the seven guest rooms is

furnished in antiques and has a private bathroom and ocean view. The dining room, which is open to the public, is a must-stop for every visitor (see *Where to Eat*). $79 (Canadian) per couple includes a full breakfast.

McLaughlin's Wharf Inn B&B (506-662-8760), Seal Cove. A rehabbed vintage-1863 wharf building offers exceptional common space and pleasant rooms. $79 (Canadian) includes breakfast.

WHERE TO EAT

The Inn at Whale Cove (506-662-3181), 25 Whale Cove Cottage Road, near North Head. Open nightly in-season, 6–8:30. Reservations required. The dining room in the early-19th-century cottage seats just 30 people. It's candlelit and decorated with vintage willowware. Chef-owner Laura Buckley uses local ingredients imaginatively. Saturday night features a five-course set meal. Fully licensed.

Compass Rose (506-662-8570), North Head. Open May through October for lunch and dinner. The harbor view is unbeatable, and even without it the dining room would strike you as unusually pleasant. Lunch on a hearty fish chowder or chicken Caesar salad. Dinner might be seafood lasagna or pan-fried haddock; leave room for double chocolate cheesecake.

The Lobster Deck, North Head at Fishermen's Wharf. Great fish chowder.

SELECTIVE SHOPPING

Roland's Sea Vegetables (506-662-3866), 174 Hill Road (marked from the Dark Harbor Road) is a must-stop. Dulse and other seaweeds are hand-harvested at Dark Harbor, then dried and packaged. We wish we had bought more bottles of dulse flakes.

Island Artisans (506-662-3625), North Head. Open seasonally. A mix of quality crafted items and art. Inquire about summer art workshops.

V. WESTERN MOUNTAINS AND LAKES REGION

Sebago and Long Lakes Region
Oxford Hills and Lewiston/Auburn
Bethel Area
Rangeley Lakes Region
Sugarloaf and the Carrabassett Valley

KIM GRANT

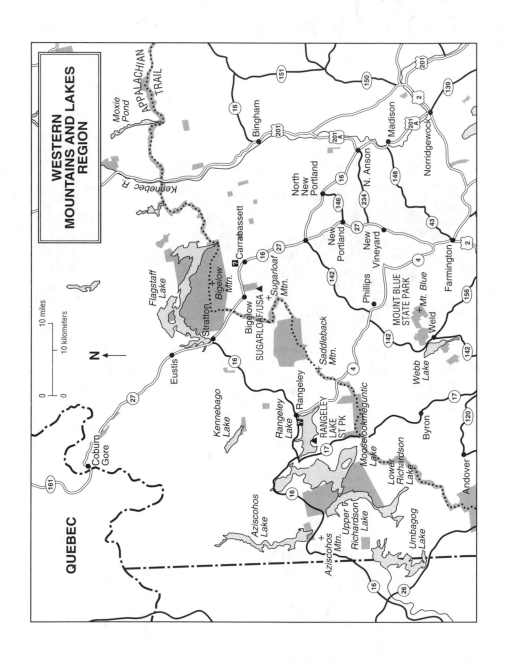

WESTERN
MOUNTAINS AND LAKES
REGION

QUEBEC

APPALACHIAN
TRAIL

Moxie
Pond

Kennebec R.

Bingham

151

150

201
201A

Madison

201
A

Norridgewock

139

2

North
New
Portland

16

146

234

148

N. Anson

Carrabassett

16

27

New
Portland

27

New
Vineyard

43

Flagstaff
Lake

Bigelow
Mtn.

Stratton

Bigelow
SUGARLOAF/USA

Sugarloaf
Mtn.

142

Phillips

4

Farmington

2

MOUNT BLUE
STATE PARK

Mt. Blue

Weld

156

Saddleback
Mtn.

142

Eustis

16

27

Coburn
Gore

161

Kennebago
Lake

Rangeley
Lake

Rangeley

4

RANGELEY
LAKE
ST PK

17

Mooselookmeguntic
Lake

Webb
Lake

142

17

Byron

120

Aziscohos
Lake

16

Aziscohos
Mtn.

Upper
Richardson
Lake

Lower
Richardson
Lake

Andover

Umbagog
Lake

16

26

10 miles

10 kilometers

N

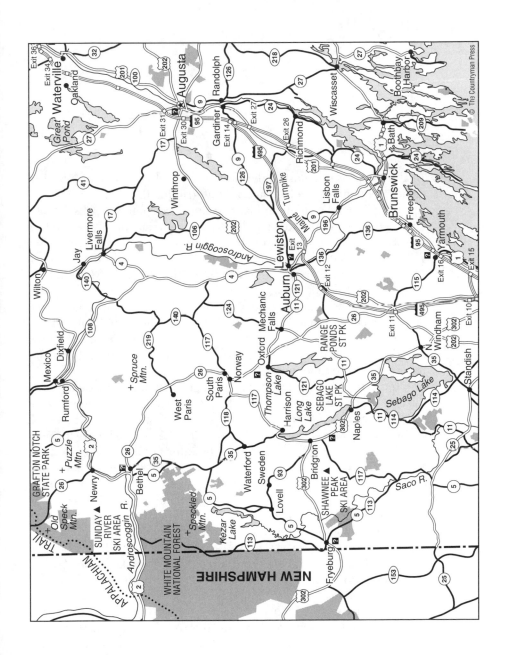

© The Countryman Press

Western Mountains and Lakes Region

Inland Maine is the most underrated, least-explored piece of New England, frequently perceived as an uninterrupted flat carpet of firs.

Larger than Vermont and New Hampshire combined, it is actually composed of several distinct and unique regions and distinguished by a series of almost continuous mountain ranges, more extensive than New Hampshire's White Mountains and higher than Vermont's Green Mountains, but lacking a name (why aren't they the Blue Mountains?).

In contrast to the coast, inland Maine was actually more of a resort area a century ago than it is today. By the 1880s trains connected Philadelphia, New York, and Boston with large resort hotels in Rangeley and Greenville, and steamboats ferried "sports" to "sporting camps" in the far corners of lakes. Many of these historic resorts survive but today require far more time to reach, unless you fly in.

Today inland Maine seems even larger than it is because almost a third of it lies beyond the public highway system, a phenomenon for which we can blame Massachusetts and its insistence that Maine sell off the "unorganized townships" (and divide the profits) before it would be permitted to secede in 1820. In the interim most of this land has been owned and managed by lumber and paper companies, and while debate currently rages about the future of these woodlands (somewhere between a third and almost half of inland Maine), the reality of the way public roads run—and don't run—continues to physically divide Maine's mountainous interior into several distinct pieces.

One of these pieces is the Western Mountains and Lakes Region, extending from the rural farmland surrounding the lakes of southwestern Maine, up through the Oxford Hills and into the foothills of the White Mountains and the Mahoosuc Range around Bethel, then on into the wilderness (as high and remote as any to be found in the North Woods) around the Rangeley lakes and the Sugarloaf area—east of which public roads cease, forcing traffic bound for the Moosehead Lake region to detour south into the farmland of the Lower Kennebec Valley.

The five distinct areas within the Western Mountains and Lakes Region are connected by some of Maine's most scenic roads, with farm-

Birches near Sugarloaf

houses, lakes, mountains, and unexpected villages around each bend. Many of these views are not generally appreciated because the area is best known to skiers, accustomed to racing up to Sunday River and Sugarloaf (Maine's most popular ski resorts) by the shortest routes from the interstate. They don't know what they are missing. The roads around Rangeley offer views so spectacular, stretches of two of them (Routes 4 and 17) are included in a newly designated National Scenic Byway.

In summer and fall we suggest following Route 113 through Evans Notch or heading north from Bridgton to Bethel by the series of roads that thread woods and skirt lakes, heading east along Route 2, continuing north to Rangeley via Route 17 through Coos Canyon and over the spectacular Height o' Land from which you can see all five Rangeley lakes and the surrounding mountains. From Rangeley it's just another 19 scenic miles on Route 16 (better known as Moose Alley) to the Sugarloaf area. You can return to Route 2 by continuing along Route 16 to Kingfield, then taking Route 142 through Phillips and Weld. (Also see *To See—Scenic Drives* in "Rangeley Lakes Region.")

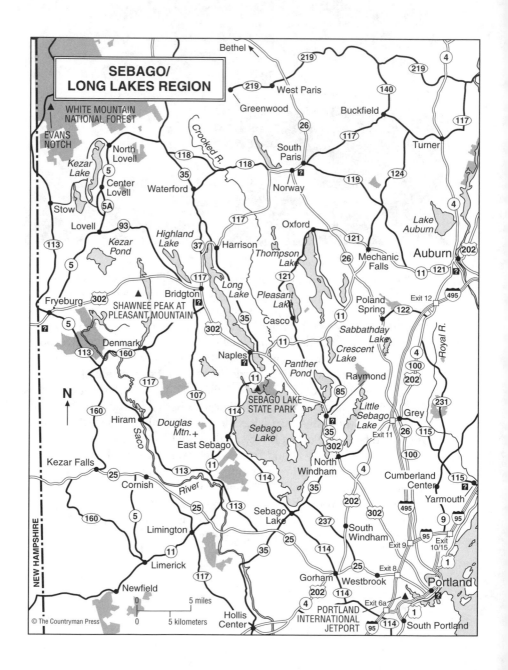

SEBAGO/ LONG LAKES REGION

WHITE MOUNTAIN NATIONAL FOREST

EVANS NOTCH

Bethel

219

219   West Paris

Greenwood

140

26   Buckfield

117

North Lovell

Kezar Lake

Center Lovell

5A

Stow

Lovell

93

Kezar Pond

Highland Lake

37   Harrison

118

118   South Paris

117   Norway

119   Mechanic Falls

121

124   Turner

4

Lake Auburn

4

Auburn   202

26

Oxford

Thompson Lake

121

Pleasant Lake

121

Poland Spring

122

Exit 12   495

Royal R.

Waterford

35

Fryeburg

302

SHAWNEE PEAK AT PLEASANT MOUNTAIN

Bridgton

117

Long Lake

35

302   Casco

11

11

Denmark   160

117

107

N

160

Hiram

Douglas Mtn.

East Sebago

Kezar Falls

25

Cornish

5

Limington

11

Limerick

Newfield

117

Naples

11

Panther Pond

Raymond

85

SEBAGO LAKE STATE PARK

114

Sebago Lake

North Windham

4

Sabbathday Lake

Crescent Lake

Little Sebago Lake

35

302

Grey

26   115

231

100

Cumberland Center

115

Yarmouth

Saco River

113

11

114

35

Sebago Lake

237

202

302

495

9   95

25

35

114

South Windham

Exit 9

95

Exit 10/15

1

Gorham   Westbrook

202   114

Exit 6a

PORTLAND INTERNATIONAL JETPORT

4

Hollis Center

25   Exit 8

1

Portland

95   114   South Portland

NEW HAMPSHIRE

© The Countryman Press

0   5 miles

0   5 kilometers

100   4   202

Sebago and Long Lakes Region

Fifty lakes can be seen from the summit of Pleasant Mountain, 10 within the town of Bridgton itself.

These lakes are what draw summer visitors. They swim and fish, fish and swim. They cruise out in powerboats or paddle canoes and kayaks. On rainy days they browse through the area's abundant antiques and crafts stores. In winter visitors ski, downhill at Shawnee Peak (alias Pleasant Mountain) or cross-country almost anywhere.

Before the Civil War visitors could actually come by boat all the way to Bridgton from Boston. From Portland, they would ride 20 miles through 28 locks on the Cumberland & Oxford Canal, then across Sebago Lake, up the Songo River, Brandy Pond, and Long Lake to Bridgton. The first hotel atop Pleasant Mountain opened in 1850, and in 1882 the "2-footer" narrow-gauge opened between Hiram and Bridgton, enabling summer visitors to come by train as well.

Today, as in the 1880s, most visitors waste little time getting onto or into water. The Naples Causeway is the base for water sports and departure point for cruises on Long Lake and through the only surviving canal lock. Sebago, Maine's second largest lake, is its most popular waterskiing area.

This southwestern corner of the state offers plenty on land too: golf, tennis, mineral collecting, and such fascinating historic sights as Willowbrook in Newfield.

Fryeburg, just west of the lakes in the Saco River Valley, is the region's oldest community and the site of the state's largest agricultural fair. It is also headquarters for canoeing the Saco River. Sandy-bottomed and clear, the Saco meanders for more than 40 miles through woods and fields, rarely passing a house. Too shallow for powerboats, it is perfect for canoes and kayaks. There is usually just enough current to nudge along the limpest paddler, and the ubiquitous sandbars serve as gentle bumpers. Tenting is permitted most places along the river, and there are public campgrounds. Outfitters rent canoes and provide shuttle service.

In summer most families come for a week to stay in lakeside cottages—of which there seem to be thousands. Motels, inns, and B&Bs still fill on weekends with parents visiting their children at camps—of which there seem to be hundreds. As more travelers discover the beauty and tranquility of the region, the number of these types of lodging, while nowhere near the glut of such establishments along the coast, is expanding every year.

GUIDANCE

Greater Bridgton–Lakes Region Chamber of Commerce (647-3472; www.mainelakeschamber.com), Box 236, Bridgton 04009. The chamber maintains a walk-in information bureau on Route 302. Request a copy of the "Greater Bridgton–Lakes Region Map and Guide." Year-round information is also available from the Bridgton town office (647-8786).

Naples Business Association (693-3285), P.O. Box 412, Naples 04055, publishes a map/guide to the Sebago–Long Lakes region just south of Bridgton; it also maintains a seasonal information bureau next to the town's historical-society museum on Route 302.

Windham Chamber of Commerce (892-8265), P.O. Box 1015, Windham 04062, maintains a seasonal information booth on Route 302 and publishes a booklet guide.

Fryeburg Information Center (935-3639), Route 302, Fryeburg 04037. The Maine Tourism Association staffs this state-owned log cabin on the New Hampshire line. Pamphlets on the state in general, western Maine in particular.

GETTING THERE

By air: The **Portland International Jetport,** served by several minor carriers, is a half-hour to an hour drive from most points in this area. Rental cars are available at the airport. (See *Getting There* in "Portland Area.")

By car: From New York and Boston, take I-95 to the Westbrook exit (exit 8), then Route 302, the high road of the lakes region. For Newfield and south of Sebago area, take Route 25 from I-95 at Westbrook (exit 8).

MEDICAL EMERGENCY

Bridgton Hospital (647-8841), South High Street, Bridgton.
Stephens Memorial Hospital (743-5933), 181 Main Street, Norway.

VILLAGES

Bridgton has experienced a new wave of antiques-shop openings, including two country auction houses, making it a good way stop for browsers. Main Street has a cluster of interesting shops, restaurants, and lodgings available within walking distance. Take time for a detour to the pretty campus of Bridgton Academy, a few miles from the center of town.

Cornish. In recent years this pretty little town has been making great efforts to attract more visitors. The colonial and Victorian homes lining Main and Maple Streets were moved here by teams of about 80 oxen in the 1850s after the arrival of a new stagecoach route. It's halfway between Portland and the Mount Washington Valley in New Hampshire. Pick up a copy of the local pamphlet, which includes a detailed map and business listings, at several area businesses.

Fryeburg is an interesting town that sees its share of traffic as travelers pass through en route to North Conway, New Hampshire, and the White Mountains. The traffic clog when the **Fryeburg Fair** (Maine's largest, most popular agricultural fair; see *Special Events*) is in town can back up for more than an hour. The village itself is small and unassuming, with a smattering of historic homes (some now inns—see *Lodging*) and businesses. As noted in the chapter introduction, canoe trips down the Saco originate here as well.

TO SEE

MUSEUMS
Willowbrook at Newfield (793-2784), off Route 11, Newfield. Open May 15 through September 30 daily 10–5. Admission charged. This is a quiet, peaceful place that shouldn't be missed. Although it's off the beaten track, the drive through the quiet countryside is well worth it. Devastated by fire in 1947, the village was almost a ghost town when Donald King began buying buildings in the 1960s. The complex now includes 37 buildings displaying more than 11,000 items: horse-drawn vehicles, tools, toys, a vintage 1894 carousel, and many other artifacts of late-19th-century life. Linger in the ballroom, ring the schoolhouse bell, picnic in the area provided. A restaurant and ice cream parlor for light lunches, an old-time country store, and a Christmas gift shop open most of the year are located on the premises.
The Jones Museum of Glass and Ceramics (787-3370), Douglas Hill (off Route 107), Sebago. Open mid-May through mid-November, Monday through Saturday 10–5 and Sunday 1–5. $5 adults, $3 students. More than 7,000 works in glass and china. Displays include ancient Egyptian glass, Chinese porcelains, Wedgwood teapots, and French paperweights. There are also gallery tours, frequent lecture-luncheon seminars, and identification days (visitors bring their own pieces to be identified).
HISTORIC BUILDINGS AND MUSEUMS
Daniel Marrett House, Route 25, Standish. Tours mid-June through September 1, Tuesday, Thursday, Saturday, and Sunday noon–5. Admission charged. Money from Portland banks was stored in this Georgian mansion for safekeeping during the War of 1812. Built in 1789, it remained in the Marrett family until 1944; architecture and furnishings reflect the changing styles over 150 years, and the formal gardens bloom throughout the summer.
Parson Smith House (892-5315), 89 River Road, South Windham. Open mid-June through Labor Day, Tuesday, Thursday, and Sunday noon–5; admission. A Georgian farmhouse with an exceptional stairway and hall; some original furnishings.
Narramissic, Ingalls Road (2 miles south of the junction of Routes 107 and

117), Bridgton. Open July and August, Wednesday through Saturday
10–3; other hours by special arrangement. $3 adults, $1 children. A
Federal-period home and a Temperance Barn in a rural setting; includes a blacksmith shop, the scene of frequent special events, including the annual antiques show in late July; check with the **Bridgton
Historical Society Museum** (647-3699), Gibbs Avenue, which also
maintains a 1902 former fire station. The collection (open same hours)
includes slide images of the old narrow-gauge railroad.

Naples Historical Society Museum (693-6790), village green, Route 302,
Naples. Open July and August, Tuesday through Friday 10–3. The brick
complex includes the old jail, great memorabilia, and slide presentations on the Cumberland & Oxford Canal, the Sebago and Long Lake
steamboats, and vanished hotels like the Chute Homestead.

Hopalong Cassidy in the Fryeburg Public Library (935-2731), 98 Main
Street, Fryeburg. Open year-round, varying days; the library is housed
in an 1832 stone schoolhouse and is decorated with many paintings by
local artists. It also contains a collection of books, guns, and other
memorabilia belonging to Clarence Mulford, creator of Hopalong
Cassidy. The **Fryeburg Historical Society Museum** (935-4192) is
next door, also open seasonally and by request at the library.

OTHER HISTORIC SITES

Songo Locks, Naples (2.5 miles off Route 302). Dating from 1830, the last
of the 27 hand-operated locks that once enabled people to come by
boat from Portland to Harrison. It still enables you to travel some 40
watery miles. The boat traffic is constant in summer.

TO DO

AIR RIDES

Western Maine Flying Service (693-3129), Naples Causeway. Operates
daily in-season; scenic flights.

Parasailing (693-3888), Naples Causeway.

BICYCLING

Shawnee Peak (647-8444), Route 302, Bridgton, offers lift-accessed riding,
a terrain park, and rental mountain bikes. Open weekends in-season.

Sportshaus (647-5100) 61 Main Street, Bridgton, rents mountain bikes by
the day or week.

BOAT EXCURSIONS

Songo River Queen II (693-6861), Naples Causeway. Operates daily July
through Labor Day; reduced schedule in spring and fall. Offers a 2½-
hour Songo River ride and a 1-hour Long Lake cruise. The 90-foot-
long stern-wheeler was built in 1982; snack bar and rest rooms. The
ride is across Brandy Pond and through the only surviving lock from the
1830 canal. It is a pleasant ride down the Songo River, which is about as
winding as a river can be, to the mouth of Sebago Lake. The distance is

The Songo River Queen II

just 1.5 miles as the crow flies, but 6 miles as the Songo twists and turns. **Mail-boat rides** (1½ hours) are also offered daily in-season except Sunday. This pontoon boat offers varied rides on Songo and Long Lakes (no toilets on board).

BOAT RENTALS

Available regionwide. Inquire at local chambers. (Also see *Canoeing*.)

CANOEING AND KAYAKING

Saco River Canoe and Kayak (935-2369), P.O. Box 111, Route 5, Fryeburg (across from the access at Swan's Falls). Fred Westerberg, a Registered Maine Guide, runs Saco River Canoe and Kayak with the help of his wife, Prudy, and daughters, Beth and Chris. They offer shuttle service and canoe and kayak rentals, which come with a map and careful instructions geared to the day's river conditions.

Saco Bound (603-447-2177 or 447-3801), Route 302, Center Conway, New Hampshire (just over the state line, south of Fryeburg). The largest canoe outfitter around. Offers rentals, guided day trips during the summer, whitewater canoeing on the Androscoggin River, a campground at Canal Bridge in Fryeburg, and a shuttle service. Its base is a big glass-faced store stocked with kayaks and canoes, trail food, and lip balm. Staff members are young and enthusiastic.

Canal Bridge Canoes (935-2605), Route 302, Fryeburg Village. Pat and Carl Anderson offer rentals and a shuttle service.

Woodland Acres (935-2529), Route 160, Brownfield. Full-facility camping, canoe rentals, and a shuttle service.

FISHING

Fishing licenses are available at town offices and other local outlets; check marinas for information. Salmon, lake trout, pickerel, and bass abound.

GOLF AND TENNIS

Bridgton Highlands Country Club (647-3491), RR 3, Box 1065, Bridgton, has an 18-hole course, snack bar, carts, and tennis courts. Nine-hole courses include **Allen Mountain Golf Course** (452-2282), Bush Row Road, in Denmark Village; **Lake Kezar Country Club** (925-2462), Route 5, Lovell; and **Naples Country Club** (693-6424), Route 114, Naples.

Tennis at Brandy Pond Camps (693-6333), Old Route 114, Naples; also at **Bridgton Highlands Country Club.**

HIKING

Douglas Mountain, Sebago. A Nature Conservancy preserve with great views of Sebago and the White Mountains. The trail to the top is a 20-minute walk, and there's a ¾-mile nature trail at the summit; also a stone tower with an observation platform. Take Route 107 south from the town of Sebago and turn right on Douglas Mountain Road; go to the end of the road to find limited parking.

Pleasant Mountain, Bridgton. Several summits and interconnecting trails, the most popular of which is the Firewarden's Trail to the main summit: a relatively easy, 2½-mile climb from base to peak through rocky woods.

✍ **Jockey Cap,** Route 302, Fryeburg. Watch for the Jockey Cap Motel beside a general store. The arch between them is the entrance to one of New England's shortest hikes to one of its biggest rewards. A 10-minute climb up the path (steep near the top) accesses a bald, garnet-studded summit with a sweeping view of the White Mountains to the west, lesser peaks and lakes to the east and south, all ingeniously identified on a circular bronze monument designed by Arctic explorer Admiral Peary (see Admiral Peary House under *Lodging—Bed & Breakfasts*).

HORSEBACK RIDING

Secret Acres Stables (693-3441), Lambs Mill Road (1 mile off Route 302), Naples, offers trail rides and lessons. **Mutiny Brook Stables** (583-6650), Sweden Road, South Waterford, offers rides on 400 acres of private trails. No riders under the age of 7.

MINI-GOLF

✍ **Steamboat Landing** (693-6429), Route 114, Naples. Open weekends Memorial Day through late June, then daily through Labor Day 10–10 (1–10 Sunday). A lovely 19-hole course with a Maine theme in a wooded setting.

✍ **Maplewood Miniature Golf and Arcade** (655-7586), Route 302 (across from State Park Road), Casco. Eighteen holes and a full arcade with video games, pinball, snacks.

✍ **Seacoast Adventure Park** (892-5952), Route 302, Windham. Elaborate mini-golf, go-carts, bumper boats, arcade, and the Skycoaster, a ride that hauls you high into the air, harnessed in on a bungee cord, then lets you swing.

SWIMMING

✍ **Sebago Lake State Park** (693-6613, June 20 through Labor Day; 693-6231 otherwise), off Route 302 (between Naples and South Casco). A great family beach, with picnic tables, grills, boat ramp, lifeguards, and bathhouses. There is a separate camping area (see *Campgrounds*).

The town of Bridgton maintains a tidy little beach on **Long Lake** just off Main Street, another on **Woods Lake** (Route 117), and another on **Highland Lake.** The town of Fryeburg maintains a beach, with float, on the **Saco River,** and **Casco** maintains a small, inviting beach in its picturesque village.

WINTER SPORTS

CROSS-COUNTRY SKIING

Five Fields Farm X-C Ski Center (647-2425), Route 107, 6 miles south of Bridgton. Open daily 9–5. Trails looping around the 70-acre working apple orchard, and connecting to logging roads. You can snowshoe to the top of Bald Pate Mountain for spectacular views. Full- and half-day rates, rentals, warming hut.

Harris Farm Cross Country Ski Center (499-2678), Buzzell Road, Dayton. Open Monday through Friday 9 AM–dusk; Saturday, Sunday, and holidays 8 AM–dusk. This 500-acre dairy and tree farm offers miles of groomed trails from easy to difficult, over hills, by ponds and streams, and through the woods. Rentals available.

DOWNHILL SKIING

Shawnee Peak at Pleasant Mountain (647-8444), Route 302, Bridgton. An isolated 1,900-foot hump, 1 mile west of the center of town. Maine's oldest ski area has a vertical drop of 1,300 feet and offers 37 trails with 100% snowmaking capacity, a double, two triples, and a quad lift, plus a handle tow. Open until 9 PM (until 10 Friday and Saturday), night skiing is big here. Ski and snowboard instruction, rentals, child care, and base lodge with pub. A self-service guest house is available (private baths) $69 per person weekends, $49 weekdays, 2-night minimum, includes lift ticket.

GREEN SPACE

The **Lakes Environmental Association (LEA)** has been working for more than 30 years to preserve the clear, unsullied look of the lakes in the western region. Trails and a boardwalk lead through the **Holt Pond Nature Area,** an undeveloped watershed with a bog pond, a river, and wetlands. **The Stevens Brook Trail** follows the water body from Highland Lake to Long Lake. Tour the LEA's **Harry & Eunice Bradley Lake Center** in Bridgton to see the water-testing lab, buffer gardens, and educational displays.

Kezar Falls, reached from Lovell Road off Route 35, is a small, pretty waterfall on the Kezar River.

LODGING

RUSTIC RESORTS

The Western Lakes area offers unusual old resort complexes, each with cabin accommodations, dining, and relaxing space in a central, distinctively Maine lodge. In contrast to similar complexes found farther north, these are all geared to families or to those who vacation here for reasons other than hunting and fishing.

✐& **Migis Lodge** (655-4524; www.migis.com), P.O. Box 40, South Casco 04077 (off Route 302). Open early June through Columbus Day weekend. Six rooms in the two-story main lodge, and 29 cottages scattered throughout the pines on 97 acres. All cottages have fireplaces, and guests enjoy use of the private beach, tennis, lawn games, waterskiing, sailboats, canoes, and boat excursions. Children under 4 are not permitted in the dining room during the high season (July through Labor Day), so the resort provides a supervised dining and playtime 6:30–8:30 PM; older children are also welcome to join in. $380–450 per couple (cottages) includes three meals; $390 per couple in lodge rooms; children's rates; 15 percent service charge.

Quisisana (925-3500; off-season, 914-833-0293; www.quisisanaresort.com), Lake Kezar, Center Lovell 04016. Mid-June through August. One-week minimum stay in high season. Founded in 1917 as a place for music students and music lovers to relax in the pines by one of Maine's clearest lakes. Each evening climaxes with performances in the lakeside hall: musical theater, opera, and concerts performed by staff recruited from top music schools. There are 75 guest rooms in all, from rooms in two lodges to one- to three-room cottages (some with fireplaces) scattered through the woods and around the soft beach. Waterskiing, boats, and fishing guides are available, croquet, tennis, and swimming. The white-frame central lodge includes a big, homey sitting room and the kind of dining room you don't mind sitting in three times a day, especially given the quality of the food. $130–175 per person double occupancy.

✐ **Aimhi Lodge** (892-6538; www.aimhilodge.com), Smith Road, North Windham 04062. Open late June through late August. For more than 80 years, this classic complex has operated in the same family. Little has changed, though the 23 cottages on Little Sebago Lake have been updated and modernized; they have one to three rooms, Franklin stoves, screened porches, and a dock. Down-home cooking; turkey every summer Sunday since the 1930s (at least), and Friday lobster bakes. Facilities include game rooms (with a sitting area for adults and a billiard table), lawn games, a beach, sailboats, canoes, tennis, supervised children's activities, and fishing. $27–145 per person per day (children less), including all three meals.

INNS

✐& **Tarry-a-While** (647-2522; 1-800-451-9076; www.tarryawhile.com), Ridge Road, Bridgton 04009. Open June through Labor Day. Marc and Nan

Stretch have redone this turreted, vintage-1897 summer hotel, giving it a classic Maine ambience. Set on 25 lakeside acres, it offers 27 rooms (22 with private baths) divided among the inn, cottages, and a two-bedroom apartment. A beach, social hall, canoes, rowboats, kayaks, and tennis are all part of the resort, and an 18-hole golf course is next door. $70–135 double includes a large continental breakfast. Dinner is served in the restaurant (see *Dining Out*).

Oxford House Inn (935-3442; 1-800-261-7206; www.oxfordhouseinn.com), 105 Main Street, Fryeburg 04037. Open year-round, this spacious 1913 house in the middle of Fryeburg has a view across the Saco River to the White Mountains. The public restaurant is popular for dinner (see *Dining Out*), but there is ample space for inn guests to relax. John and Phyllis Morris offer four upstairs guest rooms, all large and nicely decorated, with private baths. Request one with a view. $95–125 includes a full breakfast.

Center Lovell Inn (925-1575; 1-800-777-2698; www.centerlovellinn.com), Route 5, Center Lovell 04016. Closed November and April. Since 1993, Janice and Richard Cox have run this striking old inn with a cupola and a busy public dining room (see *Dining Out*). Janice's mother, Harriet, and her husband, Earle (known to guests as Mom and Pop), are on hand to help out . There are four guest rooms on the second floor (the two with shared bath are a suite), nicely furnished with antiques and art. In the 1835 Harmon House there are five cozy rooms, some with private bath. $143–183 double MAP; $71–103 no meals included.

The Cornish Inn (625-8501; www.cornishinn.com), P.O. Box 266, Main Street, Cornish 04020. Open year-round. Right in the center of this quaint town, this inn offers 16 cozy guest rooms with private baths and furnishings reminiscent of a simpler time. Common areas include a parlor and tavern, and a great front porch. Dinner is served some evenings in the public dining room. $75–125 in summer; less off season.

BED & BREAKFASTS

 ♾ **Noble House** (647-3733; www.noblehousebb.com), Box 180, Bridgton 04009. Open year-round. There is a suitably formal feel to the grand piano, crystal, and Oriental rugs in the parlor of this former senator's manor, set among stately oaks and pines. Back beyond the kitchen, however, is a comfortable den/breakfast room, and the welcome guests receive from Steve and Sherri Matte is anything but stiff. Nine guest rooms (six with private baths) are divided between the original house and newer doubles and suites in the former ell (three with whirlpool bath); all are furnished with antiques. The private beach (with a hammock, canoe, and dock) on Highland Lake is just across the road; in winter, both downhill and cross-country skiing are nearby. $90–149 double includes a full breakfast and use of canoes and a pedal boat. $15 additional per child.

 ♾ **Acres of Austria** (925-6547; 1-800-988-4391; www.acresofaustria.com),

RR 1, Box 177, Fryeburg 04037. Candice and Franz Redl have created a wonderful haven at the end of a secluded dirt road on 65 acres, . A very Austrian feel, as the name might suggest. The common rooms include a dining area with a central fireplace, a spiral staircase, and window seats; the cozy lounge is another inviting place to relax. Six guest rooms, all with private baths. Many of the inn's furnishings and decorative touches are from Vienna. Special packages are offered as well. Dinner is available to guests in the off-season with at least 3 days' advance notice. $89–159 includes a full breakfast; less off-season.

Admiral Peary House (935-3365; 1-800-237-8080; www.admiralpearyhouse. com), 9 Elm Street, Fryeburg 04037. If he returned today we suspect that Robert E. Peary, Maine's famed Arctic explorer, would be pleased with what's happened to the house in which he lived with his mother after graduating from Bowdoin College and before surveying the Panama Canal. Common space includes a large wicker-filled screened porch overlooking a perennial garden; a spacious, informal living room with barnboard walls and a large hearth, equipped with TV, a billiard table, a stereo, and games; and more formal spaces (a handsome dining room, living room, and library) in the front of the house, beyond an open kitchen. Six large guest rooms each with private bath and air-conditioning. The top-floor North Pole Room, with its king brass bed, features mountain views. Amenities include an outdoor spa, bicycles, and a well-maintained clay tennis court; innkeepers Nancy and Ed Greenberg are avid tennis players. $108–138 in-season includes a full breakfast; from $80 off-season. In winter a 7-night contract can be used anytime except holidays (not necessarily consecutive nights) for $455, and a romantic 2-night package is $149. Snowshoe rentals are available, and there are complimentary trails.

Sebago Lake Lodge (892-2698; www.sebagolakelodge.com), P.O. Box 110, White's Bridge Road, North Windham 04062. A rambling old white inn on a narrows between Jordan Bay and the Basin, seemingly surrounded by water. Debra and Chip Lougee, both Maine natives, have refurbished the rooms to create eight units with kitchens (one is a suite with an enclosed porch) and four standard rooms with kitchen privileges. A light buffet breakfast is set out in the gathering room, a pleasant space to read, play games, or watch TV. There are also 12 moderately priced cottages. Facilities include an inviting beach, picnic tables, and grills; fishing-boat, rowboat, canoe, and motorboat rentals. Fishing licenses are available, and pets are allowed in cottages. $68 for a room, $98–160 per housekeeping unit in high season. Cottages $600–1,500 per week.

The Inn at Long Lake (693-6226; 1-800-437-0328; www.innatlonglake.- com), P.O. Box 806, Naples 04055. Built in 1906 as an annex to the (vanished) Lake House Resort, this four-story clapboard building is now a warm, romantic inn. Ed and Nicky Pinkham offer 16 guest rooms from "cozy deluxe" to two-room suites. Each has private bath, TV, and air conditioner. $120–160 in summer, $90–110 off-season, includes full breakfast.

COTTAGES

The **Greater Bridgton–Lakes Region Chamber of Commerce** (see *Guidance*) publishes a list of more than two dozen rental cottages, and many in this area are also listed in the "Maine Guide to Camp & Cottage Rentals," free from the **Maine Tourism Association** (see *Information* in "What's Where in Maine").

One set of cottages that deserves special mention is **Hewnoaks** (925-6051), RR 2, Box 65, Lovell 04051. Six unusually attractive, distinctive cottages built as an artists' colony and imaginatively furnished (in no way are these your usual summer camps) are scattered on a landscaped hillside above pristine Lake Kezar. Moderately priced.

CAMPGROUNDS

See *Canoeing and Kayaking* for information about camping along the Saco River. In addition to those mentioned, the **Appalachian Mountain Club** maintains a campground at Swan's Falls. The **"Maine Camping Guide,"** available from the **Maine Campground Owners Association** (782-5874), 655 Main Street, Lewiston 04240, lists dozens of private campgrounds in the area.

Sebago Lake State Park (693-6613; 693-6611 before June 20 and after Labor Day), off Route 302 (between Naples and South Casco). Open through mid-October. On the northern shore of the lake are 1,300 thickly wooded acres with 250 campsites, many on the water; the camping area has its own beach, hot showers, a program of evening presentations, and nature hikes. For information about reservations, call 1-800-332-1501, or 207-287-3824 from outside the state.

Point Sebago (655-3821), RR 1, Box 712, Casco 04015. More than just a campground: 500 campsites, most with trailer hook-ups, on a 300-acre lakeside site, plus 160 rental trailers ranging from small trailers to large models of near mobile-home size. Campers have access to the beach, marina, dance pavilion, children's daycare, teen center, excursion boats, soccer and softball fields, horseshoe pitches, 10 tennis courts, video-game arcade, general store, and combination restaurant/nightclub/gambling casino, as well as a full daily program.

WHERE TO EAT

DINING OUT

Center Lovell Inn (925-1575), Route 5, Center Lovell. Open for breakfast and dinner daily in high season, Friday through Sunday off-season (reservations required for breakfast). Chef-owner Richard Cox's specialties include an appetizer of smoked pheasant ravioli and entrées like veal Piccata. There are two pleasant dining rooms, and the wraparound porch is also used in summer. $13.95–23.95.

&⬤ **Tarry-a-While Restaurant** (647-2522), Highland Road, Bridgton. Open for dinner Wednesday through Sunday, 5:30–9. The timber-beamed dining room in this old lakeside summer hotel overlooks Highland Lake and Pleasant Mountain. The menu includes appetizers like mushroom tartlets and a variety of entrées, including braised sea bass, and steamed fresh lobster stew made with coconut milk and Thai spices. Children's menu available. Entrées $12.95–22.95.

Venezia Ristorante (647-5333), Bridgton Corners, Routes 302 and 93, Bridgton. Open Tuesday through Sunday 5–9 PM in summer, Thursday through Sunday in winter. Dependable, moderately priced Italian dishes.

Tom's Homestead (647-5726), Route 302, Bridgton. Lunch and dinner are served (closed Monday) in this 1821 historic home. The menu includes fresh seafood and andouille sausage jambalaya and steak *au poivre*, as well as vegetarian entrées.

Oxford House Inn (935-3442; 1-800-261-7206), 105 Main Street, Fryeburg. Open for dinner every night in summer and fall, Thursday through Sunday in winter and spring. Reservations required. The dining rooms are the former living room and dining room of a handsome 1913 house. Mountain views from the back dining rooms. Hors d'oeuvres might include hot buttered Brie with fresh fruit; specialties include veal Oxford and champagne-poached salmon with fresh herb sauce. $19–24.

Cornish Inn (625-8501), Main Street, Cornish. Open for dinner; Nights vary according to season. A pleasant old inn with a creative menu and comfortable atmosphere. Dinner choices range from chicken to seafood, and include both soup and salad. For those with lighter appetites, many of the same dishes are offered as lighter portions, with salad only, at a lower cost. This is the only place we've seen a calamari steak among the entrées, so we had to try it—and we're glad we did. The inn has full bar service and a few reasonably priced wines available by the bottle or the glass.

EATING OUT

Auntie M's (625-3889), Route 25, Cornish. Open for breakfast and lunch, Monday through Saturday; breakfast-only on Sunday. Good, hearty home-cooked food. Their specialty is "the rhino burger": fresh vegetables (not soy or fillers) formed into a patty.

Bray's Brew Pub (693-6806), Routes 302 and 35, Naples. Open year-round for lunch and dinner daily. Mike and Rich Bray brew American ales, as they are known in the Pacific Northwest, using North American grains and malted barley, Oregon yeast, and Washington hops. Specials might include lobster stew, Maine crabcakes, and mussels stewed in beer. The dinner menu runs from grilled salmon to petit filet mignon; pub menu served all day.

& **Mountain View Family Restaurant** (935-2909), 107 Main Street, Fryeburg. Open from 6 AM through dinner. The Mutrie family have tacked this pine-paneled dining room onto the back of their Village

Variety, with large windows overlooking the White Mountains. For breakfast, try the Belgian waffles with blueberries; go with a special like fried haddock at dinner. Burgers and sandwiches are fine, and don't pass up the pies.

ENTERTAINMENT

FILM
Magic Lantern (647-5065) 69 Main Street, Bridgton, presents film classics and first-run cartoons. **Windham Hill Mall** (892-7000), Route 302, has a cinema that shows first-run movies. **Bridgton Drive-In** (647-8666), Route 302, shows first-run movies in summer.

MUSIC
Sebago–Long Lakes Region Chamber Music Festival (627-4939), Deertrees Theatre and Cultural Center, Harrison. A series of concerts held mid-July through mid-August.

The **Saco River Festival Association** (625-7116) holds a chamber music festival in Cornish in the summer months. Call for a brochure detailing performances.

THEATER
See **Deertrees Theatre and Cultural Center** under *Entertainment* in "Oxford Hills and Lewiston/Auburn."

SELECTIVE SHOPPING

ANTIQUES SHOPS
Route 302 seems to be regaining its 1950s and 1960s reputation as an antiques alley, and Bridgton has had nine new shops open in the past year.

The Smith Co. (625-6030), Main Street, Cornish. Specializes in country-store fixtures and memorabilia—including old Coca-Cola collectibles, and advertising signs.

BOOKSTORES
Bridgton Books (647-2122), 74 Main Street, Bridgton. Extensive stock, books on tape, stationery, music.

CRAFTS SHOPS
Craftworks (647-5436), Upper Village, Bridgton. Open daily. Fills a former church and two neighboring buildings. Selective women's clothing, pottery, books, linens, handmade pillows, crafted jewelry, and more.

Frances Riecken Pottery (928-2411), Center Lovell. Ceramic cookware, porcelain, and other functional pots, made for more than 40 years in this studio on Kezar Lake.

The Maine Theme (647-2161), 36 Main Street, Bridgton. Open daily. Two floors of New England–crafted work and widely assorted gifts.

The Bag Lady (625-8421), Old Pike Road, Cornish. A combination of factory store (luggage and totes), antiques, and collectibles in a huge old building.

One of several opportunities for bargain hunters in Naples.

SPECIAL SHOPS

The Shops at South Casco (655-5060), Route 302, South Casco. A three-building complex. **Cry of the Loon** encompasses 10 rooms in an 1800s farmhouse and barn, with a variety of unique pottery, glassware, and other handmade crafts. **The Nest** is a Victorian house offering country furniture and other items for your decor, including rugs and tapestries. In **The Barn** you'll find whimsical delights, from cast-iron toys to wine racks. Downstairs in the **Blueberry Pantry** there are free tastings of gourmet foods.

Sportshaus (647-5100), 61 Main Street, Bridgton. Open daily. Known for its original Maine T-shirts; also a selection of casual clothes, canvas bags, tennis rackets, downhill and cross-country skis, athletic footwear, swimwear, and golf accessories. Canoe, kayak, sailboat, water-ski, and mountain bike rentals in summer; ski shop in winter.

The Sheep Shop (647-3584). 2056 High Street. Bridgton Yarn, hand knits, spinning supplies, wool blankets, and other specialty items.

SPECIAL EVENTS

July: **Independence Day** is big in Bridgton and Naples. **Bridgton** holds their annual **Pondicherry Days** that week, which includes a lobster/clambake at the town hall, a road race, a concert, an arts and crafts fair, and fireworks. In **Naples** the fireworks over the lake are spectacular.

Late July or early August: The 3-day **Lakes Region Antique Show** is held at Narramissic (see *To See*), and a major **crafts fair** at the old town hall is sponsored by the **Bridgton Arts and Crafts Society.**

August: **Windham Old Home Days** *(beginning of the month)* include a parade, contests, and public feeds. In Lovell the **Annual Arts and Artisans Fair** *(midmonth)* is held on the library grounds—chicken barbecue, and book and crafts sale.

October: **Fryeburg Fair,** Maine's largest agricultural fair, is held for a week in early October, climaxing with the Columbus Day weekend. This is an old-fashioned agricultural happening—one of the most colorful in the country.

December: **Christmas open house and festivals** in Harrison and Naples.

Also see *Special Events* in "Oxford Hills and Lewiston/Auburn."

Oxford Hills and Lewiston/ Auburn

Over the years many of Maine's small towns have banded together to form distinctive regional identities. One such area, a rolling gem- and lake-studded swatch of Oxford County, is known as the Oxford Hills. Technically made up of eight towns, the region seems to stretch to include many of the stops along Route 26, the region's traffic spine, as visitors pass through from Gray (an exit on the Maine Turnpike) to Bethel, an area with both summer attractions and winter ski resorts.

Its commercial center is the community composed of both Norway and South Paris, towns divided by the Little Androscoggin River but joined by Route 26. Off Route 26 is a quiet part of the Western Lakes and Mountains Region, with startlingly beautiful villages like Waterford and Paris Hill, and genuinely interesting places to see such as the country's last living Shaker community at Sabbathday Lake.

The Oxford Hills are best known for their mineral diversity. The area's bedrock is a granite composed of pegmatite studded with semiprecious gemstones, including tourmaline and rose quartz. Several local mines invite visitors to explore their "tailings" or rubble and take what they find.

Lewiston and Auburn (Maine's "L.A."), just east of the Oxford Hills, are the "cities of the Androscoggin" but for most visitors are seen as "the cities on the Turnpike," the exits accessing routes to the Rangeley and Sugarloaf areas. Both are worth a stop. By the 1850s mills on both sides of the river had harnessed the power of the Androscoggin's Great Falls, and the Bates Mill boomed with the Civil War, supplying fabric for most of the Union army's tents.

Today Lewiston is best known as the home of prestigious Bates College (founded 1855), an attractive campus that's the summer site of the nationally recognized Bates Dance Festival. The Bates Mill is now a visitor-friendly complex housing shops and restaurants, and both Lewiston and Auburn offer interesting restaurants, shopping, and a number of colorful festivals—some, like Festival de Joie, reflecting the rich cultural diversity of the residents.

VILLAGES

Harrison. Once a booming lakeside resort town, Harrison is now a quiet village resting between two lakes. Main Street has a popular restaurant, and a clock tower in the process of being restored. In the 1930s many of the country's most popular actors came to perform at the Deertrees Theatre, which is again offering theater, dance, music, and children's shows to the area. "Old Home Days" and "Christmas in Harrison" festivities celebrate the town's cultural heritage.

Norway. Making up part of the commercial center of the region, the downtown is quiet and quaint. L. M. Longley's hardware store has items from days gone by, the town is home to Maine's oldest newspaper, and there are interesting art exhibits held by the Western Maine Art Group in the Matolcsy Art Center. The Norway Sidewalk Arts Festival in July features close to 100 artists exhibiting along Main Street.

Paris. A town divided into sections so different they don't feel like the same town at all. Paris Hill has views of the White Mountains and a number of historic houses and buildings, including the Hamlin Memorial Library. The buildings in Market Square are brick, many with stamped-tin ceilings. Main Street, the commercial center, is a row of the nondescript businesses found in many town centers.

Oxford. Home of the Oxford Plains Speedway, which attracts stock-car racing fans throughout the season, and the Oxford County Fairgrounds (host to several annual events). Oxford is also the largest manufacturing base in the area, including manufactured homes, information processing, textiles, and wood products.

GUIDANCE

Oxford Hills Chamber of Commerce (743-2281; www.oxfordhills. com), 6 Western Avenue, South Paris 04281, publishes a directory to the area.

Androscoggin County Chamber of Commerce (783-2249; www.androscoggincounty.com), 179 Lisbon Street, Lewiston 04243.

GETTING THERE

For the Sabbathday Lake–Poland Spring–Oxford area, take I-95 to Gray (exit 11) and Route 26 north. Auburn is exit 12 and Lewiston is exit 13 on the Maine Turnpike.

MEDICAL EMERGENCY

Bridgton Hospital (647-8841), South High Street, Bridgton. **Stephens Memorial Hospital** (743-5933), 181 Main Street, Norway. **Central Maine Medical Center** (795-0111), 300 Main Street, Lewiston. **St. Mary's Regional Medical Center** (777-8120), Route 126, Lewiston. Both Lewiston hospitals have 24-hour emergency rooms. Dial **911** for police or ambulance.

TO SEE

The International Sign. At the junction of Routes 5 and 35 in the village of Lynchville, some 14 miles west of Norway, stands Maine's most photographed roadside marker, pointing variously to Norway, Paris, Denmark, Naples, Sweden, Poland, Mexico, and Peru—all towns within 94 miles of the sign.

FOR FAMILIES

Maine Wildlife Park (657-4977), Route 26, Gray. Open mid-April through Veteran's Day daily 9:30–5:30 (no one admitted after 4 PM). $3.50 adults, $2 ages 4–12, ages 3 and under free. What started as a pheasant farm has evolved into a wonderful haven for animals that have been injured and cannot survive in the wild. The goal is to try to prepare them to return to the wild, but while they are here it is a great opportunity to see animals you might otherwise never see. The park provides habitats that are as natural as possible, allowing visitors to observe the animals as they might live in the wild. Nature trails and picnic facilities round out the experience. Animals you may see include moose, lynx, deer, black bears, wild turkeys, eagles, and many more.

Beech Hill Farm & Bison Ranch (583-2515), 630 Valley Road, Waterford. Paul and Marcia Hersey are raising a breeding herd of North American bison on their ranch. They offer tours, hayrides among the herd, and a trading post with bison meat and a variety of gifts. Worth a stop.

GALLERY

Creative Photographic Art Center of Maine, Bates Mill Complex, Lewiston. The center contains more than 40,000 square feet of exhibit space for photographic works and serves as the base for the International/National Certification Program for the International Freelance Photography Association. The center also offers an associate of arts degree and a one-year residency certificate program.

HISTORIC BUILDINGS

State of Maine Building from the 1893 World's Columbian Exposition in Chicago, Route 26, Poland Spring. Open July and August daily 9–1; June and September weekends 9–1. Admission charged. A very Victorian building that was brought back from the 1893 World's Columbian Exposition in Chicago to serve as a library and art gallery for the now-vanished Poland Spring Resort (today the water is commercially bottled in an efficient, unromantic plant down the road). Houses the **Poland Spring Preservation Society,** with museum displays from the resort era on the second floor and art on the third. While you are there, peek into the **All Souls Chapel** next door for a look at its nine stained-glass windows and the 1921 Skinner pipe organ.

Hamlin Memorial Library and Museum (743-2980), off Route 26, Paris Hill. Open year-round, Tuesday through Friday 11:30–5:30, Saturday

KIM GRANT

Sabbathday Lake Shaker Community and Museum

10–2; also Wednesday 7–9 PM. The old stone Oxford County Jail now houses the public library and museum. Worth a stop for the American primitive art; also local minerals and displays about Hannibal Hamlin (who lived next door), vice president during Abraham Lincoln's first term. This stop may not sound very exciting, but the setting is superb: a ridgetop of spectacular early-19th-century houses with views west to the White Mountains.

MUSEUMS

Sabbathday Lake Shaker Community and Museum (926-4597; www.shaker.lib.me.us), 707 Shaker Road (Route 26) , New Gloucester (8 miles north of Gray). Open Memorial Day through Columbus Day daily except Sunday, 10–4:30; admission charged. Welcoming the "world's people" has been part of summer at Sabbathday Lake since the community's inception in 1794.

Founded by Englishwoman Ann Lee in 1775, Shakers numbered 6,000 Americans in 18 communities by the Civil War. Today, with fewer than 10 Shaker Sisters and Brothers, this village is the only one that still functions as a religious community. These men and women continue to follow the injunction of Mother Ann Lee to "put your hands to work and your heart to God." Guided tours are offered of the 17 white-clapboard buildings; rooms are either furnished or filled with exhibits to illustrate periods or products of Shaker life. **The Shaker Store** sells Shaker-made goods, including oval boxes, knitted and sewn goods, homemade fudge, yarns, souvenirs, antiques, Shaker-style furniture, and Shaker herbs. During warm-weather months, services are held at

10 AM on Sunday in the 18th-century meetinghouse on Route 26. Sit in the World's People's benches and listen as the Shakers speak in response to the psalms and gospel readings. Each observation is affirmed with a Shaker song—of which there are said to be 10,000. This complex includes an extensive research library housing Shaker books, writings, and records; open to scholars by appointment. Inquire about special workshops, fairs, and concerts.

Olin Arts Center at Bates College (786-6255), Campus Avenue, Lewiston. Open Tuesday through Saturday 10–3, Sunday 1–5. Hosts a variety of performances, exhibitions, and special programs. Also inside the building, the museum houses a fine collection of artwork, including the Marsden Hartley Memorial Collection. Lovers of the artist won't want to miss this small but excellent collection of bold, bright canvases by Hartley, a Lewiston native (call ahead to find out what's on display).

SCENIC DRIVES

Along Route 26. Patched with ugly as well as beautiful stretches, the 46 miles between Gray (Maine Turnpike exit 11) and West Paris don't constitute your ordinary "scenic drive," but this is the way most people head for Bethel and the White Mountains (see map on page 502). The following sights are described in order of appearance, heading north:

Sabathday Lake Shaker Community and Museum, New Gloucester (8 miles north of Gray), both sides of the road, a must-stop (see *Museums*).

State of Maine Building from the 1893 World's Columbian Exposition in Chicago (see *Historic Buildings*). An abrupt right, up through the pillars of the old Poland Spring Resort.

✏ In Oxford two exceptional **farm stands** make ice cream from the milk of their own cows. Northbound, don't miss hilltop **Crestholm Farm Stand and Ice Cream** (on your right), which has a petting zoo (sheep, goats, pigs, ducks, more) as well as cheeses, honey, and great ice cream; also a nice view. Southbound, it's **Smedberg's Crystal Spring Farm** (see *Where to Eat—Snacks*).

✏ In South Paris road rash sets in big-time after the light; it's easy to miss **Shaner's Family Dining** (see *Eating Out*).

Across from Ripley Ford, look for the **McLaughlin Foundation Garden & Horticultural Center** (see *Green Space*).

The **Oxford Hills Chamber of Commerce** (743-2281), 6 Western Avenue, is open year-round, and you can pick up the magazine guide to this area.

Paris Hill is posted just beyond the second light in South Paris. The road climbs steadily up to Paris Hill common, a spacious green surrounded on three sides by early-19th-century mansions, with the fourth commanding a panoramic view of hills and valley and the White Mountains in the distance. Look for **Hamlin Memorial Library and Museum** (see *Historic Buildings*).

Christian Ridge Pottery (see *Selective Shopping—Special Shops*) is marked from Christian Ridge Road, a way back to Route 26.

✎ **Snow Falls Gorge,** 6 miles south of the center of West Paris on Route 26, left as you are heading north. A great picnic and walk-around spot, a rest area with tables and a trail by a waterfall that cascades into a 300-foot gorge carved by the Little Androscoggin. **The River Restaurant** (see *Dining Out*), just across the way, is recognized as one of the best "dining out" as well as "eating out" bets in the area.

✎ **Trap Corner** in West Paris (junction Route 219) is rockhounding central (see Perham's of West Paris under *To Do—Rockhounding*).

✎ **Trap Corner Store and Restaurant** (674-2482) Route 26, West Paris, open daily from 5 AM (6 AM on Sunday) is a good road-food stop.

Greenwood Shore Rest Area, Route 26 just north of Bryant Pond. A good waterside spot for a picnic.

STOCK-CAR RACING

Oxford Plains Speedway (539-8865), Route 26, Oxford. Weekend stock-car racing, late April through September.

TO DO

GOLF

Paris Hill Country Club (743-2371), Paris Hill Road, Paris, nine holes, founded in 1899, is the epitome of old-shoe; rental carts, snack bar. **Norway Country Club** (743-9840), off Route 117 on Norway Lake Road, nine holes, long views. **Summit Golf Course** (998-4515), Summit Spring Road, Poland Spring.

HIKING

✎ **Streaked Mountain.** This is a relatively easy hike with a panoramic view, good for kids. From Route 26 take Route 117 to the right-hand turnoff for Streaked Mountain Road and look for the trailhead on your left. The trail follows a power line up to an old fire tower at just 800 feet. The round trip takes about 1½ hours. Look for blueberries in-season.

Singlepole Mountain. Also off Route 117, nearer South Paris (see the *Maine Atlas and Gazetteer*, published by DeLorme), is a walk up a dirt road (bear left) through the woods to a summit with a view of Mount Washington and the Mahoosuc Mountains.

Also see **Bear Mountain Inn** under *Lodging—Bed & Breakfasts.*

MOUNTAIN BIKING

Paris Hill Area Park, near the common. You can bike the ridge roads radiating from here; inquire about routes in Hamlin Memorial Library and Museum (see *Historic Buildings*).

Lost Valley Ski Area (784-1561), Lost Valley Road, Auburn, opens its trails to bikers and organizes events in biking season.

ROCKHOUNDING

Perham's of West Paris (674-2341; 1-800-371-GEMS). Open 9–5 daily. Looking deceptively small in its yellow-clapboard, green-trim building (right side of Route 26, heading north), this business has been selling gemstones since 1919. Aside from displaying an array of locally mined amethyst, tourmaline, topaz, and many other minerals, as well as selling gem jewelry, Perham's offers maps to five local quarries in which treasure seekers are welcome to try their luck. Whether you're a rock hound or not, you'll want to stop by this mini-museum.

Rochester's Eclectic Emporium (539-4631), Route 26, Oxford. Nick Rochester displays a 54-carat amethyst that he found locally and steers visitors to local mines.

SWIMMING

Range Pond State Park (998-4104), Empire Road, Poland. Another great family beach, which offers a grass lawn above the beach, perfect for spreading out a picnic blanket. Snack bar, changing rooms, bathrooms, swimming, and fishing.

Pennesseewasee Lake in Norway is well off the road, but public and equipped with lifeguards.

In addition, most camps, cottages, and lodges have their own waterfront beaches and docks, and there are numerous local swimming holes.

WINTER SPORTS

CROSS-COUNTRY SKIING

Carter's X-C Ski Center (539-4848), Route 26, Oxford. Extensive acreage used to grow summer vegetables is transformed into a ski center during the winter. Equipment rentals, lessons, 10 km of groomed trails, some lighted trails for night skiing, and food.

Lost Valley Ski Area (784-1561), Lost Valley Road, Auburn. Mid-September through mid-March. Trails and rentals. $8 fee.

SNOW TUBING

Mountain View Sports Park (539-2454), Route 26, Oxford. Open Thursday through Sunday. A lighted 1,000-foot slope, tubes, helmets, and a T-bar are the ingredients of this low-tech, low-cost sport.

GREEN SPACE

The McLaughlin Foundation Garden & Horticultural Center (743-8820; www.mclaughlingarden.org), 97 Main Street, South Paris. Garden open May through October, dawn to dusk. In 1936 Bernard McLaughlin, who had no formal horticultural training, began planting. He welcomed visitors to his garden, set on his farmstead with stone walls and a massive barn. The 2-acre floral oasis feels delightfully out of place in this commercial center. After his death in 1995, a nonprofit organization was formed to preserve the home, barn, and garden. It's especially beautiful in lilac season (over 100 varieties). An informative guide to the gardens is available. The gift shop is open year-round, and a tearoom serving beverages and light lunches is open in summer.

LODGING

INNS

☙&The Waterford Inne (583-4037; www.waterfordinne.com), Box 149, Waterford 04088. This striking mustard-colored 1825 farmhouse with its double porch is sequestered up a back road, set on 25 acres of fields and woods. Mother and daughter Rosalie and Barbara Vanderzanden have been welcoming guests since 1978, offering nine tasteful, spacious rooms. Seven have private baths, and two share. The standout is the Chesapeake Room, with a fireplace and a second-story porch. A full breakfast is included in $80–110 per room; dinner is available (see *Dining Out*) at an additional cost. Pets are accepted, with a $10 pet fee.

Kedarburn Inn (583-6182), Route 35, Waterford 04088. London natives Margaret and Derek Gibson offer olde English hospitality in their seven guest rooms, five with private baths. Decor in their 1850s home is warm and pretty, with Margaret's specialty quilts throughout. We particularly like the room with a double bed and loft with two twin beds, a nice spot for families. The crafts shop on the ground floor is filled with items made by local artists as well as Margaret's quilts and crafts. $75–125 double in-season, including breakfast. Dinner is available in the restaurant, Peter's (see *Dining Out*), and English afternoon tea is served by reservation.

Lake House (583-4182; 1-800-223-4182; www.lakehousemaine.com), Routes 35 and 37, Waterford 04088. Open year-round. A graceful old stagecoach tavern and inn, the first building in Waterford "flat." It has been an inn, a sanatorium for ladies, a hotel, and a private residence. Michael Myers offers seven spacious guest rooms, including a two-room suite and a one-room cottage, all with private baths. The Grand Ballroom is particularly nice, with soft green walls, hardwood floors, and a claw-foot tub on a raised floor surrounded by a curtain. Rooms have phones, coffeemakers, hair dryers, and bathrobes, among other amenities. The whole place has an elegant 1700s feel. You don't have to leave the premises to find great food at dinner (see *Dining Out*). Lake Keoka is across the street. $110–175 includes breakfast.

BED & BREAKFASTS

Bear Mountain Inn (583-4404; www.bearmtninn.com), Routes 35 and 37, South Waterford 04081. Open year-round. Set on 52 acres on Bear Pond, this farmhouse has welcomed guests for more than 150 years. Lorraine Blais offers 10 rooms with bear-theme names and decor. The Great Grizzly suite offers a Jacuzzi, gas fireplace, private entrance, and deck. The Sugar Bear Cottage has a wood-burning fireplace, kitchenette, and claw-foot tub. A 45-minute hiking trail to the top of Bear Mountain begins across the street. Private beach with docks and canoes, kayaks, and pedal boats available to guests. $90–250 per room includes a full breakfast.

Farnham House B&B (782-9495; www.farnhamhouseb-b.com), 520 Main Street, Lewiston 04240. Open year-round. Barbara Fournier offers five rooms with a touch of elegance in this pleasant house built in 1900. Her main business comes from Bates College, just a block away, but anyone is welcome. The second-floor Deck Room is particularly nice, with (as you might suspect) a private deck. $50–100.

🖉 **Greenwood Manor Inn** (583-4445; www.greenwoodmanorinn.com), P.O. Box 551, Tolman Road, Harrison 04040. Open year-round. A former carriage barn with nine guest rooms (private baths) and a dining and lounging area overlooking gardens. The inn is situated on a hillside sloping to the tip of Long Lake, with croquet and a game room in a former icehouse. Children under 2 stay free, but there are no cribs. $120 double, $100 single; includes a full breakfast.

Wolf Cove Inn (998-4976; www.wolfcoveinn.com), 5 Jordan Shore Drive, Poland 04272. A romantic, quiet lakeside hideaway. Ten rooms, each named for a flower or herb, delicately decorated in simple, exquisite ways. The Calla Lilly Room is a suite overlooking Tripp Lake, with gas fireplace, whirlpool for two, CD player, and TV. Some private baths. $85–250 in-season includes a full breakfast.

OTHER LODGING

🐾 **Wadsworth Blanchard Farm Hostel** (625-7509), RR 2, Box 5992, Hiram 04041. Open May through October. An attractive Hostelling International (HI) facility that's an 18th-century farmstead, and handy to canoeing on both the Saco and Ossippee Rivers. Sally Whitcher and Edward Bradley offer two dorms, one with four beds, the other with six. There's also one private room with a queen bed; access to the kitchen is included in all rates. $12 for members, $15 for nonmembers; children 12 and under half price.

🖉 **Papoose Pond Resort and Campground** (583-4470), RR 1, Box 2480, Route 118, North Waterford 04267-9600 (10 miles west of Norway). Family geared for 40 years, this facility is on 1,000 wooded acres with a half mile of sandy beach on mile-long Papoose Pond. Cabins with or without baths, housekeeping cottages, bunkhouse trailers, tent sites, (some with electricity, water, and sewage). Also available are a dining shelter, kitchen, and bathhouse. Amenities include a recreation hall, store, café, movie tent, sports area, canoes, rowboats, sailboats, paddle-boats, kayaks, fishing equipment, and a vintage-1916 merry-go-round.

WHERE TO EAT

DINING OUT

The Waterford Inne (583-4037), Waterford. Ask for directions when you call to reserve. Open for breakfast and dinner daily, by reservation. Meals are served in the common rooms of this classic country inn. The restaurant is small, and the owners honor special requests and work around dietary needs if possible. Favorites include appetizers of Vidalia onion pie or carrot vichyssoise, and marinated lamb or grilled scallop entrées. $32 prix fixe. BYOB.

Peter's (583-6265), Route 35, Waterford. Peter and Emma Bodwell offer good fare in the dining rooms of the 1858 Kedarburn Inn (see *Lodging*). Specialties include stuffed artichoke hearts, steak *au poivre*, and fresh seafood specials. Entrées $8–19.

  ♿ **Lake House** (583-4182; 1-800-223-4182; www.lakehousemaine.com), Routes 35 and 37, Waterford. Open from 5:30 PM daily. The atmosphere is casual, but the dining is elegant. Two cozy dining rooms with linen tablecloths, fresh flowers, and oil lamps. The menu is varied and the wine list extensive. Owner-chef Michael Myers prepares all meals to order. This is a place to linger and enjoy, from breadsticks to coffee and dessert. Order the bananas Foster for two just for the pleasure of watching it prepared tableside. Dinner entrées average $27.

  ♿ **Maurice Restaurant** (743-2532), 109 Main Street, South Paris. Open for dinner daily, lunch weekdays, Sunday brunch. Though the main focus here is French cuisine, they also offer pasta and beef dishes. Entrées include scampi, veal flambé, and roast duck à l'orange. Extensive wine list. Reservations recommended. $12–17.

  ✪ **The River Restaurant** (743-7816), nestled beside Snow Falls, Route 26, West Paris. Open for lunch and dinner daily except Monday. Known for its creative fine dining at a reasonable price. Specialties include seafood pasta, spinach fettuccine with wine cream sauce, lobster, scallops, and shrimp. Entrées $10.95–15.95.

  ♿ **Sedgley Place** (946-5990), off Route 202, Greene. Reservations required. A lovely Federal-style house with a well-known dining room. Five-course dinners with entrées that change weekly but always include prime rib, a fish, a poultry, and a fourth selection. Prix fixe.

  ♿ **Trolley House Restaurant** (743-2211), 110 Main Street, Norway. Open for lunch and dinner daily except Sunday. Two attractive high-ceilinged dining rooms decorated with old photo blowups. The menu features Angus beef and seafood, with daily specials. Dinner entrées $8.95–16.95.

DaVinci's (782-2088), Bates Mill Complex, Lewiston. Open for lunch and dinner. Brick-oven pizza, classic Italian entrées.

Village Inn (782-7796), 165 High Street, Auburn. Casual dining. Seafood is the specialty here, especially their fried clams. $7.95–14.95.

Korn Haus Keller (786-2379), 1472 Lisbon Street, Lewiston. The specialty here is chicken cordon bleu. Other menu options include lobster pie, seafood, and beef. $8.95–16.95.

Marois (782-9055), 249 Lisbon Street, Lewiston. It is a surprise to find this fine-dining spot smack in the middle of downtown Lewiston. Well known and popular among locals. Greek and French specialties. $7–15.

EATING OUT

*   **Olde Mill Tavern** (583-4992), Maine Street, Harrison. Open daily 11–11. Popular with local residents . Featuring "family-style dinners" (for two or more) like whole roasted chicken at $7.95 per person, and a choice of "big plates" (which run as high as $19.95 for rack of lamb) and "small plates," like Mill Tavern meat loaf and fajita chicken salad; also "hand-carved sandwiches," flatbreads, and Sunday brunch.

*   **Cole Farms** (657-4714), Route 100/202, Gray. Open 5 AM–10:30 PM daily except Monday. Maine cooking from family recipes. Fried seafood, hot chicken sandwiches, daily specials like New England boiled dinner. Everything from soups and chowders to ice cream and pastries is made on the premises. No liquor. New playground and picnic area for outside dining.

    Chopsticks (783-6300), 37 Park Street, Lewiston. One of the best Chinese restaurants we have found, with all the usual choices.

*   **Val's Root Beer** (784-5592), 925 Sabattus Street, Lewiston. Seasonal. Open daily 11–8 except Sunday, when they open at noon. Fifties-style drive-in with carhops and *Happy Days* theme. Burgers, hot dogs, and the like, and their specialty, homemade root beer. During the week (except Friday) you can get a burger, fries, and root beer for less than $3. Popular summer hangout among locals.

    Chickadee (225-3523), Route 4, Turner. A longtime local favorite, serving lunch and dinner daily. Specialties include seafood and beef.

*   **Shaner's Family Dining** (743-6367), 193 Main Street, South Paris. Open for breakfast, lunch, and dinner. A large, cheerful family restaurant with booths; specials like fried chicken, liver and onions, and chicken pie; creamy homemade ice cream in a big choice of flavors.

SNACKS

*   **Crestholm Farm Stand and Ice Cream** (539-2616), Route 26, Oxford. Farm stand, cheeses, honey, ice cream, and a petting zoo: sheep, goats, pigs, ducks, more.

*   **Smedberg's Crystal Spring Farm** (743-6723) sells its One Cow Ice Cream (there are actually a couple of dozen cows) in a dozen flavors.

ENTERTAINMENT

---

*   **Celebration Barn Theater** (743-8452), 190 Stock Farm (off Route 117 north of South Paris). In 1972 theater and mime master Tony Montanaro founded a performance-arts school in this big old red racing-horse barn high on Christian Ridge. Summer workshops in acrobatics, mime, and juggling by resident New Vaudeville artists, Friday and Saturday in July and August; tickets are reasonably priced.

    Deertrees Theatre and Cultural Center (583-6747), Deertrees Road, Harrison. A 300-seat historic theater, built as an opera house in 1936, saved from being used as an exercise for the local fire department in the

5599

1980s, and restored to its original grandeur. The Deertrees Foundation operates the center as a nonprofit performing-arts center, host to the Sebego–Long Lake Music Festival concert series, and venue for a number of performances: dance and music, theatrical productions, children's shows. Also check out fine art and sculpture in the **Backstage Gallery,** open an hour before showtime, intermisson, and by appointment.

The Public Theatre (782-3200; 1-800-639-9575), 2 Great Falls Plaza, Auburn. Professional Equity theater featuring high-quality productions of Broadway and off-Broadway shows.

L/A Arts (1-800-639-2919), 49 Lisbon Street, Lewiston. A local arts agency bringing exhibitions, community arts outreach, presentations, music series, and educational programs to the area.

The Maine Music Society (782-1403), 215 Lisbon Street, Lewiston, is home to both the **Maine Chamber Orchestra** and the **Androscoggin Chorale.** A variety of performances throughout the year.

Bates Dance Festival (786-6161), Schaeffer Theater, Bates College, Lewiston. Runs mid-July through mid-August. Student and faculty performances.

SELECTIVE SHOPPING

ANTIQUES
Mollyockett Marketplace (674-3939), Route 26, junction Route 219, West Paris. Open Thursday through Monday, May through November, on winter weekends. A two-story group shop; items priced to sell.

BOOKSTORES
Books 'n' Things (743-7197), Oxford Plaza, Route 26, Oxford. Billing itself as "Western Maine's Complete Bookstore," a fully stocked store with a full children's section.

Downtown Bookshop (743-7245), 200 Main Street, Norway. Closed Sunday. A source of general titles, stationery, cards, and magazines.

GEM SHOPS
See *To Do—Rockhounding.*

SPECIAL SHOPS
United Society of Shakers (926-4597), Route 26, New Gloucester. Open Memorial Day through Columbus Day; sells Shaker herbs, teas, handcrafted items.

Christian Ridge Pottery (743-8419), 210 Stock Farm Road, Paris Hill (marked from Route 26 and from Christian Ridge Road). Open Memorial Day weekend through December, 10–5 daily except noon–5 Sunday. One of Maine's major potters, known for its functional, distinctive stippleware in ovenproof, microwavable designs: coffee- and teapots, bowls, and more; also specialty items like apple-baking dishes. Seconds are available.

RICK WEBB

Launching at the Great Falls Balloon Festival in Lewiston

Stone Soup Artisans (783-4281), Vernon and Center Streets, Auburn. Open Tuesday through Saturday 10–5. An outstanding artists' and artisan's cooperative.

OUTLETS

Bates Mill Store (784-7626; 1-800-552-2837), 49 Canal Street, Lewiston. Open year-round; weekdays 9–4, Saturday 9–1. A genuine outlet for Bates bedspreads, towels, sheets, blankets.

Marden's (786-0313), Northwood Shopping Center, Route 202, Lewiston. Like Reny's (see *Selective Shopping—Special Shops* in "Damariscotta/ Newcastle and Pemaquid Area") this is a Maine original, the first store in a Maine chain. A mix of clothing, staples, furnishings—whatever happens to be in stock. Always worth checking.

For more shops in this region, also see *Selective Shopping* in "Bethel Area."

SPECIAL EVENTS

May: **Maine State Parade** *(first Saturday).*—the state's biggest parade; theme varies annually. **Lilac Festival** at McLaughlin Foundation Gardens.

July: The **Oxford 250 NASCAR Race** draws entrants from throughout the world to the Oxford Plains Speedway; Harrison celebrates **Old Home Days. Founders Day** on Paris Hill *(midmonth).* **Bean Hole Bean Festival** in Oxford draws thousands. **The Moxie Festival**, downtown Lisbon, *(second weekend)* features live entertainment, plenty of food, and Moxie (Maine's own soft drink). The **Norway Sidewalk Arts Festival** has more than 100 exhibitors.

August: **Gray Old Home Days** *(beginning of the month)* includes a parade, contests, and public feeds. **Festival de Joie,** Lewiston, *(first weekend)*—music, dancing, and cultural and crafts displays. **Great Falls Balloon Festival,** Lewiston *(fourth weekend)*—music, games, hot-air launches.

September: **Oxford County Agricultural Fair** in West Paris *(usually held during the second week)*.

December: **Christmas open house and festivals** in Paris Hill.

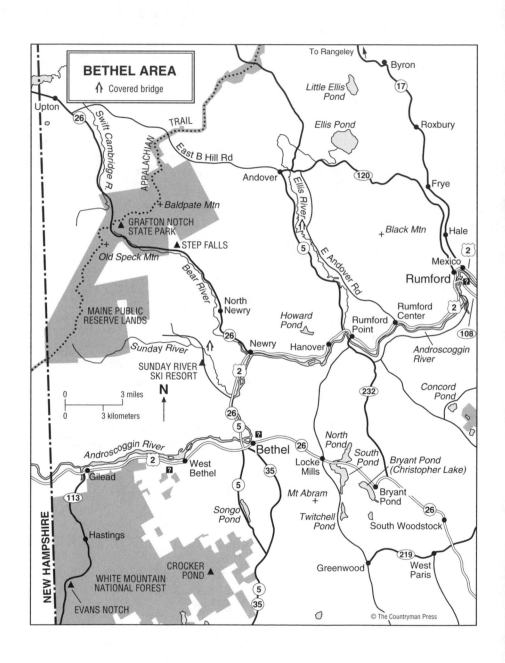

BETHEL AREA

⬆ Covered bridge

Upton

Little Ellis Pond

Ellis Pond

To Rangeley

Byron

17

Roxbury

Swift Cambridge R.

26

APPALACHIAN TRAIL

East B Hill Rd

Andover

120

Frye

Ellis River

E Andover Rd

Black Mtn

Hale

2

Mexico

+ Baldpate Mtn

GRAFTON NOTCH STATE PARK

▲ STEP FALLS

+ Old Speck Mtn

Bear River

5

Rumford

Rumford Center

2

108

MAINE PUBLIC RESERVE LANDS

North Newry

Howard Pond

Rumford Point

Androscoggin River

Sunday River

⬆

26

Newry

Hanover

SUNDAY RIVER SKI RESORT

2

232

Concord Pond

0   3 miles

N

0   3 kilometers

26

5

?

Bethel

North Pond

South Pond

Bryant Pond (Christopher Lake)

Androscoggin River

2

Gilead

?

West Bethel

26

Locke Mills

Bryant Pond

35

26

5

Mt Abram +

Songo Pond

Twitchell Pond

South Woodstock

113

NEW HAMPSHIRE

Hastings

WHITE MOUNTAIN NATIONAL FOREST

▲ EVANS NOTCH

CROCKER POND ▲

5

35

Greenwood

219

West Paris

© The Countryman Press

Bethel Area

Bethel is a natural farming and trading site on the Androscoggin River. Its town common is the junction for routes west to the White Mountains, north to the Mahoosucs, east to the Oxford Hills, and south to the lakes.

When the trains from Portland to Montreal began stopping here in 1851, Bethel also became an obvious summer retreat for city people. But unlike many summer resorts of that era, it was nothing fancy. Families stayed the season in the big white farmhouses, of which there are still plenty. They feasted on homegrown and home-cooked food, then walked it off on nearby mountain trails.

Hiking remains a big lure for summer and fall visitors. The White Mountain National Forest comes within a few miles of town, and trails radiate from nearby Evans Notch. Just 12 miles northwest of Bethel, Grafton Notch State Park also offers short hikes to spectacles such as Screw Auger Falls and to a wealth of well-equipped picnic sites. Blueberrying and rockhounding are local pastimes, and the hills are also good pickings for history buffs.

The hills were once far more peopled than they are today—entire villages have vanished. Hastings, for example, now just the name of a national forest campground, was once a thriving community complete with post office, stores, and a wood alcohol mill that shipped its product by rail to Portland, thence to England.

The Bethel Inn, born of the railroad era, is still going strong. Opened in 1913 by millionaire William Bingham II and dedicated to a prominent neurologist (who came to Bethel to recuperate from a breakdown), it originally featured a program of strenuous exercise—one admired by the locals (wealthy clients actually paid the doctor to chop down his trees) as well as by the medical profession. The inn is still known for at least two forms of exercise—golf and cross-country skiing.

Bethel is best known these days as a ski town. Sunday River, 6 miles to the north, claims to offer "the most dependable snow in North America." Powered by its snow guns (powered in turn by water from the Sunday River), the family-geared resort has doubled and redoubled its trails, lifts, and lodging regularly since 1980, when it was acquired by Les Otten. Otten's American Skiing Company owns nine ski resorts throughout the U.S. Six of these are major ski resorts in the Northeast, including Killington in Vermont and Sunday River's longtime Maine competitor, Sugarloaf. So it happens that Bethel is now the address of one of the world's largest ski-resort-operating companies (see *To Do— Downhill Skiing*). Mount Abram, a few miles south of the village, by contrast, remains an old-fashioned family ski area.

Skiers tend to see Bethel as "a quick hit" that you simply get to— and out of—without stopping on the way to the snow-covered trails. In summer it's a very different story. As it has been since settlement, Bethel is a natural way station—between the White Mountains and the coast, and between the lake resorts and children's camps to the south and Rangeley to the north (see the introduction to "Western Mountains and Lakes Region").

Bethel is also home to Gould Academy, a coed prep school with a handsome campus, and is the summer home of NTL Institute for Applied Behavioral Science, enrolling roughly 1,000 participants from around the world. Hidden away in the Newry woods, Outward Bound's Hurricane Island School also contributes to the mix that's Bethel: Several former instructors now offer visitors outdoors-geared activities such as dogsledding, llama trekking, kayaking, and horseback riding.

For Bethel, tourism has remained the icing rather than the cake. Its lumber mills manufacture pine boards, furniture parts, and broom handles. Three dairy farms ship 7,000 gallons of milk per week. Brooks Bros. is still the name of the hardware store, not a men's clothier.

GUIDANCE

Bethel Area Chamber of Commerce (824-2282; www.bethelmaine. com), P.O. Box 1247, 30 Cross Street, Bethel 04217, publishes an excellent area guide and maintains a large walk-in information center with rest rooms in the depot-style Bethel Station, off Lower Main Street (Route 26). Open year-round, weekdays 9–5, varying hours on weekends. See *Lodging* for reservations services.

The Maine Tourism Association (824-4582) and **White Mountain National Forest Service** (824-2134) also maintain a joint information center, with rest rooms, on Route 2/5/26 just outside town; open most days, but hours vary. It's stocked with information on all areas in Maine and offers detailed information about camping, hiking, and other outdoor activities in the national forest and other nearby natural areas.

GETTING THERE

By air: **The Portland International Jetport,** served by several minor carriers, is 75 miles from Bethel. All major car rentals are available at the airport (see *Getting There* in "Portland Area"). **Bethel Air** (824-4321) offers air taxi/charter service; the **Bethel Airport** (824-4321) has a paved 3,150-foot runway.

Bethel Express (824-4646). Van limo shuttle will pick up at Portland Jetport or other transportation hubs. **Northeast Charter & Tour** (1-

888-539-6328) is a 14-passenger van service that runs to the Portland International Jetport; Boston's Logan Airport; Manchester, New Hampshire, and all of New England.

By car: Bethel is a convenient way stop between New Hampshire's White Mountains (via Route 2) and the Maine coast. From Boston, take the Maine Turnpike to Gray, exit 11; Bethel is 55 miles north on Route 26. For more than a dozen suggested stops along the way, see *To See—Scenic Drives* in "Oxford Hills and Lewiston/Auburn."

MEDICAL EMERGENCY
Bethel Family Health Center (824-2193).
Sheriff's Department/Bethel Rescue: 911.

TO SEE

HISTORIC HOMES AND MUSEUMS
Bethel Historical Society's Regional History Center (824-2908), 10–14 Broad Street, Bethel. Open year-round Tuesday through Friday 1–4 and weekends (same hours) in July and August. $3 adults, $1.50 children. More than a dozen period rooms, exhibition galleries, crafts demonstration areas, a research library, and a museum shop. **The Dr. Moses Mason House** is an exquisite Federal-style mansion built in 1813; this house is proof of the town's early prosperity. Restored to the grandeur of Dr. Moses Mason's (one of Bethel's most prominent citizens in the 1800s) time, it has magnificent Rufus Porter murals in the front hall, fine furnishings in nine period rooms, and well-informed guides to tell you about the items you see throughout the house. An exhibit hall and the research library are also in this house. Next door is the **O'Neil Robinson House,** acquired by the society and opened as a museum in 1999. Built in 1821, it was remodeled in the Italianate style in 1881 and houses the main offices of the society, changing exhibits in several rooms, and the museum shop.

COVERED BRIDGES
Artists' Covered Bridge, Newry (across the Sunday River, 5 miles northwest of Bethel). A weathered town bridge built in 1872 and painted by numerous 19th-century landscape artists, notably John Enneking. A great spot to sun and swim. Other swimming holes can be found at intervals along the road above the bridge.

Lovejoy Covered Bridge, South Andover, roughly a quarter mile east of Route 5. Built across the Ellis River in 1867, another local swimming hole (it's more than 7 miles north of Route 2).

SCENIC DRIVES
Ask for a brochure detailing a 67-mile driving tour of the Bethel area at the chamber. Also pick up the auto-tour brochure prepared by the Bethel Historical Society, which leads you past several historic sites in the area.

Evans Notch. Follow Route 2 west to Gilead and turn south on Route 113 (see map on page 502), following the Wild and then the Cold River south through one of the most spectacular mountain passes in northern New England. (Also see *To Do—Camping* and White Mountain National Forest under *To Do—Hiking*.)

Grafton Notch State Park. A beautiful drive even if you don't hike (see *To Do—Hiking*). Continue on beyond Upton for views of Lake Umbagog; note the loop you can make back from Upton along the old road to Andover (look for the vintage-1867 **Lovejoy Covered Bridge** across the Ellis River), then south on Route 5 to Route 2.

Patte Brook Multiple-Use Management Demonstration Area, a 4-mile, self-guided tour with stops at 11 areas along Patte Brook near the national forest's **Crocker Pond** campground in West Bethel. The tour begins on Forest Road No. 7 (Patte Brook Road), 5 miles south of Bethel on Route 5. A glacial bog, former orchards and homesites, and an old dam and pond are among the clearly marked sites.

Rangeley and Weld loops. See the introduction to "Western Mountains and Lakes Region" for a description of these rewarding drives. You can access both by following Route 2 north from Bethel along the Androscoggin River, but back-road buffs may prefer cutting up the narrow rural valleys threaded by Rumford Road or Route 232 from Locke Mills; both join Route 2 at Rumford Point.

OTHER SITES

Mount Zircon Bottle. Walk down Broad Street and you'll see this historic bottle-shaped lunch stand, built after the company's second bottling plant opened in 1922.

TO DO

AIRPLANE RIDES

Bethel Air (824-4321) North Road, Bethel. Offers scenic flights of the area with views of the Bethel and Appalachian Mountain areas year-round by appointment only. They also offer flight instruction and air-taxi service.

BICYCLING

The **Bethel Area Chamber of Commerce** (see *Guidance*) can offer several suggested scenic rides where you will encounter little traffic.

Also see *Mountain Biking*.

CAMPING

In the **Evans Notch area** of the White Mountain National Forest there are five campgrounds: **Basin** (21 sites), **Cold River** (12 sites), **Crocker Pond** (7 sites), **Hastings** (24 sites), and **Wild River** (11 sites). All accept reservations for May 13 through October 11 through the National Recreation Reservation Service: 1-800-280-2267, Monday through Friday (Pacific time; from the East Coast, phone weekdays noon–9 PM or Saturday and Sunday 1–6 PM). For information, phone the **Evans Notch Ranger Station** (824-2134), West Bethel Road (Route 2), Bethel.

Also check with the **White Mountain National Forest Service** information center (see *Guidance*) about wilderness campsites, and see *Lodging* for commercial campgrounds.

CANOEING AND KAYAKING

Popular local routes include the **Ellis River** in Andover (13 easy miles from the covered bridge in South Andover to Rumford Point); the **Androscoggin River** has become far more accessible in recent years with 10 put-in points mapped and shuttle service offered between Shelburne on the New Hampshire line and the Rumford boat landing; the **Sunday River** (beginning at the covered bridge) also offers great whitewater trips in spring. A chain of water connects **North, South,** and **Round Ponds** and offers a day of rewarding paddling, with swimming holes and picnic stops en route. See the "Upper Androscoggin Valley Interpretive Map," produced by the Appalachian Mountain Club and available at no charge from the White Mountain National Forest Service information center (see *Guidance*).

Bethel Outdoor Adventures and Campground (824-4224; 1-800-533-3607), Route 2, Bethel (see *Lodging—Campgrounds*), offers shuttle service, canoe and kayak rentals, guided trips, and kayak clinics. **Mahoosuc Guide Service** (824-3092) offers guided trips on the Allagash, Penobscot, and St. John Rivers. **Sun Valley Sports** (1-877-851-7533) offers guided (and nonguided) kayak and canoe tours and rentals on the Androscoggin River and on local lakes and ponds. They also offer ATV tours. The **Telemark Inn** (836-2703) also offers guided canoeing (see *Lodging—Inns*).

CHAIRLIFT RIDES

Sunday River Ski Resort (824-3000) offers scenic chairlift rides, weather permitting, Memorial Day through Columbus Day weekend.

FISHING

Temporary nonresident licenses are available at the **Bethel, Newry,** and **Woodstock town offices;** also at **Dave's Store** in Andover, **Bob's Corner Store** in Locke Mills, **Bethel Outdoor Adventures** in Bethel, and **Sun Valley Sports** (824-7533; 1-877-851-7533), Sunday River Road. Fly-fishing is a growing sport here, especially along the Androscoggin, which is increasingly known for the size of its trout. Also see **L'Auberge** under *Lodging—Bed & Breakfasts*.

FOR FAMILIES

✍ **Sunday River Mountain Adventure Center** (824-3000; 1-800-543-2SKI), South Ridge Base Lodge, Sunday River Ski Resort, Newry. Open weekends Memorial Day through Labor Day daily in July and August. Includes a skateboard/in-line skating park and climbing wall.

✍ **The BIG Adventure Center** (824-0929), Route 2 and North Road (adjacent to the Norseman), Bethel. Summer hours, 11–11 daily; winter hours, Monday through Friday 2–10 PM and weekends 11–10. Indoor laser tag, indoor rock gym, two-lane water slide, outdoor 18-hole miniature golf.

GOLF

Bethel Inn and Country Club (824-2175), Broad Street, Bethel. An 18-hole championship-length course and driving range. Mid-May through October the inn's **Guaranteed Performance School of Golf** (PGA) offers 3- and 5-day sessions (classes limited to three students per PGA instructor); golf-cart rentals are available.

HIKING

White Mountain National Forest, although primarily in New Hampshire, includes 41,943 acres in Maine. A number of the trails in the **Evans Notch** area are spectacular. Trail maps for the Baldface Circle Trail, Basin Trail, Bickford Brook Trail, and Caribou Trail are available from the **Evans Notch Ranger District** (824-2134), West Bethel Road (Route 2), Bethel; open Monday through Friday 8–4. Pick up detailed maps from the chamber of commerce (see *Guidance*).

Grafton Notch State Park, Route 26, between Newry and Upton. From Bethel, take Route 2 east to Route 26 north for 7.8 miles. Turn left at the Getty station (Newry Corner) and drive toward New Hampshire for 8.7 miles. **Screw Auger Falls** is 1 mile farther—a spectacular area at the end of the Mahoosuc Range. Other sights include **Mother Walker Falls** and **Moose Cave,** a half-mile nature walk. The big hike is up **Old Speck,** the third highest mountain in the state; up Old Speck Trail and back down the Firewarden's Trail is 5½ miles.

Wight Brook Nature Preserve/ Step Falls can be found just before the entrance to Grafton Notch State Park. From Newry Corner, drive 7.9 miles. On your right will be a white farmhouse, followed by a field just before a bridge. There is a road leading to the rear left of the field, where you may park. The well-marked trail is just behind the trees at the back. Please respect the private property adjoining the trail and falls. This scenic area on Wight's Brook, maintained by The Nature Conservancy, has been enjoyed by local families for generations.

In Shelburne there are hiking trails on **Mount Crag, Mount Cabot,** and **Ingalls Mountain,** and there are more trails in **Evans Notch.** For details, check the Appalachian Mountain Club's *White Mountain Guide*, and John Gibson's *50 Hikes in Coastal and Southern Maine* (Backcountry Guides).

Mount Will Trail. Recently developed by the Bethel Conservation Commission, this 3¼-mile loop is a good family trip; many people choose to climb only to the North Ledges (640 vertical feet in ¾ mile), yielding a view of the Androscoggin Valley, which only gets better over the next 1½ miles—climbing over ledges to 1,450 feet and then descending the South Cliffs. The trailhead is a chained-off logging road on Route 2, just 1.9 miles beyond the Riverside Rest Area (which is just beyond the turnoff for Sunday River).

HORSEBACK RIDING

Deepwood Farm (824-2595), Albany Township, a family-oriented business, offers regular riding programs April through November: lessons, sleigh rides, trail rides, and 3- and 5-day summer camps for youngsters ages 6–10.

LLAMA TREKKING

Telemark Inn (836-2703), 10 miles west of Bethel. Treks offered April through October. Primarily for guests of the Telemark Inn, but treks ranging from 1 to 4 days into the surrounding wilderness are available to nonguests as well. Steve Crone offered the first llama treks in New England, and we took one of the first that he offered. The llamas carry your gear, but you walk beside them. Rates: from $85 adults, $65 children for 1 day to $575 adults, $425 children for 4 days.

MOUNTAIN BIKING

Bethel Inn and Country Club (824-6276), Broad Street, Bethel, rents 21-speed mountain bikes by the half day, full day, or for 2 days.

Sunday River Mountain Bike Park (824-3000; 1-800-543-2SKI), South Ridge Base Lodge, Sunday River Ski Resort, Newry. Two chairlifts access 60 miles of bike trails. Lift and trail passes and rental bikes are available at South Ridge Base Lodge. Lodging, lift, and meal packages are also available.

Bethel Outdoor Adventures (824-4224), Route 2, Bethel, offers scheduled, guided mountain bike tours as well as custom tours and rentals.

Mahoosuc Mountain Sports (824-3786), Route 26, Locke Mills, also rents mountain bikes.

ROCKHOUNDING

This corner of Oxford County is recognized as one of the world's richest sources of some minerals and semiprecious gems. More than a third of the world's mineral varieties can be found here. Gems include amethyst, aquamarine, tourmaline, and topaz. Mining has gone on around here since tourmaline was discovered at Mount Mica in 1821. Jim Mann's **Mt. Mann** (824-3030) on Main Street, Bethel, includes a mineral museum. In the cellar kids (of all ages) can explore "Crystal Cave": a dimly lit "mine" in which rock hounds can fill their cardboard buckets (for a nominal fee) and then identify them back in the museum. **Perham's of West Paris** (674-2341; 1-800-371-GEMS), open 9–5 daily, offers maps to several local quarries. (Also see *To Do—Rockhounding* in "Oxford Hills and Lewiston/Auburn.") The **Annual Gem, Mineral, and Jewelry Show** (second weekend in July at Telstar High School) is a mega–mineral event with guided field trips to local quarries.

SWIMMING

There are numerous lakes and river swimming holes in the area. It is best to ask the chamber of commerce (see *Guidance*) about where access is currently possible. Reliable spots includ:

Artists' Covered Bridge. Follow SUNDAY RIVER SKI RESORT signs north from Bethel, but bear right at two Y intersections instead of turning onto either of the ski-area access roads. Look for the covered bridge on your left. Space for parking, bushes for changing.

Wild River in Evans Notch, Gilead, offers some obvious access spots off Route 113, as does the **Bear River,** which follows Route 26 through Grafton Notch.

WINTER SPORTS

DOGSLEDDING

Mahoosuc Mountain Adventures (824-2073), Bear River Road, Newry 04261. Polly Mahoney and Kevin Slater offer combination backcountry skiing and mushing trips. You can be as involved with the dogs as you want: an hour, a day, or a 3-day, 2-night trip.

Winter Journeys (928-2026), Lovell, offers half-, full-, and multiday B&B dogsled trips.

Skijoring: Skiing behind dogs is a specialty at the **Telemark Inn** (see *Lodging—Inns*).

CROSS-COUNTRY SKIING

Sunday River Inn and XC Ski Center (824-2410), RFD 3, Bethel. A total of 40 km of double-tracked trails loop through the woods, including a section to Artists' Covered Bridge (see *To Do—Swimming*). Thanks to the high elevation, careful trail prepping, and heavy-duty grooming equipment, snow tends to stick here when it's scarce in much of Maine. The center offers guided night skiing, rentals, instruction, and snacks.

Bethel Inn Nordic Center (824-2175), Bethel. Redesigned trails meander out over the golf course and through the woods, offering beautiful mountain views, solitude, and challenges suitable for all levels. Skating and classic trails, rental equipment, and lessons available.

Carter's X-Country Ski Center (539-4848), Intervale Road (off Route 26 south of the village), Bethel. Call to find out which days they are open. Dave Carter, a member of one of Bethel's oldest families and a long-time cross-country pro, maintains some 65 km of wooded trails on 1,000 acres, meandering from 600 up to 1,800 feet in elevation; an easy loop connects two lodges and runs along the Androscoggin River. Reasonably priced equipment rentals and lessons. They have an additional center on Route 26 in Oxford.

Telemark Inn (836-2703), West Bethel. These 20 km of high-elevation wooded trails and unlimited backcountry skiing terrain frequently represent the best cross-country skiing in the area—but Steve Crone issues a limited number of passes a day, preserving the wilderness feel of his resort for Telemark Inn guests. So call before coming and inquire about skijoring (see *Dogsledding*) behind huskies!

Great Glen Trails Outdoor Center (603-466-2333). Just 35 minutes from Bethel, south of Gorham, New Hampshire, on Route 16. Exquisitely groomed trails, lessons, retail and rentals, and views of Mount Washington.

Also see **Mahoosuc Mountain Adventures** under *Dogsledding*, and

In summer a chairlift takes mountain bikers to the top at Sunday River Resort

contact the **Bethel Ranger Station** (824-2134) for details about cross-country trails in the **White Mountain National Forest** (see *To Do—Hiking*).

DOWNHILL SKIING

Mount Abram Ski Resort (875-5000), Locke Mills. Under new ownership in 2001 and operating on a limited schedule at press time. Open 9–4 Thursday through Sunday and holidays, but call to check. This remains a friendly family-owned and -geared ski area: 35 trails and slopes, with some pleasant surprises, including two black-diamond trails and a "cruiser" trail. The vertical drop is 1,030 feet. Facilities include 78% percent snowmaking; two double chairlifts, and three T-bars; an expanded "barn red" lodge with lounge, snack shop, nursery; and ski rentals, PSIA ski school, special programs. Family-friendly rates: $33 adults, $25 seniors, $20 juniors, under 5 free. Half-day tickets are $26 adults/$13 juniors.

Sunday River Ski Resort (824-3000; resort reservations, 1-800-543-2SKI), Newry 04217. Sunday River has become synonymous with snow. Owner Les Otten now heads the American Skiing Company, which includes Killington, the mammoth Vermont ski resort for which the 23-year-old Otten first came to 12-trail Sunday River as assistant to the manager.

At Sunday River 127 trails and glades now lace eight interconnected mountain peaks, including the Jordan Bowl. Challenges include a 3-mile run from a summit and White Heat—"the steepest longest widest lift-served expert trail in the East." The trails are served by 18 lifts: 9 quad chairlifts (4 high-speed detachable), 4 triple chairlifts, 2 doubles, and 3 surface lifts. The vertical descent is 2,340 feet and the top elevation is 3,140 feet. Snowmaking covers 92 percent of the skiing and riding terrain. There are also 3 half-pipes (one an in-ground competition half-pipe), and 5 terrain parks, including a full-length park on Aurora Peak. Facilities include 3 base lodges and a Peak Lodge, ski shops, and several restaurants; a total of 6,000 (see *Lodging*). The Discovery Center ski school offers Guaranteed Learn-to-Ski in One Day and Perfect Turn clinics, Munchkins for ages 4–6, Mogul Meisters for ages 7–12, a Junior Racing Program, and a Maine Handicapped Skiing Program. A half-pipe is lit for snowboarders at the White Cap Base Lodge. Lift tickets are $98 adults and $62 juniors for 2 days on weekends; less midweek. Many lodging packages available.

ICE SKATING
In winter a portion of Bethel's common is flooded, and ice skates can be rented from the cross-country center at the Bethel Inn. Skate rentals are also available at the public skating rink at Sunday River's White Cap Base Lodge.

SLEIGH RIDES
Telemark Inn, Sunday River Inn, and the **Bethel Inn and Country Club** (see *Lodging—Inns* and *Ski Lodges and Condominiums*) all offer sleigh rides.

SNOWMOBILING
Local enthusiasts have developed a trail system in the area. Contact the Bethel Area Chamber of Commerce (see *Guidance*) for information on where to get maps. Maine and New Hampshire also maintain 60 miles of trails in the Evans Notch District. **Sun Valley Sports** (824-7553; 1-877-851-7533) on the Sunday River Road and **Bethel Outdoor Adventures** (824-4224) in Bethel rent snowmobiles.

GREEN SPACE

The Mahoosuc Land Trust (824-3806; www.megalink.net/~mlt), P.O. Box 981, Bethel 04217. Formed in 1988 to preserve land in the Mahoosuc Range and the Androscoggin Valley, the trust owns islands, shoreland, and floodplain land, and easements on land in the eastern foothills and on the banks of a large pond.

LODGING

All listings are in Bethel 04217 unless otherwise noted.
The **Bethel Area Chamber of Commerce** maintains a lodging reservations service: 824-3585; 1-800-442-5826; www.bethelmaine.com.
Sunday River Ski Resort maintains its own toll-free reservation number: 1-800-543-2SKI, good nationwide and in Canada; the service is geared toward winter and condo information but also serves local inns and

Bethel Inn and Country Club

B&Bs. Many other condos and rental homes are available in the Bethel area through **Maine Street Realty & Rentals** (824-2114; 1-800-824-6024), **Rentals Unlimited** (824-4044; 1-800-535-2220), **Connecting Rentals** (824-4829), and **Four Seasons Realty & Rentals** (875-2414). Also see **Lake House** and the **Kedarburn Inn** under *Lodging—Inns* in "Oxford Hills and Lewiston/Auburn."

INNS

Bethel Inn and Country Club (824-2175; 1-800-654-0125; www.bethelinn.com), Bethel 04217. This rambling, yellow wooden inn and its annexes frame a corner of the town common. The lobby and parlor are large and formal, but inviting. The downstairs **Mill Brook Tavern** is comfortably old-fashioned. The formal dining room is truly elegant (see *Dining Out*). The 60 rooms in the inn and guest houses vary in size and view (request a larger room in back, overlooking the mountains), all with phones and private baths. The new wing is modern and spacious, with plenty of amenities. Families should opt for one of the 40 one- and two-bedroom town houses on the golf course. Facilities include a recreation center with a pool, two saunas, an exercise room, a game room, and a lounge. The pool is outdoors but heated to 91 degrees for winter use. The 18-hole golf course, with 7 holes dating from 1915 and 11 more added by Geoffrey Cornish, is a big draw, with golf-school sessions offered throughout the season. Facilities also include a Har-Tru tennis court, a boathouse with canoes, and a sandy beach on Songo Pond, as well as an extensive cross-country ski network (see *To Do—Golf* and *Winter Sports—Cross-Country Skiing* and *Sleigh Rides*). A day-camp program, free to inn guests, is offered for children in the summer

ELIZABETH ROUNDY RICHARDS

months. From $99 in the inn; town houses, $210–340. Many packages are available, especially off-season. Children ages 15 and under, free in room with parent.

✍ **Telemark Inn** (836-2703; www.telemark.com), RFD 2, Box 800, Bethel 04217. It is a challenge to describe this unusual retreat, set among birch trees 2.5 miles off the nearest back road and surrounded by national forest. The feel is that of a North Woods sporting camp—with a herd of llamas (see *To Do—Llama Trekking*) and a team of huskies. Steve Crone is an avid naturalist who knows where to find beaver dams and peregrine falcon nests in the wilderness accessible from his own property. Hiking, canoeing, and mountain biking are also offered, and winter brings exceptional cross-country skiing and the opportunity to try "skijoring" (skiing behind huskies). Meals are served family-style at the round cherrywood table supported by tree trunks. Built in classic "Maine rustic" style as a millionaire's retreat, the inn has five rooms sharing two baths and accommodates 12 to 17 guests, with plenty of common space, including a large semi-enclosed porch and a living room with a magnificent mineral-studded fireplace. $95 per couple, $75 single with breakfast; $25 for each additional person.

🐾✍&**Philbrook Farm Inn** (603-466-3831), 881 North Road, Shelburne, New Hampshire 03581. Open year-round. Twenty miles west of Bethel, just over the New Hampshire line. The long, meandering farmhouse, owned by the same family since 1861, sits above a floodplain of the Androscoggin River with the Mahoosuc Range at its back. Each of the 19 guest rooms in the house is different, all wallpapered and most furnished with the kind of hand-me-downs that most innkeepers scour the hills for. Second-floor rooms have private baths; third-floor rooms share. Common rooms meander on and on (there's a working Estey organ in the parlor), and the dining room is large and paneled; the family-style meals are as old-fashioned as the rest of the place (fish on Friday, ham and beans on Saturday night; BYOB). There are also four seasonal efficiency cottages (each different), plus two without kitchens. Pets are allowed in the summer cottages. Hiking is possible everywhere, and in winter there are miles of cross-country trails (untracked) as well as snowshoeing possiblities. $125–145 per couple MAP, plus a 15 percent service charge.

& **The Victoria** (824-8060; 1-888-774-1235; www.thevictoria-inn.com), 32 Main Street, Bethel 04217. Open year-round. The decor is high Victorian: lace, pillows, tasseled lamps. Each room has a phone along with a TV and a wet bar hidden away in a massive armoire. A full breakfast is included in the rates, which vary with the season, from $95 up; inquire about the suite with Jacuzzi. There is a restaurant on site (see *Dining Out*) as well.

🐾 **Sudbury Inn** (824-2174; www.thesudburyinn.com), Lower Main Street, Bethel 04217. A nicely restored village inn built in 1873 to serve train travelers (the depot was just down the street). New owner Bill White was general manager of operations at the Bethel Inn before he and his wife, Nancy, purchased this property. They offer 10 guest rooms and 7 two-room suites, all different shapes and decors. All have private baths, televisions, and air-conditioning. The dining room is the home of Randall Smith, 1998 Chef of the Year in Maine (see *Dining Out*). **Suds Pub** (see *Eating Out*) is a year-round evening gathering spot. Pets are accepted in a few of the rooms. April through November, $65–105; ski season, $80–165 double; includes breakfast.

❄ **The Briar Lea Inn and Restaurant** (824-4717; 1-877-311-1299; www.briarleainnrestaurant.com), Route 2/26, Bethel 04217. Open year-round. Gary Brearley has turned this 150-year-old farmhouse into an attractive six-room inn, with private baths, cable TV, phones, and eclectic decor. The restaurant is open to the public (see *Dining Out*). The living room with its polished floors and deep blue wallpaper is particularly attractive, as is the neighboring breakfast room. $73–103; pets $10 extra.

BED & BREAKFASTS

Blue Mountains Country Inn (369-0309), 141 Jed Martin Road, Rumford Point 04279. An inviting Victorian farmhouse set on 42 acres. Bob and Carol Nichols offer large guest rooms with pine floors and queen beds, all furnished with antiques. Each has a sitting area and a private bath. There is also a two-room suite with shared bath, good for families (older children only, please). $85 for rooms for two, $140 for four-person suite; includes a full breakfast served family style.

Black Bear B&B (824-0908; www.bbearbandb.com), 829 Sunday River Road, Newry 04261. Open year-round. A large, attractive house less than 2 miles from Sunday River. A good place to escape the crowds after skiing all day. Common areas include two TV/music rooms, both with fireplaces. Hot tub, snacks and hot beverages, Internet access and telephone use, a day cabin on the river, and a full country breakfast are also included in the rates, which begin at $70 per night.

✎ **Chapman Inn** (824-2657; 1-877-359-1498; www.chapmaninn.com), P.O. Box 1067, Bethel 04217. A find for both families and singles. Fred Nolte and Sandra Frye bring years in the hospitality business and new energy to this comfortable, rambling white wooden inn on the common. Floors have been refinished and rooms refurnished (Fred's hobby is making furniture). Six units now have private baths and four share; there's cable TV and air-conditioning in some rooms, and phones in all rooms. Options range from two apartments with full kitchens to a dorm in the attached barn. Common space includes an attractive living room and, in the barn, a game room with a pool table and two saunas. Handy to cross-country trails at the Bethel Inn, also to village shops and restaurants. Summer: $59–89 per couple for a room or apartment, $10 less for singles, $25 per person for the dorm, breakfast included. Winter: $75–105.

Holidae House (824-3400; 1-800-882-3306), P.O. Box 545, Bethel 04217.

A gracious Main Street house (the first in Bethel to be electrified), built in the 1890s by a local lumber baron. Scott and Sandy Dennis offer guest rooms are furnished in comfortable antiques and have cable TV, phones, and private baths; there's also a studio and a three-bedroom apartment. Air-conditioning and whirlpool bath available. $92–125 double includes breakfast. Efficiencies $65 and up off-season to $150 in-season for four in the apartment that sleeps 8 to 10 (each extra person is $25). There's a great little bookstore in the attached garage (see **Books 'n' Things** under *Selective Shopping—Special Shops*).

Douglass Place (824-2229), Route 2, Bethel 04217. A handsome 20-room home that once took in summer boarders. Barbara Douglass, who raised four daughters here, graciously welcomes guests. There are four guest rooms—one with a queen-sized bed and three with twin beds—a game room (with piano, pool table, and table tennis), a Jacuzzi, and a big homey kitchen where breakfast is served. Attractive living and dining rooms, grounds, a screened gazebo with comfy chairs (a perfect reading spot), and a large barn. $50–60 includes continental breakfast with homemade muffins and fresh fruit.

L'Auberge (824-2774; 1-800-760-2774; www.l'aubergecountryinn.com), Mill Hill Road, Bethel 04217. A former barn built in the 1850s for a long-vanished mansion. It was moved to its present location in the 1890s and has served as a carriage house and barn for an old mill, servants' quarters for the Bethel Inn, and a theater (one suite bears evidence of this use, with a balcony to nowhere). The property especially lends itself to groups because of its splendid living room but also works well as a low-key inn. The five guest rooms and two suites are furnished with antiques. Hidden away just off the common, it's literally around the corner from village shops and restaurants but set far enough back to feel much farther, with no traffic noise. $74–125 per night for a double with breakfast. Dinner is also available to guests. Innkeeper Tom Rideout, former owner of legendary Bosebuck Mountain Camps on Aziscohos Lake, is a Registered Maine Guide whose services fishermen might like to employ.

Crocker Pond House (836-2027; www.bethelmaine.com/crockerpond), 917 New Bethel Road, Bethel 04217. Off by itself on the Shelburne–Bethel Road (5 miles from downtown Bethel), facing south toward Evans Notch, this is a long, shingled, one-room-deep house designed and built by the architect and builder Stuart Crocker. It's a beauty, filled with light and grace, and very quiet. Hiking and snowshoeing or just peace are what it offers (no in-room phones or TVs). There is also a scenic farm pond. $75–90 per room includes a full breakfast in-season.

The Norseman Inn and Motel (824-2002), P.O. Box 934 , Route 2, Bethel 04217. An old farmstead with 9 light, pleasant guest rooms and 22 more units in the old barn. Guests in the house have access to the big, comfortable living room, with its fireplace made from local stones, and the dining room, with a similar hearth where breakfast is served. The motel units are spacious; amenities include a laundry room and game room, a deck and walking trails. $59–128 includes continental breakfast (seasonal).

SKI LODGES AND CONDOMINIUMS

ⓢ **Sunday River Ski Resort** (824-3000; resort reservations, 1-800-543-2SKI), P.O. Box 450, Bethel 04217, now offers more than 6,000 "slope-side beds." There are condominium complexes, ranging from studios to three-bedroom units. Each complex has access to an indoor pool, Jacuzzi, sauna, laundry, recreation room, and game room; **Cascades** and **Sunrise** offer large common rooms with fireplaces, and **Fall Line** has a restaurant. **Merrill Brook Village Condominiums** have fireplaces, and many have whirlpool tubs. **South Ridge** also offers fireplaces in each unit, which range from studios to three bedrooms. The 68-room **Snow Cap Inn** has an atrium with fieldstone fireplaces, an exercise room, and an outdoor Jacuzzi, and the **Snow Cap Ski Dorm** offers reasonably priced bunks. The 230-room **Summit Hotel and Conference Center** has both standard and kitchen-equipped units and a health club with tennis courts, pool, and conference facilities; it offers rooms and studios as well as one- and two-bedroom efficiency units. The 195-room **Jordan Grand Hotel** is off by itself but linked by ski trails as well as road, circled by the mountains of the Jordan Bowl; facilities include a health club, a swimming pool, and restaurants. Hotel prices: $95–787. In winter, condo units are based on ski packages from $99 per night or $370 per person for 5 days.

ⓢ&. **Sunday River Inn** (824-2410), RFD 3, Bethel 04217. Just down the road from the big ski resort but its antithesis: a homey, very personal place. Steve and Peggy Wight have been welcoming guests since 1971, catering to cross-country skiers (see *Winter Sports—Cross-Country Skiing* for details about its well-maintained trail system) and to Elderhostel groups in other seasons. A large fireplace, a selection of books, and quiet games are in the living room, and an adjacent room can be used for small conferences. A game room, sauna, and wood-heated hot tub just outside the back door are also available to guests. The 18 rooms (most with shared baths) range from dorms to private rooms in the inn or adjacent chalet. $45–85 per person includes two meals and cross-country ski passes; children's rates. Inquire about cluster house sites in the **Red House Farm Village** across the road.

🐾 **Pine-Sider Lodge** (665-2226), 481 Gore Road, Bryant Pond 04219-6113. Bill and Ernestine Riley designed and built Pine-Sider for families and groups. The lodge offers six housekeeping apartments sleeping four to eight people. Each unit has a living room, dining area, kitchen, and bath. There is a common ski storage area. In summer there are canoes, paddleboats, a johnboat, and a Sunfish sailboat available for guest use. $375–425 per week in summer; $98–158 per night in ski season.

CAMPGROUNDS

🐾✒ **Littlefield Beaches** (875-3290), 13 Littlefield Lane, Greenwood 04255. Open Memorial Day through October. A clean, quiet family campground surrounded by three connecting lakes. Full hook-ups, a laundry room, miniature golf, a game room, swimming. $19–25 daily; seasonal rates available; reduced rates in June and September.

🐾✒♿**Bethel Outdoor Adventures and Campground** (824-4224; 1-800-533-3607; www.betheloutdooradventure.com), Route 2, Bethel. Jeff and Patty Parsons have moved their base (see Bethel Outdoor Adventures under *To Do—Canoeing and Kayaking*) from West Bethel to their campground. RV and tent sites on the Androscoggin River (where you can swim), within walking distance of downtown shops and restaurants. Sites are $14–20 per night.

Pleasant River Campground (836-2000), Route 2, West Bethel Road, Bethel. Wooded sites, rest rooms, pool, playground, and many recreational possiblities (canoeing, kayaking, biking, and hiking to name a few).

Also see **Papoose Pond Resort and Campground** under *Other Lodging* in "Oxford Hills and Lewiston/Auburn."

Also see *To Do—Camping* for **noncommercial campgrounds** in the White Mountain National Forest.

SPECIAL LODGING

✒♿ **The Maine Houses** (1-800-646-8737; www.themainehouses.com), Bryant Pond (reservations: P.O. Box 1138, Yarmouth, ME 04096). Geared toward groups. Two of the three houses are located on Lake Christopher, the third just a short walk away. Unique, self-service guest houses perfect for small groups or large reunions. The Maine House has eight bedrooms, 6½ baths, a steam room, and a wraparound porch. In the Maine Farmhouse there are seven bedrooms, each with a private bath and a fireplace. The building is divided into three sections, lending itself to use by smaller groups. The Maine Mountainview House features seven bedrooms, seven full baths, an indoor spa, and a fireplace. All three have fully equipped kitchens, access to the lake, canoes, and outdoor sports equipment, cable TV, VCRs, and all bedding and towels.

CANINE ACCOMMODATIONS

🐾 **Nanny's Doggy Day Care** (824-4225), Route 2, West Bethel. Sunday River Ski Area does not permit pets in its condos or condo hotels, and few local lodging places do; this unusually plush kennel fills a need.

🐾 **Doggie and Kitty Motel** (836-3647), Route 2, West Bethel. Daycare or overnight boarding, private heated kennels, exercise area.

WHERE TO EAT

DINING OUT

♿ **Bethel Inn and Country Club** (824-2175; 1-800-654-0125), Bethel Common. Serves breakfast and dinner. An elegant formal dining room with a Steinway, a hearth and large windows overlooking the golf course and hills, with a year-round veranda. The menu offers a choice of a dozen entrées, including broiled marinated duck breast, rack of lamb, and maple-walnut-scented venison medallions; $15–22 including salad, starches, and vegetable. Leave room for dessert.

Briar Lea Inn and Restaurant (824-4717), Route 2/26, Bethel. The inn's pleasant dining room serves breakfast and dinner daily, lunch on weekends. One breakfast specialty is Moose Biscuit Benedict (eggs Benedict with a twist—served on a moose-head-shaped biscuit, with bacon and smoked tomato). Dinner entrées include pork chops served with cabernet demiglaze, roasted root vegetables, and artichoke potato pancakes; old-fashioned chicken potpie; and beef Stroganoff. $9.95–17.95.

Sudbury Inn (824-2174), Main Street, Bethel. Dinner 5–9 PM, seasonally. Attractive (and large) dining rooms and sunporch in a 19th-century village inn. Begin with the grilled seafood bisque or potato and wild mushroom lasagna. Specialty entrées include roast duckling and lobster Sudbury (lobster with tomato and fresh tarragon butter sauce). $14–20.

The Victoria (824-8060; 1-800-774-1235), 32 Main Street, Bethel. A fine dining experience in three dining rooms, two with working fireplaces. Appetizers might include stuffed portobello mushrooms; entrées range from bistro meat loaf to nut-encrusted pork chops. Entrées $15–23.

Sunday River Resort operates several "fine-dining" restaurants: **Legends** (824-5858) at the Grand Summit Resort Hotel, **Rosetto's Ristorante** (824-5094) at the White Cap Base Lodge, **Walsh & Hill** (824-5067) at Fall Line Condominiums, and **Grand Avenue Grille** (824-5000) at the Jordan Grand.

EATING OUT

Breau's (824-3192), just west of Bethel on Route 2. Will deliver, and the pizza is good. Homemade clam "chowdah," chili, burgers, subs, salads, and "lobstah" rolls are also on the extensive menu . Open from 7 AM for a full breakfast. **Breau's 2** is in Locke Mills.

Bottle & Bag (824-3673), just the other side of the bridge, east of downtown Bethel on Route 2. A local favorite for breakfast and lunch: hearty omelets, soups, and salads as well as a grill and sandwiches, pasta. Daily lunch specials for $3.95. Freshly made breads, desserts, beers.

🐾 **Café di Cocoa** (824- 5292), 125 Main Street, Bethel. Open daily for lunch and dinner. Cathy di Cocoa's cheerful eatery specializes in vegan and vegetarian dishes using local organic produce. In summer try the Fire and Ice chilled southwestern tomato soup. In winter join them for a Saturday-night ethnic dinner party (by reservation only). Porch dining in summer, full bakery, juice and espresso bars. They don't serve liquor, but you can bring your own ($2-per-party corking fee).

Great Grizzly Bar and Steakhouse (824-8391) and **Matterhorn Wood-Fired Pizza and Fresh Pasta** (824-6271), Sunday River Road, are good options for casual dining in winter.

Jacqui's Restaurant (875-2250), Route 26, Locke Mills. Handy to Mount Abram, open for lunch and dinner weekdays, breakfast too on weekends; closed for dinner on Sunday. Road food with a consciously 1950s decor.

Suds Pub, downstairs at the **Sudbury Inn,** Main Street, Bethel. Open year-round, 4:30–10 PM daily. Entertainment Thursday through Saturday; otherwise, a friendly pub with 5 draft and 25 bottled beers, and a reasonably priced pub menu.

The Sunday River Brewing Co. (824-4ALE), junction of Sunday River Road and Route 2, North Bethel. Open from 11:30 daily for lunch and dinner. Dining areas surround brewing kettles and tanks. Patrons can choose from a variety of house brews to wash down soups and salads, burgers, and pizza. Often has live entertainment evenings.

ENTERTAINMENT

Casablanca Cinema (824-8248), a four-screen cinema in the new Bethel Station development (Cross Street), shows first-run films.

The **Mahoosuc Arts Council** (824-3575) presents the Libbie Goodridge Kneeland Memorial Summer Series, Sunday afternoon concerts on the Bethel Common in memory of a longtime Bethel teacher.

Also see the **Suds Pub** and **Sunday River Brewing Co.** in *Eating Out,* and *Entertainment* in "Oxford Hills and Lewiston/Auburn."

SELECTIVE SHOPPING

ANTIQUES

Playhouse Antiques (824-3170), 46 Broad Street, specializes in antiques from Bethel-area homes.

ARTISANS

Bonnema Potters (824-2821), Lower Main Street, Bethel. Open daily 8:30–5:30. Distinctive stoneware, noteworthy for both design and color: lamps, garden furniture, dinnerware, and the like produced and sold in Bonnema's big barn. Seconds are available.

Christian Ridge Pottery. See *Selective Shopping—Special Shops* in "Oxford Hills and Lewiston/Auburn."

GEM SHOPS

As noted in *To Do—Rockhounding,* this area is rich in semiprecious gems and minerals. Jim Mann at **Mt. Mann** (824-3030), Main Street, Bethel, mines, cuts, and sets his own minerals and gems. **Mt. Mica Rarities** (875-3060), Route 26 in Locke Mills, is also a source of reasonably priced Maine gemstones. **Sunday River Gems** (824-3414), Sunday River Road, Newry, offers handcrafted pieces with Maine gems, gemstone carvings, and more. Also see *To Do—Rockhounding* in "Oxford Hills and Lewiston/Auburn."

SPECIAL SHOPS

Books 'n' Things (824-0275; 1-800-851-3219), 85 Main Street, Bethel. A full-service bookstore attached to an attractive inn (see Holidae House under *Lodging—Bed and Breakfasts*).

Maine Line Products (824-2522), Main Street, Bethel. Made-in-Maine products and souvenirs, among which the standout is the Maine Woodsman's Weatherstick. We have one tacked to our back porch, and it's consistently one step ahead of the weatherman—pointing up to predict fair weather and down for foul. A second store, an expanded version of this old landmark, recently opened in Locke Mills: even more pine furniture, toys, wind chimes, buckets, birdhouses.

Groan and McGurn's Tourist Trap and Craft Outlet (836-3645), Route 2, West Bethel. Begun as a greenhouse—to which the owners' specially silk-screened T-shirts were added. Now there is so much that an ever-changing catalog is available.

Mountain Side Country Crafts (824-2518), Sunday River Road, Newry. Made-in-Maine gifts.

Philbrook Place, 162 Main Street, Bethel, includes an interesting assortment of enterprises including **The Toy Shop** (824-8697); **True North Adventure** (824-2201), featuring sleeping bags, maps, footwear, clothing; **Wild Rose** (824-3563), with eclectic clothing; **Benevolent Bear** (824-8303), for gifts; and **Vine & Cupboard** for gourmet foods, wine, and kitchenware.

Ruthie's Clothing (824-2989), Main Street, Bethel. Great selection of women's clothing.

For more shops in this region, also see *Selective Shopping* in "Oxford Hills and Lewiston/Auburn."

SPECIAL EVENTS

February: **Bethel Winter Festival**—free cross-country and alpine ski lessons, dogsled and sleigh rides, skijoring, contests. **Androscoggin River Tour & Race** at Carter's X-Country Ski Center, Bethel. Special events every weekend at ski areas.

March: **Sunday River Langlauf Races** at the Sunday River Ski Touring Center *(first Saturday)*—for all ages and abilities.

First Saturday in April: **Pole, Paddle and Paw Race**—a combination ski and canoe event at the end of ski season.

June: **Bethel Antiques Show & Sale; Rotary Club Auction.**

July: **Bethel Historical Society Fourth of July Celebration. Bethel Open Air Art Fair** *(first Saturday).* **Strawberry Festival,** Locke Mills Union Church (date depends on when strawberries are ready; announced in local papers). **The Annual Gem, Mineral, and Jewelry Show** at Telstar High School *(second weekend)*—exhibits, demonstrations, and guided field trips to local quarries. **Mollyockett Day** *(third*

Saturday) festivities include a road race, parade, bicycle obstacle course, fiddler contest, fireworks, to honor an 18th-century medicine woman who helped the first settlers. **Annual Maine State Triathlon Classic,** Bethel *(last Saturday)*.

August: **Andover Old Home Days** *(first weekend)*. **Sudbury Canada Days,** Bethel *(second weekend)*—children's parade, historical exhibits, old-time crafts demonstrations, bean supper, and variety show.

September: **Bethel Harvest Fest** *(third weekend)*.

Columbus Day weekend: **Blue Mountain Arts & Crafts Festival** at Sunday River Ski Area.

December: A series of Christmas fairs and festivals climax with a **Living Nativity** on the Bethel common the Sunday before Christmas. **New Year's Eve** on the Bethel common—music, storytelling, fireworks.

Rangeley Lakes Region

Rangeley Lake itself is only 9 miles long, but the "Rangeley Lakes Region" includes 112 lakes and ponds, among them vast sheets of water with names like Mooselookmeguntic, Cupsuptic, and Aziscohos.

Though the area has been heavily developed with cottages, condos, and houses on the water, it retains the feel of an earlier time. Minimalls and urban sprawl have not found their way to this region yet, and we hope they never do. Part of the charm of Rangeley Village is that you won't find chain stores: no McDonald's, Wal-Mart, or Rite Aid; the bookstore, Christmas shop, restaurants, and lodging places are all owned and operated by local folk.

The scenery in this area is so magnificent that segments of the two roads leading into Rangeley, Routes 4 and 17, have been designated National Scenic Byways. In summer be sure to approach the town of Rangeley via Route 17 and pull out at the Height o' Land. Below you, four of the six major Rangeley lakes glisten blue-black, ringed by high mountains. Patterned only by sun and clouds, uninterrupted by any village or even a building, this green-blue sea of fir and hardwoods flows north and west to far horizons.

A spate of 1863 magazine and newspaper stories first publicized this area as "home of the largest brook trout in America," and two local women ensured its fishing fame through ensuing decades. In the 1880s Phillips native Cornelia "Fly Rod" Crosby pioneered the use of the light fly-rod and artificial lure and in 1897 became the first Registered Maine Guide; in 1924 Carrie Stevens, a local milliner, fashioned a streamer fly from gray feathers and caught a 6-pound, 13-ounce brook trout at Upper Dam. Stevens took second prize in *Field & Stream*'s annual competition, and the Gray Ghost remains one of the most popular fishing flies sold.

The Rangeley area is still reaping the rewards of these breakthroughs, which lured entire families, not just sports, to adopt the Rangeley Lakes as their second homes. Hundreds of these families are still here, devoting energy and skill, as well as money, to community projects ranging from restoring the theater and expanding the library to preserving more than 34,000 wooded acres.

The Rangeley Lakes Historical Society is papered with photographs and filled with mementos of the 1880s through the 1930s, an era in

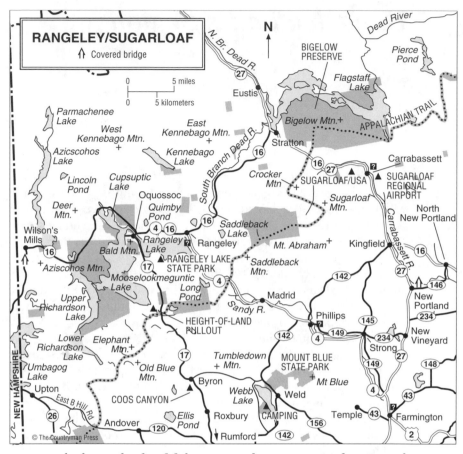

which trainloads of fishermen and visitors arrived in Rangeley every day throughout the summer, to stay in wooden summer hotels and numerous sporting camps on islands and outlying lakes.

In the 1940s and 1950s hotels closed and burned, and in the 1980s many sporting camps were sold off as individual "condominiums," but the resort has continued to evolve as a magnificent, low-key destination.

Landlocked salmon now augment trout in both local lakes and streams, and fly-fishing equipment and guides are easy to come by. Moose-watching, kayaking, and canoeing, as well as hiking and golf, are big draws. There are more shops and restaurants, events, and entertainment here than at any time since the 1930s.

Still, Rangeley is a town of 1,500 year-round residents, and "downtown" is a short string of single-story frame buildings along the lake. The village of Oquossoc, 7 miles west, is just a scattering of shops and restaurants on a peninsula between Rangeley and Mooselookmeguntic Lakes. Sure, the summer population zooms to 6,000, but both year-round homes and camps are hidden away by the water, and much of that water is itself sequestered in woodland.

Saddleback, Rangeley's 4,116-foot, 40-trail mountain, is New England's best kept ski secret, averaging 500 skiers on weekends, half the number of snowmobilers in town to take advantage of one of Maine's most extensive and best-groomed trail networks. Because the area's snow is so dependable, a separate and well groomed cross-country system has also evolved, and both backcountry ski and snowshoeing options abound.

The big news about this western neck of the Maine Woods is that it's being preserved. Within the past decade some 52 square miles have been protected through cooperative ventures involving state agencies, paper companies, and the Rangeley Lakes Heritage Trust.

GUIDANCE

Rangeley Lakes Region Chamber of Commerce (864-5364; 1-800-MT-LAKES; www.rangeleymaine.com), P.O. Box 317, Rangeley 04970. Open year-round, Monday through Saturday 9–5. The chamber maintains a walk-in information center in the village, publishes a handy "Accommodations and Services" guide and an indispensable map, keeps track of vacancies, and makes reservations.

GETTING THERE

By air: **Mountain Air Service** (864-5307). Inquire about services.

By car: From points south, take the Maine Turnpike to exit 12 (Auburn), then take Route 4 to Rangeley. In the summer the slightly longer (roughly a half hour) but more scenic route is to turn off Route 4 onto Route 108 in Livermore, follow it to Rumford, and then take Route 17 to Oquossoc (see *To See—Scenic Drives*). From the Bethel area, take Route 17 to Rumford. From New Hampshire's White Mountains, take Route 16 east.

MEDICAL EMERGENCY

Rangeley Region Health Center (864-3303), Dallas Hill Road, Rangeley. (After hours, call 1 800-398-6031). **Rangeley Ambulance:** 911.

TO SEE

MUSEUMS

In Rangeley

Rangeley Lakes Region Historical Society, Main and Richardson Streets, Rangeley. Open mid-June through late September, Monday through Saturday 10–noon; until 2 on Monday, Wednesday, and Saturday, or when flag is out. This is a great little museum occupying a former bank building in the middle of town. It features photographs and local memorabilia from Rangeley's grand old hotels, sporting camps, trains, and lake steamers. Note the basement jail cell.

❧ **Wilhelm Reich Museum** (864-3443), Dodge Pond Road, off Route 4/16 between Rangeley and Oquossoc. Open July and August, Wednesday through Sunday 1–5, Sunday in September 1–5. Admission charged.

The 175-acre property, Orgonon, is worth a visit for the view alone. Wilhelm Reich was a pioneer psychoanalyst (1897–1957) with controversial theories about sexual energy. A short documentary film profiles the man and his work. The museum occupies a stone observatory that Reich helped design; it contains biographical exhibits, scientific equipment, paintings, and a library and study that remain as Reich left them. Inquire about special programs. The wooded trails on the property are open daily 9–5.

✑ **Rangeley Lakes Region Logging Museum** (864-3939/5595), Route 16, 1 mile east of Rangeley Village. Open July and August weekends 11–2 or by appointment. Founded by woodsman and sculptor Rodney Richard, the museum features paintings about logging in the 1920s by local artist Alden Grant; also traditional wood carving and logging equipment. Inquire about Logging Museum Festival Days.

In Phillips

Phillips Historical Society (639-3352), Pleasant Street, P.O. Box 216, Phillips 04966. Open the first and third Sunday, June through September, and the third week in August for Old Home Days; also by appointent. The library and historical society are both in an 1820 house in the middle of the village. Exhibits include a significant Portland Glass collection, pictures of the town's own resort era (it had three hotels) and of the Sandy River Railroad (see *To Do—Railroad Excursion*).

Weld Historical Society (585-2586), Weld Village. Open July and August, Wednesday and Saturday 1–3, and by appointment. The 1842 house is filled with period furniture, clothing, and photographs. The original Town House (1845) features farming, logging, and ice-cutting tools.

Also see *Scenic Drives*, below.

SCENIC DRIVES

The roads in this area offer such great scenery that sections of Routes 4 and 17 are included in a newly designated National Scenic Byway.

Phillips/Weld/Byron/Oquossoc/Rangeley loop

Route 4 to Phillips and Route 142 to Weld. Follow Route 4 from Rangeley 12 miles south to **Small's Falls** (see *Green Space*) and on to Phillips, once the center of the Sandy River–Rangeley lakes "2-footer" line, now a quiet residential area. Plan to come the first or third Sunday of the month, or on foliage weekends, to ride the rails behind the steam train (see *To Do—Railroad Excursion*). Stop at the **Phillips Historical Society** (see above), and ask directions to **Daggett Rock,** a massive 50-foot-high boulder that the glaciers deposited several miles from town (off Route 142), having knocked it off Saddleback Mountain (the nearest place that matches it geologically). It's a pleasant mile's walk and has been the local sight-to-see in Phillips for more than a century. From Route 4 near Phillips, it's 12 miles on Route 142 to **Weld,** a quiet old lake village with several good hiking options, including **Tumbledown**

Mountain and **Mount Blue.** You can also swim in **Lake Webb** at **Mount Blue State Park.**

Weld to Byron. From Weld, it's 12 miles to Byron. Drive 2 miles north on Route 142 to the STATE BEACH sign; turn left, go 0.5 mile, and turn right on the first gravel road. This is Byron Road, well packed. Soon you follow the Swift River (stop and pan for gold) down into **Coos Canyon;** the picnic area and waterfalls are at the junction with Route 17 (see *To Do—Gold Panning* and *Swimming*). This is said to be the first place in America where gold was panned.

Route 17 to Oquossoc. From the picnic area, drive north on Route 17 for 10 miles to the **Height o' Land** (the pullout is on the other side of the road), from which the view is a spectacular spread of lakes and mountains; the view from the **Rangeley Lake Overlook** (northbound side of the road, a couple of miles farther) offers another panorama.

From Oquossoc, it's a beautiful drive west along the lakes on Route 16 to Errol. Roughly 20 miles west of Rangeley, be sure to detour 0.3 mile to see the **Bennett Covered Bridge** (1898–1899), spanning the Magalloway River in Wilsons Mills; follow signs to the Aziscohos Valley Camping Area.

Whether you are coming from Bethel or following the above loop, pick up Route 17 just beyond the **Mexico Chicken Coop Restaurant** (364-2710) on Route 2. Despite its exterior, this is a good way stop for Italian food, chicken, a huge salad bar, and fresh pastries.

TO DO

BIKING
Rangeley Mountain Bike Touring Co. (864-5799), Main Street, Rangeley, offers a range of rental bikes and local touring maps. Inquire about the 12½-mile Railroad Loop Trail.

BOAT EXCURSIONS
Expeditions North (864-3622), Route 17, Oquossoc, offers party boat tours of Rangeley Lake daily in July and August. Ten-person limit per tour.

Horsefeather Guide Service (864-5465), Rangeley Avenue, Oquossoc. Master Maine Guide "Mac" Macdonald leads tours of half or full days on any of the area's big lakes.

BOAT RENTALS
Check with the chamber of commerce (see *Guidance*) about the more than a dozen places in town that rent motorboats, canoes, sailboats, and waverunners. **River's Edge Sports** (864-5582), Route 4, Oquossoc, rents canoes and kayaks and offers shuttle service. **Oquossoc Marine** (864-5477), Route 4, Oquossoc, offers the largest choice of motorboats. Be sure to get out on a lake one way or another.

CAMPING
Wilderness camping is a part of what this area is about. The chamber of

commerce (see *Guidance*) lists more than a dozen sources of information about remote campsites. The **Stephen Phillips Preserve** (864-
2003), Oquossoc, maintains 42 campsites with fireplaces, picnic tables,
and toilet facilities; $10 per site per couple, $5 teenagers or extra person, $2 children. Also see **Rangeley Lake State Park** under *Green
Space*. **Aziscohos Valley Camping Area** (486-3271) in Wilsons Mills
also offers easy boat access to Aziscohos Lake and the Magalloway River.

CANOEING AND KAYAKING

Rangeley is the departure point for an 8-mile paddle to Oquossoc. On Lake
Mooselookmeguntic a 12-mile paddle south to Upper Dam is popular,
and many people portage around the dam and paddle another 8 miles
down Upper Richardson Lake and through the Narrows to South Arm
(also see *Camping*). Kayaks can be rented from **Rangeley Mountain
Bike Touring** (see *Biking*) and **River's Edge Sports** (see *Fishing*);
also see *Boat Rentals*.

A section of the 700-mile **Northern Forest Canoe Trail,** which follows
the ancient water route of Native Americans traveling from New York
to Fort Kent, comes through Umbagog Lake, the Richardson Lakes,
and Mooselookmeguntic and Rangeley Lakes before hitting a long portage to the South Branch of the Dead River. This section takes 2 to 5
days to complete. A map, produced by **Native Trails Inc.** (P.O. Box
240, Waldoboro 04572), is available for $5.95 from the Rangeley Lakes
Heritage Trust (864-7311).

If you don't know how to canoe, sign on with **Rich Gacki** (864-5136) for a
guided early-morning paddle down the Kennebago River. Chances are
you will see deer, ospreys, beavers, otters, and mink as well as moose
(see *Moose-Watching*).

FISHING

As noted in the introduction to the "Rangeley Lakes Region," it's fishing
that put Rangeley on the map. Both brook trout and landlocked salmon
remain plentiful, and while early spring and September remain the big
fishing seasons, summer months now also lure many fishermen with
fishfinders, downriggers, rods, and reels. Rangeley has, however, always been best known as a fly-fishing mecca, and both local sporting
stores, **River's Edge Sports** (864-5582), Route 4 in Oquossoc, and the
Rangeley Region Sport Shop (864-5615), Main Street, Rangeley,
specialize in fly-tying equipment; they are also sources of advice on
where to fish and with whom (a list of local guides is posted). Request a
list of members of the **Rangeley Region Guides & Sportsmen's
Association,** P.O. Box 244, Rangeley 04970. The group traces its origins to 1896. The current chamber of commerce guide also lists local
Registered Maine Guides as well as camps that specialize in boats,
equipment, and guides. Guiding service averages $150 per half day,
$250 for a full day. Nonresident fishing licenses, available from sporting
stores, are $10 per day, $35 for 7 days.

FEE-FISHING

Dunham's Pure Water Hatchery & Fee Fishing Pond (639-2815), Mount Blue Road (off Route 4), Avon (between Phillips and Strong). Open year-round, 7–7. A great spot for kids and nonfishermen to try their hand at catching rainbow or brook trout. You never miss. Equipment supplied. Fish are hatched in 23 pools housed in Bruce Dunham's barn and two haylofts. Dunham also sells seafood and a variety of fish.

GOLD PANNING

Coos Canyon, on Route 17, 23 miles south of Oquossoc (see *To See— Scenic Drives*), is said to be the first place in America where gold was panned. The Swift River churns through a beautiful natural gorge, and there are picnic tables as well as gold-panning lessons and equipment ($5) at the **Coos Canyon Campground Store** (364-3880).

GOLF

Mingo Springs Golf Course (864-5021), Proctor Road (off Route 4), Rangeley. A historic (since 1925), par-70, 18-hole course with lake views; instruction, carts, and club rentals.

Mini Golf Course (864-5799), 53 Main Street, Rangeley. Middle of the village: nine holes.

HIKING

The Rangeley regional map published by the chamber of commerce (see *Guidance*) outlines more than a dozen well-used hiking paths, including a portion of the Appalachian Trail that passes over **Saddleback Mountain.** The longest hike is up **Spotted Mountain** (4½ miles to the top), and the most popular is the trail to the summit of **Bald Mountain** (3 miles round-trip); both yield sweeping views of lakes, woods, and more mountains. Other favorites are Bemis Stream Trail up **Elephant Mountain** (6 hours round-trip) and the mile walk in to **Angels Falls**—which is roughly 4 miles off Route 17; be sure to use a current trail guide.

In Weld the tried-and-true trails are **Mount Blue** (3¼ miles) and **Tumbledown Mountain** (a particularly varied climb with a high altitude).

HORSEBACK RIDING

Horseback Riding at Bald Mountain Camps (864-3671). Trail rides are $40 per hour. Riding lessons and children's riding camp ($20 per day) also available.

MOOSE-WATCHING

Rich Gacki (864-5136) in Oquossoc offers guided canoe trips departing the **Rangeley Inn** most days at 5 AM. This is a 3-hour expedition; reservations are required by 6 PM the previous day. Breakfast at the Rangeley Inn is included in the price of the tour.

Route 16 north from Rangley to Stratton is a good bet for seeing moose at dusk; your chances improve if you drive all the way to dinner at the **Porter House** in Eustis (see *Dining Out* in "Sugarloaf and the Carrabassett Valley").

RAILROAD EXCURSION

Sandy River & Rangeley Lakes Railroad (779-1901). Runs on the first and third Sunday of each month, June through October; runs continuously through Phillips Old Home Days in late August and Fall Foliage Days in late September and early October, and on other special occasions. $3 adults, $2 children ages 6–12. From 1873 until 1935, this narrow-gauge line spawned resort and lumbering communities along its 115-mile length. Begun as seven distinct lines, it was eventually acquired by the Maine Central, which built shops and a large roundhouse in Phillips. Since 1969 volunteers have been working to rebuild a part of the railroad, producing a replica of the old steam locomotive and the roundhouse, and laying a mile of track so that you can rattle along in an 1884 car just far enough to get a sense of getting around Franklin County "back when." Two original railroad buildings remain—Sanders Station and a freight shed. A depot houses railroad memorabilia, and rolling stock now include five boxcars and two cabooses.

SUMMER PROGRAMS

Rangeley Parks and Recreation Department Summer Programs (864-3326), open to everyone vacationing in town, include lessons in fly-casting and -tying, golf, canoeing, swimming, tennis, and much more.

SWIMMING

Rangeley Lake State Park offers a pleasant swimming area and scattered picnic sites (see *Green Space*). Day-use fee; free under age 12. There is also a town beach with lifeguards and a playground at **Lakeside Park** in the village of Rangeley. Almost all lodging places offer water access.

Mount Blue State Park also has a nice swimming area (see *Green Space*).

Coos Canyon, Route 17, Byron. See *To See—Scenic Drives* and *Gold Panning*. It's terrifying to watch kids jump from the cliffs and bridge here, but there's several inviting pools among the smooth rocks and cascades.

WINTER SPORTS

DOWNHILL SKIING

Saddleback Mountain (864-5671; snow phone, 864-3380; www.saddlebackskiarea.com), off Dallas Hill Road, Rangeley. This is a very big downhill ski area with a very small, fiercely loyal following. Saddleback itself, 4,116 feet high and webbed with 40 trails serviced by just two double chairs and three T-bars, forms the centerpiece in a semicircle of mountains rising above a small lake. Top-to-bottom snowmaking augments more than 200 inches of annual snowfall to keep the slopes open from November into April. Trails and slopes include glade skiing, a 2½-mile beginner trail, and an above-treeline snowfield in spring. The vertical drop is 2,000 feet. Most trails are a shade narrower and twistier than today's average, but most intermediate runs such as Haymaker and

A peaceful trek through the woods near Rangeley

White Stallion are memorable cruising lanes. Experts will find plenty of challenge on Bronco Buster, Powderkeg, and the Nightmare Glades terrain, and there is plenty of backwoods skiing. Facilities include a cafeteria, lounge, ski school, shop, rentals, nursery, and mountain warming hut. Expansion here was blocked for 26 years by an impasse with the National Park Service over the segment of the Appalachian Trail that passes over Saddleback. Among President Clinton's eleventh-hour moves to expand National Park holdings this issue was resolved and at this writing the remaining 11,000-acre Saddleback property—a semicircle of mountains rising from a small lake—is for sale. $47 adults, $30 juniors weekends and holidays; $30 midweek.

CROSS-COUNTRY SKIING

The Rangeley Lakes Cross-Country Ski Club (864-4309; www.travelmaine.com/rangeleyxcski) offers 75 kilometers of interconnecting trails on 2,500 varied acres with some superb mountain views, well groomed for diagonal stride and skating. Inquire about clinics and special events. Access is from Route 4 and from the lodge (maps, rentals and food) on Taylor Road near the airport. $10 pass, $7 after 1 PM.

Nordic Touring at Saddleback (864-5671). At this writing the network is ungroomed but the trails at 2,400 feet are marked and offer great backcountry skiing.

Mount Blue State Park (585-2347) offers extensive cross-country skiing trails (see *Green Space*).

SNOWMOBILING

Snowmobiling is huge in this region of the state. **The Rangeley Snowmobile Club** (www.rangeleysnowmobile.com), subsidized by the town, maintains 150 miles of well-marked trails connecting with systems throughout Maine and Canada. Snowmobile rentals are available from **Dockside Sports Center** (864-2424; 1-800-941-2424), **Rev-It-Up Sport Shop** (864-2452), and **River's Edge Sports** (864-5582).

SNOWSHOEING

Marked trails abound on local conservation land and rentals are available at the **Alpine Shop** (864-3741). Snowshoeing/ski touring guide **Walter L. Pepperman II** (864-5561) offers treks, also skijoring.

GREEN SPACE

Lakeside Park in the middle of the village of Rangeley is a great spot with picnic tables, grills, a playground, portable toilets, and a boat launch.

& **Rangeley Lake State Park** (864-3858) covers over 700 acres, including 117 acres on the shore. Open May 15 through early October. There are 40 scattered picnic sites, a pleasant swimming area, a boat launch, and a children's play area; $2 per person.

Mount Blue State Park (585-2347), off Route 156, Weld. Open May 30 through October 15. This 6,000-acre park includes Mount Blue itself, towering 3,187 feet above the valley floor, and a beachside tenting area (136 sites) on Lake Webb. The lake is 3 miles wide and 6 miles long, good for catching black bass, white perch, pickerel, trout, and salmon. There are boat rentals, and a recreation hall complete with fireplace. The view from the Center Hill area looks like the opening of a Paramount picture. Despite its beauty and the outstanding hiking, this is one of the few state camping facilities that rarely fill up. $1.50 per person.

& **Small's Falls,** Route 4, 12 miles south of Rangeley. The Sandy River drops abruptly through a small gorge, which you can climb behind railings. A popular picnic spot. You can follow the trail to **Chandlers Mill Stream Falls,** equally spectacular.

Hunter Cove Wildlife Sanctuary, off Route 4/16, 2.5 miles west of Rangeley Village (across from Dodge Pond). A 95-acre Maine Audubon Society preserve with color-coded trails leading to the cove (boat launch). Good for old and small legs, rich in bird life and bugs. Bring insect repellent, waterproof footwear, and a picnic (tables are near the parking lot, and benches are scattered throughout).

Rangeley Lakes Heritage Trust (864-7311), Route 4/16, Oquossoc, open weekdays 9–4:30, Sunday 9–1. Since the trust's founding in 1991, over 10,000 acres have been preserved, including 20 miles of lake and river frontage, 10 islands, and a 2,443-foot mountain. Request the map/guide and inquire about the guided hikes and nature-study programs offered.

The Stephen Phillips Memorial Preserve Trust (864-2003) has preserved many miles of shore on Mooselookmeguntic and maintains a number of campsites (see *To Do—Camping*).

Also see *Lodging—Campgrounds.*

KIM GRANT

Rangeley Lake

LODGING

INNS AND LODGES

& **Rangeley Inn and Motor Lodge** (864-3341; 1-800-MOMENTS; www.
rangeleyinn.com), Rangeley 04970. Open year-round. A blue-shingled,
three-story landmark, partly an annex to a vanished grand hotel that
stood across the road, overlooking the lake; the classic old hotel lobby
dates from 1907. David and Rebecca Schinas are the new owners of this
landmark, which is the physical and social heart of the village. The 52
guest rooms are divided between the main building (12 with claw-foot
tubs, some with water views, all crisply decorated and comfortably
furnished) and 15 nicely decorated motel units, some with kitchenettes,
whirlpool baths, and woodstoves, overlooking Haley Pond. Occasionally
patronized by bus groups, so check if you want to avoid them. $84–119
double EP. All meals and special packages available.

🐾🐶&**Kawanhee Inn** (585-2000; www.lakeinn.com), Route 142, Weld 04285.
(In winter contact Sturgis Butler and Marti Strunk: 778-4306 evenings;
7 Broadway, Farmington 04938.) Dining room open mid-June through
Labor Day; lodging from May through October 15; cottages available
from mid-May through mid-October. A traditional Maine lodge set atop
a slope overlooking Lake Webb. Nine large comfortable rooms with
added insulation (five with private, four with shared baths). Request a
lake view. The 10 one- and two-bedroom cabins each have a screened
porch, fireplace, kitchen, and bath. All but Pine Lodge (really a house
hidden away in the pines down the road from the inn) have lake views.
Meals are served in the large pine dining room and on the screened

veranda overlooking the water (see *Dining Out*), and the open-beamed, pine-paneled living room has a massive central fireplace, a pool table, and numerous corners in which to read and talk. There is a beach and dock; canoes are available, and the local hiking is outstanding. Be sure to hear Sturgis play taps. Rooms $75–120 double; cabins $600–895 per week plus 15 percent service charge; less in shoulder seasons. Room rates include continental breakfast.

☀️& **Bald Mountain Camps** (www.baldmountaincamps.com; 864-3671; 1-888-392-0072), P.O. Box 332, Oquossoc 04964. Open mid-May through mid-September. This is the surviving part of a complex that dates from 1897. Nicely old-fashioned, with fireplaces in 15 cabins and a log-style dining room, a safe sand beach, tennis courts, horseback riding, and lawn games. Right on Mooselookmeguntic Lake and exuding the kind of hospitality found only under long-term ownership. Stephen and Fernlyn Philbrick are your hosts. **Grey Ghost Outfitters** offers fly-fishing and hiking adventures from here as well. $110 adults, meals included; less for children and during May and June; some pets accepted.

☀️& **Country Club Inn** (864-3831; www.countryclubinnrangeley.com), P.O. Box 680, Rangeley 04970. Open year-round except April and November. Surrounded by an 18-hole golf course and overlooking the lake, built by a millionaire sportsman in the late 1920s, this place has the feel of a private club. Massive stone fireplaces face each other across a living room with knotty-pine walls, plenty of books, and puzzles. Twenty rooms each have picture windows and private bath. In winter you can cross-country ski from the door, and in summer there's an outdoor pool. $107 B&B for two; $153–163 MAP. Off-season rates available.

Loon Lodge (864-5666), Pickford Road, Rangeley. A classic, early-1900s log lodge on Rangeley Lake with a pub, expansive living room with fireplace, fine dining (see *Dining Out*) and traditional lodge rooms, with and without baths, $65–85 per couple.

BED & BREAKFASTS

🎗 **Lake Webb House** (585-2479), P.O. Box 127, Route 142, Weld 04285. Open year-round. A pleasant, welcoming old farmhouse with a big porch, near the lake and village. Cheryl England makes the quilts that grace the beds in her three guest rooms (four in summer) and also sells them. The rooms share two bathrooms, but one has a private half bath as well. $65–75 double ($40 single) includes a full breakfast. Cheryl also operates the **Morning Glory Bake Shop** (behind the house), good for breads, moose cookies, and whoopie pies.

🎗 **Piper Brook Bed & Breakfast** (864-3469; piperbrook@powerlink.net), P.O. Box 139, Rangeley 04970. Just 3 miles from town, up and up a fairly rough road (but don't be discouraged). The expansive view is great for wildlife sightings (moose, bears, and more), and the place has a country-elegant feel. Four large guest rooms, two with private baths and two that share. $65–85 (for a room with a king-sized bed, whirlpool, and view).

North Country Inn (864-2440; 1-800-295-4968; www.northcountrybb. com), P.O. Box 429, Main Street, Rangeley, 04970. Just before the summer season in 2000 Jerry and Karen Leech purchased this inn. The four rooms with private baths are pretty and comfortable.The parlors are inviting, but the best spot in the house is the vast front porch with a spectacular lake view. $85–95 includes a full breakfast.

Russell Cove Bed & Breakfast (864-9067), P.O. Box 398, Rangeley 04970. Linda Nowell offers four guest rooms (shared baths), comfortably furnished with a mix of antiques, attic treasures, and Victorian nostalgia. Common areas include a Victorian parlor and a cozy television room. $69–79 includes a full breakfast. Nowell is also the contact person for renting privately owned cottages in the Russell Cove Association.

SPORTING CAMPS

Geared to serious fishermen in May, June, and September, and to families in July and August, these are true destination resorts, but don't expect organized activities.

🐾✒ **Bosebuck Mountain Camps** (446-2825; www.bosebuck.com), Wilsons Mills 03579. Open year-round. Accessible by boat or a 14-mile private gravel road, the camps are sited at the remote end of Aziscohos Lake. We have not visited since ownership changed in 1998. The lodge houses a dining room overlooking the water and a sitting room filled with books;. The nine cabins have woodstoves, electric lights, flush toilets, and showers, powered by a generator that runs 8 hours a day. Three full meals are included in the rate: $135 per person per night; $100 per night July and August with 3-night minimum. Dogs welcome. Family rates in July and August ($97 per person), when fishing eases off.

🐾✒🖑 **Grant's Kennebago Camps** (864-3608; 282-5264 in winter; 1-800-633-4815), P.O. Box 786, Rangeley 04970. Open after ice breaks up and through September. A serious fly-angler's haven located 9 miles up a private dirt road on Kennebago Lake. Large, excellent meals are served in the comfortable dining room with terrific lake views. Knotty-pine cabins are rustic, with woodstoves, screened-in front porches overlooking the water, and docks. Boat and canoe rentals available; also sailboat, Windsurfer, and mountain bikes available to guests at no charge. Floatplane rides and moose runs are offered. $110 per day for adults ($130 if you only stay 1 or 2 days) includes all meals. Children under 12, $35 per day. $15 pets.

🐾✒ **Lakewood Camps** (summer, 243-2959; winter, 392-1581; www. lakewoodcamps.com), Middledam–Richardson Lake, Andover 04216. Open after ice-out through September. The specialty is landlocked salmon and trout; fly-fishing in 5 miles of the Rapid River. Twelve truly remote cabins; meals feature fresh-baked breads, cakes, and pies. Access is from Andover. This is very much the same place described in Louise Dickinson Rich's *We Took to the Woods*. $92 per person (2-day minimum), double occupancy, includes three full meals; $40 children under

12, $15 under age 5. $15 pets. Tax and gratuity not included.

COTTAGES AND CONDOS

Rangeley still has an unusual number of traditional family-geared "camps" and second homes available for rental year-round. Check with the chamber of commerce (see *Guidance*) for listings and local rental agents.

Clearwater Sporting Camps (864-5424; www.clearwatercampsmaine. com), Oquossoc 04964. Open from ice-out through November. Four cottages, all different, are scattered on private waterfront ledges along Mooselookmeguntic Lake. Michael and Tina Warren also offer boat rentals, a boat launch, swimming, and guide service, specializing in fly-fishing. $100 per day double; $660 per week.

Mooselookmeguntic House (864-2962), Haines Landing, Oquossoc 04964. The grand old hotel by this name is gone, but the eight log cabins are well maintained and occupy a great site with a beach and marina. Many of the one- and two-bedroom cabins are on the water and have fireplaces or woodstoves. $375–625 per week.

North Camps (864-2247), P.O. Box 341, Oquossoc 04964 (write to E. B. Gibson). Open spring through hunting season. Twelve cottages on Rangeley Lake among birches on a spacious lawn. Cottages have fireplaces or woodstoves, screened porches, and access to the beach, tennis, sailboats, fishing boats, and canoes. Weekly rentals only in July and August. rentals are available by the week only. Nightly rates and rates that include all three meals are available in spring and fall. $325–645 weekly.

The Terraces Housekeeping and Overnight Cottages (864-3771; www. etravelmaine.com/terraces). Open ice-out through Columbus Day weekend. Comfortable cottages with large decks terraced on a steep embankment on Rangeley Lake. $475–725 per week.

Saddleback Ski and Summer Lake Preserve (864-5671), Box 490, Rangeley 04970. There are two condo complexes at the ski resort, and most units are exceptionally luxurious, with views over the lake. From three to five bedrooms, many with hot tubs, cable TV; all have access to the clubhouse with its game room. $285–495 in winter, but inquire about 3-day ski/stay packages; much less in summer.

CAMPGROUNDS

For reservations in the following state parks, call 287-3821.

Rangeley Lake State Park (864-3858), between Routes 17 and 4, at the southern rim of Rangeley Lake. Some 50 campsites are well spaced among fir and spruce trees; facilities include a beach and boat launch, picnic sites, and a children's play area. $16 for nonresidents. There are also a number of private campgrounds and wilderness sites accessible only by boat; inquire at the chamber of commerce (see *Guidance*).

Mount Blue State Park (585-2347), Weld. Campsites tend to get filled up later than those in better-known parks (see *Green Space*).

Coos Canyon Campground (364-3880) is only about a half hour from Rangeley, but at these sites you feel as though you are in the middle of the woods. At $10 per night, the rates can't be beat either. There's a small store and a shower house, but no flush toilets.

WHERE TO EAT

DINING OUT

Also see *Where to Eat* listings in "Sugarloaf and the Carrabassett Valley." **Porter House** in Eustis is a popular dining destination for Rangeley visitors.

The Gingerbread House (864-3602), Route 4/16, Oquossoc. Open for breakfast, lunch (except Sunday), and dinner. An ice cream parlor since the turn of the 20th century, preserved and expanded. The old marble soda fountain is still here, but there's a hearth and a wing and deck facing the pine trees in back. Lunch might be a crabcake sandwich, and you can still just come for ice cream (try chocolate truffle). At dinnertime the tables are draped in linen, and the menu ranges from spicy peanut noodles and pasta of the day to grilled duck breast and filet mignon with a béarnaise sauce. $8.95–23.95.

Loon Lodge (864-5666), Pickford Road, Rangely. Open for dinner, reserve. Candlelight dining in a series of log and book-walled rooms, lake views. The menu is large, ranging from Grandma's turkey pot pie ($13) to a superb "two texture duckling" ($21) and specials like South Texas antelope.

Rangeley Inn (864-3341), Main Street, Rangeley. Closed mid-April through late May; otherwise, open for breakfast and dinner daily. An attractive, old-fashioned hotel dining room with a high tin ceiling and a reputation for fine dining. Choices might range from chicken in creamy champagne sauce to filet mignon. All dinners include soup or salad. $10.95–21.95

Kawanhee Inn (585-2000), Route 142, Weld. Open for breakfast and dinner daily mid-June through September. A traditional lodge is the setting for candlelight meals in the open-beamed dining room or screened porch overlooking Lake Webb. The menu might include baked chicken breast stuffed with onion, feta, and spinach, served with creamy Parmesan sauce, a Caesar salad with grilled shrimp, and a selection of pasta. Entrées include salad, vegetables, and warm breads. Maine lobster available every night. $11.95–19.95.

Country Club Inn (864-3831), Rangeley. Open for breakfast daily and for dinner Wednesday through Sunday in summer and fall; weekends in winter by reservation only. The inn sits on a rise above Rangeley Lake, and the dining room windows maximize the view. The menu might include roast duck with a Bing cherry sauce, salmon and haddock chowder, and veal. Entrées $11.95–18.95.

Bald Mountain Camps (864-3671), Bald Mountain Road, Oquossoc. Dinner by reservation is available to nonguests in this classic sporting-camp dining room by the lake. The set menu varies with the night. Friday might be steamed lobster or baby back ribs or grilled chicken served with corn fries and "Maine Guide" desserts. BYOB.

EATING OUT

People's Choice Restaurant (864-5220), Main Street, Rangeley. Open daily 6 AM–9 PM. Lunch choices include sandwiches and burgers, and the dinner specialty is pork chops, a half chicken, and a slab of ribs. The lounge features Saturday bands and the largest dance floor around (everyone comes; see *Entertainment*).

Tavern Dining at the Rangeley Inn (864-3341), 51 Main Street, Rangeley. Every town should have a pub like this, with reasonably priced pub grub like steakburgers (with bacon and cheese); good chowder.

✍ **Our Place Café** (864-5844), Main Street and Richardson Avenue, Rangeley. Open for breakfast and lunch; Sunday for breakfast only. The favorite place in town for breakfast (great omelets); friendly service.

Red Onion (864-5022), Main Street, Rangeley. Open daily for lunch and dinner. A friendly Italian American dining place with a sunroom and *Biergarten;* fresh-dough pizzas and daily specials.

Parkside & Main (864-3774), 76 Main Street. Open 11–11 in summer; in winter open Sunday through Thursday 11:30–9, Friday and Saturday until 10. An attractive dining room with plenty of windows and a deck overlooking the lake. Large menu with burgers, homemade soups and chowders, seafood, and daily specials.

The Four Seasons Café (864-2020), Route 4, Oquossoc. Don't be put off by the Budweiser sign. Inside there is a bar, along with a woodstove, tables with checked green cloths, and a big menu with Mexican dishes, salads, good soups, sandwiches, and vegetarian specials. Fresh-dough pizzas are also a specialty, and Sunday brunch features omelet du jour with homefries ($4.25).

✍ **Pine Tree Frosty** (864-5894), middle of Main Street, Rangeley. Try the lobster roll packed full of meat; all this and Gifford's ice cream.

Lakeside Convenience (864-5888), Main Street, Rangeley. Great fried chicken, usually in at 9 AM and sold out by 2 PM.

ENTERTAINMENT

✍ **Lakeside Youth Theater** (864-5000), Main Street, Rangeley. A recently renovated landmark that offers first-run films, matinees on rainy days when the flag is hung out, art films on Thursday nights. Live comedy shows in summer; off-season shows on weekends.

People's Choice Restaurant (864-5220), Main Street, Rangeley. The lounge section is separate from the dining part of this popular restaurant, and on Saturdays year-round its large dance floor is jammed with couples dancing to live bands.

Rangeley Friends of the Performing Arts sponsors a July and August series of performances by top entertainers and musicians at local churches, lodges, and the high school. For the current schedule, check with the chamber of commerce (see *Guidance*).

SELECTIVE SHOPPING

Alpine Shop (864-3741), Main Street, Rangeley. Open daily year-round. The town's premier clothing store, with name-brand sportswear and Maine gifts. Check out its bargain basement across the street (down Main Street a ways).

Blueberry Hill Farm (864-5647), Dallas Hill Road, off Route 4 east of Rangeley. Stephanie and Don Palmer offer two large rooms of antiques, featuring fine quilts, baskets, furniture, and glass; also crafts and used books, a Wildlife Studio and antique fly-rods, reels, and Don Palmer's own hand-carved decoys.

Books, Lines, and Thinkers (864-4355), Main Street, Rangeley. Open year-round; hours vary depending on season. Wess Conally offers a good selection of art as well as books and music; also antiques.

First Farm (864-5539), Gull Pond Road, Rangeley. Open seasonally, Monday, Tuesday, Friday, Saturday 10–5. A mile north of town, marked from Route 16. Kit and Linda Casper's farm and store have become a Maine legend.

Frost Country (864-3473), Route 4 at South Shore Drive, Rangeley. Joan Frost's own painted furniture is worth a stop, and the quality of other crafted items—quilts, paintings, wooden loons, jewelry—is also high.

✍ **The Mad Whittler** (864-5595), Main Street, Rangeley. Rodney Richard sculpts animals and folk characters using a chain saw and jackknife, and his son Rodney Richards Jr. executes his own whimsical creations with similar tools; chances are one or the other will be there working away. Look for the "open" flag.

✍ **Ecopelagicon, A Nature Store** (864-2771), 3 Pond Street, Rangeley. In the middle of town but with windows on Haley Pond. An attractive store featuring ecological gifts, toys, music, and books.

Also see **River's Edge Sports** and **Rangeley Region Sport Shop** under *To Do—Fishing*.

SPECIAL EVENTS

All events are in Rangeley unless otherwise noted.

January: **Rangeley Snodeo**—snowmobile rally and cross-country ski races.

March: **Bronco Buster Ski Challenge** at Saddleback.

July: **Independence Day** parade and fireworks, silent auction, cookout; **Old-Time Fiddlers Contest;** and **Logging Museum Festival Days. Heritage Day Fair** in Weld Village (*final Saturday*).

August: **Sidewalk Art Show; Annual Blueberry Festival; Outdoor Sporting Heritage Days;** and **Phillips Old Home Days** (*third week*).

October: **Rangeley Lakes Logging Museum Apple Festival** (*first Saturday*).

December: **Walk to Bethlehem Pageant,** Main Street, Rangeley.

Sugarloaf and the Carrabassett Valley

The second highest mountain in the state, Sugarloaf/USA faces another 4,000-footer across the Carrabassett Valley—a narrow defile that accommodates a 17-mile-long town.

Carrabassett Valley is a most unusual town. In 1972, when it was created from Crockertown and Jerusalem townships, voters numbered 32. The school and post office are still down in Kingfield, south of the valley; the nearest drugstore, chain supermarket, and hospital are still in Farmington, 36 miles away. There are just around 325 full-time residents (males outnumber females and the average age is 34), but there are now more than 5,000 "beds." Instead of "uptown" and "downtown," people say "on-mountain" and "off-mountain."

On-mountain, at the top of Sugarloaf's access road, stands one of New England's largest self-contained ski villages: a dozen shops and more than a dozen restaurants, a seven-story brick hotel, and a church. A chairlift hoists skiers up to the base lodge from lower parking lots and from hundreds of condominiums clustered around the Sugarloaf Inn. More condominiums are scattered farther down the slope, all served by a chairlift. From all places you can also ski down to the Carrabassett Valley Ski Touring Center, Maine's largest cross-country trail network.

More than 800 condominiums are scattered among firs and birches. To fill them in summer, Sugarloaf has built an outstanding 18-hole golf course; maintains one of the country's top-rated golf schools; fosters a lively special-events program; promotes rafting, mountain biking, and hiking; and even seriously attempts to eliminate blackflies.

Spring through fall the focus also shifts off-mountain to the backwoods hiking and fishing north of the valley. Just beyond the village of Stratton, Route 27 crosses a corner of Flagstaff Lake and continues through Cathedral Pines, an impressive sight and a good place to picnic. The 30,000-acre Bigelow Preserve, which embraces the lake and great swatches of this area, offers swimming, fishing, and camping. Eustis, a small outpost on the lake, caters to sportsmen and serves as a P.O. box for sporting camps squireled away in the surrounding woodland.

Kingfield, at the southern entrance to the Carrabassett Valley, was founded in 1816. This stately town has long been a woodworking center and produced the first bobbins for America's first knitting mill; for some time it also supplied most of the country's yo-yo blanks. It is, however, best known as the one time home of the Stanley twins, inventors of the steamer automobile and the dry-plate coating machine for modern photography. The Stanley Museum includes fascinating photos of rural Maine in the 1890s by Chansonetta, sister of the two inventors. Kingfield continues to produce wood products and also offers outstanding lodging and dining.

The Carrabassett River doesn't stop at Kingfield. Follow it south as it wanders west off Route 27 at New Portland, then a short way along Route 146, to see the striking vintage-1841 Wire Bridge. Continue on Route 146 and then west on Route 16 if you are heading for The Forks and the North Woods; to reach the coast, take Route 27 south through Farmington, a gracious old college town with several good restaurants and an unusual opera museum.

GUIDANCE

Sugarloaf Area Chamber of Commerce (235-2100), RR 1, Box 2151, Carrabassett Valley 04947. The chamber is well stocked with brochures on the area as well as statewide information. It also offers an areawide year-round reservation service (235-2500; 1 800-THE-AREA) for lodging places on and off the mountain. Sugarloaf's toll-free reservations and information number for the eastern seaboard is 1-800-THE-LOAF; you can also call 237-2000, or log onto www.sugarloaf. com. Pick up a copy of "Maine's Western Mountains and Lakes Region," an area guide available locally.

GETTING THERE

By air: **Portland International Jetport** (779-7301), 2½ hours away, offers connections to all points. **Rental cars** are available at the airport. (See *Getting There* in "Portland Area.")

By car: From Boston it theoretically takes 4 hours to reach the Carrabasset Valley. Take the Maine Turnpike to exit 12 (Auburn), then Route 4 to Route 2, to Route 27; or take I-95 to Augusta, then Route 27 the rest of the way. (We swear by the latter route, but others swear by the former.)

GETTING AROUND

In ski season the **Valley Ski Shuttle Bus** runs from the base lodge to the Carrabassett Valley Ski Touring Center and Route 27 lodges.

MEDICAL EMERGENCY

Franklin Memorial Hospital (778-6031), 1 Hospital Drive, Farmington. Sugarloaf/USA has its own emergency clinic (237-2000), and the **Mount Abram Regional Health Center** (265-4555), Depot Street, Kingfield, has both a full-time nurse and a physician's assistant. **Dr. Christopher Smith** (265-5088), Kingfield's kindly country doctor, responds after business hours.

sponds after business hours.

TO SEE

MUSEUMS

Stanley Museum (265-2729), School Street, Kingfield. Open year-round Tuesday through Sunday 1–4 (closed weekends November through April). $2 adults, $1 children. Housed in a stately wooden school donated by the Stanley family in 1903, this is a varied collection of inventions by the Stanley twins, F. O. and F. E. (it was their invention of the airbrush in the 1870s that made their fortune). Exhibits range from violins to the steam car for which the Stanleys are best known. Three Stanley Steamers (made between 1905 and 1916) are on exhibit; also fascinating photos of rural Maine in the 1890s and elsewhere through the 1920s by Chansonetta Stanley Emmons, sister of the two inventors.

Nordica Homestead Museum (778-2042), Holley Road (off Route 4/27), north of Farmington. Open June through Labor Day, Tuesday through Sunday 10–noon and 1–5; also September and October by appointment. Adults $2, children $1 . This 19th-century farmhouse is the unlikely repository for the costumes, personal mementos, and exotic gifts given to the opera star Lillian Norton, who was born here (she later changed her name to Nordica).

Nowetah's American Indian Museum (628-4981), Route 27, New Portland. Open daily 10–5; no admission charge. Don't dismiss this place as just another tourist trap. Nowetah Timmerman, a member of the Susquehanna and Cherokee tribes, displays Native American artifacts from the United States, Canada, and South America. A special room holds over 300 Maine baskets and bark containers; also quill embroidery, trade beads, and more.

Red School House Museum (778-4215), Route 2/4, Farmington. Open Tuesday through Friday 9–4. A schoolhouse built in 1852 and used as a school until 1958. Old desks, books, and memorabilia; also houses the **Greater Farmington Chamber of Commerce.**

Wilton Farm & Home Museum (645-2091), Canal Street, Wilton. Open Saturdays in July and August, 1–4 PM and by appointment. A Civil War–era building housing displays of items owned by the Bass family, Bass shoes, period costumes, display on Sylvia Hardy ("The Maine Giantess"), and a large collection of Maine bottles, among other things.

HISTORIC SITES

Kingfield Historical House (265-2729), School Street, Kingfield. Open during Kingfield Days in July or by appointment. A Victorian-style house built in 1891, and operated by the Kingfield Historical Society. Furnished to the era in which it was built. Personal possessions and information about Maine's first governer, William King (also where Kingfield got its name). There's a country store in the barn with arti-

The Wire Bridge in New Portland

facts from the turn of the century.

Dead River Historical Society (246-2271), Routes 16 and 27, Stratton. Open weekends in summer 11–3. Displays memorabilia from the "lost" towns of Flagstaff and Dead River, flooded in 1950 to create the present 22,000-acre, 24-mile Flagstaff Lake. When the water is low you can still see foundations and cellar holes, including that of a round barn in the Dead River.

Wire Bridge, on Wire Bridge Road, off Route 146 (not far) off Route 27 in New Portland. Nowhere near anywhere, this amazing-looking suspension bridge across the Carrabassett River has two massive shingled stanchions. The bridge is one of Maine's 19th-century engineering feats (it was built in 1841). There's a good swimming hole just downstream and a place to picnic across the bridge; take a right through the ball field and go 0.5 mile on the dirt road. Note the parking area and path to the river.

FOR FAMILIES

❧ **The Western Maine Children's Museum** (235-2211), Route 27, Carrabassett Valley. Open Saturday, Sunday, and Monday 1–5. $2.50 per person. Plenty of hands-on exhibits include math and science tables, a dress-up corner, a big indoor sand pile, computers, and a cave with real crystals.

❧ **Sugarloaf Outdoor Adventure Camp** (237-6909), Riverside Park, Route 27, Carrabassett Valley. Runs weekdays mid-July through August. Begun as a town program and now operated by Sugarloaf. Open to visitors (reservations required); designed for ages 4–14: archery, swimming, biking, golf, climbing, camping, fly-fishing, and arts and crafts. Inquire about the teen adventure program.

🖉 **The Deer Farm** (628-5361), Millay Hill Road, North New Portland (posted from Wire Bridge Road; see Wire Bridge under Historic Sites). Open daily until sunset. $1 admission entitles visitors to grain with which to feed Scott Oliver's herd of varied deer.

🖉 **Sugarloaf Dorsets Sheep Farm** (265-4549), Freeman Ridge Road (300 feet from Kingfield town line on Route 27 headed north). On the site of a turn-of-the-century sheep farm. Come see lambs being born or just stop to pet the animals.

SCENIC DRIVES

Route 142 from Kingfield to Phillips (11 miles) runs through farmland backed by Mount Abraham (see map on page 524). Stop at the **Phillips Historical Society** and **Daggett Rock** (see *To See—Scenic Drives* in "Rangeley Lakes Region") and continue to **Mount Blue State Park** (see *Green Space* in "Rangeley Lakes Region"); return to Kingfield via New Vineyard and New Portland, stopping to see the **Wire Bridge** (see *Historic Sites*).

Route 16 though North New Portland and Emden is the most scenic as well as the most direct route from Kingfield to the Upper Kennebec Valley and Moosehead Lake.

TO DO

BOATING

See *Fishing* for rental canoes, kayaks, and motorboats.

CANOEING AND KAYAKING

The **Carrabassett River** above East New Portland is a good spring paddling spot, with Class II and III whitewater. The north branch of the **Dead River** from the dam in Eustis to the landing after the Stratton bridge is another good paddle, as is the upper branch of the **Kennebago River.**

Canoe and kayak rentals are available from **Red Oak Sports** (778-5350) in Farmington.

FISHING

Thayer Pond at the **Sugarloaf Outdoor Center** (237-6830), Route 27, is a catch-and-release pond open to the public, with fly-fishing lessons, canoe rentals, and fee fishing. The village of Stratton, north of Sugarloaf/ USA, serves as the gateway to serious fishing country. **The Dead River Sport Shop** (246-4868) rents canoes and offers a large selection of gear and locally tied flies; **Northland Cash Supply** (246-2376) is a genuine backwoods general store that also carries plenty of fishing gear; **T&L Enterprises** (246-4276) rents motorized boats and canoes; and the **White Wolf Inn** (246-2922) rents canoes and kayaks. In Eustis both **Tim Pond Wilderness Camps** and **King & Bartlett Fish & Game Club** (see *Lodging—Sporting Camps*) are traditional fishing enclaves. In Farmington **Red Oak Sports** (778-5350) rents boats, and **Aard-vark Outfitters** (778-3380) offers a wide selection of fly-fishing gear.

Fly-fishing near Sugarloaf

GOLF

Sugarloaf/USA Golf Club (237-2000), Sugarloaf/USA. This spectacular, 18-hole, par-72 course, designed by Robert Trent Jones Jr., is ranked among the nation's best, as is its golf school (now affiliated with Mount Snow's long-established Original Golf School). Inquire about weekend and midweek golf programs and packages.

Junior Golf Camp (237-2000), Sugarloaf/USA (5 midweek days), designed for ages 12–18, is offered several times between mid-June and mid-August.

HIKING

There are a number of 4,000-footers in the vicinity, and rewarding trails up **Mount Abraham** and **Bigelow Mountain.** The Appalachian Trail signs are easy to spot on Route 27 just south of Stratton; popular treks include the 2 hours to **Cranberry Pond** or 4-plus hours (one way) to **Cranberry Peak.** The chamber of commerce (see *Guidance*) usually stocks copies of the Maine Bureau of Parks and Lands' detailed map to trails in the 35,000-acre **Bigelow Preserve,** encompassing the several above-treeline trails in the Bigelow Range (the trails are far older than the preserve, which dates from 1976 when a proposal to turn these mountains into "the Aspen of the East" was defeated by a public referendum).

West Mountain Falls on the Sugarloaf Golf Course is an easy hike to a swimming and picnic spot on the South Branch of the Carrabassett River. Begin at the Sugarloaf Clubhouse.

Poplar Stream Falls is a 51-foot cascade with a swimming hole below. Turn off Route 27 at the Valley Crossing and follow this road to the abandoned road marked by a snowmobile sign. Follow this road 1.5 miles.

Check in at the Sugarloaf/USA Outdoor Center, then head up **Burnt Mountain Trail,** a 3-mile hike to the 3,600-foot summit. At the top you'll have a 360-degree view of mountains, Sugarloaf's Snowfields, and Carabassett Valley towns. The trail follows a streambed, through soft- and hardwoods.

MOOSE-WATCHING

Moose Cruises (237-6830) depart from the Sugarloaf/USA Outdoor Center, July through September, Wednesday and Saturday evenings: View a video while sipping complimentary champagne, and ride the "Moose Express" van to likely moose-watching spots.

MOUNTAIN BIKING

Sugarloaf/USA offers 50 miles of marked trails ranging from flat to vertical. Pick up maps, rentals, and information at the **Ride On! Bike Shop** (237-6998) at the Village Center. A popular ride begins here at the bottom of the lifts and is a steady downhill all the way down the access road and along the old narrow-gauge railway bed to the Carrabassett Valley Town Park. On Friday, Saturday, and Sunday you even avoid the schlep back up by hopping the **Bike Shuttle. The Sugarloaf/USA Outdoor Center** (237-2000), Route 17, is also a source of maps, info, and rentals and is the hub of a trail system designed for cross-country skiers that also serves bikers well. More adventurous bikers can, of course, hit any number of abandoned logging roads. Inquire about guided tours.

A 19.5-mile loop begins at Tufulio's Restaurant (see *Eating Out*). Park there, cross the Carriage Road bridge, and turn left onto Houston Brook Road. This road will lead you into the **Bigelow Preserve** on double-track logging roads. When the road forks, heading uphill with a hard right, stay instead to the left on the single-track trail. You'll go past Stratton Brook Pond and the Appalacian Trailhead. When you reach Route 27, head south to Bigelow Station. Follow the Narrow Gauge Trail back to Tufulio's. This is a good trip for intermediate-level bikers.

SWIMMING

Cathedral Pines, Route 27, Stratton. Just north of town, turn right into the campground and follow signs to the public beach on Flagstaff Lake; changing rooms, playground. Free.

Among the **Carrabassett River**'s popular swimming holes:

Riverside Park, Route 27, 0.5 mile south of Ayotte's Country Store, features a natural water slide and a very small beach, ideal for small children. Look for a deeper swimming hole off Route 27, 0.5 mile south of Riverside Park on the corner of the entrance to **Spring Farm.**

Also see **Wire Bridge** under *To See—Historic Sites.*

WHITEWATER RAFTING

An easy day trip. See outfitters under *To Do—Whitewater Rafting* in "The Upper Kennebec Valley and Moose River Valley" and reserve a ride: phone 1-800-RAFT-MEE.

Sugarloaf/USA (1-800-765-RAFT) has entered into a partnership with **Northern Outdoors,** providing rafting trips and packages.

WINTER SPORTS

CROSS-COUNTRY SKIING
Sugarloaf/USA Outdoor Center (237-6830), Route 27, Carrabassett Valley. Open in-season 9 AM–dusk. This is Maine's largest touring network, with 105 km of trail loops, including race loops (with snowmaking) for timed runs. Rentals and instruction are available. The center itself includes the **Klister Kitchen,** which serves soups and sandwiches; space to relax in front of the fire with a view of Sugarloaf; and a rental area.

Titcomb Mountain Ski Touring Center (778-9031), Morrison Hill Road (off Route 2/4), Farmington. A varied network of 25 km of groomed trails and unlimited ungroomed trails; used by the University of Maine at Farmington.

DOWNHILL SKIING
Sugarloaf/USA (general information, 237-2000; snow report at ext. 6808; on-mountain reservations: 1-800-THE-LOAF; www.sugarloaf.com). Sugarloaf Mountain Corporation was formed in the early 1950s by local skiers, and growth was steady but slow into the 1970s. Then a boom decade produced one of New England's largest self-contained resorts, including a base village complete with a seven-story brick hotel and a forest of condominiums. Sugarloaf has been expanding and improving snowmaking and services ever since. Snowmaking now even covers its snowy cap. In 1996 Sugarloaf was absorbed by the Bethel-based American Skiing Company. The winter of 2000–2001 marked the mountain's 50th season.

Trails number 126 and glades add up to 45 miles. The vertical drop is a whopping 2,820 feet. The 14 lifts include a gondola, a detachable quad, a triple chair, eight double chairs, and one T-bar. Facilities include a Perfect Turn Development Center, a Perfect Kids school, a ski shop, rentals, a base lodge, a cafeteria, a nursery (day and night), a game room, and a total of 22 bars and restaurants. The nursery is first-rate; there are children's programs for 3-year-olds to teens; also mini-mountain tickets for beginners. In 2000, 1-day lift rates were $49 adults, $45 young adults, $32 juniors and seniors. Also multiday, early- and late-season, and packaged rates. Under age 6, lifts are free.

ICE SKATING
Sugarloaf /USA Outdoor Center (237-6830) maintains a lighted rink and rents skates.

SNOWMOBILING
Snowmobile trails are outlined on many maps available locally; a favorite destination is **Flagstaff Lodge** (maintained as a warming hut) in the Bigelow Preserve. **Flagstaff Rentals** (246-4276) and **T&L Enterprises** (246-2922), both in Stratton, rent snowmobiles. Inquire about guided tours.

LODGING

On-mountain

Sugarloaf/USA Inn and Condominiums (237-2000; 1-800-THE-LOAF; www.sugarloaf.com), Carrabassett Valley 04947. Some 330 ski-in, ski-out condominiums are in the rental pool. Built gradually over more than 20 years (they include the first condos in Maine), they represent a range of styles and sites; when making a reservation, you might want to ask about convenience to the base complex, the **Sugarloaf/USA Sports and Fitness Club** (to which all condo guests have access), or the golf club. The 42-room **Sugarloaf Inn** offers attractive standard rooms and fourth-floor family spaces with lofts; there's a comfortable living room with fireplace, a solarium restaurant (see **The Seasons** under *Dining Out*); the front desk is staffed around the clock; the inn is handy to the health club, also to the mountain. Packages $59–109 per person in win-ter, from $99 in golf season.

    ᴖ **Grand Summit Resort Hotel & Conference Center** (1-800-527-9879), RR 1, Box 2299, Carrabassett Valley 04947. So close to the base complex that it dwarfs the base lodge, this is a massive, seven-story, 120-room brick condominium hotel with a gabled roof and central tower. Rooms are large and well furnished, and most have small refrigerators and microwaves. There are two 2-bedroom suites, each with a living room and kitchen. Also available are two palatial tower penthouses, each with three bedrooms, three baths, and a hot tub. There's a library and a health club with a large hot tub and plunge pool, sauna, and steam room. Midwinter $139–144 per night for a one- or two-bedroom, $224–650 for suites; less in summer; multiday discounts.

Off-mountain

INNS AND BED & BREAKFASTS

🐾✓ **The Herbert** (265-2000; 1-800-THE-HERB), P.O. Box 67, Kingfield 04947. Open year-round. This three-story hotel was billed as a "palace in the wilderness" when it opened in 1918 in the center of Kingfield. The "fumed oak" walls of the lobby gleam. Soak up the warmth from richly upholstered chairs and enjoy music from the grand piano. New owner-ship in summer 2000 hasn't changed the comfortably old-fashioned feel of the place. The attractive dining room is frequently filled, and the fare is exceptional (see *Dining Out*). The 28 rooms and four suites are furnished with antiques, and many bathrooms feature Jacuzzis. $49–165.

Three Stanley Avenue (265-5541), Kingfield 04947. Designed by a younger brother of the Stanley twins, now an attractive B&B next to the more ornate One Stanley Avenue, also owned by Dan Davis (see *Dining Out*). We like Number 1, with its ornate sleigh bed and claw-foot tub, and Number 4 is good for a family (one double, one twin bed). Although there's no common room, guests are welcome to use the elegant sitting room with flocked wallpaper and a grandfather clock next door at One Stanley Avenue. In summer the lawns and woods are good for walking.

Breakfast is included. $50–60, less midweek and summer.

☸ **River Port Inn** (265-2552; rivport@somtel.com), Route 27, Kingfield 04947. An 1840 roadside house on the edge of town (and on snowmobile I-84) has just two suites, each with its own bath. One sleeps six and has a private Jacuzzi. The other is an extended-stay suite, sleeping four with a kitchen and private entrance. There's also a living room, and a big, friendly dining area in which guests tend to linger over home-baked breakfast fare. $100 per night for two includes continental breakfast. Well-behaved pets are welcome.

☸占 **Tranquillity Bed & Breakfast** (246-4280), P.O. Box 9, Stratton 04982. Open Memorial Day through November. Guy and Fran Grant have transformed an old barn into an informal lodge with three guest rooms with private baths, and an attractive living/dining room overlooking Flagstaff Lake. The boat ramp is just across Route 27. $55 per couple, full breakfast included. $45 for singles.

MOTEL

☸ **Spillover Motel** (246-6571), P.O. Box 427, Stratton 04982. An attractive, two-story, 19-unit (11 nonsmoking) motel just south of Stratton Village. Spanking clean, with two double beds to a unit, color cable TV, phone. $58–74, $5 for each additional person; includes continental breakfast; $5 pets.

SPORTING CAMPS

☸占 **Tim Pond Wilderness Camps** (243-2947; in winter, 897-4056; www. timpondcamps.com), Eustis 04936. Open from ice-out through November. Located on a pond where there are no other camps, and down a road with gated access, these log cabins are quiet and private. Eleven cabins, each with a fieldstone fireplace or woodstove; three meals are served in the lodge. Recreational opportunities include mountain biking, moose-watching, swimming, canoeing, fishing, and boating on this clear, remote lake surrounded by 4,450 acres of woodland; also good for hiking. $110 single per night (plus 15 percent gratuity) includes three meals; family rates in July and August.

King & Bartlett Fish and Game Club (243-2956; buzz@somtel.com), Eustis 04936. A century-old sporting camp catering to fishermen and hunters, set on its own 34,000 acres—including 18 ponds and lakes and four streams. Each of the 12 log cabins can sleep two to six people; all have lake views, full baths, and daily maid service. Meals are served in the central lodge. $165 per person per night, $850 for 6 nights includes all meals. Inquire about family rates and Registered Maine Guide service.

CAMPGROUNDS

☸ **Cathedral Pines Campground** (246-3491), Route 27, Eustis 04936. Open mid-May through September. Three hundred town-owned acres on Flagstaff Lake, with 115 tent and RV sites set amid towering red pines. Recreation hall, beach, and canoe and paddleboat rentals.

☸ **Deer Farm Camps & Campground** (265-4599; www.deerfarmcamps.com), Tufts Pond Road, Kingfield, 04947. Open year-round; campground in summer only, housekeeping cabins all year. Fifty wooded tent and RV sites near Tufts Pond (good swimming); facilities include a store, playground, and hot showers. $13 tent sites, $14 with electric; water hookups. $225 per week for cabins.

For a list of rental units ranging from classic old A-frames to classy condos, contact the **Sugarloaf Area Chamber of Commerce** (see *Guidance*).

WHERE TO EAT

DINING OUT

🖊️& **Porter House** (246-7932), Route 27, Eustis. Dinner Wednesday through Sunday year-round. A country farmhouse located 12 miles north of Sugarloaf, drawing patrons from Rangeley, Kingfield, and beyond. The four small dining rooms are lit by fire and candlelight. Sip a drink while you study the menu, which (of course) includes Porter House steak (market price). Entrées begin at $9.95 for a char-grilled boneless skinless chicken breast Dijon or a garden-vegetable patty; children's menu available. All breads, soups, and desserts are homemade. Full bar and wine list. Your chef-hosts are Beth and Jeff Hinman.

& **One Stanley Avenue** (265-5541), Kingfield. Closed May through December; otherwise, open after 5 PM except Monday. Reservations are a must. Small, but generally considered one of the best restaurants in western Maine. Guests gather for a drink in the Victorian parlor, then proceed to one of three intimate dining rooms. Specialties include veal and fiddle-head pie, and saged rabbit with raspberry sauce. Owner-chef Dan Davis describes his methods as classic, the results as distinctly regional. $15–30 includes fresh bread, salad, vegetables, starch, coffee, and teas, but it's difficult to pass on the wines and desserts.

The Herbert (265-2000), Main Street, Kingfield. Fine dining Thursday through Sunday for dinner; lunch pub fare 7 days. Dinner entrées include seafood, vegetarian, and chicken choices. This elegant old hotel dining room gleams with cut glass; service is friendly; dress is casual; and the wine list is extensive.

Hug's Italian Cuisine (237-2392), Route 27, Carrabassett Valley. Open Tuesday through Sunday, November through April. A small eatery featuring northern Italian–style delicacies such as Shiitake mushroom ravioli with walnut pesto Alfredo sauce.

The Seasons (237-6834), Sugarloaf Inn, Carrabassett Valley. Breakfast daily, and dinner 6–9. Request a table in the glass-walled section of the dining room. The menu ranges from lobster (served nightly) to prime rib on Thursday. Entrées begin at $12.95.

EATING OUT

🍴 **Longfellows Restaurant & Riverside Lounge** (265-4394), Main Street, Kingfield. Open year-round for lunch and dinner (from 5 PM). An attractive, informal dining place in a 19th-century building decorated with photos of 19th-century Kingfield. Great for lunch (homemade soups, quiche, crêpes, and a wide selection of sandwiches); a find for budget-conscious families at dinner. Children's plates are available.

The Shipyard Brewhaus at the Sugarloaf Inn (237-6837), Sugarloaf Access Road. Open 4:30–9:30. A grand old ornate bar with Shipyard brews on tap occupies a pleasant corner of the inn (the former library), an appealing setting for reasonably priced pub fare, including pizzas and burgers, salad, and lobster bisque.

& **Mainely Yours** (246-2999), Stratton Village. Open 5 AM–9 PM Monday through Friday, 6 AM–10 PM Saturday, 7–4 Sunday. Better known as "Cathy's Place" (owner Cathy Preda is a well-known local chef) and decorated with renditions of Elvis, this is the best road food around. Breakfast specials start at $1.25, and Tuesday night features 2-for-1 dinners.

& **Tufulio's Restaurant & Bar** (235-2010), Route 27, Carrabassett (6 miles south of Sugarloaf). Open for dinner from 4:30 daily. A pleasant dining room with large oak booths, specializing in every kind of pizza, a wide selection of pastas, and microbrews. Children's menu and game room.

The Wirebridge Diner (628-6229), Route 27, New Portland. Open 6 AM–2 PM except Monday. A classic diner with wooden booths and stained glass, originally opened in Haverhill, Massachusetts, moved to Waterville, Maine, in the 1940s, here in the 1960s: great onion rings and sandwiches. Ask directions to the Wire Bridge (see *To See—Historic Sites*).

& **The Woodsman,** Route 27, Kingfield (north end of town). Pine paneled, decorated with logging tools and pictures, a friendly barn of a place. Good for stacks of pancakes, great omelets, endless refills on coffee, homemade soups and subs, local gossip.

Theo's Microbrewery & Pub (237-2211). Home of the Sugarloaf Brewing Company's pale ale. Burgers, steaks, salads, and pastas also served. Monday is 2-for-1 pizza night.

In Farmington

F. L. Butler Restaurant & Lounge (778-5223), Front Street. Open for lunch weekdays, dinner Monday through Saturday, Sunday 10–8. Steaks, a variety of fish dishes, and Italian dishes served in a brick-walled tavern. $6.95–16.95. A good way stop en route to Sugarloaf.

Soup for You! (779-0799) 36 Broadway, Farmington. The name is cleverly adapted from a line from a popular *Seinfeld* episode, and this small restaurant offers homemade soup, sandwiches that bear the name of *Seinfeld* characters, and salads. Juice bar, and cappuccino and espresso too.

The Granary Brewpub (779-0710), 147 Pleasant Street. Open daily 11–10. Home of the Narrow Gauge Brewing Company, obviously popular with local college students and faculty, and featuring a large menu of soups, sandwiches, and moderately priced entrées like chicken stir-fry and ribs.

The Homestead Bakery Restaurant (778-6162), 20 Broadway (Route 43). Open for all three meals. Dinner is Italian. The best place in town for breakfast and lunch, and a good dinner stop en route to Sugarloaf.

Gifford's Ice Cream (778-3617), Route 4/27. Open seasonally from 11 AM. Nearby Skowhegan is home base for this exceptional ice cream that comes in 40 flavors. Foot-long hot dogs also served.

SELECTIVE SHOPPING

Ritzo & Royal Studio Gallery (265-4586), at the "Brick Castle," Route 27 on the northern fringe of Kingfield. Open Thursday through Sunday 11–5:30. An exceptional selection of locally crafted jewelry, rugs, pottery, furniture and other woodwork, glass, and Patricia Ritzo's own paintings.

Kingfield Wood Products (265-2151), just off Depot Street, Kingfield. Open Monday through Friday 7–4, Saturday and Sunday 10–4. A trove of small and interesting wooden items made on the spot: wooden apples and other fruit, toys, and novelty items, all under 3 inches in diameter.

Sugarloaf/USA Sports Outlet (265-2011), Main Street, Kingfield. Open daily. Sports equipment and clothing carried with the season.

Devaney, Doak & Garret (778-3454), 193 Broadway, Farmington. Open daily. A bookstore worthy of a college town, one with a good children's section. Music and comfortable seating invite lingering.

Maiden Clay Tiles (778-6036), 248 Broadway, Farmington. Hand-painted tiles in a variety of beautiful custom designs .

Mainestone (778-6560), 161 Front Street, Farmington. Ron and Cindy Gelinas craft much of the jewelry—all made from Maine-mined gems—and carry the work of other local craftspeople.

SPECIAL EVENTS

January: **White White World Winter Carnival**—broom hockey, chili cookoff, bartenders' race, and discounts at Sugarloaf/USA.

March: **St. Patrick's Day Leprechaun Loppet**—a 15 km, citizens' cross-country race at Sugarloaf/USA Outdoor Center.

April: **Easter Festival** at Sugarloaf—costume parade, Easter egg hunt on slopes, and sunrise service on the summit. **Reggae Festival** weekend.

June: **Family Fun Days,** Stratton—Games and children's events, live entertainment, fireworks.

Late July: **Kingfield Days Celebration**—4 days with parade, art exhibits, potluck supper.

August: **Old Home Days** in Stratton, Eustis, and Flagstaff. **Weekend jazz series,** Sugarloaf/USA.

September: **Franklin County Fair,** Farmington.

October: **Skiers' Homecoming Weekend,** Sugarloaf Mountain.

December: **Yellow-Nosed Vole Day,** Sugarloaf Mountain. **Chester Greenwood Day,** Farmington, honors the local inventor of the earmuff with a parade and variety show in Farmington.

VI. THE KENNEBEC VALLEY

Augusta and Mid-Maine
The Upper Kennebec Valley and Moose River Valley,
Including The Forks and Jackman

KIM GRANT

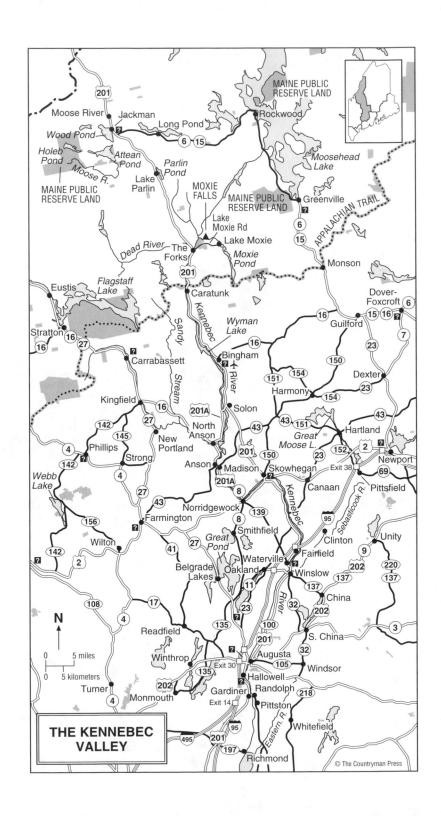

THE KENNEBEC
VALLEY

© The Countryman Press

Augusta and Mid-Maine

Augusta, the capital of Maine, rises in tiers above the Kennebec River at its head of shipping navigation. This position provided a good hunting and fishing ground for the area's earliest inhabitants, the Norridgewock and Kennebec tribes of the Algonquians. In 1625 the Pilgrims sailed to this spot and traded "seven hundred pounds of good beaver and some other furs" with the Native Americans for a "shallop's load of corn." They procured a grant to the Kennebec, from Gardiner to a waterfall halfway between Augusta and Waterville, with a strip of land 15 miles wide on either side of the bank. At the Native American village of Cushnoc (present-day Augusta), they built a storehouse and, with the proceeds of their beaver trade, were soon able to pay off their London creditors.

With the decline of the fur trade and rising hostilities with the Native Americans, these settlers sold the tract of land to four Boston merchants for just 400 pounds. The merchants had plans—farming, timber, and shipyards. War halted these plans, however, and the settlers fled, but they returned in 1754 when the British built Fort Western. The area was selected as the capital in 1827, and a statehouse, designed by Charles Bulfinch and built of granite from neighboring Hallowell, was completed in 1832. During the mid–19th century, this area boomed: Some 500 boats were built along the river between Winslow and Gardiner, and river traffic between Augusta and Boston thrived. The era is still reflected by the quaint commercial buildings lining the river downstream in Hallowell and Gardiner, both good places to shop and dine.

Today Augusta is seeing a great deal of economic growth. Retail sales have grown above the state average, and new businesses continue the sprawl effect by the civic center, with Staples, Barnes & Noble, and other retail giants moving in. Augusta was the second largest labor market in Maine in 1998, and the growth continues with new industries like Envision Net, which brought 500 jobs to the area, and was projecting another 500 by the end of 2000.

The cultural side of the state capital is also on the rise, with such nearby attractions as the Theater at Monmouth and Johnson Hall in Gardiner. In summer a concert series entertains residents and visitors alike at the waterfront park. Galleries are popping up in great numbers in surrounding areas. Augusta is also home to one of the most interesting state museums in the country; exhibits vividly depict many aspects of Maine landscape, industry, and history.

This Lower Kennebec Valley is rolling, open farmland, spotted with lakes. Just north of the city the seven lakes in the Belgrade Lakes region form an old resort area, blessed with cottage colonies that need not advertise and plenty of recreation, from mail-boat excursions and canoe rides to relaxation plain and simple. East of the city, the China Lakes form another low-profile haven. Good summer theater can be found in Waterville (upriver), Monmouth (another old resort area west of town), and Skowhegan (also known for its art school). In the past few years attractive old homes and family farms throughout this region have opened their doors to guests—who are discovering not only the beauty of the immediate area but also that "Mid-Maine" is the only true hub in this sprawling state, handy to many parts of the coast, the Western Mountains and Lakes, and the North Woods.

GUIDANCE

Kennebec Valley Chamber of Commerce (623-4559), P.O. Box E, University Drive, Augusta 04332. The office is off I-95 (the exit for Route 27) in the civic center complex. This is a year-round source of information, primarily on the area from Augusta to Gardiner.

Belgrade Lakes Region, Inc., P.O. Box 72, Belgrade 04917, maintains a seasonal (late June through September) information booth on Route 27 and also publishes a pamphlet guide to the area.

China Area Chamber of Commerce (445-2890), Box 317, South China 04358. Open year-round.

Mid-Maine Chamber of Commerce (873-3315), P.O. Box 142, Waterville 04903. Open year-round.

GETTING THERE

By air: The **Augusta State Airport** is served by U.S. Airways Express, which is operated by **Colgan Air** (623-7527).

By bus: **Vermont Transit** (1-800-451-3292) serves Augusta and Waterville.

By car: You don't have to take the Maine Turnpike to reach the Augusta area; from points south, I-95 is both quicker and cheaper (I-95 and the Maine Turnpike merge just south of Augusta). If you are not in a hurry, the most scenic route to Augusta from points south is to follow the Kennebec River up Route 24 through Bowdoinham and Richmond.

MEDICAL EMERGENCY

Maine General Medical Center, 6 East Chestnut Street, **Augusta** (626-1000); also 150 Dresden Avenue, **Gardiner** (626-1700). **Mid-Maine Medical Center** (873-0621), North Street, Waterville. **Redington-Fairview General Hospital** (474-5085), Fairview Avenue, Skowhegan.

VILLAGES

Richmond. If you follow the Kennebec River from Brunswick to Gardiner, you will be rewarded with views of Merrymeeting Bay and then of rolling farmland sloping to the river. Richmond, at first glance, seems to be just another small mill town, but its onion-domed churches recall its Russian population, which numbered as many as 500 in the 1950s and 1960s. Cross the bridge in the middle of the village to find the Pownalborough Court House, which we have described under *To See–Historic Homes* in "Wiscasset."

Hallowell. This village is much the same as it was over 100 years ago. The store names may be different, but the Water Street commercial blocks, with two- and three-story vintage mid-19th-century buildings, are definitely worth a stroll. Also note the restaurants described under *Where to Eat.*

Gardiner. Located where the Kennebec and Cobbossce Rivers meet, this old industrial (shoe, textile, and paper) town has been nicely restored. Nineteenth-century Main Street remains a great place on which to stroll and eat; also see Johnson Hall under *Entertainment.*

Winthrop is one of several towns in the area that boast a number of lakes and ponds within the town. In recent years a smattering of interesting shops and galleries have popped up, and the drive through this scenic area is worth it.

TO SEE

State House (287-2301), State Street, Augusta. Open year-round, Monday through Friday 8:30–4:30. Much modified since the original design by Charles Bulfinch (it seems like this building is always under construction), its size has actually doubled. A 180-foot dome replaced the original cupola. There are markers that will lead you on a self-guided tour, but guided tours are available.

Blaine House (287-2121), State Street, Augusta. Open year-round for tours, Tuesday through Thursday 2–4. This 28-room mansion built in the 1830s by a Captain James Hall of Bath started as a Federalist house, went through a Victorian and Italian period in the late 1800s, and was remodeled to its current semicolonial style by John Calvin Stevens. James Blaine, a Speaker of the U.S. House of Representatives, a U.S. senator, and twice secretary of state, owned the house at one time; he was known as the "plumed knight" when he ran for the presidency in 1884, battling "Rum, Romanism, and Rebellion." His daughter gave the mansion to the state in 1919, and it has since served as home for Maine governors.

Colby College (872-3000), Waterville (2 miles from exit 33 off I-95; marked). Founded in 1813, Colby College is the 12th oldest liberal arts college in the nation. It enrolls close to 1,700 students from almost every state and more than 25 countries. Its campus is set on more than 700 acres, with traditional brick and ivy-covered buildings, and there are several attractions worth noting, including the **Colby College Museum of Art** (see *Museums*); **Perkins Arboretum and Johnson Pond,** a 128-acre arboretum and bird sanctuary with nature trails and a picnic area; the **Portland String Quartet,** in residence here, with several concerts throughout the year as well as a summer string-quartet institute; the **Strider Theater,** a 274-seat theater offering a variety of programs and performances throughout the year; and the **Harold Alfond Athletic Center,** which includes a track, four tennis courts, an Olympic-sized pool, an ice arena, a large gymnasium, and fitness rooms.

A well-organized booklet guides you through a walking tour of the campus; be sure to pick one up at the admissions office.

MUSEUMS

✒️♿ **Maine State Museum** (287-2301), State Capitol Complex, State Street (Route 201/27), Augusta. Open weekdays 9–5, Saturday (and most holidays) 10–4, and Sunday 1–4. Free. Turn into the parking lot just south of the capitol building. This outstanding museum isn't even marked from the street!

Without question, this is the best state museum in New England. Allow at least an hour. The exhibit *12,000 Years in Maine* traces the story of Maine's Native Americans with reproductions of petroglyphs and genuine ancient artifacts. This fascinating exhibit also dramatizes early European explorations and 19th-century attempts to explore the state's antiquities. Elsewhere, the museum re-creates a variety of Maine's landscapes and traditional industries: fishing, agriculture, granite quarrying, ice harvesting, shipbuilding, and lumbering. *Made in Maine* depicts more than a dozen 19th-century industrial scenes: textile mills and shops producing shoes, guns, fishing rods, and more. What makes these scenes most fascinating is their incredible, lifelike quality and the attention to detail. The 1846 narrow-gauge locomotive Lion stands like a mascot in the lobby. The fourth-floor addition houses changing exhibits.

Colby College Museum of Art (872-3228), Colby College, Waterville. Open 10 AM–4:30 PM Monday through Saturday, Sunday 2–4:30. Free. Founded in 1959, this wonderful museum has a permanent collection of 18th-, 19th-, and 20th-century art that is displayed in spacious, appealing galleries. An 11-gallery addition houses some 150 works from the permanent collection, which had previously remained in storage. Three exhibit 18th-century work, two house 19th-century paintings and sculpture, another is for impressionist paintings, two for primitive 19th-century work, and two galleries are devoted to 54 works by John Marin, who spent most of his summers in Maine; much of his work in oils and watercolors reflects Maine subjects, from Mount Katahdin to seascapes.

The Schupf Wing at the Colby College Museum of Art

The Paul J. Schupf wing rotates over 400 paintings and sculptures by artist Alex Katz. The museum also offers special exhibits, gallery talks, a museum shop, lectures, and receptions throughout the year.

🖉 **Children's Discovery Museum** (622-2209), 265 Water Street, Augusta. Open Monday through Friday 9–2, Saturday 10–4, and Sunday 1–4; extended hours during school vacation and summer. $3 per person (under age 1, free). An excellent hands-on museum, with displays that include a life-sized board game that teaches about the Atlantic salmon; a stage where kids can videotape a performance and then watch themselves on TV; post office, diner, and supermarket play areas; a construction site complete with real equipment; and a weather station and communications center with computers and a ham radio.

HISTORIC SITES

Old Fort Western (626-2385), City Center Plaza, 16 Cony Street, Augusta. Open Memorial Day through July 4, 1–4 daily; July 4 through Labor Day 10–4 weekdays, 1–4 weekends; Labor Day through Columbus Day 1–4 weekends only. Groups and school programs year-round. $4.50 adults, $2.50 children. The original 16-room garrison house has been restored to reflect its use as a fort, trading post, and lodge from 1754 to 1810. The blockhouse and stockade are reproductions, but the main house (barracks and store) are original. The fort is designated as a National Historic Landmark and the oldest surviving wooden fort in New England. Costumed characters answer questions and demonstrate 18th-century domestic activities. Many annual special events.

Redington Museum and Apothecary (872-9439), 64 Silver Street, Waterville. Open mid-May through September, Tuesday through Saturday 2–6, and by appointment. $2 admission; $1 ages 18 and under. The local historical collection: furniture, Civil War and Native American relics, a children's room, period rooms, and a 19th-century apothecary.

Monmouth Museum (933-4444), Monmouth (at the intersection of Routes 132 and 135). Open Memorial Day through September, Tuesday through Sunday 1–4; year-round by appointment (933-2287 reaches the answering machine; or call Annie Smith, 933-2752). $3 adults, $1 children. A collection of buildings: 1787 Blossom House, stencil shop (1849), blacksmith shop, freight shed, and carriage house.

Waterville-Winslow Two Cent Bridge, Front Street, Waterville. One of the only known remaining toll footbridges in the country. Toll-taker's house on Waterville side. Free.

Fort Halifax, Route 201, Winslow (1 mile south of the Waterville–Winslow Bridge at the junction of the Kennebec and Sebasticook Rivers). Just a blockhouse remains, but it is original, built in 1754—the oldest blockhouse in the United States. There is also a park with picnic tables here.

Cumston Hall, Main Street, Monmouth. Open weekdays year-round during business hours. Vintage 1900, this ornate wooden building would look more at home in India than Mid-Maine. Monmouth native Harry H. Cochrane not only designed but also decorated the building with murals, detailing, and stained glass. He also composed the music and conducted the orchestra at the building's dedication. It houses the town offices, library, and the Theater at Monmouth, a repertory company specializing in Shakespeare (see *Entertainment*).

Arnold Historical Society Museum (582-7080), off Route 17, Pittston. Open July and August, Saturday, Sunday, and holidays 10–4, and by appointment. $1.50 adults, $.50 per children over age 6. An 18th-century house in which Benedict Arnold and Aaron Burr stayed for a couple of nights in the fall of 1775 on their way to attempt to capture Quebec. The army camped on Swan Island in Richmond (see *Green Space*), and about 600 men and supplies continued upriver in *bâteaux*—the flat-bottomed boats that are exhibited here in the barn. The house is furnished to period, and picture panels depict the Arnold expedition.

✒ **Norlands Living History Center** (897-4366), RD 2, Box 1740, Livermore 04254. Take Norlands Road off Route 108 between Livermore and Livermore Falls. Open July and August daily 10–4 for general tours of all buildings. $4.50 adults, $2 students. Also open by reservation year-round for live-in weekends and weeklong programs. An incredible 450-acre living-history complex re-creates life in the late 19th century. The working farm with barn and farmer's cottage, church, stone library, and Victorian mansions of the Washburn family are open to visitors. This is the genuine 1870–1890 rural experience; visitors become scholars in the one-room schoolhouse and hear the story of the famous Washburn sons. Those living-in assume the identity of a 19th-century character, carrying out chores (cooking, mending, working the farm) just as they would have if they had been living here then. Chris's husband and oldest son went for a weekend and have never been the same. Try it. Come for a special weekend like Heritage Days in June, or Christmas in early December. Three-day live-in weekends are also offered in February, April, May, and November.

SCENIC DRIVES

If you are in the mood to just take a drive in the country, passing through picturesque villages and an occasional country store or downtown area, there are plenty of options in this region. One loop we particularly like is to take Route 9 through **Hallowell,** stopping to browse in the shops, then on through **Gardiner** and continuing on Route 9 until it intersects with 132 to **Monmouth.** Visit the museum or venture into Cumston Hall (see *Historic Sites*), then head back toward through **Winthrop** to **Augusta** on Route 135.

There are a number of pleasant loops through the Belgrade Lakes region as well.

Also see *To See—Scenic Drives* in "Belfast, Searsport, and Stockton Springs."

TO DO

BALLOONING

Sails Aloft (623-1136), Augusta, offers sight-seeing flights in central and Midcoast Maine. Starts at $150 per person.

BOAT EXCURSIONS

Great Pond Marina (495-2213; 1-800-696-6329), Belgrade Lakes Village. Operates the mail boat on Great Pond (the inspiration for the book and movie *On Golden Pond*); the mail-boat ride costs $7 adults, $5 seniors, $4 children. Also moorings, boat rentals (canoes, sailboards, sailboats, fishing boats), and service.

Cobbossee Cruises (622-9409), Pond Road, Manchester, offers 2-hour cruises on Cobbossee Lake.

FISHING

The **Belgrade Lakes** are known as a source of smallmouth bass. **Day's Store** (495-2205) in Belgrade Lakes Village devotes an entire floor to fishing gear. Boat rentals are available.

FOR FAMILIES

✐ **Inside Out Playground** (877-8747), Sterns Cultural Center, 93 Main Street, Waterville. Indoor playground includes a toddler area, wooden pirate-ship structure, toy cars and trucks. Open year-round; great for rainy days.

GOLF AND TENNIS

Belgrade Lakes Golf Club (495-GOLF), Belgrade, is a new 18-hole golf course, designed by renowned English golf architect Clive Clark. Just

off Route 27 with views of both Great and Long Ponds. Fees vary with
season. Call for current fees and tee time.

Natanis Golf Club (622-3561), Webber Pond, Vassalboro, offers a 27-hole
course; tennis courts. **Waterville Country Club** (465-7773), Waterville (off I-95). Eighteen holes, clubhouse, carts, and caddies.

KAYAKING

Kennebec Valley Kayak (377-2788) offers a variety of day trips and clinics. Trips include paddling on lakes in the Kennebec Valley, a Kennebec
River paddle, and full-moon paddles.

SWIMMING

Peacock Beach State Park, Richmond (just off Route 201, 10 miles south
of Augusta). A small, beautiful sand beach on **Pleasant Pond;** lifeguards
and picnic facilities. $1 adults, free under age 12.

Public beaches include **Sunset Camps Beach** on North Pond in Smithfield
and **Willow Beach** (968-2421) in China. Although public access is limited at the Belgrade and China Lakes, every cottage cluster and most
rental "camps" there are on the water.

Lake St. George State Park (589-4255), Route 3, Liberty. A pleasant,
clean, clear lake with a sandy beach and changing facilities; a perfect
break if you are en route from Augusta and points south to the coast.

CROSS-COUNTRY SKIING

Natanis Golf Club (622-3561), Webber Pond, Vassalboro, has groomed
trails and rental equipment. **Pine Tree State Arboretum** (see *Green
Space*) also has lots of space for good skiing.

GREEN SPACE

Capitol Park, across from the State Capitol Complex, is a great place for a
picnic. Also located here is the **Maine Vietnam Veteran's Memorial,**
three triangular structures with a cutout section in the shape of soldiers
that visitors can walk through.

Maine State Veteran's Memorial Cemetery on the Old Belgrade Road,
Augusta, is a pleasant, peaceful place.

Pine Tree State Arboretum (621-0031), 153 Hospital Street, Augusta.
(At Cony Circle—the big rotary across the bridge from downtown Augusta—turn south along the river; it's a short ways down on the left,
across from the Augusta Mental Health Institute.) Open daily dawn to
dusk. Visitors center open 8–4 weekdays. There are 224 acres, with trails
through woods and fields.More than 600 trees and shrubs (including
rhododendrons and lilacs), as well as hostas and a rock garden. Cross-
country ski trails too.

Swan Island, Richmond. A state-owned wildlife management area. Day
use and overnight camping; prior reservations (287-1150) necessary for
both, since only 60 visitors are allowed on the island at any one time. $3
day visit, $5 overnight camping. The landing is in Richmond Village,

where Department of Inland Fisheries and Wildlife employees transport visitors to the island. Tours are available in an open slat-sided truck;
plenty of area for walking. The southern portion is restricted, but staff
will accompany you on a tour (also see *Lodging—Campgrounds*).

Jamies Pond Wildlife Management Area (623-4021), Meadow Hill
Road, Hallowell. These 550 acres of woodlands, managed by the Maine
Department of Inland Fisheries and Wildlife, include trails good for
walking and cross-country skiing, and a 107-acre pond.

Also see *To Do—Swimming.*

LODGING

BED & BREAKFASTS

   Maple Hill Farm (622-2708; 1-800-622-2708; www.MapleBB.com), RR 1,
Box 1145, Hallowell 04347. This pleasant old house, not far from the
turnpike and downtown Augusta, sits on 130 acres of fields and woods
with trails, a spring-fed swimming hole, and a small abandoned quarry.
Scott Cowger and Vincent Hannan offer eight rooms furnished in a
pretty country style. All have phones, televisions, clock radios, air-
conditioning, and private baths. Some have whirlpool tubs, private decks
and/or fireplaces. As you meander up the driveway by the big red barn,
watch for chickens (which provide the morning eggs) happily pecking by
the side of the road. Other animals on the farm include five goats, three
sheep, two llamas, two cows (one a dwarf), a pony, and a cat. The carriage
house has been transformed into a roomy function space. Full breakfast
served in the dining room/art gallery is included in the $90–160 double
rate; $10 less for singles; off-season rates available.

   Home-Nest Farm (897-4125), Baldwin Hill Road, Box 2350, Kents Hill 04349.
Closed March and April. This is a wonderful old family estate. The main
house, built in 1784, offers a panoramic view of the White Mountains. Lilac
Cottage (1800) and the Red Schoolhouse (1830) are available for rent as
separate units. The property has been in host Arn Sturtevant's family for six
generations. Arn can relate some interesting family tales while showing you
Civil War memorabilia. $60–120 includes breakfast.

   Independence Farm (622-0284; roried@powerlink.net), RR 1, Box 6857,
Webber Pond Road, Vassalboro 04989. This 1820s farmhouse overlooks
Webber Pond. Now that their eight children are grown, Patricia (a
craftsperson with her own store in Hallowell) and Robert Riedman raise
llamas on their 55-acre spread, as well as geese, chickens, and a dog. Two
large guest rooms have private baths, and a third small room can be
rented along with one of the others. It is frequently used for children,
who are very welcome here. Pets are also sometimes accepted, by prior
arrangement only. There's a canoe for summer use, and in winter cross-
country ski rentals and trails are available at the nearby 27-hole golf
course. $55 double includes a full farm breakfast.

Richmond Bed and Breakfast and Sauna (737-4752; 1-800-400-5751), off Route 197, Richmond 04357. Open year-round. A handsome Federal home with five guest rooms with shared bath, kitchen privileges, Finnish-style sauna, hot tub, and pool. The six saunas on the premises are rented by the hour. Visitors should be aware that clothing is optional here, and there are those who opt not to wear any. In fact, daytime nude sunbathing and swimming is available for $5 per person, and evening use of the hot tub, sauna, and pool is $15 per person. Open 6–10 PM (5–9 PM in winter). Use of all facilities is included for overnight guests. $65–85 double includes continental breakfast.

HOTEL

&.✿**Best Western Senator Inn and Spa** (622-5804; 1-800-528-1234; www.senatorinn.com), Western Avenue, Augusta. A longtime local hot spot for political figures, this property, with 125 guest rooms and suites, extends farther back from the road than you'd expect. Back-wing rooms are quieter and more private. Walking and cross-country skiing trails, indoor and outdoor pools and hot tubs, fireplace rooms available. In-room amenities include clock radios, coffeemakers, irons, and telephones. The three-story spa contains exercise machines, a saltwater pool, face and body salons, yoga, step and water aerobics classes, and spa luncheon packages. Seven conference rooms and a guest laundry are also part of the facility. $79–249 depending on room and season includes a cooked-to-order breakfast in the dining room.

CAMPS AND COTTAGES

&. **Bear Spring Camps** (397-2341), Route 3, Box 9900, Oakland 04963. Open mid-May through September. A family resort and fishing spot with 75 percent repeat business. Serious anglers come in early May for trout and salmon, and in July there's still bass. Each of the 32 cottages has a bathroom, hot and cold water, a shower, heat, an open fireplace, and its own dock and motorboat. There's a tennis court, a golf driving range, and a variety of lawn games. The swimming is great (the bottom is sandy). Meals are served in the main house. Weekly rates from $550 per couple in shoulder months to $1,975 for eight in high season, including all meals.

✍ **Castle Island Camps** (495-3312), Belgrade Lakes 04918. Open May through mid-September. In winter contact Horatio Castle, 1800 Carambola Road, West Palm Beach, FL 33406 (407-641-8339). A dozen comfortable-looking cottages clustered on a small island (connected by bridges) in 12-mile Long Pond. This is the second generation of Castles to maintain the camps, geared to fishing (the pond is stocked; rental boats are available). Meals are served in the small central lodge. There is an open fireplace in the community building, and a recreation room with pool tables, table tennis, and darts. Weekly and children's rates are available, and include all meals.

✿✍**Alden Camps** (465-7703; www.aldencamps.com), RFD 2, Box 1140, Oakland 04963. Vesta (Alden) Putnam and her husband, George, have run these camps, founded by A. Fred Alden in 1910 with just one rental unit, since 1956. They now offer 18 rustic cottages scattered among the pines on the shores of East Lake. Activities include fishing, golf nearby, swimming, waterskiing, boating, tennis, hiking, and several playing fields. Children are welcome, and pets can be accommodated for an extra fee. $90–135 daily; $540–810 weekly in high season includes all three meals.

CAMPGROUNDS

Steve Powell Wildlife Management Area (Swan Island), in Merrymeeting Bay off Richmond. State-owned Swan Island is managed as a wildlife preservation area in Merrymeeting Bay, a vast tidal bay that's well known among birders. Limited camping in primitive Adirondack shelters is available, along with a motorboat shuttle from Richmond, through the Department of Inland Fisheries and Wildlife (287-1150).

Lake St. George State Park (589-4255), Route 3, Liberty, offers 38 campsites and a boat launch ($13 for nonresidents).

WHERE TO EAT

DINING OUT

Slate's (622-9575), 167 Water Street, Hallowell. Breakfast, lunch, and dinner Tuesday through Friday, brunch and dinner Saturday, brunch-only on Sunday. Coffeehouse atmosphere in three adjoining storefronts with brick walls, tin ceilings, changing art, a great bar, and a patio in back. The brunch menu is huge and popular. The dinner menu changes daily but might include scrod baked with Brie and fresh blueberries, or cashew chicken on rice. Live music Friday and Saturday night, and during Sunday brunch. $8.95–14.95.

Michelle's (629-9151; 1-888-236-5236), 144 Water Street, Hallowell. Open for lunch during the week, brunch on Saturday and Sunday, dinner daily. Creative Fench cuisine, with many crêpe choices, escargots, and steak. $7.95–18.95

Village Inn (495-3553), Route 27, Belgrade Lakes. Open April through December, 5–9 PM Monday through Saturday, and Sunday 11:30 AM–8 PM. New owners Allen and Doris Danforth are continuing the traditions of this rambling old place with a lake view and early-bird specials. The specialty is duckling, roasted for up to 12 hours and served with a choice of sauces. Entrées $9.95–16.95.

Johann Sebastian B. (465-3223), 68 Fairfield Street, Oakland. Open Friday and Saturday for dinner most weekends (call to check). Reservations suggested. A Victorian house in the Belgrade Lakes area with three fireplaces and interesting woodwork. The menu includes German specialties, homemade European pastries, and a good selection of beer and wine. $11–21.50.

River Café (622-2190), 119 Water Street, Hallowell. Open for dinner Monday through Saturday. Downstairs lounge open Saturday as well, 4 PM–whenever. Mediterranean American specialties. Reservations required for dinner. $10.95–16.95.

Senator Restaurant (622-5804), 284 Western Avenue, Augusta. Open daily 6:30 AM to 10 PM. A big all-American dining room (buses are welcome) within the Senator Inn complex. Seafood specialties include seafood medley (shrimp, haddock, crabcake, and scallops), filet and seafood béarnaise, and crabcakes; excellent salad bar. Entrées $13.95–22.95.

EATING OUT

The A-1 Diner (582-4804), 3 Bridge Street, Gardiner. Open Monday through Saturday for all three meals, brunch only (8 AM–1 PM). A vintage-1946 Worcester diner with plenty of Formica, blue vinyl booths, blue and black tile, a 14-stool, marble-topped counter, and a neon blue and pink clock with the slogan TIME TO EAT. The kind of place where everyone seems to know one another. You won't find typical diner fare here, however. The breakfast menu includes banana-almond French toast and a wide variety of omelets, as well as eggs and hash; there are always 13 specials, 12 desserts, and four soups and chili. Beverages range from herbal tea to imported beers and wines. But you can always get tapioca pudding, and the route to the rest room is still outside and in through the kitchen door.

✒ **North Park** (621-9776), 330 Civic Center Drive, Augusta. A new dining/entertainment complex open 11–11 (till midnight on Friday and Saturday). Choose your atmosphere; all venues serve the same extensive menu. You can have dinner while seeing a movie, or dine in the main dining area with its five 10-foot TV screens (on five different channels, with audio controls at each table), the center café, or the billiard room. **Marty's Midway** offers a variety of video games, motion simulators, and carnival-style choices like skeeball and supershot basketball.

Burnsie's Homestyle Sandwiches (622-6425), 1 Hichborn Street, Augusta, between the Capitol and the rotary. Open 7:30–3 weekdays only. This is the perfect place if you're visiting the Maine State Museum. Keep your car parked where it is and walk up past the Capitol to this out-of-place house, a source of Dagwoods, Reubens, and a variety of other sandwiches, many named for local legislators. Although there is no seating in the shop, if it's a nice day the picnic tables in the park just across the river, adjoining Fort Western, offer the best view in town.

🍴 **Roseland,** Route 201/200, approximately 4 miles north of Augusta. A popular family-style restaurant with such favorites as turkey dinner or ham steak. Good for kids; casual, comfortable atmosphere.

Augusta House of Pancakes, Western Avenue, Augusta. What began as a favorite breakfast spot is now good for all meals. Popular with locals, reasonable prices.

Charlie's Pizza (622-3600), 190 Western Avenue, Augusta (in the very small King's Court Shopping Center, which is off the eastbound lane).

KIM GRANT

The A-1 Diner in Gardiner

In that lineup of fast-food places and shopping malls, it's great road food: calzones, pizza, specials, and sandwiches—clean, fast, a local favorite.

Railway Café (737-2277), 64 Main Street, Richmond. Open Monday through Saturday 6:30 AM–8 PM, later Friday and Saturday, Sunday 7–4. Minutes off I-95, this pleasant restaurant makes a great road-food stop: A wide choice of morning omelets and lunchtime sandwiches, burgers, salads, and pizzas, and a huge, reasonably priced dinner menu, including "Just for Kids." Allow a few minutes to walk around this historic Kennebec River town (see *Villages, Green Space,* and *To Do—Swimming*).

Kafe Kino (873-6526), adjacent to the Railroad Square Cinema, Waterville. Open Tuesday through Sunday for dinner, lunch on Saturday and Sunday. A good place to go before or after a show. The menu includes pasta, sandwiches, and international entrées. Rotating art show, live music occasionally, extensive wine list.

COFFEE HOUSES

Jorgensen's Café (872-8711), Main Street, Waterville. A large, funky café with at least a dozen flavored coffees, as well as tea and espresso choices. The deli serves quiche, soups, salads, and sandwiches with several delicious bread options. Coffee and tea supplies, gourmet foods.

Java Joe's (622-1110), Water Street, Augusta. Cozy place with baked goods, an interesting lunch menu, and the usual coffee and espresso drinks.

Kennebec Coffee Co., Water Street, Hallowell. Soft golden walls and comfy couches and chairs. Plenty of coffee choices as well as terrific muffins, bagels, light lunch options.

ENTERTAINMENT

✐ **Theater at Monmouth** (933-2952), P.O. Box 385, Monmouth. Performances Wednesday through Sunday in July, Tuesday through Sunday in August; matinees and children's shows vary. Housed in Cumston Hall, a striking turn-of-the-20th-century building designed as a combination theater, library, and town hall. A resident company specializes in Shakespeare but also presents contemporary shows throughout the season.

Waterville Opera House (873-7000), 93 Main Street, Waterville, presents a number of shows throughout the year, including music performances and theater productions. It is also the site of several shows during the Maine International Film Festival.

Gaslight Theater (626-3698), 1 Winthrop Street, Hallowell, has several productions per season.

Johnson Hall (582-3730), Water Street, Gardiner. A beautifully restored historic space where workshops, dances, and other performances occur frequently.

Railroad Square Cinema (873-6526), Main Street, Waterville. Heading north on Route 201 (College Avenue), turn left between Burger King and the railroad tracks. Art and foreign films in a very popular, casual atmosphere. Rebuilt after a fire, now in a separate building with a café (see Kafe Kino under *Eating Out*).

SELECTIVE SHOPPING

The mid-19th-century commercial buildings along **Water Street in Gardiner** have hatched some interesting shops.

The heart of Belgrade Village is **Day's Store** (495-2205). Open year-round, recently expanded to serve as general store; state liquor store; fishing license, gear, boot, and gift source; and rainy-day mecca. **Maine Made Shop** (495-2274), open late May through Labor Day, stocks pottery, books, and Maine souvenirs.

ANTIQUES SHOPS

The picturesque riverside lineup of shops in Hallowell harbors fewer antiques dealers than it did a few years ago, but it is still a worthwhile browsing street. **Lovejoy Antiques,** 122 Water Street, is a 70-plus-dealer mall with a wide range. **Hatties Antiques,** 148 Water Street, specializes in fine antique jewelry, antique lamps, clocks, and art glass.

ART GALLERIES

A dozen galleries in public buildings and private homes, within a short drive of each other, are listed in an art-tour brochure promoting the area as the **Kennebec Valley Art District.** Pick up the brochure at the chamber of commerce (see *Guidance*).

BOOKSTORES

✒ **Children's Book Cellar** (872-4543), 5 East Concourse, Waterville.

Leon H. Tebbets Bookstore, 164 Water Street, Hallowell, is a book lover's delight: 36,000 closely packed titles (closed Sunday in winter).

Barnes & Noble Booksellers (621-0038), the Marketplace at Augusta, directly across from the Augusta Civic Center. A full-service bookstore with music and computer software sections, as well as a café.

FACTORY OUTLETS

Carleton Woolen Mills Factory Outlet (582-6003), Griffin Street, Gardiner. Fabrics, woolens, and notions.

Cascade Fabrics, Oakland. Open Monday through Saturday 8:30–4:30. A genuine mill store.

Dexter Shoe Factory Outlet (873-6739), Kennedy Memorial Drive, Waterville.

SPECIAL EVENTS

✒ *July:* **The Whatever Family Festival**, held the week surrounding the Fourth of July, Capitol Park. Children's performances, soapbox derby, Learn the River Day, entertainment, carnival, and more. **China Connection**—public supper, pageant, road race, pie-eating and greased-pig contests in China. **Old Hallowell Days** *(third week).* **Annual Scottish Games & Gathering of the Scottish Clans,** sponsored by the St. Andrew's Society of Maine, Thomas College, Waterville.

The Upper Kennebec Valley and Moose River Valley,
Including The Forks and Jackman

Commercial rafting on the Kennebec began in 1976 when fishing guide Wayne Hockmeyer discovered the rush of riding the whitewater through dramatic 12-mile-long Kennebec Gorge. On his first ride through the gorge, Hockmeyer had to contend with logs hurtling all around him, but, as luck would have it, 1976 also marked the year in which environmentalists managed to outlaw log runs on the Kennebec.

Fourteen rafting companies now vie for space to take advantage of up to 8,000 cubic feet of water per second released every morning from late spring through mid-October from the Harris Hydroelectric Station. No more than 1,000 rafters, however, are allowed on the river at a time. In order to compete, outfitters based in and around The Forks have added their own lodging; several of these operations have evolved into year-round sports-based resorts, thanks to the popularity of snowmobiling and the recent availability of rental machines. It's this booming sport, combined with hunting, fishing, and rafting seasons, that explains the tripling of "beds" in and around The Forks over the past several years.

The Forks, sited at the confluence of the Dead and Kennebec Rivers, is technically just a "plantation" (an unorganized township) with a sign announcing its population: 30. In reality the village includes The West Forks (population around 50), north of the Route 201 bridge. The only obvious landmarks remain the old Marshall Hotel with its electrified yellow COCKTAILS sign, and Berry's General Store with its stuffed wildlife. Look more closely, however, and you will see Crab Apple's vast new lodge and restaurant/lounge tucked up behind the Marshall Hotel, and Berry's (which has added an ATM) is now flanked by Appleton's (breakfast and pizza) and a slick new Dead River Outfitter Shop. Several B&Bs and the gracious new Inn by the River are within walking distance.

Empty as it seemed when rafting began, this stretch of the Upper Kennebec had been a 19th-century resort area. A now-vanished, 100-room, three-story Forks Hotel was built in the middle of The Forks in

1860, and the 120-room Lake Parlin Lodge soon followed on nearby Lake Parlin. Caratunk, The Forks, and Jackman were all railroad stops, and "rusticators" came to fish, hike, and view natural wonders like 90-foot Moxie Falls. During Prohibition the area was also known for its steady flow of liquor. A half-dozen remote sportsmen's camps on fishing ponds date from this period.

The entire 78-mile stretch of Route 201 north from Solon to the Canadian border has recently been christened The Old Canada Road Scenic Byway, one among less than 100 in the entire country. Solon, with its Greek Revival meetinghouse, old hotel, and general store, still seems a part of the long-settled valley, but Bingham (just 8 miles north) has the feel of the woodland hub it is. A couple of miles north of Bingham is the 155-foot-high hydro dam, built in the 1930s by Central Maine Power, which walls back the river, raising it more than 120 feet and creating wide, shimmering Wyman Lake. The lake gradually narrows as Route 201 follows it north and is best viewed from the rest area at its northern end. Drive slowly and carefully along this twisty road. It's frequented by both speeding lumber trucks and lumbering moose.

North of The Forks, Route 201 traverses lonely but beautiful wilderness. Wildlife abounds: More than 100 species of birds have been seen in the region, and this section of the Kennebec is the only U.S. river supporting five types of game fish. The route is known as the Arnold Trail because Benedict Arnold came this way in 1775 to Quebec City, which—it's worth noting—is just 86 miles north of Jackman.

Jackman and Moose River form a community (divided by a brief bridge) on Big Wood Lake. In warm weather you notice that something is missing here and don't realize what it is unless you revisit in winter (November through April). It's snow. Snow fills in the gaps of this shrunken old border community with its outsized French Canadian Catholic Church and matching (defunct) convent, some good restaurants, motels, and reasonably priced camps. It's also the base for exceptional canoeing and kayaking. A former rail junction, it's now a major hub of Maine's snowmobiling network. From Route 201, we urge you to branch off on Route 15/6, the lonely 31-mile road that follows the Moose River east to Moosehead Lake.

Most American (as opposed to Canadian) visitors approach this area from I-95 and follow Route 201 north through Hinckley (see L. C. Bates Museum under *To See—Museums and Historic Sights*) over the dam and past the giant wooden statue of an Indian in Skowhegan. Those who would rather shadow the Kennebec north can follow its curve through the gracious old town of Norridgewock and on up Route 201A through Anson and Emden (just across a bridge from Solon), where petroglyphs evoke a culture that dates back several thousand years (see Skowhegan Indian and Norridgewock Monument under *To See—Museums and Historic Sights*).

GUIDANCE

Upper Kennebec Valley Chamber of Commerce (672-4100), P.O. Box 491, Bingham 04920. Look for the information center on Route 201 in the middle of town.

Skowhegan Chamber of Commerce (www.skowheganchamber.com; 474-3621), P.O. Box 326, Skowhegan 04976, maintains a year-round information center on Russell Street (Route 201) in the middle of town.

Jackman–Moose River Chamber of Commerce (668-4171; www. Jackmanmaine.org) maintains a seasonal information center (with rest rooms) in Lakeside Town Park and a year-round office in downtown Jackman.

GETTING THERE

By car: The obvious route from points south and west is I-95 to exit 36, then Route 201 north all the way to The Forks. The approach from the Rangeley and Sugarloaf areas, Route 16, is a beautiful drive.

MEDICAL EMERGENCY

Bingham Area Health Center (672-4187); **regional ambulance service** (672-4410). **Jackman Region Health Center** (268-6691) is on Route 201, Jackman. **Redington-Fairview General Hospital** (474-5085) offers 24-hour emergency care (for ambulance service, dial **911**).

TO SEE

NATURAL BEAUTY SPOTS

Moxie Falls (90 feet high) is said to be the highest falls in New England. The view is striking, and well worth the detour from The Forks (see *To Do—Hiking*).

Attean View. Heading north toward Jackman from The Forks, only one rest area is clearly marked. Stop. The view is splendid: Attean Lake and the whole string of other ponds linked by the Moose River, with the western mountains as a backdrop. There are picnic tables.

MUSEUMS AND HISTORIC SIGHTS

Listed south to north

✒ **L. C. Bates Museum** (238-4250; www.gwh.org), Route 201, Hinckley. Open Wednesday–Saturday 10–4:30, Sunday 1–4:30, and by appointment. $2 adults, $1 students and children. Across the road from the Kennebec River, one in a lineup of brick buildings that are part of the campus of the Good-Will Hinckley School (founded in 1889 for "disadvantaged chidden"), this ponderous Romanesque building houses a large and wonderfully old-fashioned collection, with stuffed wildlife, paintings by noted American impressionists, and some significant Wabanaki craftsmanship, with examples ranging from several thousand years old to early-20th-century items. The annual summer art exhibit, usually incorporating work by faculty and/or students at the nearby Skowhegan School of Painting, is a bonus. The extensive grounds include nature trails.

Moxie Falls, Upper Kennebec River

Margaret Chase Smith Library Center (474-7133), 54 Norridgewock Avenue, Skowhegan. Open year-round Monday through Friday 10–4. Turn left at the first traffic light heading north out of town. Set above the Kennebec, an expanded version of Senator Smith's home, this research and conference center houses records, scrapbooks, news releases, tape recordings, and memorabilia from over three decades in Chase's public life.

Wabanaki cultural landmarks. Wabenaki heritage is particularly strong along this stretch of the Kennebec River. Your clue might be the 62-foot high **Skowhegan Indian,** billed as "the world's largest sculptured wooden Indian." He stands in the downtown parking lot, visible (and accessible) from Route 201. To seek out genuine evidence of longtime Indian habitation, however, requires some sleuthing. There are two sites, one commemorating an early-18th-century Indian mission village and the second consisting of genuine Indian petroglyphs. To find the first from Skowhegan, follow Route 201A along the Kennebec for just a few miles to Norridgewock. If you are interested only in the petroglyphs, you can remain on Route 201 into Solon.

French Jesuit Sebastian Rasle established the mission in Norridgewock, insisting that Native American lands "were given them of God, to them and their children forever." Rasle and his mission were wiped out by the English in 1724. **Norridgewock Oosoola Park** features a totem pole topped by a frog (this is a good picnic spot and boat-launch site). The site of the village itself is marked by a pleasant riverside picnic area in a pine grove.

Continue on Route 201A toward Madison across the bridge and up a steep hill. Turn left at the top of the hill onto the **Father Rasle Monument** Road (also known as Ward Hill Road); continue 3 miles.

The **petroglyphs** (pictured in the Maine State Museum) are in Emden on an arrowhead-shaped rock that juts into the Kennebec. From Route 201 in Solon turn at the sign for the Evergreens Campground. Cross the Kennebec and turn south on Route 201A; the trail to the river is just down the road; it's not marked but easy to see. If you are coming from the mission village site, continue straight ahead; the road hugs the river all the way to Solon. Also see the L. C. Bates Museum, above.

South Solon Meeting House, off Route 210, Solon. Open year-round. An 1842 Greek Revival building with murals and frescoes by WPA and Skowhegan School artists.

Jackman Moose River Historical Museum, Route 201, Jackman. Open Memorial Day through Labor Day but hours vary due to volunteer staffing. Housed in the big old (former) mansard-roofed Catholic school (you can't miss it): photographs and artifacts dating back to the early 1800s, including pictures of Captain James Jackman, for whom the town is named.

TO DO

CANOEING AND KAYAKING

The Moose River Bow Trip is a Maine classic: a series of pristine ponds form a 34-mile meandering route that winds back to the point of origin, eliminating the need for a shuttle. The fishing is fine, 21 remote campsites are scattered along the way, and the put-in is accessible. One major portage is required. Canoe rentals are available from a variety of local sources. Several rafting companies rent canoes and offer guided trips, but the kayaking specialists here are Registered Maine Guides Amy and Leslie McKendry at **Cry of the Loon Outdoor Adventures** (668-7808; www.cryoftheloon.net) in Jackman. Canoe rentals are also plentiful in Jackman.

FISHING

Fishing is what the **sporting camps** (see *Lodging*) are all about. The catch is landlocked salmon, trout, and togue. Rental boats and canoes are readily available. Camps also supply guides, and a number of them are listed on the Jackman chamber's web site (see *Guidance*).

GOLF

Moose River Golf Course (668-5331), Route 201, Moose River (just north of Jackman). Mid-May through mid-October; club rental, putting green, nine holes.

HIKING

Hiking possibilities abound in this area. The standout is **Moxie Falls,** a 90-foot waterfall considered the highest in New England, set in a dramatic gorge. It's an easy ⅔-mile walk from the trailhead (it can be very muddy and wet). Turn off Route 201 onto Moxie Road on the south side of the bridge across the Kennebec in The Forks. Park off the road at the trailhead sign on your left.

MOOSE-WATCHING

The best time to see a moose is dawn or dusk. Favorite local moose crossings include Moxie Road from The Forks to Moxie Pond; the Central Maine Power Company road from Moxie Pond to Indian Pond; the 25 miles north from The Forks to Jackman on Route 201; and the 30 miles from Jackman to Rockwood on Route 6/15. Drive these stretches carefully; residents all know someone who has died in a car-moose collision.

MOUNTAIN BIKING

Local terrain varies from old logging roads to tote paths. Rentals are available from many rafting outfitters (see below).

WHITEWATER RAFTING

See the introduction to this chapter. Wimps like us have no reason to fear the 12-mile run down the **East Branch of the Kennebec River** from Harris Dam. The only scary Class IV and V whitewater is at Magic Falls, which comes early in the trip, and after that it's all fun. We have also tried the slightly more challenging run on the **Dead River,** available less often (releases are less frequent) but offered by most outfitters. The safety records for all outfitters are excellent, or they wouldn't be in this rigorously monitored business. April through October all offer the basics: a river ride with a hearty cookout and a chance to view (and buy) slides of the day's adventures. Variables include the morning put-in time, the equipment (take only a self-bailing raft), whether you eat along the river or (frequently more comfortable) back at camp afterward, the comfort level of the lodging, and the size and nature of the group you will be rafting with. Note that some outfitters are on lakes or ponds, good for kayaking and canoeing. Most offer hot tubs. Rates run $70–80 on weekdays, $100–110 on weekends. **Raft Maine** (1-800-723-8633; www.raftmaine.com) is the group to which all outfitters belong.

✎ *Note:* Although whitewater rafting began as a big singles sport, it is becoming more and more popular with families, who frequently combine it with a visit to Quebec City. Minimum age requirements vary, but weight is also a consideration (usually no less than 90 pounds). We identify the outfitters who cater to kids and/or offer "Lower Kennebec" trips geared to children as young as 6 with our ✎ sign.

✎ **Northern Outdoors, Inc.** (663-2244; 1-800-765-7238; www. northernoutdoors.com), P.O. Box 100, The Forks 04985. Open year-round. Suzie Hockmeyer now heads up Northern Outdoors, the Kennebec's first and still its biggest outfitter. Its Outdoor Adventure Center includes an attractive open-timbered lodge with high ceilings, a huge hearth, comfortable seating, a cheerful dining room (see *Dining Out*), a bar, a pool, a private lake, platform tennis, volleyball and basketball, a sauna, and a giant hot tub. Accommodations vary from riverside camping to lakeside cabins, from lodge rooms to "logdominiums" (condo-style units with lofts and a kitchen/dining area). In addition to rafting, they offer sportyak adventures, fishing trips, rock climbing, a ropes course, canoe and kayak clinics. In winter the lodge caters to snowmobilers with snowmobile rentals and guided tours.

🖊 **Adventure Bound** (1-888-606-7238), specializing in youth groups, has its own base lodge and cabin-tent village. While Northern Outdoors still favors families with children, the atmosphere is almost peaceful since youth groups have been siphoned off into this entirely new resort.

New England Outdoor Center (723-5438; 1-800-766-7238; www. neoc.com), P.O. Box 669, Millinocket 04462. Matt Polstein's is also one of the oldest, largest, and classiest rafting operations. Lodging accom-modations include the 17-room **Sterling Inn** in Caratunk, a 19th-century stage stop that dates from 1816 and offers attractive country-inn–style guest rooms and delightful common rooms. Across the road on quiet Silver Cove (where Wyman Lake turns back into the Kennebec River and there's a good swimming beach), by the Osprey Center Base Lodge (housing a shop, changing rooms and showers, and a common area), are cabin tents and "guest houses" (sleeping up to 10 people) with a full kitchen. Amenities include an outdoor Jacuzzi, sand volleyball, a dining pavilion, and kayak rentals. The Sterling Inn charges $42 per person, breakfast included, year-round.

Wilderness Expeditions (534-2242; 1-800-825-WILD), P.O. Box 41, Rock-wood 04478. Wilderness maintains a base camp in The Forks, with a pleasant central lodge, campsites, riverside cabin tents, and cottages. Facilities include swimming pool, hot tub, and volleyball court. Meal packages are available. This is an offshoot of The Birches Resort in Rockwood, a beautifully sited, full-service resort (see *Lodging—Rustic Resorts* in "Moosehead Lake Area"); some packages combine Kennebec and Dead River rafting with stays at The Birches Resort. Wilderness also offers rooms in the Dew Drop Inn, a B&B in Caratunk across from Pleasant Pond.

🖊 **Crab Apple White Water** (663-4491; 1-800-553-RAFT), The Forks 04985. A family-owned operation that won't stop growing! Its base camp, **Crab Apple Acres** (see *Winter Sports—Cross-Country Skiing*), began with an 1830s Cape with a fanlight over the door and flowery wallpaper in the seven guest rooms. The original Cape is still there as an option, but Crab Apple long ago added a neighboring annex with luxury motel-style units (with wet bars, fridges, Jacuzzis, and decks). More of the same and a large lodge with a restaurant were added a couple of years ago. "Funyaks" (inflatable kayaks) and half-day "float trips" are also offered.

Maine Whitewater (672-4814; 1-800-345-MAIN), Gadabout Gaddis Air-port, P.O. Box 633, Bingham 04920. Jim Ernst operates the second oldest rafting company on the river, but he can claim the longest rafting

Rafting the Kennebec

experience, having begun to guide in 1968 on the Grand Canyon. His Bingham base complex includes a restaurant and lounge, game room, hot tub, private airport, llamas, bike rentals, and campground. Inquire about Jim's 12-foot airboat, which may or may not be offering tours on the Kennebec this season.

Unicorn Rafting Expeditions (668-07629; 1-800-UNICORN), Route 201, Lake Parlin 04945, has many packages for families at its Lake Parlin Resort, which offers nine lakefront cabins sleeping 4 to 10; also campsites and cabin tents. Facilities include a main lodge with fieldstone fireplace, lounge, pool table, hot tub, and heated swimming pool. Packages combining mountain biking, canoe trips, and/or "funyaking" are offered. Guided fishing expeditions, too. Lower Kennebec River trips are offered for families with children as young as age 6. Inquire about 4-day "family adventures" that include canoeing, camping, and mountain biking.

North American Whitewater Expeditions (1-800-727-4379; www. nawhitewater.com), P.O. Box 64, Route 201, West Forks 04985. The co-owners, river guides Liz Mallen and Peter Doste, have been in business since 1984, offering rafting in Connecticut's Housatonic and Vermont's West Rivers, also the Deerfield in western Massachusetts as well as the Dead and the Kennebec in Maine. Equipment is first-rate, as is the guiding and lodging in an attractive B&B right in The Forks.

Magic Falls Rafting (1-800-207-7238; www.magicfalls.com), P.O. Box 9, The Forks 04985, has a base camp that includes a pleasant B&B (12 rooms), cabin tents, and rooms in and campsites on the banks of the Dead River in The Forks. They also now own the **Marshall Hotel** (see

Eating Out)and the riverside cabins across the road on the river. In addition to rafting they offer "funyaks" (an inflatable cross between a canoe and a kayak) and rock climbing.

Windfall Rafting (668-4818; 1-800-683-2009), P.O. Box 505, Moose River 04945. Based in a classic 1890s schoolhouse in Moose River (just north of downtown Jackman), Windfall has been in business one way or another since 1982. The Blake brothers book you into the gamut of what's available in Jackman, from motel rooms through camps and campsites to splendid **Sky Lodge** (now available only to groups of 12 or more). Windfall also offers inflatable-kayak trips on the Kennebec's East Outlet.

WINTER SPORTS

CROSS-COUNTRY SKIING

Crab Apple Acres (663-4491; 1-800-553-RAFT) offers a dedicated network of cross-country trails in The Forks, and the endless network of snowmobliing trails is also good for cross-country. The **Inn by the River** (see *Other Lodging*) caters to cross-country skiers.

SNOWMOBILING

Snowmobiling is huge in this region, with more than 100 miles of Interconnecting Trail System (ITS) trails over mountains, rivers, and lakes and through woods with connections to Sugarloaf, the Moosehead area, and Canada. Rentals and guided trips are available from all the major rafting companies, also from the **Marshall Hotel** (see *Eating Out*) and the **Dead River Outfitter Shop** (see *Selective Shopping*). Check with the Jackman–Moose River Chamber of Commerce (see *Guidance*) and Sled Maine (1-877-2SLED-ME; www.sledme.com). Sled rental prices run around $150 per day single, $175 double, plus insurance.

LODGING

SPORTING CAMPS

While these camps were originally geared exclusively to fishermen, they now also welcome families and hikers.

Harrison's Pierce Pond Sporting Camps (672-3625, radiophone—let it ring and try again; if it doesn't work, call 603-279-8424; Columbus Day through May 15 call 603-524-0560), Box 315, Bingham 04920. Open May through Columbus Day. Sited on the Appalachian Trail, 20 miles from Bingham; 15 of those miles are along a dirt road. Fran and Tim Harrison have brought new life to this classic 1930s log sporting camp, set on a hillside and overlooking a stream with a waterfall in the distance. Nine-mile-long Pierce Pond is a short walk across the stream and through the woods. Five of the nine log cabins have a half bath, and there are three full-facility bathhouses on the premises. Fly-fishing is the heart of this sporting camp. Rates include three abundant meals per day (lunch is generally packed). Word has gotten out about Fran's cooking, and some people actually drive the bumpy road for Sunday turkey or Friday lobster. $65–74 per person per day, or $400–450 per week, includes all meals (based on double occupancy and a 2-night minimum); half price for children; 3-night minimum in high season; lower rates July 7 through August 6; also group rates. Guides and boat rentals available.

✎ **Cobb's Pierce Pond Camps** (628-2819 in summer; 628-3612 in winter), North New Portland 04961. There are 12 guest cabins accommodating from two to eight people; each has a screened porch, woodstove, bathroom, and electricity. Home-cooked meals and between-meal snacks are served in the main lodge. This traditional sporting camp dates from 1902, and the Cobb family has been running it for more than four decades; 90 percent of the guests are repeats. It's the kind of place that doesn't advertise. It has a loyal following among serious fishermen; sand beaches nearby. Guiding services available. $71–78 per person per day includes three meals; children's rates.

✎ **Attean Lake Lodge** (668-3792; 668-7726 in winter; www.atteanlodge.com), Jackman 04945. Open Memorial Day weekend through September. Sited on Birch Island in Attean Lake, surrounded by mountains. The resort is easily accessible from Jackman; you phone from the shore, and a boat fetches you. It has been in the Holden family since 1900; 15 log cabins, luxurious by sports-lodge standards, with full baths, Franklin fireplaces, kerosene lamps, and maid service daily. There is a relatively new central lodge (the old one burned) in which meals are served. Fishing boats, kayaks, and canoes are available. A great place for canoeing, kayaking, sailing, and hiking. $200–240 per couple includes meals; children's rates and weekly rates available.

✎ **Hardscrabble Wilderness Cabins and Sporting Lodges** (243-3010; www.hardscrabble.org), P.O. Box 459, Jackman 04945. A classic sporting camp dating from around 1900 on the north shore of remote Spencer Lake. The complex includes a handsome lodge and five fully modernized log cabins. Facilities include mountain biking, horseshoe pits, swimming, hiking, and a variety of boats (canoes are complimentary). Families are welcome, and food is a point of pride. $145 per adult per night, $50 children over 2; includes breakfast and dinner; packed lunch is available.

OTHER LODGING

Inn by the River (663-2181; www.innbytheriver.com), Route 201, HCR 63, Box 24, West Forks 04985. Open year-round. Bill and Cori Cost, longtime teachers and rafting guides, have rebuilt—from scratch when it proved impossible to save the old building—a traditional inn on a bluff above the Kennebec. It's well done. The Great Room with its fireplace and piano opens onto a porch and gardens. Guest rooms have private baths and are all nicely furnished. Trails out the back door lead up into the woods and in winter connect with much of Maine via snowmobile. You might want to reserve dinner (see *Dining Out*). There's also a pub for guests. $90–120 includes breakfast during rafting and snowmobiling season; otherwise, $65–110.

Mrs. G's Bed & Breakfast (672-4034; 1-800-672-4034 or 1-888-267-4833), Box 389, Meadow Street, Bingham 04920. A tidy house on a side street in the middle of town. Frances Gibson (Mrs. G) delights in orienting guests to the full range of local hiking, biking, rafting, and cross-country skiing possibilities. There are four cheerful guest rooms, also a delightful loft dorm room with nine beds, perfect for groups; shared baths. $32.50 per person includes a fabulous full breakfast and state tax. Canoe available.

Also see the **Sterling Inn,** run by New England Outdoor Center, under *To Do—Whitewater Rafting*. Most lodging described for the outfitters under *Whitewater Rafting* is available to nonrafters.

🐾 **Sky Lodge** (668-2171; www.skylodge.net), Route 201, Moose River 04945 (2 miles north of Jackman). Unfortunately the grand old lodge itself is now rented only to groups, but the 12 motel units across the road are available on a per-night, per-couple basis ($49–59 in winter, less in summer), as are several log cabins. Accommodates up to six people ($130–140 in winter, less in summer).

Bishop's (668-3231; 1-888-991-7669; www.bishopsmotel.com), 461 Main Street, Jackman. This spanking-new two-story motel attached to **Bishop's Store** has clean and spacious rooms and all the bells and whistles it takes for AAA to give it three diamonds.

WHERE TO EAT

DINING OUT

Lakewood Inn Restaurant (474-7176; www.lakewoodtheater.org). Open Tuesday through Saturday, Memorial Day through mid-October, for lunch and dinner. The old inn that once served the likes of Humphrey Bogart and Vincent Price and was on the verge of being razed when it was restored and reopened as an elegant restaurant—in time to celebrate the centennial year of the adjoining summer theater. The inn itself dates back to 1925 and features three fieldstone fireplaces.

Moose Point Tavern (668-4012), Jackman. Open daily in summer 5–9; otherwise, Friday, Saturday, and Sunday—but check. Built on the shore of Big Wood Lake in the 1890s as the main lodge for Henderson's Sporting Camps, now destination dining for much of this neck of the woods and operated by former rafting guide Carolann Ouellette. Entrées range from a "Big Wood" burger with fries to roast duck and curried peanut butter sauce with apples and smoky blue filet mignon ($7.25–18.25).

Inn by the River (663-2181) Route 201, West Forks. The attractive dining room and cooked-to-order dinners are open to the public. The country-inn atmosphere is more intimate than at other local options. Entrées from $8.95 (for chicken cordon bleu) to $17.95 (for haddock stuffed with shrimp). Fully licensed.

Northern Outdoors (663-4466; 1-800-765-RAFT), Route 201, The Forks. The pine-sided dining room in the lodge is open daily year-round for all three meals. Informal, with great photos of The Forks in its big-time logging and old resort days adorning the walls. There's a brewpub, and the food is good. Entrées $6–14.

✎ **Crab Apple on the Kennebec** (1-800-553-7238), Crab Apple Acres, just off Route 201, The Forks. Open daily for dinner Memorial Day through Labor Day; otherwise, Wednesday through Sunday. The large new base lodge includes both a pub and a more formal restaurant. Dinner options range from vegetable pasta Alfredo ($10.95) to prime rib and Yorkshire pudding ($16.69). Children's menu.

Harrison's Pierce Pond Sporting Camps (672-3625), Bingham. We don't want to understate the taxing trip into Harrison's (see *Lodging—Sporting Camps*), but if you happen to be spending a few days in this area and want a very special meal, it's worth the ride for the turkey dinner on Sunday, baked stuffed pork on Monday, steak teriyaki "Juline" on Tuesday, and so on. Lobster is served on Friday night. Breakfast served to Appalachian Trail hikers daily 7:30 with reservation; dinner is served promptly at 5:30, with reservations required at least 1 day in advance. Moderately priced.

EATING OUT

Listed south to north

Heritage House Restaurant (474-5100), Madison Avenue, Skowhegan. Open Tuesday through Friday for lunch and daily for dinner. Locally rated as the best place to eat.

Old Mill Pub (474-6627), 41-R Water Street, Skowhegan. Open daily for lunch and dinner. A picturesque old mill building set back from the main drag with a seasonal deck overlooking the Kennebec. A friendly bar and scattered tables; sandwiches (a good Reuben), quiche, and specials for lunch; spinach lasagna or stir-fry shrimp for dinner; early-bird specials 4–6; music Fridays.

❧ **Thompson's Restaurant** (672-3245), Route 201, Bingham. Open daily 6 AM–8:30 PM. This inviting spot remains our favorite never-fail road-food stop in the Upper Valley. It's been in business since 1929 and still has an old-fashioned look, with deep booths. The menu includes homemade doughnuts, fresh fish, and often favorites like pea soup, baked beans, and custard pie. Look for the purple awning.

Valley View Market (672-3322), Route 201, Bingham. Source of good take-out sandwiches if you are running late or want to eat by the lake.

The Marshall Hotel (663-4455), The Forks. Open for dinner most nights; live bands on weekends. A genuine old hotel with rooms still upstairs, but a better place to eat than to sleep.

Appleton's (663-2114), Route 201, The Forks. Open 6:30 AM–9 PM during rafting season. Pizzas, subs, and "breakfast burgers"; Gifford's ice cream.

Four Seasons Restaurant (668-7728), Jackman. Open 5 AM–9 PM. One big room, booths, good road food, blackboard specials.

ENTERTAINMENT

✐ **Lakewood Theater,** the Cornville Players (474-7176; www. lakewoodtheater.org), RFD 1, Box 1780, Skowhegan. Late May through mid-September. A community group performs in Maine's century-old summer theater. Broadway plays most evenings and occasional matinees; Saturday-morning children's performances.

Skowhegan Drive-in (474-9277), Route 201 South. A genuine 1950s drive-in with nightly double features "under the stars" in July and August; weekends in June.

The Skowhegan Cinema (474-3451), 7 Court Street, is another period piece, dating from the 1920s; films nightly.

SELECTIVE SHOPPING

General stores in Solon and on up through Jackman are generally the only stores, ergo community centers. Our favorite is **Berry's** in The Forks (open 6 AM–9 PM), source of fishing/hunting licenses and liquor, lunch, flannel jackets, rubber boots, and groceries as well as gas. Stuffed birds and other wildlife are scattered throughout the store, most of it shot by Gordon Berry, who has been behind the counter for 36 years. Until the rafting/snowmobiling boom hit, Berry notes, he and his parents could manage the place alone; now it takes a staff of up to 10.

Dead River Outfitter Shop (1-800-727-4379), Route 201, West Forks. A Quonset hut has been refaced in logs and filled with about every kind of clothing and equipment that might come in handy for rafting, snowmobiling, cross-country skiing, and hiking. In winter, snowmobile rentals and service as well as guided tours are offered.

SPECIAL EVENTS

June and July: During its 9-week sessions the prestigious **Skowhegan School of Painting and Sculpture** (474-9345) sponsors a lecture series on weekday evenings that's free and open to the public.

August: **Skowhegan State Fair,** one of the oldest and biggest fairs in New England—harness racing, a midway, agricultural exhibits, big-name entertainment, tractor and oxen pulls.

September: **Oosoola Fun Day,** Norridgewock, includes the state's oldest frog-jumping contest (up to 300 contestants) around a frog-topped totem pole; also canoe races, crafts fair, flower and pet contests, live music, barbecue. **Fly-in,** Gadabout Gaddis Airport, Bingham. **Annual Fall Festival,** Jackman *(late September).*

November: **Annual Hunter's Supper,** Jackman.

VII. NORTHERN MAINE

The North Woods
Moosehead Lake Area
Katahdin Region, Including Lower Piscataquis
Bangor Area
Aroostook County

Driving the logging roads of Aroostook County

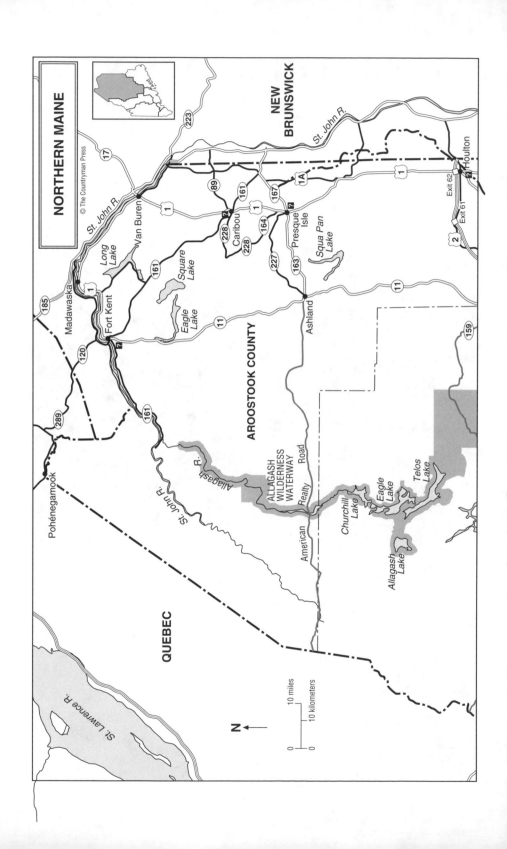

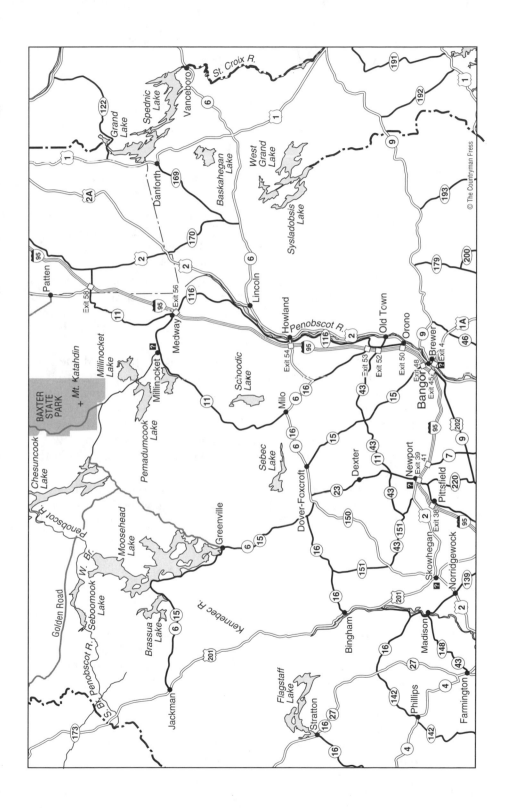

© The Countryman Press

The North Woods

Like "Down East," Maine's "North Woods" may seem a bit of a mirage, always over the next hill. In fact, 17.6 of Maine's 22 million acres are forested, and much of that woodland lies in what we've described in this book as the "Western Mountains and Lakes Region."

Still, one particular tract of forest tends to be equated—mostly by out-of-staters—with the North Woods. That section is the 6.5 million acres bordered to the north and west by Canada, which on highway maps shows no roads. This is the largest stretch of unpeopled woodland in the East, but wilderness it's not.

Private ownership of this sector, technically part of Maine's 10.5 million acres known as the unorganized townships, dates from the 1820s when Maine was securing independence from Massachusetts. The mother state, her coffers at their usual low, stipulated that an even division of all previously undeeded wilderness be part of the separation agreement. The woods were quickly sold by the legislature for 12½   to 38 cents per acre, bought cooperatively by groups to cut individual losses.

The vast inland tracts, mostly softwood, increased in value in the 1840s when the process of making paper from wood fibers was rediscovered. It seems that the method first used in A.D. 105 had been forgotten, and New England paper mills were using rags at the time.

By the turn of the century pulp and paper mills had moved to their softwood source and assumed management responsibility and taxes for most of the unorganized townships. Mergers and sales have fragmented the ownership of the North Woods considerably in recent years, and much of the land is now owned by out-of-state companies. North Maine Woods, Inc., a consortium of more than 20 landowners, now pays the lion's share of the area's land tax and the cost of maintaining thousands of miles of private gravel roads, the ones not shown on the state highway maps but open to visitors who pay a fee and promise to abide by the rules (rule number one: Drive slowly and pull over to permit logging trucks to pass).

Recent years have seen an increase in selling off the forestland, sometimes to developers rather than to those involved in the paper industry. In the last two years alone the ownership of over 5 million acres was transferred, often to several different owners. This results in fragmented forests, with high potential for overdevelopment, especially as the paper industry wanes and the demand for outdoor recreation areas is rising. This isn't to say that the forests aren't being used for industry, however. Some of the largest landowners remain Great Northern Paper/Bowater in the areas surrounding Millinocket, and other timber and woodlands management companies from Chesuncook west to Quebec as well as to the south. The out-of-state ownership and shifting focus have conservationists ready for action.

Though recent projects have protected close to 2 million acres, the conservationists have just begun. Restore: The North Woods is a grassroots organization working to create a North Woods national park, an idea that has met with great disagreement throughout the state. Opponents fear what creating a national park (and therefore bringing under federal control a large portion of northern Maine) will do to the lifestyle in that region. Proponents fear the alternative. Another idea being tossed into the mix is that of a state park, an idea that seems to be quietly gaining support among environmental agencies.

Whatever the result, this is an issue that will only gain more attention in coming years. At the moment there are two North Woods preserves that have been set aside to provide a wilderness experience to the general public. These are 200,000-acre Baxter State Park and the 92-mile ribbon of lakes, ponds, rivers, and streams designated the Allagash Wilderness Waterway. Yet even the Allagash has stirred controversy in the past year. Amid pressure from sportsmen's groups, the Department of Conservation plans to open up more vehicle access along the waterway, despite strong opposition to this plan. Baxter, on the other hand, is simply strained by the wave of visitors who arrive each year seeking a wilderness experience.

Already the private roads have multiplied since the end of log drives in the 1970s and changed the look and nature of the North Woods. Many remote sporting camps, for a century accessible only by water, and more recently by air, are now a bumpy ride from the nearest town.

Many of the sporting camps themselves haven't changed since the turn of the 20th century. Some have hardly altered since the 1860s, the era when wealthy "sports" first began arriving in Greenville by train from New York and Boston, to be met by Native American guides. The genuine old camps are Maine's inland windjammers: unique holdovers from another era. Many simply cater to descendants of their original patrons.

There are three major approaches to this "North Woods." The longest, most scenic route is up the Kennebec River, stopping to raft in The Forks (see listings under *To Do—Whitewater Rafting* in "The Upper Kennebec Valley and Moose River Valley"), and along the Moose River to the village of Rockwood at the dramatic narrows of Moosehead Lake, then down along the lake to Greenville, New England's largest seaplane base. (You can, of course, also drive directly to Greenville, exiting from I-95 at Newport.)

From Greenville, you can hop a floatplane to a sporting camp or set off up the eastern shore of Moosehead to the woodland outpost of Kokadjo and on to the Golden Road, a 96-mile private logging road running east from Quebec through uninterrupted forest to Millinocket. As Thoreau did in the 1850s, you can canoe up magnificent Chesuncook Lake, camping or staying in the tiny old outpost of Chesuncook Village. With increased interest in rafting down the West Branch of the Penobscot River through Ripogenus Gorge and the Cribworks, this stretch of the Golden Road has become known as the West Branch region.

For those who come this distance simply to climb Mount Katahdin and to camp in Baxter State Park, the quickest route is up I-95 to Medway and in through Millinocket; it's 18 miles to the Togue Pond Gatehouse and Baxter State Park.

Northern reaches of Baxter State Park and the lakes beyond are best accessed from the park's northern entrance via Patten. Both Ashland and Portage are also points of entry, and Shin Pond serves as the seaplane base for this northernmost reach of the North Woods.

GUIDANCE

North Maine Woods (435-6213; www.northmainewoods.com), Box 421, Ashland 04732, is a consortium of more than 20 major landowners that manages the recreational use of more than 3 million acres of commercial forest in northwestern Maine. It publishes map/guides that show logging roads and campsites, as well as a canoeist's guide to the St. John River, a pamphlet about the organization that tells a bit of history and details the regulations and fees, and a list of outfitters and camps that are licensed and insured to operate on the property.

Maine Sporting Camp Association, P.O. Box 89, Jay 04239, publishes a booklet guide to its members. See *Sporting Camps* in "What's Where in Maine."

Moosehead Lake Area

As Route 15 crests Indian Hill, you see for a moment what Henry David Thoreau described so well from this spot in 1858: "A suitably wild looking sheet of water, sprinkled with low islands . . . covered with shaggy spruce and other wild wood."

Moosehead is Maine's largest lake, 40 miles long with more than 400 miles of shoreline, much of it owned by lumber companies. Greenville is the sole "organized" town.

Around the turn of the century you could board a Pullman car in New York City and ride straight through to Greenville, there to board a steamer for the Mount Kineo House, a (long-gone) palatial summer hotel on an island halfway up the lake. Greenville began as a farm town, but it soon discovered its best crops to be winter lumbering and summer tourists—a group that, since train service and grand hotels have vanished, now consists largely of fishermen, canoeists, whitewater rafters, and hunters, augmented in winter by snowmobilers, cross-country skiers, ice fishermen—and moose-watchers.

Unlike 1890s "sports" (the game hunters and trophy fishermen who put Moosehead Lake on the world's resort map), many current outdoors enthusiasts want to watch—not kill—wildlife and to experience "wilderness" completely but quickly; that is, by plunging through whitewater in a rubber raft, pedaling a mountain bike over woods trails, or paddling an hour or two in Thoreau's trail or in search of a moose.

Moosehead has become Maine's moose mecca. Experts debate whether the name of the lake stems from its shape or from the number of moose you can see there. In 1992 the Moosehead Lake Region Chamber of Commerce launched Moosemainea, an off-season (mid-May through mid-June) festival that courts Moosemaniacs with a series of special events. Moose sightings during that month now average 3,500.

Immense and backed by mountains, Moosehead Lake possesses unusual beauty and offers a family a wide choice of rustic, old-fashioned "camps" at reasonable prices and an increasing number of attractive, even "romantic" rooms in inns and B&Bs. The town remains a lumbermen's depot with a salting of upscale, offbeat shops. Greenville, New England's largest seaplane base, has three competing flying services ready to ferry visitors to remote camps and campsites in the working woodland to the north and east.

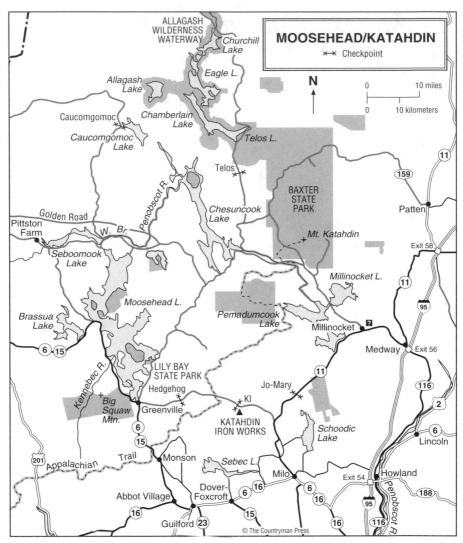

The community of Rockwood, a half-hour drive north of Greenville on the lake's west shore, is even more of an outpost: a cluster of sporting camps and stores between the lake and the Moose River. Hidden away here on the lake, overlooking Kineo, is the lake's leading resort, The Birches. An authentic old sporting camp with traditional lakeside cottages, it's set in 11,000 acres stretching back to Brassua Lake.

Rockwood sits at the lake's narrows, across from its most dramatic landmark: the sheer cliff face of Mount Kineo, a place revered by Native Americans. According to local legend, the mountain is the petrified remains of a monster moose sent to Earth by the Great Spirit as a punishment for sins. It was also the Native Americans' source of a flintlike stone used for arrowheads. The Mount Kineo House once stood at the foot of this outcropping. First opened as a tavern in 1847, it evolved by 1884 into one of the largest hotels in America, accommodating 500 guests and maintaining its own farm as well as a golf course, yacht club, and stables.

Then came World War I, followed by the Great Depression. The hotel burned in 1938. Its annex has also recently vanished, leaving just a ghostly staff building, a huge elm tree, and a row of shingled Victorian-style summer homes, many of which are available as private rentals. Kineo is an islandlike peninsula, most of it now owned by the state, and the climb to the abrupt summit is one of the most rewarding hikes in all of New England.

Most Greenville visitors explore Moosehead's eastern shore at least as far as Lily Bay State Park, and many continue to the outpost village of Kokadjo (population: not many), prime moose-watching country. It's another 40 miles northeast over paper company roads to Chesuncook Lake and to Ripogenus Dam, from which logging roads lead north into the Allagash and east to Baxter State Park and Millinocket. We also strongly suggest driving or flying up to Pittston Farm to sample the fare and feel of a genuine lumber camp and driving—better yet skiing or dogsledding—to Little Lyford Pond Camps and on into Gulf Hagas, a gorgeous stretch of the Appalachian Trail.

GUIDANCE

Moosehead Lake Region Chamber of Commerce (695-2702 or 695-2026; www.mooseheadarea.com), P.O. Box 581, Greenville 04441. A four-season resource. The walk-in information center up on Indian Hill (Route 15 south of town) is open daily in summer; 6 days a week from October through May.

Moosehead Vacation and Sportsmen's Association (534-7300), P.O. Box 366, Rockwood 04478, is a source of year-round information about the Rockwood area.

GETTING THERE

By air: **Folsom's Air Service** (see *Getting Around*) offers charter service to Bangor, Augusta, and Portland.

By car: From points south, take the Maine Turnpike to exit 39 (Newport). Proceed up Route 7 to Dexter, continue north on Route 23 to Sangerville (Guilford), then up Route 15 to Greenville. Note the longer, more scenic route up through The Forks and Jackman to Rockwood described in the introduction to "The Upper Kennebec Valley and Moose River Valley."

GETTING AROUND

By air: **Folsom's Air Service** (695-2821), Greenville. Billed as "Maine's largest seaplane operator," founded by Dick Folsom in 1946, now headed by his son Max. Until recently Folsom's radiophone was the only link with the outside world for many camps. Inquire about "Float-plane Adventures," ranging from 15-minute flights ($20 per person) to hour-long moose watches ($60 per person), and "Fly 'n' Dine" packages at remote Pittston Farm and Northern Pride Lodge, Folsom's will also taxi you to a wilderness lake for a day of fishing, canoeing, or hiking ($50–100 per person).

Currier's Flying Service (695-2778), Greenville Junction, offers day trips; scenic flights, including Allagash, Mount Katahdin, Mount Kineo, and others; and service to camps. They will book camps and guides or set up guided backcountry, cross-country ski trips.

Jack's Flying Service (695-3020) caters to Allagash canoe trips, offers fly-in to housekeeping cottages , and sight-seeing flights.

By boat: The **Kineo Shuttle** (534-8812) from Rockwood runs in summer (every hour, 8 AM–5 PM), transporting visitors to the golf course and hiking trails. **Rockwood Cottages** (534-7725) also runs a shuttle, especially useful after 5 PM.

By car: If you plan to venture out on the network of private roads maintained by the lumber companies, be forewarned that it may be expensive, in terms of both gate fees and damage to your car's suspension. You need a car with high clearance, and preferably four-wheel drive.

MEDICAL EMERGENCY

Charles A. Dean Memorial Hospital and ambulance service (695-2223), Prithan Avenue, Greenville. Emergency aid is also available from **Maine State Police Headquarters** (1-800-452-4664).

TO SEE

Moosehead Marine Museum (695-2716; www.katahdincruises.com), P.O. Box 1151, Greenville. Home for the S/S *Katahdin*, a restored vintage-1914 steamboat that cruises daily July through Labor Day, weekends Memorial Day through late September. Three- and six-hour cruises offered. Private charters available. One of 50 steamboats on the lake at its height as a resort destination, the *Katahdin* was the last to survive, converted to diesel in 1922 and in the 1930s modified to haul booms of logs, something we can remember her doing in 1976, the year of the nation's last log drive. This graceful 115-foot, 150-passenger boat was restored through volunteer effort and relaunched in 1985. The museum's displays depict the lake's resort history from 1836.

Eveleth-Crafts-Sheridan House (695-2909), Main Street, Greenville. Guided tours offered June through early September, Wednesday through Friday 1–4. $2 adults, $1 children. Home of the **Moosehead Historical Society,** a genuinely interesting 19th-century home, with displays on the region's history, including early hotels and steamboats, a lumbering exhibit, and changing exhibits on the "sunporch."

SCENIC DRIVES

Along the western shore

Follow **Route 6/15** north through Greenville Junction. If **Squaw Mountain's** chairlifts are running (see *To Do*), the ride is well worth taking for the views. Continue to **Rockwood** and take the shuttle (see *Getting Around*) to **Mount Kineo;** allow the better part of a day for exploring this dramatic spot (see *To Do—Hiking*). From Rockwood, you can continue north for 20 miles to the North Maine Woods checkpoint (gate fee for out-of-staters). **Pittston Farm,** a short distance beyond, was once the hub of Great Northern's operations for this entire western swath of North Woods. It's now a lodge known for lumber-camp-style cooking (see *Eating Out*). Note that from Rockwood you can also continue on to Quebec City (via Jackman).

Along the eastern shore

Lily Bay State Park (695-2700), 8 miles north of Greenville, offers a sandy beach, a grassy picnicking area, and camping.

Kokadjo, 18 miles north of Greenville, is a 100-acre parcel of independently owned land on First Roach Pond, in the center of lumber-company-owned forest. Most of the buildings here were once part of a lumbering station and are now camps attached to the **Kokadjo Trading Post** (see *Eating Out*); **Northern Pride Lodge** (see *Lodging—Inns*) rents canoes and boats. Continuing north, the road turns to dirt and is fairly bumpy for the first few miles. The road surface improves when you pass the (now-unstaffed) gate entering paper-company land, and is fairly smooth (but you must now pull over to let lumber trucks pass); it improves even more in a dozen miles when you hit the **Golden Road** (see the introduction to "The North Woods"), where you turn right (east).

Cushing's Landing, at the foot of Chesuncook Lake, is worth a stop. The woodsman's memorial here was created from a post in the doorway of a Bangor tavern; it is decorated with tools of the trade and an iron bean pot. This is also the logical boat launch for visiting **Chesuncook Village,** one of the few surviving examples of a 19th-century North Woods lumbermen's village, now on the National Register of Historic Places. In summer, access is by charter aircraft from Greenville or by boat from Chesuncook Dam. In winter you can come by snowmobile. Writing about the village in 1853, Henry David Thoreau noted, "Here immigration is a tide which may ebb when it has swept away the pines." Today a church, a graveyard (relocated from the shore to a hollow in the woods when Great Northern raised the level of the lake a few years ago), an inn, and a huddle of houses are all that remain of the village (see **Chesuncook Lake House** under *Lodging—Inns*).

Ripogenus Dam, just east of Chesuncook Lake, is the departure point for a number of whitewater rafting expeditions (see *To Do—Whitewater Rafting and Kayaking*). This is one of the two major centers for whitewater rafting in Maine—the other is The Forks (see listings under *To Do—Whitewater Rafting* in "The Upper Kennebec Valley and Moose River Valley"). Beginning at the dam, the West Branch of the Penobscot drops more than 70 feet per mile—seething and roiling through Ripogenus Gorge—and continues another 12 miles, with stretches of relatively calm water punctuated by steep drops. You can get a view of the gorge by driving across the dam. **Pray's Store** (723-8880), a short distance from the dam, is open year-round and sells most things you might need.

The **Telos Road** leads to the **Allagash Wilderness Waterway,** a 92-mile-long chain of lakes, ponds, rivers, and streams that snakes through the heart of the North Woods. The traditional canoe trip through the Allagash takes 10 days, but 2- and 3-day trips can be worked out. Brook trout, togue, and lake whitefish are plentiful. For details, see *Canoeing the Allagash* in "What's Where in Maine," and *To Do—Canoe and Kayak Rentals* and *Trips,* below.

TO DO

AIRPLANE RIDES

See descriptions of scenic flights offered by flying services under *Getting Around.*

BOAT EXCURSIONS

See **S/S *Katahdin*** at the Moosehead Marine Museum under *To See.*

A variety of outfitters in the area offer excursions, including **The Birches Resort** and **Evergreen Lodge Bed and Breakfast,** which offer pontoon-boat cruises (see *Moose-Watching*). Check with the chamber of commerce (see *Guidance*) for current options.

Also see *Canoe and Kayak Rentals* and *Trips* for guided excursions, and *Fishing* for guided fishing trips.

CANOE AND KAYAK RENTALS

Northwoods Outfitters (695-3288; www.maineoutfitter.com), Main Street, Greenville, is a full-service outfitter. They rent Old Town canoes and Hydra kayaks; guided moose safaris and other guide service available.

Moose River Landing (534-2897) and **Rockwood Cottages** (534-7725) rent canoes, kayaks, and motorboats.

Song in the Woods (876-4736), Abbot, offers canoe adventures, from half-day tours to 4 or more days.

Note: Most sporting camps also rent canoes or kayaks, and all the flying services will ferry canoes into remote backcountry (see *Getting Around*).

CANOE AND KAYAK TRIPS

✐ **Allagash Canoe Trips** (695-3668), Greenville. A family business since 1953, offering professional guides and top equipment. Weeklong expeditions into the Allagash Wilderness Waterway, on the West Branch of the Penobscot, and on the St. John River. Also special teen trips.

Wilderness Expeditions (534-2242/7305; 1-800-825-WILD), P.O. Box 41, Rockwood 04478. Based at The Birches Resort, offering a variety of guided kayak trips, including a 3-day/2-night tour up Moosehead Lake that retraces Thoreau's exact canoe route north from Greenville to Northeast Carry (35 miles).

Moosehead Adventures (695-4434), Greenville. Registered Maine Guides Edie and Darrell Miles and Eric Sherman offer guided kayak tours (novices welcome) on Moosehead Lake, ranging from 3 hours to overnight.

CHAIRLIFT RIDES

🌂 **Chair Lift Ride at Big Squaw Mountain Resort** (695-1000), Route 6/15 between Greenville and Rockwood; generally weekends in summer and fall, but call ahead. Spectacular view of lake and mountains.

FISHING

Troll for landlocked salmon and brook trout in Moosehead Lake, and fly-fish in the many rivers and ponds—rental boats and boat launches are so plentiful that they defy listing.

There are two prime sources of fishing information: the **Inland Fisheries and Wildlife** office (695-3756), Greenville, and the **Maine Guide Fly Shop and Guide Service** (695-2266), Main Street, Greenville. At the Fly Shop, Dan Legere sells 314 different flies and a wide assortment of gear; he also works with local guides to outfit you with a boat and guide or to set up a river float trip or a fly-in expedition. The resurgence of fly-fishing as a popular sport is reflected in the variety of gear and guides available in this shop. Deep lake trolling is, however, also popular, and Chris DiPala of **Mt. Kineo Guide Service** (534-7743), with a 25-foot Sea Ray equipped with numerous rods, reels, sonar, and digital down-riggers, can guarantee a catch, even midday in mid-August. For a list of local boat rentals as well as a list of local guides, check with the **Moosehead Lake Area Chamber of Commerce** (see *Guidance*). Also see listings under *Lodgings—Rustic Resorts,* all of which are on water and cater to fishermen.

Ice fishing begins January 1 and ends March 30. Icehouse rentals are available locally. Inquire at the chamber.

GOLF

Mount Kineo Golf Course (534-8812) . A spectacularly sited nine-hole course at Kineo, accessible by frequent boat service from Rockwood; carts and club rentals.

Big Squaw Mountain Resort on Moosehead Lake (695-3609), Route 15, Greenville. A nine-hole course with lounge and restaurant.

HIKING

There are two stellar, not-to-be-missed hikes in this area.

Mount Kineo, an islandlike peninsula, has trails to the back side of the famous cliff that rises 763 feet above the water and the apron of land once occupied by the Kineo House resort. Most of the island (8,000 acres) is now state owned, and trails along its circumference and up the back of the cliff are maintained. Take the **Indian Trail,** which heads straight up over ledges that are a distinct green: This is one of the world's

TIMOTHY ELLIS, JR.

Gulf Hagas

largest masses of rhyolite, a flintlike volcanic rock. This trail is shaded by red pines, oaks, and a surprising variety of hardwoods. The view down the lake from the fire tower is spectacular. **The Bridle Trail** is easier for the descent, and a good option on the way up for small children. A carriage trail also circles the island, which is accessible from Rockwood by frequent water shuttle (see *Getting Around*). Bring a picnic or lunch at the Kineo House.

Gulf Hagas, billed as the "Grand Canyon of Maine," is just 15 miles east of Greenville via the airport road (see *To Do—Hiking* under "Katahdin Region" for details). In winter this is the far more accessible approach and a fabulous adventure (see *Winter Sports—Dogsledding* and Little Lyford Pond Camps under *Lodging—Rustic Resorts*).

Other good hikes include:

Borestone Mountain Sanctuary, 10 miles out the Eliotsville Road from Route 6/15 at Monson. A good hike for families. At Sunrise Pond, halfway up the 3-mile trail, there's an information center (open June 1 through October 1, 8 AM–dusk) maintained by the National Audubon Society. At the summit, the 360-degree view is quite a sight.

Check local sources for details about hiking **Little** and **Big Spencer Mountains** and **Elephant Mountain,** and walking into **Little Wilson Falls,** a majestic 57-foot cascade in a forested setting.

Song in the Woods (876-4736), P.O. Box 127, Abbott 04406, offers hiking adventures from half-day tours to 4 or more days.

HORSEBACK RIDING AND WAGON RIDES

Northern Maine Riding Adventures (564-3451/2965), P.O. Box 16, Dover-Foxcroft. Judy Cross-Strehlke and Bob Flury-Strehlke, Registered Maine Guides and skilled equestrians, offer 1-hour trail rides, centered-riding clinics, and day trips from their four-season facility; also overnight treks based at their camp in the backwoods around Katahdin Ironworks. Special-needs riders are welcome.

Rockies Golden Acres (695-3229), Greenville, offers 1½- to 2-hour trail rides through the woods to Sawyer Pond; mountain views. Call after 7 PM, or leave a message.

MOOSE-WATCHING

"Moosemainea," sponsored by the Moosehead Lake Chamber of Commerce mid-May through mid-June, is the largest, most colorful moose-watching event in New England; but chances are you can spot the lake's mascot any dawn or dusk, especially if you go on a guided moose-watching tour.

Greenville's three flying services offer moose-watching both strictly from the air and by flying into prime spots (see *Getting Around*).

Moose Cruises aboard pontoon boats are offered mornings and evenings both by the **The Birches Resort** (534-7305) and **Evergreen Lodge Bed and Breakfast** (695-3241; 1-888-624-3993).

Bullwinkle's Guide Service (695-4338), **Northwoods Outfitters** (695-3288), and **Moose Country Safaris and Dogsled Trips** (876-4907) offer early-morning and evening moose cruises using vehicles and canoes.

MOUNTAIN BIKING

Northwoods Outfitters (695-3288), Main Street, Greenville, rents bikes and has trail information available.

The Birches Resort (534-7305; 1-800-825-WILD), Rockwood, offers mountain bike rentals for use on its extensive cross-country ski network.

Northern Pride Lodge (695-2890) in Kokadjo also rents mountain bikes by the half day and day.

RECREATIONAL FACILITY

Greenville Athletic Complex. A new, large complex that includes a variety of recreational options: an outdoor rink for skateboarding/roller hockey in summer, ice hockey in winter; a ¼-mile, 8-foot-wide paved in-line skating track; sand volleyball court, a ¼-mile running track, outdoor tennis courts, a basketball court, ball fields, and a creative playground for little ones.

SCUBA DIVING

Diving to the wrecks in Moosehead is an increasingly popular activity in the area. **All Resource Divers** (1-800-828-1102) can outfit you and give tips on area diving.

SPECIAL LEARNING PROGRAMS

Maine Journeys (285-3332), 113 Christian Hill Road, Charleston, offers workshops at their homestead in making wood-and-canvas canoes, brown ash baskets, maple toboggans, mukluks (winter moccasins), and corroked knives (these are all-purpose wood-carving tools). The two-day to week-long courses are for individuals or small groups, for all ages,

and are taught in the workshop attached to the homestead. Meals are
included, as is indoor sleeping bag space, and most materials. They also
offer guided wilderness canoe trips and handcrafted products for sale.

SWIMMING

See **Lily Bay State Park** under *To See—Scenic Drives*.

Red Cross swimming beach, halfway between Greenville Village and the
Junction, is a good beach on the lake, with lifeguards.

WHITEWATER RAFTING AND KAYAKING

Moosehead Lake is equidistant from Maine's two most popular rafting
routes—Kennebec Gorge and Ripogenus Gorge. **Wilderness Expeditions** (534-2242; 1-800-825-WILD), P.O. Box 41, Rockwood 04478,
based at The Birches Resort in Rockwood (see *Lodging—Rustic Resorts*), is a family-run business specializing in half-day whitewater rafting trips on the Kennebec at East Outlet (minimum age is 7); also longer
expeditions on the Kennebec from a base camp in The Forks and on
the Penobscot from another base near Baxter State Park. Also see the
entries under *To Do—Whitewater Rafting* in "The Upper Kennebec
Valley and the Moose River Valley" and "Katahdin Region" chapters.

WINTER SPORTS

Northwoods Outfitters (695-3288) is a full-service retail shop, selling and
renting cross-country and downhill skis, snowboards, snowshoes; offers
a list of trails good for exploring.

DOGSLEDDING

Song in the Woods (876-4736), Abbot 04406. Stephen Medera and his
team of huskies offer not only sled rides but also short (from $15 for a
half hour) to full-day trips on which you actually do the driving. After
the first tangle around a tree, we were amazed at how smoothly the
dogs responded to our commands on the 10-mile woods road (it's much
smoother in winter than summer) into Little Lyford Pond Camps (see
Lodging—Rustic Resorts). Inquire about moonlight rides and inn-to-
inn multiday adventures.

Moose Country Safaris and Dogsled Trips (876-4907) is the musher for
the Lodge at Moosehead Lake (see *Lodging—Inns*).

CROSS-COUNTRY SKIING

Formal touring centers aside, this region's vast network of snowmobile trails
and frozen lakes constitutes splendid opportunities for backcountry skiing. We've skied from the cabins at Chesuncook Lake House and Northern Pride Lodge in Kokadjo (see *Lodging—Inns*), which are all open in
winter for cross-country skiers as well as snowmobilers.

✐ **A Fierce Chase** (997-3971), Elliotsville Road, Monson. Open weekends
and school vacations 8 AM to sunset. Ten km of cross-country ski trails for
both classical and skate skiing. Ski rentals and lessons available. Trail fees
$7 adults, $5 students (9–18), children ages 8 and under free.

Birches Ski Touring Center (534-7305), Rockwood. The Birches Resort maintains an extensive network of trails, taking advantage of an 11,000-acre forested spread across the neck between Brassua and Moosehead Lakes. You can ski to Tomhegan, 10 miles up the lake, or out past the ice-fishing shanties to Kineo. Rentals and instruction; snowshoes, too.

Little Lyford Pond Camps (see *Lodging—Rustic Resorts*) offers a network of groomed trails connecting with backcountry trails, including the Appalachian Trail and leading into Gulf Hagas.

Chesuncook Lake House and **Medawisla** (see *Lodging—Inns*) also cater to cross-country skiers.

DOWNHILL SKIING

Big Squaw Mountain Resort (695-1000), Route 15, Greenville. Though the state is changing the mountain's name to Moose Mountain, the resort has elected to keep the name it has always had. A ski resort since 1963, with one of New England's first base-area hotels, owned by Scott Paper (1970–1974) and then sold to the state, under whose ownership it languished for 11 years. It has had its ups and downs under private ownership since. Even in summer you are struck by the small number of trails streaking such a big mountain: just 22 trails, but with a 1,750-foot drop. Skiers have terrific views of Moosehead Lake and Mount Katahdin. Lifts include a double chair, a triple chair, a T-bar, and a pony lift. Other facilities include a base lodge and cafeteria, ski school, ski shop, and lodging in 54 rooms. Weekend lift tickets: $24 adults; $18 students and seniors. All ages $15 midweek. On-mountain motel-style rooms begin at $49 per couple midweek ($5 per extra person).

SNOWMOBILING

Snowmobiling is huge in this area. The chamber of commerce (see *Guidance*) publishes and sells a map of area snowmobile trails, which also offers information on area businesses catering to snowmobilers. Their winter 1999–2000 issue of "Moosehead Snowline" lists eight separate snowmobile clubs in the area. **Moosehead Riders Snowmobile Club** proudly proclaims the area the "hub" of snowmobiling and offers a 24-hour trail-condition report (695-4561). Its clubhouse is open Saturday and Sunday in winter. The club also sponsors guided tours. Interconnecting Trail System (ITS) routes 85, 86, and 87 run directly through the area, and there are many locally groomed trails as well. The Moosehead trail goes around the lake, avoiding formerly dangerous ice-out situations. Route 66 is a trail that runs east to west from Kokadjo to Jackman. Snowmobile rentals are available from **Evergreen Lodge Bed and Breakfast** (1-888-624-3993) in Greenville, **Kokadjo Trading Post** (695-3993) in Kokadjo, **Greenwood Motel** (695-3321) in Greenville Junction, and **The Birches Resort** (1-800-825-9453) and **Old Mill Cabins** (534-7333) in Rockwood. Inquire about guided tours.

LODGING

INNS

 ♿ **Greenville Inn** (695-2206; 1-888-695-6000; www.greenvilleinn.com), Norris Street, Box 1194, Greenville 04441. Open all year (B&B November through May). A true lumber baron's mansion set atop a hill just off Main Street, with a sweeping view of Moosehead Lake. Rich cherry, mahogany, and oak paneling, embossed walls, working fireplaces, and an immense leaded-glass window depicting a single spruce tree—all contribute to the sense of elegance. There are four second-floor rooms plus a Master Suite, with a fireplace, original fixtures in the bathroom, and a view; a more rustic suite is in the carriage house (ideal for families). Six cottages offer private baths, TV, and mountain views. The dining room, open to the public, is considered the best in northwestern Maine (see *Dining Out*). Your hosts are Elfi and Susie Schnetzer. $135–165 for rooms in-season (includes European breakfast buffet); $145–175 cottages, $175–235 suites; less mid-October through late May; $20 per extra person.

 ♿ **The Lodge at Moosehead Lake** (695-4400; www.lodgeatmooseheadlake. com), Box 1175, Lily Bay Road, Greenville 04441. Closed early November through Christmas, and mid-March through mid-May. Jennifer and Roger Cauchi have transformed a vintage-1916 hunting lodge into a phenomenon. Each of the 11 guest rooms (4 with lake views) has been designed with immense care around a theme. Spectacular carved four-poster beds depict each theme (moose, bear, loon, totem). All rooms have cable TV, gas fireplaces, and baths with Jacuzzi tubs. A carriage house holds three more luxurious suites. Roger delights in playing concierge, arranging fishing, hiking, or rafting trips, and whatever else guests may desire. Common areas are comfortable and vast, including a downstairs billiards room, where a puzzle is always in progress. A full breakfast is served in the glass-walled dining room, and dinner is also available to guests some evenings (ask when you book). $175–395 double occupancy includes breakfast.

 ✎ **Northern Pride Lodge** (695-2890), HCR 76, Box 588, Kokadjo 04441. Open year-round. Built as a hunting lodge for lumber baron Sir Harry Oaks, now a friendly lodge with five guest rooms, each with enough beds for a family or group; shared baths. The living room has a hearth, stained-glass windows, and a sense of opulence; the dining room, on a glassed-in porch overlooking First Roach Pond, is open to the public by reservation. There are also 24 campsites, rental canoes, motorboats, moose-watching trips, and mountain bikes. In winter the lodge caters to snowmobilers and cross-country skiers. $80 per couple May through November; $70 per couple December through April (includes breakfast). $59 per night for single; rates with all three meals are also offered.

Chesuncook Lake House (745-5330), Box 656, Route 76, Greenville

04441. Open year-round. An unpretentious 1864 farmhouse built on the site of an older log cabin that served as the center for the lumbering camp (see Chesuncook Village under *To See—Scenic Drives*). New owners David and Luisa Surprenant are carrying on a long-standing tradition of hospitality with four guest rooms (shared bath). Guests can be shuttled in by boat or snowmobile, or hike, fly, or canoe in. This is a peaceful, magical spot. $110 person per night includes all three meals.

BED & BREAKFASTS

The Blair Hill Inn (695-0224; www.blairhillinn.com), Lily Bay Road, P.O. Box 1288, Greenville 04441. Set high above Moosehead Lake at the top of Blair Hill, this is an expansive Victorian mansion (vintage 1891) that has been restored to its original granduer (with the discreet addition of modern conveniences) by Dan and Ruth McLaughlin. The eight rooms all have private baths with custom-made bath products; four have wood-burning fireplaces. Our favorite is a less expensive room on the third floor with three lake-filled windows. There's wicker and a hot tub on the 90-foot veranda (overlooking the lake), where wine is served from the well-stocked wine cellar, and a feel of unstuffy luxury throughout. $200–300 includes a full breakfast.

Lakeview B&B (695-2229; www.lakeview.com), P.O. Box 1102, Greenville 04441. A modern home high on the hill west of town, with splendid views over meadows to the lake. There's a ground-level suite with a sitting room, and two rooms with king-sized beds, private baths, air-conditioning, and TV. Ruth and Dick Files are longtime local residents who enjoy sharing their knowledge of the area. $75–125.

RUSTIC RESORTS (TRADITIONAL SPORTING CAMPS)

The Birches Resort (534-7305/2241; 1-800-825-WILD; www.birches. com), P.O. Box 41, Rockwood 04478. Open year-round. The Willards have turned this 1930s sporting camp into one of the most comfortable and satisfying family-geared resorts in Maine. It's sited in a birch grove overlooking Mount Kineo. Sixteen hand-hewn log cabins are strung along the lake, each with a porch, a Franklin stove or fireplace in a sitting room, and one to three bedrooms. All of the cabins have kitchens (some don't have ovens), but three meals are available in summer. The main lodge includes a cheerful open-timbered dining room (see *Dining Out*), an inviting lobby with a trout pool, and a living room with hearth room. Upstairs are four guest rooms with decks overlooking the lake (shared bath); there are also "cabin tents" near the lodge and several yurts scattered throughout the resort's 11,000 acres. Facilities include an outside hot tub and sauna; Windsurfers, sailboats, kayaks, canoes, fishing boats, and mountain bikes are available. Moose Cruises and guided kayak, hiking, and biking tours are offered, as well as cross-country skiing rentals and expeditions. From $40 double in the lodge. Housekeeping

The Birches Resort

cottages are $129–155 per night, $695–995 per week in summer (less off-season) without meals. Cabin tents begin at $22 single per day. A variety of rafting, canoeing, and other packages are also available.

🐾✔ **Little Lyford Pond Camps** (280-0016; www.littlelyford.com), Box 340, Greenville 04441. Open year-round. Reservations are required. Sited in a sheltered alpinelike valley, these camps were built in the 1870s as a logging-company station on a tote road. The nine shake-roofed log cabins (without plumbing or electricity) sleep from one to four. Each has a private outhouse. Arlene and Bob LeRoy offer three meals and plenty of hospitality in the main lodge; facilities also include a cedar sauna and hot showers. Gulf Hagas is a short hike away, and cross-country ski trails are maintained. In winter you can ski, fly, or dogsled in. The camps are 3.5 miles off the Appalachian Trail and 12 miles via a gated logging road from Greenville. In summer 2000 four llamas were being trained, and llama treks will be offered in future seasons. $85 per person includes all meals (with an emphasis on vegetarian) and use of canoes. Two neighboring ponds offer an abundance of native brook trout, and fly-fishing lessons are offered. We came in March via dogsled and enjoyed exceptional cross-country skiing into Gulf Hagas and around the camps.

🐾✔ **Nugent's Chamberlain Lake Camps** (695-2821), HCR 76, Box 632, Greenville 04441. Open year-round. The original camps on this site were built in the 1930s by Al and Patty Nugent. Since 1987 John Richardson and Regina Webster have rebuilt many of the old cabins, and built a couple of new ones, but retained the old-fashioned feel. This is one of the area's most remote camps, nicely sited on the Allagash Wilderness Waterway, 50 miles north of Millinocket between Baxter State Park and

Allagash Mountain. It's best reached via floatplane (see *Getting Around*); otherwise, it's a 4-mile boat or snowmobile ride up Chamberlain Lake. The eight housekeeping cabins have the traditional front overhang and outhouses; they sleep 2 to 16. Boats are available. AP, MAP, or housekeeping plans available. $22–60 per person.

Medawisla (radiophone year-round: 695-2690), HCR 76, Box 592, Greenville 04441. Open year-round. The LeRoys offer six fully equipped cabins with woodstoves, flush toilets, and hot showers. Each can sleep 2 to 10 people. These camps cater to a quiet clientele. We love the "reading room," a spot outside overlooking a dam that was once the only road in. Meals available October through March. Boats and canoes are available. The loons on the sound track from the movie *On Golden Pond* were taped here. $45–100 per day double, housekeeping; weekly rates are $270–600.

✎ **West Branch Ponds Camps** (695-2561), P.O. Box 1153, Greenville 04441. A 10-mile drive from the main road at Kokadjo. Open after ice-out and through September; inquire about winter season. First opened as a moose-hunting lodge in the 1880s; the newest log cottage was built in 1938. Directly across the pond is the majestic bulk of Whitecap Mountain. The camps are rustic; some of the furnishings are a bit worn, but that all adds to the authentic feel. All cabins have heat, electricity, bath; three have Franklin stoves. Andy and Carol Stirling are third-generation owners, and Carol is well known for her cooking. Motorboats and canoes are available. The square central lodge (with a bell on top) has plenty of books and comfortable corners. $58 per person per day includes three meals and use of a canoe; children are half price.

❦ **Maynard's in Maine** (534-7703), just off Route 6/15 over the bridge in Rockwood 04478. Open May through hunting season. "The only thing we change around here is the linen," says Gail Maynard, who helps run the sportsmen's camp founded by her husband's grandfather in 1919. Overlooking the Moose River, a short walk from Moosehead Lake, Maynard's includes a dozen tidy moss-green frame buildings with dark Edwardian furniture, much of it from the grand old Mount Kineo Hotel. The lodge is filled with stuffed fish, moose heads, and Maynard-family memorabilia, and furnished with stiff-backed leather chairs. Two meals a day are served, plus one "packed." $50 per person with three meals ($55 if you stay less than a week).

CAMPS

Tomhegan Wilderness Resort (534-7712; www.tomhegan.com), P.O. Box 308, Rockwood 04478. Open year-round. A 10-mile ride up a dirt road from Rockwood Village; 1½ miles of frontage on Moosehead Lake. Nine hand-hewn cottages along a wooden boardwalk with kitchens and living rooms, rocking chairs on the porches, full baths, woodstoves, and gas grills; efficiency apartments are available in the lodge. Very remote and peaceful; deer are frequently seen at close range. Boats and canoes

A camp on Moosehead Lake

are available; cross-country skiing and snowmobiling in winter. Cabins range $695–$1,010 per week; lodge apartments begin at $85 per night.

Rockwood Cottages (534-7725), Box 176, Rockwood 04478. Open year-round. Ron and Bonnie Searles maintain clean, comfortable housekeeping cottages with screened-in porches overlooking the lake and Mount Kineo just across the narrows. They are happy to advise about exploring Kineo and this less developed end of the lake. Boat and motor rentals, as well as canoe rentals; hunting and fishing licenses are available, and guests have free docking. There's also a sauna, a barbecue area, and an impressive moose head. $65 per couple, $15 per additional person; $425 per couple per week, $75 per additional person.

Beaver Cove Camps (695-3717; 1-800-577-3717; www.beavercove. camps.com), P.O. Box 1233 Greenville 04441. Open year-round. Eight miles north of Greenville on the eastern shore of Moosehead Lake are six fully equipped housekeeping cabins, each with full kitchen and bath. Owner Jim Glavine is a Registered Maine Guide specializing in fly-fishing. Guided hunting and snowmobile or ski touring also offered. $70 per night or $420 double per week.

Spencer Pond Camps (radio service: 695-2821), Star Route 76, Box 580, Greenville 04441. Open May through mid-November. Bob Croce and Jill Martel maintain the traditions of this long-established cluster of six housekeeping camps (sleeping 2 to 10) in an unusually beautiful spot, accessible by logging road from Lily Bay Road. The hosts are warm and helpful, with plenty of suggestions for enjoying the wilderness. Guests are welcome to fresh vegetables from the garden. Gas and kerosene lights and hand-pumped water; each cottage is stocked with cooking utensils and dishes and has a private shower room (Sunshower) and outhouse. A terrific base for birding, hiking, and mountain climbing. Canoe rentals available. $40–50 per couple; weekly rates available.

CAMPGROUNDS

Lily Bay State Park (695-2700), 8 miles north of Greenville. Ninety-three sites, many spaced along the shore; boat launch and beach.

Seeboomok Wilderness Campground (534-8824), HC 85, Box 560, Rockwood 04478-9712. Accessed by logging roads (some 28 miles from Rockwood), a peaceful, special place. Sites for both RVs and tents, Adirondack shelters on the water, and six comfortable cabins with flush toilets, gaslights, basic utensils (no linens). Photos in the camp store (where there's a lunch counter) document this as the site of a World War II POW camp. Richard Sylvester Jr. and his wife, Jeannine, are accommodating hosts who can direct you to hiking, canoeing, fishing, and wildlife haunts. $10–14 per night, $10 for Adirondack shelters, $30–80 for cabins; weekly rates available.

Maine State Bureau of Forestry (695-3721) maintains free (first-come, first-served) "authorized sites" (no fire permit required) and "permit sites" (permit required) scattered on both public and private land along Moosehead Lake and on several of its islands.

OTHER LODGING

On the way to Greenville

    ♿ **Brewster Inn** (924-3130; www.bbonline.com/me/brewsterinn), 37 Zion's Hill, Dexter 04930. Open year-round. Dexter is a proud old Maine town, and this is its proudest house—fit for the governor who built it. Michael and Ivy Brooks have furnished the nine guest rooms (including two suites) with antiques and bright fabrics; request one overlooking the formal garden, the one with a whirlpool for two. $59–99 per couple includes breakfast.

    🐾 **The Guilford Bed & Breakfast** (876-3477; www.guilfordbandb.com), P.O. Box 88, Elm Street, Guilford 04443. Harry and Lynn Anderson offer wonderful hospitality in their lovely post-Victorian home. A good spot to stop if you are traveling Route 11 en route to the Moosehead or Katahdin regions. Common areas are inviting, especially the bright living room with fireplace and the wraparound porch. Four rooms have private baths, two share. $55–75 includes a full breakfast.

Shaw's Boarding House (997-3597), Pleasant Street, Monson. Open year-round. A short walk from the Appalachian Trail and patronized 99 percent by hikers (snowmobilers in winter), Shaw's is a phenomenon in its own right, famed for the size of its breakfasts ($4.50) and dinners ($8). Beds are in a mix of private ($20 per person) and bunk rooms ($15 per person) in several adjoining buildings, with and without kitchen facilities.

WHERE TO EAT

DINING OUT

Greenville Inn (695-2206; 1-888-695-6000), Norris Street, Greenville. Dinner served nightly by reservation from 6 PM. Elfi Schnetzer has turned over the kitchen to her daughter Susie, who continues to delight diners with appetizers like country pâté with black peppercorn, and an ever-changing selection of entrées. Leave room for dessert, maybe plum streudel *linzertorte*. $17–28.

The Birches Resort (534-2242), Rockwood. Open year-round: daily in summer, sporadically after that (call for times). This popular resort (see *Lodging—Rustic Resorts*) has one of the area's most attractive dining rooms—log-sided with a massive stone hearth, a war canoe turned upside down in the open rafters, and hurricane lamps on the highly polished tables. The menu offers grilled or baked options; specialties include prime rib and pork tenderloin with chutney. $11–16.95. Reservations suggested. There's also an inviting pub.

Northern Pride Lodge (695-2890), Kokadjo. The dining room in this classic lumber baron's hunting lodge (see *Lodging—Inns*) is a modified sunporch overlooking First Roach Pond. Dinner is served to the public by reservation. Entrées $14.95–18.95.

Blue Moose (695-0786), Main Street, Greenville. Open for dinner 5:30–8:30 Monday through Saturday in summer, Thursday through Saturday off-season. We've heard rave reviews of this new fine-dining experience. The menu changes often, with an emphasis on fish and healthy grilled options. $7.95–21 (for the seafood feast).

EATING OUT

Pittston Farm (call Folsom's Air Service: 695-2821). Open year-round except for the last 2 weeks in April. "Authentic" only begins to describe this classic outpost, a wilderness farm built around 1910 as a major hub of Great Northern's logging operations. Sited at the confluence of the North and South Branches of the Penobscot River a little more than 20 miles north of Rockwood, the white-clapboard lodge and its outlying barns and fields are now owned by Ken Twitchel (a veteran lumbercamp cook) and his wife, Sonja. Visitors are welcome for all-you-can-eat meals, which include thick, tasty soups and at least two kinds of meat, several vegetables (some grown outside), a salad bar, and freshly baked rolls, bread, and pastries. Reasonably priced buffet suppers are served at 5 and 6 PM; reservations are appreciated. Folsom's will fly you in and back from Greenville for $50–60 per person including the meal. Lunch is also a buffet, or it might be short-order. Upstairs lodging is available, with a number of quilt-covered beds; shared baths.

Kokadjo Trading Post (695-3993), Kokadjo. Open 6 AM–11 PM; open earlier during hunting season. Fred and Marie Candeloro offer a cozy dining room/pub room with a large fieldstone fireplace and a view of First Roach Pond.

Maynard's Dining Room (534-7703) off Route 6/15, Rockwood. Dine (6–8) much as your grandparents would have here in the traditional old lodge dining room overlooking the Moose River. Choices vary with the night; $9.95 includes juice or soup, salad, choice of potato or veggie, bread, dessert, and beverage; BYOB.

In Greenville

Flatlander's Pub (695-3373), Pritham Avenue, Greenville. Open except Tuesday, 11 AM "'til close." We've always enjoyed this place, but had a recent complaint. Hamburgers, chicken wings, deli sandwiches; homemade chili, a good pea soup, and pies. Nice atmosphere; in the middle of town.

The Boom Chain (695-2602), Pritham Avenue, Greenville. Open 6 AM–2 PM. A good bet for breakfast; a local gathering spot.

Kelly's Landing (695-4438), Greenville Junction. Open 7 AM–9 PM. A breakfast bar and large salad bar, fried seafood platter, roast chicken, sandwiches. A big, cheerful place with tables on the deck by the lake. Inquire about motel rooms with lakeside decks upstairs.

Auntie M's Restaurant (695-2238), Main Street, Greenville. Open for all three meals but best for breakfast; homemade soups and specials. We love this place. Everything always tastes good.

Grave's Seafood (695-2001), Pritham Avenue, Greenville. Open 9–9 daily in summer, 11–8 off-season. Fresh fish market and extensive take-out menu, including hand-picked lobster rolls; fried, grilled, or boiled seafood baskets; sandwiches; burgers; and salads. Cooked lobsters and steamers to go; chowders, soups, and daily specials.

ENTERTAINMENT

East Sangerville Grange Coffeehouse. Call Mr. Paperback (564-3646) in Dover-Foxcroft for schedule information and tickets. A major stop on New England's folk-music circuit.

SELECTIVE SHOPPING

Indian Hill Trading Post (695-3376), Greenville. Open daily year-round, Friday until 10 PM. Huge—a combination sports store, supermarket, and general store, stocking everything you might need for a week or two in the woods.

Moosehead Traders (695-3806), Moosehead Center Mall, Route 15 in downtown Greenville. The most upscale shop in the North Woods: furs, moose antlers, and moose antler furnishings (like chandeliers), antiques, books, and many tempting gifts. The ear is not for sale.

Great Eastern Clothing Store, a trendy emporium, has replaced the old landmark Indian Store in the Shaw Block, and **Northwoods Outfitters** (695-3288), selling sporting gear and wear (see *To Do—Canoe and Kayak Rentals*), now occupies the space vacated by Greenville's other old commercial landmark, Sanders Store.

Maine Mountain Soap and Candle Co. (695-3926), Route 15, downtown Greenville. The real thing. Good soap.

The Corner Shop (695-2142), corner of Main and Pritham (across from Great Eastern Clothing), Greenville; gifts, books, magazines.

Sunbower Pottery (695-2870), Scammon Road, Greenville, home of the "moose mug"; locally made gifts, artwork.

SPECIAL EVENTS

February: **Winter Festival,** Greenville—snowmobile events and poker runs.

Mid-May–mid-June: **Moosemainea** month, sponsored by the chamber of commerce, takes place throughout the area. It's big; see "What's Where in Maine."

July: The **Fourth of July** is big in Greenville, with a crafts fair, food booths, music, parade, fireworks, and street dance.

August: **Forest Heritage Days**—Greenville. Crafts fair and many forestry-related events.

September: The **International Seaplane Fly-In Weekend,** Greenville.

Katahdin Region,
Including Lower Piscataquis

Mile-high Mount Katahdin is the centerpiece not only for Baxter State Park but also for a surprisingly large area from which it is clearly visible. Like a huge ocean liner in a relatively flat sea of woodland, the massive mountain looms above the open countryside to the east, the direction from which it's most easily accessible.

Though the mountain and park are unquestionably its biggest drawing card, the Katahdin Region offers its share of wooded lake country and represents one of the most reasonably priced destinations in Maine for families who want to get away together to hike and fish. The quest to reach the top of Maine's highest peak makes this the most popular hike in the region, but those seeking a milder experience shouldn't dismiss the area. Between the lower peaks within the park and at Gulf Hagas, about a half-hour drive away, plenty of less difficult (and sometimes more satisfying for wilderness lovers) treks are available. Whitewater rafting on the West Branch of the Penobscot has risen in popularity over the past few years, with rafting companies building extensive base camps near the Togue Pond Gatehouse to Baxter State Park and in nearby Millinocket. Winter recreation, especially snowmobiling, has become a huge draw to the area.

Like Acadia National Park, Baxter State Park's acreage was amassed privately and given to the public as a gift. In this case it was one individual—Governor Percival Baxter—who bought all the land himself, after unsuccessfully attempting to convince the state to do so during his political term. At the time (1931), no one seemed able to conceive why Maine, with all its forest, needed officially to preserve a swatch of woods as wilderness.

Decades of subsequent logging and present concerns for the future of this woodland have heightened the value of Governor Baxter's legacy and his mandate—the reason camping and even day-use admission to the park are strictly limited—to preserve at least these 201,018 acres of Maine's North Woods as wilderness.

The restaurants and beds nearest to Baxter State Park are in Millinocket, a lumbering outpost built by the Great Northern Paper

Company around the turn of the 20th century. Though much of Great Northern's land has been sold off in recent years, they retain the forests around Millinocket and the town is still centered on the paper mills and the logging industry that feeds it. Route 11 from Millinocket into Lower Piscataquis County is a nice drive, and some of the towns along the way make good resting places for those heading to Katahdin Iron Works, Gulf Hagas, or to the Moosehead region.

GUIDANCE

The **Baxter State Park** information phone is 723-5140, or you can write to park headquarters, 64 Balsam Drive, Millinocket 04462. For details about making reservations, see *Green Space*. The attractive visitors center, which offers picnic tables, rest rooms, and a selection of guides to the park, is 1 mile east of Millinocket on Route 11/157.

Katahdin Area Chamber of Commerce (723-4443; www. katahdinmaine.com), 1029 Central Street, Millinocket 04462. The chamber maintains a seasonal information center on Route 11/157 east of Millinocket; it serves as a year-round source of information about the motels and restaurants that are chamber members.

Northern Katahdin Valley Regional Chamber of Commerce, P.O. Box 14D, Patten 04765, publishes a brochure focusing on the Patten area and points north and east.

GETTING THERE

The most direct route is I-95 to exit 56 at Medway (50 miles northeast of Bangor), and 10 miles into Millinocket. From here, it's about 10 miles to Millinocket Lake, and from there another few miles to the Togue Pond entrance to Baxter State Park.

GETTING AROUND

Katahdin Air Service Inc. (723-8378), P.O. Box 171, Millinocket. Available May through November to fly in to remote camps and shuttle in canoes and campers; will also drop hikers at points along the Appalachian Trail. **Scotty's Flying Service** (528-2626) at Shin Pond also serves wilderness camps.

MEDICAL EMERGENCY

Millinocket Regional Hospital (723-5161), 200 Somerset Street, Millinocket.

***

TO SEE

***

The Katahdin Iron Works. Open May through mid-October, 6 AM–8 PM. Turn at the small sign on Route 11, 5 miles north of Brownville Junction, and go another 6 miles up the gravel road. This state historic site is really not worth the effort unless you plan to continue on down the gravel road to hike in Gulf Hagas or to camp (see *To Do—Hiking* and *Lodging—Campgrounds*). The spot was a sacred place for Native Americans, who found the yellow ocher paint here. From the 1840s

Katahdin Iron Works

until 1890, an ironworks prospered in this remote spot, spawning a village to house its 200 workers and producing 2,000 tons of raw iron annually. Guests of the Silver Lake Hotel (1880s–1913) here came on the same narrow-gauge railroad that carried away the iron. All that remains is a big old blast furnace and an iron kiln. Tours and books on the ironworks are offered by local author and backwoods guide Bill Sawtell (965-3971).

Lumberman's Museum (528-2650), Shin Pond Road (Route 159), Patten. Open mid-May through Columbus Day, July and August, Tuesday through Sunday 10–4; the rest of the season, Friday through Sunday only. $3.50 adults, $1 children. The museum, which encompasses more than 4,000 displays housed in nine buildings, was founded in 1962 by bacteriologist Lore Rogers and log driver Caleb Scribner. Exhibits range from giant log haulers to "gum books," the lumberman's scrimshaw: intricately carved boxes in which to keep spruce gum, a popular gift for a sweetheart. There are replicas of logging camps from different periods, dioramas, machinery, and photos, all adding up to a fascinating picture of a vanished way of life. This road leads to the Matagamon Gate, the northern, less trafficked corner of Baxter State Park.

A. J. Allee scenic overlook, some 15 miles beyond the Medway exit. The view is of Mount Katahdin rising massively from woods and water.

The Golden Road, a 96-mile logging road owned by private companies, runs from Millinocket to Quebec; 35 miles are paved, the rest gravel, but it is better maintained than most of the logging roads found in the North Woods. It is the best way to travel from Millinocket to Greenville, with plenty of woods and river views. The chances of spotting a moose on this road are high. Great Northern's outdoor classroom and hiking trail is along this road (see *To Do—Hiking*). Day use is free to Maine-registered vehicles, $4 for out-of-state vehicles. Overnight camping is $5 per night per person.

The Ambajejus Boom House, Ambajejus Lake. Open year-round, $2 donation. Accessible via boat or snowmobile, or even by walking if you don't mind getting your feet wet. Ask for directions at the Katahdin Area Chamber of Commerce (see *Guidance*). Riverman Chuck Harris has single-handedly restored this old boom house, former quarters for log drivers, as a museum about life during the river drives. Exhibits include tools, paintings, and photographs among the artifacts of the river-driving years.

TO DO

BOAT EXCURSION
Katahdin View Pontoon Boat Rides (723-5211/9712), 210 Morgan Lane, Millinocket. Seasonal sight-seeing cruises on a 24-foot pontoon boat along Millinocket Lake and into Mud Brook. Approximately 2 hours; the sunset cruise is a little longer and very popular (reservations suggested). Departs from Big Moose Cabins, Millinocket.

CANOEING AND KAYAKING
This area is often used as a starting point for trips on the Allagash (see *To Do—Canoeing* in "Aroostook County") and St. John Rivers. Good canoeing on the East and West (not for beginners) Branches of the Penobscot as well.

New England Outdoor Center (723-5438; 1-800-766-7238), Route 157, Millinocket, offers a canoe and kayak school, guided tours, and rentals.

Penobscot River Outfitters (746-9349 in Maine; 1-800-794-5267 outside the state), Route 157, Medway 04460. Old Town rentals; specializes in 1- to 7-day canoe trips on the East and West Branches of the Penobscot.

Katahdin Outfitters (723-5700), in Millinocket, offers rentals, planning, transport, and shuttle for trips on the Allagash, St. John, and Penobscot Rivers.

Canoe rentals are also available in Peaks-Kenny State Park (see *Lodging— Campgrounds*).

For a more complete list of guide services, contact the **North Maine Woods office** (435-6213) in Ashland.

FISHING

We've been told that **Dolby Flowage** is good for bass fishing, and the West Branch of the Penobscot offers good salmon and trout fishing. **New England Outdoor Center** (723-5438) offers guided fishing trips. Licenses are available at many of the stores in the area, including the Katahdin General Store in Millinocket and North Woods Trading Post on Millinocket Lake.

HIKING

Baxter State Park. Ever since the 1860s—when Henry David Thoreau's account of his 1846 ascent of "Ktaadn" began to circulate—the demanding trails to Maine's highest summit (5,267 feet) have been among the most popular in the state. Climbing Katahdin itself is considered a rite of passage in Maine and much of the rest of New England. The result is a steady stream of humanity up and down the Katahdin trails, while other peaks, such as 3,488-foot Doubletop, offer excellent, little-trafficked hiking trails and views of Katahdin to boot. Many hikers base themselves at **Chimney Pond Campground** and tackle Katahdin from there on one of several trails. *50 Hikes in the Maine Mountains* by Cloe Chunn (Backcountry Guides) details many of Baxter's trails far better than we can here.

We finally climbed Katahdin in the summer of 1999. Arriving at the gate at 5 AM (when it opens), we were the 47th car in line. The parking area for the **Knife's Edge Trail** was already full. If you want to go this route, arrive very early. We climbed the **Abol Trail,** up the face of an old rockslide. It was steep and slow going, and we had to watch every step for loose rocks. Bring plenty of water—the need for rest stops will be frequent. When we reached the plateau at **Thoreau Spring,** we could clearly see where we were headed. This last mile wasn't as steep, and had a well-beaten path to the peak. The top of the mountain is anything but peaceful, with hordes of climbers celebrating the feat of reaching this peak; for some, it's the end of the long trek from Georgia on the Appalachian Trail. There's often a line of hikers waiting to take pictures by the sign marking the top. Our descent, down the **Hunt Trail,** took longer than the climb up. Take it slow and easy and watch your step carefully. Make sure you bring plenty of water— you'll need just as much on the way down. The round-trip climb of close to 10 miles took us 10 hours, moving at a fairly steady pace. We're glad we did it, but this climb seems more about challenging terrain and bragging rights than the peace and tranquility of many other hikes. With the hundreds of people trekking up the trails, it didn't feel like the wilderness. Still, the view from the top is well worth the effort it takes to get there, and the feeling of satisfaction at having completed the task outweighs the need for solitude at the top.

We also did the **Sentinel Mountain Trail,** said to be the easiest climb up a mountain peak in the park. It was approximately 6½ miles round-trip, a moderate climb with lots of rocks and roots on the path. The trail can be wet and muddy, but the trees were so thick that even in a light rain we didn't get soaked. At one point on the trail you have to cross a brook on a wooden log bridge about 2 or 3 feet above the water. It's sturdy, but not great for people who aren't crazy about heights. The last bit of this trail is steeper, leading to the peak, where there is a loop trail. We were there on a foggy day, so our view wasn't great, but we assume it is better when the weather is clear. From the same starting point (Kidney Pond Camps), you can choose the **Daicey Pond Trail,** a flat loop around the pond that we hear is a good spot to see moose. Just before Kidney Pond Camps is the **Doubletop Mountain Trail.** We were also told that the **South Turner Mountain Trail** from Roaring Brook via Sandy Stream Pond is a good wildlife-watching trail. In all, there are 46 mountain peaks and 175 miles of well-marked trails in Baxter. Allow 3 to 5 days at a campground like Trout Brook Farm Campground in the northern wilderness area of the park, or base yourself at Russell Pond (a 7- or 9-mile hike in from the road, depending on where you begin) and hike to the **Grand Falls** and **Lookout Ledges.** A free "Day Use Hiking Guide" is available from the park headquarters (see *Green Space*).

Gulf Hagas is most easily accessible (3.1 miles) from the Katahdin Iron Works (see *To See*). Billed as the Grand Canyon of Maine, this 2½-mile-long canyon with walls up to 40 feet high was carved by the West Branch of the Pleasant River. At the beginning of the trail you will need to cross the river in ankle- to calf-high water. Bring water shoes for the crossing, or be prepared to take off your shoes and wade barefoot (be aware that the rocks are very slippery; find a good walking stick to help with balance). Once you are over the river, you will approach the trail through a 35-acre stand of virgin white pines, some more than 130 feet tall. A landmark in its own right (known as the Hermitage), this area is preserved by The Nature Conservancy of Maine. The trail then follows the river, along the Appalachian Trail for a ways, but turns off along the rim of the canyon toward dramatic **Screw Auger Falls** and on through the Jaws to **Buttermilk Falls, Stair Falls,** and **Billings Falls.** We started early in the day and found ourselves alone for most of the hike. The trail winds through the woods, almost always moving either up or down, with a series of small side paths. Don't skip these turnouts—they are where you see the views of the falls and the gorge. The hike back is

The Chimney Pond Trail is a popular approach to Mount Katahdin

more flat, with a series of logs laid down to cover the mud in some spots. The Gulf Hagas trails are much less traveled than those at Katahdin; when we were there, the caretaker told us that only 140 people had been through that day. Many don't take the whole trek but make it only to the first waterfall for a swim and a picnic. It's a different kind of hike—no mountain peaks but plenty of scenic views nonetheless. Allow 6 to 8 hours for the hike and plan to camp at one of the waterside campsites within the **Jo Mary Lake Campground** (see KI-Jo Mary Multiple Use Forest under *Lodging—Campgrounds*).

Great Northern's River Pond Outdoor Classroom and Hiking Trail is a 5¾-mile loop through both harvested and unharvested forest. Eleven sites along the way help visitors understand the multiple uses of this forest, and offer a chance to observe wildlife in its natural habitat. A handy brochure (available at Great Northern headquarters) outlines the sites in detail. For those not wishing to hike, most sites can be reached by car from the Golden Road (see *To See*).

SCENIC FLIGHT

Katahdin Air Service, Inc. (723-8378), offers several scenic flights daily, ranging from a 15-minute flight along the base of Mount Katahdin ($20 per person) to a day exploring Henderson Pond and Delosconeag Lake ($70 per person). Inquire about fly-and-dine packages.

SWIMMING

Peaks-Kenny State Park in Dover-Foxcroft is a great family beach, with lawns, playground equipment, and a roped-in swimming area. Hiking trails and camping.

WHITEWATER RAFTING

Rafting on the West Branch of the Penobscot has gained increasing popularity in recent years. It has been deemed the ultimate challenge in Maine rafting, best for experienced rafters (to run the whole river you must be at least 15). Class V rapids include Exterminator, Nesowadnehunk Falls, and the Cribworks. Several whitewater rafting companies maintain bases near the Togue Pond entrance to Baxter State Park; there are mid-May through mid-September departure points for day trips. Rates are $70–80 during the week, $100–110 on weekends.

New England Outdoor Center (723-5438; 1-800-766-7238; rafting@neoc.com) has a beautiful facility in Millinocket and offers a range of options to rafters. The campground offers tent and cabin-tent sites, fire rings, and a shower house. Nearby **Twin Pine Camps,** on Millinocket Lake, are traditional sporting camps set in the woods, with an indoor pool and hot tub among the facilities. The lodge at **Rice Farm** has a popular restaurant, wraparound deck with water views, hot tub, changing room and showers, and a complete outfitters shop.

Northern Outdoors (1-800-765-RAFT) and **Wilderness Expeditions** (1-800-825-WILD; wwld@aol.com) share the **Penobscot Outdoor Center** on Pockwockamus Pond, where facilities include a bar, restaurant, hot tub, sauna, canoes, kayaks, and Windsurfers; lodging is at campsites and in cabin tents.

Unicorn Rafting (1-800-UNICORN) has a new base in Millinocket; they also offer a 6-day Penobscot expedition tracing Thoreau's journey in the Maine woods.

WINTER SPORTS

CROSS-COUNTRY SKIING AND SNOWSHOEING

Katahdin Country Skis and Sports (723-5839), 1 Colony Place, Millinocket, offers rental skis. Trail maps for close to 60 miles of free groomed and backcountry trails are available here and from the local chamber of commerce (see *Guidance*).

Katahdin Lake Wilderness Camps (see *Lodging—Remote Rustic Camps*) caters exclusively to cross-country skiers.

SNOWMOBILING

Snowmobiling is huge in this region, just as it is in Moosehead. There are over 350 miles of groomed trails in the region, and more than 10 snowmobile clubs in the area to consult. A snowmobile map is available at the chamber (see *Guidance*), showing the Interconnecting Trail System (ITS) trails and containing advertisements for many snowmobiling-geared businesses. On the Baxter State Park Road next to the Northern Timbercruisers Clubhouse, check out the **antique snowmobile museum,** which details the history of early riding in the region.

New England Outdoor Center has a fleet of 50 snowmobiles for rent, and lodging at their Rice Farm base. They offer half-day, full-day, and overnight guided snowmobile excursions, from tours through Baxter State Park, a maple sugar farm, and throughout Piscataquis, Penobscot, and Aroostook Counties, among other places.

GREEN SPACE

BAXTER STATE PARK

This 201,018-acre park surrounds Mount Katahdin, the highest peak in the state (5,267 feet). There are only two entry points: **Togue Pond Gate** near Millinocket, by far the most popular, is open 6 AM–9 PM, May 15 through October 15. **Matagamon Gate,** in the northeast corner of the park, is open 6 AM–9 PM. Nonresident vehicles pay an $8 day-use fee at the gate ($25 for the season). Vehicles with Maine plates are admitted free. Day-trippers should be aware that the number of vehicles allowed in the park is restricted because of limited parking; arrive early to avoid being turned away.

The list of rules governing the park is long and detailed. No motorcycles, motorized trail bikes, or ATVs are allowed in the park. Bicycles can be used on maintained roads only. Snowmobiles are allowed in only particular areas of the park. Pets are not allowed in the park. The list goes on and on; be sure to pick up a copy at park headquarters or the chamber of commerce (see *Guidance*) and read it through before heading in.

The park is open daily, but note the restricted camping periods and the special-use permits required from December 1 through March. Orchids, ferns, alpine flowers, and dozens of other interesting plants here delight botanists. Geologists are intrigued by Baxter's rhyolite, Katahdin granite, and many fossils. Birds and wildlife, of course, also abound. Rental canoes are available at several locations in the park.

Camping is only permitted May 15 through October 15 and December through April 1. As a rule, campsites are booked solid before the season begins; don't come without a reservation. In all there are 10 widely scattered campgrounds. **Daicey Pond** and **Kidney Pond** both offer traditional cabins with beds, gas lanterns, firewood, and table and chairs ($17 per person per night minimum; $30 for a two-bed cabin, $40 for a three-bed cabin, and $50 for a four-bed; children ages 1–6 are free, 7–16 are $10 per person). **Six more campgrounds,** accessible by road, offer a mix of bunkhouses, lean-tos, and tent sites (bunkhouses $7 per person per night; lean-tos and tenting space $6 per person per night; minimum $12 for both). There are two more backcountry, hike-in campgrounds, at **Chimney Pond** and **Russell Pond,** which are among the most popular. Beyond that there are several **backcountry sites,** available by reservation for backpackers. Some of these sites have restrictions, so be sure to contact the park before planning your trip.

Summer-season reservations (accepted only for the period between

May 15 and October 15; dates vary a little according to campground opening and closing dates; request information from park headquarters) must be made in person or by mail with the fee enclosed (check or cash), posted no earlier than December 26 of the year before you are coming (Baxter State Park, 46 Balsam Drive, Millinocket 04462). Send a stamped, self-addressed envelope if you want to receive a confirmation. No refunds.

Also see **KI-Jo Mary Multiple Use Forest** under *Lodging—Campgrounds.*

LODGING

Note: For details about a choice of motels handy to I-95, check with the Katahdin Area Chamber of Commerce (723-4443).

INNS AND BED & BREAKFASTS

Katahdin Area B&B (723-5220; 1-800-725-5220), 94–96 Oxford Street, Millinocket 04462. Open year-round. Five clean, comfortable rooms with private baths and cable TV. Also a two-bedroom suite (sleeps five) with private bath and sitting area. Washer/dryer available for guest use; off-street parking. $40–55 includes a full breakfast.

Carousel B&B (965-7741), Back Brownville Road, Brownville 04414. Open mid-May through November. Exquisite murals adorn the walls throughout the house. One room has a private bath and a double bed. The other two, one with twins, one with a queen, share a bath. This is the most convenient lodging to **Gulf Hagas.** Betty Friend is warm and welcoming. $45 for private bath, $40 shared includes a full breakfast.

Big Moose Inn Cabins & Campground, Inc. (723-8391; www.bigmoosecabins.com), Millinocket Lake, Millinocket 04462. Open June through October but will open the lodge in winter for groups. A classic old summer inn has been a family-run business since 1976, offering 11 simple guest rooms with double or twin beds, 11 cabins, and a 40-site campground. Beautifully situated on the water, with lake swimming; not far from the Togue Pond entrance to Baxter State Park. Also a base for whitewater rafting. The dining room is open to the public (see *Where to Eat*). $35 per person for rooms in the inn.

REMOTE RUSTIC CAMPS

❧ **Katahdin Lake Wilderness Camps** (723-4050; www.katahdinlakecamps.com) Box 398, Millinocket 04462. Open all year, and located at the end of a private 3½-mile tote trail from Roaring Brook Road in Baxter State Park; it's an hour's walk. Al Cooper will meet you in summer with packhorses, or you can fly in from Millinocket Lake (Katahdin Air Service: 723-8378). In winter you can ski in from the Abol Bridge Store on the Penobscot River just outside Millinocket. Ten log cabins (with one to eight people per cabin) and a main lodge built on a bluff overlooking the lake; firewood, linens, kerosene lamps, and shower houses; several also have gas stoves for housekeeping. Hiking tours, sandy beaches, fly-fishing lessons; boats and canoes available. Fishing in the 717-acre lake from May through July yields native brook trout. $125 per day includes all three meals. Pets are allowed, with a $10 fee. Catering exclusively to cross-country skiers in winter.

    ᵴ **Bradford Camps** (746-7777; www.bradfordcamps.com), Box 729, Ashland 04732. Open following ice-out through November. Sited at the Aroostook River's headwaters, Munsungan Lake. Virtually inaccessible by land (unless you want to weather 47 miles on logging roads), this unusually tidy lodge has well-tended lawns and eight hand-hewn log cabins on the waterfront, all with full private baths. $105 per person per night includes meals, but boat and motor are extra. Family rates in July and August.

    🐾 **Shin Pond Village** (528-2900; www.shinpond.com), RR 1, Box 280, Patten. Ten miles down Route 159 from Patten. Open year-round. Craig and Terry Hill run this recreational facility, which offers 30 campsites, six housekeeping cottages, and three guest suites. Set on a hill above Shin Pond, and there are nice views of Mount Chase. There is a snack bar and a nice little crafts shop. The north entrance to Baxter State Park isn't far. Cottages accommodate three to eight people and have full bath, linens, towels, and cookware. Canoe rentals in summer; snowmobile rentals in winter. Camping is $14.95 per night; cottages are $59–99 depending on number of people.

    🌿🐾 **Frost Pond Camps** (radiophone: 695-2821; www.frostpondcamps.com), Box 620, Star Route 76, Greenville 04441. Off the Golden Road across Ripogenous Dam. Gene Thompson and Maureen Raynes are the new owners of these seven traditional North Woods housekeeping cottages (five on the waterfront) and 10 campsites on the shore of Frost Pond. Cabins have gaslights, refrigerators, and stoves and are heated by woodstoves in spring, fall, and winter. One has plumbing, the others each have a clean pit toilet. A great base for exploring the wilderness. $25–30 per person per night for cabins, $18 per night for campsites.

CAMPGROUNDS

KI–Jo Mary Multiple Use Forest (695-8135). Open May through October, a 200,000-plus-acre tract of commercial forest stretching almost from Greenville on the west to the Katahdin Iron Works on the east, and north to Millinocket. Seasonal checkpoints are open 6 AM–8 PM (Thursday through Saturday until 10 PM in May, June, and August; 10:30 PM in July). Primitive sites. Good fishing, hunting, and plenty of solitude. The **Jo Mary Lake Campground** (723-8117) is located within the forest but offers modern facilities with flush toilets, hot showers.

Gulf Hagas (see *To Do—Hiking*) boasts 50 miles of the Appalachian Trail, 96 lakes, and 125 miles of brooks, streams, and rivers within its boundaries, not to mention 150 miles of roads over which lumber trucks have rights-of-way. It also offers over 60 authorized campsites, some on rivers and lakes. The day-use fee (for those ages 15 to 70) is $4 for residents, $7 for nonresidents; the camping fee is a flat $4 per person. For reservations (valid only at least a month in advance), write North Maine Woods, Box 382, Ashland 04732.

Peaks-Kenny State Park (564-2003), Route 153, 6 miles from Dover-Foxcroft. Open mid-May through September for camping and for swimming in Sebec Lake.

Mattawamkeag Wilderness Park (746-4881; www.mwpark.com), Mattawamkeag (off Route 2; a half-hour drive from the I-95 Medway exit). Fifty campsites, 11 Adirondack shelters, bathrooms, hot showers, small store, recreation building, picnic facilities, 15 miles of hiking trails, 60 miles of canoeing on the Mattawamkeag River with patches of whitewater, and bass, salmon, and trout fishing.

Scraggly Lake Public Lands Management Unit (contact the Bureau of Public Lands, Presque Isle: 764-2033). A 10,014-acre forested preserve laced with ponds and brooks. It has 12 "authorized" campsites (no fire permit needed). Scraggly Lake is good for salmon and brook trout; a half-mile hiking trail loops up Owls Head.

🐾✔ **Katahdin Shadows Campground** (746-9349; 1-800-794-5267; www.katahdinshadows.com), Route 157, Medway 04460. This is a full-service, family-geared four-seasons campground with a central lodge, a swimming pool, a hot tub, a dock, weekend hayrides, a big playground, athletic fields, free morning coffee, a "community kitchen," tent and hook-up sites, hutniks, and well-designed cabins with kitchen facilities. Rick and Debbie LeVasseur also offer canoe and boat rentals, hiking, cross-country skiing, and snowmobiling information. Pets are welcome. They own the motel across the road as well, a clean, cozy place where pets are also welcome. $18–23 for tent sites, cabins $29–65, motel $44 double (less for single; more for additional guests).

For camping in Baxter State Park, see *Green Space*.

WHERE TO EAT

Appalachian Trail Café (723-6720), 210 Penobscot Avenue, Millinocket. Open for all three meals year-round. Good home cooking; reasonable prices.

  ♿ **Big Moose Inn Cabins & Campground, Inc.** (723-8391), Millinocket Lake, 8 miles west of Millinocket on the Baxter State Park Road, between two lakes. Open for dinner Wednesday through Saturday, June through early October. A popular place; reservations suggested. A pleasant Maine woods atmosphere with choices like seafood casserole, grilled or blackened swordfish, and pineapple-glazed baked ham. $10.95–18.95.

Angie's Restaurant (943-7432), Milo. Open for all three meals. Great road food, homemade sandwich bread, wooden booths, blue frilly curtains, dinner specials ranging from liver and onions to salmon steak.

   ℷ **River Drivers' Restaurant** (723-5438) at New England Outdoors Center's Rice Farm. Open for dinner year-round. Hearty fare, with seafood, steak, and pasta specialties.

   ✑ **Schootic In/Penobscot Room** (723-4566), 70 Penobscot Avenue, Millinocket. Open for lunch and dinner. George and Bea Simon are third-generation owners. Menu choices include pizza, calzones, seafood, and prime rib. Banquet facility seats up to 40 people. Children's menu. $4.95–14.95.

SPECIAL EVENTS

July: **Fourth of July celebration** in Millinocket features a weekend full of activities and a fireworks display.

August: **Annual Wooden Canoe Festival**—wooden canoe show, parade, demonstations, and more.

September: **End of the Appalachian Trail Festival.** A celebration at the end of the Appalachian Trail, includes outdoor displays, Native American trail blessing, entertainment, demonstrations, outdoors skills contest, and more. **Annual Art Festival,** Millinocket.

October: For 3 weeks before Halloween, the scariest, most elaborate **haunted trolley ride** in Maine, sponsored by Jandreau's Greenhouse, Millinocket.

February: **Winterfest**—snowmobile parade, bonfire, cross-country ski events, dogsled demos, pig roast.

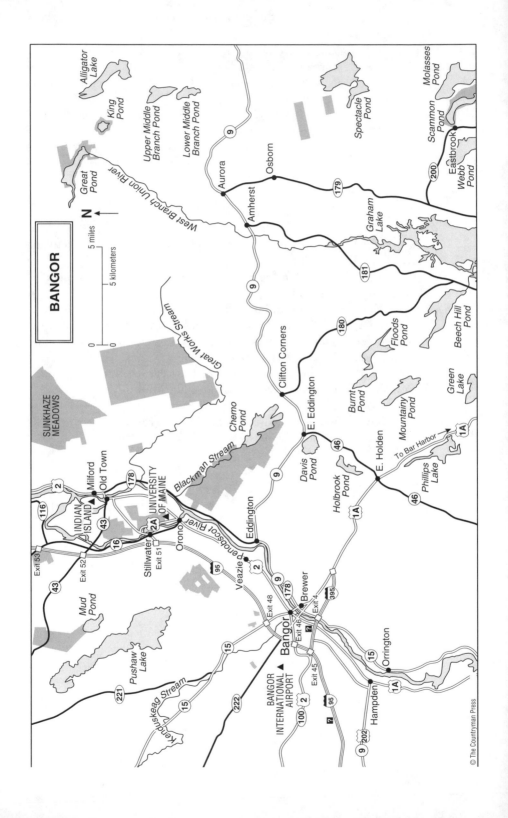

BANGOR

N

5 miles

5 kilometers

© The Countryman Press

Bangor Area

It is no coincidence that the year 1820—when big-city merchants began buying timberland along the upper reaches of the Penobscot River—was also the year in which the Massachusetts District of Maine became a state and planted a white pine in the center of its official seal.

By the 1830s the Penobscot River was filled with pine logs, all of which were processed in the sawmills just above Bangor, where they were loaded aboard ships. By 1834–1836 land broker offices were springing up as land speculation reached its peak. Townships and lots were sold sight unseen several times over. In 1835 it was reported that two paupers who had escaped from Bangor's almshouse had each cleared $1,800 by speculating in timberland (the land offices worked around the clock) by the time they were caught the next morning.

By the 1850s Bangor was the world's leading lumber port, handling over $3 million in lumber in its peak year. During this boom, a section of the city came to be known as the Devil's Half Acre, where loggers flooded in after a long winter's work (and with a long winter's pay) to frequent the numerous taverns and brothels.

The Bangor of today is substantially different. The only Paul Bunyan around now is the 31-foot-high statue next to the chamber of commerce office. A 1911 fire wiped out the business district, and the end of the logging boom combined with urban renewal to leave the Devil's Half Acre a distant memory. Still, Bangor is one of Maine's largest cities, and Bangor International Airport is the departure point for craft (admittedly air instead of sailing) bound for faraway points on the globe. The Bangor area also makes for a good resting spot for those venturing into the northern part of the state, to either the Baxter State Park region or the vast expanse of Aroostook County.

Two neighborhoods actually hint at the city's past grandeur. One is the West Market Square Historic District, a mid-19th-century block of shops. The other is the Broadway area, studded with the Federal-style homes of early prominent citizens and lumber barons' mansions. Across town, West Broadway holds a number of even more ornate homes, including the turreted Victorian home of author Stephen King (look for the bat-and-cobweb fence).

GUIDANCE

Bangor Region Chamber of Commerce (947-0307; www. bangorregion.com), 519 Main Street, P.O. Box 1443, Bangor 04402-1443 (just off I-95/exit 45 to 495 east/exit 3B; across from the Holiday Inn), maintains a seasonal visitors information office in Paul Bunyan Park on lower Main Street (Route 1A). The **Bangor Convention and Visitors Bureau** (947-5205; www.bangorcvb.org) is located at 115 Main Street and is also a helpful source of information.

The Maine Tourism Association maintains two rest area/information centers on I-95 in Hamden between exits 43 and 44: northbound (862-6628) and southbound (862-6638).

GETTING THERE

By air: **Bangor International Airport** (942-0384; www.flybangor. com) is served by Delta Air Lines, Northwest Airlink, and U.S. Airways Express. **Rental cars** are available at the airport.

By bus: **Greyhound** (942-1700) offers daily service to the downtown terminal. **Concord Trailway**s (945-5000; 1-800-639-5150) has express trips, complete with movies and music, daily from Portland and Boston. **Cyr Bus Line** offers daily scheduled service all the way to Caribou, with stops in between.

By car: I-95 from Augusta.

GETTING AROUND

The Bus (947-0536) runs Monday through Saturday to Brewer, Bangor, Hampden, Veazie, Orono, and Old Town.

MEDICAL EMERGENCY

Eastern Maine Medical Center (973-7000), 489 State Street, Bangor. **St. Joseph Hospital** (262-1000), 360 Broadway, Bangor.

VILLAGES

Hampden. Adjacent to Bangor, but offering a more rural setting. The academically excellent Hampden Academy and a well-known truck stop (see Dysart's under *Eating Out*) are found here.

Orono. A college town, housing the University of Maine, but still a small town, where almost everyone knows everyone else. Downtown there are some nice shops and local dining landmarks, and on campus a multitude of cultural activities are available.

Old Town. Definitely a mill town, also the home of the famous Old Town Canoe factory. There's a great little museum worth visiting.

Indian Island. In 1786 the Penobscot tribe deeded most of Maine to Massachusetts in exchange for 140 small islands in the Penobscot River; they continue to live on Indian Island, which is connected by a bridge to Old Town. The 1970s discovery of an 18th-century agreement that details the land belonging to the tribe (much of it now valuable) brought the island a new school and a large community center, which attracts crowds to play high-stakes bingo (call 1-800-255-1293 for the schedule). The **Indian Island Reservation,** the Penobscot homeland for more than 5,000 years, is presently home to 500 tribal members. A **Penobscot Nation Museum** (827-4153), 6 River Road, is open Monday through Thursday noon–5 and Saturday and Sunday 10–2. The museum occupies the former Indian Agent's office, one of the first things you see after crossing the bridge. Curator James Neptune greets visitors, explaining that the birch table is by the legendary Passamaquoddy craftsman Tomah Joseph—who taught Franklin Roosevelt to paddle a canoe—and that the beaded deerskin dress belonged to Indian Island's Molly Spotted Elk, a dancer, actress, and writer known around the world in the late 1930s. Most items in this authentic and informal collection—which includes a 150-year-old birch-bark canoe and some exquisite beaded work, war bonnets, war clubs, and basketry—have a human story. Inquire here about where to buy Penobscot craftswork. The island is accessible from Route 2, marked from I-95, exit 51.

Winterport. An old river town, once home of many sea captains and now a quiet little area with a historic district. Walking-tour brochure available from area businesses.

TO SEE AND DO

MUSEUMS
Cole Land Transportation Museum (990-3600), 405 Perry Road (junction I-95 and I-395), Bangor. Open May 1 through October 30 daily 9–5. $3 adults, $2 seniors, under 18 free. A collection of 200 antique Maine vehicles going back to the 19th century: snowplows, wagons, trucks, sleds, rail equipment, and more.

Hose 5 Fire Museum (945-3229) 247 State Street, Bangor. Open by appointment. A working fire station until 1993, now a museum with firefighting artifacts from the area. Three fully restored fire engines, wooden water mains, and plenty of historical pictures. Free, but donations gladly accepted.

University of Maine Museums, Route 2A, Orono. **Hudson Museum** (581-1901), **Maine Center for the Arts** (open Tuesday through Friday 9–4, Saturday and Sunday 11–4) is an exceptional anthropological collection including a special section on Maine Native Americans and Maine history. General tours for the public are offered in July and August on Tuesday and Thursday at 1 PM. **University of Maine Museum of Art** (581-3255), 109 Carnegie Hall (open weekdays 9–5, Saturday 1–4), shows a fraction of its 4,500-work collection, which includes an extensive selection of 19th- and 20th-century European and American prints by Goya, Picasso, Homer, and Whistler and modern American paintings by George Inness, John Marin, Andrew Wyeth, and others.

A sculpture on Market Square in Bangor

Tours are available by prior arrangement, and tours on tape are also available. **Page Farm & Home Museum** (open daily May 15 through September 15, 9–4; closed Sunday and Monday off-season). Free. Historical farm implements and household items from 1865 to 1940.

Old Town Museum (827-7256), North 4th Street Extension, Old Town. Open early June through the end of August, Wednesday through Sunday 1–5. A former waterworks building houses a great little museum with exhibits on the Penobscot tribe and on local logging; early area photos; an original birch-bark canoe; well-informed guides.

Maine Forest and Logging Museum (581-2871), Leonard's Mills, off Route 178 in Bradley (take Route 9 north from Brewer; turn left onto 178 and watch for signs). Open during daylight hours. "Living History Days" on two weekends, one in mid-July and another in October, with people in period attire yarding logs with horses or oxen and performing various duties using 18th-century tools. The museum is located on the site of a 1790s logging and milling community, and includes a covered bridge, water-powered sawmill, millpond, saw pit, stone dam, barn, and trapper's line camp. Special events throughout the season include Children's Day and Woodsmen's Day.

HISTORIC HOMES AND SITES

Bangor Historical Society Thomas A. Hill House (942-5766), 159 Union Street (at High Street), Bangor. Open April through mid-December, Tuesday through Friday 12–4 (also Saturday, June through September). $5 adults; children and members free. Downstairs has been restored to its 19th-century grandeur with Victorian furnishings and an elegant double parlor, while changing exhibits of city memorabilia are housed upstairs in this Greek Revival house. Architecture buffs might also want to check out the neighboring **Isaac Farrar Mansion** (941-2808), 166 Union Street, open weekdays 9–4 ($1 admission). A restored English Regency lumber baron's mansion with marble fireplaces, mahogany paneling, and stained-glass windows.

Mount Hope Cemetery in Bangor is one of the nation's oldest garden cemeteries, designed by noted Maine architect Charles G. Bryant. Hannibal Hamlin's grave is here.

FISHING

Bangor Salmon Pool. Located 2 miles south of Bangor, Route 9, Brewer. A gathering spot for salmon traveling upstream in the Penobscot River to spawn.

FOR FAMILIES

✐ **Maine Discovery Museum** (941-0942), 74 Main Street, Bangor. Slated to open in January 2001, this is the second largest children's museum in New England, with three floors of excitement. Exhibits include an indoor river, world cultures area, book town, and much more. There will also be a gift shop and special events throughout the year. $5 per person.

GOLF

Bangor Municipal Golf Course (945-9226), Webster Avenue; 27 holes. **Penobscot Valley Country Club** (866-2423), Bangor Road, Orono; 18 holes. **Hermon Meadow Golf Club** (848-3741), Newberg Road, Hermon; nine holes.

SWIMMING

✐ **Jenkins' Beach.** Popular beach on Green Lake for families with children. Store and snack bar.

Violette's Public Beach and Boat Landing (843-6876), East Holden (between Ellsworth and Bangor). $2 admission. Also on Green Lake, a popular spot for college students and young adults. Swim float with slide, boat launch, and picnic tables.

DOWNHILL AND CROSS-COUNTRY SKIING

Mt. Hermon Ski Area (848-5192), Newburg Road, Hermon (3 miles off I-95 from exit 43, Carmel; or off Route 2 from Bangor). Popular local ski area, with two T-bars and 17 runs (the longest is 3,500 feet); rentals available; base lodge, night skiing, snowboarding.

Hermon Meadow Ski Touring Center (848-3471), Newburg Road, Hermon. Approximately 6 miles of groomed trails on a golf course.

See also **Sunkhaze Meadows** under *Green Space*, below.

GREEN SPACE

Sunkhaze Meadows (827-6138), Milford. Just north of Bangor, this 9,337-acre refuge includes nearly 5 miles of Sunkhaze Stream and 12 miles of

tributary streams. Recreation activities include canoeing, walking logging trails, and hunting and fishing in accordance with Maine laws. Also
excellent bird-watching and cross-country skiing opportunities. The refuge office is on Route 2 in Old Town, and is open 7:30–4 weekdays.

A brochure titled **"Trails in the Bangor Region"** is available at the chamber
visitors center and lists close to a dozen trails for biking, walking, picnicking, running, hiking, cross-country skiing, and other outdoor activities.

LODGING

🐾♿ **The Phenix Inn** (947-0411), 20 Broad Street, Bangor 04401. A historic inn
located in the heart of downtown Bangor. The 32 rooms are each
decorated a bit differently, some with mahogany beds. All have antique
brass water faucets, private baths, air-conditioning, and TVs. There are
two suites, one with a Jacuzzi bath, and an extended residency apartment. Innkeeper Paul Johnson is helpful and friendly. Continental
breakfast is served in the pretty breakfast room. $80–160 in-season.

🐾 **Best Inn** (947-0566), 570 Main Street, Bangor 04401. A 50-room motel that
is clean, comfortable, and convenient. **Geaghan's,** the on-site restaurant, isn't your typical motel dining: It's an Irish pub with a local
following. Rates are $59.95–79.95, including continental breakfast.
Children under 18 stay free.

♿ **Highlawn Bed and Breakfast** (866-2272; 1-800-297-2272), 193 Main
Street, Orono 04773. Betty Lee and Arthur Comstock have hosted guests in
their majestic white house with front columns for over 15 years. Six of the
17 rooms in this 1803 house are pretty guest rooms, but only 3 are rented
at a time, which means each has a private bath. Full breakfast (maybe
pancakes or omelets) is included in their $50–70 year-round rates.

The Lucerne Inn (843-5123; 1-800-325-5123; www.lucerneinn.com), RR
3, Box 540, Holden 04429. A 19th-century mansion on Route 1A, overlooking Phillips Lake in East Holden. Best known as a restaurant (see
Dining Out), it also has 25 rooms with private baths, working fireplaces,
heated towel bars, whirlpool baths, phones, and TVs. $99–159 in-sea-
son includes continental breakfast. Lower rates off-season.

Note: Bangor also has many hotels and motels, mainly located by the mall
and near the airport.

WHERE TO EAT

DINING OUT

J. B. Parkers (947-0167), 167 Center Street, Bangor. Open for lunch Monday through Friday, dinner Monday through Saturday. Upscale dining,
with with entrées ranging from seafood to beef. Also a variety of vegetarian and pasta dishes. On Thursday and Friday evenings they also
offer live music. $10–21.

The Lucerne Inn (843-5123; 1-800-325-5123), Route 1A, East Holden (11 miles out of Bangor, heading toward Ellsworth). Open for dinner daily, as well as a popular Sunday brunch. A grand old mansion with a view of Phillips Lake. Specialties include shrimp Niçoise and veal Normandy. $11.95–19.95.

Pilot's Grill (942-6325), 1528 Hammond Street (Route 2, 1.5 miles west of exit 45B off I-95), Bangor. Open daily 11:30–9:30 (until 8 on Sunday). A large, long-established place with 1950s decor and a huge all-American menu. $7–15.

EATING OUT

City Limits (941-9888), 735 Main Street, Bangor. Open for lunch and dinner daily. A large, casual place serving Italian specialties and seafood. Great breadsticks.

Captain Nick's (942-6444), 1165 Union Street, Bangor. Open daily for lunch and dinner. A large, locally popular place with good seafood and steaks.

✎ **Governor's** (947-7704), 643 Broadway in Bangor; and Stillwater Avenue in Stillwater (827-4277). Open from early breakfast to late dinner. The Stillwater restaurant is the original in a statewide chain. Popular at all meals, large breakfast menu, hamburgers to steaks; specials like German potato soup, fresh strawberry pie, ice cream.

Momma Baldacci's (945-5813), 12 Alden Street, Bangor. A longtime family-owned and -operated restaurant open for lunch and dinner, and serving Italian specialties at reasonable prices.

Dysart's (942-4878), Coldbrook Road, Hermon (I-95, exit 44). Open 24 hours. Billed as "the biggest truck stop in Maine," but it isn't just truckers who eat here. At breakfast you'll see drivers, families, and businesspeople among the patrons. Known for great road food and reasonable prices. Homemade bread and seafood are specialties.

Pat's Pizza (866-2111), Mill Street, Orono. A local landmark, especially popular with high school and university students and families. Now franchised throughout the state, but this is the original with booths and a jukebox, back dining room and downstairs taproom, plus Pat and his family still running the place. Pizza, sandwiches, Italian dinners.

BREWPUB

Bear Brew Pub (866-BREW), 36 Main Street, Orono. A downstairs, dark dining room with a cozy atmosphere and a creative menu that includes Parmesan pesto scallops over pasta, and crabmeat primavera. Also offers sandwiches, pizza, and burgers. The beer is all brewed on the premises, along with root beer, cream soda, and ginger ale.

COFFEEHOUSES AND SNACKS

✎ **The Store & Ampersand** (866-4110), 22 Mill Street, Orono. A combination health food store, coffee bar, and gift shop. Great for snacks (try the big cookies) and specialty items. Kids love to browse the gift shop.

New Moon Café (990-2233), 21 Main Street, Bangor. Spacious and open with a tile floor and interesting art on the walls. Offers a wide variety of coffee and espresso drinks, smoothies, Italian sodas, sandwiches, wraps, and desserts. Live music many nights.

Intown Internet Café (942-0999; café@ime.net), 56 Main Street, Bangor. Several flavored coffees, breakfast and lunch, but the real focus here is the Internet access. Seven computers available for e-mail access, surfing the web, word processing, and more.

ENTERTAINMENT

☞ **Maine Center for the Arts** (581-1755), at the University of Maine in Orono, has become the cultural center for the area. Hosts a wide variety of concerts and events, from classical to country-and-western, children's theater, and dance. Many performances are held in Hutchins Concert Hall, Maine's first concert hall.

☞ **Penobscot Theatre Company** (947-6618), 183 Main Street, Bangor. This company has been putting on quality shows for more than 20 years. They recently purchased and renovated the Bangor Opera House (Main Street, Bangor) and now offer performances in both facilities throughout their 9-month season. In summer the company sponsors the Maine Shakespeare Festival and the Creative Arts Program for young people.

Maine Masque Theater (581-1963), Hauck Auditorium, University of Maine, Orono. Classic and contemporary plays presented October through May by University of Maine theater students.

☞ **Theatre of the Enchanted Forest** (945-0800), 9 Central Street, Bangor. Children's theater.

Bass Park (942-9000), 100 Dutton Street, Bangor. Complex includes **Bangor Auditorium, Civic Center, State Fair,** and **Raceway** (featuring harness racing Thursday through Sunday, May through July). Band concerts in the park by the Paul Bunyan statue on Tuesdays in summer.

Bangor Symphony Orchestra (942-5555). The symphony began in 1895 and is still going strong, with performances at the Bangor Opera House from October through May.

SELECTIVE SHOPPING

BOOKSTORES

Betts' Bookstore (947-7052), 584 Hammond Street, Bangor, is a full-service bookstore specializing in Maine and Stephen King titles.

Mr. Paperback. Bangor is home base for this eastern Maine chain, with a stores at the Airport Mall (942-9191). All are fully stocked stores with Maine sections.

BookMarc's (942-3206), 10 Harlow Street, Bangor. A great little full-service bookstore, with a cozy café.

Borders Books and Music (990-3300), off Hogan Road at Bangor Mall.

Part of a large chain, but a great place to find what you are looking for and grab an espresso at the same time.

See also **The Briar Patch** under *Special Shops.*

CANOES

Old Town Canoe & Kayak Factory Outlet Store (827-1530), 130 North Main Street, Old Town. Varieties sold include fiberglass, wood, Kevlar, Crosslink, and Royalex. Factory-tour video shows how canoes are made.

SPECIAL SHOPS

Winterport Boot Shop (989-6492), 264 State Street, Twin City Plaza, Brewer. Largest selection of Redwing workboots in the Northeast. Proper fit for sizes 4–16, all widths.

✐ **The Briar Patch** (941-0255), 27 State Street, Bangor. A large and exceptional children's book and toy store.

Snow & Neally (947-4242), 60 Summer Street, Bangor. An attractive showroom for the high-quality gardening tools that this family business has been producing since 1864.

✐ **The Grasshopper Shop** (945-3132), West Market Square, Bangor. So many items, they now have two stores across the street from each other. Trendy women's clothing, toys, jewelry, gifts, housewares.

The Bangor Mall, Hogan Road (just west off the I-95, exit 49, interchange). The centerpiece of a whole range of satellite malls and stores. Since this is precisely the kind of strip most visitors come to Maine to escape, we won't elaborate, but it certainly has its uses.

SPECIAL EVENTS

April: **Kenduskeag Stream Canoe Race.**

July: **Bangor State Fair,** Bass Park—agricultural fair with harness racing.

Late July–early August: **Maine Shakespeare Festival**—three shows performed in rotation outside on the bank of the Penobscot River; food vendors, bleachers, plenty of lawn space.

August: **WLBZ Downtown Arts Sidewalk Festival.**

September: **Paul Bunyan Festival Days,** at Paul Bunyan Park, featuring crafts, food, entertainment.

Aroostook County

Aroostook is Maine's largest and least-populated county, simply referred to as The County within the state. Almost the size of Massachusetts, this region has long suffered the misconception that the only thing to see is potato fields. In truth, The County is rich in cultural traditions, friendly faces, and interesting heritage, including a Swedish colony and Acadian settlements. Tiny, fascinating historical museums can be found scattered from the southern part of The County to the northern tip of the state, treasure troves of information on the areas and the people who first settled here.

Acadians trace their lineage to French settlers who came to farm and fish in Nova Scotia in the early 1600s and who, in 1755, were forcibly deported by an English governor. This *grand dérangement,* dispersing a population of some 10,000 Acadians, brutally divided families (a tale told by Longfellow in "Evangeline"). Many were returned to France, only to make their way back to a warmer New World (Louisiana), and many were resettled in New Brunswick, from which they were once more dislodged after the American Revolution when the British government gave their land to loyalists from the former colonies.

In a meadow overlooking the St. John River behind Madawaska's Tante Blanche Museum, a large marble cross and an outsized wooden sculpture of a voyageur in his canoe mark the spot on which several hundred of these displaced Acadians landed in 1785. They settled both sides of the St. John River, an area known as Mattawaska ("land of the porcupine"). Not until 1842 did the St. John become the formal boundary dividing Canada and Maine.

The 1842 Webster-Ashburton Treaty settled the Aroostook War, a footnote in American history recalled in the 1830s wooden blockhouses at Fort Kent and Fort Fairfeld. Until relatively recently this bloodless "war" was the area's chief historic claim, but the valley's distinct Acadian heritage is gaining increasing recognition.

In 1976 a "Village Acadien" consisting of a dozen buildings was assembled just west of Van Buren. It's an interesting enough little museum village, but it only begins to tell the story evinced in the very shape of the St. John Valley towns—the houses strung out like arms from cathedral-sized Catholic churches at their centers.

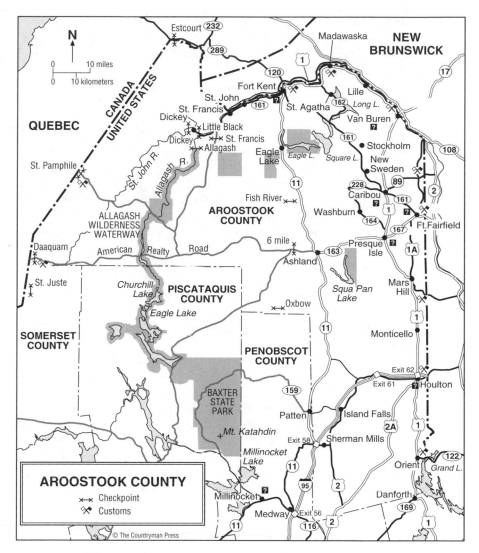

The County can not be easily categorized. Within the boundaries there are three distinct regions, each with a unique feel. The Upper St. John Valley at the top of The County, a broad ribbon of riverland backed by woodland to the west and by a high, open plateau to the east, has its own distinctly Acadian look, language, and taste. Central Aroostook—the rolling farmland around Fort Fairfield, Presque Isle, and Caribou—is generally equated with the entire county. It, too, has its appeal, especially around Washburn and New Sweden, sites of two of New England's more interesting museums. Houlton, the northern terminus of I-95 and the county seat, is in southern Aroostook, a mix of farmland, lonely woods, and lakes.

Four million of Aroostook's 5 million acres are wooded—land that includes many major mountains, most of the Allagash Wilderness Waterway, and more than 1,000 lakes. Many visitors actually enter The County in canoes, paddling up the Allagash River, which flows north and empties into the St. John River at Allagash, a minuscule hamlet that's become widely known as Mattagash to readers of novels (*The Funeral Makers, Once upon a Time on the Banks,* and *The Weight of Winter*) by Allagash native Cathie Pelletier. Local residents will tell you that the names of Pelletier's characters have been changed only as slightly as that of her town, and that the interplay between Catholics and Protestants (descendants of Acadian and Scottish settlers, respectively) chronicled in her books remains very real. From the 1940s to the 1960s French was a forbidden language in local schools, and students were punished for speaking it anywhere on school grounds.

Aroostook County still produces 1½ million tons of potatoes a year, but the family farms—once the staple of The County's landscape and social fabric—are fading, replaced by consolidated spreads that grow other crops, notably broccoli, barley, and sugar beets. The family potato farm is already the stuff of museum exhibits. Our favorites are in the New Sweden Museum, which commemorates not only family farms but also one of the most interesting immigration stories in American history.

The tourist experience in The County is far different from that along the coast. There are often many miles between attractions, interesting shops, and sights, and part of the experience is that of driving the peaceful country roads. Route 1 looks different in this region, passing through small downtown centers with long stretches of rolling farmland in between. You shop in craftspeople's and farmers' homes; ask locally for directions to the best places to walk, ski, and fish; feast on fiddleheads, *ployes* (buckwheat crêpes), and *poutine* (fries with cheese and gravy) rather than lobster. B&Bs are smaller (often just two or three rooms), with a more personal feel. The hospitality we've encountered here is overwhelmingly warm, and hosts are genuinely excited about sharing what The County has to offer.

Winter brings predictable snowfall and is the big draw. Most visitors come in this season—to snowmobile, cross-country ski, snowshoe, or dogsled. Fort Kent is becoming a base for biathlon training, with world-class coaches. Biathlon competitions are also being held here, as are annual sled-dog races. Winter driving, we're told, is less daunting here than elsewhere in the Northeast because, thanks to the region's lowest temperatures, the snow is drier (no ice) as well as more plentiful. Summer temperatures also tend to be cooler than elsewhere, and in early July the potato fields are a spread of pink and white blossoms. Fall colors, which usually peak in the last weeks of September at the end of potato harvest, include reddening barley fields as well as maples.

Aroostook is said to mean "bright," actually the best word we can think of to describe the entire county, since the luminosity of its sky—broader than elsewhere in New England—is The County's single most striking characteristic, along with its location. Bounded by Canada on two sides and the North Woods on the third, Aroostook is so far off any tourist route that many New England maps omit it entirely. Maine pundits are fond of noting that Portland is as far from Fort Kent, the northern terminus of Route 1, as it is from New York City.

The conventional loop tour around The County is I-95 to its terminus at Houlton, then Route 1 north to Fort Kent and back down Route 11. We suggest doing it in reverse.

Canada's proximity means that residents of The County are often as likely to travel across the border to dine or shop as they are to venture into other parts of the state. For this reason, we are including a few Canadian recommendations within this chapter.

GUIDANCE

As noted in the chapter introduction, The County is divided into three distinct regions. For details about northern Aroostook (the Upper St. John Valley), contact the **Greater Fort Kent Chamber of Commerce** (834-5354), P.O. Box 430, Fort Kent 04743. A walk-in information center at the blockhouse, staffed by the Boy Scouts, is open seasonally. For central Aroostook, contact the **Presque Isle Chamber of Commerce** (764-6561), P.O. Box 672, Presque Isle 04769; and for southern Aroostook, the **Houlton Chamber of Commerce** (532-4216), 109-B Main Street, Houlton 04730. The County has recently been making efforts to market itself as a tourist destination, with color brochures inviting people to "discover the other Maine." This campaign is headed by the **Northern Maine Development Commission** (1-800-427-8736), which will send you fact sheets that list lodging, dining, and recreational options for all three regions.

The big walk-in information center in The County is maintained by the **Maine Tourism Association,** just off I-95 in Houlton (532-6346). *Note:* The North Maine Woods information office on Route 1 in Ashland is described under *Guidance* in "The North Woods."

GETTING THERE

By car: Our most preferred route is to take I-95 to Benedicta or Sherman Mills, then Route 11 up through Patten, Ashland, and Eagle Lake to Fort Kent, from which you can explore west to Allagash and east along the Upper St. John Valley to St. Agatha and/or Van Buren. Stop at the New Sweden Museum, for a meal in Caribou, and for a final overnight in the Houlton area. An alternate route through The County, especially if you are beginning Down East, is to follow Route 1 through rolling hills and past scenic lakes (Grand Lake is breathtaking from the top of one hill), through tiny town centers, to Houlton. From here, continue through Presque Isle and Caribou to Van Buren, then follow Route 1 along the St. John River to Fort Kent. Return on Route 11 to

Sherman Mills, where you can pick up I-95 south.

By plane: Regularly scheduled service to Presque Isle/Northern Maine Regional Airport is limited to **U.S. Airways Express** (1-800-428-4322) and **Business Express** (1-800-345-3400). **Aroostook Aviations** (543-6334), formerly Pine State Air, no longer offers regularly scheduled service but is available for charters. **Scotty's Flying Service** (528-2626), Shin Pond, is a commercial seaplane operation geared to shuttling canoeists, hunters, and anglers to remote lakes and put-in places along the St. John, Allagash, and Aroostook Rivers.

By bus: **Cyr Bus Lines** (532-6868), Houlton, runs daily between the Greyhound terminal in Bangor and Caribou, with stops in between.

MEDICAL EMERGENCY

Northern Maine Medical Center (834-3155), 143 East Maine Street, Fort Kent. **Aroostook Medical Center** (768-4000), 140 Academy Street, Presque Isle. **Houlton Regional Hospital** (532-9471), 20 Hartford Street, Houlton.

TO SEE

MUSEUMS

A brochure detailing The County's historical museums and attractions is available from most area chambers of commerce. Following are those we found of particular interest (in order of suggested routing). As most of these museums are entirely run by volunteers, and there are many miles in between each museum, you should always call before visiting to be sure they are open.

See *To See* in "Katahdin Region" for details about **The Lumberman's Museum** in Patten.

Fort Kent Historical Society Museum (834-5121), Main and Market Streets, Fort Kent. Open Tuesday through Friday in summer, 1–4 PM. The former Bangor & Aroostook Railroad depot is filled with local memorabilia and exhibits on the economic and social history of the area, focusing on lumbering and agriculture.

Fort Kent Blockhouse Museum, off Route 1, Fort Kent. Open Memorial Day through Labor Day, usually 9–dusk, and maintained by the town and the local Boy Scout troop. This symbol of the northern terminus of Route 1 is a convincingly ancient, if much restored, two-story 1830s blockhouse with documents and mementos from the Aroostook War. Be sure to wander down to the Fish River behind the blockhouse, a pleasant walk to picnic and tenting sites.

Madouesk Historic Center and Acadian Cross Shrine (728-4518), Route 1, Madawaska. Open early June through Labor Day, weekdays 10–3, and Sunday morning. The complex includes the **Tante Blanche Museum** (local memorabilia) and, if you follow the dirt road behind the museum to the river, the 18th-century **Albert Homestead,** plus the *Voyageur* statue and stone cross described in the introduction to this chapter.

Acadian Village & Levasseur-Dube Art Museum (868-2691/5042), Route 1, Van Buren. Open mid-June through mid-September, noon–5 daily. The 16 buildings include a school and store, a barbershop, a train station, old homesteads with period furnishings, a gallery, and a reconstructed 18th-century log church. $3.50 adults, $1.50 children.

Ste. Agathe Historical Society Museum (543-6911), 433 Main Street, St. Agatha. Open late June through early September, Tuesday through Sunday 1–4. The oldest house in this unusually pleasant village on Long Lake, the Pelletier-Marquis home dates just from 1854; it's filled with a sense of the town's unusually rich ethnic and social history.

✎ **New Sweden Historical Society Museum** (896-5844), just east of Route 161, New Sweden. Open late May through mid-October, Tuesday through Friday noon–4; weekends 1–5. Entering the community's reconstructed Kapitileum (meetinghouse), you are faced with the imposing bust of William Widgery Thomas, the Portland man sent by President Lincoln to Sweden in 1863 to halt the sale of iron to the Confederacy. Thomas quickly learned Swedish, married two countesses (the second after her sister, Thomas's first wife, died), and eventually devoted his sizable energies to establishing a colony of Swedish farmers in Maine. In 1870 the House of Representatives authorized the project, granting 100 acres of woodland to each Swedish family. A pink granite memorial in a pine grove behind the museum complex commemorates the arrival and hardships of those who settled here between 1870 and 1875. Despite the severe climate and thin soil (Thomas had been struck by the similarities between Sweden and northern Maine), New Sweden prospered, with 1,400 immigrants in 1895 and 689 buildings, including three churches, seven general stores, and two railroad stations. New Sweden's annual festivals draw thousands of local descendants. The museum remains a cultural touchstone for Swedes living throughout the Northeast, and the town continues to attract visitors from Sweden, even an occasional immigrant. Also check out nearby Thomas Park, with a picnic area, the monument and cemetery behind the museum, and the other historic buildings in New Sweden, including the Larsson Ostlund Log Home, Lars Noak Blacksmith and Woodworking Shop, and the one-room Capitol Schoolhouse.

The Salmon Brook Historical Society (455-4339), Route 164, Washburn. Open in summer on Wednesday 8–11 AM and Sunday 1–4 PM. The pleasant 1852 **Benjamin C. Wilder Farmstead** (13 rooms of 1850–1900 period furnishings) and the **Aroostook Agricultural Museum** (potato-harvesting tools and trivia housed in the neighboring barn) offer a sense of life and potato farming in the late 19th century. Washburn's Taterstate Frozen Foods claims to have invented the frozen french fry.

✒ **Nylander Museum** (493-4209), 393 Main Street, Caribou. Open June through September, Wednesday through Sunday 1–5. A small but intriguing museum displaying permanent collections of fossils, minerals and rocks, shells and other marine life, butterflies and moths, birds, and early-man artifacts, most collected by Swedish-born Olof Nylander; also changing exhibits, and a medicinal herb garden in the back with over 80 specimens.

Caribou Historical Center (498-2556), Route 1, Caribou. Open June through August, Wednesday through Sunday 11–5. A log building filled with local memorabilia from the mid–19th century to the 1930s, including antiques, historical papers, photographs, home furnishings, and tools. Also a replica of an 1860s one-room school with a bell in the cupola.

Northern Maine Museum of Science (768-9482), Folsom Hall, University of Maine at Presque Isle. Open during university hours. Interesting exhibits, including an herbarium (library of plant species), a coral-reef environment, an extensive display of plant and shell specimens collected by Leroy Norton (a well-known local amateur naturalist), topographic maps, and Aroostook potato varieties, among much more. Be sure to pick up a copy of the museum guide.

The Presque Isle Air Museum (764-2542), 650 Airport Drive, Presque Isle. The Presque Isle Historical Society has created this museum as a testament to the rich history of air travel in Presque Isle. During World War II, Presque Isle became the departure point for planes and equipment going overseas. An Army Air Field was created, and more planes left PIAAF bound for Europe than from any other U.S. base. In the early 1960s the missle wing was deactivated and the base was closed. Though the museum is small, the story of the airport and the artifacts they do have are interesting.

Aroostook County Historical and Art Museum (532-4216), 109 Main Street, Houlton. Open Memorial Day through Labor Day, weekdays 1–4 and by appointment. Same building as the Houlton Area Chamber of Commerce, and if there is enough staff, someone from the chamber will take you up. A large, well-organized, -labeled, and -maintained collection of local memorabilia.

Oakfield Railroad Museum (757-8575), Station Street, Oakfield. This 1910 Bangor & Aroostook Railroad station is one of three remaining wood-framed railroad stations between Searsport and Fort Kent. Exhibits include photographs from the early days of the railroad, vintage signs and advertising pieces, maps, newspapers, a rail motor car, and a C-66 caboose.

Webb Museum of Vintage Fashion (862-3797 or 463-2404), Route 2, Island Falls. Open June through early October, Monday through Thursday 10–4. $3 adults, $2 seniors, $1 children under 12. Fourteen of the 17 rooms in this Victorian-era house are filled with some 6,000 articles of clothing amassed by Frances Stratton—hats, jewelry, combs, and mannequins dressed to represent the specific people to whom their outfits once belonged. It's a spooky, fascinating place, chronicling life in a small town as well as what its inhabitants wore from the 1890s to the 1950s. Each room has its own theme, and the collection rotates each year. *Note:* This museum can be accessed either from Route 11 (it's 9 miles east of Patten) or from I-95.

CHURCHES

As noted in the introduction to this chapter, tall, elaborate, French Canadian–style Catholic churches form the heart of most Upper St. John Valley villages: **St. Leonard** in Madawaska, **St. Louis** in Fort Kent (with distinctive open filigree steeples and a fine carillon), **St. David's** in the village of St. David, and **St. Luce** in Frenchville. When the twin-spired wooden church dominating the village of Lille was condemned, it was purchased by local resident Don Cyr (895-3339), who converted it into **Association culturelle et historiqe du Mont-Carmel,** an Acadian cultural center and a setting for concerts and workshops. On Labor Day weekend the center sponsors the **Lille Classical Impressionist Music Festival.**

OTHER ATTRACTIONS

✎ **A. E. Howell Wildlife Conservation Center and Spruce Acres Refuge** (532-0910), Lycette Road (off Route 1), North Amity (14 miles south of Houlton). Open May through November, 9–sunset; $5 adults, $2 youth 13–18, children 12 and under free. Art Howell, one of the best-known and -respected of Maine's more than 90 wild-animal "rehabilitators," nurtures bald eagles, bears, foxes, otters, and many more creatures that have been wounded and are being readied, if possible, for return to the wild. The center has 64 acres of woods with a picnic area and a pond stocked with fish for children; also a camping area for environmental groups. No dogs, please.

SCENIC DRIVES

Flat Mountain. The single most memorable landscape that we found in all of Aroostook is easily accessible if you know where to turn. The high plateau is well named Flat Mountain and is just above but invisible from Route 1 east of Fort Kent. Ask locally about the road through the back settlements from Frenchville to St. Agatha, a lake resort with several good restaurants.

Watson Settlement Covered Bridge. Follow Main Street through Houlton's Market Square Historic District (a "Walking Tour Guide" to this area is available from the chamber of commerce) until it turns into Military Street (dating from the Aroostook War). Turn north on Foxcroft Road; in 2 miles note your first view of Mars Hill Mountain (the area's only mountain, at 1,660 feet). The mountain's ownership was disputed in the Aroostook War; it is now a ski area. At roughly 3.5 miles, note the road on your left descending to a small iron bridge across the Meduxnekeag River; the covered bridge, built in 1902, is midway down this hill. The road rejoins Route 1 ten minutes north of Houlton.

Driving Route 1 from Presque Isle to Houlton, you will see a **scale model of the solar system.** The community project is headed by Kevin McCartney, a professor at the University of Maine at Presque Isle and director of the Northern Maine Museum of Science. The solar system is a scale model, both in diameter of planets and in distance between planets, of 1:93,000,000. Jupiter, the largest planet, is 5 feet in diameter. Pluto, just an inch in diameter, is located at the Maine Tourism Association's Information Center in Houlton (see *Guidance*) An informational brochure details where the planets are and facts about the planets and moons.

TO DO

CANOEING

Allagash Wilderness Waterway. This is considered *the* canoe trip in Maine, and after a 3-day expedition we have to agree. The whole trip, 92 miles of lake and river canoeing, takes far longer than 3 days. We put in at Round Pond and paddled the shorter 32-mile trip to Allagash Village. The first step in any Allagash trip is the planning. Though it's possible to shuttle your own vehicles, leaving one at the beginning and one at the end, we recommend using a transportation service, which will bring you, your gear, and your canoes into your put-in spot and retrieve you at take-out. This simplifies the parking issue; also, you won't have to go back into the woods to retrieve your car at the end of the trip, and the transportation companies are experienced in negotiating the bumpy dirt roads that can lead to blown tires and rocks thrown at the windshield. **Norman L'Italien** (398-3187), P.O. Box 67, St. Francis, 04774, was well informed, helpful, and friendly. After we checked in at the gate (road-use fee of $4 per person; overnight camping fee $4 per person per night), his driver dropped us off at the bridge just above Round Pond and told us to call when we were off the river. Norman also operates **Pelletier's Campground** in St. Francis, a good spot to stay the night before your departure. Keep in mind that the trip to the area from Sherman Mills, where you leave I-95, is at least 3 hours, head up the night before your trip. Plan to arrive in daylight if you need to set up tents.

We found the river itself to be serene, unspoiled, and spectacular. Paddling and floating with the current, sunlight twinkling off the water, you'll feel you're truly in a wilderness paradise. Even when the sun hid behind the clouds, the river wasn't the least bit gloomy or less beautiful. We were there on Labor Day weekend, and the weather and bugs cooperated quite nicely, but come prepared for both rain and pests. Blackflies, mosquitoes, and no-see-ums can be brutal, so bring plenty of bug

STACI BUCK

The Allagash Wilderness Waterway

repellent, maybe even protective netting. On our trip, however, bugs were not a problem, and we slept out underneath the stars 2 of the 3 nights. Remember that there are no stores around the next corner; if you leave it at home, you do without. Pack light, but bring enough spare clothing so that if some gets wet, you'll still be comfortable. Pack in waterproof backpacks, or seal items in plastic bags to prevent soaking should your canoe tip. Bring extra garbage bags to wrap around sleeping bags and pillows. Don't forget a camera and extra film. **Allagash Falls** are particularly nice, and the portage around them is an easy half-mile hike. The trail and picnic area are well maintained. This is actually a good place to cook a solid meal, using up your heaviest supplies before carrying your stuff around the falls. The trip after the falls to Allagash is just one more overnight, and if you plan remaining meals accordingly, you can lighten your load around the portage.

Campsites on the waterway are clean and comfortable, with plenty of space for a group to spread out. Sites are available on a first-come, first-served basis, so the earlier in the day you begin paddling, the better choice you have. The river was far from crowded, even on a holiday weekend. We saw less than 15 people outside our group on our 3-day journey. The rangers keep track of who is on the river, so there's no need to be nervous that you will be too isolated should something happen. If you are not an experienced canoeist, don't worry: A 3-day trip is easily manageable without putting too much strain on infrequently used muscles. Paddling the whole waterway takes 7 to 10 days, and it is best to be flexible, especially on your end date, in case wind or rain delays your trip.

If you are not comfortable venturing out on your own, several area guides can take you down the river. Following are a few suggestions. Contact **North Maine Woods** (see *Guidance* in "The North Woods") for other options.

Allagash Guide Service (398-3418), Allagash, rents paddles and canoes, and also offers transport and car pickup.

Allagash Canoe Trips (695-3668). Warren Cochrane and his father founded this company in 1953. He, his son, and other guides continue to lead trips, providing all equipment and meals. Trips vary in length.

Maine Canoe Adventures/Cross Rock Inn (398-3191), Route 162, Allagash. Gorman Chamberlain offers 5- to 7-day trips on the St. John and Allagash Rivers; also guided trips into the nearby Debouille area, departing from his lodge. There are three guest rooms, a tenting area, and canoe rentals.

Note: The map/guide to the Allagash and the St. John Rivers ($4.95, available locally and from DeLorme 846-7000) is useful.

FARM TOUR

Knott-II-Bragg Farm (455-8386), Box 150, Wade 04786. Open June through October, Tuesday through Saturday 9:30 AM–6 PM. $5 adults, $3.50 children; family rates available. Natalia Bragg gives a fantastic tour of the farm, including the herb gardens and flower gardens. Old-time skills are a way of life here, and Natalia will describe such things as making butter, soap, and maple syrup, as well as give detailed explanations of the uses for the oils she makes from her herbs. Fee fishing is available in Copper Penny Pond, and the gift shop sells items made on the farm, from soaps and oils to cedar "twig" handcrafted furniture. Natalia is warm, friendly, and fascinating. Ask for a copy of the tourist guide to Washburn that she put together, detailing all businesses in the northern Maine community.

FISHING

The catch is so rich and varied that it is recognized throughout the country. Salmon grow to unusual size, and trout are also large and numerous. The 80-mile Fish River chain of rivers and lakes (Eagle, Long, and Square Lakes) is legendary in fishing circles. Fish strike longer in the season than they do farther south, and fall fishing begins earlier. Contact the Maine Department of Inland Fisheries and Wildlife in Ashland (435-3231; in-state, 1-800-353-6334).

GOLF

The County's topography lends itself to golf, and the sport is so popular that most towns maintain at least a nine-hole course. The most famous course, with 18 holes, is **Aroostook Valley Country Club,** Fort Fairfield (476-8083); its tees are split between Canada and Maine. The 18-hole **Jo-Wa Golf Course** (463-2128) in Island Falls and the **Presque Isle Country Club** (764-0439) are also considered above par.

HIKING

See the **Debouille Management Unit** and **Aroostook State Park** under *Green Space.*

Fish River Falls. Ask locally for directions to the trail that leads from the former Fort Kent airport down along the river, an unusually beautiful trail through pines. Note the swimming holes below the falls. **The Dyke in Fort Kent** is also worth finding: a half-mile walk along the Fish River. The trail up **Mount Carmel** (views up and down the river valley) begins on Route 1 at the state rest area near the Madawaska–Grand Isle town line.

WINTER SPORTS

CROSS-COUNTRY SKIING

The same reliable snow that serves out-of-state snowmobilers allows residents to take advantage of hundreds of miles of trails maintained exclusively for cross-country skiing by local towns and clubs. Any town office or chamber of commerce (see *Guidance*) will steer you to local trails.

Maine Winter Sports Center (328-0991). The name is deceiving, as there isn't really a center. The organization, funded by the Libra Foundation, has developed a network of community trails for use by schoolchildren and local residents. They also have two Nordic skiing facilities, used for training, with world-class coaches. The facility in Fort Kent includes a biathlon range and links to the recreational trails, and a lodge is being built. In Presque Isle a similar facility is planned, though not yet constructed. At present there is an access road and parking lots, and the first trails have been created. The center also operates an alpine ski area at Mars Hill, called Big Rock.

Kate McCartney at the Old Iron Inn in Caribou (492-4766) has compiled a brochure of northern Maine cross-country trails, which lists nine centers dedicated to the sport, including phone numbers, rates, and locations.

SNOWMOBILING

Snowmobiling is the single biggest reason that visitors come to The County. It is the easiest way to see some of the more remote sporting camps and wilderness areas, since riding over well-maintained trails is often smoother than bumping down logging roads in summer. Trails lead from one end of The County to the other and are far too numerous for us to detail here. Call any Aroostook County chamber of commerce (see *Guidance*) for a "Trail Map to Northern Maine" detailing 1,600 miles of trails maintained by The County's 40-plus snowmobile clubs and including locations of clubhouses, warming huts, and service areas. On the back of the map are ads for several companies that cater to snowmobilers, from rentals and service to lodging and dining.

GREEN SPACE

Debouille Management Unit, including Debouille Mountain and several ponds, is a 23,461-acre preserve managed jointly by the state and North Maine Woods (charging gate and camping fees; see *Guidance* in "The North Woods"), accessible by gated logging roads from St. Francis and Portage. Campsites are clustered around ponds (good for trout) and near hiking trails leading to the distinctive summit of Debouille Mountain. For details, contact the Bureau of Public Lands in Presque Isle (764-2033).

Aroostook State Park (768-8341), marked from Route 1, just 4 miles south of Presque Isle. Open May 15 through October 15. A 600-acre park with swimming and picnicking at Echo Lake; also 30 campsites (June 15 through Labor Day only) at 1,213-foot Quaggy Joe Mountain—which offers hiking trails with views from the north peak across a sea of woodland to Mount Katahdin. Note the monument in the small **Maxie Anderson Memorial Park** next door; a tin replica of the *Double Eagle II* commemorates the 1978 liftoff of the first hot-air balloon to successfully cross the Atlantic.

Aroostook Valley Trail and **Bangor and Aroostook Trail** (493-4224). A 7½-mile recreational trail system connecting Caribou, Woodland, New Sweden, Washburn, Perham, Stockholm, and Van Buren. Many bogs, marshes, wetlands, and streams are along these trails, which are owned by the Maine Bureau of Parks and Lands. Several parking lots and rest areas on the trails. Good for biking, walks, cross-country skiing, and snowmobiling.

Fish River Falls. See *To Do—Hiking*.

New Brunswick Botanical Garden (506-735-3074), Route 2, St.-Jacques, New Brunswick. Open June through mid-October, daily 9–dusk. More than 50,000 varieties are represented in this spread of rose gardens, rhododendrons, annuals, and perennials designed by a team from the Montreal Botanical Garden. There's a gift shop and snack bar as well.

Also see **Allagash Wilderness Waterway** under *To Do—Canoeing*.

LODGING

HOTELS

The Northeastland Hotel (768-5321; 1-800-244-5321), 436 Main Street, Presque Isle 04769. Built in 1934 in the heart of downtown, this 50-room, two-story hotel remains a favorite with business and pleasure travelers alike. Guest rooms are unusually large, sparely but nicely furnished and spotless, equipped with a full, mirrored closet, phone, coffeemaker, iron, and blow dryer (the only clock is on the TV). The hotel **Coffee Shop** serves all three meals (full liquor). Double rooms (two queen beds) are $67 year-round, no charge for children; single $62.

🐾 **Caribou Inn and Convention Center** (498-3733; 1-800-235-0466;

www.caribouinn.com), junction of Routes 1 and 164, Caribou 04736. This is The County's largest, most modern facility, a sprawling 73-room motor inn with an indoor pool, hot tub and fitness center, and the full-service **Greenhouse Restaurant.** Rooms are large and suites have kitchenettes. We haven't had the best feedback but it fills a need. Quiet in summer and fall but noisy on winter weekends as this is snowmobiler central. $66–112; children stay free.

BED & BREAKFASTS

& **Daigle's Bed & Breakfast** (834-5803; www.mainerec.com/daigles.html), 96 East Main Street, Fort Kent 04743. This cheery modern house features a sunny, glass-walled, flower-filled dining room in which guests tend to linger over Doris Daigle's generous breakfast. The five guest rooms range from small with shared bath, to a spacious double with twin beds, to a room decorated in red and black with a refrigerator, TV, and phone. Guests are also welcome to join Elmer and Doris in the evening for drinks and snacks by the living room fireplace. $55–85 double.

River Watch (728-7109; jcayer1@juno.com), 31 Riverview Street, Madawaska 04756. A small place in the heart of the St. John Valley, offering guest rooms with private baths. Breakfast, which could be Belgian waffles, a smoked salmon omelet, or double decker French toast, is included in the rates.

Auberge du Lac (728-6047), Birch Point Road, St. David. Open year-round. This small place is very quiet and private. The Ouellettes live downstairs, leaving visitors in two guest rooms to share a large, comfortable living room with a fireplace and a picture window overlooking Long Lake. Across the street is a stretch of land on the water with Adirondack chairs. $65 double includes a full breakfast. Grace also offers dinners to guests and to the public, by reservation only.

The Yellow House Bed & Breakfast (757-8797; yellowhousebandb@pocketmail.com), 1040 Ridge Road, Oakfield 04763. Located 1.5 miles off I-95 (exit 60) between Island Falls and Houlton, this vintage-1862 homestead has been in George Clark's family since then. His wife, Gina, has worked as an international tour guide and enjoys helping guests explore The County. $40 for singles, $75 double, and $100 for a family; private baths. Full country breakfast is served in the travel library or in a glass atrium. They have also added a 37-jet theraputic spa on their outdoor deck (sheltered). Alcohol-, smoking-, and pet-free.

🐾 **Old Iron Inn** (492-4766 ; www.oldironinn.com), 155 High Street, Caribou. Kate and Kevin McCartney offer four rooms (two with private baths, the other two sharing a bath and a half) decorated with antiques, including an impressive collection of old irons throughout the inn. The hosts are well informed and happy to help plan a vacation in The County. After a visit or two, guests will feel like old friends. Evening conversation is stimulating and interesting; Kevin always has an interesting project in the works, and Kate's energy seems endless. Specialized libraries of

Lincoln, aviation history, and mysteries, as well as subscriptions to 40 magazines, offer plenty of reading material to guests. Once a month the McCartneys host a music night, free and open to all (see *Entertainment*). $49–59 includes a full breakfast.

☙ **Rum Rapids Inn** (455-8096; www.mainerec.com/rmrapids), Route 164, Crouseville 04738 (not far from Presque Isle). One of the oldest houses in The County (vintage 1839), this inn is set in 15 acres on the Aroostook River. Clifton (Bud) and Judy Boudman offer candlelight dinners as well as two rooms (private baths) with all the comforts of home, including robes, TV/VCR with movie selections, and an honor-system snack bar. In the afternoon, complimentary beverages are offered, and you can relax in the theraputic hot tub in the solarium or curl up on the screened porch. Bud is happy to help with travel plans in Maine and the Maritimes. Dinners are open to the public by reservation only, and they only book one party per night. It's a multicourse event, and there are 17 entrée choices (each party can choose only 2), including Tuscan primavera (a delicious pasta dish), steamed Maine lobster, and roast beef with Yorkshire pudding. Entrées $23–42. Overnight guests are offered the "chef's table" option ($14.50) if they would like to have dinner at the inn. Room rates start at $78 double, including a full Scottish breakfast.

SPORTING CAMPS

Allagash Gardners Sporting Camps (398-3168), Box 127, Allagash 04774. Open May through December. Five tidy camps along a ridge overlooking the confluence of the St. John and Allagash Rivers across the road from Roy and Mande Gardner's welcoming old farmhouse. B&B and hiking, hunting, camping, and fishing guide service also offered. $30 double; $100 per week.

☙♿ **Moose Point Camps** (435-6156), Portage 04768. Open May 10 through early December. Ten hewn log camps on the east shore of Fish Lake (5 miles long and connecting with other lakes linked by the Fish River). The central lodge features a library, a large stone fireplace, and a dining room overlooking the lake where meals are served (BYOB). The camps are 17 miles from Portage, up a paper company road. $365 per person per week or $75 per person per day in spring and summer; ask about children's rates and hunters' packages. Boats and canoes available.

☙ **Libby Sporting Camps** (435-8274; www.libbycamps.com), P.O. Box 810 Ashland 04732. Open ice-out through November. One of the area's original sporting camps, which has been Libby owned and operated for more than 110 years. Features hearty meals in the lodge and guides to take you to 40 lakes and ponds from the eight cabins (each with its own bath). Also 10 outpost cabins on remote ponds and streams. Sited at the headwaters of the Aroostook and Allagash Rivers. There is a seaplane based at the camps, available for day and overnight trips. $130 per person per night includes all meals, boats, motor, and canoes. Pets are accepted, with an additional fee.

MOTEL
Long Lake Motor Inn (543-5006), Route 162, St. Agatha 04772. Ken and Arlene Lermon pride themselves on the cleanliness and friendliness of this motel overlooking Long Lake. There is a lounge, and continental breakfast is included in $49 for standard room ($43 single); $68 for the suite, which has a Jacuzzi.

WHERE TO EAT

DINING OUT
✎ **Sirois' Restaurant** (834-6548), 84 West Main Street, Fort Kent. Henry Sirois operates this hospitable, homey restaurant with an extensive menu. Choices range from chicken to seafood, steaks, and Italian specialties. $6.95–18.95. Children's menu $2.95–3.95.

  Long Lake Sporting Club (543-7584; 1-800-431-7584), Route 162, Sinclair. Open daily year-round. Sit down in the lounge with a drink, order, and then go to your table when your meal is ready. Specialties include appetizer platters (wings, mozzarella sticks, ribs, and shrimp), steaks, seafood, jumbo lobsters (3½-pound hardshells), and barbecue ribs. Right on Long Lake, with terrific views, dancing on Saturday night, a large deck, and a full-service marina. $8.95–16.95.

  Lakeview Restaurant (543-6331), Lakeview Drive, St. Agatha. Open daily for breakfast, lunch, and dinner. Set on a hilltop with a view across the lake and valley. Steak, seafood, and barbecued baby back ribs are the specialties. Live entertainment on summer weekends. Most entrées are around $10.

Daniel's (868-5591), 52 Main Street, Van Buren. A large restaurant and lounge open for lunch and dinner. At lunch choose from sandwiches and light entrées like chicken stir-fry. The dinner menu includes linguine with white clam sauce, and filet mignon, and pressure-fried chicken dinners (party boxes available to go). Dinner entrées $8.75–13.95.

Green Acres (493-4700), Route 1 south of Caribou. Open for dinner Monday through Saturday. A family dining room, specializing in steak and seafood.

Eureka Hall (896-3196), Stockholm. Open for dinner on weekends; reservations recommended. A new gourmet dining spot, with steak, seafood, local organic produce, and homemade breads and desserts.

York's (506-273-2847), Perth Andover, New Brunswick, Canada. Open seasonally for lunch and dinner. A large, popular dining room overlooking the St. John River. Home cooking, from steak to lobster and duck. Huge portions.

For special private dining experiences, also see **Rum Rapids Inn** and **Auberge du Lac** under *Lodging—Bed and Breakfasts.*

EATING OUT

Lil's (435-6471), Route 1, Ashland. Open 6 AM–8 PM. A counter and orange vinyl booths, homemade bread, pizza, outstanding sandwiches and pies, daily specials.

Ma & Pa's Sunrise Café (543-6177), Cleveland Road, St. Agatha. Open daily year-round 5:30 AM–8 PM. Our favorite kind of eatery: a counter, tables, and a view. Features local items as specials, like chicken stew and *ployes* (buckwheat crêpes).

Doris's Café (834-6262), Fort Kent Mills, open for breakfast and lunch; everything prepared from scratch.

Pierrette's Kitchen (834-6888), 57 East Main Street, Fort Kent. The large menu includes specialty pizzas (try potato or pesto pizza) and sandwiches, "road-kill chili," and *poutine* (fries with cheese and gravy) in a bright, friendly atmosphere. Fantastic cakes.

The Dicky Trading Post, (398-3157), St. Francis. Open 5 AM–7 PM. A combination general store (with stuffed bobcat and lynx), sporting-goods shop, and Formica-topped coffee shop.

Stan's Grocery, Route 161 north of Jemtland. Home of Stan's 10-cent cup of coffee, to be savored in a back booth of this indescribable store, the center for the surrounding summer community on Madawaska Lake. The pay phone next to the piano is roto-dial.

Frederick's Southside Restaurant (498-3464), 217 South Main Street, Caribou. Good homestyle cooking, generous portions, reasonable prices.

Rib Crib (493-7750), 21 Bennett Drive, Caribou. If you're craving barbecue, this is the place to get it. Ribs, ribs, and more ribs—from a quarter rack to a full rack, dinners, or pulled pork sandwiches. Sides of corn, beans, and coleslaw.

Winnie's (769-4971), 79 Parsons Street, Presque Isle. A small, local favorite for more than 50 years. Their lobster stew has made a name for itself and is now sold frozen as Leblanc's Gourmet Lobster Stew. Burgers, seafood rolls, sandwiches.

The Courtyard Café (532-0787), 59 Main Street, Houlton. A great little place that has a more cosmopolitan feel than you might expect in Houlton. Great sandwiches, daily specials, coffee, and sweets.

Elm Tree Diner (532-3181), Bangor Road, Houlton. Open early and late, an outstanding classic diner for over 50 years. Everything is made from scratch; daily specials.

ENTERTAINMENT

Monthly music nights are put on at the Old Iron Inn (see *Lodging—Bed and Breakfasts*), and everyone is welcome. A different style of music each month.

SELECTIVE SHOPPING

Main Street Emporium, Main Street, Houlton. A nicely renovated old building with several small gift shops and a nice little café (see the Courtyard Café under *Eating Out*).

Bradbury Barrel Co. (429-8188; 1-800-332-6021), P.O. Box A, 100 Main Street, Bridgewater 04735. Showroom of white-cedar barrels of all sizes as well as other wood products. Mail-order catalog. Tours of the company are available by prior arrangement.

Fish River Brand Tackle (834-3951). Call for directions. Tackle made by Don Baker—one of his big metal flashers secured the $10,000 grand prize in the Lake Champlain Fishing Derby in 1994.

Bouchard Family Farm (834-3237), Route 161, Fort Kent. Stop by the family kitchen and buy a bag of *ploye* mix. *Ployes* are crêpelike pancakes made with buckwheat flour (no eggs, no milk, no sugar, no oil, no cholesterol, no fat—*c'est magnifique*).

✐ **Goughan Farms** (496-1731), Route 161, Fort Fairfield. Open weekdays 10–5, Sundays 12–5. Pick-your-own strawberries; also a farm stand and animal barn.

SPECIAL EVENTS

✐ *February:* **Mardi-Gras** in Fort Kent—the 5 days before Ash Wednesday bring a parade, ice sculptures, kids' day, Franco-American music, and exhibitions.

Early March: **The Can Am Sled Dog Race.** Triple Crown 60- and 250-mile races, starting and ending at Fort Kent.

June: **Acadian Festival** in Madawaska, with parade, traditional Acadian supper, and talent revue. **"Midsommar"** *(the weekend nearest June 21)* is celebrated at Thomas Park in New Sweden and at the New Sweden Historical Society Museum (see *To See—Museums*) with Swedish music, dancing, and food.

July: **Maine Potato Blossom Festival,** Fort Fairfield, features a week of activities, including mashed-potato wrestling, Potato Blossom Queen pageant, parade, entertainment, dancing, industry dinner, and fireworks.

August: **Northern Maine Fair,** Presque Isle. **Potato Feast Days** in Houlton has arts and crafts, potato-barrel-rolling contest, potato games, carnival, and more.

Index

652

666

678

680